MONSTROUS ADVERSARY

LIVERPOOL ENGLISH TEXTS AND STUDIES, 40

Edward de Vere, 17th Earl of Oxford, 1575, unknown artist, from a lost original. Currently housed in National Portrait Gallery, Welbeck Abbey.

MONSTROUS ADVERSARY

The Life of Edward de Vere, 17th Earl of Oxford

ALAN H. NELSON

LIVERPOOL UNIVERSITY PRESS

First published 2003 by
Liverpool University Press
4 Cambridge Street
Liverpool
L69 7ZU

British Library Cataloguing-in-Publication Data
A British Library CIP record is available.

ISBN 0-85323-678-x *cased*
     0-85323-688-7 *limp*

Typeset in Garamond by
Koinonia, Bury, Lancashire
Printed and bound by CPI Group (UK) Ltd, Croydon, CR0 4YY

'...my Monsterus adversarye Oxford (who wold drinke my blud rather then wine as well as he loves it)...'

Charles Arundel, 1581

Contents

List of Illustrations

Maps (after p. 236)

1 Essex, showing places of particular significance to the Earl of Oxford.

2 Norden's map of London. From John Norden, *Speculi Britanniae. ... Middlesex* (1593: STC 18635), copy BL Maps C.7.b.23(1), opp. p. 26. By permission of the British Library.

3 Norden's map of Westminster. From John Norden, *Speculi Britanniae. ... Middlesex* (1593: STC 18635), copy BL Maps C.7.b.23(1), opp. p. 42. By permission of the British Library.

4 Norden's map of Middlesex. From John Norden, *Speculi Britanniae. ... Middlesex* (1593: STC 18635), copy BL Maps C.7.b.23(1593). By permission of the British Library.

Figures (after p. 236)

1 A sixteenth-century childbirth, with astrologers. From Jacob Rueff, *De Conceptu* (1587), copy BL 1173.l.4. By permission of the British Library.

2 A suit of armour from the 'Almain Armourer's Album'. By permission of the Victoria and Albert Museum.

3 Van den Wyngaerde's two sketches of Greenwich Palace, 1558, details showing the 'little house' in which Oxford is resorted to have conjured. By permission of the Ashmolean Museum, Oxford.

4 'Ser George Howarde Knight Master of the Qwenes Maiesties Armory Anno Domini 1561'. From Sir George Howard MS on long-term loan from the Earl of Dartmouth to the Royal Armouries, H.M. Tower of London. By permission of the Earl of Dartmouth.

5 Satan. From Folger Shakespeare Library MS V.b.26, p. 172. By permission of the Folger Shakespeare Library.

6 'Tilting table', 1571. From Oxford, Bodleian Library. MS Ashmole 845, f. 164. By permission of the Bodleian Library.

List of Abbreviations

Place of publication is London unless otherwise noted.

APC (PRO) *Acts of the Privy Council*, ed. John Roche Dasent, 32 vols (1890–1964)

Arber Edward Arber (ed.), *A Transcript of the Registers of the Company of Stationers of London; 1554–1640 A.D.*, 5 vols (1875–94)

BLD *Black's Law Dictionary*, 4th edn (St Paul, MN 1961)

CBP [Calendar of Border Papers:] General Register Office (Scotland), *Calendar of Letters and Papers Relating to the Affairs of the Borders of England and Scotland*, 2 vols (1894–96)

Chamberlain, *Letters* *The Letters of John Chamberlain*, ed. Norman Egbert McClure, 2 vols (Philadelphia, 1939)

Colvin H. M. Colvin (ed.), *A History of the King's Works*, 4 vols in 2 parts (London: HMSO, 1982)

Commons *The House of Commons, 1558–1603*, ed. P. W. Hasler, 3 vols (1981)

Cooper Charles Henry Cooper and Thompson Cooper, 2 vols, *Athenae Cantabrigienses* (Cambridge, 1858–1913)

Correspondance *Correspondance Diplomatique de Bertrand de Salignac, de la Mothe Fénélon, Ambassadeur de France en Angleterre de 1568 à 1575*, 7 vols (Paris and London, 1838–40)

CP [Cecil Papers:] *A Calendar of the Manuscripts of the most Honourable the Marquis of Salisbury ... at Hatfield House*, 24 vols, HMC (1883–1976)

CPR (PRO) *Calendar of the Patent Rolls [1547–82]*, 19 vols (1924–86), continued as *(Draft) Calendar of Patent Rolls*, List and Index Society (Kew, 1990–), vols 241 (1584–85), 242–43 (1585–87), 247 (1587–88), 255 (1588–89), 272 (1591–92), 282 (1592–93), 286 (1582–83), 287 (1583–84), etc.

CSP (PRO) *Calendar of State Papers*

    Carew Calendar of the Carew Manuscripts, Preserved in the Archiepiscopal Library at Lambeth [1515–1623], 6 vols (1867–73)

    Colonial *CSP Colonial Series [1509–1739]*, 45 vols (1860–1994)

    Foreign *CSP Foreign Series [1547–89]*, 24 vols (1861–1969)

    Ireland *CSP Relating to Ireland [1171–1670]*, 13 vols (1860–1912)

    Rome *CSP Relating to English Affairs, Preserved Principally at Rome in the Vatican Archives and Library [1558–78]*, 2 vols (1916–26)

    Scotland *CSP Relating to Scotland and Mary Queen of Scots [1547–1603]*, 13 vols (Edinburgh, 1898–1952)

Spanish   *Calendar of Letters, Despatches, and State Papers Relating to the Negotiations between England and Spain Preserved in the Archives at Simancas and Elsewhere [1554–1603]*, 6 vols (1862–90)

Venice   *CSP and Manuscripts, Relating to English Affairs Existing in the Archives and Collection of Venice [1202–1675]*, 38 vols (1864–1923)

CSPD (PRO)   *Calendar of State Papers, Domestic*

LPH8   *Letters and Papers, Foreign and Domestic, of the Reign of Henry VIII*, 21 vols (1862–1910)

1547–1625   *CSPD Series, of the Reigns of Edward VI, Mary, Elizabeth[, and James]*, 12 vols (including addenda) (1856–72)

Edward VI   *CSPD Series of the Reign of Edward VI, 1547–1553*, rev. edn C. S. Knighton (1992)

Mary I   *CSPD Series of the Reign of Mary I, 1553–1558*, rev. edn C. S. Knighton (1998)

CUA   Cambridge University Archives

CUL   Cambridge University Library

Diary (Burghley)   see Murdin (below)

DCAD (PRO)   *A Descriptive Catalogue of Ancient Deeds in the Public Record Office* (1890–1915)

DCPR (PRO)   Draft Calendar of Patent Rolls: see *CPR*

DNB   *Dictionary of National Biography*, ed. Leslie Stephen and Sidney Lee, 21 vols (1921–22)

EB   *Encyclopaedia Britannica*, 11th edn, 28 vols (1910–11)

Ekwall   Ekwall, Eilert, *The Concise Oxford Dictionary of Place-Names* (Oxford, 1947)

Emden   Emden, A. B., *A Biographical Register of the University of Cambridge to 1500* (Cambridge, 1963)

ERO   Essex Record Office (Chelmsford unless noted otherwise)

Foster, *Alumni Oxonienses*   Foster, Joseph (ed.), *Alumni Oxonienses. The Members of the University of Oxford, 1715–1886*, 4 vols (Oxford and London, 1888)

Fowler   William Plumer Fowler (ed.), *Shakespeare Revealed in Oxford's Letters: The Pre-Armada Letters, 1563–1585, and The Post-Armada Letters, 1590–1603, of Edward de Vere, Seventeenth Earl of Oxford* (Portsmouth, NH: Peter E. Randall, 1986)

G-BL   BL MS Add. 36,768 ('Order of the Garter' manuscript)

GLE   *Grand Larousse Encyclopedique*, 10 vols (Paris, 1960–64)

Golding (L.T.)   Louis Thorn Golding, *An Elizabethan Puritan* (Freeport, NY, 1937; rpt. 1971)

HBC   *Handbook of British Chronology*, ed. E. B. Fryde, 3rd edn (Cambridge, 1996)

HMC   Historical Manuscripts Commission

HMC Hastings   *Report on the Manuscripts of the late Reginald Rawdon Hastings, Esq.*, 2 vols (1928–30)

Inquisitiones (PRO)   *Inquisitiones post mortem of the Tudor Period for the City of London*, pt. ii, British Record Society, xxvi (1901)

Journals   *Calendar of the Journals of the House of Lords: from the Beginning of the Reign of King Henry VIII ...*, 2 vols (1810–26)

Kingsford   John Stow, *A Survey of London*, reprinted from the text of 1603, intro. and notes by Charles L. Kingsford, 2 vols (Oxford: Clarendon Press, 1908)

LIB   Libels: see Editorial Procedures and pp. 489–91

LL   Oxford's Letters: see Editorial Procedures and pp. 487–89

LMA   London Metropolitan Archive (Clerkenwell, London)

Machyn   Henry Machyn, *The Diary of Henry Machyn, Citizen and Merchant-Taylor of London [1550–63]*, Camden Society, 42 (1847)

Miller   J. Thomas Looney, *Shakespeare Identified in Edward De Vere, Seventeenth Earl of Oxford* [1st edn 1920], 3rd edn, ed. Ruth Loyd Miller, with *The Poems of Edward De Vere* [and other essays], 3 vols (Port Washington, NY, 1975)

Morant   Philip Morant, *The History and Antiquities of the County of Essex*, introd. by G. H. Martin (1748; rpt. East Ardsley, England: EP Publishers, 1978)

MSC   Malone Society Collections, 15 vols to date (1908–93), Oxford

Murdin   Murdin, William, *Collection of State Papers ... left by William Cecill lord Burghley*, 2 vols (1740–59)

New Grove   Stanley Sadie (ed.), *New Grove Dictionary of Music and Musicians*, 20 vols (1981)

Nicolas   Nicholas Harris Nicolas, *Memoirs of the Life and Times of Sir Christopher Hatton* (1847)

Nicholl   Charles Nicholl, *The Reckoning: The Murder of Christopher Marlowe* (1992)

Nichols   John Nichols, *The Progresses and Public Processions of Queen Elizabeth*, 3 vols (1823)

Nichols, *James*   John Nichols, *The Progresses, Processions, and Magnificent Festivities, of King James the First*, 4 vols (1828)

Nungezer   Edward Nungezer, *A Dictionary of Actors and of Other Persons Associated with the Public Representation of Plays in England before 1642*, Cornell Studies in English, 13 (New Haven, 1929)

OCEL   Oxford Companion to English Literature, 5th edn, ed. Margaret Drabble (Oxford, 1985)

OED   Oxford English Dictionary, 2nd edn, 20 vols (Oxford, 1989)

OLD   Oxford Latin Dictionary, ed. P.G.W. Glare (Oxford, 1982)

Ogburn   Ogburn, Charlton (the younger), *The Mysterious William Shakespeare: The Myth and the Reality* (New York, 1984)

Pearson   Daphne Pearson, 'Estates and Lawsuits of Edward de Vere' (Sheffield University PhD dissertation, 2000)

Peerage   G. E. Cokayne et al., *The Complete Peerage of England, Scotland, Ireland, Great Britain, and the United Kingdom*, 12 vols (1910–59)

PRO   Public Record Office, Kew

RCHM, *Essex*   Royal Commission on Historical Monuments, *An Inventory of the Historical Monuments in Essex*, 4 vols (1916–23)

REED   Records of Early English Drama (Toronto: University of Toronto Press). Collections to date: *Bristol*, ed. Mark C. Pilkinton (1997); *Cambridge*, ed. Alan H. Nelson (1989); *Chester*, ed. Lawrence M. Clopper (1979); *Coventry*, ed. R. W. Ingram (1981); *Cumberland, Westmorland, Gloucestershire*, ed. Audrey Douglas and Peter Greenfield (1986); *Devon*, ed. John M. Wasson (1986); *Dorset and Cornwall*, ed. Rosalind C. Hays and C.E. McGee, and Sally L. Joyce and Evelyn S. Newlyn (1999); *Herefordshire, Worcestershire*, ed. David N. Klausner (1990); *Kent: Diocese of Canterbury*, ed. James M. Gibson (2002); *Lancashire*, ed. David George (1991); *Newcastle upon Tyne*, ed. J.J. Anderson (1982); *Norwich, 1540–1642*, ed. David Galloway (1984); *Shropshire*, ed. J. Alan B. Somerset (1994); *Somerset [including Bath]*, ed. James Stokes and Robert J. Alexander (1996); *Sussex*, ed. Cameron Louis (2000); and *York*, ed. Alexandra F. Johnston and Margaret Rogerson (1979)

SRP   James F. Larkin and Paul L. Hughes (eds), *Stuart Royal Proclamations*, 2 vols (Oxford: Clarendon Press, 1973–83)

Star   Ogburn, Dorothy and Charlton, *This Star of England: "William Shake-speare", Man of the Renaissance* (New York, 1952)

STC   *A Short-Title Catalogue of Books Printed in England, Scotland, and Ireland ... 1475–1640*, comp. A. W. Pollard and G. R. Redgrave; 2nd edn Katharine F. Pantzer, 3 vols (1976–91)

Stiffkey   A. Hassall Smith (ed.), *The Papers of Nathaniel Bacon of Stiffkey*, vol. 1, 1566–77, Norfolk Record Society 46 (Norwich, 1979)

Stone   Stone, Lawrence, *The Crisis of the Aristocracy, 1558–1641* (Oxford, 1965)

Strype   Strype, John, *Annals of the Reformation and establishment of religion, and other various occurrences in the Church of England, during Queen Elizabeth's happy reign* (1709; rpt. New York, B. Franklin [1966])

SWM   Steven W. May: (ed.), *The Poems of Edward DeVere, Seventeenth Earl of Oxford, and of Robert Devereux, Second Earl of Essex, Studies in Philology*, 77, part 5 (1980)

TE   Kinney, Arthur, *Titled Elizabethans: A Directory of Elizabethan State and Church Officers and Knights, with Peers of England, Scotland, and Ireland, 1558–1603* (Hamden, CT, 1973).

TRP   Paul L. Hughes and James F. Larkin (eds), *Tudor Royal Proclamations*, 3 vols (New Haven, 1964–69)

VCH, *Essex*   *The Victoria History of the County of Essex*, 10 vols to date (Westminster, 1903–66)

Venn   John Venn and J. A. Venn, *Alumnae Cantabrigienses; A Biographical List of all known Students, Graduates and Holders of Office at the University of Cambridge*, 4 vols (1922–26)

Venn, *Register*   *The Annals of Gonville and Caius College, by John Caius*, ed. John Venn (Cambridge, 1904)

Visitations of Essex   *The Visitations of Essex*, ed. Walter C. Metcalfe, Publications of the Harleian Society, 13–14 (1878–79)

Walsingham, *Diary*   *Journal of Sir Francis Walsingham, from Dec. 1570 to April 1583*, ed. Charles T. Martin, Camden Society Miscellany, vol. 6, no. 104 (1870)

Ward   Bernard M. Ward, *The Seventeenth Earl of Oxford, 1550–1604, From Contemporary Documents* (1928)

WCA   Westminster City Archives

WKCRO   West Kent County Record Office (Maidstone)

Williams   Williams, Franklin W., Jr, *Index of Dedications and Commendatory Verses in English Books before 1641* (1962)

Wing   *Short-Title Catalogue of Books Printed in England, Scotland, Ireland, Wales, ... 1641–1700*, comp. Donald Wing, 2nd edn, 3 vols (New York: Index Society, 1972–88)

Wood, *Athenae*   Anthony Wood, *Athenae Oxonienses: An Exact History of all the Writers and Bishops who have had their Education in the University of Oxford: to which are added the Fasti, or Annals of the said University*, ed. Philip Bliss (1813–20)

Acknowledgements

I first became involved in the 'authorship controversy', and thus with the 17th Earl of Oxford, in 1993, during a San Francisco 'Humanities West' conference on 'Shakespeare in London'. There I was challenged by Oxfordians who questioned whether I was not a 'typical academic with a closed mind' who would not deign to read what they wrote. In self-defence I promised to read everything they would send my way. Since then I have rarely been embarrassed by an empty mailbox – domestic, departmental, or electronic.

Over the past decade I have had the pleasure of examining numerous documents, and making or renewing numerous friendships. I am indebted for countless suggestions and favours to David Kathman, Steven W. May, and above all to Daphne Pearson. I owe thanks for more particular assistance to Jonathan Bate, Nicholas Davidson, A. J. Davies, Elizabeth A. Freidberg, Donna Hamilton, Paul Hammer, Simon Healey, Arthur Kinney, Jane Lawson, Irvin Matus, Thomas McCoog, SJ, Michael Questier, Marvin Rosenberg, Terry Ross, Conrad Russell, David Harris Sacks, Jason Scott-Warren, Dana Sutton, William J. Tighe, and James Turner.

Among new acquaintances who (I think) will gladly accept the epithet 'Oxfordians' I owe most to Nina Green, though we have never met except through e-mail: she has put me on to so many documents that I have lost count, and asked (and still asks) questions which test both my memory and my complacency. Others who contributed to this project directly or indirectly include Katherine Chiljan, Francis Edwards, SJ, Gary Goldstein, Ron Hess, Stephanie Hughes, Peter Moore, Richard Roe, Wayne Shore, Joseph Sobran, Richard Whalen, and Professor Daniel Wright. Mark Sacharoff kindly provided me with publications by A. Bronson Feldman through the latter's son Owen. Friends entranced by the 'authorship controversy' who would probably resist carrying a label include Alison Beaton, Carol Sue Lipman, and Virginia Renner.

Editors from the Records of Early English Drama (REED) series who entertained questions about Oxford's players and musicians include Robert Alexander, Anne Brannen, Jane Cowling, Audrey Douglas, John R. Elliott, Jr, Mary Erler, James M. Gibson, Peter Greenfield, Alexandra F. Johnston, Rosalind Hays, Anne Lancashire, Cameron Louis, Sally-Beth MacLean, Edward McGee, John McKinnell, Evelyn S. Newlyn, Barbara Palmer and John Watson, Mark C. Pilkington, J. A. B. Somerset, and James Stokes.

I am grateful to the administration and staff of the Bodleian Library, Oxford, the British Library, the College of Arms, the Cambridge University Library, the Essex Record Office (Chelmsford and Colchester), the Family History Centre, the Folger Shakespeare Library, Hatfield House, the Huntington Library, the Institute of Historical Research, Senate House, London, the Lambeth Palace Library, the London Metropolitan Archive, and the Public Record Office (Chancery Lane and Kew). Among members of staff I have incurred a special obligation to Robin Harcourt-Williams (Hatfield House), Colin Johnston (Bath Record Office), Elisabeth Leedham-Green (Cambridge University Archives), Malcolm Underwood (St John's College, Cambridge, Archives), Laetitia Yeandle (Folger Shakespeare Library), and Robert Yorke (College of Arms).

Libraries and institutions which have supplied photographs are acknowledged in the List of Illustrations (pp. ix–x). For permission to publish transcriptions I am grateful to the following: Bath Record Office; Bibliothèque Nationale, Paris; Bodleian Library, University of Oxford; The British Library; Cambridge University Archives; Syndics of Cambridge University Library; Canterbury Cathedral Archives (Dean and Chapter); College of Arms; Essex Record Office (ERO); Folger Shakespeare Library; Hertfordshire Record Office (Hertford); London Guildhall Library; Hackney Archives Department (HAD); Hatfield House (Lord Salisbury); Huntington Library, San Marino, California; Kingston Borough Archives; Trustees of the Lambeth Palace Library; London Metropolitan Archives (LMA); Public Record Office (PRO); The President and Fellows of Queens' College, Cambridge; The Masters, Fellows, and Scholars of St John's College, Cambridge; Archivio di Stato, Venice; West Kent County Record Office (WKCRO); and the City of Westminster (Archives).

Initial work on this biography was undertaken during the course of a long-term Fellowship at the Folger Shakespeare Library, 1994–95, awarded for an altogether different project. I am grateful to both the Folger and to the National Endowment for the Humanities, which funded the Fellowship. I am grateful to the University of California, Berkeley, for sabbatical leave (further subsidized by a Humanities Research Fellowship), and for assistance, through Enabling Grants, from the Academic Senate Committee on Research, toward the acquisition of photocopies and microfilms, and of the photographs and maps which appear in this book.

My more than usually faulty memory will doubtless have caused me to forget obligations to individuals and institutions – for any such oversight I apologize in advance of having it called to my attention. Faults of omission, commission, and illogic are entirely my own. Finally, I am happy to make a public declaration of gratitude to my wife, Judith, whose patience both I and the 'authorship controversy' have sorely tried.

Editorial Procedures

The documents that lie at the heart of this biography are, with few exceptions, freshly transcribed from original sources. To preserve the flavour of the originals I retain original spellings (in which u is essentially interchangeable with v, i with j and y) and something of the original format. I print the archaic 'thorn' (þ or y) as th, and long-s as s. I silently expand abbreviations; incorporate scribal corrections, additions, and interlineations; suppress cancellations; restore missing text; and insert letters, words, and comments, as needed for clarity, within square brackets. Dates are normalized to a calendar year beginning 1 January (rather than 25 March).

More pedantically accurate transcriptions of many of the same documents are posted on my website: http://socrates.berkeley.edu/~ahnelson/. I will add more documents as I complete full transcriptions: but as websites are not forever, I will deposit printouts and other items in the Edward de Vere Collection at Concordia University, Portland, Oregon; and the Massachusetts Center for Renaissance Studies at the University of Massachusetts, Amherst.

For items in the *Calendar of State Papers* I have recorded both the 'article' and the folio number:

> *CSPD*, 1581–90, p. 395 (PRO SP12/199[/38], f. 71)

The document, noted and partly described in the *Calendar of State Papers*, volume 1581–90, page 395, survives in the Public Record Office, Kew. SP12/199 is a typical guard-book into which documents – often letters – have been bound. This is the thirty-eighth document, and the citation is from leaf 71 (as marked by a mechanical stamping-machine). The reader may consult *CSPD*, 1581–90 in almost any major library, or SP12/199 on microfilm at the PRO, and in specialist libraries elsewhere.

I will maintain a webpage for corrections of factual errors, along with announcements of newly discovered or overlooked documents. An example of the latter was brought to my attention by Nina Green too late for inclusion in this volume:

> By a Deed of Covenant [PRO C.54/626, No.45], the 16th Earl conveyed some of his lands (there was a statutory limit of two-thirds) in trust, to various members of his family, but temporarily away from his principal heir [i.e. Oxford: NG]. The trustees were the Duke of Norfolk and lord Robert Dudley – later Earl of Leicester.

Similarly, I hope to announce the whereabouts, and to post transcriptions, of three 'grammar-school' documents in Oxford's hand, noted in Chapter 66: these are currently accessible to me only in a published photograph, and nineteenth-century transcripts in the Essex Record Office, Chelmsford.

.

Introduction

The life of Edward de Vere (1550–1604) was almost exactly contemporaneous with the latter half of the sixteenth century, and just overlapped the reign of Elizabeth I at both ends. As 17th Earl of Oxford he was among England's premier noblemen – very few approached being the seventeenth of anything. But he held no office of consequence, nor performed a notable deed. He served, it is true, as Lord Great (or High) Chamberlain, but that office was purely ceremonial, and quite distinct from that of Lord Chamberlain.[1]

Oxford neglected to serve others for the simple reason that his first aim in life was to serve himself. Of his estates he wrote to his father-in-law, the famous Lord Burghley:[2]

> I haue no help but of myne owne, and mine is made to serue me, and myself not mine.

That is to say: I have no resource but my own properties; they are meant to serve me, I am not meant to serve them.

Feudal rank was theoretically based on the very opposite principle: that noblemen held property first by royal grant and then by inheritance precisely in exchange for service. Movers and shakers of the Elizabethan age embraced this principle with zeal. Some, like Sir Francis Walsingham, happily bankrupted themselves in the effort. Others, including Lord Burghley and Sir Christopher Hatton, accumulated apparent wealth, but gave such bountiful service that by any reasonable measure they were under-compensated for their pains.

Though lack of service would make Oxford virtually irrelevant to historians of the Elizabethan reign, he remains an object of curiosity for cultural and literary historians. He was a leader of fashion, a court poet of modest ability, and a patron of writers and performers. Additionally, he lived a life so privately scandalous and so richly documented that his biography opens a window onto secret passages of Elizabethan life and manners. Oxford has also been touted, for the past eighty years, as the author of the poems and plays of William Shakespeare. It has become a matter of urgency to measure the real Oxford against the myth created by partisan apologists, and all too often embraced without critical rigour by the popular press – even by justices of the United States Supreme Court.

Oxford's character has been estimated differently by different observers. Contemporary praise came mostly from would-be protégés such as Gabriel Harvey (1578):

> Your British numbers have been widely sung, while your Epistle testifies how much you excel in letters, being more courtly than Castiglione himself, more polished. I have seen your many Latin things, and more English are extant; of French and Italian muses, the manners of many peoples, their arts and laws you have drunk deeply.

The poet and adventurer Thomas Churchyard described Oxford as 'a noble man off sutch worth, as I wyll employe all I haue to honor hys worthynes'. But Gilbert Talbot entertained his father, the Earl of Shrewsbury, with a more back-handed compliment: 'My Lord of Oxforth is lately growne into great credite ... if it were not for his fyckle hed he would passe any of them shortly'. The same Gabriel Harvey who complimented Oxford in public called him in private 'a passing singular odd man'. Henry Howard, the future Earl of Northampton, railed against Oxford as having 'ane addell heade and a railing tounge'; while the unbridled Charles Arundel called him 'my Monsterus adversarye ... who wold drinke my blud rather then wine as well as he loves it'. In 1595 John Carey (a future Lord Hunsdon) congratulated Burghley on the wedding of Oxford's daughter Elizabeth, adding: 'thimperfections of her father shall be no blemishe to her honour'.

Opinion following Oxford's death was similarly divided. Sir George Buc, who had interviewed Oxford on at least one occasion, wrote (with the inevitable pun on 'Vere' and Latin *veritas*, meaning 'truth'),[3]

> ... certainly the earl was a devout and a magnificent and a very learned and religious nobleman, and so worthy in every way, as I have heard some grave and discreet and honourable persons (who knew this earl from his youth and could very well judge of the hopefulness and the springtimes of young men) say and affirm that he was much more like to raise and to acquire and to establish a new earldom than to decay and waste and lose an old earldom. And in a word, he was a Vere in deed as in name, *vere nobilis*. For he was verily and truly noble and a most noble Vere.

Oxford's kinsman Percivall Golding said of him,

> ... I will only speak what all men's voices confirm; he was a man in mind and body absolutely accomplished with honourable endowments

Most seventeenth-century commentators, by contrast, treated Oxford with open contempt. Sir Robert Naunton (1563–1635) characterized him as driven by 'emulation', or envy:

> ... and for my Lord of Oxford's jest of [Sir Walter Ralegh] ... we all know it savoured more of emulation ... than of truth.

Fulke Greville described Oxford's speech during a famous quarrel with Sir Philip

Sidney as being 'like an Echo, that still multiplies by reflexions'. Most amusingly disrespectful of all is John Aubrey, the anecdotalist (p. 305):

> The Earle of Oxford, making of his low obeisance to Queen Elizabeth, happened to let a Fart, at which he was so abashed and ashamed that he went to Travell, 7 yeares. On his returne the Queen welcomed him home, and sayd, My Lord, I had forgott the Fart.

That the story is almost certainly apocryphal does not diminish the contempt.

Of all posthumous accounts of Oxford, none had a greater impact on modern historians – combining praise and blame in approximately equal measure – than Sir William Dugdale's *Baronage of England* (1675–76). Dugdale carries his account of the de Vere family over from John de Vere, the 16th Earl (i, pp. 199–200):

> To whom succeeded Edward his son and Heir; who in 29 Eliz. was one of the Peers by special Commission appointed to try Mary Queen of Scots (then Prisoner in England,) for her life. And in Anno 1588. (31 Eliz.) one of the chief persons in the Queens Fleet, imployed against the great Navy of Spaniards, then threatning an Invasion; which thereupon was dissipated, and destroyed by the English Forces. ...

> This Edward, being an intire friend to Thomas Duke of Norfolk; when he discerned [Norfolk's] Life in danger, upon what was laid to his charge; touching the Q. of Scots (whereof our Historians of that time do give some account) earnestly interceded with the Lord Treasurer Burghley (his Wives Father and one of the chiefest States-men of that time) for the preserving him from destruction; but prevailing not, grew so highly incensed against Burghley, knowing it was in his power to save him; that, in great indignation, he said, he would do all he could to ruin his Daughter: and accordingly, not only forsook her Bed, but sold and consumed that great Inheritance, descended to him from his Ancestors; leaving very little for Henry his Son and Successor. ...

Dugdale's account survives essentially intact in Sidney Lee's entry in the *Dictionary of National Biography*.

In 1920 the amateur literary historian J. Thomas Looney (pronounced 'Loanee') transformed the popular image of Oxford in his *Shakespeare Identified in Edward De Vere, Seventeenth Earl of Oxford*, now in its third edition. Eight years later, in 1928, appeared the only documentary biography of Oxford until the present, Bernard M. Ward's *The Seventeenth Earl of Oxford, 1550–1604, From Contemporary Documents*. Ward embraced Looney's hypothesis that Oxford was Shakespeare, but confined overt speculation to interstitial chapters which he called interludes. According to his own account (pp. ix–x), Ward spent five years hunting down documents illustrating Oxford's life, primarily in the British Library, the Public Record Office, and among the Cecil Papers at Hatfield House. Even critics of the 'Oxfordian' hypothesis – that Oxford was Shakespeare – consider Ward a worthy (if partisan) historian, and frequently cite him as an authority. I share their respect.

Ward has his faults, however, which may be gathered under four heads: too great an adulation for his subject; a Victorian sensibility concerning sex (especially homosexuality); inadequate respect for primary documents; and inadequate foot-noting.

Ward is inclined to assume rather than prove Oxford's identity as Shakespeare, insisting on Oxford's (relative) worthiness regardless of circumstance. When Oxford turned state's evidence against his erstwhile friends in December 1580, Ward celebrates his patriotism, but does not question his betrayal of friends.[4]

Ward was no more than a man of his time in his reserved attitude towards homosexuality. Where anyone who casts half an eye over the libel manuscripts in the PRO will encounter the words 'sodomy' and 'buggery', Ward retreats into circumlocution, for example, '"notable dishonesty of life" of a criminal nature' (p. 212). In this he follows the PRO *Calendar*, where the same actions are para-phrased as 'unnatural offences', 'unnatural propensities', and 'unnatural crimes'.[5] Solid information is thus suppressed in the interest of good form, and also, in Ward's case, to protect Oxford's reputation.

Ward not only dismisses primary evidence, but tends to modernize spelling, replace original punctuation with his own, substitute his own words to make an original more comprehensible to the modern reader, and overlook authorial cor-rections and emendations. He rarely reveals that the text in an original document is damaged, and fails to acknowledge original readings which are for one reason or another obscure and hence of uncertain meaning. Though Ward may have been capable of reading difficult hands, whether personally or through an amanu-ensis, serious doubts must arise from his failure to have noticed (or at least recorded in print) that two sheets among the 'libel documents' are in Oxford's own hand and idiosyncratic spelling.[6]

Finally, while Ward usually acknowledges his sources, he occasionally presents an argument or cites a document without providing a necessary footnote.

While Ward put the most positive possible spin on every aspect of Oxford's career, orthodox historians who cite him tend to remain unpersuaded. Among the many who have protested against the use of rose-coloured glasses and the misinterpretation or misapplication of evidence, Conyers Read, the magisterial biographer of Sir Francis Walsingham and Lord Burghley, put it best in his criticism of a particularly egregious argument by Oxfordian idolators: 'Their idea of what constitutes valid historical evidence is widely at variance with my own'.[7] Other historians ignore Oxford altogether, or dismiss him as 'the detestable Earl of Oxford'.[8] Meanwhile, members of the literary establishment are inclined to dismiss both Oxford and Oxfordians as thorns in their flesh.

The biographer who is not persuaded that Oxford wrote the works of Shakes-peare must nevertheless pay tribute to those who are, for it is often his amateur admirers who have discovered new evidence about the man and his milieu.

Though Looney discovered little more than was known to Sidney Lee, Ward put a great deal of flesh on the bones. But Ward missed Oxford's capture by pirates in 1576; his fathering of an illegitimate son, born in 1581; and his preoccupation from 1595 to 1599 with the mining of tin. (Ward thought that Oxford had by then retired from public life.) Though E. K. Chambers in *Sir Henry Lee* (1936) was the first to report Oxford's affair with Anne Vavasor, the Oxfordian Charles Wisner Barroll published supplementary details in 1941 and 1942. Also worthy of mention is the amateur historian Gwynneth Bowen, one of many contributors to partisan publications bearing such names as *Shakespeare Fellowship Newsletter, Shakespeare Authorship Review*, or *The Shakespeare Oxford Society Newsletter*. I dismiss from serious consideration *This Star of England* (1952) by Dorothy Ogburn and Charlton Ogburn the elder, and *The Mysterious William Shakespeare* (1975) by Charlton Ogburn the younger, neither of which contains anything substantial in the way of original documentary research.

My main purpose is to introduce documents from Oxford's life, many of them written in Oxford's own hand. Since documents alone do not make a biography, however, I have felt duty-bound to point out their significance for an accurate estimation of Oxford's character. If I judge Oxford harshly from the outset, it is because I neither can nor wish to suppress what I have learned along the way. True believers will of course spin Oxford's reprehensible acts into benevolent gestures, or will transfer blame from Oxford to Burghley, Leicester, Queen Elizabeth, or even to Oxford's much-abused wife Anne. I beg the open-minded reader to join me in holding the mature Oxford responsible for his own life, letting the documentary evidence speak for itself.

Edward de Vere was born on 12 April 1550. To understand him we must first try to understand the provincial world into which he was born, and the woman who bore and the man who begat him.

PART I

Roots
1548–1562

1 Oxford's Essex

On 12 April 1550 a son was born to John de Vere, 16th Earl of Oxford, probably at Castle Hedingham in rural Essex.[1] Noting the time of birth, the Earl consulted his astrologers (Fig. 1). The news was dire:[2]

> The mathematicians that calculated the nativity of this Earl Edward told the Earl his father that the earldom would fall in the son's time.

The earldom did in fact shrink almost to nothing during the life of the child now born.

The lands that supported the Oxford earldom lay not in Oxfordshire, but in Essex, just east of London and its adjoining county of Middlesex. Losses by 1594, ten years before Edward's own death, may be appreciated from John Norden's 'Historical and Chorographical Description of the County of Essex'.[3] Norden begins with a general description:

> This shire is moste fatt, frutefull, and full of profitable thinges, exceeding (as farr as I can finde) anie other shire for the generall commodities, and the plentie. Thowgh Suffolke be more highlie comended of some[,] wherwith I am not yet acquaynted: But this shire seemeth to me to deserue the title of the englishe Goshen[,] the fattest of the Lande: comparable to Palestina, that flowed with milke and hunnye. But I can not commende the healthfulnes of it: And especiallie nere the sea coastes, Rochford, Dengre, Tendering hundredes and other lowe places about the creekes, which gaue me a most cruell quarterne feuer. But the manie and sweete commodities counteruayle the daunger. ... (p. 7)

The principal Oxford estates lay in the north-east quadrant of the shire:

> ... aboute the hundredes of Waltham, Onger, Becontre, and muche of the libertie of Hauering, are for the moste parte woodes and woodie groundes, and foreste, as the moste part of Essex in time paste hath bene. This forest is well replenished with deere red and fallow, whoe seeme noe good neighbors to the foreste inhabitantes: but the kindnes which they receyue of the forest, may worke their patience towardes the game. Ther is also nere Hatfeylde Broadokes a chace called Hatfeylde Chace[,] a grounde well replenished with fallow deare. This shire seemeth not anie

> wher altogether destitute of wood, thowgh no wher well stored. / It is full of parkes.
> ... (p. 9)

The sea-coasts to the east and south were noted for their ease of navigation:

> The seacoaste is here and ther furnished with harbours for shipping, wherof the
> principall is Harwiche, which is a towne fitlie seytuate [=situate(d)] for seafaring
> men. Small boates come up as farr as Colchester, and up to Maldon. ... (p. 10)

> There are within this shire manie riuers of name, amonge which theis are
> principall, as Colne that watereth all the Colnes, and so passing to Colnechester, it
> thence hasteth to the ocean. ... (p. 11)

The principal Oxford properties lay along the River Colne, which, rising east of
Ridgwell, flows south-east through or near Great Yeldham, Castle Hedingham
(left bank), Sible Hedingham, Halstead, Colne Endgaine (left bank), Earls Colne
(right bank), White Colne (left bank), Wakes Colne, Colchester (tidal), Wivenhoe (left bank), and thence to the sea (Map 1).

Norden names some dozen Essex properties lost to the earldom by 1594:

> Stansted Mountfichet ... This mannor came ... by the youngest dowghter of
> Richarde Mountfichet, to Hugh de Plaiz, by mariage of whome came Elizabeth
> Countess of Oxon, who was dowghter to Sir John Haward, Knighte, by whom the
> lande cam to therles of Oxforde. (p. 25)

> Wyuenhoo ... somtyme a stately seate of the Earls of Oxforde. (p. 28)

> Berwyke Hall ... Somtyme Earl of Oxfordes, now Jerome Weston's, Esq. (p. 29)

> Crippinge Hall ... somtyme Earl of Oxfordes, now the heyre of Christian Turnor.
> (p. 31)

> Henningham [=Hedingham] Castle.[4] A uerye stately howse, mounted on a hill,
> havinge 3 parkes. sometyme Earl of Oxfords now Lord Burghleys, Lord high
> Treasoror of England. (p. 37)

> Stansted Mountfichet hall. Sometyme Earl of Oxfords now Edward Hubberds.

> Tilbery hall. Israell Amyas. [Sometime Earl of Oxford's]

> Wakes hall. William Tyffyn, apprentice at the common law; sometyme Earl of
> Oxfords (p. 38)

> Wyuenhoo hall, decayde. A stately howse; sometyme Earl of Oxfords (p. 39)

> ... Dodinghurste. sometime therle of Oxfords now [Richard] Stoneley. (p. 40)

Castle Hedingham remains among the most magnificent and best-preserved
Norman keeps in Europe, its attendant village among the most charming in
England.[5] Rising five storeys from its base, its corner turrets making a sixth
storey, with walls 12 feet thick at the base and 10 feet thick at the top, the castle
proclaims itself in all directions. Despite its Great Hall with a fine fireplace and a

ceiling supported by the widest Norman arch in existence at 26 feet, the castle
must always have been short on human comforts.

Domesticity reigned at Earls Colne, where a priory established by Godfrey de
Vere, son of the 1st Earl, was appropriated by the 15th, under Henry VIII;[6] and at
Wivenhoe, brought to the earldom by Joan, daughter of John Walton, who
married the 12th Earl in 1425. Here a gatehouse served as a landmark for its
'lading place' which, relatively impervious to silt, could accommodate ships of
sea-going draught.[7]

The Oxford estates were described by the antiquary John Leland in 1540:[8]

> Mr. Sheffeld told me that afore the old Erle of Oxford tyme, that cam yn with King
> Henry the vii. [i.e., the 13th Earl], the Castelle of Hengham was yn much ruine, so
> that al the building that now ys there was yn a maner of this old Erles building,
> except the gate-house and the great dungeon toure.

> Mr. Sheffelde told me that a litle beside Colne Priorie yn Estsax [=Essex], wher the
> Erle[s] of Oxford usid to be buried, was a manor place of theirs, the dikes and the
> plotte wherof yet remayne, and berith the name of the Haulle Place.

> Syns the ruine of this manor place the Erles hath buildid hard by the priory.

So the 13th Earl had refurbished the castle and the great houses, which in 1550
stood proud and in good repair.

2 Progenitors

Edward de Vere's mother, Margery, Countess of Oxford, was the daughter of Sir
John Golding, of the tiny rural village of Belchamp (pronounced 'Beecham') St
Paul's, Essex.[1] Sir John's wife, Elizabeth, was the daughter and co-heir of Thomas
Tonge of West Malling, and the widow of Reginald Hammond. Elizabeth bore
Sir John two sons and two daughters: Thomas, William, Margery, and Elizabeth.
Dying on 27 November 1527, she was soon replaced by Ursula Marston, daughter
and co-heir of William Marston of Horton, Surrey. Ursula bore Sir John four
sons and three daughters: Henry, Arthur, George, Edmond, Mary, Dorothy, and
Frances. Thus Golding aunts and uncles would lie thick on the land.

At the time of her marriage in 1548, Margery Golding was twenty-two at the
least. Sir John's death the previous year released her from the oversight of both
biological parents.[2] Margery must have been very beautiful, very sexy, or both, for
– as we will soon discover – the 16th Earl married her under circumstances that
imply reckless passion.

Sir John Golding's heir maintained family dignity by securing a knighthood,
like his father before him. Sir Thomas would serve as sheriff of both Essex and

Hertfordshire in 1563, and of Essex alone in 1569. He and his uterine siblings retained roots in Essex and East Anglia, sustaining or improving their lot by marriage. Margery's half-brother Arthur, born in 1536, would achieve lasting fame as an Elizabethan man of letters, his professed Puritanism well disguised in his sensuous translation of Ovid's *Metamorphoses*.

Edward's paternal grandmother was Elizabeth née Trussell,[3] daughter of Edward Trussell of Cublesdon, Staffordshire, and Margaret Don (or Done), of the family that would later produce the poet John Donne. Through Margaret, a grand-daughter of Leonard Hastings and Alice Camoys, Edward de Vere was connected to the blood royal, for Alice was the daughter of Elizabeth Mortimer, who was the daughter of Edmund Mortimer, Earl of March, who was the son of Edward III. Thus Edward III was Edward de Vere's father's mother's mother's mother's father's father, or (more simply) his great-great-great-great-great-grandfather. Nevertheless, contention for the English throne lay with the earls of Hertford, Derby, Huntingdon, Westmorland, and Northumberland, but never the earls of Oxford.[4]

The John de Vere who became the 16th earl was born in or about 1516.[5] On 2 July 1536, about the age of twenty, he married Dorothy Neville, second daughter of Ralph Neville, 4th Earl of Westmorland. On the same occasion, in a dynastic triple marriage celebrated at Holywell in Shoreditch, London residence of the earls of Rutland, Henry Manners, aged about nine, later 4th Earl of Rutland, married Margaret Neville, fourth daughter of the same Earl of Westmorland; and Henry Neville, aged about eleven, later 5th Earl of Westmorland, married Anne, second daughter of Thomas Manners, 1st Earl of Rutland.[6] King Henry VIII himself graced the post-prandial festivities.[7]

From the 16th Earl the male line can be traced back ten generations to the 1st Earl, and three generations beyond that. While the 17th Earl owed a mere 1 part in 2000 of his genetic makeup to the first, and 1 part in 8000 to the earliest known Vere, by the myth of nobility the blood-line was mystically renewed in each generation. His ancient male lineage determined not so much who the 17th Earl was, as who he *thought* he was.

The earls of Oxford included many whose reputations survived into the sixteenth century: Aubrey III, 1st Earl of Oxford, who came to England with William the Conqueror in 1066, possibly the original builder of Castle Hedingham;[8] Robert, 3rd Earl of Oxford, one of the peers who forced King John to sign the Magna Carta; Robert, 9th Earl of Oxford, scandalous favourite of Richard II;[9] Richard, 11th Earl of Oxford, a commander at Agincourt, 25 October 1415;[10] John, 12th Earl of Oxford, beheaded six days after his eldest son Aubrey suffered the same fate, under Edward IV, on Tower Hill, 26 February 1462.

The 13th Earl, another John, the 12th Earl's second son, led a life of fabulous adventure. Born in 1443, and thus a minor when his elder brother and father were executed, at his majority he achieved a reversal of his father's attainder, was restored to the title, and created a knight of the Bath. Sent to the Tower in November 1468, he was released before January 1469, but soon offended Edward IV by supporting Henry VI. Vainly opposing Edward at the battle of Barnet, John fled to France. In 1473 he attempted a return via St Osyth on the south coast of Essex, but retreated before superior odds, fetching up at St Michael's Mount off Cornwall. Forced to surrender, he was shipped off to Hammes near Calais, now attainted in his own person.

In 1478 the Hammes prisoner 'lyepe [=leapt] the wallys and wente to the dyke and in-to the dyke to the chynne, to whatt entent I cannott telle – some sey to stele awey and some thynke he wolde have drownyd hym-selfe, and so it is demyd [=deemed, judged]'.[11] Plucked up half-dead, he was returned to prison, but escaped in August 1484, with Richard III seated on the English throne. Landing with Henry Richmond at Milford Haven in 1485, the Earl took command of the right wing at Bosworth, when it counted more than at Barnet. Again his attainder was reversed, and land and offices rained down upon him. He received command again in 1492; again came military success, lands, and offices.

Lady Fortune, having raised the 13th Earl to the top of her wheel, uncharacteristically kept him there. Despite a notorious check at Castle Hedingham in 1498, when he is said to have been heavily fined for too openly keeping a private army, he served as high steward for the trial of the Earl of Warwick in November 1499. Confirmed in the king's favour, he lived until 10 March 1513; having achieved seventy years against the odds, he was buried at Earls Colne. Lacking an heir, he was succeeded by John Vere, son of his brother George and of Anne, daughter of Thomas Howard, 2nd Duke of Norfolk.

The 13th Earl's failure to produce an heir was widely regarded as divine punishment for ambition. Sir George Buc, a contemporary of the 17th Earl, retails a prophecy that in fewer years than the 13th Earl had lived – that is, before 1583, seventy years after his death in 1513 – the earldom would be wasted, and ancestral bones would lie scattered in the fields.[12]

The 14th Earl, similarly childless, was succeeded by another cousin and yet another John, a great-grandson of the 11th Earl through his father John de Vere (his mother was Alice Kilrington *alias* Colbroke) and his grandfather Sir Robert de Vere. (The identity of the 15th Earl's mother – Edward's great-grandmother – has yet to be established.) Born about 1482,[13] the 15th Earl was active in the service of Henry VII in 1507, achieving a knighthood on 25 September 1513 under Henry VIII at Tournai following the Battle of the Spurs. He served as Sheriff of Essex and Hertfordshire, and as Keeper of Colchester Castle in 1515–16, 1519–20, and 1524–25. He attended Henry VIII at the Field of the Cloth of Gold in 1520, and at royal events thereafter.

The 15th Earl's marriage to Elizabeth Trussell yielded four sons and four daughters:[14] John, father of Edward de Vere; Aubrey, father of Hugh, John, Anne, Bridget, and Jane Vere; Robert, father of John and Mary Vere;[15] Geoffrey, father of John, Francis, Robert, and Horace (or Horatius/Horatio) Vere; Frances, who married Henry Howard, Earl of Surrey (the poet); Anne, who married Edmund Sheffield (also a poet); Elizabeth, who married Sir Thomas Darcy; and Ursula, who may have died young. The most distinguished of these names would be Geoffrey Vere's sons Francis and Horace, 'The Fighting Veres'.[16]

A charming vignette of the 15th Earl survives in a letter addressed by the young Gregory Crumwell to his father in 1531:[17]

> Father, I beseach you when you meet the Right Honorable Lord of Oxford, to give thanks unto his Lordship, for when he came to a town called Yeldam, to the persons thereof to hunt the fox, he sent for me and my cousins, and made us good cheer; and let us see such game and pleasure as I never saw in my life.

As we shall learn, this love for children extended to cooperation with Christopher Swallow, vicar of Messing, Essex, in founding a grammar school at Earls Colne about 1520, with the Earls of Oxford as patrons.

On 3 November 1529 Henry VIII walked in procession, 'Therle of Oxford great Chamberleyn bearing the trayne'.[18] In April 1533 the 15th Earl served as a commissioner for the deposition of Queen Catherine. On 1 June, again as 'high chamberlaine of England', he carried the crown in the coronation procession of Anne Boleyn; then, at the dinner that followed, he carried a white staff, the material sign of his office:[19]

> on the right side of her chair stoode the [Dowager] Countesse of Oxford ... in the middest [i.e., at the end of the table] betweene the Archbishop [of Canterbury] and the Countesse of Oxford stoode the Earle of Oxford with a white staffe all dinner time.

Three years later, on 15 May 1536, the same Earl sat among his peers at the trial of the same Queen – a close relative – for treason. On 3 January 1540 he and his eldest son accompanied King Henry to Blackheath to receive Anne of Cleves.

On 21 March 1540 the 15th Earl died at Earls Colne, and was buried on 12 April at the parish church of Castle Hedingham. A handsome tomb presents the Earl and his Countess in prayer, surrounded by their eight offspring.[20] The funeral hearse – not a wheeled cart but a wooden scaffold – bore a large tapestry powdered with icons of the Order of the Garter, to which the Earl had been elected in 1527.[21] The first Protestant in his line, the 15th Earl won a place in the popular mind as 'the good earl'.

Comfortably past his twenty-first birthday at the time of the 15th Earl's death, the 16th Earl assumed his inherited wealth and his title without the complications of minority that were to bedevil his son. In 1541 he received livery (in effect, delivery) of lands that descended to him through his mother. In 1544 he served

Henry VIII at Boulogne as captain in the rear guard. Eighty years later, in 1624, Gervaise Markham, in *Honour in his Perfection* (sigs. C3v–4v), celebrated an exploit of the 16th Earl during a pause in the Boulogne campaign: he nonchalantly killed a boar with his dancing-rapier, much to the chagrin of his French hosts. A fine story! But from its late publication, and the fact that about 1557 George Cavendish attributed the same action to Henry Radcliffe, 2nd Earl of Sussex (1506?–57), in 1542,[22] we may suppose that both accounts were myth and not history.

The report of an extraordinary wager reveals the 16th Earl's passion for gambling:[23]

> ... John Lucas, master of the Requeste whoe beinge a great Gamster wonne of the Earle of Oxford the wardshipe of [Mistress] Roydon at dice, with whome he matched his yongest sonne.

Mary Roydon was the daughter and heir of Christopher Roydon of Roydon Hall, Essex. Lucas, having won the girl at dice, married her to his youngest son, John, from his second marriage. Not one to bear a grudge, in his will of 1552 Oxford would remember 'my trustie & faythefull friende & Cownsaillour Iohn Lucas Esquyour'.

Keeping up a family tradition traceable to 1492, Earl John maintained a company of players.[24] On 5 February 1547, a week after the death of Henry VIII, Bishop Stephen Gardiner complained to Sir William Paget from Southwark:[25]

> ... Tomorrow the parishioners here and I have agreed to have solemn dirige for our late sovereign, and certain of Oxford's players intend to have, as they say, a solemn play, on the other side of the borough. It seems a marvellous contention that some should profess mirth and some sorrow at one time. I follow the common determination to sorrow until our late master [=Henry VIII] is buried. What these lewd fellows mean in the contrary I cannot tell and reform, and therefore write to you who, by means of the lord protector, may procure uniformity in the commonwealth. I have spoken with [Sir Robert] Acton, justice of the peace, whom the players smally regard, and pressed him to answer whether he dare let them play or not. To the play he answers neither yes nor no, but to the assembly he pleads no to the players until he has contrary command. But his no is not much regarded, mine less. If you will not meddle, send word and I will myself sue the protector.

Gardiner thus dismisses Oxford's men as 'lewd fellows'.

On 7 February 1547 Oxford's application to furnish water at the coronation of the young King Edward on the 20th was approved, as was his request to carry the royal rod.[26] But while Oxford 'held Water vnto the King, which the Earle of Huntingdon before tasted', it was Warwick who now served as Great Chamberlain, Oxford's claim to the office having been rebuffed.[27] He nevertheless received a knighthood at the coronation, more in deference to the will of the deceased Henry VIII than by the favour of the new boy-king (*Peerage*). He also served as one of twelve chief mourners for the old King, and would serve in 1553 as a mourner for Edward VI.[28]

The 16th Earl's wife Dorothy bore him two daughters: Katherine, born about 29 September 1538; and Faith, who died in swaddling clothes.[29] Katherine was an uncharacteristic product of the Oxford line, for her mother was an earl's daughter. After Dorothy's death in 1548, Earl John took a commoner as his next wife. The difference in lineage between the pure-bred Katherine and her mongrel half-brother would have serious repercussions following the 16th Earl's death in 1562.

3 Doubtful Marriage

The 16th Earl's second marriage is recorded in the parish register of St Andrew in the village of Belchamp St Paul's, Essex, under the year 1548:[1]

> The weddinge of my Lorde Ihon Devere Earle of Oxenforde and Margery the daughter of Ihon Gouldinge Esquier the firste of Auguste.

Despite the routine character of the entry, the marriage was so desperately irregular that it would prompt doubts and suspicions as to the legitimacy of the 17th Earl.

The circumstances of the marriage were the subject of depositions taken on 19 and 20 January 1585 before Sir John Popham, Queen Elizabeth's attorney general, and Thomas Egerton, her solicitor general.[2] Twenty questions (interrogatories) were put to each of five examinants on behalf of Richard Masterson, gentleman, complaining against Hugh Key concerning property in Ashton, county of Chester, leased by the 16th Earl to Hugh and to Hugh's mother Margaret Key for the duration of either of their lives, or for eighty years (if either should live so long). After the 16th Earl's death in 1562, the 17th Earl sold the reversion of this property to Christopher Hatton, who provided a lease to Masterson, who entered the property while Key was still in occupancy. Key held that any contract issued by the 17th Earl was flawed as he was not a legitimate heir.

The five examinants were Rooke Green Esq., of Little Sampford, Essex, then about 62 years of age, son of Sir Edward Green of Sampford Hall;[3] John Anson, clerk, 60 years of age and above, parson of Weston Turvill, Buckinghamshire;[4] Richard Enowes of Earls Colne, Essex, about 92 years of age (hence born about 1493), sometime servant of the 16th Earl;[5] Thomas Knollis of Cottingham, Northamptonshire, aged 58 years and above;[6] and William Walforth of Finchingfield, Essex, yeoman, 60 years of age and above, the 16th Earl's servant for twenty years, and his gamekeeper at Hedingham Park.[7] All five confessed ignorance concerning the Ashton property, but more or less extensive knowledge concerning the 16th Earl's marriages. All defended the legitimacy of the 17th Earl, and must thus be considered sympathetic witnesses.

The deponents agreed that the 16th Earl had married Dorothy Neville in or about 1536.[8] Rooke Green 'knoweth well that they lyved long after the same marriage in good lyking together, and came often together to this Examinantes fathers house [in Little Sampford]' (A.6). About January 1546, however, Dorothy left her husband by reason of 'the vnkynde dealing of the earl' (C.6, D.5–6). Richard Enowes reported that the Duke of Norfolk (Thomas Howard) had ordered the Earl to attempt a reconciliation, but that Dorothy 'said she wold never goe home agayne amongst such a bad companye as were about the Earle of Oxforde at that tyme' (C.6).

With Dorothy out of the way, John entered into a bigamous marriage with Joan Jockey of Earls Colne (D.9–10). Enowes dates this marriage 'about Corpus Christi tyde at Whit Colne Churche' (C.9) – about 31 May 1546. Dorothy 'wrott to Mr Tyrrell then the same Earles Comptroller' – evidently George Tyrrell, whom we shall meet again – 'to knowe yf it were true, that the said Iohan [=Joan] were marryed to the same Earle'; when Tyrrell confirmed her worst fears, Dorothy took it 'verey grevouslie' (C.10).

John Anson reported that John kept yet another woman, named Anne, at Tilbury Hall near Tilbury-juxta-Clare, less than four miles north-west of Castle Hedingham (B.9–10).[9] Rooke Green similarly deposed that 'about fortie yeares past he sawe a woman nere Tylbery Hall of whom it was then reported to this Examinant that the said Iohn Earle of Oxforde kept her' (A.11). None of the examinants reports Anne's surname, but Knollis and Walforth agreed that she had been a servant to Mr Cracherode (D-E.11), Oxford's tenant at Tilbury Hall;[10] following the conclusion of her affair with Oxford, this Anne married one Phillips (B.11, 17).

Dorothy died on about 6 January 1548, at a parsonage located half a mile from distant Salisbury (B-E.8). The examinants agreed that before Dorothy's death, John had made a clean break from his other entanglements: 'all theise women were shaken of[f] by the same Earle of Oxforde by the aduise & workinge of his Counsell before the said lady Dorothie dyed' (B-C.11). Presumably the Earl simply abandoned Anne, who had no claim on him. His separation from Joan Jockey, a more dangerous alliance because sanctified by marriage (however irregular), was expedited by an act of gut-wrenching violence. One day, when the Earl had left Joan Jockey alone, a gang of five approached her residence in Earls Colne: these were Sir Thomas Darcy, Lord Sheffield, John Smith, Richard Enowes, and another servant (name unknown). The servants broke in Joan's door, then pinned her down while Smith 'spoyled' or 'disfigured' her: in point of fact, 'Iohn Smyth cutt her nose' (C-E.13). Presumably Smith either cut her nose clean off, or cut the skin at the base of the nostrils into flaps to give her a permanently grotesque appearance – traditional punishment for 'unsocial' behaviour.[11] Though Joan Jockey survived the attack, the Earl definitively 'put her away'. Walforthe believed that Joan Jockey was still alive in 1585 (E.17), but none of the examinants could depose as to her current whereabouts.

The mutilation of Joan Jockey was very much a family matter. The chief thugs – Sir Thomas Darcy and Lord Sheffield – were brothers-in-law to the 16th Earl. Darcy, subsequently Baron Darcy of Chiche (Essex), was born in 1506,[12] and was thus about forty-two at the time of the attack. His mother was Elizabeth, daughter of Sir Henry Wentworth of Nettlestead, Suffolk; he took to wife Elizabeth, third daughter of the 15th Earl of Oxford. At the time of the attack Darcy held the office of Lord Chamberlain of the Household. Edmund Sheffield, born in 1521 and thus about five years younger than the 16th Earl, was the son of Sir Robert Sheffield and of Jane, daughter of Sir George Stanley, Lord Strange of Knockyn. After Sir Robert's death in 1531, Edmund became a ward first of Lord Rochford, and later, on 2 January 1538, of the 15th Earl of Oxford. While attached to Cromwell, Edmund became notorious for his unruliness, dispatching an 'undutiful' letter to the Earl of Oxford, dated July 1538 from prison. Despite his insolence, at some time unknown he married Anne, the 15th Earl's second daughter. By the will of Henry VIII, Sheffield was created Baron Sheffield of Butterwick at the start of the reign of Edward VI. Under his recently bestowed title, he accompanied the Earl of Northampton on an expedition to quell Ket's Rebellion in Norfolk, where he was killed – at Norwich – in August 1549. A poet of the same generation as Henry Howard, Earl of Surrey, Sheffield was praised by Thomas Fuller: 'Great his skill in music, who wrote a book of sonnetts according to the Italian fashion' (*DNB*, under Sir Robert Sheffield). Sheffield's poems have not survived.

The 16th Earl's exact role in the attack on Joan Jockey is uncertain. Either his two brothers-in-law acted to destroy an alliance that they regarded as a threat to their own interests; or the Earl cooperated in an effort to drive away a woman who had become a liability. That the Earl was somehow complicit is suggested by the fact that Enowes and Smith stayed in his service, as revealed by the Earl's will of 1562, while he remained on exceedingly good terms with Darcy, as revealed in his will of 1552:[13]

> to my right entierbeloved Brother in Lawe Sir Thomas Darcy knight Lorde Darcy of Chyche and Lorde Chamberleyn of the Kinges mooste Honorable Howsehold oon Hundred powndes of lawfull money and oone of my best horses.

Earl John also appointed Darcy as one of the three executors of this will.

Dorothy's death left the Oxford earldom in peril, for John had neither a male heir nor a wife who might produce one. On 1 February 1548, some three weeks after Dorothy's death, Lord Protector Somerset extorted an agreement from John promising Lady Katherine Vere, aged nine, to Somerset's seven-year-old son Henry, Lord Seymour, who thus stood to acquire the Oxford estates. Since Katherine and Henry were minors, control of the lands was vested in a syndicate comprised of Somerset, Sir Michael Stanhope, Sir Thomas Darcy, and John Lucas. The promise of marriage was enforced by a bond dated 26 February, with a penalty of

£6000; it was further enforced (but eventually reversed) by subsequent acts of Parliament. The agreement was enshrined in a will drawn up as an indenture tripartite, signed by John, and witnessed by Darcy; by Thomas Golding (Margery's eldest brother), Anthony Stapleton, and Robert Kelweye, all esquires; and by Thomas Almot, Thomas Larke, Roger Golding, and Robert Scoroth, all gentlemen.[14]

For John the indenture was an obnoxious burden which he doubtless accepted only because he had put himself in Somerset's power. Perhaps psychological pressures took their toll, for on 3 February John received '[d]ispensation to eat meat during Lent and at other prohibited times, also for four other persons invited to his table', paying 16s 8d for the privilege.[15] Such dispensations were usually claimed and granted only for illness.

Despite his apparent malaise, word soon spread that the Earl was conducting an amour with Dorothy Fosser of Haverhill, Suffolk, then residing in the Green household in Little Sampford. On 27 June Sir Thomas Darcy composed a letter from Castle Hedingham, apparently addressed to William Cecil:[16]

> Aftre right harte commendacions these shall bee to aduertyse yow that accordynge to my late conuercacion had with yow in my lordes graces galerye at Westmynstre / I haue by all means that I can inquiryd of the mater beytwen my lorde of Oxenford and the gentilwoman with whom hee is in love namyd mrs Dorothe late woman to my ladie Katheryn hir doughter / And vpon comunicayon had with them bothe / I haue founde and do perceyve them to bee in the same case that they wer in when my said lorde of Oxenforde was before my lordes grace And non other savynge that the bannes of matrimonye betwen them wer twise proclamyd in on[e] daye / other treatys or solempne conuercacyon hathe not ben befor wytnesse But onlye be in secrett betwen them twayn
>
> Syr if ye shall stande with my lordes graces pleassure to haue this mater further steyd (as my lorde of Oxenfordes honour welthe and preseruacyon consideryd) I thynke yt verey expedyent and maye righte well bee Then I beseche yow I maye bee therof aduertysyd, and that yee will move his grace to dyrecte his lettres to Mr Edward Grene of Stampford in whose house the said Dorothe dothe now contynew / commandynge him by the same neyther to suffre my said lorde of Oxenford to haue accesse to hyr ne [=nor] shee vnto hym / And that noo privey messengers maye goo betwen them whyche as I supose wilbee the sureste wey to stey them / And vppon further communicatyon with my lorde Wentworthe for a maryage to bee had betwen my said lord of Oxenford and on[e] of his daughters / And as they vppon sighte with other treatyce maye agree soo to procede in that same Syr vppon your motyon to be made vnto my lordes grace concernynge the premysses I praye yow I maie bee aduertysyd of by this berer of his pleasure in the same Whyche knowen I shal righte gladly indevour my syellff to accompplyshe by thayd [=the aid] of the blessed Trynyte whoo haue yow in his contynewall preservacyon ...

Dorothy Fosser was not only Countess Dorothy's maid and young Katherine's servant, but also Dorothy's god-daughter (and namesake) (A.16; C.16). Darcy's

letter betrays a private interest: he wished the Earl to marry one of the several daughters of Lord Wentworth, Darcy's first cousin on his mother's side. Meanwhile,
members of the Golding family conspired with the Earl in a plot of their own.

Despite Darcy's urging cessation of communication between John and Mistress
Dorothy, John managed to spirit her out of Green's house. We may suppose that
the liaison was consummated before Dorothy returned to her home in Haverhill,
awaiting John's arrival at the parish church where their banns had been announced and where they were to be married on Thursday, 2 August.

On Wednesday, 1 August, while her friends expected John to make his way to
Haverhill to marry Dorothy Fosser the next day, he rode instead to Belchamp St
Paul, where he wed Margery Golding without royal consent, pre-contract, or
banns – not at the parish church, but in the Golding residence. The priest who
conducted the ceremony was not the local vicar, Stephen Lufkin,[17] but the vicar
of SS. Peter and Paul of Clare, Suffolk, three miles to the north. The compliant
vicar, either John Reiston or John Metton,[18] received for his present effort and
prospective bother a gift of £10 per annum for life (B.14, D-E.15).

The clandestine marriage elicited the wrath of Protector Somerset. On 13
September Oxford was forced to sign a bond for £500:[19]

> Uppon condicion that if the same Erle forbere at any time betwene this and the
> Feast of Christenmas next to make any annuitie of any his castles, manours, landes
> and tenementes to any person whatsoever, or to dispose during that tyme any plate,
> juelles, stuf, or other thing in his possessyon without speciall licence of the Lord
> Protectour, except in tyme of extreme sycknes it shalbe laufull for him to dispose of
> the movables for declaration of hys last will, onles his Grace shall within that tyme
> take furder order with him; and also during the sayd tyme use the advise for
> thordre of his landes and howsehold of Sir Thomas Darcy and others his officers
> which he hath at this present, not chaunging any of them of himself oneles the sayd
> Lord Protectour, informed of just falt in any of them, shall accord to the same …

Probably Somerset meant to keep Oxford from transferring property to the no-
account Margery, to the detriment of Katherine and Somerset's son Henry.

The irregular circumstances of the 16th Earl's marriage help to explain the
words of a sympathetic eighteenth-century historian:[20]

> Edward Seymour, Duke of Somerset, Protector of the Realm, out of his extreme
> avarice and greedy appetitie did under color of justice convent before himself for
> certain criminal causes John Earl of Oxford and so terrify him that to save his life he
> was obliged to alienate to the said Duke by deed all his estates, lordships, castles,
> manors, &c.

The 'criminal causes' may have included any or all of the Earl's 'bad companye',
the bigamous marriage to and mutilation of Joan Jockey, Oxford's unauthorized
marriage to Margery Golding, and his breach of promise to Dorothy Fosser,
whom he eventually agreed to compensate with a payment of £10 per annum (A.16).

In his will of 21 December 1552, Oxford ordered his executors to

> recompens compound & satysfie or cause to be recompensed compownded or
> satysfied all & singuler wronges Iniuryes & trespasses by me at any tyme before my
> decesse commytted perpetrated or doon or by me procured to be commytted
> perpetrated or doon the same being proved by sufficyent wytnesse before or vnto
> my said Executours or the more part of them to be true & vnsatysfyed at the tyme
> of my said decesse.

The words 'or by me procured to be commytted perpetrated or doon' were added
by interlineation. To his credit – though probably not to her benefit – the 16th
Earl may have suffered pangs of conscience over Joan Jockey.

The legitimacy of the second marriage turned not on whether Oxford and
Margery Golding had observed ceremony, for indeed they had,[21] but on whether
their marriage was valid. The implied impediments were two: first, as the Earl
had married Joan Jockey, his marriage to Margery Golding was bigamous; second,
as the Earl was pre-contracted to Dorothy Fosser, his marriage to Margery Golding, which in any case lacked banns, was clandestine.

Arguments supporting legitimacy were several: John's marriage to Joan Jockey
was bigamous and thus not a true marriage either before or after Countess
Dorothy's death; Anne was kept at Tilbury Hall without benefit of marriage; no
divorce had severed John's marriage with Dorothy Neville either before or after
his marriage to Joan Jockey; Anne subsequently married one Phillips, which
proves that she was not married to John; his pre-contract with Dorothy Fosser
did not constitute a marriage; she in any case subsequently married John Anson,
the second of the five examinants.

Had he still been alive, Henry VIII would scarcely have looked kindly on such
a squalid marriage by one of his earls; Queen Elizabeth would at a minimum have
locked the couple in the Tower. Somerset could threaten but not command the
16th Earl. In any case, he held power only until 1 October 1549; any residual hold
was weakened with his execution in 1552 and terminated on 22 January 1553.[22]

Richard Enowes testified that he himself was 'one of theym that with the rest
of the Earles men did fett [=fetch] the same Margery after the marriage to
He[d]yngham Castle' (C.14–15). It was probably there, about 20 July 1549 (give
or take a week), that Margery conceived her first child.

4 Infancy and Childhood

Margery's pregnancy coincided with a disturbance in nearby Norfolk known to
historians as 'Ket's Rebellion'. In July 1549 Oxford was put on alert,[1] in August (as
noted) Edmund Sheffield was killed at Norwich, while on 5 October Somerset

dispatched an order from Hampton Court to his 'servant' Golding – evidently Thomas:[2]

> ... for the confidence we have in you, being our servant, we will and require you to solicit and give order for our very good Lord the Earl of Oxford's things, servants, and ordinary power, that he himself and the same also, be in good readiness, whatsoever shall chance to require his service for the King's Majesty; whereof, if any occasion shall chance, we will signify by our letters. Thus we commit the order of the whole unto your good discretion, and will you to use herein convenient secrecy.

On 16 October Oxford's name appeared in a memorandum of troops levied for service.[3] But the rebellion was soon contained, and order restored in East Anglia.

Edward de Vere was born on Saturday 12 April 1550, probably at Castle Heding-ham. On 17 April the Privy Council authorized a baptismal cup as a royal gift:[4]

> The kynges maiestes pleasure by our advise is that ye delyver vnto Phillip Manwaring gentleman Vssher to the Kinges maiestie one standing cup guilte with a cover weing twentye and seven ounces quarter by hym to be delyuered as the kinges maiestes guyft at the Christening of our very goode Lorde the Erle of Oxfordes Sonne / And these our lettres shalbe your sufficient warraunte and discharge therin Youen [=Given] at the Kinges maiesties mannour at Grenewich the xvijth of Aprell the iiijth yere of his highnes moast prosperous Reigne King Edward the sixte 1550.

Baptism was probably ministered not long after the date of this order, the choice of name – new to the de Veres – doubtless honouring the young King. Like Oxford heirs before and after, the child was styled Lord Bolbec, derived from Isabel de Bolebec, wife of the 3rd Earl.[5]

Lord Bolbec grew up in rural Essex, his nurses and servants supervised by the lusty Countess Margery. The literal fabric of his life may be inferred from a schedule of household goods accompanying Earl John's will of December 1552,[6] listing 'trussing' beds, 'sparvers' (bed-canopies), counterpoints, quilts, tapestries, linens, featherbeds, and sheets and blankets. There was a 'Sparvar of Estate of redd satten powdered with blewe bores & Letters and my olde Lordes Armes' (the blue boar was the earldom's symbol); 'twoo Counterpoyntes of Venus & Cupid'; 'a Counterpoynt of Tapissarie having Saynte George in it'; 'a Counterpoynt of Tapissarie with twoo graye Howndes in it and Huntyng Storyes'; and 'a Counter-poynt of Course Counterfett Arres with a great Lyon in it'. Among the fabrics assigned to Lord Bolbec himself were 'a trussyng bedd hangyng made of a Sparvar of Russett & yellowe Satten paned with my Lorde Cursons Armes with Curteyns of Lyke colored Sarcenett'; 'Seven peces of Hangynges of Counterfett Arres and Morrans for the greate Chambre at Hedingham'; 'fower peces of hangynges of Counterfett Arres of the Storye of Tullius Hostilius'; 'fyve peces of Counterfett Arres the grounde grene powdered with blewe borys & Crosbowe Rackes and twoo small peeces cutt owte of the same'; and 'a greate Herce Clothe of blacke velvett with Angelles Molettes & garters'. The angels, mullets, and 'garters' had doubtless adorned his grandfather's 'hearse'. A little coffer called 'Jack of Bullen' may have accompanied the 16th Earl to Boulogne. The 'Armorye Harnesses & weapon to the same' must have been particularly intriguing to Lord Bolbec.

Lady Katherine's place of residence during her brother's infancy is unknown. Had Dorothy Fosser married the 16th Earl on 2 August 1548, she would have been twice Katherine's mother: as the servant who had looked after her in her childhood, and subsequently as her step-mother. Instead, Katherine's Neville aunts and uncles may have served as her guardians.

On 2 March 1552, as Lord Bolbec approached his second birthday, his father became involved in a violent incident at court:[7]

> The Lord of Abergavenny was committed to ward for striking the Earl of Oxford in the chamber of presence.

A Patent Roll entry of 6 April supplies more details:[8]

> Whereas Henry Nevyle lord Bergevenny ... within the precinct of the Royal Palace of Westminster, namely within the king's chamber of presence, struck a certain nobleman a blow with his right hand which drew blood; for which by law he ought to suffer the loss of his right hand and imprisonment during the king's pleasure; Pardon, at the instance of divers magnates and nobles and in consideration of his frail youth (*juventutem fragilem*) to the said Henry Nevile lord Bergevenny of all affrays within the king's palace and other offences to date.

Evidently Neville remained under arrest for more than a month. (Perhaps he had criticized Oxford's treatment first of Dorothy, born a Neville, and now of Katherine, her daughter.)

On 21 December Oxford signed his second but first surviving will. Since Tudor wills were often deferred until death seemed imminent, he may have felt himself in mortal danger (though he was to live another ten years). He may also have meant to alter the will extorted from him by the recently executed Somerset. Finally, he had both a male heir, and a marriageable daughter. The will names Katherine without reference to her deceased mother, but with a clear reference to an act of Parliament made earlier in her behalf; it puts Katherine on notice that she must not contract a marriage distasteful to her father.

On 22 January 1553 the indenture of 1548 was revoked, thus voiding the requirement that Katherine must marry Henry, Lord Seymour.[9] The old indenture is alluded to in a letter of 25 November 1555 from Thomas Blagrave to Sir Edmund Peckham:[10]

> ... as the Lorde of Oxforde with fyve hundreth markes by him receivid of the duke [of Somerset] in tender of a maryage which (lyke as therle of Westminsters landes) was not performed but after the deth of the duke vndon & ffrustrate ...

By 1558 Katherine had married Edward, Lord Windsor, evidently with her father's acquiescence (*Peerage*, xii, p. 798).

Early in 1553 Countess Margery found herself in a skirmish over legal instruments establishing the jointure (or marriage settlement) of Margaret Arundel, sister of the unfortunate Catherine Howard and widow of the recently executed Sir Thomas Arundel. Northumberland addressed Lord Darcy and Sir William Cecil:[11]

> [The Countess of] Oxford, having almost finished her suits in the town, desired me to know what she should do touching Lady Arundel's jointure. She has received a letter from one of the council for its delivery to Lady Arundel. But although she is her niece and gave 500 marks to her marriage, she will not deliver the jointure without command of the majority of the board, for it may be prejudicial to the king in claiming her thirds. She should therefore have a letter from the board for its delivery to your lordships, with thanks that she so well considered her duty and truth. It seems Lady Arundel's great labour and suit is to get the jointure out of her sight to obtain her thirds, which some have consented to that have written alone to that effect.

We shall learn more about Lady Arundel – and her son Charles – in due course. On 1 March 1553,[12]

> the king kept his parliament within his pallace at Westminster. The[y] proceded from the gallery into the closet, thorough the closett into the chapell to service, every man in their robes as at this day. Therle of Oxford bare the sword, and the marquis of Northampton as great chamberleyn went jointly with him on the right hand. The lord Darcy beinge lord chamberleyn bore the king's trayne, and was assisted by sir Andrew Dudley, chief gentleman of the privy chamber.

King Edward was now suffering from the illness that would take his life on 6 July. On 16 June Oxford and 25 fellow peers signed letters patent nominating Lady Jane Grey as successor; but on 19 July, less than two weeks after the King's death, Oxford declared instead for Mary. Appointed to the Queen's Privy Council on 3 September, on the 30th he bore the sword before Mary in her progress through London, and performed the same service at her coronation on 30 November.

Not much enamoured of his new monarch despite public demonstrations of loyalty, Oxford was 'vehemently suspected' of active participation in the anti-Marian plot of Sir Henry Dudley and Richard Uvedale in 1556.[13] Meanwhile, in Essex he held posts of honour and power: joint lord lieutenant 25 September 1550 and 24 May 1553; joint lord justice and lieutenant 4 May 1551 and 7 May 1552; justice of the peace 18 February 1554; lord lieutenant 17 January 1558 and 1 May 1559. None of these offices constituted a heavy administrative burden.

The most compelling contemporary description of Oxford, far more worthy of credit than Markham's tale of the boar-hunt in Boulogne, is provided by Stow:[14]

> The late Earle of Oxford, father to him that now liueth, hath beene noted within these fortie yeares, to haue ridden into this Citie, & so to his house by London

stone, with 80 Gentlemen in a liuery of Reading Tawny, and chaines of gold about their necks before him, and 100 tall yeomen in the like liuery to follow him without chaines, but all hauing his cognisance of the blew Bore, embrodered on their left shoulder.

The 'house by London stone', which Lord Bolbec may have visited occasionally as a child, also went under the name of 'Vere House'.[15] Stow's figure of 180 retainers may be too high: 59 are listed by name in the Earl's will of 1552, 89 in his will of 1562.

Active throughout Mary's reign as the principal magnate of Essex, Oxford apprehended Protestant rebels and traitors in the years 1554 through 1556, and was commended on 15 June 1555 for supervising the burning of heretics.[16] In his personal life he still kept 'bad companye', eliciting a reprimand from by the Privy Council on 13 January 1556:[17]

> A … lettre to Sir Edward Walgrave and Serjaunte Browne to examyne the trueth of onne Rooke's cace, an innekeper of Braynetree, being a reteyner to therle of Oxford, of whome the Lords are enfourmed that notwithstanding a notoriouse and manifest felonie by the saide Rooke of late committed by the heigh waie, and being pursued and taken did afterwardes confesse the same, he shulde, nevertheles, contynue in howsholde with the saide Earle of Oxeforde and waite upon his table …

Waldgrave and Browne were to declare 'whether this be trewe or no, and to certifie their knowleage'. Rooke (or Booke) was the alias of Thomas Robinson, a notorious highwayman.[18] Unrepentant, Oxford kept the man on salary and remembered him in his will of 1562. Discord within the Earl's marriage may be implied by a lawsuit brought against him by Margery in the early months of 1558.[19]

The Earl's estrangement from the Queen may have meant that Lord Bolbec saw more of his father during the mid-1550s, and engaged in manly sport; nevertheless, the son never developed a passion for the hunt, being more attracted to such literary endeavours as were practised by his half-uncle Arthur Golding. Another joy must have been the occasional visit from his father's players, who presumably entertained the family during major holidays.

No record of birth or baptism survives for Margery's second child, Lady Mary Vere, but as she is not mentioned in the 16th Earl's will of December 1552, nor in a codicil of 28 January 1554, we may surmise that she was born late in 1554 at the earliest. A mere girl, she had no power to push her brother from centre-stage.

5 The Education of Lord Bolbec

In October 1558 Lord Bolbec entered Queens' College in Cambridge, where his father, though not a university man, had personal contacts.[1] A key was ordered for the boy's room, and one Otte, a smith, hired to repair the lock:[2]

Item pro clavi ad ostium cubiculi domini Bulbecke vjd
Item Otte fabro pro resartione ser' interioris ostij eiusdem cubiculi xd

On 14 November the young lord's name was entered on the University's matriculation register:[3]

Dominus Edwardus Bulbecke impubes

The previous March five boys had matriculated as *impubes* ('immature'),[4] and now, in November, four, including two others from Queens'.[5] The following May eight matriculated, aged nine to twelve.[6] No other boy from the period was quite as young as Lord Bolbec, but then no other was the son of an earl.

Boys were admitted to Cambridge colleges not because they were intellectually precocious, but because their families could afford to lodge them under the supervision of college dons, just as other well-heeled boys joined noble or royal households. Though *impubes* might receive instruction, they were not academically accountable. Indeed, 'fellow commoners' (as they were called) were 'not in general considered as over full of learning' – at least in later years.[7] Lord Bolbec doubtless applied himself to such studies as were set for him, above all (one must imagine) to the mastery of Latin prose and verse.

In January 1559 the boy's name was entered on the books of St John's College:[8]

For the admission of my lord Bulbecke into the fellowes commons 13s 4d

Though he secured dining rights at this second college, he remained resident in Queens':

f. 258v (January expenses):
Pro duobus pedestri novi vitri et vndecim particulis novi vitri in cubiculo Domini Bulbecke ijs iiijd
Pro septem novis particulis et duobus rotundis particulis ibidem xijd
Pro inseren' tribus pedis in novo plumbo in eodem cubiculo xd

f 259v (March expenses)
Pro inseren' tribus pedibus vitri in novo plumbeo in superiore cubiculo Domini Bulbecke xvd

These payments are for the repair of window-glass, which might have been broken from the inside or the outside. Either way, the young lord's presence spelled trouble for the college.

On 23 November 1558 Thomas Peacock, a staunch Roman Catholic, became President of Queens'. This was nine days after Lord Bolbec's matriculation and six days after the death of Peacock's co-religionist patron, Queen Mary. The following July Peacock would resign to avoid expulsion (Venn). Queens' had shrunk to eleven senior fellows, of whom only three were priests, and nine junior fellows, of whom only three were on the foundation.[9] Probably not much instruction occurred under the circumstances.[10]

If instruction was scarce, entertainment was not. Queens' promulgated statutes this very year reinforcing its traditional performance of two plays each year, whether comedies or tragedies, *privatim* (before a restricted audience), or *publice* (in the college hall), between 20 December and Lent. Although college books record none this year, there can be little doubt that plays were performed. Meanwhile, Trinity College staged five plays, while Christ's and St John's had Christmas Lords. On 11 November Cambridge received a visit from a professional acting company, the Queen's Men.[11]

Lord Bolbec's name disappears from college records after March 1559, nor did he receive a BA with his classmates in Lent 1562. His subsequent education seems to have been supervised by Sir Thomas Smith, as recalled in a letter to William Cecil (by then Lord Burghley) dated 25 April 1576, in which Sir Thomas wished Edward well, 'for the love I beare hym, bicause he was brought vp in my howse'; two years earlier, on 3 August 1574, Cecil wrote to Walsingham: 'I dout not but Mr Secretary Smith will remember his old love towardes the Erle whan he was his scollar.'[12]

Sir Thomas, following his second marriage in 1554, to a widow with an estate at Theydon Mount, commissioned a new residence there. Presumably, therefore, it was in rural Essex that Lord Bolbec received tuition for the next three years, rubbing shoulders with Sir Thomas's illegitimate but dearly beloved son and namesake. Born 15 March 1547, Thomas Smith would meet an untimely death in Ireland on 18 October 1573 (*DNB*, under Sir Thomas Smith).

Lord Bolbec's tutor from the age of eight was Thomas Fowle, of St John's College, Cambridge, who had attained his BA in 1550, and his MA in 1553.[13] Under Mary, Fowle lost his college fellowship, and secretly served as a Protestant minister in or near London. From 4 May 1558 he received £10 per annum 'for his service in teaching Edward de Vere ... Vicount Bulbecke'.[14] On 4 November 1562 he was collated to the rectory of Aldham, Essex, and installed as canon of Norwich Cathedral on 22 November 1563, rarely setting foot in Norwich except to collect his stipend. In 1570 he joined a mob of Norwich prebendiaries who, 'disaffected to the established order as regards matters ecclesiastical, entered into the choir of that cathedral, forcibly broke down the organs and committed certain other disorders of the like outrageous character'. Fowle served in 1572 on a commission against Catholic Recusants in Norfolk, and in 1573 joined John Hansdon and John Grundye in supervising 'prophesyings' at Bury St Edmunds, Suffolk – extremist Protestant activities soon suppressed by royal authority. Fowle's 'after-life' suggests that Lord Bolbec was tutored during his formative years by a religious fanatic of violent temper.

6 Long Live the Queen

On 1 September 1558, as Queen Mary lay on her deathbed, the Privy Council required of Oxford that 'divers villages appointed to the watching of the Blockhouse of West Tilbury ... contynue to be charged with town watches and beacon watches'.[1] Following Mary's death on 17 November, Oxford may have escorted Elizabeth from Hatfield to London on the 23rd.[2] Like most peers, he switched loyalties with alacrity.

On 23 January 1559 the French ambassador described Elizabeth's coronation of 15 January:[3]

> The banquet being ended, the collation (*la collatione*) was brought by three Earls – Bedford, Oxford ['Oxette'], and Montague. Shortly afterwards her Majesty rose, and by a covered way returned to her Palace of Whitehall by water; everybody in a like manner returning home.

Oxford successfully (though unjustly) asserted a hereditary claim to the Lord Great Chamberlainship.[4] Sir George Howard – whom we shall meet again – jousted in celebrations held on the 17th:[5]

> They could not finish it on the first day, the challengers, viz. the Duke of Norfolk, Sir George Howard, and Lord Robert Dudley, having as many hits as the adventurers. The judges therefore could not award the prize, which, as they jousted for love, was a diamond.

A draw contributed to the harmony of the occasion. Margery served as a Queen's Maid of Honour,[6] and, as noted by Ward (p. 12), seems to have spent the year 1559 at court. About this time the aged Countess Anne, widow of the 14th Earl, died at Lambeth.[7]

On 22 April 1559 Oxford sat at the trial of Lord Wentworth for his surrender of Calais. That autumn he welcomed John, Duke of Friesland, broker of a marriage between his brother Prince Eric of Sweden and the Queen:[8]

> [The Prince landed at Harwich] about the end of September, and was there honorably received by the Earl of Oxford and the Lord Robert Dudley, and by them conducted from thence to London. [The Prince] had in his own train about fifty persons well mounted; the Earl of Oxford also, and the Lord Robert Dudley were followed with a fair attendance both of gentlemen and yeoman.

Oxford treated the Duke to 'great sport' in the valley of the Stour.

The use of debased Swedish coin by the Duke's men caused a local stir, mentioned in a letter dictated and signed by Oxford and dispatched from Colchester on 1 October:[9]

> After my hartie commendacions to your Lordships / This morning I receiued your letters. And towchinge the proclamacion, I called on Sir Thomas Smyth to talke

with the duke by the waye. And at Colchester he gave to hym the Copie of the proclamacion done in to Latten. /

ffurst for the deceite of the Quenes Subiectes he speaketh verye fair(?) And saith he is verie sorie that enye of his men ben so lewde to put forth eny soche coynes as was Declared vnto hym by Mr Smyth.

And saith altho they haue the bignes they be no Dallers nor be not acceptid so in Sweden but are callid a duble marcke and thother a marcke, and so an half marke, and thes are curraunt onlie in there owen Countrie wheare everie man knowth them. And that they onelie be Dalers which haue the Image of Christ on the one side /

thother (saith he) were forbidden paine of deathe to be browght with me and to be vtterid forth. And suerlie they wear but Shipmen or soldiars and soch Lewde fellowes that vtterid them.

And I am sorie saith he that I harde not of this before / but if Therle will cawse them which so haue ben deceived to com to London and bringe the money to me, I will paye them that they shalbe no Loseres. / and rather beare there charges then they shold not com.

Yt was aunswerid to him againe that that was verye honorablie spoken. / And rather yt might haue ben sayd(?), that they might well haue there amendes in there handes, for their folishenes which wold take soche strange money and make nother the Lord Lieutenant nor his cownsell privie.

Naye saith he yt ys but reason and saith(?) that they shold be payd who of symple men was deceived. But I desire no action(?) of such Lewde men of myne shold bringe the money of Sweden in to Slaunder and contempte./

ffor the proclamacion he saith, it is a verie reasonable and Honorable proclamacion

and he thanketh the Quenes Maiestie that it pleaside her highnes to remember hym and that his coyne shold be exchaunged to the valor./

And he saith he is content So that he maie haue other money for it for els he hath none to Laye out but of that coyne and wold gladlie promes that none shold be vttered but onelie the trewe Daleres.

So this night he is com to Colchester / with xj cartes and xliiij Horse. And of his owen horse about xxx. I must be faine to make shift and Laye out money for them this night, seing the proclamacion is now knowen abrode they will take none of his coyne. / And if they shold[,] as y perceive, the pore men shold be great Losers./

He Liketh the countrey verie well. And I haue prepared for hym and his vncle handsome ambling geldinges and will do still for his iorney. / So that I do not doubt to bringe hym to London as was to fore appointed, on Wednisdaye at night betymes / And thus I bid your Lordships hartelie fare well /

On the same day, Sir Thomas Smith sent an enthusiastic report to Sir William Cecil:[10]

Sir: To show eny more of the contentacion of the duke with all thyngs hitherto I nede not / I assure yow if he were neuer so great a prynce he may be well content with his Interteignement here.

And I like hym better euery daye becawse he begynneth more and more to learne oure maneres And as we call it merilie in England, to be a good felow. I meane to leave of[f] his high lokes & pontificale. In eny thyng that is movid as towchyng thies maters as yow perceive by the lettres to my Lords of the Cownsell he awnswered gentilly & wiselie /

Our contrey he liketh but to[o] well / My Lord [=Oxford] here omytteth nothyng that should be nedefull or mete for hym / I do assure yow I thynk no man in England either in Queen Maries tyme or eny other could do so myche and so redilie with threatenyngs Imprisonementes & paynes as my Lord doth here with the love that the gentlemen & the hole contrey beryth to hym. / Whether the Antiquitie of his Awnceteres or his owne gentlenes or the dexteritie of those that be about doth make it(?) or rather all thies / I thynk yow could not wish it to be done better.

Marie [=Marry,] for this money for ther daleres seying [=seeing] thei are made bullion / it must nedes com hither at the fardest to morowe / Ye shall as ye knowe pynche the earle and vs all to[o] myche else / for ye haue not written what valor the trew daler is estemed at the mynt /

Otherwise for his comyng my lords [=the Privy Council] nede take no thowght / He liketh his conduction so well / that he will now go and tarie even as my lorde willeth let his halberderes & gard folow hym / & hath with hym viij fotmen araid [=arrayed] in black velvet ierkyns after the maner of England / as I perceive som of his hath sene about London / & endeth a faster pase [=pace] then he was wont to go[e] on hawkyng / the most care he hath is· for his great horse / And yet I do not dowte we shall learne then to go thies small iorneys well enough

Thus Oxford and Smith brought harmony out of chaos.

In April 1560 Oxford was named Lord Lieutenant of Essex. On 15 June, attempting to quash rumours circulating through Essex and Hertfordshire, he wrote to the Privy Council from 'Hedingham castell', accusing Thomas Holland, rector of Little Burstead, of 'uttering malicious words against the Queen':[11]

My moste hartie comendacions to your good Lordships remembered / It may please the same to vnderstande that the xth of this presente there was sente vnto me from two Iustices of Essex, one Thomas Hollande parson of litill Bursted for certeyne gret disordres and moste slaunderous crymes by hym maliciously vttered ageinst the Quene her excellente maiestie / and forasmoche as (the same beinge but woordes) the ponishement of the lawe extendethe but to the losse of his eares or Cli [=£100] fyne so farre as I can lerne and yet the haynousnes of thoffence mought haue tended verie moche to withdrawe the hartes of her maiesties subiectes from their allegiaunce and due obedyence it standethe doubtfull vnto me what might therof be construed The prieste I haue examyned diuerse and sondry tymes. and bothe by lenitie and otherwise haue sought to make hym confesse the articles deposed by sondry persons which herewith I sende vnto your good lordships but cannot by any meanes get hym therunto / onely this he saiethe that beinge at London before the laste Christenmas he met with one in Chepeside that was sometyme vicar of Storford in Hertfordshire whose name or dwellynge place he is vtterly ignoraunt of. Who tolde hym that there was one gone to the tower for saieng [=saying] the quenes maiestie was with childe / other confession I can in no wise get of hym / whearfore I haue thought good to aduertise your Lordships of the circumstances herof. and to desire your letters I may vndrestande from you what your order shalbe in this matter whether ye will haue hym ponished here in the countrie and in what sorte, or whether ye will haue hym examyned before your Lordships or otherwise delyuered in the open session of oyer and termyner or generall gaole delyuery ...

Noting that he had acted both with leniency and 'otherwise', Oxford seems to concede that he had tried force, and now hoped for permission to try torture.

In August 1561, from Thursday the 14th to Monday the 18th, Queen Elizabeth visited Castle Hedingham, evidently departing on Tuesday the 19th.[12] Lord Bolbec, now eleven, was doubtless an eager witness. On 21 September the Queen sent the Duke of Norfolk and the earls of Oxford and Rutland orders for the reception of the King of Sweden;[13] but Sweden never came to England.

7 The Earl is Dead

On New Year's Day 1562 Earl John gave Queen Elizabeth £10 'in a red silk purse, in dimy soveraigns'; similarly, Margery gave £5 'in a red purse, in dimy soveraignes'. Conversely, Elizabeth gave Oxford 'oone guilt cup with a cover', and Margery a smaller version of the same.[1]

On 1 July the Earl put his signature to a marriage contract, called an indenture of covenants, between his twelve-year-old son, on the one part, and Elizabeth or Mary Hastings, younger sisters of Henry Hastings, Earl of Huntingdon, on the other part.[2] The indenture provided that on his eighteenth birthday (which would fall on 12 April 1568) Edward should choose for wife whichever of the two Hastings sisters he might prefer at the time. Witnesses to the indenture were John Wentworth, Thomas Golding, John Gibon, Henry Golding, John Booth, Jasper Jones, and John Lovell, of whom 'Iohn Wentworth', 'Thomas Goldyng', and 'Henry Goldyng' attached signatures. Though ethically reprehensible by modern standards, the practice of arranging a marriage, and even of offering a young son the choice between two prospective brides, was conventional among the higher nobility of sixteenth-century England.[3] Not that such negotiations inevitably achieved their intended goal: often as not, youth had its way.

About the same time, an entail was executed on behalf of the earldom:[4]

> the Erldome of Oxinford and the honors, castles ... of the same Erldome together
> with the Offyce of Greate Chamberlayneshipp of England ... have of longetyme
> contynued remayned and bene in the name of the Veeres from heire male to heire
> male by tytle of an ancyent entayle thereof ... shoulde and myght contynew go
> remayne and be in the name of the Veeres from heire male to heire male forever yf
> yt maye please Almyghtye God so to permytt and suffer.

Since most honours and properties passed to the male heir in any case, the point
of this legal exercise may have been to assure that the office of Great Chamberlain
was included in the inheritance. Under Elizabeth the office would transfer
without question, but rights to the office would become a matter of dispute in
subsequent years.[5]

On 3 August John de Vere, 16th Earl of Oxford, died, in his mid-forties, at
Castle Hedingham (*Peerage*). From his arrangements for his son's future marriage
on 1 July, his attempt to clarify the entail of the earldom, and his signing an
elaborate will on 28 July (as discussed below), it is clear that he saw death coming.
His burial is recorded in the parish register of Castle Hedingham:[6]

> Iohn De Vere earle of Oxenford was buried the 31 of August 1562.

The Londoner Henry Machyn recorded in his diary:[7]

> The xxxj day of August was bered [=buried] in Essex the good erle of Oxford, with
> iij haroldes of armes, master Garter, master Lancostur, master Rychmond, with a
> standard and a grett baner of armes, and viij baner-rolles, helmet, crest, targett, and
> sword, and cott armur, and a herse with velvett and a palle of velvett, and a x dosen
> of skochyons, and with mony mornars in blake, and grett mone [=moan] mad[e]
> for hym.

The passing of the 16th Earl was noticed in another contemporary document:[8]

> This John Vere, erl of Oxford, dysseased [=deceased] at his castell of Hemyngham
> in Essex on Monday the 3 of August, in the 4 yere of the quene our soveraigne lady
> Elizabeth, &c. 1562, and was beryed on tewsday the 25 [in fact, the 31st] of August
> next enshewing [=ensuing], at the Parishe churche of Hemyngham. He married
> first Doraty, doughter of Raff erle of Westmerland, and had issue Kateren wyff to
> Edward lord Wyndesor; secondly, Margery, doughter of Golding, syster to Sir
> Thomas Goldinge, and had issue Edward erl of Oxford, and Mary.

The Earl's last will and testament reveals a great deal about himself and the
estate his son would come to inherit.[9] Its beginning is conventional:

> In the name of God Amen. I Iohn de Veer Erle of Oxinforde, Lorde greate
> Chamberlayne of Englonde Vicounte Bulbeck &c, being of hole and parfecte
> mynde, and by the grace of almightie God in parfect Love and Charitie with all the
> worlde, doe make ordayne and declare this my presente testament and laste will the
> xxviij of Iulij in the yere of our Lorde God 1562 ...

The Earl had not identified himself as Lord Great Chamberlain in his earlier will of 1552: evidently he did so now in an attempt to include the title in the inheritance.

The Earl's religious sentiments are compatible with his Protestant faith, but are not pietistic:

> And ... I commytt my soule vnto the eternall God my maker, and creator, and to Iesus Criste his only sonne my sauiour and redemer, by the merites of whose death and passion I doe stedfastly beleve to haue remission of all my synnes.

The 15th Earl had been buried at Castle Hedingham; the 16th chooses the more domestic atmosphere of Earls Colne, with charity to the local poor. He repeats a request from his 1552 will that his household remain intact for one full month after his death, and that his servants receive their full quarter-wages.

Bequests begin with £50 for the poor boxes of named parishes:

> Castill Hedingham, Sibley Hedingham, nether Geldham Tilbury next Clare, Wivenhoe, and Gestingthorp Lammershe, Toppisfilde, Cockfield, Erles Colne Colne Wake, White Colne, Gaines Colney St Swythins parrish at London stone, Lavenham Este Bergholte, Tadingstone, Aldham Swaffham Bulbeck ...

Similarly, he sets £10 aside for 'the reperacion of the Highe Waye Leading from Erles Colne to Cogeshall'. Thus the Earl acknowledges his principal estates, and his obligation to maintain the road between Earls Colne and Coggeshall.

The Earl next makes provision for Margery, confirming her control of lands in her marriage jointure; he also gives her silver and gold plate, including gifts from monarchs – probably including Edward's baptismal cup. She receives all her personal clothing, and 'all suche householde stuf as ys contayned in a scedule written in paper hereunto annexed'. The will does not discourage Margery from re-marriage.

Edward receives 1000 marks (£666–13–4) in cash, all plate not given else-where, and all armour and weapons, whether powder weapons (such as muskets), or thrusting or cutting weapons (such as spears and swords). Lady Katherine and Lord Windsor receive 300 marks (£200). Each of Margery's gentlewomen, up to the number of six, receives £6–13–4. Lady Mary receives 2000 marks (£1333–13–4), payable on the day of her marriage (she was now only six or seven years old). Presumably Katherine had already received her marriage portion.

The Earl makes bequests to collateral relations, including his brother Aubrey Vere's sons Hugh and John and daughters Anne, Bridget, and Jane; his brother Robert Vere's daughter Mary (not named); and his brother Jeffrey's sons Francis and Horatio (also not named). He also makes provision for his servants, who clearly mean much to him:

> Item I will giue and bequeath to every one of my seruauntes whiche be written and named in a scedule hereunto annexed which shalbe and contynue in my service at the tyme of my deceace, all suche some and sommes of monney as to hym ys

Lymmyted and appointed to be payed in the same scedule, the same to be payed to every of my saide servauntes by myne executors of this my laste will and testamente, within as short a tyme after my decease as they conuenyently maye.

The schedule names 23 gentlemen, 44 yeomen, and 22 grooms.

The Earl makes provision for his three surviving sisters, Elizabeth, Frances, and Anne Vere, named as Lady Darcy, Ladye Surrey, and Lady Sheffield – the last two now widows. He remembers his friends from court, giving Sir Nicholas Bacon (his good lord) and Sir William Cecil (his right trusty and loving friend) £10 and a great horse each, requesting their aid in assuring that his provisions and bequests will be carried out. For his servant Robert Christmas, who had been at his side since at least 1552, he transmutes the remaining years of a twenty-one-year lease on the manor of Walborne, Norfolk, into an outright gift. The residue of his goods, chattels, jewels, apparels, and obligations receivable the Earl bequeathes to his executors for the payment of such debts and obligations as are named in the body of his will. Among the properties specifically set aside for these purposes are the principal estates of the earldom:

the Mannors of Tedinstone and Aldham with theire appurtenaunces in the Countie of Suff and all and singuler my messuages Landes tennementes and hereditamentes in Tadingstone Aldeham and Hadley in the saide Countie of Suff and the Mannours of Walborne in the Countie of Norf And all and singuler my Landes tennementes and hereditamentes in Walborne or elce where in the saide Countye of Norffolk and my mannors of Wyvenhoo Newars Badelswyke, Muche Canfield, Muche Bentley, Dudhinghurste, Lammersh, and Colne Wake with theire appurtenaunces, in the Countie of Essex, and all and singuler my landes tennementes and hereditamentes in Wyvenhoo Newyeres, Badelswyke, Alresforde, Grenested, Estdolylond Muche Canfield, Little Canfield High Roding, Hatfielde Regis Muche Bentley Frating Dudinghirst Shenfield Lamersh Muche Henney, Alphumpstone Wakes Colne within the saide Countie of Essex.

These properties are sequestered for twenty years.

Earl John appoints as his executors Margery ('my righte Loving and welbe-loued Wief'), Edward (now twelve), Sir John Wentworth, Henry Golding, Robert Christmas, and John Turner. The supervisors are Thomas Howard, 4th Duke of Norfolk, and Robert Dudley, Earl of Leicester, each recompensed with a horse or a gelding. The Earl duly signed his will with his distinctive signature ('Oxenforde'), a form that would be retained for two further generations. Witnesses were Henry (or Harry) Walker; Roger Ponder, clerke; John Ludnam, Jasper Jones, John Lovell, Thomas Coe, William Hill, and Edmund Freake – all but Walker and Coe included in the list of servants (Coe had been named as a gentleman servant in Oxford's 1552 will).

Of the two appended schedules, the first, signed 'Oxenforde', reserves to Margery various household items including beds, complete with hangings and fittings. The second schedule specifies monetary bequests to the 89 'Gentlemen', 'Yeoman', and 'Grooms'. Several of these will reappear in the life of Edward de Vere: Henry Golding, Robert Christmas, John Turner, John Lovell, George Tyrrell, Edward MacWilliam, and – if this name is to be identified with the subsequently famous dramatist – John Lyly.

The will was probated on 29 May 1563, on the oath of Robert Christmas, gentleman, to whom administration is granted, with power reserved to Margery Countess of Oxford, Edward Lord Bolbec, Sir John Wentworth and Henry Golding, John Turner renouncing. On 22 July 1563 Margery would similarly renounce.

Of the servants mentioned in the 1562 will, one of the more notable for Lord Bolbec must have been Richard Bull, yeoman and armourer, who kept[10]

> all his Armour & Artillarye beinge or Remaininge aswell at or within his house of Hedinghame & Colne as els where within the Realme of Englande

Thus Castle Hedingham and Earls Colne harboured armour and artillery.

Though the 16th Earl of Oxford faithfully performed administrative, military, and judicial duties in his home county of Essex, he never approached the centre of power under Henry, Edward, Mary, or Elizabeth; unlike his father, he neither sat on the Privy Council nor wore the Garter. His inconsequence is remarked by David Loades, Mary Tudor's biographer:

> Oxford, whose transfer of allegiance [to Mary in 1553] had been of considerable importance, never became a councillor, or received any other position of trust …

Though the Earl 'recovered his hereditary … office of lord great chamberlain', that office was 'purely ornamental'.[11] His son, now twelve, would suffer the same fate of inconsequence.

PART II

Youth
1562–1571

8 London Wardship

The 16th Earl's household remained intact for precisely one calendar month after his death. Then, on 3 September 1562, his servants rode the forty-odd miles to London, bringing the heir to a new home, as described by Machyn:[1]

> The iij day of September cam rydyng owt of Essex from the funeral of the yerle of Oxford his father the yonge yerle of Oxford, with vij-skore horse all in blake [=black] throughe London and Chepe and Ludgatt, and so to Tempulle bare, and so to (blank), betwyn v and vj of the cloke at after-none.

Machyn's figure of seven-score (140) retainers is fewer than Stow's 180, but more than the 89 listed in the 1562 will.

The entourage that reached Temple Bar between 5:00 and 6:00 p.m. was a last tribute to the old Earl rather than a first tribute to the new: only John Turner, John Lovell, Henry Golding, Robert Christmas, George Tyrrell, and John Davye would remain to supervise the new Earl.[2] Turner, in his first official action, escorted Oxford (as I will call him henceforth) to Elizabeth's court:

> ... to John Turner gent' for bringing therle to Greenewiche xviijli vijs

Since the court left Greenwich on 6 September,[3] Oxford must have met the Queen within three days.

Like most children of the English upper classes before and since, Oxford had lived with surrogate parents from a young age, including Cambridge dons at eight, and Sir Thomas Smith at nine. Now, at twelve, he became a ward of Sir William Cecil, the Queen's Principal Secretary and Master of Wards, at Cecil House on the Strand. Wardship was an ancient and theoretically honourable device to protect the assets of a minor against depredation by rapacious relatives or executors.[4] The ultimate guardian of wards was the monarch, who traditionally farmed the responsibility to a Master of the Wards, who might farm wardships to others – for a price. Guardians had both heavy responsibilities and potential benefits. As Cecil had been a particular friend of the 16th Earl, it had probably been agreed between them that he personally would serve as guardian.

Oxford's wardship would last nine years, until 1571, when he would attain his majority. He overlapped at least three wards of high rank (Ward, p. 378): Edward Manners, 3rd Earl of Rutland (wardship 1563–70); Edmund Sheffield, 3rd Lord Sheffield (wardship 1568–85); Edward Zouch, Lord Zouch (wardship 1569–77).[5] Wards of lower rank in the Cecil household included James Baron of Ireland, possibly son of John FitzGerald *alias* Baron, Baron of Burnchurch, murdered in 1552;[6] William Carr, born 11 November 1551, son of Thomas Carr of Ford, Northamptonshire, murdered in January 1558;[7] and Thomas Grey, born 11 April 1549, son of the Sir Ralph Grey of Heton and Chillingham, Northamptonshire, who died 17 December 1564.[8] Subsequent Cecil wards included Robert Devereux, 2nd Earl of Essex (wardship 1576–87); Henry Wriothesley, 3rd Earl of Southampton (wardship late 1581 or early 1582 to 1594); Edward Russell, 3rd Earl of Bedford (wardship 1585–93); and Roger Manners, 5th Earl of Rutland (wardship 1588–97). Thus Cecil had the wardship of many of the most eminent young men of his age.

Of these wards, the 3rd Earl of Rutland, born in 1549, was a serious and studious youth who went on to a distinguished military, civil, and legal career, sadly cut short by death in 1587.[9] But the historian Lawrence Stone notes, among young nobility of the Elizabethan age (p. 582),

> a personal recklessness of behavior whose cause was more psychological than social. This private malaise was particularly common in the 1580's and 1590's as there grew up a whole new generation of high-spirited young aristocrats in open rebellion against the conservative establishment in general and Lord Burghley [i.e., Cecil] in particular. Very many, like Oxford, Rutland, Southampton, Bedford, and Essex, had been wards of the old man and were reacting violently against his counsels of worldly prudence. Such a development is hardly surprising. To listen to Polonius for a few moments in a theatre is one thing; to have to put up with him pontificating at every meal-time for years on end is another. No wonder these young men adopted a way of life of absurdly prodigal extravagance; it was the only revenge they could take on a guardian to whom waste and imprudence were deeply horrifying. The knowledge that so many of his charges had both disliked him and gone to the bad must have puzzled and saddened this well-meaning old gentleman.

Stone risks a sentiment espoused by both Oxford and his apologists: whatever went wrong was someone else's fault – usually Cecil's. (I myself assume that an individual born into power and privilege must sooner or later be held accountable for his own actions.)

Also living in Cecil's household was Thomas, Cecil's only child by his first wife, Mary Cheke; and Anne, his daughter by his second wife, the brilliant Mildred Cooke. Born 5 December 1556,[10] Anne was more than six years younger than Oxford. A year after Oxford's arrival Mildred gave birth to Robert, a sickly boy who in the course of time would outstrip every one of Cecil's wards.[11]

Cecil House lay on the north side of the Strand, between London and West-minster:[12]

> [it was originally built] of Bricke and Timber, very large and spacious, but of later time it hath beene farre more beautifully encreased by the late sir William Cicile Baron of Burghley ...

John Norden described the house thus in 1594:[13]

> Burleigh howse, the howse of the ryght honorable Lord Burleigh, Lord high Treasorer of England, and by him erected. Standinge on the north side of the Stronde, a verie fayre howse raysed with brickes, proportionablie adorned with four turrets, placed at the four quarters of the howse; within[,] it is curiouslye bewtified with rare devises, and especially the Oratory, placed in an angle of the great chamber.

> Unto this is annexed on the east a proper howse of the honorable Sir Robert Cecill, knight, and of Her Maiesties most honorable Prevye Counsayle.

Behind the house lay intricate gardens, supervised by the botanist John Gerard (1545–1612).[14] Across the Strand stood the Savoy, a religious house not fully disestablished; beyond that flowed the Thames, with something of the aspect of the Grand Canal of Venice. The nearest access point to river traffic was the wharf at the bottom of Ivy Lane (see Maps 2 and 3). In his retrospective Diary, under 14 July 1561, Cecil noted: 'The Queen supped at my House in Strond before it was fully finished' (ii, 752). Presumably the house was still unfinished a year and some months later when Oxford arrived there. On 7 September 1570, Cecil purchased land from the Earl of Bedford to enlarge his gardens.[15] In this magnificent estate, Cecil's stables alone cost him 1000 marks (£666–13–4) per annum (Ward, p. 17).

Another of Cecil's houses was Theobalds, near Cheshunt, Hertfordshire, just north of London, described thus by the German traveller Paul Hentzner in 1598:[16]

> In the Gallery was painted the Genealogy of the Kings of England; from this place, one goes into the Garden, encompassed with a Ditch full of Water, large enough for one to have the pleasure of going into a Boat, and rowing between the shrubs; here are great varieties of Trees and Plants, Labyrinths made with a great deal of Labour; a *Jet d'eau*, with its Bason of white Marble; and Columns and Pyramids of Wood and other Materials up and down the Garden. After seeing these, we were led by the Gardener into a Summer-house, in the lower part of which, built semi-circularly, are the twelve Roman Emperors, in Marble, and a Table of Touchstone; the upper part of it is set round with Cisterns of Lead, into which the Water is conveyed by Pipes, so that Fish may be kept in them; and in Summer time they are very convenient for Bathing. In another Room, for Entertainment, very near this, and joined to it by a little Bridge, was an Oval Table of red Marble. We were not admitted to see the Apartments of this Palace, there being nobody to shew it, as the Family was in Town attending the Funeral of their Lord.

In fact, when Hentzner visited in 1598, Cecil – Lord Burghley – had just died.

Confident of his grasp of pedagogy and child psychology, Cecil drew up 'Orders for the Earl of Oxfords Exercises' in his own hand.[17] The young Earl was to 'rise in such time as he may be ready to his exercises by 7 o'clock'. Then he was to follow a daily regimen:

7–7:30	Dancing
7:30–8	Breakfast
8–9	French
9–10	Latin
10–10:30	Writing and Drawing

Then Common Prayers, and so to Dinner

1–2	Cosmography
2–3	Latin
3–4	French
4–4:30	Exercises with his pen

Then Common Prayers, and so to Supper.

On Holy Days Oxford was to 'read before dinner the Epistle and Gospel in his own tongue, and in the other tongue after dinner. All the rest of the day to be spent in riding, shooting, dancing, walking, and other commendable exercises, saving the time for Prayer.' His tutor was Lawrence Nowell, Dean of Lichfield, brother of Alexander Nowell the scholarly Dean of St Paul's.[18]

On 1 January 1563 Oxford joined his adult peers in his first Parliament:[19]

Then th'erles, but ix present: th'Erle of Hertford, present Pembrooke, and px. Bedford, yonge Southampton, Warwick, yong Bath, pr. Huntington, Ireland Sussex, Cumberland, pr. Rutland, px. Worcestre, px. Derby, px. Shrewsbury, Westmerland, px. Northumberland, yong Oxford, and pr. Arundell; their robes of scarlett with iij rowes of mynyver. ...

On the neither [=nether] sack sate Doctor Huick, Spilman, clerk of the parliament, and Mr. Marten, clerk of the Crowne. And behinde them kneeled Mr Smith, Allen, Dyster, Nicasius, Cliffe and Permitter. At the side hand of the Queene sate on the ground three or ffower ladyes and noe more. And at the back of the rayle behind the cloth of estate kneeled the Erles of Oxford and Rutland, under age, the Erle of Desmond, the Lord Roos, the Lord Herbert of Cardiff and divers other noblemen's sonnes and heires.

The Queene beeing sett, the lower house was lett in. ...

Though Oxford could not yet play a formal role, he witnessed the ceremony and spectacle of the occasion.

On 30 April Countess Margery dictated a reply to letters she had received from Cecil, about the second week of March, urging her to complete the probate of her late husband's will:[20]

Good Master Secretorye I call to my remembrance / that abowght Mydlent last past I receyuid Sundrye Letters of lyke importance, to that ende I schowld vse Expedition in the probate of my late Lord & Husbondes wyll (whose Sowle God haue.) I Receyuid them by one messenger and at one instant. / wherbye I Gatheryd generallye that Complayntes had byne browght to my Lord of Norfolks grace & to my Lord Robert Dudleyge, by sundrye / that the onelye lett whye my Late Lordes wyll hathe not byn provyd or exhibytyd hathe byn onlye in me / and throwghe my delayes / And the awctors of that cowlde as well have sayid yf yt had pleasyd them that I was fullye myndyd in this Ester Terme at the furthest (by Goddys helpe) to have mad[e] my full determination eyther in takynge appon me or in Refusynge by syche good advyce as I can gett / and that done to have mad yow & my Sunne [=son (Edward)] privye what I had intendyd / And soo consequentlye my Lords Grace & my Lord Robert Dudleyghe whoo have the lyke Trust Commyttyd to them And thus muche I Intendyd & determynid in the herynge of all the rest of the executors & other of my fryndes / and Good mr Secretorye lett me be purgid with yow (and with other of the Quenes heyghnes most honorable privye Cowncell) with any Suspytion that I showld be a slander to my Lords Wyll, & not performe the Trust commyttyd vnto me as I have byn of late burdeyned [=burdened] I confesse that a great Trust hathe byn commyttyd to me, of thos thinges whyche in my Lords Lyffe tyme was kept most Secrett from me / And synce that tyme the dowghtfull declaration of my Lordes dettes hathe soo vncertenlye fallen owt, that (by syche advyce as I have allwayes hetherto fownd most sownde to me) I hade rather geve vpe the hole doynges therof to my Sune (yf by yowr good advyce I maye soo dele honourablye) then to venture further and vncertenlye, altogethers with peryll /

Evidently her late husband's debts had taken Margery by surprise; hence her desire to be relieved of the responsibility of administering the will. She continued:

And Good master Secretorye I most hartelye praye yow to consyder me in syche thinges as I have hertofore byn a Suter to yow for, whyche wer in my Late Lordes handes for the provytione of his howse / onelye desyryng yt non other wyse but to be preferryd & consyderyd for my monye before a St[r]anger, and to wayte appon yow to that end I send [< … >] vppe one of my men of purpose to gyve yow Instructions of syche thinges as I shall have gretyst want of. And what my further determynation ys towchyng the wyll yet lothe to determyn withowt yowr good advyce / for that I meane the honor or geyne (yf anye be) myght Come hollye to my Sune who ys vnder yowr Chardge. And showlde be by yowr good devyce, the sowndlyer delt withall at other mennes handes. that the honorable delyng therin myght onlye sownde to hym, I rather bend my selffe for my parte to leve the hole doynges therof to hym / And herin, and in all other thinges wherin I have byn bowld to trouble yow alwayes, I most hartelye & humblye praye yow to contynewe yowr good advyce & fryndshipe towerdes me ...

The endorsement provides a good summary of the letter itself:

... my Lady of Oxenford to my Master In answer to her delayes to prove her lately deceased Lords Will: being disposed to renounce it, & leave it to her son.

A memorandum accompanying the will notes that on 22 July Margery formally renounced her executorship, leaving administration in the hands of her son and his counsellors.

Some eight months after young Oxford entered Cecil House, Lawrence Nowell wrote to Cecil:[21]

> I clearly see that my work for the Earl of Oxford cannot be much longer required.

Perhaps Oxford surpassed Nowell's capacity to instruct him. More likely – since nothing indicates that Oxford was an enthusiastic scholar, and much indicates that he was not – Nowell found the youth intractable.

That Oxford was consumed with a sense of his own importance is suggested by 'A summary of the charges of the apparel of the Earl of Oxford, 1566' running from 3 September 1563 to 22 March 1567:[22]

> ffor the apparell, with Rapiaress and daggers for my Lord of Oxenford his person, viz.
>
> 1562 & 63   In the fyrst yeare and xxvj odd dayes, beginning the third of September, and ending xxviijth of September, Anno Reginae Elizabeth vto   CLiiijli vs vjd
>
> 1563 & 64   Item in the second yeare beginning the xxixth of September Anno vto and ending the xxxth of September Anno Reginae Elizabeth vjto   Cvjli xvs vjd
>
> 1564 & 65   Also in the third yeare beginning the last of October Anno vjto & ending the xxixth of September Anno Reginae Elizabeth vijmo   Ciiijxxli vjs xviijd
>
> 1565 & 66   More for the vth yeare beginning the xxxth of September Anno vijmo and ending the xxviijth of September Anno Reginae Elizabeth viijvo   CLxxvli xijs jd
>
> Summa of theis iiij yeares   vjC xxvijli xvs [=£627–15–0]
>
> 1566   And as by one warrant ending at Christmas   Lvjli   iiijs [=£56–4–0]

Thus, over a period of four and a half years, Oxford spent £683–19–0, a sum greater than his entire cash inheritance of £666–13–4, on apparel, rapiers, and daggers. However much he gave to his studies, he was clearly giving more time, energy, and money to his accoutrements.

Oxford's expenses were offset at least in part by monies collected by his half-uncle Arthur Golding, among others. Of two receipts exemplifying Golding's employment, with his personal signature,[23] the first (*Manerium de Colbrooke in Comitatu Devon*) is dated 22 May 1563 (f. 175):

> Received the xxijth of May in the yere aforesayd of John Dawe Baylyf there for the Collection of the half yeres Rent of the said Manor due vnto the right honorable the Erle of Oxinford at the feast of Thanunnciation of our Lady last past, the summe of fyvetene powndes

The second (*Manerium de Chrysten Malford in Comitatu Wylshyre*) is dated 26 May 1563 (f. 184):

> Received the xxvjth of May in the yere above wrytten of Ierom Balborowe Baylyf in part payment of the Revenues of the said Manour Dve vnto the right honorable the Erle of Oxinford at the feast of Thanunnciation of our Lady last past for that half yere the summe of xxli

A supplementary statement accompanies the receipts (f. 176):

> Monney received by me Arthur Goldyng to thvse of the right Honorable the Erle of Oxinford at thappointment of the right honorable Sir William Cecill knight Master of the Quenes Highnesse Court of Wardes and Lyveries.

> Received of the Baylyf of Colbrook in the County of Devonshyre the summe of xvli

> Item of the Baylyf of Christen Malford in Comitatu Wylshyre the Summe of xxli

Golding was doubtless also responsible for a valuation of lands in Herefordshire dated 24 May 1563 (ff. 177–78). Other rents were gathered by Thomas Williams and Thomas Browne, feodaries of Devon and Cornwall respectively.[24]

Golding assisted with another, far more serious matter. Edward, Lord Windsor, husband of Oxford's half-sister Katherine, sued to have the issue of the 16th Earl's marriage to Margery Golding – Edward and Mary – declared illegitimate. Though Lord and Lady Windsor must have coveted the Oxford estates, resentment may also have played a role. On 28 June 1563 Golding responded to the suit, doubtless on Cecil's instructions:[25]

> Being informed on the report of several persons that Catherine, wife of Lord Edward Windsor, Baron de Stanwell, has entered a vigorous demand and still urges that the most Reverend Matthew [Parker], Archbishop of Canterbury, shall decree that the afore mentioned lord Earl of Oxford and Lady Mary his sister be summoned to produce witnesses (if they shall think it concerns their interest) to be received, sworn and examined about certain articles touching and concerning the said Earl and his sister under protestations of 'not consenting unless &c'. Arthur Golding alleges and to the effect of all right alleges the petition of the said lady Catherine to contain grave prejudice of the lady the Queen and to touch the legitimacy of the blood and right of hereditary possessions of the said Earl and his sister and alleges the aforesaid Earl to have been and to be a minor of fourteen years and known and of record to be under the ward, tutelage and care of the said lady the Queen with all and singular his lands, tenements and hereditaments which of right are and ought to be in the possession and rule of the said lady the Queen during his minority. And for the same reason by the common law as by the statutes of the realm, and also by the privileges of the Court of Wards and Liveries no plea or controversy may be moved or any other be recited, set in motion or proposed before any ecclesiastical or secular judge, which touches directly or indirectly the person, state, things, goods, lands, possessions, tenements or hereditaments of the same in any way or in any manner during his minority in the Court of Wards and Liveries of the said lady the Queen save before the master and council for the same Court to this deputed by the strength of the law of this realm. And further he alleges that the said lady Mary the sister of the said Earl was and is a minor of

fourteen years and her right and interest to depend directly on the right and title of the aforenamed Earl. Therefore he asks that the most Reverend decree by reason of the premisses that it be superseded, until special licence in this part be obtained, according to the laws and customs in like causes in the said Court of Wards and Liveries lawfully used.

Though Golding puts the ages of both Edward and Mary at fourteen, he had just turned thirteen on 12 April, while she was ten or less at the time. Windsor's challenge was overcome, partly with Cecil's assistance,[26] but this did not stop Queen Elizabeth from taunting Oxford with bastardy (LIB-4.2/9.2).

Oxford's earliest surviving letter, dated 23 August 1563, constitutes a compliment in French to his guardian Cecil (LL-01). Although the letter – or its corrections – may have been dictated by a tutor, the handwriting is Oxford's own. His 'exercises with his pen' paid off, for unlike some of his contemporaries, including Queen Elizabeth herself, he never to the end of his life stinted his penmanship: letters and memoranda in Oxford's hand are among the most accessible of the Elizabethan age.

9 Early Teens

Countess Margery took as her second husband the Gentleman Pensioner Charles Tyrrell, sixth son of Sir Thomas Tyrrell of Heron, East Houndon, Essex, by Constance Blount, daughter of John Blount, Lord Mountjoy.[1] (Charles's prior marriage to Agnes Chitwode *alias* Odell had been annulled by the Court of Delegates on 6 April 1560.)[2] Although Margery and Charles are first identified as husband and wife in a will signed on 13 May 1566 by Charles's brother Richard of Assheton, Essex,[3] as early as 11 October 1563 Margery, thanking Cecil for his 'Gentylnes and fatherlye fryndshippe towerdes my Sunne', refers to herself and 'Mr Tyrell' as 'vs boothe'.[4] The couple retained an interest in the Manor at Earls Colne,[5] but lived principally in Kingston-upon-Thames, south-west of London. Charles's companions included 'maister Iohn Seymore esquire one of the quenes Maiesties gentlemen penciorers and Mr Richarde Kelton gentleman ... my freinde, maister Kelton of Colne'. An acquaintance was 'Mr More clerke of our bande' – another Gentleman Pensioner. Charles kept a 'chamber at London'.[6] Margery maintained friendships with the countesses of Warwick and Worcester, as with Charles's three sisters and one of their husbands: 'sister Churche'; 'brother and sister Garnisshe'; and 'sister Felton'. One of Margery's gentlewomen-servants was a 'Mrs Gardener'.

As for Oxford, on 9 January 1564 William Cecil wrote to the Countess of Rutland:[7]

> I wrote lately to you that Lord Rutland your sone in law [=step-son] might be brought up hither by my cousin Disney, your officer, and I wrote the like to him. I understand by the steward of my house near Stamford that my letters have miscarried. I therefore pray that either Mr. Disney, or any other whom you shall think meet, may forthwith conduct my said Lord hither or to a place within three miles, near Maidenhead Bridge, where Lord Oxford is. It is called Hitcham next to Burnham. In my letter to my cousin Disney, I offered this manner of journey for my Lord ...

Hitcham (Berkshire), where Oxford was recuperating from an illness, lies about twenty-five miles west of London, between Slough and Maidenhead. Oxford and Rutland would keep close company over the next three years.

In August the Queen visited Cambridge, arriving on Saturday the 5th and leaving on Thursday the 10th. St John's College accommodated Cecil, Oxford, and Rutland – for this was Cecil's alma mater.[8] Marchpane and sugar loaves were bestowed by the town on six noblemen, on Cecil (who was also chancellor of the University), and on the controller of the Queen's household.[9] Cecil had taken an interest in the preparation of sermons, disputations, and plays for the entertainment of noble visitors. As no college hall could provide a sufficient theatre, royal surveyors ordered up an enormous stage in King's College Chapel. Here three plays were performed on successive nights. First, on Sunday 6 August, came Plautus's *Aulularia*. Next was 'a tragedye named Dido', with Leicester and Cecil holding the book of the play. Both plays were performed by students from several colleges. Then came Nicholas Udall's *Ezechias*, performed by King's College only. On Wednesday the 9th, *Ajax Flagellifer* was to have been performed, again by King's alone, but as the Queen was exhausted, the performance was cancelled.[10]

The University's great commencement stage was erected in the church of St Mary the Great on the market: here, on Thursday 10 August, academic degrees 'in honor of the university' were bestowed on seventeen visitors:[11]

1. The Duke of Norfolk (Thomas Howard)
2. The Earl of Sussex (Thomas Radcliffe)
3. The Earl of Warwick (Ambrose Dudley)
4. The Earle of Oxford (Edward de Vere)
5. The Earle of Rutland (Edward Manners)
6. The Lord Robert (Robert Dudley)
7. The Lord Clynton (Edward Clynton)
8. The Lord Hunsdon (Henry Carey)
9. The Lord Chamberlayn (William Howard)
10. Sir William Cecyll, Knt.
11. Sir Francis Knollys, Knt.
12. [John] Ashley, Esquire
13. [Richard] Bartue, Esquire

14. [Thomas] Henneage, Esquire
15. Edward Cooke, Esquire
16. William Cooke, Esquire
17. Mr. William Latimer, Clerke of her Majestie's Closet, Doctor in Divinity

The University distributed these unearned degrees even as the town distributed marchpane and sugar loaves. During this same year his uncle, Arthur Golding, dedicated his translation, *Thabridgment of the Histories of Trogus Pompeius*, to Oxford, having originally intended it for the 16th Earl. Golding attributes to his nephew, now fourteen, an interest in ancient history and current events.[12] (Golding lived at Cecil House at least until 23 December 1564; in early 1565 he departed, apparently for good.)[13]

On 7 May 1565 Countess Margery dictated another letter to Cecil:[14]

> My commendations to yow remembred where as my lord of Oxinforde my sonne now the queins maiesties warde ys by law intitled to have a certain porcion of his inheritaunce from the death of my late Lorde & husbande his father and presently to his vse to be received, and as I vnderstand the porcion particulerly ys set furth by order of the quenis Maiesties honorable Cowrte of Wardes and Lyveries yf it myght stande with your pleasuer that the same pencion soe set furthe might by your order be committed to some suche of his freinds during his minoritie so as myght be trewly aunswered of the hole yssuis and profittes of the same at his full age he shuld haue good [cause] to thinke hymself muche bounde to you for the same.

Thus Margery requests that monies from family properties be guarded by friends during her son's minority:

> For otherwise when he shall come to his full age he shall not be hable either [to] furnyshe his house with stuff or other provision mete for one of his callinge neither be hable to beare the charges of the sute of his liverie, which charges weare foreseyne and provided for by my said late Lorde and husbande and his counsell lerned by suche devises as they made that his said sonne shuld thus be entitled to a porcion of his inheritaunce during his minoritie. And yf the same porcion shuld rema[i]nne in the handes of my Lorde now in his minoritie and not [be] committed to some suche persons as shuld be bounde to aunswere hym the same at his full age, The care which my said lorde his father and his counsell lerned had for the aide and reliefe of hym at his full age myght come to small effect.

Margery fears that her son's extravagance will pose a danger to the livery of his estates six years hence. She will assume responsibility herself, with the assistance of Robert Christmas and others, offering bonds to guarantee honest performance:

> which matter moveth me ernestly to become a suter to you in his behalf. And in case it myght please yow to think me being his natural mother mete to be one to haue the order receite and gouernement of the said porcion ioyned with some other of worshipp and substaunce and Robert Chrismas for the trew aunswering of the meane profittes of the same to my lorde at his full age I woulde willingly travell

[=travail, work] to procure suche persons to ioyne with me in it as shall be to your contentacion. And therwith they to be bounde in suche boundes for the trew aunswering of the said revenues and profittes as shall seme vnto yow good....

Young Oxford cannot have appreciated this interference by his mother.

On 11 November Ambrose Dudley, Earl of Warwick, married Anne Russell, eldest daughter of the Earl of Bedford, at Westminster Palace:

... the sayd Anne lying in the Courte, she came from her Chamber and went to the Queenes Majesty's great Clossett, ledd by the Erles of Oxford and Rutland, being accompaned with divers Lords and Gentlemen before her, and the Queen's Mayds of Honnor, and other young Gentlewomen after her ... And after that the sayd Bryde was com[e] to the Clossett, the Lords returned and fetched the Lord Bridegrome ... After they were both in the Clossett the Lords went for the Queene, who cam[e] to her Clossett accompanyed with the Nobility as accustomed ...

A tournament held at Westminster to celebrate the wedding must have come as a particular delight to both young earls.[15]

On 6 February 1566 William Cecil, master of the wards; Sir William Dansell, receiver; William Took, auditor; and Robert Nowell, attorney of the Court of Wards, wrote to Robert Christmas, apparently in his capacity as administrator of Oxford's Essex estates:[16]

There is a yearly rent of 66l. due to Her Majesty out of the late priory of Colne, co. Essex, parcel of the possessions of Edward, now Earl of Oxford, Her Majesty's ward, which priory is contained in a lease granted to your master, under the seal of Her Majesty's Court of Wards and Liveries. As the said rent reserved is not comprised in the lease, for lack of instructions given upon the making thereof, it has remained unpaid ever since the death of the late Earl, father of the present Earl, now upwards of three years, and amounts to 198l., for payment whereof the receiver of Essex is a suitor to us. We therefore require to order the said arrears to be forthwith paid, as also the yearly rent hereafter, and this shall be a sufficient discharge to his Lordship for payment thereof, and to the Auditor General of the Court of Wards and Liveries to allow it on his Lordship's account for the possessions of the said now Earl, so long as the same shall remain in Her Majesty's hands.

Elizabeth demanded her portion of Oxford's current revenue, which while unpaid would accumulate as debt.

In August 1566 Elizabeth paid a visit to Oxford University, modelled on her 1564 visit to Cambridge. She witnessed three plays in Christ Church hall, outfitted, if anything, more sumptuously than King's College Chapel at Cambridge:[17] *Marcus Geminus*, a Roman history play in Latin by Toby Matthew of Christ Church; *Palamon and Arcyte*, a two-part play in English, based on Chaucer's 'The Knight's Tale', by Richard Edwards, formerly of Corpus Christi College [Oxford], and now Master of the Children of the Chapel; and *Progne*, a tragedy

in Latin by James Calfhill of Christ Church. As we will discover, Richard
Edwards's name was destined to be linked with Oxford's.

On 6 September Oxford MAs were showered upon distinguished guests, as
Cambridge degrees had been two years before:[18]

1. The Earl of Oxford, Edward Vere
2. William Haward or Howard, Baron of Effingham
3. Thomas Butler, Earl of Ormond
4. Ambrose Dudley, Earl of Warwick
5. Henry Lord Strange, son of Edward Earl of Derby
6. Edward Stafford, Lord Stafford
7. John Sheffield, Lord Sheffield
8. Sir William Cecil, Secretary of State
9. (blank) Rogers, Comptroller
10. Sir Franics Knolys, Knight, Captain of the Halberdiers
11. Sir Nicholas Throcmorton, Knight
12. John Tomworth, or Tamworth, Esq. of the Privy Chamber to the Queen

Again, no academic accomplishment or desert is to be imputed to any recipient.

It was probably during this same visit that George Coryate composed Latin
verses which his peripatetic son Thomas appended to *Coryates Crudites* of 1611.
Preceded by poems to the Queen and to William and Henry Herbert, and
followed by poems to William Cecil, Ambrose Dudley, and Thomas Cecil, the
poem addressed to Oxford consists of standard themes of praise, but also contains
two lines tailored to his subject:

Tum quia Musarum tanto capiaris amore,
Auribus his modulis occinit vna tuis.

'Then, since you attract the love of the muses in such great measure, these notes
may seem unpleasing to your ears.' The compliment paid to Oxford and the
muses could refer to any of the arts, including poetry, or to learning in general.

Oxford must have visited Cambridge at least once in the late 1560s, as Gabriel
Harvey later recollected meeting him there in Spenser's *Foure Letters* of 1592 (p.
21):

... in the prime of his gallantest youth, hee bestowed Angels vpon me in Christes
Colledge in Cambridge, & otherwise voutsafed me many gratious fauours at the
affectionate commendation of my Cosen, M. Thomas Smith, the sonne of Sir
Thomas ...

An 'angel' was an old coin valued (under Edward VI) at 10s. In his 1592 *Strange
Newes*, Thomas Nash soon berated Harvey for besmirching the reputation of the
recently deceased Robert Greene (sig. E4v):

A good fellowe hee was, and would haue drunke with thee for more angels then the
Lord thou libeldst on, gaue thee in Christs Colledge ...

Harvey's tenure at Christ's lasted from Easter 1566 to the receipt of his BA in Easter term 1570.[19] We shall consider his libel of Oxford in Chapter 43.

From 30 September 1566 to 2 January 1567 the second session of Elizabeth's Second Parliament convened in Westminster Hall (*TE*). Among the lords sat four minors:[20]

> Att the formost forme on the southside sate these peeres as followeth: ... Veere Earle of Oxford warde ... Manners Earle of Rutland warde ... Bourchier Erle of Bathe ward ... Wriothesley Erle of Southampton ward ...

In the official minutes Oxford and others are listed for the opening session only, and as *infra etatem* (under-age).[21]

On 1 January 1567 Cecil presented his ten-year-old daughter Anne with a spinning-wheel accompanied by a poem, 'To Mistres Anne Cecil', in two rhyme-royal stanzas of his own devising:[22]

> As yeres do growe, so cares encreasse
> and tyme will move to loke to thrifte,
> Thogh yeres in me worke nothing lesse
> Yet for your yeres, and new yeres gifte
> This huswifes toy is now my shifte.
> To set you on woorke some thrifte to feele
> I sende you now a spynneng wheele.
>
> But oon thing firste, I wisshe and pray
> Leste thirste of thryfte might soone you tyre.
> only to spynne oon pounde a daye.
> and play the reste, as tyme require.
> Sweat not (oh fy) fling rocke in fyre
> God sende who sendth all thrifte & welth
> you long yeres & your father helth.

The sentiments of a doting father shine brightly in this slight domestic verse.

On 1 February 'Edward Vere' was admitted to Gray's Inn, Cecil's former legal establishment. As with numerous other noblemen, Oxford's may have been a mere courtesy admission.[23] Of four current Burghley wards – Oxford, Edward Manners, William Carr, Edward Zouche – only Carr is known to have paid chamber rent at Gray's Inn. Conversely, only Oxford purchased no known legal books: his tastes, as we shall discover, ran rather to Chaucer, Plutarch (in French), Cicero, and Plato. Oxford never rose to prominence at Gray's Inn,[24] and hired attorneys for his legal affairs, as revealed on 22 November 1601 (LL-35): 'For counsel, I have such lawyers, and the best that I can get as are to be had in London, who have advised me for my best course ...'

Long before his seventeenth birthday, which occurred on 12 April 1567, Oxford evinced deeply rooted habits of self-importance and fiscal extravagance, spending heavily on clothes, personal weapons, horses, and retainers. He had received the dedication of one book and the gift of two university degrees without effort on his part. Honour, like wealth, came not for what he did, but for who he was.

10 First Blood

On Wednesday 23 July 1567, at seventeen years and three months, in the back yard of Cecil House, Oxford killed a man.[1] Entering the yard between seven and eight o'clock in the evening with Edward Baynam, a Westminster tailor,[2] Oxford practised the science of defence with rapiers. Thomas Brincknell, an undercook, evidently in the Cecil household, happened by. Whether by Brincknell's unwanted interference or by Oxford's deliberate act, the Earl's foil pierced the thigh of the unarmed man, and Brincknell was dead before midnight. His body was carried to Cecil House, to await the coroner.

The next day Middlesex coroner Richard Vale convened an inquest of 17 jurymen. Cecil recalled the affair and the verdict in his retrospective Diary (ii, 764):

> Thomas Bryncknell, an under Cook, was hurt by the Erle of Oxford at Cecill-houss, wherof he dyed, and by a Verdict found *felo de se*, with running upon a Poynt of a Fence Sword of the said Erle.

The coroner's report, in Latin, may be summarized thus:[3]

> Inquisition taken in the parish of St Martins in the Fields 24 July 1567 before Richard Vale, coroner, upon a viewing of the body of Thomas Brincknell, of Westminster, yeoman, lying dead, by seventeen jurymen (named), who affirm that on 23 July 1567 between seven and eight in the evening Edward Earl of Oxford and Edward Baynam, tailor of the same city, were together in the back yard of the residence of Sir William Cecil in the same parish, meaning no harm to anyone. Each had a sword, called a foil, and together they meant to practice the science of defence. Along came Thomas Brincknell, drunk, ... who ran and fell upon the point of the Earl of Oxford's foil (worth twelve pence), which Oxford held in his right hand intending to play (as they call it). In the course of which, with this foil Thomas (Brincknell) gave himself a wound to the front of his thigh four inches deep and one inch wide, of which he died instantly. This, to the exclusion of all other explanations, was the way he died.

The report states further that Brincknell had not kept God before his eyes,[4] but rather had been driven to this act of desperation at the instigation of and seduced by the Devil.

Presumably Oxford severed Brincknell's femoral artery, which might have resulted in death within four or five minutes, but only if the wound were left to bleed freely. The fiction of instantaneous death was, however, necessary to support the fiction of suicide. A verdict of *felo de se* required that the victim, of his own volition and supplying his own momentum, deliberately ran himself on a weapon held passively by another, and died without regret. Brincknell's property was forfeit, nor was he buried in sanctified ground. Oxford, meanwhile, got off scot free. The fictive scenario, abusing common sense and justice, was notorious.[5] The 17 jurymen were, however, as compliant as the jury was packed: one juryman, William Waters, was Oxford's own servant, while the subsequently more famous Ralph (or Raphael) Holinshed was Cecil's protégé.[6] Cecil himself may have had an uneasy conscience, since his recollection of the event nearly ten years later, about April 1576, is characterized by a sense of pathos, and partly re-writes history:[7]

> I did my best to haue the Iury fynd the death of a poor man whom he killed in my houss to be found *se defendendo*.

Cecil would thus recall the verdict as self-defence by Oxford rather than suicide by the victim.

The parish register of St Margaret's, Westminster, reveals that Thomas Brincknell was one of four or five siblings, possibly the eldest. On 8 August 1563 he had married Agnes Harris, probably of the same parish; on 6 November 1564 their first-born, Quyntyn, was baptized. The absence of any burial record for Thomas is consistent with the verdict of suicide. On 3 November 1567 a post-humous son, John, was baptized, but as a 'chrisom child', evidently still-born.[8] Agnes Brincknell was thus widowed after less than four years of marriage, the mother of one child under three, six months pregnant with another. As the widow of a suicide she was deprived of all her husband's worldly possessions – few though they doubtless were. Remaining a widow until her death eleven years later on 28 July 1578,[9] Agnes received charity from her parish both before and after Thomas's death.[10] The parish buried her 'chrisom child' at its own expense.[11]

Oxford, at the age of seventeen, presumably on his own initiative, practised the art of defence with an unguarded foil, partnered by a Westminster tailor. His success in subsequent tournaments suggests that Oxford was a good swordsman, though at seventeen perhaps not fully in control. His particular tactic was reprehended years later by Camden, who attributed it to Rowland York, one of Oxford's men:[12]

> [York] was famous among the Cutters of his time, for bringing in a new kind of fight, to run the point of a rapier into a man's body; this manner of fight he brought first into England, with great admiration of his audaciousnes. When in England before that time the vse was with little bucklers, and with broad swords to strike, and not to thrust, and it was accounted vnmanly to strike vnder the girdle.

The distinction of being the first man in England known to have killed another by the 'vnmanly' thrust of a rapier beneath the girdle belongs rather to Oxford than to York.

Cecil at least felt the injustice inflicted on the 'poor man' and his family. Nor was the killing forgotten by others. In December 1580 Henry Howard would state that he himself would not deal 'with the bloudshed of [Oxford's] youth bycause it is longe past althoughe most terrible'; similarly Charles Arundel: 'I speke not of his tastinge blud in his infancie almost' (LIB-3.1/4@53; 4.2/4.13).

In the Brincknell incident, Oxford learned a lesson which largely determined the next thirty years of his life: he could commit no act, however egregious, that his powerful guardian Cecil would not personally forgive and persuade others to forget.

11 Restless Youth

Across the Channel, exiled Catholics monitored the young hothead. In a list of 'Names and Faith of English Nobles' dated 18 December 1567, Oxford appears fifth, following the Duke of Norfolk and the earls of Sussex, Leicester, and Rutland, all perceived as 'Well affected towards Catholics'.[1] Similar lists over the next thirty years (1571, 1592, 1603) would routinely (but vainly) pin Catholic hopes on Oxford.

Also about this time the adventurer-poet Thomas Churchyard seems to have become acquainted with Oxford, whom he names by title in his 1602 *A True Discourse Historical* (pp. 10–11):[2]

> ... at the time when he ariued at Dillenbrough, where Churchyard[,] being sent (from the Lord high Chamberlaine of England)[,] saw the meeting of all this mightie assemblie, and serued vnder Monsieur de Lume (Counte de la March) as Cornet-bearer to two hundred and fiftie light horsemen all that warres, which was against the Duke of Alua in his first comming to Flanders.

Cecil rather than Oxford – still a minor – presumably authorized Churchyard's travels.

The indenture signed by the 16th Earl before his death required that his son, on his eighteenth birthday, which would occur on 12 April 1568, must choose for wife either Elizabeth or Mary Hastings. The day came and went with no known interest on either side. Oxford remained at Cecil House, joined by twelve-year-old Edward, Lord Zouch, whose wardship would last until 1577.

Countess Margery died on 2 December 1568, and was buried at Earls Colne, alongside her first husband.[3] Presumably Oxford and Lady Mary attended their mother's funeral, along with Margery's second husband, Charles Tyrrell, who subsequently died at Kingston-upon-Thames, where his burial on 7 March 1570 is recorded in the parish register:[4]

> Tewsdaye the buring of Mr Charlles Terrell gentleman

Related entries appear in churchwardens' accounts for the same year:[5]

> Item Received for the grawe [=grave] of Mr Terrell vis viiid
> Item Received for the pavle clothe xiid

In his will, probated on 4 May, Charles bequeathed 'unto the Earl of Oxford one great horse that his lordship gave me'.[6] Since Oxford had given Charles a horse, and Charles returned it, the two must have been on a cordial footing.[7] Charles also remembered Lady Mary:

> Secondarilie I giue and bequeathe vnto the ladie Marie sister to thearle of Oxforde one kirtell of black velvet ymbrodered all ouer with gold and pearle. Item I will that the same ladie Marie haue the karkenott of rewbies and pearle soe as she will paie xlli for the same.

The 'karkenott' was clearly worth considerably more than the £40 Mary was asked to pay into the estate. Charles overlooked the Windsors, who had traduced Margery's first marriage and brought misery to her issue.

Charles Tyrrell's will reveals that a lease on the 'howse, mannour and priorie of Colne' had been given by an indenture 'made by the late earle deceased' to John Boothe and Thomas Coe, 'which saide Iohn and Thomas have by theire deade [=deed] signed and sealed, released over theire intereste to my late wife the counties [=countess] of Oxforde in her widowehodde'. Boothe and Coe had been with the 16th Earl in 1562, the former as a witness to the marriage indenture, the latter as a witness to his will. His father, mother, and step-father all dead before his twentieth birthday, Oxford was more than ever the child of his guardian Cecil.

On 26 February 1569 Mary Queen of Scots was moved from Bolton Castle, Yorkshire, to Tutbury, into the guardianship of George Talbot, 6th Earl of Shrewsbury. Mary's English well-wishers attempted an insurrection remembered as 'The Rising of the Northern Earls'. The earls of Northumberland and Westmorland anticipated active support from the Earl of Derby and the Duke of Norfolk, and cooperation from Thomas Radcliffe, 3rd Earl of Sussex. Sussex, however, remained staunchly loyal to Elizabeth. By December, retreating towards the Scottish border, the rebels faced a powerful southern force near Durham; by mid-January 1570 the rebellion was contained.

Meanwhile, on 22 April 1569, ten days after his nineteenth birthday, Oxford received his first vote for the Order of the Garter (G-BL). Cast by William Lord Howard of Effingham, Lord Chamberlain, one of ten electors this year, the single vote probably represented no more than an affectionate gesture by a fond and somewhat distant uncle.

On 24 November Oxford wrote to Cecil. This, his first surviving letter in English, provides the earliest clear evidence of his personality (LL-02):

Sir. Althoth [=although] my hap hathe bin so hard that yt hathe visited me of lat[e] wythe syknes yet thanks be to God throw [=through] the lokinge to [=looking-to, oversight] which I haue had by yowr care had ouer me, I find my helthe restored and myself doble behowldinge vnto yow bothe for that and many good turnes whiche I haue receiued before of yowre part. For the which althothe I haue fownd yow to not account of late of me as in time tofore yet not wythstandinge that strangnes yow shall se at last in me that I will aknowlege and not be vngrat[e]full vnto yow for them and not to deserue so ill a thowght in yow that they were ill bestowed in me. But at this present desiringe yow yf I haue done any thinge amise that I haue merited yowre offence imput[e] [it] to my yong yeares and lak of experience to know my friendes. and at this time I ame bowld to desire yowre fauoure and friendship that yow will suffer me to be imploid by yowre meanes and help in this seruice that now is in hand Wherby I shall think my self the most bownd vnto yow of any man in this court and hearafter ye shall command me as any of yowre owne Hauing no other meanes wherby to speak wythe yow my self I am bowld to impart my mynd in paper, ernestly desiring yowr Lordship that at this instant as her to fore [=heretofore] yow haue giuen me yowre good word to haue me se the wares [=wars] and seruices in strange and forren places sythe yow cowld not then obtayne me licence of the Quenes Magesti Now yow will doo me so much honor as that by yowre purches of my licence I may be called to the seruice of my prince and contrie as at this present troblous time a number arr. Thus leuing [=leaving, ceasing] to importunat [=importune] yow wythe my ernest sut[e] I commit yowe to the hands of the Almighty. ...

Apparently writing from quarantine, Oxford concedes that he had disappointed Cecil, and begs him, 'yf I haue done any thinge amise that I haue merited yowre offence', to impute any failings to his youth and 'lak of experience to know my friendes'. Probably the behaviour that gave offence was more recent than the killing of Brincknell in 1567. We have reason to suspect indeed that by this his nineteenth year Oxford had found companions in drink, riot, and sexual licence.[8]

Some of Oxford's preoccupations in his twentieth year are revealed in expense accounts certified by John Hart, Chester Herald, over three successive quarters from 1 January to 30 September 1570.[9] From an expenditure of £399–10–0 over three quarters, we may infer an annual expenditure of approximately £533. A conspicuous consumer, over nine months Oxford purchased 32 pairs of Spanish shoes, nine pantoffles (a kind of slipper), three moyles (a kind of shoe), six hats, five caps, and seven pair of garters. First-quarter entries for 1570 reveal that Oxford, together with his tutors and servants, was charged £3 per week at Cecil House (equivalent to £156 per year). The third-quarter charges of £27–13–4 (equal to about £110 per year) may suggest a reduction of his retinue. Oxford lay sick at Windsor for part of the first term, and at Charing Cross, evidently again for illness, for some of the second. From his outlays on drugs and care, at £66–16–0 nearly one-fifth of his total expenses,[10] and from his subsequent patronage of apothecaries, we may infer that Oxford was chronically sickly, hypochondriacal, or both.

Oxford's wish for military service abroad is echoed by the French ambassador Fénélon's report of 15 February 1570:[11]

> I have recently heard that the Earl of Oxford, a young lord well esteemed in this court, who has desired to see war, and importuned the Queen for permission to go to meet the Prince of Condé; after several refusals, she told him that she wished a young man of his status to meet only men of better intent; to which he replied that he then asked her permission to serve the King, and that he would happily fight against the rebels, who were then making war. Rebuked [for his presumption], he appeared before the Lords of the Council, before whom he showed himself resolved in his opinion, so that they thought this would play into the hands of the Catholics, whom they had wished to subject to a certain force; but, after having learned that the Queen had responded to him, they were all astonished, and had no further reply.

Fénélon wrote again on 21 March:[12]

> It is true that the young Earl of Oxford has frequently appeared ready, with a number of young English noblemen, to join the Prince of Condé, or certain German princes, for the purpose of observing war, but he hasn't succeeded in gaining permission from the Queen. It appears that certain individuals have advised him to go on his own, saying that he wouldn't in fact incur the Queen's wrath. In the end, however, she has expressly forbidden it and has given him letters for travel to Ireland.

... or did Fénélon mean Scotland?

Elizabeth did finally allow Oxford to join Sussex's operations in the North. Authorization for the journey occurs in a warrant dated 30 March, addressed by Cecil to Sir William Dansell, Receiver-General of the Court of Wards and Liveries:[13]

> Mr Receavour inasmuch as the Quenes Majestie sendeth at this present the Earle of Oxenford into the North partes to remain with my Lord of Sussex & to be imployed there in her Majesties service, These be to require yow to deliver vnto the said Earle or to the bearer herof for his vse the somme of *forty powndes* towardes his charges whilest he shall remain in those partes. And this shalbe your warrant and discharge in this behalf. At Hamptoncorte the xxxth of March 1570.

Your loving freind (signed) W Cecyll

> Received the daie and yere abovesaid of Sir William Damsell knight Receivour generall of the Queenes maiesties Court of wardes and Liveries accordinge to the purport of this warrant dated as appeareth the some of fortye powndes above mencioned.
>
> (*signed*) Edward Oxenford

To thandes of William Byshop

Cecil dictated the warrant to an amanuensis, who left the amount blank; Cecil then entered the amount and signed the warrant with his own hand. Oxford then carried the warrant to Dansell (or perhaps Bishop), signing for the £40 with his own hand. Oxford's purchases during the first quarter of 1570 suggest preparation for military service: a riding cloak and personal weapons, horses, and a close stool – a portable toilet – supplied by the upholsterer Philip Gunter.

By 17 April Sussex pushed up the valley of the Teviot with fearful reprisals:[14]

> burning on both hand at the least two mile, leaving neither Castle, town, nor tower unburnt till we came to Jedburgh.

Civilians suffered more than soldiers, who could move out of harm's way. Such was Sussex's design, expressed in a communication of 10 April:[15]

> ... before the lyght of this mone [=moon] be paste to leave a memory in Scotland wherof they and their chylderne shalbe affrayed to offer warre to England.

Elizabeth thanked Sussex on 11 June:[16]

> ... For, indeed, we have not known in our own time, nor heard of any former, that such entries into Scotland, with such acts of avenge have been so attempted and achieved with so small numbers, and so much to our honour, and the small loss or hurt of any of our subjects ...

As Ward notes, however (p. 48), 'We do not know for certain what part Lord Oxford played in this campaign'. In April Oxford received his second vote for the Order of the Garter, again from William Howard, one of nine electors (G-BL).

More truly indicative perhaps were Oxford's 1570 book purchases: in the first quarter, a Geneva Bible of the 1569–70 edition (now in the Folger Shakespeare Library),[17] a Chaucer, Plutarch's works in French (along with other books), and two Italian books, possibly including Francesco Guicciardini's *La historia d'Italia* (1565);[18] in the third quarter, folio copies of Tully (Cicero) and Plato, along with other books. Oxford's intellectual interests in his twentieth year seem to have been strictly humanistic.

On 29 July John Freake, MA, was presented to the rectory of Fulmer, co. Cambridge, Ely diocese, void by the resignation of Edmund Freake, MA, Queen's chaplain. By virtue of Oxford's minority, the right to appoint lay with the crown.[19] Family interests seem to have been consulted, however, since Edmund had been remembered in the 16th Earl's will.

A murky petition from an unidentified woman, entitled 'Certain conspiracies that of force I have been acquainted, touching Your Majesty', claims that Oxford attempted a political rescue on 3 August, 'the time the late Duke of norfolke was removed oute of the Tower to the Charterhouse [=Howard House]':[20]

> ... my husbande beinge prisoner in the fleet, the Earle of Oxforde provided a ship, (called the Grace of God) and tenne poundes was given erneste thervpon, and fiue

hundreth poundes more was to be paide for her, my husbandes libertie graunted and the shippe to be giuen him with two thowsande poundes in redie monie the one half to be payde here the other to be deliuered him at his ariuall with the duke in Spaine, my husbande opened these dealinges to me and offered to leaue me nine hundred poundes of the first paimente so that theare mighte no woordes growe theron. But I vtterlie renounced such gaine to receive. I had a care of the dutie I owe to your maiestie, as also I feared it woulde be the vtter destruction of my husband. So that with dutifull persuasions I caused to let the ernest be loste. And so that enterprise was dasshed. ... And sith I opened thes thinges to the Lord threasurer it is a year, euen when their last enterprise was in hand ...

The petition, evidently composed in 1574, was addressed to Cecil, then Lord Treasurer; the woman's earlier petition, now lost, may thus be dated to 1573. However doubtful the woman's references to Norfolk, it is certain that Oxford controlled ships which might carry men, money, or letters to Catholic interests abroad.

12 Best Friends

The deepest recesses of Oxford's private life over the whole of the 1570s would become the subject of detailed reports composed in December 1580 and January 1581 by three companions who began that decade as Oxford's most intimate friends. The first, Henry Howard, Oxford's elder by ten years, was born on 25 February 1540, the second son of Lady Frances Vere (Oxford's aunt) and of Henry Howard, eldest son of the 3rd Duke of Norfolk, known to posterity as the poet Surrey. In 1540 Henry VIII married Surrey's sister Catherine Howard. Triumph turned to ashes when she went to the block in 1542. A second blow fell in 1547, when Surrey himself was executed for treason. His five children – Thomas, Henry, Jane, Catherine, and Margaret – were billeted upon the Duchess of Richmond, a Protestant aunt. Young Henry was subsequently placed under the tutelage of the avid Protestant John Fox.[1]

The third Duke escaped his son's fate when Henry VIII conveniently died the night before the scheduled execution. The dukedom remained attainted until restored by Mary in 1553. Hereupon Henry, a precocious thirteen-year-old, was deposited in the household of John White, Bishop of Lincoln. Following White to Winchester in 1556, Henry's idyll vanished with the accession of Elizabeth in 1558. Restored in blood in 1559, Henry attended King's College, Cambridge, at the expense of the new Queen.

Thomas Howard became 4th Duke of Norfolk on his father's death in 1554. But while Thomas basked in the quadruple blessings of title, wealth, marriage, and social recognition, Henry survived in relative poverty and obscurity. Never interested in women or marriage, he sponged off rich relations decade after miserable decade until the accession of James in 1603. Academic life proved thoroughly congenial, however, and he 'charted a career unusual for one of his birth and rank as a scholar and teacher':[2]

> Taking his degree in 1564, he went on to read civil law at Trinity Hall. To his classical and legal training, Howard joined a knowledge of modern languages including Spanish, French and Italian and a familiarity with contemporary European literature. In his first known work, a treatise on natural philosophy, dated from Trinity Hall [a Cambridge college], August 1569, and dedicated to his sister Catherine, Howard cited, along with the works of Aristotle, Plato, Seneca and Plutarch, 'that most excellent work of the Count of Castiglione called the Courtier', an important allusion in light of his continuing ambition for a position outside the academy.

> While a Reader in Rhetoric at Cambridge, Howard lectured as well on civil law. Certainly, he was the only nobleman of the Elizabethan era to teach at a university, apparently to augment his slender income.

Howard was hands down the most learned nobleman of his time.[3] Not only his published books, but his voluminous papers now in the British Library – mostly notes for books never published – testify to his scholarly industry and acumen. He assembled a personal library which included a 1541 Italian edition of Castiglione's *Courtier*.[4] He cultivated musical and sartorial interests, consulting Cecil's servant Michael Hickes,[5] sometime between 1565 and 1570, over a teacher of the lute, and seeking 'to have a gown made in the latest fashion, with short hanging sleeves'.[6]

While Henry breathed the dank air of Cambridge in academic celibacy, Thomas married three heiresses in succession: Mary Fitzalan, heiress of the Earl of Arundel; Margaret, daughter of Lord Audley; and Elizabeth Leyburne, widow of Lord Dacre.[7] Following the latter's death in 1567, Thomas's thoughts of marriage to Mary Queen of Scots entangled him in the Rising of the Northern Earls. Committed to the Tower on 8 October 1569, he was released to Howard House in London, but re-committed on 7 September 1571. Following Thomas's execution in 1572, Henry would devote himself to the eldest son and principal Howard heir, Philip, styled Earl of Surrey, who would become Earl of Arundel in 1581.

The second of Oxford's companions was Charles Arundel. His mother was Margaret Howard, sister to the tragic Catherine,[8] whereby Charles would claim cousinship with Queen Elizabeth, Henry Howard, Oxford, Sussex, Edward Stafford (English ambassador to France 1583–90), and Anne Vavasor, whom we shall meet in due course, and numerous others.[9]

Charles's father, Sir Thomas Arundel, was second son of Sir John of the Lanherne Arundels. The Arundels, with roots in Cornwall, were so numerous by the sixteenth century that their principal branches were routinely distinguished as the 'great' Arundels of Lanherne, and the Arundels of Trerice, Tolverne, and

Wardour.[10] (The earls of Arundel were not Arundels – they were Fitzalans and Howards; nor were the Arundels earls.[11]) Sir Thomas lost his head at Tower Hill on 26 February 1552 for a conspiracy against John Dudley, Duke of Northumberland, Leicester's father (Sir Thomas's brother Humphrey having been executed before him).[12] Left behind were his widow and five offspring: Margaret, Matthew, Charles, Dorothy, and Jane. Matthew, apparently seventeen in 1552, must have been born in 1534 or 1535. As for Charles, Ward's surmise of 1538 for his birth year, or Peck's of 1540, may be close to the mark.[13] Report had it that Charles was named after the Holy Roman Emperor Charles V by Prince Philip of Spain, his godfather.[14]

Sir Thomas's attainder required the surrender of Lady Margaret's jointure, then in the hands of the Countess of Oxford.[15] On 13 February 1553 one third of the forfeited property was returned to Lady Margaret, preserving her family from destitution.[16] In due course Matthew would restore the family name, dying Sir Matthew Arundel in 1598; his son Thomas (1560–1625) became first Baron of Wardour.[17] Meanwhile, Charles lived off a small property in South Peterton, Somerset, with an annual rent of £85–7–4.[18] His first cousin, the Sir John Arundel who was born about 1527, proved a notorious Catholic who would spend years in London prisons, including much of the period from 1580 to the time of his death in 1590.[19] His recusancy brought the whole Arundel clan under suspicion.

Henry Howard and Charles Arundel were thus almost exact contemporaries, second sons of second sons, connected by birth to the Howards and to the Queen, but by the rules of primogeniture left mostly to fend for themselves. Both, moreover, were sons of fathers executed for treason, both unmarried, both Catholics, both would-be courtiers, both 'cousins' and close friends of Oxford.

A curious document entitled 'Memorialles for Charles Arundell' identifies its subject as 'Mr Allens man'.[20] Internal references to Secretary Cecil and Secretary Petre point to a date between 5 September 1550 and 1 June 1553.[21] Possibly a young Charles (if this was he) carried legal papers to London on behalf of Mr Allen, possibly the William Allen of Oxford responsible for English Catholic universities in exile (*DNB*).

Charles's early experience of family tragedy together with an apparent personal attachment to Philip of Spain must have made the accession of Mary on 19 July 1553 and her marriage to Philip on 25 July 1554 feel like a personal triumph; conversely, Mary's death in 1558 must have been a personal tragedy, as for many English Catholics. Charles even lacked the diversion of study at Cambridge, Oxford, or any of the known legal establishments in London.

The third of Oxford's close friends is more elusive. A Francis Southwell 'thelder' composed a will dated 6 October 1581 and probated on 9 February 1582 (he died on 19 November 1581).[22] Left behind were three minors: Miles, not yet twenty; Francis, perhaps nineteen; and Mary, not yet eighteen.[23] Francis the elder is probably too old and Francis the younger too young to have been Oxford's companion, but the same will names 'my Nephe Fraunces Sowthwell one of Sir Robert Sowthwell his childrene',[24] and this is probably our man.

Sir Robert Southwell, Master of the Rolls under Edward VI, died in 1559; since he fathered at least five children after Francis,[25] Francis must have been born in 1554 at the latest. He was related to the prolific and well-connected Southwells of Norfolk through his father, and to the socially prominent and financially prosperous Nevells (or Nevills) through his mother, daughter and sole heir of Sir Thomas Nevell.[26] In a letter of 11 May 1573, Gilbert Talbot, son of the Earl of Shrewsbury, declared 'one Francis Sothewell' both 'a frend of myne' and 'very great' with Dr Thomas Wilson.[27] As Master of Requests, Wilson supervised the interrogation of suspected conspirators, occasionally seeking and receiving a licence to use torture.[28]

We have already seen that when he was seventeen, Oxford took as his fencing companion a local tailor, Edward Baynam of Westminster, yeoman, and that Oxford killed an under-cook. Indeed, he and his servants indulged in violence of one form or another for almost two decades. On 4 April 1570, for example, residents of Long Melford, Sudbury, and Foxearth invaded lands owned by Oxford, but met with such resistance that the affair was brought to the attention of the Privy Council.[29] Many Oxford servants were of a low type indeed:[30]

> On a tyme My lorde oxforde beinge merye amonges his men demaynded whether hanginge were any payne or no / where vpon a semple man was desirous my Lord shoulde haue present knowledge thereof tooke his garters and made a knott and put yt about his necke / and willed one of his fellowes to drawe him vpp his backe but he drue him so ferre that he waxed blacke in the face / wher struglinge very hard and laboringe for liefe / wherevpon he lett him down / and beinge come to him selfe againe and well breathed he tolde my lorde that hange that wolde / for he woulde not haue the payne for all the worlde.

> This beinge don a wyser fellowe (as him thought) of the saied Lordes men wolde trye whether it were payne or noe / and so takinge of bothe his garters and tyinge them together / made a toppe slipinge knotte and drewe yt about his necke and drewe and drewe and still his armes still backwardes so longe that indede the drawinge still became verie blacke in the face and still drewe And so falinge at last to the grownde laye grovelinge and stryvinge for liefe by the holders was taken vpp and the gartere undon / and havinge breathed alitel / they asked him the cause why he drewe so and backwarde / he ansered that him thought before him there was a depe hole and that yf he hilde not his armes above he should haue fallen in / this is the delewcions of Sathan / wherfore yt is good to haue regarde with what weapons ye worke /

Reference may in fact be to the 16th Earl, whose wife 'wold never goe home agayne amongst such a bad companye as were about the Earle of Oxforde at that tyme'. But as the father's retainers included Thomas Robinson, the highwayman, so low types as well as high would people the life of the son.

13 Necromancer

In 1592 the English necromancer John Dee reported that he kept in his possession (and to his credit) 'The honorable Erle of Oxford his favorable letters Anno 1570'.[1] That Oxford was engaged in magic about this time is confirmed by Henry Howard's subsequent report that Oxford boasted at table of three distinct acts of necromancy (LIB-3.1/3):

> – that he had often tymes copulation with a female spirite in Sir George Howardes house at Grenwiche

> – that Charles Tyrrell apperid to him with a whippe after he was dead and his mother in a shete fortelling thinges to come

> – that he could coniure [=conjure] and had often conference with Sathan

Charles Arundel offered variations on the same three charges (LIB-4.2/2):

> – that Charles Tyrrell appereid to him with a whipp, which had made a better shew in the hand of a carman then of Hobb Gobbline, and this was in vnckle Howards at Grenewidge

> – that in the same place he had copulacion with a female spright

> – that he had often sene the devell by coniuringe with Parsons of the chappell that died, and by his direction paynetid owte a bo[o]k of prophesies; the coniuringe was in the little howse in the [tiltyard] at Grenewidge

Both lists refer to Oxford's step-father Charles Tyrrell, buried on 7 March 1570 at Kingston-upon-Thames; Howard refers also to Oxford's mother, who had died in December 1568. 'Parsons of the Chappell that died' is Robert Parsons, musician of the Chapel Royal, famously drowned in January 1570 crossing the river Trent at Newark.[2] Since the recently dead were aptest for necromantic contact,[3] the conjurations at Greenwich evidently began in the latter half of 1570, following Oxford's return from the North.

Both Howard and Arundel situate Oxford's conjuring at or near the house of Sir George Howard at Greenwich. Sir George, evidently born in the late 1520s, was the third son of Edmund Howard, and younger sibling of Catherine and Margaret Howard.[4] He alone of three brothers prospered in the wake of their sister's execution in 1542, acquiring a knighthood in 1547 and various offices in the 1550s.[5] He participated in a tournament on 25 March 1555,[6] and, as we have seen, in the coronation jousts of 17 January 1559. In this latter year the Queen appointed as her Master of the Armoury Sir Richard Southwell – yet another member of the extensive Southwell clan; but in 1561 Sir Richard resigned in favour of Sir George, who retained the mastership until Sir Richard resumed the office in 1575.[7]

Masters of the Armoury supervised both practical and ceremonial weaponry and trappings. On 30 June 1564 Sir George, whose responsibility included the 'dressing of the Queen's coursers', received an order to produce a complete suit of armour for 'Christopher Hatton, gentleman', the Queen's new favourite.[8] This very suit of armour may be depicted in the 'Almain Armourer's Album' (Fig. 2). The armour made for Henry Herbert, 2nd Earl of Pembroke, circa 1575–80, now preserved in the New York Metropolitan Museum, may be another product of his workshop.[9]

Of Sir George's private life not much is known. Evidently he never married.[10] He wielded administrative authority in and about Greenwich in 1566,[11] and was bailiff of Sayes Court, the manor-house at Deptford (just west of Greenwich).[12] He occupied a substantial property on the west side of East Greenwich Park, with 'two tenements, one barn, one stable, two gardens, and their appurtenances'.[13] Greenwich Palace was the site of the Royal Workshops and principal repository of arms and armour before their transfer to the Tower in 1580.[14] The Greenwich tiltyard, which he doubtless supervised, appears in both of Van den Wyngaerde's sketches of Greenwich Palace in 1558, while the 'little house' in which Oxford is reported to have conjured may be shown most clearly in the view from the south (Fig. 3).[15]

A man of literary pretensions, Sir George Howard devised the triumph of 'Cupid, Venus, and Mars' performed at Greenwich Palace on Twelfth Night 1553: though no text survives, a 'plat' or 'proporcion' drawn up and signed by Sir George himself is preserved among the Loseley papers now in the Folger Shakespeare Library.[16] On New Year's Day 1562 he presented to Queen Elizabeth 'a book containing thoffice of the Armery, covered with blak vellat, and bound with parssarmoryne of silver, with two plates of silver':[17] the manuscript, which survives with its original cover under the title 'Inventory of the Armouries', includes a portrait entitled 'Ser George Howarde Knight Master of the Qwenes Maiesties Armory Anno Domini 1561' (Fig. 4).[18] Sir George is the dedicatee of the second volume of William Painter's *Palace of Pleasure* (1567). He remained alive and well and the master of a fine appetite through 1576,[19] receiving New Year's 'free gifts' from the Queen as a gentleman usher through 1 January 1579.[20] He was certainly dead by 9 June 1580.[21]

Oxford's conjuring is thus to be imagined as having occurred either in Sir George's residence, or at the little house by the tiltyard, at Greenwich, perhaps as early as the summer of 1570, and probably before Sir George's mastership ended in 1575. We are free to imagine that Sir George shared in the enterprise. Oxford's infatuation with the occult may be celebrated in a verse stanza printed in the 1584 *Pandora*, a pamphlet composed by John Soowthern and dedicated to Oxford (sig. A3):

> For who marketh better than hee,
> The seuen turning flames of the Skie:
> Or hath read more of the antique.

Hath greater knowledge in the tongues:
Or vnderstandes sooner the sownes,   [sownes = sounds]
Of the learner to loue Musique.

The 'seven turning flames of the sky' are the seven planets of astronomy and astrology. Soowthern embraces Giambattista della Porta's claim that a magician 'must be a philosopher, a physician, an herbalist, know metals and distillation, understand mathematics, especially astrology, and be skillful in optics':[22]

These are the Sciences which Magick takes to her self for servants and helpers; and he that knows not these, is unworthy to be named a Magician.

Oxford may have acquainted himself with della Porta's *De i miracoli et mara-vigliosi effetti dalla natura prodotti, libri IIII* (Venice, 1562). Indeed, we have seen that he purchased Italian books in the first quarter of 1570.

The necromancy attributed to Oxford by Howard and Arundel conforms to types illustrated in contemporary documents.[23] Instructions for 'copulation with a female spirite' occur in a Folger manuscript dated circa 1580: 'the maner to maik a bande to bynd the vij sisters of the fayeres'.[24] The seven sisters of the fairies are invoked by name. Then the conjuror reads his spells facing 'est & west, south & northe'; 'Yow muste call [the sisters] before Sone [=sunrise?]: after Sone marke a circle of chalke or other wise one for her and then for your selfe':

Heare followethe the waye & maner howe youe shall call one of theese vergins of fayres afore nammed at onc[e] vnto thy beed where so ever thowe liste & have her at pleasuer. ...

This sayd goo to thy naked beed with her but laye youe one [=on] thy Ryght syde & lett [her] lye one her lefte syde & do with her what soo euer yow pleasses or canste doo for with owt doute shee is a woman + & yow nedeste not to feare her for shee shall haue no power to hurte the[e], being so bownde as is afore, to the[e] prescribed, nor the nether [=thou never?] in th[y] lyfe hadiste so pleasante a creature or lyvelye woman in beed with the[e] for bewtye & bountye nether quene nor empres in all the worlde is able to countervaile her for I have dyveres tymes provede her & have had here [=her] with me amen

then when thow haste accomplishe[d] it & fullfilled thie will & desier with her thow maiste Reason with her of any maner of thinges that thow desyreste to & in all kinde of question yow list to demmande of her but in any wysse I advyce the[e] to be well warre that yow aske her not what shee is and also I advyce the[e] to be well warre that yowe never tell deweringe [=during] the tyme shee is bownd in frendshipe to the[e], what shee doothe for the[e], to no boodye nor bye any other meanes dysclosse it for no kynde of occasion or besines howe greate or whate soever, it be, & so downing [=doing?] & ordyring thy selfe yow shall be sewer not onlye to hawe her Redye at your commaundemente, to come to lye with the[e] when soever, it is thye will to have thy pleasure on her / but allso you shalbe suere to haue thy wille fullfyled & done, in all other thinges that you leste to demande of her amen heare followethe the maner of the lycence when you will have her to departe / ...

Oxford is credited with a similar assumption that the magician's goal is not so much pleasure as knowledge – particularly knowledge of the future.

Another Folger manuscript recalls Howard's report that 'Charles Tyrrell apperid to [Oxford] with a whippe after he was dead and his mother in a shete fortelling thinges to come'. The magician must deploy an array of alphabetical letters and other signs:[25]

> This mvst be layed in the erth to vrge a late dead man to appeare & speake. ...
> These Letters before passed mvst be laied in the earth to vrdge a late dead man to speake.

The same manuscript provides advice and instruction on how 'To see spirrites et cetera', or 'To see divells or spirrites' (p. 57):

> Take the Herbe scabiosa[26] & beare it Reverently, for it defendeth the place where it is from evill thinges for with this Prophets made dead men to speake that were dead manie daies. ...

The 1570s began a long string of necromantic stage-plays, including *Clyomon and Clamydes* (early 1570s), Anthony Munday's *John a Kent and John a Cumber* (1589?), Marlowe's *Dr Faustus* (1592?), and Robert Greene's *Friar Bacon and Friar Bungay* (1594).[27] As we shall learn, Munday was Oxford's servant.

Like his stage counterparts, Oxford 'could coniure and had often conference with Sathan', or, in Arundel's more elaborate version, 'he had often sene the devell by coniuringe with Parsons of the chappell'. An appropriate picture of Satan survives in the same Folger manuscript (Fig. 5), along with instructions on how to address him (p. 172):[28]

> If you wish to invoke the spirit of Satan, make a circle with a well-burnished sword and go over it again with chalk or quick-lime – this is something I have tested. But beware that you do not do this for a trifle. And this is something that can be done at any hour; whatever hour you choose, do this at the midpoint of the hour, and be clean in dress because of the sanctity of the names. Here follows the very invocation by which you can compel the demon to appear, and he will immediately give you true responses (to your questions) ... whenever you desire to know anything for certain.

Thus knowledge is achieved by contacting devils – in this case, the master-devil, Satan.

Oxford's conjuring recalls not a highbrow like Giordano Bruno, who would live in London from 1583 to 1585,[29] but a lowbrow like the poet Thomas Watson. In 1579 Watson became involved in an intrigue which Nicholl has aptly denominated 'The Case of the King of Spain's Daughter'.[30] Anne Kirkall of Westminster, daughter of a butcher in East Cheap, suffered under the conviction that she was the natural daughter of Philip II, King of Spain, having been assured by a witch of Nottinghamshire that 'she was a Spanish bird, & that she had marks about her which would more appear hereafter'. Late in 1579 she consulted with Watson, who happened to reside in the same house. Watson flattered her: 'if you knew yourself, you would be the proudest woman in the parish'; and again: 'The best Spaniard that ever came in England was your father'.

> You have marks about you that shall appear greater hereafter. You shall have a lock of hair like gold wire in your head, and a mark in the nape of your neck like the letter M, and three moles standing triangle upon your right shoulder, and upon the reins of your back you shall have a mark of the breadth of twopence, which in time shall grow to a greater compass.

Watson was another close acquaintance of Oxford's, and dedicated his *Hekatompathia* to him in 1582.

Oxford may have retained an interest in alchemy well past the decade of the 1570s. John Manningham of the Middle Temple, in his diary under 25 October 1602, wrote:[31]

> I heard that Sir Richard Basset is much seduced, indeed gulled, by one Nicholas Hill, a great profest philosopher, and nowe abuseth this yong knight by imagined Alchymie.

Manningham cites as his informer one John Chapman. Manningham's most recent editor points out that Anthony Wood later described Nicholas Hill as an astrologer and alchemist patronized by the 'prodigal Earl of Oxford' as well as by Henry, Earl of Northumberland, otherwise known as the 'Wizard Earl'.[32] Arundel's charge that Oxford by the Devil's direction had 'paynetid owte a book of prophesies' had a curious denouement which we shall consider in Chapter 42.

14   Oxford's Letters

Oxford's letter of 24 November 1569 is one of many that survive, falling roughly into five groups: personal letters 1563 to 1604, mostly to William and (later) Robert Cecil (44); draft interrogatories, January 1581 (2); personal memoranda, 1591 to 1597 (4); letters on Cornish tin-mining 1595 to 1599 (18); memoranda on the same 1595 to 1599 (9). Seventy-four items are entirely in Oxford's italic hand, while two are partly and one entirely in the hand of an amanuensis. The total number of words surviving from Oxford's pen surpasses 50,000. Oxford's hand is almost always a clear and legible italic. Before 1569 and after the Queen's death in 1603 his signature is also italic; between these dates it contains distinctly antique letter-forms.

With respect to general habits of spelling, Oxford falls about midway between the untrained and phonetic practices of the poet Thomas Churchyard or the landlady Julian Penn (1592), and the more nearly uniform and 'modern' practices of William Cecil, Oxford's daughters Bridget and Susan, and his second wife, Elizabeth Trentham.[1]

The opening sentence of Oxford's first known letter in English (see p. 51) may be taken as representative:

> Althoth my hap hathe bin so hard that yt hathe visited me of lat wythe syknes yet thanks be to god throw the lokinge to which I haue had by yowr care had ouer me, I find my helthe restored and myself doble behowldinge vnto yow bothe for that and many good turnes whiche I haue receiued before of yowre part.

The vocabulary is recognizably English, virtually every word resolvable into a modern equivalent. Since internal punctuation is sparse (a single comma), it is necessary to parse the sentence, inferring a break or pause, for example, between 'syknes' and 'yet'. Some compounds must be read differently from their modern equivalents. Thus, for example, 'lokinge to' represents the compound 'looking-to', meaning 'oversight' or 'observation'. The clause 'yt hathe visited me of lat wythe syknes' contains an impersonal pronoun as subject, as in 'it is raining'.

Oxford's consonants are familiar, except perhaps for 'v' and 'u': historically these are one letter of the Latin alphabet, normally 'v' in initial positions, 'u' in medial positions, so that 'visited' and 'vnto', 'haue' and 'ouer', reflect contemporary practice. Distinctly odd even for the time is the 'th' (elsewhere 't' and 'the') which terminates 'althoth'. As for vowels, the y-for-i substitution in 'wythe' and 'syknes' is typical for the time; similarly, 'helthe' for health and 'doble' for double. Also typical is the use of 'silent e' without reference to the length of the preceding vowel: thus Oxford's 'hap' and 'hathe' were doubtless both pronounced with a short 'a' as in modern hap and hath, 'lat' with a long 'a' as in modern late.

The second sentence of the same letter reveals similar habits:

> For the which althothe I haue fownd yow to not account of late of me as in time tofore yet not wythstandinge that strangnes yow shall se at last in me that I will aknowlege and not be vngratfull vnto yow for them and not to deserue so ill a thowght in yow that they were ill bestowed in me.

Here is the same absence of punctuation, modern lexicon (but 'tofore' for modern heretofore), 'althothe' for although, and the indifferent use of 'silent e', as in 'late' for late but 'vngratfull' for ungrateful.

The 50,000-odd words which survive from Oxford's pen reveal several distinctive features:

Oxford had no settled way of spelling many common words: thus he could spell 'halfpenny' ('ha'penny') at least eleven different ways: 'halfpennie', 'halpenie', 'halpennie(s)', 'halpenny', 'halpennye', 'halpens', 'halpeny', 'halpenye', 'hapens', 'happenie(s)', and 'happenye'. Similarly, 'buy', 'by', 'buye', 'bvy', 'bwy', and 'bwye'.

Oxford used 'u', 'v', and 'w' interchangeably in medial and final positions, yielding, for example, three of the variants of 'buy' (see also 'law' and 'suit' below).

Oxford had no consistent way of spelling legal terms such as 'attorney' (also 'atturney', 'atturnie', 'atturnye', 'aturnye'); or 'suit' and 'suitor' and their plurals ('sut(e)', 'suter(s)', 'sutes', 'sutor', 'swt(e)', 'swter(s)', 'swtes'). Many variants result from the substitution of 'w' for 'u'. Similar substitutions result in the highly unusual spelling of law as 'lav' or 'lave' and lawyers as 'lavers'.

Oxford tended to write 'cowld' for could, 'showld' for should, and most particularly 'wowld' for would (but on one occasion, 'sowlde' for 'should').

Certain idiosyncracies suggest peculiar habits of speaking as well as writing: Oxford almost always wrote 'lek' for like, not only in the simple verb, but in such combination forms as 'misleke' and 'leklywhodes': 'leke', 'lekes', 'leket', 'lekinge', 'leklier', 'leklihode', 'lekly(e)', 'leklywhodes', 'lekwise'; also 'disleke', 'dislekinge', 'misleke', 'misleked', 'mislekes'. The same word occurs one time each as 'leake', 'leeke', and 'lick'. Oxford never used the 'like' spelling, in sharp contrast to the 'likely' used by his amanuensis, and 'liking' used by Burghley. So characteristic is Oxford's spelling in this regard that the three spellings 'cowld', 'showld', and 'wowld', along with 'lek' for 'like', are almost enough in themselves to identify a piece of writing as his.

A distinctly odder habit is Oxford's invariable use of 'oft' or 'ofte' for 'ought':

> '... they cannot and oft not to transport ...'; '... to her Magesty oft to be made ...'; 'Blokes oft to be 250*l* a peace'; 'the Marchante oft to bringe in suche an other quantite'; '... by auncient custome ofte to be 250*l* weyght ...'

He also used 'oft' meaning often, as in 'long and oft', or 'two thre and oft fowre shillinges a pound'. Conversely, Oxford used the spelling 'ought' for 'out': 'withe ought disparkinge the grounde'; 'withe ought dissemblinge my faultes'; 'as fast as I cane get me ought of towne'; 'ro[o]ted ought of yowre/fauoure'. He spelled this same word 'out', 'owt', and 'owte'.

The *Oxford English Dictionary* defines one sense of 'oft' as an obsolete or dialectal form of aught or ought, citing the rustic dialect of *Gammer Gurton's Needle* (1575), III.iii: 'Did I (olde witch) steal oft was thine?' Another example comes from Robert Greene's *Orpharion* (1599, written c. 1590), p. 57, perhaps influenced by 'oft' meaning often: 'We oft rightly to think of women, seeing so oft we seeke their favors'.[2] The *OED* head-note reveals that Oxford's substitution of the labial fricative 'f' for the gutteral 'ough' is a positive linguistic error, not just a rural dialect.

Oxford's spelling of 'like' in almost all forms as 'lek', 'likelihoods' as 'leklywhodes', and 'falsehood' as 'falswhood', reveals e-for-i and wh-for-h substitutions typical for an East Anglian dialect, reminding us that Oxford spent his formative years in rural Essex. Thus Oxford (like his contemporary Walter Ralegh) habitually spoke a provincial dialect.

Oxford's spelling suggests that he routinely misheard words and failed to correct his pronunciation by recourse to verbal roots. In this he is like the otherwise intelligent native speaker of modern English who says 'ek-cetera' for 'etcetera', or 'newk-u-lar' for 'nuclear'. The most egregious example of Oxford's mishearing is his spelling of 'stannary' as 'stammerye'. The 'stannaries' were tin mines, from late Latin *stannum*, meaning 'tin'. Clearly, Oxford misheard the n's as m's and did not make the correction (as any person actively conscious of Latin etymology would certainly have done). Mishearing will similarly account for Oxford's irregular use of 't', 'th', or 'the' to terminate 'although', 'enough', 'though', or 'through': 'allthough', 'allthought', 'allthowghe', 'althoth', 'althothe', 'although', 'althoughe', 'althoughte', 'althowgh', 'althowghe'; 'inoughe', 'inought', 'inowghe'; 'thoughe', 'thought' (thought and though), 'thowgh', 'thowghe', 'thowght' (thought and though), 'thowghte'; 'through', 'throughly', 'throught', 'throw', 'throwgh', 'throwghe', 'throwght'. Oxford also put a 't' at the end of 'prop', spelling it 'propt'; similarly, he wrote 'slypte' for 'slip', and 'hightnes' for 'highness'. Yet another linguistic error based on mis-hearing is Oxford's writing of so and so many pounds 'of year' rather than 'a year'; and 'any kind away' for 'any kind of way'.

The following is a list of misspellings based on mishearings: 'agers' for 'agents', 'churge' for 'church', 'dept' for 'debt', 'lenghe' for 'length', 'lyggates' for 'ingots', 'my thinkes' for 'methinks', 'reame' for 'realm', 'sticken' for 'sticking'. Three words in particular are written both oddly and without regard to their historical origins: 'accept' for 'except', 'impodent' for 'impudent', 'obsurdite' for 'absurdity' (compare Latin *exceptare, impudens, absurdus*). Certain spellings are wildly egregious, even by Elizabethan standards: 'leveid' for 'lived'; 'necescessarye' for 'necessary', 'privoy' for 'privy', 'prouerd' for 'proverb', 'yowse' for 'use'. (Presumably 'necescessarye' is the consequence of Oxford's having lost track of the syllabification of 'necessary' – perhaps through inattention.)

Oxford's tendency to mishear words is particularly marked for proper nouns: 'Gurley' for 'Gurlyn', 'Hulbert' for 'Hubbard/Hubert', 'Wesmester' for 'Westminster', 'Wiwehole' and 'Wiuenghole' for 'Wivenhoe'. Oxford's propensity for intruding an extraneous 'l' into Hubbard or Wivenhoe (note conversely his dropping of the 'l' from 'realm') marks him as particularly defective in his habits of pronunciation.

Four odd spellings of latinate words also occur, albeit rarely, among Oxford's contemporaries: 'importunate' for 'importune' (verb), 'interested' for 'interested' (adjective), 'satisfise' for 'satisfy' (verb), 'subieste' for 'suggest' (verb). *OED* lists all four under individual headings (the last two under 'satisfice' and 'subjestion'), giving cross-references to more normative forms. Shakespeare concordances provide no instances of 'importunate' (verb) against 17 of 'importune'; one of 'interessed' against none of 'interested'; one of 'satisfice' against 79 of 'satisfy' (including grammatical variants); and none of 'subjeste' against 30 of 'suggest' and its grammatical variants. Clearly Oxford's language was not the language of Shakespeare (except in one instance of 'satisfice' for satisfy); similarly, Oxford's language was not the language of Burghley or other well-established Londoners.

When writing Latin, particularly legal Latin, Oxford frequently made serious grammatical errors and sometimes misspelled words.[3] The following Latin (or Anglo-Latin) phrases and clauses in Oxford's letters in his own hand are grammatically and otherwise correct: *praeter spem*; *in medio rerum omnium certamine et discrimine*; *finis coronat opus*; *nemo sit*; 'wryte [=writ] of *elegit*'; *de bene esse*; *de bene esse quantum in nobis est*; *de bene esse quantum in Regina est*. (The legal phrase *de bene esse* refers to a provisional royal grant.) The following phrases, by contrast, are seriously defective:

de benne esse quantum in nos est: Oxford spells *bene* correctly several times (see above); the doubling of the 'n' here is a clear error in spelling, in a language for which the rules of spelling were taught in schools and universities. The replacement of *nobis* (ablative following 'in') by *nos* (accusative) is an egregious error in grammar and a mis-writing of a legal commonplace.

leuare facias: The correct legal term is *levari facias* (BLD). The difference between the incorrect *levare* and the correct *levari* is the difference between the active and the passive form of the infinitive. This is a distinction taught in first-year Latin and doubtless observed in the Inns of Court. Oxford thus has made an error not only in first-year Latin, but in legal Latin.

fyre facias: The correct legal term (BLD, under *facias*), is *fieri facias*. Once again Oxford has incorrectly used the active rather than the passive infinitive. He has then compounded his error by writing 'y' in place of 'ie' in *fieri*: not only is this an incorrect spelling, but 'y' is a letter borrowed from Greek, and seldom if ever appears in legal Latin. (Perhaps Oxford heard *fieri* pronounced by lawyers and attempted to give a phonetic representation of what he heard others speak).

summum totale: The standard medieval and Renaissance Latin for 'the sum of all (the foregoing)' is *summa totalis*, which occurs thousands of times in household and institutional accounts. The correct nominative singular of this feminine noun is *summa*; its plural (not normally used in a situation like this) is *summae* or (in medieval Latin) *summe*. Oxford treats the noun incorrectly as a neuter singular. He also mistakes the declension of *totalis*.

Oxford's Latin is thus extremely puzzling. At best one might argue that his spelling was as idiosyncratic as his spelling of English, though Latin masters permitted very small leeway in conventions of spelling. At worst one might argue that although Oxford may have carried some Latin phrases in his head along with their correct spelling, he did not retain the basic grammar lessons of his youth. Like Chaucer's Summoner, he could parrot legal phrases which he had overheard but of which he had little expert understanding or knowledge. Oxford's errors in Latin confirm, at any rate, his indifference to etymology. Only a person ignorant of or indifferent to Latin could spell 'impudent' as 'impodent' or (worse) 'impotent'. On the evidence of his own letters written in his own hand, therefore, we must conclude that Oxford was neither a Latin scholar, nor even a fully competent practitioner of his native English.

PART III

Emancipation
1571–1574

15 Majority and Marriage

At the approach of his twenty-first birthday, Oxford was poised to escape the constraints of wardship. The Queen proposed a celebratory tournament at Greenwich in Lent (Ash Wednesday fell this year on 28 February), as noted by the French ambassador on 23 January:[1]

> They say that the day after tomorrow [the Queen] will go down to Greenwich for the rest of the winter, where the tournament-place is already in preparation for this coming Lent, in which Oxford and Sir Charles Howard will be among the combattants.

But the tournament was postponed to the beginning of May.

In March Oxford's name appeared among 'Friends' in a Catholic memorandum; two months later a similar list was compiled in respect of the Ridolfi plot:[2]

> 1. Friendly: – Duke of Norfolk, Marquis of Vincestri, Earls of Arandel, Oxford, Huestmorland, Nortumberland, Scialusberi, Darbi, Vorcestrie, Cumberland (a child), Pembruc, Sudampton, Viscount Montacute, Baron [ ] Award ...

Norfolk of course was still a prisoner, Northumberland and Westmorland still outlaws.

On Monday 2 April, ten days from his majority, Oxford walked in procession for the opening of the Queen's Third Parliament, which would sit until 29 May:[3]

> The procession to Westminster was led by the fifty Gentlemen Pensioners all mounted and carrying their gilt battle-axes. After them followed, in order, the Knights of the Bath, the Barons of the Exchequer, the Judges, the Master of the Rolls, the Attorney and Solicitor General, the Lords Spiritual, the Lords Temporal, and finally the Archbishop of Canterbury. Then came the officers of State; the Marquess of Northampton with the Hat of Maintenance; the Lord Admiral Clinton, who was acting Lord Steward for the day; the Earl of Oxford, Lord Great Chamberlain; and the Earl of Worcester, who deputised as Earl Marshal in the enforced absence of the Duke of Norfolk.[4]

As the service at Westminster Abbey concluded, the procession made its way to Westminster Hall:

the lordes all on foote in order as afore, and over [the Queen's] head a rich canopie was caried all the way from Westminster Church; shee being entred into the over house of the parliament and there sittinge in princely and seemely sort under a highe and rich cloth of estate, the robe supported by the Earle of Oxenford, the Earle of Sussex kneelinge holdinge the sword on the left hand, and the Earle of Huntington standinge houldinge the hatt of estate, and the lordes all in their roomes on eich side of the chamber, that is to say, the lordes spirituall on the right hand, and the lordes temporall on the left side, the judges and her learned councell beinge at the woolsackes in the middest of the chamber, and at her Highnes' feete on eich side of her kneelinge one of the groomes or gentlemen of the Chamber, their faces towardes her, the knightes, cittizens and burgesses all standing belowe the barrs.

Prominent in the assembly was William Cecil, now Lord Treasurer and Baron Burghley. Oxford is recorded as present on April 2, 4, 6–7, 9–12, and May 7, 28 (first session); and as absent on April 5, 14, 19–21, 25–26, 28, 30, May 1–3, 5, 8–10, 12, 14–15, 16–17 (two sessions each), 19 (two sessions), 21–26 (two sessions each), 28 (second session), 29 (two sessions).[5] In all he was present for 10 of 50 sessions, while on 10 April he was appointed to a committee 'touching matters of religion'.[6]

Burghley anticipated Oxford's milestone birthday:[7] 'Apryll 12 Edward Comes oxon' erit annorum 21.' Oxford finally became a serious candidate for the Order of the Garter, garnering a first-place vote from each of the ten electors (G-BL). Though Elizabeth was not persuaded to make the appointment, she sanctioned the celebratory tournament:[8]

> The first, second, and third of May 1571 was holden at Westminster, before the Queen's Magesty, a solemn joust at the tilt, tournay, and barriers. The challengers were Edward Earl of Oxford, Charles Howard, Sir Henry Lee, and Christopher Hatton, Esq., who all did very valiantly; but the chief honour was given to the Earl of Oxford.

The defenders were Lord Stafford, Thomas Cecil, Robert Colsell, Thomas Knyvet, Thomas Bedingfield, and Thomas Coningsby.[9]

> This Triumph continued three days. The first at Tilt; the second at Tournay; and the third at the Barriers. On every of the Challengers Her Majesty bestowed a prize, for the receiving whereof they were particularly led, armed, by two ladies into the Presence Chamber; Oxford himself receiving a tablet of diamonds.

The elaborate 'tilting table', equivalent to a modern score-card, is reproduced here as Fig. 6.[10]

The French ambassador reported on 8 May:[11]

> The Earl of Oxford has joined Sir Charles Howard, Henry Law, and Mr. Hatton to make up the four defenders, against twenty-seven other gentlemen of good families, challenging; and the judges of the tourney were the earls of Worcester and Sussex, the Lord Armiral, and Lord Sidney – and no mishap has occurred.

On 14 May George Delves in a letter to Rutland reveals that while receiving the 'chief honour', Oxford had not in fact won:[12]

> Lord Oxford has performed his challenge at tilt, tourney, and barriers, far above expectation of the world, and not much inferior to the other three challengers ... The Earl of Oxford's livery was crimson velvet, very costly; he himself, and the furniture, was in some more colours, yet he was the Red Knight ...

Oxford's performance was handicapped in deference to his inexperience, and in celebration of his majority. Delves wrote again on 24 June:[13]

> ... There is no man of life and agility in every respect in the Court but the Earl of Oxford.

Oxford's success at court thus surpassed his success in the tournament.

From 12 April Oxford was technically free from Burghley's control. In addition, he was now entitled to £666–13–4 and moveable properties, as specified in his father's will:

> ... all the reste of my plate not giuen and bequeathed in this my laste will and testamente, together with all suche other householde stuf, armor artillary, and weapons, as are not appointed, and bequeathed to my sayde Wyef / All whiche plate stuff and other thinges to be deliuered vnto hym by my saide executors at his full age of xxj yeres / yf he shall soe longe lyve.

Perhaps Oxford had already inherited considerable 'household stuff' from his mother. It may be doubted, however, given the reluctance of the law to move faster than a snail, that Oxford took practical control of his lands on his very birthday; formal certification of his freedom, moreover, was deferred until 1572. Properties set aside to pay off his father's debts would remain beyond his reach until 1582.

Under the wardship system, approximately one-third of the value of a titled minor's inheritance reverted to the Crown. Oxford had built up obligations to Burghley, who had to settle with the Queen in his turn. Thus, though his freedom was notably increased, he remained in financial leading-strings, and never got clear of the Cecils – father and son – to the end of his days.

Lured like moths to his apparent new-found wealth, a financial syndicate approached Oxford with an offer of £12,000 per annum for financial control of his 'stately Erledome'.[14] Though he might thus have enjoyed a life of great comfort, he opted instead for a life of reckless expenditure, which he would sustain for some fifteen years only by treating his lands as liquid assets.

In a public display of extravagance, Oxford organized a martial spectacle for the French ambassador in June:[15]

> ... as in (the Queen's) park at Wesminster there was a (military) salute and review of certain 'harquebuziers' which the Earl of Oxford and the captains Orsey and

Leyton organized there; [the Queen] said that she was happy to be able to provide such pleasures to Monsieur ...

A strong dose of reality hit on 1 July, when Oxford received the Queen's demand for £3000 for his wardship and £4000 for 'suing his livery' – the formal recognition of a nobleman's majority which conferred the powers attaching to his title. Lacking ready cash, Oxford signed an obligation to pay double – £14,000 – if he should fail to pay the £7000 by some specified date. Since payment of the fine would not cancel the debt, Oxford now risked a total obligation of £21,000.

Loosed from Burghley's doubtless burdensome control, with his next move Oxford put his head straight back into the noose, for he now contracted a marriage with Burghley's daughter, Anne, as intimated in a 22 July communique from the French ambassador:[16]

> [Burghley] told me openly that he was unhappy, given her age, for her to be brought to church to marry one the age of the Earl of Oxford, and that this could not transpire without criticism and regret.

On 28 July Lord St John wrote from Paris to Rutland, whose wardship in the Burghley household had ended in 1570 and who evidently had kept his own eye on Anne:[17]

> Th'Earl of Oxenforde hathe gotten hym a wyffe – or at the leste a wyffe hathe caught hym – that is Mrs. [=Mistress] Anne Cycille, wheareunto the Queen hathe gyven her consent, the which hathe causyd great wypping [=weeping], waling, and sorowful chere, of those that hoped to have hade that golden daye. Thus you may see whylst that some triumphe with oliphe [=olive] branchis, others folowe the chariot with wyllowe garlands.

The identity of the prospective bride thus occasioned raised eyebrows, and tears from disappointed young ladies.

Though not yet fifteen, Anne was, by all accounts, a nubile beauty, while Oxford was the most eligible bachelor in England. But was she fair game? And was he? In 1562 Oxford had been pledged to whichever of the two Hastings sisters he might choose in 1568; having foregone the choice, he was evidently free. On 9 August 1569, scarcely two years before, Anne had been pledged to Philip Sidney.[18] Evidently Oxford's rank trumped all else.

In his retrospective Diary (ii, p. 772) Burghley noted Anne's betrothal under 3 August, and supplied a few additional details:[19]

> The Erle of Oxford declared to the Queens Majesty at Hampton-court his Desyre to match with my Daughter Anne: wherto the Queen assented: so did the Duke of Norfolk, being then a Presoner in his own House, called Howard-house.

So Oxford both sought and received royal consent. Norfolk, despite his imprisonment, retained a voice in dynastic alliances.

Taking pen in hand on 15 August, Burghley explained matters at length to the presumably disappointed Rutland:[20]

> I think it doth seem strange to your Lordship to hear of a purposed determination in my Lord of Oxford to marry with my daughter; and so before his Lordship moved it to me I might have thought it, if any other had moved it to me himself. For at his own motion I could not well imagine what to think, considering I never meant to seek it nor hoped of it. And yet reason moved me to think well of my Lord, and to acknowledge myself greatly beholden to him, as indeed I do. Truly, my Lord, after I was acquainted of the former intention of a marriage with Master Philip Sidney, whom always I loved and esteemed, I was fully determined to have of myself moved no marriage for my daughter until she should have been near sixteen, that with moving I might also conclude. And yet I thought it not inconvenient in the meantime, being free to hearken to any motion made by such others as I should have cause to like. Truly, my Lord, my goodwill serves me to have moved such a matter as this in another direction than this is, but having more occasion to doubt of the issue of the matter, I did forbear, and in mine own conceit I could have as well liked there as in any other place in England. ...

Burghley evidently means that his personal choice would have been Rutland. He continues:

> Percase your Lordship may guess where I mean, and so shall I, for I will name nobody. Now that the matter is determined betwixt my Lord of Oxford and me, I confess to your Lordship I do honour him so dearly from my heart as I do my own son, and in any case that may touch him for his honour and weal, I shall think him mine own interest therein. And surely, my Lord, by dealing with him I find that which I often heard of your Lordship, that there is much more in him of understanding than any stranger to him would think. And for my own part I find that whereof I take comfort in his wit and knowledge grown by good observation.

Like many an Elizabethan father, Burghley is sufficiently cognizant of the risks of childbearing not to wish his daughter married before she had achieved physical maturity.[21] In the event, the wedding was deferred until after Anne's fifteenth birthday, which would occur on 5 December.

Much is surely implied in Burghley's back-handed compliment to his prospective son-in-law: 'there is much more in him of understanding than any stranger to him would think'. But why should any stranger think Oxford deficient in understanding? Even apart from the killing of Thomas Brincknell in 1567, we have noted Oxford's letter of 24 November 1569 asking Burghey to attribute his faults to 'my yong yeares and lak of experience to know my friendes', and his necromantic experiments – including sexual experiments – at Greenwich. The perceptive Rutland would understand Burghley's reservations. Burghley, however, puts the best face on things: 'I find that whereof I take comfort in his wit and knowledge.'

On 17 August Sussex wrote to Rutland:[22]

I doubt not you hear of a marriage concluded between my Lord of Oxford and my Lord of Burghley's daughter. ...

Marriage was thus agreed, but consummation still lay four months off.

In psychological and sexual limbo, Oxford attended on the Queen's progress to Hertfordshire and Essex:[23]

On the 30th of August, the Queen and court being at Audley End, the French ambassador came from thence to Cambridge, accompanied by Lord Burghley Chancellor of the University, the Earls of Oxford, Bedford, Hertford, the Lord Buckhurst, Sir Thomas Smith, Sir George Carew, Sir Charles Howard, Mr. Thomas Cecil, and others. Lord Burghley was met by the bedels near the Spital House, where he left his coach and took horse, and proceeded to Trinity College, where Dr. Whitgift the Vicechancellor, was in waiting to welcome the illustrious visitors. From this College to Corpus Christi, the various members of the University were ranged along the streets according to their several degrees and ranks. A dinner was provided in Trinity College at the expence of the University, and the Chancellor and his visitors inspected the several Colleges and University buildings, and appear to have been particularly gratified at Peterhouse by Dr. Perne's study or library, supposed to be the worthiest in all England. There were disputations in the schools and at Trinity College, and the Earl of Hertford, the Lord Buckhurst, Sir George Carew, Sir Charles Howard, and Mr. Thomas Cecil (afterwards Earl of Exeter), were admitted Masters of Arts.[24]

University accounts contain records of gloves distributed on the occasion:[25]

Item ... twoe payer gyven to the Lorde Oxford & Semer vij s viij d

'Semer' was Edward Seymour, third surviving son of Lord Protector Somerset. Born in 1548, the child was christened Edward despite the fact that his elder brother bore the same name (DNB). He received the University's MA routinely bestowed on noble visitors.

When Burghley wrote to Walsingham, now serving as English ambassador in Paris, on 2 September, he mentioned Oxford merely in passing, being chiefly interested in royal marriage prospects:[26]

... Monsieur de Foix hath had good entertainment in all external offices, well used by her Majestie, defrayed for his diet at the time he hath been near the Court; and in coming and returning, my Lord of Buckhurst hath very courteously and honourably accompanied him, during his being here; and to increase his honour, I caused my Lord of Oxford to attend on him in sundry places; and by the way from London hither to Walden, he dined at my house, as I doubt not but he and the Resident Ambassador have seen my hearty devotion to the marriage; and indeed, so is my judgment therein confirmed; as I am not ashamed to utter my self; howsoever, it may be perilous to me when it shall not take place; you see also, how openly I deal with you. ...

On 21 September Hugh Fitz-William wrote to the Countess of Shrewsbury:[27]

They say the Queen will be at my Lord of Burghley's house beside Waltham on Sunday next, where my Lord of Oxford shall marry Mistress Anne Cecil his daughter.

The Queen and her court visited Theobalds on 21–22 September,[28] but the wedding was still three months off. September 27 and 28 found Oxford at Warwick and Kenilworth Castle with Robert and Ambrose Dudley, earls of Leicester and Warwick, along with the Earl of Hertford, Sir Henry Sidney, Sir John Spencer, Sir Henry Lee, Sir Richard Knightley, the lord and lady marquesse of Northampton,[29] the lords Barkley, Dudley, and Chandos, 'and many other Lords Knights and gentlemen'.[30]

By 1 November an attempt was made to set Oxford's full financial obligations down on paper:[31]

> Fine for wardship was 2,000*l.* payable in 10 installments ending 10 May, 1581. The mean rates of the Earl within age, 48*l.* 19s. 9–1/2d., payable All Saints Day, 1571. Fine for livery, 1,257*l.* 18s. 0–3/4d., payable in 13 installments ending All Saints Day, 1583.

While Oxford's debt for wardship plus livery had been reduced to £3257, other bills were coming due.[32] To get a handle on his finances, particulars were drawn up of his lands in Essex.[33] Burghley had agreed to provide Anne with a dowry of £3000, which Stone characterizes as a 'record sum'.[34] Oxford's financial condition was nevertheless dire.

Walsingham entered in his Diary under Wednesday, 8 November:[35]

> Tow [=Two] of my lord of Oxfordes men came out of England, Mr. Fant and Mr. Clapton, by whom I received lettres from my Lord of Burghley.

Oxford's servants were William Faunt and John Clopton (or Clapton, *alias* Wotton).[36] Perhaps the latter was the son or relative of Roger Clopton, a gentleman remembered in Earl John's 1562 will.

On 22 November Lord Hunsdon wrote to Burghley that he was 'glad to hear of the Earl of Oxford's marriage so soon'.[37] Burghley's letter to Walsingham on 19 December establishes an approximate date for the nuptials:[38]

> I can write no more for lack of leasure, being occasioned to write at this time divers waies, and not unoccupied with feasting my friends at the marriage of my daughter, who is this day married to the Earl of Oxford to my comfort, by reason of the Queenes Majestie, who hath very honourably with her presence and great favour accompanied it.

George Golding, Oxford's auditor, reports more circumstantially that the marriage occurred on 16 December, 'Being sondaye':[39]

> Edward de Veer, Erle of Oxenforde dyd the xvjth day of December 1571 anno xiiijto Regine Elizabethe mary the Lady his wyfe named Anne Cecill one of the

daughters of Sir William Cecill Knyghte Lorde of Burghley at the Court then being at Whithall by Weastmester The same day yere and place the Lord Herberde sonne and heyre of the Erle of Worcester dyd marry the Lady Hastinges sister to Henry Erle of Huntington.

In this joint wedding – reminiscent of the 16th Earl's wedding in 1536 – the second bride was the very Elizabeth Hastings whom the marriage indenture of 1562 named as Oxford's optional intended. The second groom was Edward Somerset, born about 1550 and thus almost exactly Oxford's age (*Peerage*, under Worcester). Elizabeth Hastings had cause – though she may not have appreciated it yet – to thank her lucky stars.

Giles Fletcher the elder celebrated Oxford's marriage with an eclogue in Latin hexameters, *In nuptias clarissimi D. Edouardi Vere, Comitis Oxoni, et Ann Cecili optimae ac illustrissimae feminae. Æcloga Callianissa. Dec. [1571]*, addressed to the father-in-law, the groom, and the bride. The poem is translated thus by Ward:[40]

> Fortunate art thou as a father-in-law, witnessing the marriage of thy daughter, and happy art thou as a son-in-law, and thou maiden in thy husband, and, last of all, happy bridegroom in thy bride. Not as an oath-breaker doth Hymen join these bands, for both the bridegroom and the bride possess that which each may love, and every quality which may be loved. For like a river swelling the banks, by means of intercourse and sympathy love will arise, and the glory of rank, and children recalling the qualities of both parents; for the valour of the father and the prudence of the mother will come out in the offspring. ... Hail to thee, Hymen, hail!

> But if at any time with fiery energy he should call up a mimicry of war, he controls his foaming steed with a light rein, and armed with a long spear rides to the encounter. Fearlessly he settles himself in the saddle, gracefully bending his body this way and that. Now he circles round: now with spurred heel he rouses his charger. The gallant animal with fiery energy collects himself together, and flying quicker than the wind beats the ground with his hoofs, and again is pulled up short as the reins control him.

> Bravo, valiant youth! 'Tis thus that martial spirits pass through their apprenticeship in war. Thus do yearling bulls try the feel of each other's horns. Thus too do goats not yet expert in fighting begin to butt one against the other, and soon venture to draw blood with their horns.

> The country sees in thee both a leader pre-eminent in war, and a skilful man-at-arms. Thy valour puts forth leaves, and begins to bear early fruit, and glory already ripens in thy earliest deed.

On 4 January 1572 Sir William Fytzwylliam wrote to Burghley from Ireland:[41]

> Congratulations on the marriage of the Lady Anne Cecil to Edward de Vere, Earl of Oxford.

But not everyone was as pleased with Oxford's marriage as Burghley, Fletcher, and Fytzwylliam. On 21 December, Guerau De Spes, the Spanish ambassador, reported to his master, the King of Spain:[42]

> In the meanwhile Lord Burleigh is celebrating with great festivity at the palace, the marriage of his daughter with the earl of Oxford. The son of the earl of Worcester is married also to the sister of the earl of Huntington, which means taking two families away from the Catholics.

On 22 December the French ambassador Fénélon composed his report:[43]

> Last Tuesday I had audience with the Queen; and on Wednesday she took me with her to dine with Lord Burghley, who was celebrating the marriage of his daughter with the Earl of Oxford ...

He continued:

> Madame, there have been four marriages in this court this week, including those of the Earl of Huntington with the daughter of the Earl of Worcester, and the eldest daughter of the Lord Chamberlain with Lord Dudley – arranged for the accommodation of certain noblemen who were caught up in the affairs of the Duke of Norfolk; and I believe that this has been to reassure them. The others were of the daughter of Lord Burghley with the Earl of Oxford, and of a young, rich widow with Lord Paget, which also were celebrated with pleasure and contentment, and with the approbation of the Court. And, having been arranged at the festivity of those of the aforesaid Earl of Oxford, the Queen of England has wished me to say, that with so many marriages at one time, each of them presages well ...

The 'affaires du duc de Norfolc' were also the subject of a French communique dated 10 December, mentioning Sir Ralph Lane:[44]

> The good affection that the nobility of this realm bear towards the King will be shown in a letter that one of them, Sir [Ralph] Lane, wrote to me in Italian, the contents of which, as well as certain other matters Sir Lane confided in me, will be explained to the King by de Sabran; and he will also tell him of a certain proposal recently made by the Earl of Oxford to some of his friends, and what came of it.

The proposal may have concerned a plan to rescue the Duke of Norfolk, who was still under arrest awaiting the Queen's pleasure.

Oxford and Anne evidently took up residence in the Savoy, a religious house directly across the Strand from Burghley House (formerly Cecil House). Stow provides a brief history of the house, latterly a hospital, concluding thus:[45]

> This Hospitall of Sauoy was againe new founded, erected, corporated and endowed with landes by Queene Mary, the thirde of Nouember: in the fourth of her raigne one Iackson tooke possession, and was made maister thereof in the same moneth of Nouember. The Ladies of the Court, and Maydens of honour (a thing not to be forgotten) stored the same of new with beddes, bedding, and other furniture, in very ample manner, &c. and it was by patent so confirmed at Westminster, the 9. of May, the 4. and 5. of Philip and Mary.

Oxford rented an above-stairs apartment, described in 1573 as 'certaine lodginges within the said hospitall, with a garden belonginge to the Master of the Savoye'.[46]

The young couple may well have made the first excursion of their marriage to Castle Hedingham, as well as to Wivenhoe, where, as we will discover shortly, Oxford communed with his 'country muses'. Apparently they entered Essex via Old Ford, a village on the River Lea, which divides Middlesex from Essex.[47] This itinerary may be inferred from a letter written by Henry Lok to Burghley in 1590,[48] recalling a debt unpaid to him since 'his Lordships and his Ladies ... first being at Owldfoord and Hiningam Park' – the reference is clearly to Oxford and Anne.

It is difficult to believe that the happiness of the couple was complete. Anne was a virgin only just fifteen, having been adored and protected by doting parents, while Oxford was a buck in his twenty-first year with more than his share of experience – both worldly and otherworldly.

16 Country Muses

In 1573 Thomas Bedingfield, one of the Queen's Gentlemen Pensioners, published his translation of a consolatory essay by Girolomo Cardano under the title *Cardanus Comforte* (STC 4607). Prefaced is a letter from Bedingfield, 'To the Right Honourable and my good Lorde the Earle of Oxeforde, Lorde great Chamberlaine of Englande', dated (by modern reckoning) 1 January 1572, purveying the polite fiction that Bedingfield had hoped to keep his work unpublished (sigs. A2–2v):[1]

> My good Lord, I can geeue nothinge moore agreable to your minde, and my fortune, then the willinge performance of such seruice as it shall please you to commaunde mee vnto. And therefore rather to obeye then boaste of my cunninge, and as a newe signe of myne olde deuocion, I doe presente the booke your Lordeship so longe desired. With assured hope that how so euer you mislike or allowe therof, you will fauourably conseale myne imperfections which to your Lordshippe alone I dare discouer, because most faithfully I honor and loue you. My long discontinuance of study, or rather the lacke of grounded knowledge did many times discorage me, yet the pleasure I tooke in the matter did counteruaile all dispayre, and the rather by encouragement of your Lordship who (as you wel remember) vnwares to me found some parte of this worke, and willed me in any wyse to procede therin. My meaning was not to haue imparted my trauayle to any, but your honour hath power to countermaund myne intencion. Yet I most humbly beseech you either not to make any pertakers thereof, or at the least wise those, whoe for reuerence to your Lordship or loue to mee, will willingly beare with myne errors. A nedelesse thing I know it is to comforte you, whom nature and fortune

> hath not onelye not iniured, but rather vpon whom they haue bountifully bestowed their grace: notwithstandinge sith you delighte to see others acquited of cares, your Lordship shall not doe amisse to reade some part of Cardanus counsell: wherein consideringe the manyfolde miseries of others, you may the rather esteeme your owne happye estate with encrease of those noble and rare vertues which I know and reioyse to be in you. Sure I am it would haue better beseemed me to haue taken this trauaile in some discourse of Armes (being your Lordships chiefe profession & mine also) then in Philosophers skill to haue thus busied my selfe: yet sith your pleasure was such, and your knowledge in eyther great, I do (as I will euer) most willinglye obeye you. ...

Thus Bedingfield represents himself as self-effacing but overruled by a superior. He introduces another polite fiction, suitable to an earl perhaps, but not to this earl: that his chief profession is military.

Bedingfield's letter is followed by a reply from Oxford in the form of a letter addressed 'To my louinge frende Thomas Bedingfeld Esquyer, one of her Maiesties gentlemen Pentioners' (sigs. A3–4). Oxford begins by deprecating Bedingfield's purported desire not to publish:

> After I had perused youre letters good maister Bedingfeld, findinge in them your request farre differing from the desert of your labour, I could not chose but greatly doubt, whether it were better for me to yelde to your desyre, or execute myne owne intention towardes the publishinge of youre Booke. For I do confesse the affections that I haue always borne towardes you coulde moue mee not a little. But when I had throughlye considered in my mynde of sondrye and diuers argumentes, whether it were best to obeye myne affections or the merites of your studyes. At the length I determined it better to denye your vnlawfull request, then to graunte or condiscende to the concealment of so worthy a worke.

Oxford goes on to praise philosophy, 'of whiche youre booke is plentifully stored', and declares it an unpardonable error 'to haue murthered the same in the wast[e] bottomes of my chestes' – like other men of his day, Oxford kept miscellaneous papers in chests. The balance of the missive repeats *ad nauseam* the argument that neither wisdom nor virtue nor desert should remain hidden. Oxford signs off 'From my newe countrye Muses at Wiuenghole' – a spelling of Wivenhoe apparently unique to himself.

Oxford's letter is followed by a pretentious exercise in cross-rhyming, finished off with a couplet – a kind of stretched-out sonnet. Entitled 'The Earle of Oxenforde to the Reader', this was Oxford's first poem to appear in print (sig. A4v):

> The labouring man, that tilles the fertile soyle,
> And reapes the harvest fruite, hath not in deede
> The gaine but payne, and if for all hys toyle
> He gets the strawe, the Lord will have the seede.
> The Manchet fyne, falles not unto his share[;]
> On coursest cheat, his hungrye stomacke feedes[.]

The Landlord doth, possesse the fynest fare[;]
He pulles the flowers, the other pluckes but weedes.
The Mason poore that buildes the Lordlye halles
Dwelles not in them, they are for hye degree[;]
His Cotage is, compact in paper walles
And not with bricke, or stone as others bee.
The idle Drone, that labours not at all
Suckes vp the sweete, of honnye from the Bee[.]
Who worketh most, to their share least doth fall,
Wyth due desert, reward will neuer bee.
The swiftest Hare, vnto the Mastiue slowe
Oft times doth fall, to him as for a praye:
The Greyhounde thereby, doth misse his game we know
For which he made, such speedy hast awaye.
So hee that takes, the payne to penne the booke
Reapes not the giftes, of goodlye golden Muse
But those gayne that, who on the worke shal looke
And from the soure, the sweete by skill doth chuse.
For hee that beates the bushe the byrde not gets,
But who sittes still, and holdeth fast the nets.

This poem comes oddly from a man who himself dwelt in 'Lordlye halles' built by hired hands – in short, from the exploiter rather than the exploited.

Oxford's letter and poem are followed by a prose dedication, 'Thomas Churchyarde gentleman, to the Reader' (sig. A5–5v), and by a poem, 'Thomas Churchyarde in the behalfe of the Booke' (sig. A6–6v). Like the items supplied by Bedingfield and Oxford, these too smack of literary posturing. Clearly, neither Bedingfield the gentleman nor Oxford the nobleman nor Churchyard the poet-adventurer had the slightest compunction about seeing their words in print. The title-page itself openly proclaims Oxford's involvement: *Cardanus Comforte ... published by commaundement of the right honourable the Earle of Oxenford*. A second edition appeared in 1576 (STC 4508).

17 Country Matters

On 14 January 1572 George Golding 'of London, gentleman' was appointed auditor for Oxford's estates, replacing Thomas Wyseman, Esq., of Shipley, Sussex, who had inherited from his father John the post granted 'by John, Earl of Oxford, for two lives, 10th Dec. 1540'.[1] George was Arthur Golding's next younger brother.

Camden attributed to this same month a plot 'to kill certain of the Privy Council and to free the Duke of Norfolk', implicating William Herle, among others.[2] When Herle embarked at Gravesend on 19 March, his ship nearly foundering off the coast of Holland,[3] his shipmates included the soldier-poet George Gascoigne, the desperado Rowland York, and Edward (Ned) Denny. Both York and Denny were – or shortly became – Oxford's men. 'Gascoigne's Voyage into Hollande, Anno 1572. Written to the Right Honourable the Lorde Grey of Wilton', tells us perhaps more than we want to know about the group's adventures in the Netherlands:[4]

> As for the yong Nunnes, they be bright as glasse,
> And chaste forsooth, met v: and anders niet.   ['with you and nobody else']
> What sayde I? what? that is a misterie,
> I may no verse of such a theame endite[.]
> Yong Rowlande Yorke may tell it bet than I,   [bet=better]
> Yet to my Lorde this little will I write,
> That though I haue my selfe no skill at all
> To take the countnance of a Colonel,
> Had I a good Lieutenant general,
> As good Iohn Zuche whereuer that he dwel,
> Or else Ned Dennye (faire mought him befal),
> I coulde haue brought a noble regiment
> Of smugskinnde Nunnes into my countrey soyle.

The 'yong Nunnes' were prostitutes. Gascoigne's open use of names is breath-taking.

Back in England, Norfolk took steps on 28 January to settle his affairs:[5]

> Although my hap hath been such that my kin have had cause to be ashamed of me, their kinsman; yet I hope when I am gone nature will so work in them that they will be in good will to you, as heretofore they have been to me. Amongst whom I will begin as high as I unworthy dare presume, with my cousin Oxford.

As Norfolk approved Oxford's marriage to Anne Cecil, he now referred his son and heir Philip Howard to Oxford for comfort and protection.

On 18 March John Lee sent a semi-secret dispatch to Burghley from Antwerp (the italicized words were originally in cypher):[6]

> ... *The Papists in the Low Countries* arre yn summe good hope, that summe attempte wyll bee shortly tacken yn hande, agaynste *the Queen* for that yt ys geven them to vnderstande, that the Frenche Kynge mannethe owtte twenty shyppes of warre, for the wyche [i.e., for the purpose?], and how that *the Duke of Alva* hathe sente yn to [G]ermany / as troythe [=truth] ys / to tayke vpp certayne bandes, bothe of fouttemen and horsmen. further they affyrme, that ther was lyke to haue byn a mutteny the xxvijth of the laste munnethe [=27 February], when yt was thowght that *the Duke of Norfolk* sholde haue passed, so that they bee fully perswaded, that *the Queen* dares procede no further theryn, at aull, affyrmynge that *the Duke of Norfolk* haythe secret frendes, and those, of the beste, and suyche [=such] as may doo very muyche wythe *the Queen* and how that the erlle of Oxforde (who haythe

byn a moste humbell sutter [=suitor] for hym) haythe conceued summe grette dysplessuer agaynste yower honour for the same, wheruppon he haythe (as they say here) putte away fromme hym, the countes hys wyffe. What other vayne Imagynatyons they haue conceiued, of *the Queens* goynge to see the erlle of Sussex, and what wordes were spoken vnto hym by *the Queen* I spare to wrytte ...

Thus within three months of his marriage rumour had reached as far as Antwerp that Oxford, who pleaded for Norfolk's life, had separated from Anne, driven by anger against Burghley.

Though Lee dismisses rumours as 'vayne Imagynatyons', a memo in Burghley's hand confirms that the marriage was in trouble:[7]

at Grenewich no bord wagis for ij gromes, vsher, page, chamber keepar

after the co[o]kes not payd.

horsis lent to Smith befor the prograss

new nag[g]es [=horses] for xiijli [=£13] sent to Thebaldes vnshod no mony to defray

knokt vp at j a clok [=1:00 a.m.]. wakid

kept out of his chamber at dyner & supper by York & other within

When Momerancy [=Montmorency] cam no mony to bye befor he was landid.

not speak a word nor cowntenance in fathers howse.

so many Cli [=hundred pounds] spent, of xM [=10,000] come to his hand sins mariadg

never one tokin of Lov[e] in gowne button, agrets [=aigrettes?].[8]

a hose garter askid agen [=asked again, demanded back].

no pillyon [=woman's light saddle] to come from Wyvnho, but of pore[?] golding fustian.

his man to demand a note of her small plate in her own hand, gyven her & he never speak him selfe. linin spoylled, very fyne, & damask.

wemen ij gotten with child. men intertaining them in chamber & not dar fynd fawt [=fault] because they wer great abowt him.

iijMli. [=£3000] sins Ester lyeng at Grenwitch.

Chang[e] of men to kepe purse

The names Theobalds, York, and Wivenhoe connect the complaints to Oxford. Burghley charges that Oxford suffered York – doubtless Rowland – to bar Anne from his private chamber, keeping a virtual bawdy-house in which two women became pregnant, lording it over Anne, who dared not find fault with their conduct.

François Duc de Montmorency, leader of the French Huguenots,[9] landed at Dover on or about 5 June 1572, and was installed as Knight of the Garter (along with Burghley) on the 17th.[10] Montmorency's visit had been delayed by illness. As early as 7 April Fénélon wrote to France:[11]

> ... I have arranged with Lord Burghley that, if the aforesaid Count is unable to travel, then it is necessary that it should be Burghley and his son-in-law Oxford (now the premier Earl and Great Chamberlain of England) who should undertake this commission – to which Burghley agreed.

Thus Fénélon wanted Burghley and Oxford to supervise Montmorency's visit, and indeed Burghley's efforts are acknowledged in contemporary letters.[12] (Oxford's refusal to support Anne's purchase of apparel – mentioned in the memorandum – apparently occurred during Montmorency's stay.) Burghley complains also that Oxford stinted on Anne's maintenance during the Court's stay at Greenwich – which we know from other sources to have been from 3 February to 23 November 1573.[13] Oxford, on the other hand, spent more than £3000 on himself 'sins Ester lyeng at Grenwitch'.

A century later (1675–76) William Dugdale echoed Lee:[14]

> This Edward [=Oxford], being an intire friend to Thomas Duke of Norfolk, when he discerned his life in danger, ... earnestly interceded with the Lord Treasurer Burghley ... for the preserving him from destruction; but prevailing not, grew so highly incensed against Burghley, knowing it was in his power to save him; that, in great indignation, he said, he would do all he could to ruin his daughter: and accordingly, not only forsook her bed, but sold and consumed that great inheritance, descended to him from his ancestors; leaving very little for Henry his son and successor.

Though Dugdale (like Lee) probably placed too much weight on the Norfolk affair, his characterization of the marriage and of the dispersal of Oxford's inheritance is accurate enough.

On 21 March 1572 Sir Thomas Smith wrote to Dr Thomas Wilson from Blois, apparently referring to the Garter election:[15]

> ... I thank you for your news of the chancellorship of the order, yet I know not what it is, and I am afraid my lord of Oxford spake rather as he would have it to be than that he knew it to be so given. ...

Evidently Oxford presumed on his own election. Although he received votes from seven of the nine electors this year, he did not receive an appointment from the Queen (G-BL).

On 4 May Oxford witnessed the creation of Walter Devereux as Earl of Essex and Edward Fynes *alias* Clinton as Earl of Lincoln.[16] On 8 May, at the opening of the first session of her Fourth Parliament, which would sit until 30 June, Elizabeth was conveyed to Whitehall:[17]

... and her Maieste beinge sett in her Coche the gentlemen pensioners with theyre axes, the Sargentes set were on horsback, and the Esquiries with others on foote on eache side of her highnes Coche in good order. next to her Maieste Rod therle of Kent with the Cape [=cap, hat] of mayntenaunce & therle of Rutland bearinge the Sword next before. then therle of Oxeford Lord great Chamberlen of England, & with him therle of Worcester being for that tyme appoynted to be Erle Marshall caryed the Rodd next before. ...

Oxford's presence is recorded in the minutes for May 8, 10(?), 12, 15, 17, 21, June 3, 6, 10, 24, 26; he was absent on May 14, 16, 19, 22–24, 28–31, June 2, 4, 5 (two sessions), 7, 9, 11, 25, 27 (two sessions), 28 (two sessions), 30 (2 sessions).[18] In all he attended 11 of 35 sessions, including the opening (but not the closing) of Parliament: he was one of 11 Lords appointed as 'triers of petitions from England, Ireland, France, and Scotland', while on 12 May he was appointed to a committee 'touching the Queen of Scots' which convened at 8:00 the next morning at the Star Chamber.

On 28 May Sir Thomas Gresham wrote to Burghley:[19]

It may licke [=like] you to undirstond, that I have in Redynes 2000 Marks [=£1333–13–4] for to paye to my Lorde of Oxefford, whensoever it shall please your Lordeshipe to seand for it. And I shall provid[e] his Reaseit wyth as moche Spead as I can. ...

This may have been an instalment on the inheritance granted in the 16th Earl's will. On 30 May the licence Oxford had anticipated for most of his conscious life was finally issued:[20]

Licence for Edward Deveere, Earl of Oxford, son and heir and elder issue male of John Deever, late earl of Oxford, to enter upon his lands; issues from the time when Edward attained the age of 21.

Meanwhile, on 28 May the newly created Earl of Lincoln embarked from Dover, for the marriage on 18 August of Marguerite de Valois to Henri de Bourbon – the Protestant Prince of Navarre.[21] Lincoln's entourage included several of Oxford's friends ('filz aisné' means 'eldest son' – and heir):[22]

My Lord Talbot	Filz aisné du conte de Shreusbery.
My Lord Clinton	Filz aisné dudict Sieur conte de Lincoln
My Lord Dacres	Sieur et baron dudict Lieu
My Lord Sande	Sieur et baron dudict Lieu
My Lord Riche	Sieur et baron de Leez ...

Le Sieur Edouard Hastings, frere du conte de Huntington, du sang royal.
Le sieur Henry Borough, filz aisné de my Lord Borough
Monsieur Giles Briges, filz aisné de my Lord Chandos chevalier de Lordre
Le sieur Arthus Champernon chevalier viceadmiral du paye de Deuon.
Monsieur Philipee Sidney filz aisné de monsieur Sidney chevalier de Lordre, president du conseil au paye de Gales [=Wales].

Le sieur Ierosme Bowes chevalier gentilhome de La maison et chambre de la Royne
Monsieur Charles Arundel de La Maison D'Arundel du paye de West
Monsieur Middelmore gentilhomme ordinaire de la chambre de la Royne.
Monsieur Scudamore
Monsieur Rauf Bowes   gentilzhommes de la maison et
Monsieur Leke   chambre de la Royne
Monsieur Paston
Monsieur Chent capitaine

Charles Arundel 'of the house of Arundel of the West Country' is easily
recognized.[23] 'My Lord Talbot' was Gilbert Talbot, the acute reporter and critic
of Court life. Henry Borough was another dining companion of Oxford's (he
would be killed in a duel in January 1578), while Philip Sidney would become an
important rival. Sir Arthur Champernowne was the brother of Katherine
Champernowne, step-mother to Sir Walter Ralegh: the latter would become an
intimate of Oxford's circle during the second half of the decade.[24] Osborn
suggests that Lincoln's party left London about Tuesday 27 May, and reached
Paris on Sunday 8 June.[25] A report by the French ambassador reveals that Leicester and Oxford were meanwhile appointed to receive Montmorency, who would
sail to Dover on the very ship which had just brought Lincoln to Calais:[26]

> ... with another group of nobility, from Gravesend, to accompany them up the
> Thames, to this city, where the earls of Leicester and Oxford greeted them
> disembarking at Somerset House, one of the Queen's residences ...

Oxford must thus have been stationed in London from the closing days of May.

On 2 June Thomas Howard, 4th Earl of Norfolk, was executed on Tower
Hill.[27] Probably it suited the Queen and Privy Council to have a number of
noblemen abroad, and to have Oxford where he could be watched. Oxford
attended the House of Lords, as we have seen, on 3 June, and probably met
Montmorency in London on the 6th or 7th. Oxford did not participate in a
tournament at the barriers on 14 June at Whitehall,[28] but may have borne the
sword of state before the Queen on the 18th at Windsor.[29]

In mid-July the Queen's progress took her to Havering-atte-Bower, Essex, a
property sometimes attached to the Oxford earldom.[30] On the 22nd, at Theo-
balds, Oxford was assigned two rooms in the west end of the second storey, next to
Rutland. Accommodations were likewise arranged for Leicester, Hatton, Warwick,
Heneage, 'Mr Alphonso', Burghley himself, and the ladies Carey, Stafford,
Marquess [of Northampton], and Strange – but not for Countess Anne.[31]

On 12 August the Queen came to Warwick Castle. About 3:00 on the same
afternoon:[32]

> ... her majesty ... in her coache acompanyed with her Lady of Warwick in the same
> coche & many other Ladyes & Lords attending namely the Lord Burghley lately
> made Lord Tresorer of Englond The Earle of Sussex lately made Lord Chamberleyne

to her Majesty The lord Howard of Effingham lately made lord pryvy seale The Earle of Oxford Lord gret chamberlyn of Englond Therle of Rutland Therle of Huntingly [*sic*] lately made president of the North Therle of Leycester Master of the horse and many other bishops lords ladyes & great estates ...

On Sunday 18 August:

... it pleasid her to have the countrey people resorting to see the daunce in the Court of the castell her Maiesty beholding them out of her chamber wyndowe which thing as it pleased well the country people so it seemed her Maiesty was much delightyd and made very myrry.

... there was devised on the tempel diche a forte made of slender tymber coverid with canvais in this fort were apointid divers persons to serve as soldiers and therefore so many harnesses as myght be gotten within the towne were had wherewith men were armed & apointid to shewe themselfs Some others apointed to cast out fire woorks as squibbes & balles of fyre Agaynst that fort was another castlwise prepared of like strength wherof was governor the Earle of Oxford a lusty Jentleman with a lusty band of gentleman Between these forts or against them were placed certen battering pieces to the nomber of xij or xiij brought from london and xij skore chambers or mortys pieces brought also from the towne at the chardge of therle of Warwik These pieces & Chambers were by traynes fyred & so made a great noise as though it had bene a sore assault having some intermission in which tyme therle of Oxford & his soldiers to the nomber of xx with qualivers & harqbuzues likewise gave divers assaults Then the fort shoting agayn & casting out divers fyers terrible to those that have not bene in like experience valiant to such as delighted therein and inded straung to them that understood it not ffor the wild fyre falling into the Ryver of Aven wold for a tyme lye still and than agayn rise & flye abrode casting fourth many flasshes and flambes wherat the quenes maiesty tok great pleasure till after by mischaunce a poore man or two were much trowblid ffor at the last whan it was apointed that the overthrowing of the fort should be A Dragon flieng casting out huge flames & squibs lighted upon the fort and so set fyre thereon to the subversion thereof But whether by negligence or otherwise it happed that a ball of fyre fell on a house at the end of the bridge wherein one henry cowy otherwise called myller dwellid and sett fyre on the same house the man & wief being both in bed & on slep which burned so as before any reskue could be the house & all things in it utterly perished with much ado to save the man & woman besides that house an other house or two nere adioynyng were also fyred but reskued by the diligent & carefull help as well of therle of Oxford Mr Fulk Grevile & other gentlemen & Townesmen which repared thither in greater nomber than could be orderid And no mervaile it was that so litle harme was done for the fire balles & squibbes cast upp did flye quiet [=quite] over the castell and into the myds of the towne falling downe some on houses some in courts & baksides and some in the streats as farre as almost of Saint Mary church to the great perill or ells great feare of the Inhabitants of this borough And so as by what meanes is not yet knoen foure houses in the towne & suburbes wer on fyer at once wherof one had a ball cam thorough both sides & made a hole as big as a mans head & did no more harm This fyere appeased it was tyme to goo to rest And in the next morning it pleasid her Maiesty to have the poore old man & woman that had ther house burnt brought unto her whom so brought her Maiesty recomfortid very much And by her great bounty & other courtiers There was given towards their losses that had taken hurt xxvli xijs viijd or therabouts which was dispensed to them accordingly.

Fortunately, damage was confined to property.

Within a month news trickled and then poured in from France of the horrors of the massacre on St Bartholomew's Day (24 August), triggered by the very marriage which the English party had meant to celebrate.[33] Writing to Burghley on some date in September, Oxford, as was his wont, put his own affairs first (LL-03):

My Lorde, I haue vnderstoode by yowre Lordshipes letters, that Roberte Christmas, acordinge to my appointment, hathe repaired to yowre good Lordship abought my causes, and as yowre Lordship thinkes good therin, as touchinge a new suruaye, so do I determine shalbe done for bothe, as yowre Lordship perceiues; and also mi selfe I haue ben greatlye abusd in the former, by suche as I pute in trust tofore, but for that is past now I haue no other remidie but to loke better to amend the fault in the rest of my delinges hearafter. and as for my timber at Colne Parke; therin, I had no other meaninge saue onlie to make, as it weare, a yearlie rente, so as I may, withe ought disparkinge the grounde. But now for the suruaier whiche yowre Lordship hathe named, I must get him by yowre Lordships meanes, and for yowre Lordships sake, for I ame vtterly vnaquantted withe him

Oxford does not name the surveyor recommended by Burghley, but it may have been Israel Amyce, who was to play an important role in Oxford's life.

And as for those large leases, whiche yowre Lordship hathe bene aduertised ofe, to be graunted by me, I doo assure yowre Lordshipe withe ought dissemblinge my faultes to yow to whome I perceiue my self so muche to be bownd vnto for yowre singouler care ouer my weldoinge: I must confess my negligence and to[o] littell care withe the two [=too] muche trust I haue put to some ouer myn owne doinges; it may be I am greatly abused, but as yet till I searche into those things now vpon yowre Lordships most gracious admonissiones I doo nott know. But It is leklier [=likelier] to be as yowre Lordship dothe gesse then otherwise, and if it be not so it is more by good hape [=hap, fortune] then of my prouidence.

The deuice of makinge fre my copihoulders mi Lord I neuer thought of otherwise then amotion [=a motion, proposal] mad[e] to me by Robert Christmas wherin amonge the other thinges I bad him tell it yowre Lordship at whose lekinge or dislekinge I was to be ruled in ani thinge. knowinge if it weare a thinge fitt or vnfite for me I showld by yowre Lordships good aduise quiklye vnderstand, and so I left it to be not done, or taken in hande, and thuse [=thus] sir for these matters bothe in this as in all other thinges I am to be gouerned and commanded att yowre lordshipes good deuotion.

Thus Oxford was already involved in surveys of his lands, disparking (the cutting down of woods), and the disposal of lands by lease or copyhold. Finally he turns to the subject of Burghley's safety:

I wowld to god yowre lordship wowld lett me vnderstand sume of yowre newes, whiche here dothe ringe doutfullie in the eares of eurie man of the murder of the admirall of Fraunce and a number of noble men and worthie gentelmen, and suche as greatlye haue in there liue times [=lifetimes] honored the Queens Magestie oure mistris, on whose tragedies we haue an number of Frenche Æneases[34] in this citte that tels of theare owne ouerthrowes withe teares fallinge from ther eies, a piteous thinge to heare but a cruell and far more greuous thinge we mus[t] deme it thane [=then, therefore] to see. all rumores here are but confused, of those tropes [=troops] that are escaped from Paris, and Rohan [=Rouen] where Monsieur hath also bene, and leke a vesper Sicilianus[35] as they sey that crueltie spredes ouer all fraunce. wherof yowre Lordship is better aduertised then we are here. And sithe the world is so full of treasones, and vile instrumentes, daylie to attempt new and vnloktfor thinges, good my Lord, I shall affetiouslye,[36] and hartely desire yowre Lordship to be carfull bothe of yowre self and of her Magestie that yowre friendes may longe enioie yow and yow them. I speake bycause I am not ignorant what practises haue bene made against yowre persone latlye by Madder,[37] and later as I vnderstand by forren practises, if it be tru. And thinke yf the admiral in fraunce was a ey[e]sore or beame in the eyes of the papistes, that The lord tresorer of England is a bloke [=block, impediment] and a crosebare in ther way, whose remoue, they will neuer stikte to attempte, seinge they haue preuailed so well in others.

This estatte hathe depended on yow a great while, as all the world dothe iuge [=judge], and now all menes eyes, not beinge ocupid any more on these lost lordes, are as it weare one [=on] a soden bent and fixed on yow, as a singular hope and piller wherto the religion hath too [=to] leane. And blame me not thought [=though] I am boulder withe yowre Lordship at this present then my custome is, for I am on[e] that count my self a follower of yowres now in all fortunes; and what shall hape [=hap, occur by fortune] to yow I count it hap to my selfe; or at the least I will make my self a voluntarie partaker of it.

Thus my Lord I humbli desire yowre Lordship to pardone my yowthe, but to take in good part my zeale and affection towardes yowre Lordship As on whome I haue builded my fowndation ether to stand or fall. And good my Lord think I do not this presumptiouslie / as to aduise yow that am but to take aduise of yowre Lordship but to admonishe yow as one withe whome I wowld spend my blud and lyfe so muche yow haue made me yowres. and I do protest ther is nothinge more desired of me then so to be taken an[d] accounted of yow. thus withe my hartie comendationes and yowre daughters we leaue yow to the custodie of Almightie God.

This letter is remarkable as one of only two from Oxford's pen expressing as much concern for another – here Burghley – as for himself. The second he would write following the death of Queen Elizabeth in 1603.

Oxford wrote again on 22 September, having remained in London while Anne went ahead to Wivenhoe (LL-04):

My Lorde, I receiued yowre letters, when I rather loked to haue sene yowre selfe here, then to haue harde [=heard] from yow: but sithe it is soo, that yowre Lordship is other wise, affaired withe the busines of the common wellthe, then to be disposede to recreat yowre selfe, and repose ye amonge yowre owne, yet we do hope, after this yow hauinge hade so great a care of the Queens Maiesties seruice, yow will begine to haue sume respect of yowre owne healthe, and take a plesure to duele [=dwell] where yow haue taken paine to builde; My wife (whome I thowght showld haue taken her leue [=leave] of yow, if yowre Lordship hade come, till yow wowld haue otherwise commanded, is departed vnto the contrie this day: my selfe, as fast as I cane [can] get me ought of towne, doo followe. Where <…> I be any way imploide, I am content and desiroues so[?] <… serv>ice, wher by I may show my selfe dutifull to her. otherwise if it wer<…> that respecte, I thinke ther is more troble then credite to be gotten in suche gouermentes. if ther were any seruice to be done abrode, I hadd rather serue there, then att home, wher yet sume honor were to be gotte; if ther be any settinge forthe to sea, to whiche seruice I beare most affectione, I shall desire yowre Lordship to giue me and gett me that fauoure and credite, that I myght make one. whiche if therbe no suche intention, then I shalbe most willinge to be imploide on the sea co[a]stes, to be in a redines withe my contrie man against any invasione. ...

Desirous of travelling abroad, Oxford would yet be satisfied with military service on the English coasts.

By 31 October, the date of his next surviving letter, Oxford was in 'Wiwehole', and on friendly terms with Burghley (LL-05):

My lord, yowre last letters, whiche be the first I haue receiued, of yowre lordshipes good opinion conceiued towardes me, (whiche god graunt so longe to continue) as I wowld be bothe desirowes and diligent to seke the same, haue not a littell, after so many stormes passed of yowre heui [=heavy, disapproving] grace towardes me, lyghtned and disburned my carfull minde. And sithe I haue bene so littell behouldinge to senister reportes, I hope now, withe yowre Lordships indiferent iugment, to be more plausable vnto yow then her to fore [=heretofore], throught [=through] my carfull dedes, to please yow, whiche hardly, eyther throwght [=through] my yowthe, or rather misfortune hether to I haue donne. But yet, least those, (I can not tell how to terme them,) but as bakfriendes vnto me, shall take place againe to vndo yowr lordshipes beginninges of welconceiuinge of me, I shall most ernestlye desire yowre Lordshipe to forbere to beleiue to[o] fast, least I growinge so slowlie into yowre good opinion may be vndeseruedly of my parte, roted ought of yowre fauoure. The whiche thinge, to allwayes obtayne, (if yowre lordshipe doo but equally consider of me) may se by all the meanes possible in me, I doo aspire. thought [=though] perhapes by reasone of my yowthe, yowre grauer and seuerer yeres will not iuge the same, Thus therfore hopinge the best in yowre lordshipe, and feringe the worst in my selfe, I take my leaue, least my letters may become lothsume and tedious vnto yow to whome I wishe to be most grat[e]full ...

Oxford concedes that Burghley has received 'senister reportes' – from Burghley's memorandum we know exactly what was reported – but Oxford dismisses the informants as 'back-friends'. (I leave it to the reader to judge how appropriate it is for a young man of twenty-two, a member of the House of Lords, and married, to be pleading 'my yowthe' or 'misfortune' as excuses for misconduct.) Oxford added a postscript:

> This bearer hathe sum ne[e]d of yowre Lordships fauoure, whiche when he shall speake withe yowre Lordship I pray yow, for my sak[e] he may finde yow the more his furtherer and helper in his cause.

The bearer is unfortunately not identified.

On 8 December William Homberston wrote, evidently to Burghley, from Bury St Edmunds:[38]

> Maye it please your honorable Lordship to be advertysed that after my departure from London I travayled to wyvenhoe to my Lord of Oxenford who very honorably was contented to here me and semed wyllyng to concent to all thynges I colde devyse for his benefyte. I praye god good execucion maye followe accordyngly ffrom thence Lewen and I traveled to Colne where I had appoynted certeyne menne to meete vs to see the woodes in the parke and in fyne sold there vjxx [=120] okes for iijC xxli [=£320] at liijs viijd [=£4–13–8] the tree which is lxxvli [=£75] more then they were valued by the Comyssioners at the last Surveye / The cause whie I sold no moe, or rather whie I sold eny at all I wyll declare to your honour at my returne to London with my poore opynyon touching other Therle his causes.
>
> Thole [=The whole] somme of the woodes sold at this present is aboue a thowsand poundes / yf this maye be well employed, toward the payement of his dettes, I shall thynke my travayle well bestowed / ...

'Lewen' was probably William Lewin, who will appear again in 1575. Oxford had begun to liquidate his properties, including his woods, to pay off his debts.

18 Murder

On 1 January 1573 Lady Mary Vere received a New Year's gift from the Queen.[1] Now about eighteen, Lady Mary was beginning to be noticed at court.

By 3 February the Privy Council had taken up residence at Greenwich.[2] On Wednesday 18 March, Queen and Court arrived for the Maundy Thursday cele-bration.[3] Before the month was out Burghley dispatched a shattering message to Walsingham in Paris:[4]

> Here hath been a murther committed about Shooters-hill, somewhat to the reproof of this place; and herein I have used such care, as the party is taken, being one Brown an Irish man, who had served, and is put from my Lord of Oxfords seruice.

On 25 March, the Wednesday after Easter, George Brown murdered George Saunders, a London merchant, on Shooters-hill near Greenwich. Brown was in fact a Yorkshireman who had seen service in Ireland. On 26 March the Privy Council took action:[5]

> A letter to the Mayor of London to cause diligent inquirie to be made for a murdre donne the day before upon one Saunders, an honest merchant man, one Browne being vehemently suspected.

On 30 March the Council took up the subject once more:[6]

> A warraunt to the Tresorer of the Chamber for vli [=£5] to the Mayor of Rochester for bringing of George Browne, prisoner, to the Coourte for the murdering of Saunders, a merchant of London.

By now Brown had been captured. Again on 1 April:[7]

> A letter to the Knight Mershall to deliver unto the Lieutenant of the Towre George Browne, to be furder ordered as he shall receve from the Lords of the Counsell.

> A letter to the Lieutenant to receve him and to kepe him in suer custodie, without havinge conference with any, saving the Master of the Rolles, Mr. Justice Sowthcote and Manwoode, or any two of them, whom they have appointed to examine him, willing him to assiste them by bringing or putting him to the racke or otherwise.

> A letter to the Master of the Rolles, Justice Southcote and Justice Manwoode, or any two of them, to examine George Browne and all others suspected to be contrivers of the murdre of Saunders, upon suche instructions as shalbe given them by the bretheren and frindes of the said Saunders, to put Browne to tortures if they finde cause, to committe suche to pryson as they shall finde touched with the facte, and to admitte the brethern and frindes of Saunders to be presente at the examinacion, and to minister interrogatories if they finde cause.

Brown was put to torture; by 13 April he required medical attention:[8]

> A letter to the Lieutenant of the Towre to send for a phisicion for George Browne to loke unto him, and to suffer Anne Drurye's doughter or sume other woman to cume unto her and lye in her chamber, so that they be by him searched and examined that they bringe in nothing that may do harme.

> A letter to the Master of the Rolles undelaiedly to gyve order that all thinges may be in redines for the furniture [=furnishing] of George Browne's inditement, so that thereupon justice may ensue.

The Anne Drury named in the first letter was, as we shall learn, a co-conspirator.

So sensitive were the authorities to the murder that a pamphlet entitled *Brief Discourse of the late murther of master George Saunders* was immediately published for 'the avoiding of miscredite' – in effect, damage control. The author was Oxford's uncle and Burghley's protégé Arthur Golding.[9] A second edition appeared in 1577, contemporaneously with a briefer narrative by yet another Burghley protégé, Raphael Holinshed, in his oft-reprinted *Chronicles*. Holinshed explains that Brown 'cruelly murthered' not only George Saunders of London, but also John Bean of Woolwich, 'whiche murther was commytted in maner as followeth' (pp. 1805–06):

On Tuesday in Easter Weeke (the xxiiijth of Marche) the sayde George Browne receyuing secrete intelligence by letter from Mistresse Anne Drurie, that Maister Saunders shoulde lodge the same night at the house of one Maister Barnes in Woolwich, and from thence goe on foote to Saint Mary Cray. The next morning he lay in waite for him by the way, a little from Shooters hill, and there slue both him and Iohn Bean seruant to maister Barnes, but Iohn Bean hauing x or xj woundes, and being left for dead, by Gods prouidence did reuiue againe, and creeping awaye on all foure, was founde by an olde manne and his Maiden, and conueyed to Woolwich, where he gaue euident markes of the Murtherer.

Immediately vpon the deed doing, Browne sent Mystresse Drurie worde thereof by Roger Clement (among them called trustie Roger) hee himself repayred forthwith to the court at Greenwich, & anon after him came thither the report of the murther also. Then departed he thence vnto London, and came to the house of Mystresse Drurie, where though hee spake not personallye with hir, after conference had with hir seruaunt trustie Roger, she prouided him xx pounde that same day, for the which she layde certaine Plate of hir owne, and of Mistresse Saunders to gage.

The next morning Mistress Drury employed 'Trusty Roger' to carry another £6 to Brown, who, having fled to Rochester, was soon captured. Under torture Brown confessed 'that hee had oftentymes before pretended and sought to doe the same, by the instigation of the sayde mystresse Drurie, who had promised to make a maryage betweene him & mystresse Saunders (whome hee seemed to loue excessiuely).' Brown was executed in Smithfield, his body 'hanged vp in Chaynes neare vnto the place where he had done the fact'.

In the meane time mistresse Drurie & hir man being examined, as well by their owne confessions, as by falling out of the matter, and also by Brownes appeachment thought culpable, were committed to warde. And after mistresse Saunders being deliuered of child, and churched, (for at the tyme of hir husbandes death she looked presently to lie down) was vpon mistresse Druries mans confession, and other great likelihoodes, likewise committed to the Tower, and on Wednesday the sixt of May, arraigned with mistresse Drurie at the Guildhall. The effect of whose inditement was, that they by a Letter written had beene procurers of the sayde murther, and knowing the murther done, had by money and otherwyse relieued the murtherer, whervnto they pleaded not giltie. Howbeit they were both condemned as accessaries to maister Sanders death, and executed in Smithfield the xiij of May, beeing Wednesday in the Whitsonweeke, at which time they both confessed themselues guiltie of the fact. Trustie Roger, mystresse Druries man was arraigned on Fryday the viij of May, and being there condemned as accessarie, was executed with his mistresse, at the time and place aforesayd.

> Not long after, Anthonie Browne brother to the forenamed George Browne, was
> for notable felonies conueyed from Newgate to Yorke, and there hanged.

In sum, on 25 March George Saunders and John Bean were murdered by Oxford's
man George Brown, who was hanged for the crime at Smithfield on 20 April.
Mistress Saunders (the wife of George Saunders), Mistress Anne Drury, and Roger
Simms (*alias* Roger Clement, *alias* Trusty Roger) were hanged as accessories on 13
May. Convicted of independent felonies, Brown's brother Anthony was later
hanged at York.[10]

Further details of the murder, and of the hanging of Trusty Roger, are recorded in the Middlesex County archives, with reference to the date of 25 March:[11]

> True Bill that, at Eltham co. Kent in the highway leading from Woolwyche to St.
> Mary Cray, George Browne late of London gentleman assaulted George Saunders
> late citizen and merchant-taylor of London, and murdered him: And That,
> knowing him to have committed the said murder, Roger Symes late of the parish of
> St. Gabriel in Fanchurche Streate yoman, on the 26th of March, 15 Eliz., and at
> divers subsequent times received, comforted, and aided the same George Browne.
> Putting himself 'Guilty', Roger Symes was sentenced to be hung.

Among the authorities taking testimony on 6 May was Jasper Fisher, whom we
shall meet again.

The murder of George Saunders recalls the more notorious murder of Arden
of Feversham in 1551, reported in Holinshed's *Chronicle* (1577), then dramatized
and published as a play in 1592.[12] This fresh murder was reported by Oxford's
servant Anthony Munday in *A View of Sundry Examples. Reporting Many Straunge
Murthers* (1580), sigs. B1v–2v, and subsequently dramatized and published as *A
Warning for Fair Women* (1599), as performed by the Lord Chamberlain's Men –
Shakespeare's company.[13]

19 Mayhem

Untouched by the crimes of his servant George Brown, on 22 April Oxford
received votes from ten of the twelve electors for the Order of the Garter,
including Burghley in his first year of membership in the Order (G-BL).
Elizabeth did not make the appointment.

On 30 April Roger, Lord North, eccentric, powerful, and cultured Lord
Lieutenant of Cambridgeshire, wrote to Burghley from his country residence at
Kirtling of a rural intrigue with a set of characters as odd as himself.[1] One was a
runaway servant of Oxford's surnamed Booth, probably 'my seruant William
Bothe' named in Oxford's letter of 27 November 1575 (LL-08). A second was
Josias Bird, MA, fellow of Benet (now Corpus Christi) College, Cambridge, son

of Samuel Bird of Walden, Essex.[2] A third was Oxford's gentleman-servant Richard Thimbleby.[3] North wrote as follows:

> My singvlar good Lord: I ame more redy then able to do you plesvre: but when I may here [=hear] of anything that conserneth you: my eares shalbe yours.

> Sir I have h[e]ard yow do seke to have on[e]: Booth: some time sarvant to my Lord of Oxford for what purpose I know not: what I have learned your Lordship shall here.

> this Booth: did lie at an alehowse yn Chesterton by Cambridg before Easter and after: disgised yn a shepperds cloke: an old hatt and an yll paire of hose: he called him self Sturdye: this Booth repaired to one Bird a Master of art yn Benet Colledge: with whom I have spoken: and what I have learned of him followeth.

> Speches past [=passed] by Booth to Mr Bird of Benet Colledg

> 1 Booth being asked whie he went so disguised: and laye yn sutch an ale howse saith my Lord tresorer doth lay waite for me yn every place and I darr not be seen:

> 2 yt was time for me to goe from my Lord of Oxford: for saith he: there was poison bowght: to poison me withall

> 3 he told Bird that my Lord cowld not like my Lady [=Countess Anne] adding words rather of his lewdnes then dishonorable to my Lady saieng she was a child.

> Bird ys able to say more but he fereth my Lord of Oxford and some displesure to follow:

> Sir this man went away the 14 of Aprill from oure sheer [=shire, county]; and where he ys I know not: but you maye learne: my Lord of Oxford hath a mane [=man] called Thimbilbe: whoe came to Chesterton by Cambridg on Easter day vnto Booth: from thence they went to Cambridge: yf your Lordship cane speke with Thimbilbe he can tell your Lordship what ys becom of him: for he hath conveied him awaye: when Thimbilbe came to him: he said Booth be of good cheer: my Lord our Master will convey the[e] over ynto Spaine presently:

> My good Lord I know not whether I troble you: which yf I do lett my love procver [=procure] my pardon: But yf ther be any matter yn yt: I will assver your Lordship apon knowlage from you: yf ever he put foot yn his old hawnt I will have him: or yf you will have him yt ys certain that he ys gone: either to Colme Parke yn Essex: wher he lurketh: or ynto Norfolke to a brother yn lawes howse that he hath whom I know not.

> all the servis that I can do your Lordship yn any theng command me: and yf therbe any matter yn this letter to sarve any torne [=turn]: yt shalbe abidden by: I like not that poison that was bowght I pray God yt was not for a better creature then for him self: ons [=once] he hath confessed yt.

> thus I committ your Lordship to God and my self to your Lordships devotion: remaining redi to all the servis you cane employe me: Beseching your good

Lordship to lett Bird be as Littell seen yn yt as may be: but he shall not goe from any thing: and perhapp your Lordship may learne more then I. I humbly commend me.

There is much in this letter to digest. First, Booth left Oxford's employment, fearing Oxford meant to poison him. Booth went into hiding from before 22 March (Easter Sunday) to 14 April, in Chesterton, a village which bore approximately the same relationship to Cambridge that Southwark bore to London – a place of nefarious activity. Disguising himself as a shepherd and taking a false name, he seems to have been hiding more from Burghley than from Oxford. (Perhaps Burghley wanted to keep him from telling tales; or perhaps he was a security risk.) Discovered at Chesterton by Thimbleby, the two men visited Josias Bird of Benet College, who pumped Booth for information. Thimbleby convinced Booth that Oxford would protect him, if necessary by conveying him to Spain. Leaving Chesterton on 14 April, Booth subsequently lurked in Colne Park, Essex, or took shelter with his brother-in-law in Norfolk.

Booth's report to Bird, conveyed by North, that Oxford 'cowld not like my Lady', substantiates the report of 18 March 1572 that Oxford 'putte away fromme hym the countes hys wyffe'. That older report attributed Oxford's rejection of Anne to a political difference with Burghley over the execution of the Duke of Norfolk; now the failure of the marriage is attributed to Oxford's 'lewdnes' – nothing 'dishonorable' to Anne, who 'was a child'. North hints at sexual incontinence on Oxford's part: 'Bird ys able to say more but he fereth my Lord of Oxford and some displesure to follow'. Just as Booth feared that Oxford meant to have him poisoned, so Bird feared retaliation from Oxford for saying too much. North himself feared for Bird's safety: 'Beseching your good Lordship to lett Bird be as Littell seen yn yt as may be'. As for Oxford, he had now gained a reputation for abandoning his wife, for sexual profligacy, for lethal hostility to servants who fell out with him or strangers who told on him, and for an ability to spirit men across the sea to Spain.

On 1 May Antonio de Guaras wrote to the Duke of Alva at Brussels, concerning a conversation with Burghley:[4]

> ... and he said to me that, if his friends knew that he held a pension from the King it would be his undoing, and in no manner acceptable; and he said that he thought that, if there were no pension, he would not refuse help for the marriage of madame his daughter, who was married to the count of Oxford, that my lady his wife would not refuse the demonstration of the good will of the King.

If we are to trust this report, Burghley refused the offer of a direct pension from the King of Spain on the grounds that he would be compromised if it were discovered by his friends; but he would welcome a pension given in support of the marriage of Anne and Oxford; nor would Lady Burghley refuse such an offer.

On 11 May Gilbert Talbot, long since returned from Paris, sent a screed of gossip to his father:[5]

> ... My Lord Tresurer, even after the ould manner, delythe with matters of the state only, and beareth himself very upryghtly. My Lord Lecester is very muche with her Maiestie, and she sheweth the same great good affection to him that she was wonte; of late he hath indevored to please hir more then hertofore: There are twoe sisters nowe in the Courte that are very farr in love with him, as they have been longe; my Lady Sheffeld, and Frances Haworthe; they (of lyke stryving who shall love him better) are at great warres together, and the Queine thinketh not well of them, and not the better of him; by this meanes there is spies over him. My Lord of Sussex goeth with the tyde, and helpethe to backe others; but his owne credite is sober, consydering his estate: He is very diligent in his office, and takethe great paynes. My Lord of Oxforth is lately growne into great credite; for the Queens Maiestie delitethe more in his parsonage, and his dalunsinge, and valientnes, then any other: I thinke Sussex dothe back him all that he can; if it were not for his fyckle hed he would passe any of them shortly. My Lady Burghley unwisely hathe declared herselfe, as it were, geliouse, which is come to the Quene's eare; whereat she [=the Queen] hathe bene not a litell offended with hir, but now she is reconsiled agayne. At all theise love matters my Lord Treasurer winketh, and will not meddle in any way. ...

Evidently the Queen had taken to flirting with Oxford. While Lady Burghley became jealous, doubtless on behalf of her neglected daughter, Lord Burghley, deferring to rank and privilege, was content to let the flirtation take its course. Most acute of all is Gilbert's characterization of Oxford: 'if it were not for his fyckle hed he would passe any of them shortly'.

On Thursday 21 May Oxford's potentially lethal hostility to disaffected servants flared up once more. William Faunt and John Wotton *alias* Clopton[6] complained to Burghley from Gravesend that they had been hounded out of London and attacked with calivers – light muskets – by three of Oxford's servants:[7]

> The dutyful regard we owe to youer honor, and the due consyderatyon we have in this case, dothe staye vs to addresse oure complaynte to any but to youer lordshype / because the matter dothe neare touche the honor of my Late good Lord and master of whom publykely to heare complaynt (of raginge deameanore) would greaue youer honor and my sealfe to make it, if ther were any other meanes for oure securytye / So it is Righte honorable wootton and my sealfe, rydynge peasably by the hyghe way, from Grauesend to Rochester, had thre calyvers charged with bullettes dyscharged at vs by thre of my Lord of Oxenfordes men / Danye Wylkyns Ihon Hannam, and Deny the Frenche man vhoe lay preuylye in a diche awaytynge oure cummynge wythe full intente to murder hus [=us] yet (notwythestandyng they all dyschargyng vppon vs so neare that my saddell hauynge they [=the] gerthes broke fell withe my sealfe from the horse and a bullet wythein halfe a foote of me) hit plesed God to delyuer vs from that determyned myschefe whervppon they mounted one [=on] horse backe and fled towardes London wythe all possyble

spede / The consyderatyon hereof dothe warne vs to provyde for oure safty /
insomuche we playnely see oure lyves are soughte for / otherwayse the fornamyd
partyes would not haue pursued vs from London / vho in lyke maner yesterday
besett oure lodgynge / for viche cause and to procure my Lordes fauor in tyme we
lefte the citty an[d] chose the cuntrey for oure safeguard / where we fynd oure
sealfes in no lesse perryll of spoyle then before and nowe seynge that neyther cytty
nor cuntrey is a suffycyente protectyon from theyre malyce we humbly appeale to
youer honor / vhom we neuer knue but a mayntener of Iustyce and punysher of
abuses or ells generally to the counsell as youer honor lykethe best / they [=the]
Lawe hathe geuen vs greate advantage of them viche surely we would pursue to the
vtermost of hit / weare it not in respecte of oure Late noble Lord and master (who
withe pardon be hit spokene) is to be thoughte as procurer of that w[h]iche is done
/ and so to conclude ryghte honorable if we haue offended the Lawes of this realme
or oure Late noble Lord as (viche we haue not) ve [=we] remayne here in grauesend
to abyde condygne punyshemente from whence we dare not departe befor we be
assured of oure securytys, and order taken for them ...

The letter, in Faunt's hand, also carries the signature of Wotton. Both men had
brought Burghley's letters to Walsingham in Paris on 8 November 1571. 'Deny
the French man' was Maurice Dennis, who would become involved in Oxford's
pro-Guise adventure of 1577.

Faunt and Wotton identify themselves as former servants of Oxford,
complain of his 'raginge deameanore', and state explicitly that Oxford is 'to be
thoughte as procurer of that w[h]iche is done'. The matter was not treated
lightly. Burghley reported in his retrospective Diary under 21 May (ii, p. 774):

... Thomas [error for John] Wotton shott at with Calivers by Hammon and Denny.
The Erle of Oxfords Men near Gravesend.

We shall soon learn that the three offenders were sent to prison for their offence –
much to Oxford's disgust.

In an undated letter to the Queen about June of this year, Christopher Hatton
seems to allude to himself as a sheep, to Oxford as a boar:[8]

God bless you for ever; the branch of the sweetest bush I will wear and bear to my
life's end: God witness I feign not. It is a gracious favour most dear and welcome
unto me: reserve it to the Sheep, he hath no tooth to bite, where the Boar's tusk
may both raze and tear.

Hatton seems to be recommending himself, as a harmless drudge who would
slave on Elizabeth's behalf, over Oxford, who was capable not only of doing her
service, but of doing her (and others) harm.

On 11 June Oxford's entitlement to Vere House, on Candlewick Street at
London Stone, was validated by a royal grant rich in descriptive detail:[9]

Grant in fee simple to Edward de Veer, earl of Oxford, viscount Bulbeck,
chamberlain of England and lord Baddelesmere and Scales, of a great messuage in

the parish of St. Swithin by London Stone in Candelwikestrete in London, a great garden and a small garden adjoining the said messuage, with access therto by two great gates (whereof one extends towards Candelwicke Strete by St. Swithin's church towards the South, and the other lower down towards the North), the land between the said gates and all cottages and hereditaments adjoining and belonging to the messuages, the advowson of the rectory [and] vicarage of St. Swithin and all lands in the said parish once of Tortington priory, co. Sussex; to hold in free burgage of the city of London and by a yearly rent of 30s. The premises, being then of the yearly value of £15, were granted in tail male by patent, 8 June, 31 Henry VIII, to John Deveer, earl of Oxford, to hold by service of the twentieth part of a knight's fee and by a yearly rent of 30s; later by fine in the Common Pleas in Easter term, 15 Eliz. [=1573], the said Edward, earl of Oxford, son and heir male of John, conveyed them to the Crown.

The 15th Earl acquired Vere House in 1539, shortly before his death, and the 16th Earl had used it as a townhouse.[10] Though the 17th Earl may have known the place from his childhood, Leicester had controlled the property during his wardship.[11]

Stow described 'Vere house' or 'Oxford house' thus in 1598 (by which time Oxford had sold the property):[12]

> On the north side of [St Swithin's] Church and Churchyard, is one faire and large builded house, sometime pertayning to the prior of Tortington in Sussex, since to the Earles of Oxford, and now to sir Iohn Hart Alderman: which house hath a faire Garden belonging thereunto, lying on the west side thereof. On the backeside of two other faire houses in Walbrooke, in the raigne of Henrie the seuenth, sir Richard Empson knight, Chanceler of the Duchie of Lancaster, dwelled in the one of them, and Edmond Dudley Esquire in the other: either of them had a doore of entercourse into this Garden, wherein they met and consulted of matters at their pleasures. In this Oxford place sir Ambrose Nicholas kept his Maioraltie, and since him the said sir Iohn Hart.

The garden behind the main house constituted one of its principal amenities.

On 13 July Maisonfleur, in London, wrote to Burghley:[13]

> The Earl of Oxford has at the house of a merchant of this city thirty gilt morions, which the merchant is willing to sell if he can have licence from the Earl, which he prays him to obtain for him.

The 'thirty gilt morions' were steel helmets, perhaps part of Oxford's inheritance.

Although Oxford had acquired rights to Vere house, he retained apartments in the Savoy. On 12 August four members of the Savoy foundation wrote to Burghley with a complaint against their superior, Thomas Thurland, clerk:[14]

> ... That as you have bene a speciall Patron & protector of the said poore hospitall, So yt may please you to contynue, and to defende & delyver vs from suche iniuries as the said Thomas Thurland by his subtill practice dothe offer vnto the said hospitall, Righte Honorable, towchinge certaine lodginges within the said hospitall, with a garden belonginge to the Master of the Savoye, which the said

Thomas Thurland maketh clayme vnto, by vertue of a forged lease; which is not good, nor never herde of till after his depryvacion, we the poore Chapleines for the speciall good will that we beare to your honor, are contented that the Earle of Oxforde shall have the occupacion therof and of all other lodginges above the Stayers belonginge to the Master of the Savoye, So that he keepe them in good reparacions, vntill suche tyme as we shall have a Master / But as for the Romethes benethe the Stayers viz. The parlor, Hall, Buttry, kytchen, & woodyarde; we can not spare them beinge so necessarye for the provision of the poore & vs,
(*signed*) William Neale, Iohn Parke, Iohn Hodgeson, Thomas Chambers

The four are 'contented' that Oxford inhabit 'lodginges above the Stayers' but want the rooms 'benethe the Stayers viz. The parlor, Hall, Buttry, kytchen, & woodyarde' for the poor and for themselves. Thurland replied that he had given over the best rooms (referred to by the four as those 'benethe the Stayers') to Oxford by way of exchange (f. 76):

Charytably I have thoughte good to lett you vnderstand this my doinges which God willinge I meane to prosecute till the Quenes Maiesties returne from her progresse, whereof I requier of you all fower dyrectly to be aunswered.

first To lett you vnderstand that I have for good & resonable causes exchaunged with my Lord of Oxford the rest of my howses & Lodgings Ioyninge to the Masters Lodginge which he hathe by vertue of Mr Hudlestons Lease as particulerly by articles indented betwixte the said Earle and me ...

Evidently Thurland himself now occupied the rooms 'above the Stayers', Oxford those below, while the four chaplains were left with little or nothing. The four wrote again on 20 November (f. 85):

... whan as we the Chapleyns of the Savoye dyd commende my Lorde Threasaurer for the good will that he dyd beare vnto our poore howse for we sayd that yf he were not, we were in a shrode [=shrewed, evil] case / Than Mr Thurlande moste sclanderously & dishonestly replyed sayeinge / that the sayd Lord Threasaurer ys the greatest enemy that we have, & dothe seeke the dissolution & vndoynge of our howse, the which the sayd Lord had accomplished & browthte to passe had not the sayd Thurlande withstande him, & also the sayd Lord Threasaurer ys a contynuall suter vnto Thurlande as he sayd, for the Masters lodginge, that my lord of Oxforthe may have the same. & further he sayd that he & my lord of Oxforthe have bene at greate & highe wordes, my Lord of Oxforthe meanynge the overthrowe & distruction of the howse & Thurland the preservacion thereof / these and suche lyke sclanderouse & moste vntrwe reportes are spoken and gyven abrode by the sayd Thurlande, & for proffe that he hath spoken them yf he denye yt / we with others are readye to depose.

The vague pronominal reference makes it unclear whether Oxford was at 'greate & highe wordes' with Thurland or with Burghley; either scenario fits what by now has become an essential element of Oxford's reputation. The chaplains add by way of a postscript (f. 87):

We do moste hvmblye besyche youre honor that Mr Thurlande layte Master of the
Savoye, myght be commandyd to delyver, all the covnterpaynes of leases, books of
accovntes, & obligations, as he haithe of our houses in his handes, and like wyse we
do desier yf it be youre honors pleasure, that my lorde of Oxfurthe myght haue the
vse of certayne chambers, with a gardynge, wyche Mr thurlande doithe challenge
by vertu of a novghtye [=naughty, fraudulent] lease newer [=never] harde of before
his depryvations, theye be the necessaries roomes that are aboute our house for my
lorde of Oxfurthe

Evidently Oxford still used these tenements or suites of rooms as his London
residence.[15] He would retain control of the Savoy tenements until at least 1576,
and probably beyond. In 1573, however, the sum of £10–11–8 was demanded by
officials of the Savoy 'from Edward, Earl of Oxford' for 'part rent of two
tenements within the Hospital'.[16] Already Oxford was defaulting, even on his rent.

20 Wanderlust

In late summer 1573 Burghley's servant, Barnard Dewhurst, composed a report to
his 'singuler good Lord and Master' revealing that Oxford, having expressed his
desire as early as 1569 to travel abroad, and having been authorized to travel
(whether to Ireland or Scotland) in 1570, now meant to travel to Ireland. Because
he carried a title, arrangements had to be made for the control of his estates in his
absence, and for its disposition in the event of his death. Dewhurst incidentally
and usefully details six days of Oxford's life in his twenty-third year, from Friday
28 August to Thursday 3 September, while the Queen was on progress in Kent.[1]
Oxford spent Friday night at the Savoy, Saturday at Theobalds (arriving just at
bedtime), Sunday at Burghley House, Monday elsewhere, Tuesday at Burghley
House. On Wednesday, after dining at Burghley House, he evidently retired to the
Savoy, arising Thursday at 7:00 to catch a favourable morning tide for Gravesend. Though Anne too spent Saturday night at Theobalds, and though Oxford
'gave order' that she should be with him in Canterbury, his bedfellow at the
Savoy and travelling companion to Canterbury was Charles Arundel.

On the Monday Justice Southcote returned from the country at Oxford's
request, while Sir William Cordell, Master of the Rolls, arrived on Tuesday
afternoon, similarly summoned from the town of Oxford. Southcote, hoping to
find Oxford at the Savoy, had been intercepted by Thomas Gent, esquire,
described elsewhere as 'steward of the manors and lands of the Right Honorable
the Earl of Oxford'.[2] Reporting that Oxford was not at home to visitors, Gent
conferred with Southcote at Serjeants Inn, one of the Inns of Court. While
Dewhurst watched from a distance, Southcote and Gent inspected articles
proposed by Burghley, along with Oxford's written reply, which Gent 'tolde Mr

Iustice in secrete was Dr Atslowes device'. Dr Edward Atslowe of Downham, Essex, physician, was a Catholic recusant later subject to indictment and persecution.[3] Atslowe's 'device' was to propose John, Lord Darcy of Chiche, son of the Lord Darcy who had been involved with Oxford's father, as Oxford's spokesman, and Gent as Oxford's commissioner.

When Southcote told Gent that he would gladly see Oxford in person, Gent replied that Oxford would communicate only through a go-between. On Tuesday night Cordell and Southcote sent a man to Oxford 'to knowe his pleasure when they shoolde wayte on hym'. Oxford sent three representatives – Gent, one Baynes (otherwise unknown),[4] and Richard Thimbleby. Objecting that they could not well proceed 'onles they had som talke with my Lord', Cordell and Southcote requested that Oxford 'tary one day longer'. Oxford returned word that Cordell and Southcote should 'forbeare to comm vnto hym because he was troobled in takinge inventorie of his playte, and other thinges whiche woolde fullie occupie hym so longe as he was in the towne'. On Wednesday Cordell and Southcote cooled their heels from 'vij of the Clocke in the morning vntill ij of the clock in thafter nowne' in the vain hope of a further reply. Meanwhile, it must have occurred to these elder statesmen that if Oxford had meant to negotiate through his servants, there was no point in their having been called to London in the first place.

Oxford was not merely inconsiderate, but deep in the throes of other disputes with other men. William Ayloffe, an Essex landowner,[5] had been calling on Oxford daily at the Savoy. Oxford 'sent hym woorde he woolde sende for hym, when the Master of the Rolles came home'. Dewhurst adds: '... but did not yett that I can learne'. Lady Burghley informed Dewhurst that Oxford was irate because his men remained in prison while 'the villaynes' – Faunt and Clopton *alias* Wotton – were favourably heard at the Privy Council, backed – so Oxford suspects – by Burghley and Leicester.

Dewhurst's letter was accompanied by the promised letter from Sir William Cordell, the proposed articles with Oxford's written responses, and a letter (now lost) from Cordell to the Warden of the Fleet Prison. Cordell's surviving letter, dated 2 September from the Rolls Office, picks up Dewhurst's story from Tuesday afternoon.[6] Having come down from Oxford at the Earl's request:

> Mr Iustice Sowthecote & I sent Imediatly vnto his Lordship aduertisyng the same that wee wer bothe redye ether as yester daye or elles this mornyng what tyme & wher he shold Command vs to wayte vppon hym ...

Understanding that the Earl 'was so busied that he had no leyser', Cordell renewed his request. The answer came back that Oxford was

> soe occupyed abowte makyng of his Inventoryes of his plate & other Stuff & that Mr Charles Arundell was specially sent vnto hym to hasten his Iorney to the Court that he had no kynde of leyser.

Perusing the written proposals, Cordell expressed the opinion that

> the Substances of thosse articles wer not assured specially touchyng the assuraunces of the landes that shold discend to the next Erle for defalte of Issewe of his body & for my lady his wiffes Ioynter [=jointure] & for the payment of his detes

Gent answered that Anne would have certain of Oxford's lands '& his howse of Wyvenho' and adjoining properties to the yearly value of £669–6–8. Cordell concluded by asking to meet face to face with Burghley: clearly disgusted with having been fobbed off by Oxford, he hopes that Burghley can control his son-in-law.

That Burghley himself was the author of the twelve articles in question is obvious from Oxford's responses (not in his own hand).[7] I have 'interleaved' the two to make their relationship more apparent:

> 1. To determyne what the debtes are, and to considre howe many of them maybe moderated and made less, and howe the Creditours maye be compounded with all [=withal] for reasonable dayes of payment./

> > 1. To determyne what my debtes are certainely / yt is not possible because as yet I cannot have the sight of them all, but my debt to the Queens maiestie and those which I haue gathered together considered, I haue iust cause to thinke that the some of my debtes wilbe vjMli [=£6000] at the least / The moderacion & stallinge of them I must leave to suche as shalbe put in trust with my landes

> 2. To considre howe the same maye be payde, and what landes maye be lymitted to be answerable for the same./

> > 2. ffor the payment of my debtes, I haue assigned between iiij & vCli [=£4–500] by the yeare over and besides suche profites and improvementes as maye reasonably be raysed in my absence of my landes or otherwise /

> 3. To make estates of his landes accordinge to his owne disposicion, howe his landes shall remaine if he shold dye with out heires of his bodye and howe moche shold remaine to the yssue ffemale, if he shold haue no heires male, and what shall be assigned for his wief to lyve on in his absence, and what to be a Iointer [=jointure] for her /

> > 3. My meaninge is that the Erldome shall remaine to my heire male, & with all so moche land as I maye leave by lawe /

> > To my yssue female if I shold haue no heires male must nedes remayne certaine landes amountinge to CCxiiijli vijs jd ob qr [=£214–7–1¾] as by the partyculers appeareth /

> > ffor my wief to lyve one in my absence I haue assigned CCCli [=£300]. And for her Iointer vjC lxixli vjs viiijd [=£669–6–8] / In consideracion whereof I requyre of your Lordship for my mariage money iijMli [=£3000]. And am content to resigne over Combe againe./

> 4. Item what landes and howe moche shall remaine to the heire that shall have the Erledome /

4. The iiijth is answered in the third.

5. Item what money maye be provyded presently for him to take with him, and to make over by eschange for vj monethes, and so from vj monethes to vj monethes./

5. I haue appointed for my self to serue my turne beyonde the seas Mli [=£1000] and hope to be furnished with present money by your Lordship for my mariage money

In consideracion whereof I am content to resigne my interest & estate in Combe as I haue sayde before /

6. Item what revenewe shalbe left to these seuerall vses / first to be answerable for his charges abroade, secondly for mayntenaunce of his wief & her seruauntes & company / Thirdly for his Lordships sister and suche of his seruauntes as he will also leve behinde him, to lyve vppon his charge.

6. The vjth is answered before in parte / viz for my self I haue appointed Mli [=£1000] for my wief CCCli [=£300] for my sister Cli [=£100] and the rest of my necessary charges at home I leave to be ordered by my Commyssioners /

7. Item howe he will leave ordre for money to giue his sister in mariage, howe for his fathers will /

7. My sisters mariage money is to be levyed of suche landes as by statute are lymited to the performance of my Lord my fathers will / and the same will is to be answered in lyke manner /

8. Item to consider whome he will appoint receivour, who had nede to be a man of lyveloode /

8. ffor my Receiuour I doe appointe & nominate (*blank*)

9. Item to appointe certaine Attornyes for his sutes in Lawe /

9. ffor my Attornyes for sutes in Lawe / (*blank*)

10. Item to name some to heare the accomptes of all suche as haue had to deal with my Lordships money and paymentes and also to examyne the state of all his Leases past

10. To heare thaccomptes of all suche as haue had to deale for me and to examyne the state of Leases & patentes past I leave to my generall Commyssioners viz to (*blank*)

11. To make Inventoryes of // Plate apparell // Wardrobe stuff // Horses & geldinges
That they may be [ap]praysed savinge his horses & geldinges that shall not be vsed maye be sold

11 The makinge of Inventoryes of my plate apparell wardrobe stuff horses and geldinges and the order of all savinge suche as must serue for my wiefes necessary vse I leave to the sayd Commyssioners /

12. Item to considre howe and by what meanes his money shalbe made over to him

by Exchange from vj monthes to vj monthes and from 3 monthes to three monethes.

> 12 So doe I also leave to them to consider howe my money maye be made over vnto me from tyme to tyme /

Oxford thus estimates his debts to the Queen and other creditors at £6000, which may include £1800–13–8 owing to 'Creditors appointed by my Lord, to be paid at the ffirst payment'.[8] The heir to the earldom should be his natural male successor, who should inherit as many of his lands as possible. Oxford assigns £4–500 per annum to retire his debts, £214 for any female heir, £300 to Anne (above her jointure of £669–6–8),[9] £1000 for his travel overseas, and £100 for his sister Mary (above her marriage portion of £1333–13–4). Other outlays were to be overseen by his commissioners. To offset all these expenses (which with debt retirement and expenses for himself, Anne, and Mary, came to nearly £2000 per annum) Oxford counts on revenues from his lands, but also demands immediate payment of the £3000 marriage settlement from Burghley. In return for Burghley's cooperation Oxford declared himself 'content to resigne over Combe [=Combe Nevill, an estate received from Burghley] againe'.[10]

Burghley annotated his own copy of the same articles thus:[11]

> That his Castell of Hennyngham may be kept in repayre duryng his absence
>
> That his game of deare be not destroyed
>
> Persons nedefull to be with hym[12] / 2 Gentillmen / 2 gromes / on[e] payemaster / on[e] Cook. / a harbynger / a horsekeeper / a trencherman
>
> It wer good that what so ever landes shall be ordred to remayn to any heyres female, if my Lord shall haue non of his own body, that there might be an equall portion assigned to my Lord Wyndsors wiff [i.e., Oxford's half-sister Katherine] for if she be not speciall provyded for, all the landes in fe symple will remayn wholly to my lady Mary because she is his Lordships sistar of whole blood. and the other is the doughter of a noble houss of hir Mothars syde, and as I have h[e]ard, the Erle of Westmerland gave a gret portion with hyr.

So Burghley wished Oxford to travel with a retinue of nine, and that provision might be made for Lady Katherine as well as Lady Mary Vere.

Cordell wrote to Burghley again on 4 September, as promised:[13]

> With my moste humble deuty vnto your good Lordship I do send vnto the same herenclosed a mynute of the manors appoynted for the Countesse of Oxford your Lordships doughter as I receyvd them of Mr Gent I beleve that the Erles determyn-acion for his spedy goyng beyond the sees ys altered & as I am Crediblie Informed fully Steyed [=stayed] partely by the good advice your Lordship gaue hym by a lettre you did lately wright to his Lordship which hathe prevaylled moche with him. And ther ys one matter which ys the want of money wherof he hath some truste to be furnysshed by your Lordship Or elles of necessite he muste tarye at home /

> I have shewed vnto this be[a]rer my pore [=poor, humble] oppynyon touchyng this
> yourney [=journey] to whom yf yt shall please your Lordship to give audiens he will
> Informe yow therof for as I am lothe to trowble your Lordship with any long lettre.
> Soo yt ys trew that I haue bene very evell at ease sens [=since] my Comyng home
> which was in moste [*for* more?] haste then nedes ...

Thus Burghley had written Oxford a letter (now lost) counselling against travel.
Cordell was mistaken in thinking that Oxford's determination to travel had
permanently cooled.

Within a day or two of the events described in Dewhurst's letter, Anne joined
the Queen at Canterbury, as mentioned in a contemporary report of the Queen's
fortieth birthday feast, sponsored by the Archbishop of Canterbury, Matthew
Parker, on Monday 7 September:[14]

> ... on the left side of the high table, in a place of honour, sat four illustrious ladies:
> the Marchioness of Northampton, and the countesses of Oxford, Lincoln, and
> Warwick.

On Sunday 5 October, William Fleetwood wrote to Burghley:[15]

> ... and after all these things done as they ought to be, I meane, by God's Grace, to see
> your Honour, my Ladie, and my good Landladie, my Ladie of Oxenford, and then
> Mr. Chancellor of the Duchie, and so to Cambridge, and then hom again to my
> former affayres.

On 14 October Edward Bacon wrote to his brother Nathaniel from Gray's Inn
(*Stiffkey*):

> ... My Lord of Oxford and Mr Hatton were at great wordes in the chamber of
> presence, which matter is said to be before the Counsell.

Evidently the 'great words' had led to a challenge, but of the incident no more is
known.

On 4 November Nicholas White wrote to Burghley from Dublin, closing thus:[16]

> I will at more leysyer write to your honour myn opinion towching the worthe, and
> what I thinke of the greate brute made of my Lord of Oxfordes comyng into
> Conaght.

Oxford, however, did not reach Ireland now or ever. As of 1 December, he was
still at Greenwich:[17]

> To the Commissioners appointed in Kent against the transportacion of corne and
> vittels to suffer 100 quarters of otes to be brought to Grenewiche for the provision
> of the Earle of Oxforde.

During this same year (and again in 1576), Oxford's 'Great Park' at Hedingham
Castle was raided by two men of Yeldham and Toppesfield who shot at the wild
and fallow deer, and by five men of Gestingthorpe who killed a doe. Confessing,

the Gestingthorpe five were ordered to remain in prison for three months and afterwards to be bound over on good behaviour for seven years.[18]

The several vectors of Oxford's life by the close of this his twenty-third year trended in a decidedly negative direction. Oxford was now well established as courtier, royal favourite, poet, patron, egotist, and thug. His associates included the Queen, peers, courtiers, poets, and protégés, but also the Westminster tailor Edward Baynam, the murderous George Brown, and the violent threesome Danny Wylkyns, John Hannam, and Maurice Dennis *alias* Denny the Frenchman. Reports circulated that Oxford had deserted his young wife, first in a fit of pique, then out of lewd adventurism. He yearned for foreign travel, solo. He treated the most respectable statesmen of England with contempt, and quarrelled with his father-in-law. Not without reason had Gilbert Talbot, the astute critic of Court life, identified the chief impediment to Oxford's advancement as his own 'fyckle hed'.

21 Desperadoes

On 17 January 1574 Ralph Lane, then in Greenwich, addressed a deliberately cryptic letter to Burghley, concerning ship-traffic with Portugal and three individuals: Antonio de Guaras, a Spanish agent; one 'R. B.'; and Lane himself.[1] The Privy Council had offered a lieutenancy first to R. B., who declined, then 'soodenly resolued vppon another Agent for them, which ys Rowlande Yorck', overlooking Lane, who was considered too hot in spirit.

Rowland York, evidently the ninth of ten sons of Sir John York,[2] was a man of extraordinary notoriety, as noted by Camden in his 1615 *Annales* (p. 470), whose Latin was Englished by George Carleton in his *Thankful Remembrance* of 1624 (p. 116): 'York was a Londoner, a man of loose conversation, and actions, and desperate.' The balance of the passage has been cited above in connection with Oxford's 1567 killing of Thomas Brincknell;[3] a translation of 1625, *A True and Royal History*, gives a slightly different rendering (Book 3, p. 223):

> This Yorke, borne in London, was a man most negligent and lazy, but desperately hardy; he was in his time most famous among those who respected Fencing, hauing been the first that brought into England that wicked and pernicious fashion to fight in the Field in Duels, with a Rapier called a Tucke, onely for the thrust: the English hauing till that very time, vsed to fight with Backe-swords, slashing and cutting one the other, armed with Targets or Bucklers, with very broad weapons, accounting it not to be a manly action to fight by thrusting and stabbing, and chiefly vnder the waste.

As we have noted, it was not Rowland York but Edward de Vere who, as early as 1567, killed his man with an unmanly thrust of his rapier beneath the waist.

Rowland York's character may be judged by his subsequent actions (*DNB*). On 28 October 1580 William Herle reported to Walsingham that York had been arrested on a felony.⁴ In 1584 York was caught up in a plot to betray Ghent to the Duke of Parma. In 1586 he joined Leicester's expedition to the Low Countries, where, serving under Sir Philip Sidney, he betrayed the sconce of Zutphen to the Spanish, encouraging Sir William Stanley's more disastrous betrayal of Deventer. Scarcely more loyal to Spain than to England, his death in 1588 is variously attributed to poisoning at the hands of the Spanish, or to smallpox. In 1591 Low-Country Protestants ordered his body exhumed and set on a gibbet.

In the second paragraph of the same letter Lane turns to the subject of a young nobleman. Though the syntax may suggest otherwise, this was probably Oxford, in whom Burghley had the greatest personal interest, and whom Burghley names in his endorsement:

> Yf your lordship doo send for Guerasse ymmedyatly vppon his returne, for feare, of some mayegames to be carryede ouer by this messenger that lately ys come and to putte hym out of all doute that nothing canne eskap your intellygence touching eny my said Lords dealinges synce your interest ys sych [=such] in hym as yt ys, hyt wyll cutt of[f] not only this, but eny other advantages that forreyene factyones may seeke to take of his younge vnstayed mynd.

> Trewely, sir, besydes my deuety vnto your lordship and my affeccyone towardes hym self, the reasonable mystrust that I doo conceiue, that the acquayenting of hym to[o] mych [=much] with forreyene intellygence, (though no harme ment of his parte nor doonne) yeat the same may turne hym in tyeme to mych hurt; and a Westerne Spanysshe storme, may with summe vnhappye mate at healme, steare his noble barcke so myche to the Northewarde, that vnwares hee maye wracke, as sume of his nobellest kynred hath doonne, the moore pytye of theyre faulte, and to bee playene with your lordship yf her maiestie take not sume order sum way to ymploy hym well, hee ys lyeke ynough at one tyeme or other to ymploye hym self abroad, without his best frendes advyeses. And therefore to drawe hym from this humore lately crept into hym, yf your lordship doo thinck of sume ymployement of hym in her maiesties servyce yf yt were but to accompagnye my Lord Deputy into Ierland, and there to bestowe this summer this only mocyone of your lordship with such hoope of further ymployment hereafter in greater matters as your lordship maye adde thereto, wyll peradventure be suffycient of hyt self, to quench this vapore newely kindelled, and especially when hee shall vnderstande of your lordship that you are not ignorante of this present watche

> Thus, sir, my harty dewetyfull affeccyone vnto your lordship whom I knowe his case doothe touche, hath made me to bewray my folly in aduysing your lordship ...

Lane joined the advisers who mistrusted Oxford's interest in foreign affairs and thought he could be bought off with a trip to Ireland.

On 16 March Burghley voided a bond from Oxford for the payment of £4000, 'on condition of the performance of the covenants contained in certain indentures, or on the death of the Lady Anne, wife of the said earl and daughter of the said baron, before any proceedings taken thereon'.[5] Also in March note was taken of the value of lands assigned for Anne's jointure.[6]

On 19 March Oxford's temporary quarters at Lambeth Palace were allotted to Christopher Hatton.[7] Contemporaneous preparations for a royal visit to Archbishop Matthew Parker's palace at Croydon included room-assignments:[8]

> Sir George Howard ... The Capten of the Gard where my Lord Oxford was

One S. Bowyer, writing from Croydon on Wednesday 24 March, observed:

> The Gromes of the Privye Chamber nor Mr. Drewrye have no other waye to their Chambers but to pass thorowe that waye againe that my Lady of Oxford should come. ...

Anne was cared for separately from her husband.

In April Oxford received votes from four of the twelve electors for the Order of the Garter. Though Burghley remained loyal, the votes had declined from ten of twelve in the preceding year (G-BL). On 13 May Edward Bacon, writing to his brother Nathaniel from Gray's Inn, revealed that Oxford's name had been connected with scandal (*Stiffkey*):

> Ther was, as is reported, a most vile libell fownd in court to the evil report of most of the woemen therin slandred. Dyvers have byn examyned, as Sowthel which was with my Lord of Oxenford & dyvers others.

'Sowthel' was doubtless Francis Southwell. Although his noble companion is not accused, Charles Arundel would report in December 1580 that Oxford was given to slander, 'spareinge no woman be she never so vertuous nor any man be he never so honorable' (LIB-4.3/2).

On 27 June Burghley to wrote to Sussex, the Lord Chamberlain:[9]

> My good Lord, I heartily thank you for your gentle remembrance of my daughter of Oxinforde, who, as I think meaneth as her duty is, to wait on Her Majesty at Richmond, except my Lord her husband shall otherwise direct her.

Burghley yearned for Oxford to command Anne to join him anywhere at all, for Anne had been married two and a half years and was not yet pregnant. To the extent that Oxford had been sexually active since December 1571, it was evidently with partners other than his young, pretty, and lawful wife.

22 Flight

On 28 June 1574 Gilbert Talbot wrote to his mother, the Countess of Shrewsbury:[1]

> The young Earl of Oxford, of that ancient and Very family of the Veres, had a cause or suit, that now came before the Queen; which she did not answer so favourably as was expected, checking him, it seems, for his unthriftiness. And hereupon his behaviour before her gave her some offence. This was advertised from the Lord Chamberlain [=Sussex] to the Lord Treasurer [=Burghley], who, being Master of the Wards, had this Earl under his care; and whom he afterwards matched his daughter Anne unto. The news of this troubled that Lord; saying, 'He was sorry her Majesty had made such haste; and had answered him so, that he feared the sequel might breed offence, if he were ill counselled; that is, in case he should upon this yield to such heads as himself, which he was apt enough to do.' And then gave his favourable character of the said young Earl, that howsoever he might be, for his own private matters, of thrift inconsiderate, he dared avow him to be resolute in dutifulness to the Queen and his country. And then prayed God, that the usage of that poor young Earl might not hazard him to the profit of others.

Thus, approaching the Queen with some (unknown) suit, Oxford found himself rebuked 'for his unthriftiness'. When he dared to reply, she checked him. Burghley, however, came to his defence.

Before two days were out, Oxford betrayed his father-in-law's confidence utterly, fleeing abroad without licence. Details are supplied by George Golding, Oxford's auditor:[2]

> Edwarde de Veer Erle of Oxenforde wente ffrom the Ladye Yorkes house in Walbrook in London where he then lay for a tyme and at Allgate [w]here [he] Tooke horse Scilicet the firste day of Iuly 1574 anno xvjth Regine Elizabethe being Thursday betwene twoo and three of clocke in the morning and so to Wyvenhoo in Essex and the nexte nyghte he took ship & co[a]sted over into Flaunders arryving at Callice [=Calais]/

> Where the sayde Erle departed from the lady Yorkes betwene ij & iij of clock in the morning on Thursday primo Iulii 1574. In thafternoone of the same day there was delyuered to Robert Rose his Lordships servaunte a lease engrossed in parchemente by my clerke for xxj yeres to begyn at Michelmas 1574 of suche things as Sir Edwarde Litleton holdethe in Actontrussell [=Acton Trussell, Bastiwick, Staffs.] whiche he wolde have preferred to the said Erle to be sealed yf he had tarryed.

Lady York was Rowland's mother. Named Anne or Anna, she was the daughter of Robert Smyth of London, now a widow by the death of Sir John, master of the Mint, in or about 1569. Oxford had been living at Lady York's house in Walbrook Street, whence, between two o'clock and three o'clock in the morning of Thursday 1 July, he went east by foot to Aldgate, secured a horse, rode the forty miles to Wivenhoe, and took ship to reach Flanders via Calais.

Early confirmation of Oxford's flight occurs in a letter from Edward Bacon to his brother Nathaniel from Gray's Inn, dated 1 July (*Stiffkey*):

> My Lord of Oxford is goen beyond the sea & hath caried a great somme of mony with him. He toke shipping by his howse in Essex. My Lord Edward Seamer is with him, Edward York, on[e] Cruse, & a other. He went without leave, the cause of ther departur unknowne. Moch speache therof. The Quen is said to take it ill.

Edward York was another of the ten sons of widow York. 'My Lord Edward Seamer' was Edward Seymour. 'Cruse', otherwise unknown, was perhaps a Spaniard. On 8 July the French ambassador reported the flight:[3]

> ... And I shall only add that last Saturday the Earl of Oxford and Lord Edward Somerset decamped from here for Flanders, which has caused the court great vexation.

Saturday 3 July was evidently two days later than the actual event. In his retrospective Diary, Burghley lists the incident under 8 July, a week too late (ii, p. 775):

> The Erle of Oxford departed into Flanders without the Queens Licenss, and was revoqued [=revoked, called back] by the Queen sendyng the Gentlemen Pensioners for hym.

One of the Gentleman Pensioners sent to fetch Oxford back to England was his old friend Thomas Bedingfield.

On 8 July Walsingham wrote from the Court at Windsor to Burghley at Theobalds, rehearsing a recent conversation with the Queen:[4]

> I made her aquaynted with my Lord of Oxfordes arryvall at Calles [=Calais], whoe dothe not interprete the same in any evyll parte: she conceyvethe great hope of his returne vppon somme secret message sent him.

More ominously, Mary Queen of Scots seems to have been informed. In a letter of 4 August to the Archbishop of Glasgow she interpreted the incident as a sign of Oxford's Catholic leanings. Mary anticipated his support for the exiled Earl of Westmorland:[5]

> ... I should be very glad that he had [an official appointment], provided that two things were secured – the one his safety, of which I entertain doubts, because the remainder of those who are of his religion, and who are better supported than he would be, are beginning to withdraw, as you will hear is the case with Oxford. ...

Mary seems to have been persuaded that Oxford fled religious persecution, but she also realized that he would not be a trustworthy ally

On 6 July John Knyveton wrote from Coldharbour to his master the Earl of Shrewsbury, guardian of Mary Queen of Scots at Sheffield:[6]

> ... I can wryte of no other newes then I did yesterdaye by Nicholas Steward, savinge that where all the quenes shippes were dischardged there ys nowe again comandement

that certein of them shalbe made readie with all spede which was done vpon therle
of Oxford his departure so sodenly without lycens./ notwithstandinge[,] the
Spanyshe Imbasyder and mr Harbart with certein others haue commission to go
into the west Countrey, and to see that the kynge [of] Spayne his shippes (if any
come there) be well vsed & maye haue vyttells for their money, if thei haue suche
necessitie. ...

Thus Elizabeth partly recalled ships discharged following the dispersal of a
Spanish mini-armada, but avoided a new round of hostilities.

On 13 July Sir Thomas Smith wrote to Burghley from Richmond:[7]

Of my Lord of Oxford, for my part I can as yet learne no certayntie; but it is
commonly said, that he arrived at Calais, and was there very honorably received
and interteigned, and from thence he went in to Flandres. As far as I can yet
perceive, her Majesities grief for hym, or towards hym is som what mitigated. But I
will do what I can convenyently to understand more of hir highnes advertisements
and mynde [=mind, opinion] in this case.

On 15 July Burghley wrote somewhat defensively to Sussex:[8]

My very good Lord I most heartily thank your Lordship for your advertisementes
of my Lord of Oxfordes cause, wherin I am sorry that hir Maiesty maketh such hast
and so to answer hym, as I feare the sequele may brede offence, if he shall be evill
Counselled. My Lord, how so ever my Lord of Oxford be for his own privat[9]
matters of thrift vnconsiderat I dare avow hym to be resolvt in dutyfullnes to the
Queen and his country. /. As for my being or comming to Redyng I ment not, but
at Woodstock for so hir Maiesty appoynted me. And yet this daye I receaved a
lettre from Mr secretary Walsingham by which he semeth that the Queens Maiesty
hath a disposition to haue my Lord Kepar and me with Sir R. Sadler, to abyde at
London I know not yet why. I shall do as I am commaunded only I wish I had bene
at the Court, at this depeche [i.e., accusation], although I dout I should not haue
prevayled. I pray god the vsage of the poore yong Lord may not hazard hym to the
proffitt of others. ...

Burghley's sympathy for 'the poore yong Lord' – Oxford was now twenty-four –
is only too characteristic. He signed off 'from my houss at Thebaldes wher my
Lord of Surrey and his ij brethern ar sportyng': thus he was entertaining Philip,
Thomas, and William Howard, sons of the recently executed Duke of Norfolk
and nephews of Henry Howard.

The three Howards were the issue of Norfolk's first two marriages. By his
third marriage, to Elizabeth Dacre, the Duke had acquired three step-daughters.
Before his death he matched his three sons with their three step-sisters (still in
their childhood or infancy). Philip, betrothed to Anne Dacre, eventually became
Earl of Arundel; Thomas, betrothed to Mary Dacre (who died in her childhood),
became Lord Howard de Walden, with a residence at Audley End, from 1597, and
was created Earl of Suffolk in 1603; while William, betrothed to Elizabeth Dacre,
became master of Naworth Castle in Cumberland (*Peerage*, iv, pp. 23–24).

On 18 July Henry Killigrew, then ambassador at Edinburgh, wrote to Walsingham:[10]

> My Lord of Oxford and Lord Seymour are fled out of England, and passed by Bruges to Brussels.

Brussels was the residence of the attainted Earl of Westmorland. Edward Woodshaw's letter of 3 September from Antwerp refers to these July events:[11]

> A countryman of mine, Edward Harcourt, servant to the Earl of Arundel, tells me that he has secretly brought over to Louvaine a young gentleman, one of the next heirs apparent. Harcourt is gone to Spain; he was great when here with Lord Edward Seymour, who is going to Italy, and wants me to go with him.

Indeed Seymour did not return with Oxford, but went on to Italy, where he died before the year was out.[12] Woodshaw continues:

> There was a great triumph among the northern rebels who are here, and our Catholics at Louvaine, when they heard of the Earl of Oxford's coming over; it was said that he was flying, and that the Earl of Southampton had fled to Spain. In a council held at Louvaine, it was concluded that the Earl of Westmorland should ride to Bruges to welcome him, and persuade him not to return; but the Earls did not meet. It were a great pity such a valiant and noble young gentleman should communicate with such detestable men.

On 2 August Silvio de Porcia, writing from Augsburg, reported to his master Ptolemy Galli, Cardinal of Como:[13]

> ... By letters from Antwerp of the 24th [July] we understand that the siege of Leidem [=Leiden] was being pressed, and that Gorcom [=Gorinchem] was not wholly neglected; also that Schoonhoven, a small town in Holland, had surrendered ... The Earl of Oxford, an Englishman, having come to Flanders, without the Queen's licence, was bidden to return under very heavy penalties.

It is unlikely that Oxford reached Brussels, or that Westmorland risked a visit to Bruges. Oxford would later boast that he had taken part in the battle of Bommel, known to historians as the battle of Mook and dated 14 April 1574. Protestant troops under Count Louis of Nassau were routed by the combined forces of three Spanish generals. Though Ward (p. 98) imagines that Oxford may have gone to have a look, he missed the battle by some three months. Conceivably Oxford witnessed the siege of Leiden, which lasted from June to October 1574.[14]

Oxford's return to England was anticipated in a letter of 27 July from Sir Walter Mildmay to Burghley, written from Apthorp:[15]

> of my Lord of Oxfordes reatorne, I am glad to here. I trust this litle iorney will make hym love home the bettre heraftre. It wear greate pytie he should not goe strayt, there be so many goad [=good] thinges in hym, to serue God, and his Prince.

The event is likewise recorded in Walsingham's Diary under 28 July:[16]

I receaved lettres from the Lord Cobham of the arivall of the Earl of Oxforde at Dover.

George Golding, finishing off the memorandum cited above, provides exact details:

The sayde Erle returned and was at London agayne on Wednesdaye at nythe abowte ix of clock the xxviijthe of Iuly aforesayd. 1574

Thus Oxford returned to London about 9:00 p.m. on Wednesday 28 July.

Henry Howard later recalled Oxford's disembarkation at Dover (3.1/4@64):

[Oxford] sayd that my Lord of Lester and he [=Hatton] kept him at Douer from being sworne of the Pryuy Counsayle ...

Evidently Hatton and Leicester met Oxford at Dover, but rejected his request for a place on the Privy Council (Ward, pp. 94–97). Thus Oxford returned on the Queen's terms rather than his own. On 29 July Burghley and Anne went to London. On the 30th Oxford and Anne returned to Theobalds, where Oxford evidently remained until at least 3 August, and perhaps until the 5th:[17]

29 Iulij	Lord Burghley went to London with his doughter the Countess of Oxford
30 Iulij	The Erle of Oxford went to Thebaldes with his wiff
31 Iul	Erle of Oxford
sonday primo Aug	Erle of Oxford Mr Benyngfeld
2° Aug	Erle of Oxford / Bennyfeld [sic] / Mr Dickens & his wiff. Mr Cookes & his wiff
3 Aug	Erle of Oxford at the huntyng of the stagg ...
5° Aug	To London

On 1 August Walsingham wrote to Burghley:[18]

I fynd her maiestie gracyowsely ynowghe inclyned towardes the Earl of Oxforde, whos peace I thinke wyll be bothe easely and spedely made: for that her maiestie doothe conceyve that his obedyence in his retvrne hathe fvlly satysfyced the contempt of his departvre; and the rather than vowghe [=vow] his honourable and dvtifvll caryage of himself towardes the rebelles, and other vndvtyfvll svbiectes of her maiesties in that contreye: an argvment of his approved loyaltye which as opportvnyte shall serve I wyll not fayle to laye befor her maiestie by acquayntyng her with your Lordships letters.[19]

About this same time an unidentified but highly placed informant wrote to Burghley from Court:[20]

My very good Lord vnderstandinge of this messengers repaire vnto you thoughe there is no great matter to advertise your Lordship of yet I thought I would not turne him away without some few lines to witnes that your Lordship is not forgotten amongst your frendes here absent. The cheefest newes presentlie here, is that the Earl of Oxford latelie arrived at Dover whose returne, hath very much qualified her maiesties displeasure conceaved against him: yet I perceive her Maiestie doth not meane to wrappe vp his contempt without vsinge some kind of reprehension: that he may not thinke but that his fault is not onelie to be reproved but were also to be corrected, had he not cured the wound of his vndutifull departinge contrary to her maiesties inhibition, throughe his dutifull returne vpon her maiesties revocation. ...

On 3 August Fénélon reported that Elizabeth[21]

... is continuing her progress toward Bristol, very pleased that the Earl of Oxford returned at her commandment, even though Lord Edward [Seymour] remained abroad.

Thus Fénélon confirms that Seymour remained on the Continent.

Also on 3 August, Burghley wrote to Walsingham from Theobalds:[22]

Sir yesternight your lettres came to Master Beningfeld and me signefying hir Maiesties plesure, that my Lord of Oxford shuld come to Glocester now at hir Maiesties being ther, Whereof he being advertised by vs, was very redy to tak the Iournaye, shewyng in hym self, a mixture of contrary affections, although both resonable and commendable, the on[e] fearfull and doutfull in what sort he shall recover hir Maiesties favor because of his offence in departure as he did without licenss, the other gladfull and resolute to look for a spedy good end, because he had in his abode so notoriously reiected the attemptes of hir Maiesties evill subiectes, and in his retorn set apart all his own particular desyres of forayn travell, and come to present hym self befor her Maiesty of whose goodness towardes hym he sayth he cannot dout. Hervppon he and Mr Bennigfeld departed this afternoone to London where the Erle as I perceieve will spend only twoo dayes, or less, to mak hym some apparell mete for the Court, although I wold have had hym forborn that new chardg consideryng his formar apparrell is very sufficient, and he not provyded to increase a new chardg.

Burghley characterizes Oxford as he would have him: fearful of the Queen's sense of justice, hopeful of her sense of mercy. Amusingly, Burghley reprehends Oxford's decision to delay his trip for the sake of acquiring a new set of clothes: not only is he sufficiently provided, but the expense is more than his purse can support. Burghley continues:

But now consideryng my Lord is to come to Glocester, ther, to mak all humble meanes, to recover hir Maiesties favor, wherin he is to be helped with advise and frendes, and that I cannot be so soone as he, for that on Fryday or Satyrday next I am to attend at London for the celebration of the French kings funeralls, so as I am in dowt whyther I shall come to Glocester before Wednesday followyng, I must be bold by this my lettre, to requyre yow in my name most humbly to besech hir Maiesty, that she will regard his loyalte, and not his lightnes in sodden goyng over, his confidence in hir goodnes and clemency, and not his boldnes in attemptyng that which hath offended hir, and finally so to ordre hym both in the ordre and spede of his comming to hir Maiesties presence that hir Maiesties ennemyes and rebells which sought by manny devises to stey hym from retorning, may perceave his retorning otherwise rewarded than they wold have had hym Imagyned, and that also his frendes, that have advised hym to retorn, may take comfort therof with hym self, and he not repent his dutifullnes, in doyng that which in this tyme none hath doone, I meane of such as hath ether gon without licenss, or gon with licenss and not returned in ther due tyme. of his offence he hath examples over manny in goyng without licenss.

Burghley is repeating himself; he repeats himself yet more:

but of his dutyfulnes abrode, where he was provoked to the contrary, and of his retorning ageyn, wher he lacked not som stynges of feare, he hath no examples at all to my remembrance. and truly not for hym self only, but for to gyve some good examples, to others that ether have erred / as he did or may herafter err in lik[e] sort, I thynk it a sound Counsell to be gyven to hir Maiesty, that this yong nobleman being of such a quallite as he is for byrth, office, and other notable valleurs of body and spryte, be not discomforted, ether by any extraordynary delaye, or by any ovtward sharp or vnkynd reproff.

Burghley thus hopes the Queen will even forbear harsh language.

but if hir Maiesty will not spare from vtteryng of some sparkes of hir first offence for his first, yet that the same may in presence of some few of hir Counsell be vttered, and that hir favorable acceptyng of his submission may be largly and manifestly declared to hym to the confirmation of hym in his syngular loyalte.

Thus you see how busy I am and suerly not without some cause, for if he shall not fynd comfort now in this amendment of his first favlt, I feare the mallyce of some discontented persons, wherewith the Cowrt is overmuch sprynkled[,] will collorably sette to draw hym to a repentance rather of his dutyfullnes in thus retornyng, than to satle [=settle] in hym a contentation to continew in his dutye

Burghley fears not Oxford, but the 'discontented' among his acquaintances.

And to conclud sir I besech yow to impart such partes of this my scriblyng with my Lords of the Counsell [with] whom yow shall perceave hir Maiesty will have to deal in this case, that not only they will favorably reprehend hym for his favlt, but frankly and liberally comfort hym for his amends made both in his behavior beyond seas and in his retorning as he hath doone, and besyde this that they will be svtors to hir Maiesty for hym, as noble men for a noble man, and so bynd hym in honor, to be indetted with good will to them herafter, as in deed I know some of them hath gyven hym good occasion, though he hath bene otherwise seduced by such, as regarded nothyng his honor nor well doyng, wherof I perceave he now acknowledgeth some experience to his chardg, and I trust will be more wary of such sycophantes and parasites / you se I can not well end, nother will I end without also prayeng yow to remembre Mr Hatton to continew my Lordes frend, as he hath manifestly bene, and as my Lord confesseth to me that he hopeth assuredly so to prowe [=prove] him.

and now I end. my Lord kepar Mr Sadler and I will be to morrow at London, and on Fryday spek with the Lord Mayre for ther matters, and for redress of some disordres abovt the Cite

The 'sycophantes and parasites' feared by Burghley include Edward Seymour, Edward York, and the unidentified Cruse.

Burghley added a postscript to his already over-long letter:

I pray yow so to deale with my Lordes [=the Privy Council] that ar to deale with my Lord of Oxford, that this my lettre to yow may serve as an intercession to them from me for my Lord. and I dout not but Mr secretary Smyth will remember his old love towardes the Erle whan he was his scollar.

We have already noted the evidence that Oxford had lived with Sir Thomas Smith in his youth.

Oxford left Theobalds and London on 5 August, remaining in the west, 'absent in the progress about on[e] month'.[23] On 13 August Fénélon reported of Burghley:[24]

... thus I am assured that, even if he himself has never approved of such things, he will speak of them in a lively fashion to the Queen his mistress, whom he is travelling to meet the following day, with the purpose of restoring the Earl of Oxford, his son-in-law. This he hopes she will accept for his having acquitted himself virtuously in his behaviour, when he was in Flanders, where he communicated neither with the Earl of Westmorland nor the Countess of Northumberland, nor attempted to see nor hear them, nor any of the fugitives of this realm.

Elizabeth's progress took her to Bristol on 14 August.[25] Burghley noted in his retrospective Diary (ii, p. 776):

Erle of Oxford retourned [i.e., from abroad]; and he and I went to the Queen's Majesty to Bristoll.

Walsingham, writing in his own diary, noted under 14 and 21 August respectively (p. 20):

After dinner the counsell sat about the Earle of Oxforde. Her Majestie came to Bristowe. / The Queen removed from Bristowe to Bathe. The Earl of Oxford came before her Majestie.

An unidentified official sent Burghley word of the happy outcome:[26]

My very good Lord the perswasion I have that your Lordship is now of late so wholie dedicated to a private life, as the hearinge what course publicke affaires taketh might rather breed vnto yow discontentment then otherwise ... & amongst other thinges I am assured yow are not vnadvertisde how the Earle of Oxford is restored to her Maiesties favour. whose loyall behaviour towardes her Maiesties rebells in the low countrey, who sought conference with him, a thinge he vtterlie refused, did very much qualifie his contempt in departinge without her Maiesties leaue.

> The desire of travaile is not yet quenched in him thoughe he dare not make any
> motion vnto her Maiestie that he may with her favour accomplish his said desire.
> By no meanes he can be drawen to follow the Courte and yet there are many
> cunninge devices vsed in that behallfe for his stay. ...

Not only was Oxford's desire for travel still unquenched, he secured from the
Queen an agreement that he might travel abroad with licence – not to the Low
Countries, where trouble lurked, but to Paris, Germany, and Italy.

On his good behaviour indeed, Oxford returned to the bosom of his family.
On 16 September, two days after Holy Rood Day:[27]

> Erle of Oxford at Thebaldes retorned from the progress from Farnham

Burghley thus notes that Oxford lay in the village of Farnham Royal, near
Slough, on the 15th, and at Theobald's on the 16th – but with Anne?

PART IV

Exploration
1574–1576

23 Preparation for Travel

On 13 September 1574 Anne addressed a letter from Theobalds to Sussex, who as Lord Chamberlain was in charge of allocating lodgings at Hampton Court, whither the Queen would return from the West:[1]

> My good Lord, Because I think it long since I saw Her Majesty, and would be glad to do my duty after Her Majesty's coming to Hampton Court, I heartily beseech your good Lordship to show me your favour in your order to the ushers for my lodging: that in consideration that there is but two chambers, it would please you to increase it with a third chamber next unto it, which was reserved last time for my Lord Arundel's men, and, as I was informed by my Lord Howard, he had it when he lay in the same lodging. I shall think myself greatly bound to you for it, for the more commodious my lodging is the willinger I hope my Lord my husband will be to come thither, thereby the oftener to attend Her Majesty. Thus trusting in your Lordship's favourable consideration I leave to trouble your Lordship any further, with my most hearty commendations to my good Lady your wife. ...

Anne clearly meant to spend as much time as possible with Oxford before he left for the Continent. Her plan worked, but – as we shall see – with bitter consequences.

Burghley's chronology continues into the second half of September:[2]

19 Sonday	Lady Lennox, Earl of Oxford Erle Northumberland, the lady Northumberland.
20 Monday St Mathew even	lady Margaret Lennox, Erl of Oxford, Lord Lennox, lady Hunsdon, Bash & his wife
21 sept (St Mathew daye)	lady Lennox, Lord of Northumberland and my lady.

Burghley concludes: 'October at Hampton Court'. Some eighteen months later, in April 1576, Oxford would confess to Henry Howard 'that he lay ... with his wife ... at Hampton Court'.[3] Here Elizabeth Vere, who would be born on 2 July 1575, was conceived. Assuming a gestation time of approximately 38 weeks, conception occurred on 9 October 1574, give or take a week.

Burghley's memorandum contains a final entry:

> the Countess fell sick at Hampton Court. afor[e] Novembre

Burghley doubtless meant that towards the end of October Anne experienced morning sickness. A subsequent letter from Dr Richard Master[4] reveals that Anne consulted him about having missed her period.

News of Anne's pregnancy travelled quickly. On 7 November Sir Thomas Smith sent Lady Burghley medicinal 'water', along with a letter, from Hampton Court:[5]

> Madame I sent yesterday of my water to my lord for my lady of Oxford / Me thynks there is som dowte made of it Yf it please god / that she haue so mich naturall heate in hir / as may ioigne [=join] with it / I dout not your ladiship shall haue great comfort of it & she much help / There is nothyng in it / but such as is daily eaten & dronken / no purgacion / no spiw [=spew, vomit?] / But it hath such vertue that next to God / I ow[e] my helth to it / & so many as hath ones vsed it hath given me thanks / & do repute it a syngular thyng / Yt doth but help nature not constreyne it / Yf it be vomyted out / (eny heate beyng in the bodie) it can not be vomyted out before the chief vertue of it be dispersed / for the fenel & angelica water can be vomyted out / the rest with the first heate is dispersed / Yf hir ladiship do not fyend immediately comfort in it / Then nature is to[o] feble / I can say no more / But I wold be as sory that my ladie of Oxford should miscarye as if she were v [=5] tymes my doughter for diverse cawses & wold be as glad to do hir good as eny livyng next to your ladiship / & if those ij waters were not in it to temper it / I durst say she should not vomyte it out givyng but a sponefull yf lief were in the bodie for it should desperse streight [=immediately] & comfort Immediately the vitale spirites
>
> Let it be given a lone [=alone] & by a sponefull at a tyme till she hir self shall require more /.
>
> Pardone my folishnes madame it is my good will deservid of my Lord and yow / & the love which I bere to my lady of Oxford which cawseth me write thies [=these, this letter] & so commend yow to God ...

Thus Smith not only offers a remedy for Anne's nausea, but fears lest 'my ladie of Oxford should miscarye'. She spent November and December largely in the company of her mother, visiting Theobalds on at least two occasions, and visiting Lady Wroth on 12 December.[6]

On 27 November Edward Hubbard, charged with the oversight of Oxford's lands, wrote to Sir John Arundel in Lanherne, Cornwall, from his lodgings in Chancery Lane, London:[7]

> ... I am commanded by my lord and master the earl of Oxford to make his hearty commendations unto you, and to make answer to your letter to him but with thanks with the same. Who would have written unto your worship himself, but that sickness letted him, whereby he willed me to write ...

After the interlude at Hampton Court, therefore, and during preparations for his journey abroad, Oxford also fell sick – but soon recovered. Hubbard further informs Sir John Arundel of conferences had 'with my lord's learned counsell in the law' concerning property matters.

On 1 January 1575 Oxford presented the Queen with a New Year's gift:[8]

> Item, a very fayre juell of gold, contayning a woman holding a shippe of sparks of diamondes, upon her knee; the same fully garnished with sparcks of dyamonds, foure fayre rubyes, one large dyamond, and sundrye dyamondes with three perles pendante; and three small cheynes of golde sett with sparcks of dyamonds. Geven by therle of Oxforde ...

Oxford's name (as 'Com. Oxon.') also appears in the 'Boug de Curia', dated 20 January from Hampton Court:[9] given Oxford's impending absence, this was an entitlement rather than an actual benefit. Oxford's name also appeared about this time in a long and apparently indiscriminate list of noblemen and gentlemen who 'have served and are fit to serve in foreign employments'.[10]

In his chronology, Burghley assigned Oxford's departure to the end of January or beginning of February.[11] Among 'Licences passed to go beyond the Seas' was issued on 24 January:[12]

> The Erle of Oxford one yere, Ianuarie 1574 [=1575].

On the same day two letters of introduction were prepared for the Queen's signature at Hampton Court: one was addressed generally to all and every monarch or ruler to whom these letters might be presented, while the second was addressed specifically to the Holy Roman Emperor Maximillian II – whom Oxford did not in fact meet.[13] The description of Oxford in the second letter is the more elaborate of the two:

> An illustrious youth much adorned with many virtues, the offspring of a most ancient family of England, Edward Vere (etc.), our most beloved subject and cousin, wishes to inspect the palaces of your many princes, as also the cities and regions of your realm, to acquire knowledge of them; he himself being imbued with manners, virtue, learning.

In brief: Oxford hopes to learn from you; you can learn from him.

On the same day, Fénélon recorded his suspicion that England had some military enterprise in mind; even so he felt sure that Oxford – as usual – would take an independent course of action:[14]

> It seemed that the Earl of Oxford was the leader of that enterprise, but he took another path, having begged of the Queen his Mistress permission for a trip to Italy, and thinks to depart in a week, passing through France, spending a month in Paris; and he seems, Sire, to be much devoted to Your Majesty, but they say that he is so notoriously partial to the Queen of Scots and grand-nephew to the Duke of Norfolk, that the Queen doesn't trust him; nevertheless, he intends very humbly to

kiss Your Majesty's hands, and not to disobey any command you may give him. And because he is as it were the premier earl and Great Chamberlain of England, and thus the chief nobleman of the realm, and with more followers and the object of greater expectations than any other in the realm, he begs of you, Sire, that he may have the honour and favour of being permitted to pass through your realm; because, in addition to his merit, all England and the court would be infinitely gratified. The residents of 'Bourgoine' have promised him that he might be of service to the King of Spain, as soon as he arrives in Italy, and to be able to meet Don John of Austria, he not wanting [i.e., lacking] letters of bank and credit for that purpose; but he shows a greater inclination toward your service than that of the King of Spain.

Oxford was still in England on 30 January, when an important settlement was drawn up with the possibility in mind – real enough for the age – that he might not survive the journey:[15]

> Settlement by Edward Earl of Oxford, 'Viscount Bulbecke, and Lorde of Badles-mere and Scales,' on Thomas Earl of Sussex, Robert Earl of Leicester, Thomas Cecill, esq., Sir William Cordell Knight, and Thomas Bromley, esq., Solicitor General, as trustees, of divers manors and estates. Recites that the Earl intends, by the Queen's licence, to travel beyond the seas, that he has, as yet, no issue, and that should he die, his whole possession would pass to his sister, Lady Mary 'Veer', saving the life interest of his Countess, and those estates specially entailed on his grandfather's heirs-male. To avert this impoverishment of 'That auncient Erldome house and famylie of Oxenforde', the Earl 'remembrynge and considerynge the longe contynuaunce of his saide house and famylie in the name of the Veers, whereof he is lyneallye discended, in the grace and favour of the kings and princes in whose tymes they have lived, and in alliance and kindred with moste of the ancient nobilitie of this realme, and in the good will and good lykinge of the Cominaltie of the same realme; and having therefore a speciall desire and rare to preserve contynue and leave all or the most parte of his possessions' to such persons as in his opinion is most likely to continue the line 'most like to his noble auncestors' he entails, subject to the payment of his debts, of a marriage portion of 3,000l to each daughter he may have (failing male issue), and of his sister's portion under his father's will, the whole of his estates specified on his cousins in tail male, viz. Hugh son and heir apparent of Aubrey Vere, John son of Robert Vere, John, Francis, Robert, and Horatius, sons of Geoffrey Vere.

Annexed is a long schedule of Oxford's debts, totalling of £9096–10–8$\frac{1}{2}$, being the sum of £3457 owed 'to the Quene's maiestie' and £5639–10–8$\frac{1}{2}$ owed on 128 private accounts. Among others, Oxford was in debt to Thomas Skinner, Mercer (£537 on two accounts), 'Weber for lace delivered to William Rosewell [=Ruswell] Taylor for my lord's use' (£99–9–9), William Rosewell himself (£60), Lady Mary Vere for arrearages of her fee (£70), and George Golding gentleman for his charges (£40). Burghley was authorized to pay any debts omitted from the list. One of three trustees was Sir William Cordell, who had tried so unsuccessfully to interview Oxford in 1573. Oxford nevertheless was prepared to distribute largesse among his servants, as for example to Arthur Milles, to whom he gave 'certaine hangings & an old hearse cloth and divers other things ... vnder his Lordships owne hand and seale'.[16]

Of Oxford's initial travelling companions, only Nathaniel Baxter can be identified from independent sources.[17] Two other Englishmen, William Lewin and Ralph Hopton, would join Oxford on the Continent. (The anecdotalist John Aubrey thought Oxford's party included Nicholas Hill, who, however, was no more than five years of age at the time.)[18] Oxford probably left London during the first week of February: some eighteen months later Burghley reckoned Oxford's accounts from 'February whan my Lord went'.[19] On 7 February Edward Bacon wrote to his brother Nathaniel from Gray's Inn:[20]

> My Lord of Oxford is gone beyond the seas with licence.

24 To Italy

Oxford is first noticed in France in letters of 5 and 7 March 1575, wherein the English ambassador Dr Valentine Dale informed Burghley:[1]

> – Cannot procure the Earl of Oxford's access to the King because of the new mourning for the Duchess of Lorraine, whose death the Queen Mother takes very heavily to heart, being her dear daughter.

> – I presented my Lord of Oxford also unto the King and Queen, who used him honourably. Amongst other talk the King asked whether he was married. I said he had a fair lady. 'Il y a donc' dit-il 'un beau couple'.

In his Diary, Burghley listed the event under 6 March: 'Erle presented to the French kyng.'[2]

On 12 March Giovanni Francesco Morosini, Venetian ambassador in Paris, wrote to the Signory:[3]

> An English gentleman, whose name is the Earl of Oxford, has arrived in this city; he is a young man of about twenty or twenty-two years of age. It is said that he fled from England on account of his inclination to the Catholic religion; but having returned he received great favour from the Queen, who gave him full licence to travel and see the world, when she ascertained that he had resolved to depart under any circumstances.

Thus Oxford retained his reputation for Catholicism. Morosini's underestimation of his age and the French King's compliment confirm that age sat lightly on Oxford.

Back in England, Burghley fretted over his daughter's pregnancy. On 7 March, about the beginning of her fifth month, Dr Richard Master wrote a long and complex letter to Burghley from Richmond:[4]

After my duetie, yt may pleace your Lordship to vnderstond that hauyng her magestie thys Munday mornyng in the chamber at the galeris ende next to the grene, syttyng alone, I sayd, that the confidence I hade in my messages made me presume to come to herre in that place, for beyng at Londone with my wyffe that had bynne sicke, I h[e]ard say that my Lord tresarer hade lefthe [=left] woord at my howse, that I schold not returne vnto the Court vntyl I had spoken with hym; whervpon feryng lest he hadde byn sicke vpon hys purgatione taken the Friday, I went vnto hym and fownd hym mycle wele, sauyng for hys coughe and often nising [=sneezing] and vnderstondyng off my spedie returne to the Court, he desiryd me to say thus muche to your hyghenesse, that seyng yt hade pleasyd your magestie often tymes to inquire tenderly after my Lady of Oxfoordes helthe, yt ys now fawlen owt so (God be thanckyd) that sche ys with chyld euidently. and albeyt yt werre but an indifferent thing for herre magestie to here off, yet yt was more then indifferent for your Lordship to signifie the same vnto herre. Here with al [=Herewithall] sche arose, or rather spronge vp from the coschyns [=cushions], and sayd thes woordes. In dede yt ys a mattier that concernythe my Lords yoye [=Burghley's joy] chiefly, yet I protest to God that next to them that haue interest in yt, ther ys no bodie can be more yoyous off yt then I am. Then I went forthe and told herre that your Lordship hade a pretie lekelyhood off it vpon your cummyng from the Court after schrovetyde, but you concelyd yt, *Ne si aduersum euaderet Audires parturiunt montes et cetera*. And that now by cause your Lordship dyd fere the concelyng off yt any lenger, dowtyng lest the mattier myght other wyse cume to the Court, your Lordship thought yt gud and a pece off duetye to haue yt impartyd vnto her magestie rather by your selfe then by any other. and here agayne sche bade me make her thanckes with that woordes repetyd as before by comparyng your Lordships yoye and interest to hers. After thys, I had lesure to schew herre off my Ladies duble recknyng viz *a retentione et a consortio Comitis*,[5] and that my Ladie beyng here at schrovetyde had delt with me to prepare sum medicines *ad menses promotiones* ['to cause the menses to resume']. but I counselyd herre to stay a whyle. herre magestie asked me how the iunge [=young] Ladie dyd bere the mattier. I answeryd that sche kept yt secret iiij or v daies from al parsons & that herre face was muche fawlen & thynne with Lytle colure, and that when sche was comfortyd & counselyd to be gladsume and to reyoyce, sche woold crie alas alas how schold I reioyce, seyng [=seeing] he that schold reyoyce with me ys not here, and to say treught [=truth] [I] stond in dowt whether he passe vpon me & yt or not; and bemonyng herre case woold lament that after so longe sicknesse off bodie, sche schold enter a new grieff and sorow off mynd. At thys herre magestie schewyd great compassione as your Lordship schal here hereafter. And repetyd my Lord of Oxfords answere to me, which he made openly in the presence chamber to herre magestie viz. that yff sche werre with chyld yt was not hys, I answeryd that yt was the commone answer off Lustie curters [=courtiers] euery where so to say. I told herre also that sche [=the Queen] ought to thinke the case to be hard, when that sche [=Anne] was let blud and purgyd, the phisitiens hauing greater regard to the stocke than to the branche, but I trustyd now they werre bothe in saftie. Then sche askyng, and beyng answeryd of me, how [=who] was in the next chamber sche caulethe my Lord of Lecyter [=Leicester] and tellythe hym al. and here I told herre that thoughe your Lordship hade concelyd yt a whyle from herre yet yow lefthe

[=left] yt to herre discretione eyther to reuele yt or to kepe yt close. And here an ende was made, takyng advantage off my last woordes, that sche woold be [wroth?] with yow for concelyng yt so longe from herre. and seuerly [=surely] sche schewyd herre selfe vnfaynydly to reyoyce, and in great offence with my Lord of Oxfoord, repetyng the same to my Lord of Leceter after he came to herre. Thus muche rather to schew my gud wyl, then other wyse; desiryng your Lordship that there may a note be taken from the day off the first quicknyng, for ther off [=thereof], sumewhat may be knowen, note woorthey. ...

Anne experienced more than her share of problems. It cannot have helped that she had been abandoned by her husband, who also denied paternity. By a 'double reckoning' – calculating both from the time her periods had ceased and from the time she had lain with her husband – Anne had proof that Oxford was indeed the child's father. For further verification Dr Master recommends that Burghley note when Anne felt the first 'quickening' – just after Shrovetide, which this year began on Sunday 13 February.

In response to a letter from Burghley (now lost), Oxford clearly acknowledged paternity on 17–18 March from Paris (LL-06):

My lord yowre letters haue made me a glad man, for thes last haue put me in asseurance of that good fortune whiche yowre former mentioned doughtfullye. I thank God therfore, withe yowre Lordship that it hathe pleased him to make me a father wher yowre Lordship is a grandfather. and if it be a boij I shall lekwise be the partaker withe yow in a greater contentation. But therby to take an occasion too [=to] returne I am far of[f] from that opinion, for now it hathe pleased God to giue me a sune of myne owne (as I hope it is) mithink [=methinks] I haue the better occasion to trauell, sithe whatsoeuer becommethe of me, I leue behind me on[e] to supplie my dutie and seruice either to my prince or els my contrie.

Oxford now turns to other topics, starting with his debts:

I thanke yowre Lordship I haue receiued farther bils of credite, and letters of great curtesie from Mr Benidic Spinola. I am allso behouldinge here vnto mr Reymondo, that hathe help me greatly withe a number of fauours whom I shall desire yowre Lordship when yow haue leisur and occasion to giue him thankes, for I know the greatest part of his friendshipe towards me hathe bine in respect of yowre Lordshipe.

For feare of the inquisition I dare not pas by Milan, the Bishop wherof exersisethe such tyranie. wherfore I take the way of Germanie, where I mean to aquaint my self withe sturmius, withe home [=whom] after I haue passed my iornie which now I haue in hand I meane to pas sum time

I haue found here this curtesie, the kinge hathe giuen me his letters of recommen- dation to his embassadour in the Turks court, lekwise the venetian embassadour that is here knowinge my desire to see those parties [=parts] hathe giuen me his letters to the Duke, and diuers of his kinsmen in Venice, to procur me ther furtherances to my iornie which I am not yet assured too [=to] howld for if the Turkes cum as they be loked for vpon the coste of Italy or els where, if I may I will se the seruice, if he commethe not then perhapes I will bestowe twoo or thre monthes to se Constantinople, and sum part of Grece.

The Englishe imbassadour here greatly complainethe of the deernes [=dearness, costliness] of this contrie, and ernestly hathe desired me to craue yowre Lordshipes fauour to consider the difference of his time, from thers whiche were before him, he saiethe the charges are greater, his abilite less the court remoues long and oft, the causes of expences augmented, his allowance not beinge increased. But as concerninge thes matters, now I haue satisfisd [=satisfied] his desire I refer them to yowre Lordships discretion, that is better experienced then I perhaps enformed him in th<e…> negotiations of Embassaders.

My Lord wheras I perceiue by yowr Lordships letters, how hardly monie is to be gotten, and that my man writeth that he wowld faine pay vnto my creditours sum part of that monie whiche I haue appointed to be made ouer vnto me, good my Lord let rather my crediters beare withe me awhile and take ther dayes assigned according to that order I left, then I to want in a strange contrie, vnknowinge yet what nede I may haue of mony my self. my revenu I appointed withe the profites of my lands to pay them as I may, and if I cannot yet pay them as I wowld yet as I can I will but preferringe myne own necescite before thers, and if at the end of my travell I shall haue sumthinge left of my prouision they shall haue it amonge them, but before I will not disfurnish my self. good my lord haue an ey vnto my men that I haue put in trust. thus makinge my commendations to yowr Lordship and my Ladie I commite yow to God …

By 'my Ladie', Oxford means not Anne but Lady Burghley. Oxford appends a postscript concerning a Mr. Corbek:

My Lord this gentellman Mr Corbek, hathe giuen me great cause to leke [=like] of him bothe for his curtesies that he hathe showne me in lettinge me vnderstand the dificulties as well as the safties of my trauell, as allso I find him affected bothe to me and yowr Lordshipe I pray yowre Lordship that those whoo ar my friends may seme yowres as yowres I esteme myne, and giuen yowre Lordships good countnance and in short I rest yowres

Burghley carefully noted the sequellae under 17 March:[6]

The Erle departed from Pariss and wrot to his wiff and sent hir, his pictur and ij horsses

Oxford's Parisian 'picture' may be one of at least two extant images.[7] The 'St Albans' portrait is attributed to Marcus Geeraerts the younger (1561–1635), then a youth of fourteen or fifteen. It seems unlikely, however, that this was made in France, for Geeraerts had come to England with his father in 1568, and lived in London.[8] His inexperience produced a portrait rich in detail but poor in character: little more than simple hauteur can be read in the face. A more likely candidate, perhaps, is the 'Welbeck' portrait, thought to be a later copy of a lost original (see Frontispiece). The horses Oxford sent to Anne were, as we learn in Chapter 27, coach-horses.

Oxford declares his hope to visit not only Italy – avoiding Milan for fear of its militantly Catholic bishop – but even Constantinople and Greece. Far from drawing him to her side, Anne's pregnancy affords Oxford freedom to travel, as he is guaranteed an heir, which he presumes will be male. He also presumes on the patience of his creditors, and that he will have funds left from his journey to settle his debts.

A letter from Ambassador Dale dated 23 March reports Oxford's departure from Paris a day earlier than recorded in Burghley's memo:[9]

> Lord Oxford departed hence the 16th of this present, and took the way by Germany.

Earlier, on the 18th, Dale had written to Burghley:[10]

> ... I had all passports and commissions for post-horses and letters for my Lord of Oxford that he could require; and indeed he was well liked of, and governed himself very honourably while he was here. I got the Ambassador of Venice's letters for him, both unto the State, and unto the Ambassador's particular friends. He did wisely to cumber himself with as little company as he might.

To a second letter of the 23rd, Dale added more on the 26th:[11]

> ... I will assure your Lordship unfeignedly my Lord of Oxford used himself as orderly and moderately as might be desired, and with great commendation, neither is there any appearance of the likelihood of any other. God send him a Raphael always in his company, which I trust he verily so hath, for Mr. Lewyn is both discreet and of good years, and one that my Lord doth respect. ...

> ... Chiverny appoints to be with him to-morrow. If the skill of this painter here be liked, I suggest he would be induced to come thither, for he is a Fleming, and liketh not over well of his entertainment here. It seemeth to us he hath done my Lord of Oxford well. My Lord's device is very proper, witty and significant.

Dale reassures Burghley that William Lewin will serve Oxford as a guardian angel – though this Raphael was still lagging far behind his charge. A Cambridge graduate and Burghley's retainer, Lewin was on the verge of a meteoric career (*Commons*). Oxford's portraitist is commended once more, and the way smoothed for his visit to England.

Towards the end of April Oxford received eight votes from the eleven electors for the Order of the Garter, doubling his support from the preceding year (G-BL). Perhaps his reconciliation with the Queen counted for much; or perhaps absence made hearts grow fonder.

The small entourage soon made its way to Strasbourg, where Oxford secured an introduction to the polymath John Sturmius (1507–89), rector of its university and intellectual leader of European Protestantism (*Brockhaus Enzyklopädie*). On 26 April, according to Burghley's chronology Diary:[12]

> The Earl of Oxford departed from Strasburg.

Making his way through the Brenner Pass, Oxford encountered George Chapman – or so we may gather from a passage in the latter's 1613 *Revenge of Bussy d'Ambois* (sigs. F3v–4):

> I ouer-tooke, comming from Italie,
> In Germanie, a great and famous Earle
> Of England, the most goodly fashion'd man
> I euer saw: from head to foote in form
> Rare, and most absolute; hee had a face
> Like one of the most ancient honour'd Romanes,
> From whence his noblest Familie was deriu'd;
> He was beside of spirit passing great,
> Valiant, and learn'd, and liberall as the Sunne,
> Spoke and writ sueetly, or of learned subiects,
> Or of the discipline of public weales;
> And t'was the Earle of Oxford. ...

Chapman goes on to say that Duke Casimir offered Oxford a view of his army in the field, but that Oxford refused the offer, saying 't'was not fit / To take those honours that one cannot quit'. Indeed, Oxford 'no foote was mou'd to stirre / Out of his owne free fore-determin'd course'.

In May Sir Richard Shelley wrote to Burghley from Venice:[13]

> I sent a gentleman of mine with a letter to him [=Oxford] to give him hora buona of his welcome and safe arrival, offering him then a house furnished that should have cost him nothing, and to have provided him with the like against his coming hither to Venice, with all the fervour that I was able. ... His Lordship thanks me by a letter for my courtesy, praying me nevertheless very earnestly to forbear the sending of him either letters or messages, till he should know how I was thought of by the Queen's most excellent Majesty; which affection and wariness, albeit I liked very well in so great a subject, yet on the other side it appalled me much that I, for all my wariness and fidelity, should be in jealousy, as it were of a fugitive.

Thus Oxford declined direct surveillance along with free housing.

On 16 May Thomas Butler, 10th Earl of Ormond, addressed a letter to Burghley from Ireland, in a correspondence much dilated by the exigencies of distance:[14]

> My veray good lord I receaved your letter dated at St Iames the 17 of Aprill, this 9 of May and whear your lordship wryts [=writes] I gave you mor[e] thanks then in poer[?] you cowld desarve, hit is so that you shall indede, find me as thankfull, as ether letter or word can declare, and for my sarvis to my contry, and my good wyll to your self, I wold ther wear no more for you to dowt of. if any report have ben made of any ill dealing I shold vse to my wyfe, as your lordship wrytes, and that you are glad of the contrary, I wold the hearers of reports wold not be faster led away to beleue them, then I hope you are, or then my self have, or shall geve caws.
>
> and for your sownd aduice, that I shold be ware whome I trost abowt my wyfe I humbly thank your lordship, I wold she wear in the same cace your dawghter of

Oxford is in, to whome I wish as well as any frend she and her husband hathe, and wold his hap had bene to have sene one sonne of his, afore he had taken his travell in hand.

but no frend cowld perswade him from his will ther in, whear of God send him to reap good. I am hartely glad he hath that honorable care of my lady, to visit her with tokens and letters in this tyme, whear in, kindnes is most nedfull, God send him a good retorn, and after, a setteled mynd, to vse her as becommeth. ...

Evidently Burghley had cited Oxford as an example of a dutiful husband; and certainly Butler envied Oxford his wife's pregnancy. But Butler replies that Oxford would have done well to defer his journey until after his lineage had been assured by the birth of a son.

On 28 June Antonio de Guaras wrote to Zayas from London:[15]

I now have to add that an Englishman named Lusies [=Lewins?] left here a fortnight ago, he having been sent hither by the English ambassador in France, and immediately afterwards the earl left for Germany accompanied by a son of the Lieutenant of the Tower. This Lewins [?] is a person of great intelligence and efficiency, although he will employ his talents in a bad cause. There are signs that these men were dispatched on this enterprise. I have had good spies on Sir William Drury who left two days ago. ...

The Lieutenant of the Tower was Owen Hopton; Ralph Hopton, his son, left the party of Sir Philip Sidney (completing his tour begun in 1572) and joined Oxford's.

Back in England, as Burghley noted in his retrospective Diary under 2 July:[16]

Anne my daughter, Countess of Oxford, gave birth to a daughter, Elizabeth.

Doubtless the child was named after the Queen. Elsewhere Burghley noted medical complications:[17]

In hir sycknes whan she bred child hir charges war great; the lyk whan she was delyvered.

The very next day, 3 July, Sir Walter Mildmay, writing from London, congratulated Burghley on the birth of a grand-daughter:[18]

my veary good Lord. I thanke God hartelie with your Lordship for the good delyvery it hath pleased hym to geve my Lady of Oxford, and I thank your lordship that it like yow to let me vnderstand the same by your lettres which I receyved this mornynge / I trust God shall make hir a glad mother of many children, to your Lordships compfort and her mothers. And next vnto you twoo, no body can wisshe her more good, than I haue and ever will be[a]r / ...

Burghley's chronology assigns Elizabeth's baptism to Sunday 10 July:[19]

Elizabeth daughter of Anne Countess of Oxford baptized at Theobalds.

Four days later Queen Elizabeth, evidently standing as the child's Godmother, sent a basin and a 'lame' – a piece of plate, from the Latin *lamnella* – as a baptismal gift:[20]

> Item more gevon by her saide Maiestie and deliuerid the xiiijth of Iuly Anno predicto At the Christeninge of the Earle of Oxfourdes doughter oone Basone and a Lane [=Lame] guilt po'z [=weighing] Ciiij oz di quarter / And oone standing Cup guilt with a Couer of fflaunders making po'z liij oz di both bought of the said Robert Brandon in toto Clvij oz di di quarter

The peripatetic Oxford would not learn of the birth until 24 September.

On 4 July William Lewin wrote to Burghley, evidently from Strasbourg:[21]

> Has received two letters from him and answered the first on 12 June. Complains of his health. Though Dr. Sturmius has completed his 67th year he [=Sturmius] is stronger than he [=Lewin] is. Does not know whether his master [=Oxford] has started for Greece, or whether he still tarries in Italy, but when he can learn for certain, will inform Burghley. Hopes that his master's travels may benefit him, and expresses his readiness to obey any command of Burghley.

On 20 July Lewin wrote again from Strasbourg:[22]

> Understands that there is an English nobleman at Venice who has a companion who was with Philip Sydney. Thinks that they must be his master and Ralph Hopton, and does not expect that they will remain much longer at Venice.

On 23 September Clemente Paretti, an Italian banker, wrote to Burghley from Venice:[23]

> Right Honourable, My most humble duty remembered. I am sorry that afore this time I could not, according to duty, write to your honour of my Lord's success and good disposition in this his travel. But my daily and continual service about my Lord hath rather hindered than furthered my good intention and service which always hath been and is employed to obey your honour's commandment. At this present your honour shall understand my Lord's better disposition, God be thanked, for now last coming from Genoa his Lordship found himself somewhat altered by reason of the extreme heats; and before his Lordship hurt his knee in one of the Venetian galleys, but all is past without further harm. Of any other reports that your honour hath understood of my Lord, no credit is to be given unto. It is true that a while ago at Padua were killed unawares (in a quarrel that was amongst a certain congregation of Saffi and students) two noble gentlemen of Polonia, and the bruit ran *Gentiluomini Inglesi*. ...

Oxford had not in fact gone to Greece, but only to Genoa. Paretti's report of Oxford's injured knee may account for the lameness of his later years. Paretti thinks Burghley may have heard evil reports of Oxford, even of a killing at Padua in which two Englishmen were involved. Paretti begs Burghley to give the report no credence.

On 24 September Benedetto Spinola, in London, wrote to Burghley:[24]

Has sent his Lordship's letter by the ordinary post to Venice to be delivered into the hands of the Earl. No letters have come from thence for six weeks on account of the great pestilence at Trent, through which place the post has to pass, so that it is no marvel that the Countess has not heard from her husband. ...

On this same day Burghley's July letters finally reached Venice. In his reply Oxford dwells on matters higher in priority than the birth of a daughter (LL-07):

My good lord, hauinge loked for yowre Lordships letters a great while, at lenght when I grew to dispaire of them I receiued twoo from yowre Lordship thre pakets whiche at sundrie times I had sent this summer towards England retorned bake againe, by reason the plage beinge in the passages, none were sufferd to pass but as they came were returned bake; whiche I cam not to the knowlege of till my returne now to Venice, where I haue bene grieued withe a feuer. yet withe the help of God now I haue recouerd the same and am past the danger therof thowght [=though] browght veri weake therby, and hindred from a great deale of trauell. whiche griues [=grieves] me most, feringe my time not sufficient for my desire. for allthought [=although] I haue sene so muche as sufficethe me yet wowld I haue time to profite therby. yowre Lordship semes desirous to know how I leake [=like] Italy, what is myne intention, in trauell, and when I meane to returne; for my lekinge of Italy, my lord I am glad I haue sene it, and I care not euer to see it any more vnles it be to serue my prince or contrie. for myne intention to trauell, I am desirows to see more of Germanie, wherfore I shall desire yowre Lordship withe my Lord of Lecester, to procure me the next summer, to continue my licence. at the end of whiche I meane vndoughtedly to returne. I thought to haue sene Spaine, but by Italy, I gess the worse. I haue sent on[e] of my seruants into England, withe sume new disposition of my thinges there, wherfore I will not troble yowre Lordship in thes letters with the same. if this siknes had not happend vnto me whiche hathe taken away this chifest time of trauell, at this present I wowld not haue written for further leaue, but to supply the whiche, I dought not her Magestie will not denie me so small a fauour. by reason of my great charges of trauell and siknes I haue taken vp of Mr Baptisto Nigrone 500 crounes, which I shall desire yowr Lordship to se ther[e] [i.e., in England] repaid. hopinge by this time my monie whiche is made of the sall [=sale] of my land is all com in. lekwise I shall desire yowre Lordship that whear as I had on[e] Luc Atslow that serued [me], whoo now is become a lewd subiect to her Magestie and an euil member to his contrie, whiche had certeine leses [=leases] of me, I doo thinke accordinge to Lawe he lesethe [=loseth] them all to the Queen sithe he is become on[e] of the Romishe church and there hathe performed all such ceremonies as myght reconcile hime self to that churge [=church] hauinge vsed lewd speaches against the Queens Magesties supremice, legitimation, gouerment and particuler lyf, and is here as it were a practiser vpon owre nation, then this is my desire that yowre Lordship if it be soo as I doo take yt wowld procure those leses into my hands againe where as I haue vnderstood by my Lord of Bedford they haue hardly delt withe my tenants.

Thus far Oxford has discussed the post, the plague, his sickness, his travel, his debts, his licence to travel, his finances, his lands, his servant Luke Atslowe, and his leases. Now a quick mention of his wife and child, and back to his request for an extension of his licence:

> thus thankinge yowre Lordship for yowre good newes of my wiues deliuerie, I recommend my self vnto yowre fauoure and allthought [=although] I write for a few months more yet thowght [=though] I haue them so it may fall ought I will shorten them my self.

Not so much as a greeting to his wife, or a mention of a child – only of the 'delivery'. Doubtless Oxford was abashed that Anne had not produced a son. The fact that Oxford acknowledged the birth at all was of such moment to Burghley that in a memorandum of 1576 he wrote under 24 September:[25]

> The letter of the Earl by which he gives thanks for his wife's delivery. Mark well this letter.

Among Burghley manuscripts now at Hatfield occurs a Latin poem – here Englished – allegedly copied from the fly-leaf of a New Testament:[26]

> To the illustrious Lady Anne de Vere, Countess of Oxford, while her noble husband, Edward Vere, Earl of Oxford, was occupied in foreign travel:

> Words of truth are fitting to a Vere; lies are foreign to the truth, and only true things stand fast, all else is fluctuating and comes to an end. Therefore, since thou, a Vere, art wife and mother of a Vere daughter, and seeing that thou mayest with good hope look forward to being mother of an heir of the Veres, may thy mind always glow with love of the truth, and may thy true motto be Ever Lover of the Truth. And that thou mayest the better attain to this, pray to the Author of all Truth that His Word may teach thee; that His Spirit may nourish thy inner life. So that, thus alleviating the absent longings of thy dear husband, thou, a Vere, mayest be called the true glory of thy husband.

The words may have been Oxford's, but they are more likely to have come from such as Arthur Golding, Bartholomew Clerke, or John Brooke.

On 6 October Spinola wrote to Burghley from London:[27]

> Congratulates him on the safe arrival of the Conte at Venice from Milan. His brother, Pasqual Spinola, will shortly be at Venice, to pay his respects to him there. His brother, Jacob Spinola, has paid the 1,000l. to Mr. James Harvy, at Antwerp.

Evidently Oxford had overcome his fears and travelled to Milan after all.

On 27 November Oxford wrote to Burghley from Padua (LL-08):

> My Lord. hauinge th'oportunite to write by this bearer whoo departethe from vs her[e] in Padowa, this night, allthought [=although] I cannot make so large a write as I wowld gladly desire yet I thought it not fitt too lett so short a time slipe [=slip]. wherfore remembringe my commendationes to yowre good Lordshipe, thes shalbe to desire yow to pardon the shortnes of my letters, and to imput[e] it at this present to the hast of this messengers departure. And as concerninge myne owne matters, I shall desire yowr Lordship to make noo staye of the salles [=sales] of my land, but

that all thinges [be] accordinge to my determinationes before I came away. withe those that I appointed last by my seruant William Bothe myght goo forward, accordinge to myne order taken, witheought any other alteration. thus recommendinge my self vnto yowre Lordship againe, and to my Ladie yowre wife, withe mine [=my wife (Anne)], I leaue further to troble yowre Lordship

Oxford's chief interest is to sell land towards the settlement of his debts.

On 11 December money sent by Pasquino Spinola reached Oxford at Venice; the very next day, according to Pasquino's report, Oxford departed for Florence:[28]

The Earl of Oxford is in good health, and is resolved to see the rest of Italy if he can travel with safety, and will leave to-morrow for Florence. Has paid over to him yesterday all the money which he has been directed to do, of the which he carries with him a portion, and for the rest he has letters of Cambio payable in different places, for the repayment of which he has given orders to his receiver at London.

Possibly Oxford visited even more of Italy during the year. Edward Webbe's *Travels*, published in 1590, suggest that Oxford reached Sicily:

Many things I have omitted to speak of, which I have seen and noted in the time of my troublesome travel. One thing did greatly comfort me which I saw long since in Sicilia, in the city of Palermo, a thing worthy of memory, where the Right Honourable the Earl of Oxford, a famous man of Chivalry, at what time he travelled into foreign countries, being then personally present, made there a challenge against all manner of persons whatsoever, and at all manner of weapons, as Tournaments, Barriers with horse and armour, to fight a combat with any whatsoever in the defence of his Prince and Country. For which he was very highly commended, and yet no man durst be so hardy to encounter with him, so that all Italy over he is acknowledged the only Chevalier and Nobleman of England. This title they give unto him as worthily deserved.

Webbe apparently saw Palermo and Sicily, but not Oxford in person. Nor is it to be credited that no man in all Italy would rise to Oxford's challenge.

On 25 September Henry Percy, 2nd Earl of Northumberland, wrote to Burghley from Croydon:[29]

Is newly returned with Burghley's son from Sussex, where he was desirous to have his brother, to know his opinion of the site of the place. Asks Burghley to come and see him, and bring Lady Burghley and Lady Oxford. When he learns the time of his lordship's leisure he will wait upon him as his guide.

Sir Thomas Cecil, Burghley's son, wrote in a similar vein on 3 October:[30]

Understanding that his Lordship was unwilling to bring my Lady his mother and Lady Oxford to Croydon unless it were to satisfy the great desire of my lord, assures him that the latter will take it very thankfully, and trusts that as they are to pass so near Wimbledon they will do him and his wife the honour to visit them.

Social visits must have helped Lady Oxford endure the pain of her husband's absence. Had she known more, she would have suffered greater anguish.

25 Journey Home

On 3 January 1576 Oxford wrote to Burghley from Siena, dogged even here by his creditors (LL-09):

> My lord I am sorie too here [=to hear] how hard my fortune is in England as I perceiue by yowre Lordshipes letters, but knowinge how vaine a thinge it is to linger a necessarie mischief, (to know the worst of my self & to let yowre Lordship vnderstand wherin I wowld vse yowre honorable friendship) in short I haue thus determined, that wheares I vnderstand, the greatnes of my dett; and gredines of my crediters, growes soo dishonorable to me, and troblesume vnto yowre Lordshipe, that that land of mine which in Cornwale I haue appointed too [=to] bee sould accordinge too that first order for myn expences in this trauell be goone throught [=through] withall. And to stope [=stop] my crediters exclamationes or rather defamations I may call them I shall desire yowre Lordship by the vertue of this letter which dothe not err as I take it from any former purpose which was that allwayes vpon my letter to authorise yowre Lordship to sell any portion of my land ...

Against this last sentence Burghley noted in the margin: 'no such avthorite'.

> ... that yow will sell on[e] hundreth pound a yere more of my land where yowr Lordship shall thinke fittest, to disburden me of mye de[b]ts to her Magestie my sister or els where I am exclaimed vpon. lekwise most ernestly I shall desire yowre Lordship to loke into the lands of my fathers will, whiche my sister beinge payd and the time expired I take is to come into my hands. ...

Having pre-approved the sale of lands to a certain value, Oxford instructs Burghley to sell off additional lands worth £100 per annum (with an absolute value of perhaps £2000). Oxford apparently anticipates the inheritance he would acquire in 1582 – twenty years after his father's death, but still six years in the future.

> ... and if yowre Lordship will for not troblinge of yowre self to[o] much with my causes command, Lewine, Kelton, and myne auditor [=George Golding] to make a v[i]ew into the same, I think it wilbe the soner dispached as for Hulbert I pray yowre Lordship to displace him of his office whiche I restored vnto him before myne auditor on condition he showld rendre it vp at all times that I showld command. my reason is whi I doo the same for that he bargend withe me in Coulne [=Colne], and trusting him, therin he hathe takene more then I ment and as his owne letter whiche I haue sent to my seruant Keltone dothe showe more then him self did mean, a fit excuse for soo coseninge a part and yet thowght [=though] it was more then he ment wheras it is conditioned that all times he showld surrender the same when his monie showldbe offred to him againe in compas of certeine yeres, yet in myne absence he hathe refused the same as I vnderstand. whervpon my thinkethe [=methinketh] he diserueth verie euill at my hands. and he that in so small a matter dothe misvse the trust I haue reposed in him, I am to dought his seruice in greater causes. wherfore I doo againe desire yowre Lordship to discharge him from all dealinges of myne, vpon his accountes too [=to] the rest of my fornamed seruants. ...

Evidently Lewin had already returned to England. Oxford's servant 'Hulbert' was Edward Hubbard, who had apparently purchased lands from Oxford on the understanding that he would sell them back when asked; but now, having been asked, he would not. (Hubbard soon became one of the Six Clerks of the Court of Chancery.)[1] Oxford continued:

> ... In doinge thes thinges yowre lordshipe shall greatly plesure me. in not doinge them yow shall as muche hinder me. for allthough to depart withe land yowre Lordship hathe aduised the contrarie and that yowre Lordship for the good affection yow beare vnto me could wishe it otherwise, yet yow see, I haue non other remedie

Thus conceding that Burghley had advised him not to part with his lands, Oxford continued:

> I haue no help but of myne owne, and mine is made to serue me, and myself not mine. whervpon till all suche incombrances be passed ouer and till I can better settell my self at home I haue determined to continue my trauell the whiche thing in no wise I desire yowre Lordship to hinder. vnles yow wowld haue it thus *Vt nulla sit inter nos amicitia* [='that there should be no friendship between us']. for hauinge made an end of all hope to help my self by her Magesties seruice consideringe that my yowthe is obiected vnto me, and for eury step of myne, a bloke [=block, hindrance] is found to be layd in my way, I see it is but vayne, *calcitrare contra li buoi*.[2] and the worst of thinges beinge knowne, they are the more easier to be prouided for, to beare and support them withe patiencie [=patience]. wherfore for thinge passed amis[s] to repent them it is to[o] late, to help them, (whiche I cannot but ease them[)] that I am determined to hop[e] for any thinge I doo not, but if any thinge doo happen preter spem [='above/beyond hope'] I thinke before that time I must be so ould as my sunes [=sons], whoo shall enioi them, must giue the thankes and I am to content my self accordinge to this Englishe prouerd [=proverb] that it is my hap to sterue leke [=like] the horse, whilst the gress [grass] dothe growe.
>
> thus my good lord I doo bouldly write that yow showld not be ignorant of any thinge that I doo, for if I haue reason I make yow the iuge, and lay my self more open vnto yow, then perhapes yf I write fewer lines ore penned les store of wordes [than] otherwise I could doo. But for that it is not so easie a matter at all times to conuey letters from thes parties [=parts] in to England I am therfore the more desirous to vse larglie this oportunite. and to supplie in writinge the want of speaking, wiche the longe distance betwien vs hathe taken away. thus I leaue yowre Lordshipe to the protection of almightie god. whoome I beseche to send yow longe and happie lyfe. and better fortune to define yowre felicite, in thes yowre aged yeres, then yt hathe pleased hime to graunt in my yowthe. but of a hard beginninge we may hope a good and easie endinge.

Burghley considered this letter of peculiar importance, and noted it in his chronology: '3rd Jan. The Earl wrote to me'.[3]

Of the thousands of sentences that survive from Oxford's pen, one from this letter stands out as most characteristic, and most chilling:

> I haue no help but of myne owne, and mine is made to serue me, and myself not mine.

To paraphrase: I have only my own resources; they are made to serve me; I am not made to serve them. As noted in the Introduction, Oxford here expresses the very opposite of the feudal ideal.

In January, evidently of this year, Eleanor Bridges wrote to the Earl of Rutland:[4]

> Lady Mary de Vere, sister of the Earl of Oxford, is sworn one of the Privy Chamber. The Court is as full of malice and spite as when you left.

Evidently Lady Mary, known for her sharp tongue, was now a Queen's maid of honour.

The second session of Queen Elizabeth's Fourth Parliament sat this year from 8 February to 15 March (*TE*). Oxford is recorded as absent for all sessions, and neither appointed a proxy nor was appointed to any committee (*Journals*). On 2 March his licence to travel was renewed for one year more:[5]

> The Erle of Oxford for one yeere after thexpiration of his former licence ij marcij 1575 [=2 March 1576].

On 23 March Benedetto Spinola wrote to Burghley:[6]

> Has received a letter from his brother at Venice, of the 26th February, who informs him that the illustrious Count [=Oxford] continues in his resolution to return home by way of Lyons, and believes that he will set out after Carnival.

Shrove Tuesday, the last day of Carnival, fell this year on 6 March; as we will learn, Oxford left Venice on Monday the 5th.

Among the Burghley papers is an elaborate memorandum in Italian, endorsed by Burghley:[7]

> Note of the money that Benedict Spinola, at the instance of the Lord High Treasurer of England, caused to be paid to the Earl of Oxford, as well in France as at Venice. The payments are made partly in 1575 and partly in 1576, the total amount being 3,761*l*. 4s 5d.

Thus the Spinola brothers between them had supplied nearly £4000 for Oxford's Italian journey.

About three and a half weeks after Carnival, on 31 March, Francis Peyto wrote to Burghley from Milan concerning a genealogical chart of the royal houses of England and Scotland:[8]

> Meant to have shown this designment to the Earl of Oxford when he passed this way, but was always refused to be spoken with.

Passing through Milan on his return journey, Oxford would not give Peyto the time of day, but struck out for Paris via Lyon and the military encampments of one or another French faction. On 21 March Ambassador Dale informed Burghley of Oxford's arrival in Paris:[9]

> The Earl of Oxford has passed through all the camp, and is arrived here, and Mr. William Russell with him. It seems this year has been a time well bestowed on him.

This may have been the Mr Russell later found among Oxford's dining companions.

On 31 March Ambassador Dale wrote to Walsingham from Paris:[10]

> The camp of Monsieur approaches. The King is unready. The strangers cannot abide to linger this matter. Lord Oxford is here attending his coming.

On 3 April Giovanni Francesco Morosini, Venetian ambassador in France, wrote to the Signory from Paris:[11]

> The Earl of Oxford, an English gentleman, has arrived here. He has come from Venice, and, according to what has been said to me by the English Ambassador here resident, speaks in great praise of the numerous courtesies which he has received in that city; and he reports that on his departure from Venice your Serenity had already elected an Ambassador to be sent to his Queen, and the English Ambassador expressed the greatest satisfaction at the intelligence. I myself, not having received any information from your Serenity or from any of my correspondents, did not know what answer to give concerning this matter.

Oxford apparently left Paris on 10 April, when Ambassador Dale reported that he was sending letters to Burghley 'by Lord Oxford'.[12] Having made his way safely to Calais, as he crossed the Channel Oxford's ship was taken by pirates. Nathaniel Baxter recalled the event in his 1606 *Sidneys Ouránia* (sig. A3v):

> N   Aked we landed out of Italie,
> I   Nthral'd by Pyrats men of noe regard,
> H   Orror and death assayl'd Nobilitie,
> I   F Princes might with crueltie be scar'd
> L   O thus are excellent beginnings hard.

The Privy Council took note of the event on 15 April:[13]

> The same day Mr. Beale was dispatched towardes the Lowe Countrey upon occasion of a spoile committed upon thearle of Oxford at the seas in his passage, and for other injuries donne by them of Flusshinge against diverse of her Majesties subjectes, acording to instructions remayning in the handes of Mr. Secretary Walsingham.

> A letter to thearle of Oxford signifieng what their Lordships had donne in respect of that injurie donne unto him, that Mr. Beale should cume unto him to be informed of the manour of the oultrage and the particulars of his losses, and either to deliver him perfect instructions or to send some servante of his with him that knowe his stuffe and whereof he made moost accompt.

For his dispatche there were signed by their Lordships sundrie letters of creditt for Mr. Beale, as to the Prince of Orenge and the Admirall of Flusshinge and the Governour of Middleburghe.

On the same day Robert Beale was commissioned to negotiate with the Prince of Orange:[14]

On his arrival at Flushing he shall inform himself whether the ships of the Merchant Adventurers are released or whether they mean to detain them; and if he finds that they be departed, and in no danger of arrest, he shall deliver her message to the Prince or, in his absence, to the Governor of Zealand. If he finds that they are not released, but that there is hope of their being set at liberty, he shall let them understand that her Majesty finds her honour greatly wounded by the daily misusing of her subjects, and specially by the outrage lately committed upon the Earl of Oxford, and that in case the offenders be not severely punished, she will be forced to put in execution such remedies as she would be loth to do. In case he finds the Prince or Governors stand upon conditional terms as to have the ships arrested in the West first released, he shall let them understand that they forget themselves in standing upon conditional terms with a prince of her Majesty's quality; besides which the arrest of their ships proceeded of sundry complaints of spoils and outrages sustained by her subjects (the said Flushingers having carried in within the space of one month 30 sail of her subjects). They would then see that the cause of arrest proceeded from themselves, so are they in reason first to make satisfaction, and that by staying the ships of the Merchant Adventurers, to whom by contract they have given free passage, they have offered double injury. He is to be guided by his discretion accordingly as he shall find the state of affairs there, only it is necessary, until the ships are released, that he forbears to use threatenings, but when they are departed, he shall deliver her message to the Prince and Governors.

On 17 April, according to Burghley's retrospective Diary (ii, p. 778):

Mr. Robert Beale sent to Flushyng to demand Restitution of certen of the Merchant Adventurors ther arrested: to require Restitution of Goods taken by Flushyngers from the Erle of Oxford betwixt Dover and Calliss [=Calais].

Details are supplied in a 16 April letter from Burghley to Walsingham:[15]

... as I wrote yesterday, I found it hard to make a good distynction betwixt angre and judgment for My Lordes of Oxforde's misusage, so suerly, whan I look into the universall barbarism of the Prince's forces of the Flushyngars, which ar[e] only a rable of common pyrattes, or worss, and that mak no difference whom they outrage, I do mistrust of any good issue to the cause, though of itself it be to be favored. Yet, as it is sayd bonam causam male agendo perisse ['A good cause may be killed by bad proceeding'], I humbly thank all my Lordes for the regard of My Lord of Oxford, in whose person suerly Hir Majesty and the realme hath taken disgrace, and, if the Prince shall not yeld to hang some of the principall for such a robbery, I must saye howe so ever Hir Majesty shall bend hirself for the public cause, she ought in justyce otherwise to se it revenged. For, if justyce be denyed in such a notoriouss case, all lawes betwixt meare princes do warrant a procedyng otherwise to mak an example of avendg. And suerly, if Mr. Beale shall spek with the Prince, he may do well to advise him to thynk that such an outrage as this is, cannot tak end without more offence to hym and his than may be the hangyng of v or vj such theves, as, if he war rid of an hundred of them, his cause wold prosper better, and his frendes wold increass, which if he shall by subterfuge in answer delay, he will fele shall nether prosper, nor yet his frendes remayn obliged to hym as they have. You se my angre ledeth my judgment. And yet trust I am not herto moved more for particular than for the publick.

I nede add nothyng to your wrytynges. Mr. Beale is wise, and I pray hym, if my name be of any vallew, to use it to the Prince, as felyng my self in the person of the Erle of Oxford interested with this outrage, and so expecting the rather some honorable amendes by justice in executyng of the pyrattes.

On 21 April the French ambassador Mauvissière reported of the Queen:[16]

She too is here, and is marvellously angry that the Earl of Oxford, son-in-law of the High Treasurer and one of the premier counts of this land, on his return from Italy was left naked, stripped to his shirt, treated miserably, his life in danger if he hadn't been recognized by a Scotsman. The Queen dispatched Lord Howard to Dover to welcome and console him, for it is said that he had brought with him a great collection of beautiful Italian garments, which were taken from him, over which his regret is infinite.

Is Mauvissière suggesting that Oxford thought more of his Italian garments than of his life?

On 31 May the Prince of Orange wrote to Burghley from Campveer:[17]

Was greatly displeased when he heard from Mr. Robert Beale of the injuries which the Earl of Oxford had received at the hands of certain sea captains calling themselves Flushingers. Has taken such order that some of them are already in prison, and if they are found guilty they shall be punished in such a manner that all who have been aggrieved by them will be contented and will see how unpleasing such actions are to the States.

As we shall learn, the apparent date of Oxford's arrival at Dover was 20 April.

26 Inglese Italianato

Although he had travelled to Padua, Genoa, Milan, and Siena (and more doubtfully Palermo) between April 1575 and March 1576, Oxford devoted most of his Italian journey to Venice. In 1617 Sir Henry Wotton would recall:[1]

when he arrived in Venice, [Oxford] took no trouble to see the rest of the country, but stopped here, and even built himself a house.

The construction of a house – or apartment – would account for Oxford's huge expenditure during his year abroad.

Nathaniel Baxter recalls Oxford's life in Venice in the same 1606 poem that reported his capture by pirates. Addressed to Oxford's third surviving daughter, Susan ('To the Right Noble, and Honorable Lady Susan Vera Mongomriana'), the poem (sig. A3v) is an acrostic on a feminized version of the Oxfordian motto ('Nothing Truer than Truth'). For Baxter, 'Albania' is 'England' (sigs. A4, E2v, G2), while 'infested' means 'infected':

> V   Aliant whilome the Prince that bare this Mot,
> E   Ngraued round about his golden Ring:
> R   Oaming in VENICE ere thou wast begot,
> A   Mong the Gallants of th' Italian spring.
>
> N   Euer omitting what might pastime bring,
> I   Talian sports, and Syrens Melodie:
> H   Opping Helena with her warbling sting,
> I   Nfested th'Albanian dignitie,
> L   Ike as they poysoned all Italie.
>
> V   Igilant then th'eternall majestie
> E   Nthraled soules to free from infamie:
> R   Emembring thy sacred virginitie,
> I   Nduced vs to make speedie repaire,
> V   Nto thy mother euerlasting faire,
> S   O did this Prince begette thee debonaire.

More truthful than decorous, Baxter reveals that the 'Albanian' nobleman devoted his time in Venice to sexual adventure, at the cost of a besmirched reputation and a sexually transmitted disease.

Oxford's personal courtesan – his own 'hopping Helena' – was Virginia Padoana, as revealed in a letter from Sir Stephen Powle to John Chamberlain, 21 September 1587, from Venice:[2]

> Yf to be well neighboured be no smalle parte of happines I may repute my self highly fortunate: for I am lodged emongst a great number of Signoraes. Isabella Bellochia in the next howse on my right hand: And Virginia Padoana, that honoreth all our nation for my Lord of Oxfords sake, is my neighbour on the lefte side: Ouer my head hath Lodovica Gonzaga the Frenche kinges mistris her howse: you thinck it peraduenture preposterous in Architecture to haue hir lye ouer me. I am sorry for it, but I can not remedye it nowe: Pesarina with hir sweet entertainment & braue discoorse is not 2 Canalls of[f]. Ancilla (Mr Hattons handmayde) is in the next Campo: Paulina Gonzaga is not farre of[f]. Prudencia Romana with hir courtly trayne of Frenche gentlemen euery nighte goeth a spasso [=unemployed] by my Pergalo. As for Imperia Romana hir date is out which florished in your tyme. I must of force be well hallowed emongst so many Saints. But in troath I am a frayde they doe condemne me of heresye, for setting vp so fewe tapers on their high Altars. ...

I doe obserue Guicciardins method, that in euery Cittíes description, forgetteth not the persons that florished therin: and you hauinge hearde the names of the cheef Ladyes of account, I must put downe likewise the names of the famous mountebanckes. ...

While Chamberlain's reply does not mention Oxford, it mirrors and thus confirms Powle's salacious tone.[3]

Oxford's courtesan is twice on record as transgressing the Venetian sumptuary laws:[4]

Virginia Padoana Cortesana, sta a S. Geremia, condanada adi 5 Magio 1581 ducati 45, appar in libro a carte 1.

Virginia Padoana Cortesana, sta a S. Geremia, fo condanada adi 20 Ottobre 1595, ducati 35, appar in libro a carte 52.

Could it be that she was indebted to Oxford for her residence on the Campo Santa Geremia, at the intersection of the Canale Grande and the Canale di Cannaregio (near the modern train station)?

A typical, bare-breasted Venetian courtesan is pictured and described in Thomas Coryate's *Crudities* of 1611 (Fig. 7):[5]

... Also the ornaments of her body are so rich, that except thou dost euen geld thy affections (a thing hardly to be done) or carry with the[e] Vlysses hearbe called Moly which is mentioned by Homer, that is, some antidote against those Venerous titillations, shee wil very neare benumme and captiuate thy senses, and make reason vale bonnet to affections. ... if thou dost linger with them thou wilt finde their poyson to be more pernicious then that of the scorpion, aspe, or cocatrice.

The courtesan's 'poyson', like Baxter's 'warbling sting' (which 'poysoned all Italie'), is venereal disease. (A 'warble' is literally a raised lump in the skin caused by the gad-fly, or 'warble-fly': *OED*.)

Oxford's Italy fulfils the worst English stereotypes, as embodied, for example, in Powle's 'description of Italie to my brother Powle the elder, 20 Iune 1581':[6]

To speake in generall what I thinck of Italie, I must needs confesse, to have found a verie flowrishing cuntrie, and a fruitles people. I have seen manie bewtified Cittyes, with gorgeous buildings; but poluted and Deformed inhabitantes with vicious behaviour; fortified townes with arteficiall bulwarkes; and standinge walls; but weake Captaines with ruinous manners, that yeald vp to everie assault of sensualitie: manie relicks of dead saints, but more monuments of livinge Sarazens for religion, and divelish serpentes for life: to saie in a word, I have found an evell people, and a good land. The Italian is in behaviour civill, and sociable, & of nature couragious & merrie; he hateth all melancholik humors, & therfore delighteth in maskinge, dauncinge, musicall instruments, pleasant gardens, beautifull pictures, & daintie dames: accountinge religion but pollicie to keepe men within the compas of sum honest limittes; preachinge to be but pratlinge of fryers and moncks: all inordinate pleasures to be but solaces of nature. And therfore besides the horrible

vice of Sodomie (which is common) the father will committ incest with his owne
daughter, and that which is moste to be detested (and I blushe almoste to reporte it)
in Calabria they ordinarilie polute them selves with their goates. And yet although
he be stained with these vices, he standeth so muche on his puntillos of honor, that
he will die on him by whome he receaveth anie reproche or disgrace of this vicious
livinge.

Roger Ascham had similarly railed against Italy in *The Schoolemaster* (1570, sig.
I2), citing the old proverb, *Inglese italianato, e vn diabolo incarnato* ('an English-
man Italianate is a Devil incarnate'); while Thomas Nash would rail again in *The
Unfortunate Traveller* (1594, sig. L4v):

> Italy the paradice of the earth, and the Epicures heauen, how doth it forme our
> yong master? It makes him to kisse his hand like an ape, cringe his neck like a
> starueling, and play at hey pass repasse come aloft when hee salutes a man. From
> thence he brings the art of atheisme, the art of epicurising, the art of whoring, the art
> of poysoning, the art of Sodomitrie. The onely propable good thing they haue to
> keepe vs from vtterly condemning it, is, that it maketh a man an excellent Courtier,
> a curious carpet knight: which is by interpretation, a fine close leacher, a glorious
> hypocrite. It is now a priuie note amongst the better sort of men, when they would
> set a singular marke or brand on a notorious villaine, to say, he hath been in Italy.

Oxford, as we shall see, was a perfect instantiation of the type.

A comic Italian narrative, published in 1699, may distantly refer to Oxford:[7]

> I found myself ambassador of my illustrious country of Bologna at the court of the
> Emperor Polidor of Trebizond, and attending the great tournament celebrating his
> marriage to Irene, Empress of Constantinople. Present were many great worthies,
> Basil, King of Zelconda, Doralba, Princess of Dacia, Arcont, vaivode of Moldavia,
> Arsileus, heir of Denmark, Isuf, pasha of Aleppo, Fatima, Sultan of Persia,
> Elmond, milord of Oxford ...

> The horse of Milord of Oxford is faun-coloured and goes by the name of
> Oltramarin (Beyond-the-Sea). Edward carried a large sword (spadone). His colour
> of costume is violet. He carries for device a falcon with a motto taken from
> Terence: Tendit in ardua virtus (Valour proceeds to arduous undertakings).

> In this Tirata, Milord of Oxford ... tilted against Alvida, countess of Edenburg,
> who was mounted on a dapple grey, was armed with a Frankish lance and was
> robed in lemon colour. In the end, Edward and Alvida, alas, threw one another
> simultaneously, both landing face down in the dust!

> Nevertheless, Emperor Polidor awarded to all the knights and amazons gifts out of
> the cupboard of antiquity. To Elmond – Edward – was given the horn of Astolf ...

The Rabelaisian characterization is of a sexual adventurer.

Oxford's adventures in Italy were not only heterosexual, but homosexual and
pederastic. Henry Howard testifies (LIB-3.6.1/3):

> Touchinge buggery Auratio the Italian boye complayned howe horribly my Lord
> had abusid him, and yet wold not giue him any thinge [i.e., by way of medical
> relief].

Charles Arundel attributes the boy's departure from Oxford's service to the same
cause (LIB-4.2/6.4):

> Auracio that came with him owte of Italie made it the quarrell of his departure, as
> Henrye Locke can testefie.

Lok, as we shall learn, had been Oxford's servant as early as 1571, and perhaps
accompanied him to Italy. Orazio Coquo, the object of Oxford's affection, will
tell his own story in the next chapter but one.

27 A Stranger to his Wife

Piracy was the lesser of two shocks that attended Oxford's return from Italy. The
greater is recorded in Burghley's retrospective Diary (ii, p. 778):

> The Erle of Oxford arryved being retorned out of Italy, he was entyced by certen
> lewd Persons to be a Stranger to his Wiff.

Parted from Anne for more than a year, Oxford refused to rejoin her. For
Burghley, as always, the fault lay not with Oxford, but with certain other 'lewd
Persons' – obvious candidates including Rowland York, and Orazio Coquo.

On Holy Thursday, 19 April, 'My Lorde [=Burghley] went to London in
thaftarnowne'.[1] Burghley anticipated Oxford's return by a day:[2]

> 20 Aprillis Comes Oxon' rursus in angliam ('20 April: Earl of Oxford back in
> England')

Subsequent events are recorded in numerous letters and memoranda, mostly
in Burghley's own hand, as in a list, dated 25 April, of highly compressed recol-
lections:[3]

> assurance of a ioyntur, not so much as his thyrdes
>
> iijm [=£3000] gyven with hir [=Anne], besyde half as much otherwise expended.
>
> assurance of a portion / no more than she hath necessarely spent. for she was in
> dett, for lack of releff. she had bene long sick before that. in hir sycknes whan she
> bred child, hir charges war great; the lyk whan she was delyvered. [Left Margin:
> 'nota: no land assuerd to his daughter, though he have no other child'.] with that
> [=what] she hath my Lord is discharged, of meat and drynk for hir self, hir women
> and hir servantes, and for all manner of wages and lyveryes. she also beareth the
> charges of a gentle woman, a nurss, a rockar and a launder for hir child.[4]

Thus Anne's expenses, for herself and for baby Elizabeth, were paid out of her own resources. Burghley then recounts actions of Oxford and others, beginning with his departure in early 1575:

> no vnkyndness knowen on his part at his departure. she made hym prive [=privy, aware], that she thought she was with child, wherof he sayd he was glad. whan he was certefyed therof to Pariss, he sent hir, his picture with kynd lettres and messadges. he sent hir ij coch horsses.

> When he h[e]ard she was delyvered, he gave me thankes by his lettres for advertisyng therof.

> he never signefyed any mislykyng of any thyng vntill the 4 of Aprill at Pariss, from whence he wrote, somewhat that by reason of a man of his which was his receavor, in abusyng hym and me he had conceaved some vnkyndnes: but he prayed me to lett pass the same, for it did grow by the dooblenes of servantes.

The receiver whom Oxford accused of malfeasance was probably Edward Hubbard.[5] Burghley continues:

> I wrot[e] to Pariss to hym to hasten hym homeward/.

> I sent for my sonn Thomas Cecill, who was more than hundred myles from London to come in post, to go and mete hym at Dover, or in France, who cam, and was with hym at Dover within ij howres after my Lord Howard and others and thither carryed my commendation & his wyves [=wife's] /. and did not vnderstand from hym any poynt of mislykyng. my doughter went to Gravesend sonar [=sooner] than I wold, for my advise was that by my sonn she shuld vnderstand his contentation. but she thought long to do for my sonns answer and looked that my Lord wold be come neare London befor she cold have word, and so went with my lady Mary, who had wrytten to hir to Theobaldes, requestyng that she might go with hir/

Thus Thomas Cecil went to Dover to meet Oxford as he came off his ship, while Anne and Lady Mary went to Gravesend with the hope of catching Oxford himself or news about him.

> all this whyle I knew of no mislykyng towardes me or his wiff./ but I h[e]ard that his receavor had bene at Dover to spek with hym, and he refused it sayeng he wold speak with hym befor me./

Evidently Oxford refused to speak with Thomas Cecil until he had spoken with Edward Hubbard.

> I sent lettres to hym, to intreat hym to tak my houss for his lodgyng. wherof I had no answer. and yet I wrot twise by ij severall messyngers. but my sonn sent me word, that he found hym disposed to kepe hym self secretly ij or iij dayes in his own lodgyng. and yet that Edward York told hym secretly that his Lordship wold come first to my houss but he wold nobody knew therof. wheruppon I was very glad, but his wiff gladder. and the contrary I knew [not?], vntill he was landed, and than my

sonn told me how he did soddenly leave the bardg and took a whery, and only with Rowland York landed about Yorkes houss.

Oxford avoided his wife and sister by taking a boat (called a 'wherry') up the Thames.

Hervppon I sent to welcom hym, and with request to tak a lodgyng in my houss. but therto he answered, that he ment to kepe hym self secret ther, in his lodgyng ij or iij dayes, and then he wold come and speak with me. and the messynger did comm from his wiff, with request that if he shuld not come that night to hir fathers houss that than she wold come to hym, for she desyred to be on[e] of the first that might se hym. to it he answered nether yea nor naye, but sayd why I have answered you, meaning that he wold kepe hym self secret ij or 3 dayes, as the messyngar took it/. whervppon I thought convenient she shuld forbeare to go to hym vntill we might se how others war suffred to come to hym, or he to resort to others. Within ij howres I h[e]ard by them that had bene with hym, how manny had bene with hym. without any his mislykyng. and also that it was h[e]ard, that he ment to supp out of his lodging at Edward Yorkes. and that ther was a co[a]ch preparyng for my lady his sistar [=Lady Mary] to come to hym. Which being h[e]ard by my daughter, she very importunatly required me she might go to hym and yet I required hir to stay vntill I might send to my Lord Haward, from whom I wold know whyther he knew that my Lord hir husband wold go to the Court, for if he wold, she shuld not go vntill he had bene ther/. My Lord Haward sent me word that he as yet cold not tell, but whan he shuld know he wold send me word, wherof I had noone/

and than hearyng that my Lord Howard was at the Erles lodgyng and supper provyded at Yorkes, and my lady Mary comyng from the Court.

Rejecting Burghley's offer of hospitality, Oxford took refuge in York House, Walbrook, accompanied by Rowland York. Here Anne proposed to visit her husband, but Burghley put his foot down.

Already on 23 April Burghley addressed a letter to the Queen which in its indirections and circumlocutions (and emendations in draft) reveals a desperate struggle to face facts:[6]

Most soveraign lady, As I was accustomed from the beginning of my service to your Majesty until of late by the permission of your goodness and by occasion of the place wherein I *served your Majesty, to be frequently an intercessor for others to your Majesty, and therein did find your Majesty always inclinable to give me gracious audience; so now do I find in the latter end of my years a necessary occasion to be an intercessor *to your Majesty or rather an immediate petitioner for my self and an intercessor for another next to my self, in a cause godly, honest, and just; and therefore, having had proof of your Majesty for most favours in causes not so important, I doubt not but to find the like influence of your grace in a cause so near touching myself as your Majesty will conceive it doth. ...

To enter to trouble your Majesty with the circumstances of my cause, I mean not for sundry respects but chiefly for two; the one is that I am very loth to be more cumbersome to your Majesty than need shall compel me; the other is for that I hope in God's goodness, and for reverence borne to your Majesty, that success thereof may have a better end than the beginning threateneth. But your Majesty may think my suit will be very long where I am so long ere I begin it; and truly, most gracious sovereign lady, it is true that the nature of my cause is such as I have no pleasure to enter into it, but had rather seek means to shut it up than to lay it open, not for lack of the soundness thereof on my part, but for the *brickelness [=frailty, softened from 'inhumanitie'] of others from whom the ground work proceedeth.

My suit therefore shall be *presently to your Majesty but in general sort, that whereas I am, by God's visitation with some infirmity and yet not yet great, stayed from coming to do my duty to your Majesty at this time, and my daughter, the Countess of Oxford, also occasioned to her great grief to be absent from your Majesty's Court, and that the occasion of her absence may be diversly reported to your Majesty, as I said before, by some of ignorance by some percase otherwise, it may please your Majesty – because the ground and working thereupon toucheth me as nearly as any worldly cause in my *conceit can do *to continue your princely consideration of us both – of me as of an old worn servant that dare compare with the best, the greatest, the oldest and the youngest, for loyalty and devotion, giving place to many others in other worldly qualities, as your Majesty shall prefer any before me; and of my daughter, your Majesty's most humble young servant, as of one that is towards your Majesty in dutiful love and fear, yea, in fervent admiration of your graces to contend with any her equals, and in the cause betwixt my Lord of Oxford and her, whether it be for respect of misliking in me or misdeeming of hers whereof I cannot yet know the certainty, I do avow in the presence of God and of his angels whom I do call as ministers of his ire, if in this I do utter any untruth.

I have not in his absence on my part omitted any occasion to do him good for himself and his causes, no, I have not in thought imagined anything offensive to him, but contrariwise I have been as diligent for his causes to his benefit as I have been for my own, and this I pronounce of knowledge for myself, and therefore if, contrary to my desert, I should otherwise be judged or suspected, I should receive great injury for my daughter, though nature will make *me ... to speak favourably; yet now I have taken God and his angels to be witnesses of my writing, I renounce nature, and protest simply to your Majesty, I did never see in her behaviour in word or deed, nor ever could perceive by any other *mean, but that she hath always used herself honestly, chastely, and lovingly towards him; and now upon expectation of his coming so filled with joy thereof, so desirous to see the time of his arrival approach, as in my judgment no young lover rooted or sotted in love of any person could more excessively show the same with all comely tokens; *or when, *after his arrival, some doubts were cast of his acceptance of her true innocency, seemed to make her so bold as she never cast any care of things *past, but wholly reposed herself with assurance to be well used by him. And with that confidence, and importunity made to me, she went to him, and there missed of her expectation, and so attendeth, as her duty is, to gain some *part of her hope.[7]

And now, lest I should enter further into the matter, and not meaning to trouble your Majesty, I do end with this humble request; that in anything that may hereof follow, whereof I may have wrong with dishonesty offered *to me, I may have your Majesty's princely favour to seek my just defence for me and mine; not meaning *for respect of my old service, nor of the place whereunto your Majesty hath called me (though unworthy) to challenge any extraordinary favour, for my service hath been but a piece of my duty, and my vocation hath been too great a reward. And so I do remain constant to serve your Majesty in what place so ever your Majesty shall command, even in as base as I have done in great.

Burghley added a note: 'In some part makyng suit to wryte it new, I have I think rather shortened then enlarged it'.

On 25 April Sir Thomas Smith wrote to Burghley concerning his own failing health, concluding on a topic of more immediate concern:[8]

> I am sory to here of this vndewtifull & vnkyend dealyng of my Lord of Oxford toward your Lordship which I am suer must very mych greave your honor Seyng [=seeing] it greaveth me for the love I beare hym, biacuse he was brought vp in my howse your Lordships benefites towards hym & great cares for hym deserveth a fare [=far] other recompense of dewty & kyndnes, then I here say he now doth vse at his commyng over. What cownsellores & persuaders he hath so to behave hym self, I can not tell I am sorie for it, and sory to hear so mich of it.

Even Smith blames 'cownsellores & persuaders' rather than Oxford himself.

To help him comprehend the 'undutiful and unkind dealing of my Lord of Oxford', Burghley set down a chronology of Oxford's actions from 29 July to 5 August 1574, and from 16 September 1574 to 3 January 1576.[9] One entry among many is exceptionally informative and exceptionally puzzling:

> he confessed to my Lord Haward, that he laye not with his wiff but at Hampton Court. and that than the child cold not be his because the child was born in Iuly. which was not the space of twelve monthes

Did Oxford – or Burghley – not know that the period of human gestation is nine months?

On 24 April Robert Christmas, still one of Oxford's several receivers, secured legal protection 'for three years for [himself] and all sureties standing bound with or for him'.[10] Perhaps Christmas wished to secure himself against claims over Oxford's mountainous debts.

On 27 April Oxford wrote to Burghley from Greenwich (LL-10):

> Mi lord, all thought [=although] I have forborne, in sume respect, whiche I hould priuat to my self ether to write ore come vnto yowre Lordshipe, yet had I determined, as oportunitie should haue serued me, to haue acomplished the same in compas of a feue dayes.

> But now vrged therunto by yowre letters, to satisfie yow the soner, I must let yowre Lordship vnderstand thus muche.

That is vntill I can better satisfie or aduertise miself of sume mislekes [=mislikings], I am not determined as touchinge my wife to accompanie here [=her]. What they are because sume are not to be spoken of or written vpon as imperfections I will not deale withall, sume that otherwayes discontent me I will not blas [=blaze] ore publishe vntill it pleas me. and last of all I mean not to werie my life any more withe suche trobles and molestationes as I haue endured nor will I to please yowre Lordship only, discontent my self. Wherfore as yowre Lordship veri well writethe vnto me that yow mean if it standethe withe my lekinge to receiue her in to yowre howse, thes are lekwise to let yowre Lordship vnderstand that it dothe veri well content me, for there as yowre doughter or her mothers more then my wife yow may take comfort of her and I rid of the comber therby, shall remaine well eased of many griefes. I doo not dought but she hathe sufficient proportion for her beinge to liue vpon and to maintaine herself. This myght haue bene done throwght [=through] priuat conference before and had not neded to haue bene the fable of the world yf yow wowld haue had the patience to haue vnderstood me, but I doo not know by what ore whose aduise it was, to rune that course so contrarie to my will or meaninge, whiche made her disgraced, the world reised suspitions openly, that withe priuate conference myght haue bene more silently handled, and hathe giuen me more greater cause to misleke. Wherfore I desire yowre Lordship in thes causes now yow shall vnderstand me not to vrge me any farther. and so I write vnto yowre Lordship as yow haue done vnto me. ...

The response of the historian Conyers Read is a classic of its kind:[11]

This is the letter of a cad if ever there was one. He would not charge his wife with anything, but he was well rid of her! It is rather shocking to discover that a young, unwhipped cub like Oxford could have dared to write in these terms to the chief minister of the Queen. But such was the prestige of the Veres that socially they were above reproach. The Cecils, of course, were parvenus in comparison.

On 29 April Burghley composed a memorandum endorsed 'The convocation I had with my Lord of Oxford'.[12] The convocation seems to have been rather one-sided, mostly complaints from Oxford:

1. his monny not made over to hym accordyng to his direction

3. Favnt and Clopton not sufficiently pvnished

Denny and the rest pvnished by my meanes

2. his followars not favored by me —/—

no svte gotten for hym at any tyme // a sute that Sir Ihon Hubbard ment for incress of the taxe of the spiritualtes

his lettre shewed to the Queens Maiesty, of sett purpooss to bryng hym into hir Maiestes indignation

lettres wrytten to his servantes in Itally —/—

his wiff taken awey from hym at Wyvenho and carryed to London —/—

manny other thynges of vnkyndnes, which he is assured ar trew but he may not vtter them for harming of the partyes. nether hath he as yet fully inquired of the particularetyes thereof —/—

for his wiff, he meaneth not to discover any thyng of the cause of his mislykyng. but he will not come to hir vntill he vnderstand further of that wherof he meaneth to be advertised, and he meaneth not to vse hir but honorably. —/—

that my wiff[13] hath ever drawen his wiffes love from hym, and that she hath wished hym dead.

That at Wyvenho she caused a division in his houss, and a slander to be raysed of hym for intention of killyng of his men

The closing item probably refers to the assault on Clopton *alias* Wotton and Faunt reported on 30 May 1573. Though Oxford objected to Lady Burghley's interference, she may well have acted to protect Anne from abuse. It can come as no surprise that the mother-in-law of such a son-in-law would have wished him dead.

Burghley composed yet another version of the same complaints, endorsed 'Cavillations by the Erle of Oxford Contra Lord burghley':[14]

Iniuryes and vnkynd partes/.

The leavyng of the Issew female being heyre to be vnprovyded for of any land.

The reiectyng of his wiff at hir coming to hym, without cause shewed.

The contynvance of that cours to forbeare from his wiffes company without cause.

The deteaning of hir apparrell and all hir chamber stuff the space of 3 monthes./

The suffrance of falss reportes to be made towchyng my doughter in hir honesty.

The quarrellyng ageynst the Lord Tresorer for matters vntrew, and the most of no vallew.

That is to saye /

1. that Clopton and Favnt war by hym mayntened.
2. that Denny the French boye and others that lay in wayte to haue killed Clopton, war punished by the Lord Tresorer
3. That he had not his monny made over sea, so spedely as he desyred.
4. That his wiff was most directed by hir father and mothar.
5. That Hubbard wold not delyver to the Erle his wrytynges wherin it was supposed that he was mayntened by the Lord Tresuror.
6. That his book of entayle was not enrolled wherby the estates war voyd.

To these short and trew answers./
1. they war committed by the Lord Tresorer, and no cause cold be shewed of ther desert and they wer sett to liberty, by the Erle hym self, without knovledg of the Lord Tresorer

2. They war emprisonned by ordre from hir Maiesty gyven to hir Counsell, as they deserved./

3. he had in the space of on[e] yere ijM vijCli [=£2700] and all that sent over by the Creditt of the Lord Tresorer. whan the Erles monny cold not be had./

4. she must be most directed, by hir parentes, whan she had no houss of the Erles to go to, and in hir sicknes and chyld bed only looked to by her parentes.

5. Hubbard never denyed to delyver wrytyng to the knowledg of the Lord Tresour, but rather offred to delyver all so he might be saved harmless against my Lords Creditors, who thretned to arrest hym. and in fyne by the Lord Tresours ernest vrgyng of hym he delyvered all that war required not having such dischardg as he desyred.

6. The book of entayle was never devised by the Lord Tresour, nor yet was he a party therto, nor ever knew whyther it was enrolled or no, vntill a month after that the Erle retorned, that Hubbard told the Lord Tresour, that it was not enrolled, nether that it was to be enrolled, but that it was good without enrollment/

Burghley then adds a note of his own:

The Lord Tresorer did first assure to the Erle and his wiff and the heyres of ther twoo bodyes a mannor of jC viij [=£108] per annum. and because the Erle myght not sell the same awey he was first offended with the Lord Tresorer./ and than vppon surrendre of that estate, the Lord Tresour payd iijMli [=£3000] to and for the Erle. for which some [=sum] after xij in the hundred he might have had iijC lxli [=£360] yerly and his stock retorned/.

The marriag hath cost the Lord Tresorer from the begynning above v or vj M powndes [=£5–6000].

Burghley had given Combe to Oxford and Anne as a wedding present. Irritated that he could not simply liquidate the property, Oxford agreed to its return in exchange for cash settlement of £3000, finally paid about the time Oxford left for Italy.

On the outside of the same folded sheet appear more of Burghley's notes, evidently an outline for a letter of reconciliation:

his own good nature/.

pleasyng of Almighty God, wherin ar conteyned *omnes charitates*

Contentyng of the Queens Maiesty, as by hir dealyng with me it appereth and also with his Lordship

add also the contentation of others his honourable frendes

and that (*blank*) ought to content all his frendes, except ther be any that regard some present or futur proffitt more than his own honor

mislykynges yea hatredes hath amongst manny bene purefyed in tyme.

> The Gretest possession that any man can have, is honor good name, good will of manny, and of the best sort.

Burghley was drawing on his rhetorical and theological resources in hopes of restoring harmony.

By 16 May Anne seems to have resigned herself to a life of exile at Theobalds:[15]

> My Lady [Burghley] & my Lady Oxforde came from London at night & vij servants with them.

On 27 May Dr William Aubrey, who had served as Anne's obstetrician, replied to Burghley's appeal for more complete information.[16] Back on 7 March 1575, Dr Master had recommended 'that there may a note be taken from the day off the first quicknyng',[17] and this seems to have been the information Burghley now requested. Aubrey's entirely noncommittal reply suggests that he has been threatened into silence:

> My dutie moste humblie remembrede to your good Lordship Yf your Lordship shall herafter happen to vnderstande that I haue benn any way movede towchinge your Lorde sheepes [=Lordship's] dougter of Oxforde, I am (as I haue fownde your Lordship my vearie goode Lorde) humblie to beseeke your Lordship of your accustomede wisedome to considere that it cowlde nott ne yet cann lie in me to lette the moovinge for that it growethe from othere But howe pleasawnte the motion was or howe willinge I was or am to heere it, God knoweth it, and my selfe. And your Lordship may gesse by the nature of the mattere and by the liklehode of any good that I may therby hope to my selfe.

> My seconde humble reqweste to your Lordship is that it may please your Lordship to accompte your selfe assurede from me who beste knowethe my owne determination, that I have benn, am, and wilbe as carefull as of my lyffe to do what good I can and to be sure to do no harme; and in all things generallie, and particulerlie in this, to studie that your Lordship may fynde that I will seeke all occasiones, to do my dutie and all good offices to your Lordship and to all yours

> And for that beinge chargede to vse somme secrecie herin it importethe me to haue it to go no furthere than to your Lordship your selfe. I make bolde humblie to putte your Lordship in remembrannce to teare this or to remitte it sealede agayne to me by this berer or otherwise to dispose of it as it shall seeme beste to your good wisedome.

> I did lacke no good will to haue waytede vpon your Lordship my selfe but for respectes that your Lordship may coniecture I dyd nott thinke it conveniente as yet. thus for this tyme I humblie take my leave from your good Lordship

In four paragraphs Aubrey supplies Burghley no information at all. In the first he declares that Burghley must understand that he is prohibited from testifying on Anne's behalf, and that he can do nothing about the prohibition because it has come 'from othere' – doubtless from Oxford. Aubrey asks Burghley to guess the circumstances. In the second paragraph Aubrey declares that his first duty is to save his own life; next after that he places his duty to Burghley and to Burghley's dependents – including Anne. In the third paragraph he informs Burghley that he has been commanded to use secrecy – and he asks Burghley either to tear up the letter, or to send it back with the seal restored, or otherwise dispose of it. (Burghley merely filed it away with his papers.) Finally, Aubrey apologizes for not having gone to Burghley in person: 'your Lordship may coniecture I dyd nott thinke it conveniente as yet'. Aubrey, in short, feared Oxford's violence more than Burghley's authority – and he thought Burghley would understand.

By 12 June Burghley's list of complaints 'To be remembred' grew longer:[18]

> The tyme now past almost of ij monthes without certenty whervppon to rest
>
> Argumentes of vnkyndnes both towardes my daughter his wiff and me also
>
> Nota reiectyng of hir from his Company
>
> Nota not regardyng his child born of hir
>
> Nota his absence from the Court in respect to avoyd his offence / and hir solitary lyung [=living]
>
> reportes of my vncourteuoss or vntrusty dealyng with hym in his absence and therof no prooff, nor particularety avowed but Contrary
>
> my care to gett hym his monny whan his servantes had none
>
> my endevor to have his land sold to the most advantage, or els not to be sold my redynes in his absence to defend his titles of inheritance
>
> my dealyng with his Creditors, to stey ther clamors for ther dettes
>
> my particular svtes to hir Maiesty for his avancement to place of service, and namely to be Master of the hors as hir Maiesty can testefy
>
> Concerning the entaylyng of his landes, I had le[a]st cause of any to lyk therof, for that he barred his issew female, from that whervnto the same was inheritable
>
> for all other his Conveyances at that tyme I did not devise them nor was party to any of them that ar vnresonable.
>
> Conclusion
>
> I desyre that his Lordship will yeld to hir, being his wiff ether that love that a lovyng & honest wiff ought to haue, or otherwise to be so vsed, as all lewd and vayne speches may ceasse [=cease] of his vnkyndnes to hir. and that with his favor and permission she may both come to his presence and be allowed to come to do hir duty to hir Maiesty, if hir Maiesty shall therwith be content, and she shall bear, as she may the lack of the rest, or els, that his Lordship will notefy some iust cause of hir not deservyng such favor, and that she may be permitted to mak hir answer therto befor such as hir Maiesty may please to appoynt

Burghley compiled two more such memoranda, neither dated. The first – as currently bound – contains a list of possible actions:[19]

> To resort to the Master of the Rooles and to shew hym the memoryall.

> To shew the same to Mr [William] Ayliff: and to Mr Iustice Sovthcot

> To intreat them all, to considre such thynges as concern my dovghter the Countess, in such frendly sort as they may for that I am not so mete to press my Lord in any thyng for hir, as others may doo.

> If my Lord allott hir any good portion to mayntean hir self with all, I will order the same, that she being sometyme with me, sometyme in the Court, as much of that portion as can be spared shall be employed to provide necessary thynges for his housholld ageynst his return, wherof he hath gret lack.

> I wold gladly that he wold leave to hir the houss and demayns at Wyvenho if vppon occasion she shuld be compelled to lyve in the Country, and that she might have lodgyng in the Savoy.

> I perceave he wold mak the sonnes of the youngar vncle his heyre male if he co[u]ld,[20] which I thynke he cannot of the Erledom. but he may gyve them some portion and chardg the inheritance with some annuities &c. the doynges herof wold be kept secret for avoydyng of contention betwixt the children and so tell the Master of the Rooles.

> It wer good that a man of possessions such on as [William] Ayliff is wer his receavor.

> my Lord sayth he will committ all his trust to me, but I do not desyre that burden. only I shall be content with an authorite to call all such persons as he shall trust with his causes to accompt, and ether to reform them or to advertise my Lord.

> yow may saye to the Master of the Rooles that my Lord hath promised the Queens Maiesty to be wholly advised by me, and to vse this wiff well and honorably. and so he avoweth to me.

Burghley is still attempting to persuade Oxford to provide Anne with residences befitting a countess, the Savoy in town and Wivenhoe in the country. Burghley also reveals that Oxford wished to make the sons of his younger uncle Geoffrey (John, Francis, Robert or Horace) rather than the sons of his older uncle Aubrey (Hugh or John) his principal male heirs.

The second memorandum lists more responses to Oxford's complaints:[21]

> Manny causes to stey mi Comts [=accounts] that I have held for the Queen principally leste it might offend hir that I shuld deale sharply with hym in reproving hym of his faultes with whom hir Maiesty shewed so much favor

> as his slaunders / lyes / reprochees / only for service / relligion / scottish Quene

> Earl of Oxford vngratefullnes to me that brought hym vpp
>   carefully bountifully

toke care of his possessions
one of Cardynalls a postori
   inhvmanite towardes his wiff whom he first sought
   contempt of God and of all good ordres argving allways agaynst the articles of
   fayth
wastyng of his patrimony.

Duryng his minorety
I preservid his title to his erledom, the Lord Wyndsor attemptyng to haue made
hym illegitimat
I did my best to haue the Iury fynd the death of a poor man whom he killed in my
houss to be found *se defendendo*
I preserved his possessions from incumbrances of titles. I made a less [=lease] that
Cardinall claymed from his father of certen pastvres for his provisions to be free
which afterwardes he graunted awey.
I suffred no wood sales in any of his landes to be made nor no coppys [=copses,
small woods] but left them all voyde for hym self.
I did vse all the good meanes that I cold to haue the case aiudyed [=adjudged] for
hym for the arrerages of the landes that discended to hym over and above the
thyrdes
I did allow to hym so largely for his exhibicion that the Queens Maiesty ha [ends
abruptly]

'Cardynall' was probably William Cardinall, mentioned in subsequent lawsuits.[22]
Burghley recalls his efforts on Oxford's behalf stretching back to the attack on his
legitimacy in 1562–63, and to the killing of Thomas Brincknell in 1567 – which
Burghley mis-remembers as having been settled with a plea of self-defence.
   On 10 July Burghley composed the following memoranda:[23]

Although I both hope and assure my self, that my Lord of Oxford doth now
vnderstand that the conceptions which he had gathered to thynk vnkyndnes in me
towardes hym, war grownded, vppon vntrew reportes of others, as I have manifestly
proved them, yet because I vnderstand, that of late the same vntruthes, ar still
contynued in secret reportes to others, wherby some, which have no cause to thynk
amiss of me, may by gyving creditt to the same, thynk otherwise of me for lack of
knolledge of the truth, than I deserve, or than on[e] of my place or callyng ought to
be thought of, without manifest cause knowen. Therfor vppon such report as I
he[a]re is lately made vntruly and falsly[?] I do as followeth not only avowe the
same to be vntruthes, but the mayntenors and devisors of them to be lyers and
maliciouss backbyters, and such as will so lightly creditt such slaunders of me, to be
light in consideration and Iudgment, and if they will not heare the tryall of the
falshod therof, I must thynk them furderors of vntruthes and vnworthy for my
poore good will or frendshipp.

1. Who so ever sayth that I was the occasion or prive [=privy, secretly informed]
that in my Lord of Oxfordes absence, a certen book of his entaylyng of his landes to
his heyres males, was not enrolled in the Chancery sayth therin vtterly vntruly.

2. Who so ever sayth that I did stey my Lord of Oxfordes monny here so as he had no monny in Italy by the space of vj monthes they saye also vntruly.

Contraryly

1. I saye, and sweare that I was no devisor of that book of entayle, nor was prive to my Lords sealyng and delyvery therof, nor had any trust committed to me to enroll the same, nor yet did heare or vnderstand, duryng the tyme my Lord was absent, nor vntill almost on[e] month after his return, whyther it was enrolled or not enrolled. But after my Lords coming home, hearyng that my Lord was offended with certen other thynges in that book concerning the payement of his dettes, I did almost a month after Ester send to Edward Hvbbard who had the Custody of that book committed to hym, to know who war the deuisors of such thynges therin, as I h[e]ard that my Lord of Oxford dyd mislyk and than also asked of hym whyther it was enrolled or no and he sayd no, wherwith I was offended, as he knoweth, and yet he bare me in hand that ther was no cause why it shuld be enrolled, wherin I did not beleve hym at that tyme and so conceavyng therby that the sayd book was not of such force as I thought it to be, I did in speche with my Lord of Oxford tell hym my self, that if he mislyked of any thyng in that book, he might reform it, for the book wold not bynd hym. And yet afterwardes I was by better lerned than my self assured, and so I do thynk now, that there was no cause to enroll that book. and so eftsoones spekyng with Hubbard he told me that after my Lord of Oxfordes departure, he ment to have enrolled, and he was [informed] by them that ar best experimented, that it was not nedefull[?] to be enrolled, but that it was sufficient without enrollyng.

And so I conclude, that I am vntruly reported herin, and will so avowe it by word and oth. and therof I call God to wytness, to avendg me, if herin I do coller [=colour, misrepresent] any vntreuth.

2. Secondly I did from tyme to tyme for the whole tyme my Lord of Oxford was absente, with my creditt and my bills to Mr Spinola here in London, procure all the monny that was sent over to hym. and to prove that my Lord was not [*sic*] cared for by me, whan ther was no monny to be had of his own by sale of his landes I did, of myn own creditt and having no Counter surance of my Lord, because he shuld not be destitute, procure to be made over seas within the space of the first vj monthes ijM iijC iiijxx xli [=£2390] of which ther was not on[e] penny answered of my Lords own monny, and to prove this, Mr Spinolla vppon my bond, forbare this some, vnpayd to hym neare hand vj monthes

Item to prove that I was carefull for my Lord of Oxford to have monny and not to lack by my bills and Creditt, I having no assurance, ther was made over in the whole from February whan my Lord went, vntill Iune the sayd ijM iijC iiijxx xli. [=£2390] / and from thence vntill Septembre viijC lxjli [=£861] and from thence vntill the 4 of Novembre jM iijC iijxx jli [=£1361] / which amonteth vnto above iiijMli [=£4000] and yet befor my Lord cam home I also gave my bill for viijC [=£800] more to Atkyns who by chance cam not to his Lordship / but yet my care was not the less

And thus I conclude, that I am vniustly and vntruly charged that I did not my dilligence in procuryng of monny to be sent over. And in other thynges I may aswell be vntruly reported, wherof I will allweise [=always] be redy to try my honesty, with confusion of all lyers /

Burghley calculates that he sent Oxford £2390 from February to June, £861 from June to September, and £1361 from September to 4 November, a total of £4802. Additionally, Burghley has sent £800 which did not actually reach Oxford. All this money came directly out of Burghley's pocket. Oxford may have drawn on his own resources, but if so his total expenditure was considerably beyond the £4802 received from Burghley.

Perhaps Burghley did not broadcast his declaration, which sounded very much like a direct challenge. He did, however, meet with Oxford face-to-face on 12 July, as revealed in a letter from Oxford to Burghley on the 13th, written from 'my lo[d]ginge at Charinge Crosse. this morninge. ...' (LL-11):

My verie good lord, yesterday, at yowre Lordships ernest request I had sume conference with yow abought yowre doughter, wherin for that her Magestie had so often moued me, and for that yow delt so ernestly withe me, to content as muche as I could, I dyd agre that yow myght bringe her to the court withe condition that she showld not come when I was present nor at any time to haue speche withe mee, and further that yowre Lordship showld not vrge farther in her cause. But now I vnderstand that yowr Lordship means this day to bringe her to the court and that yow mean afterward to prosecut the cause withe further hop[e]. Now if yowre Lordship shall doo so, then shall yow take more in hand then I haue or can promes yow. for alwayes I haue and will still prefer myne owne content before others. and obseruinge that wherin I may temper or moderat, for yowre sake I will doo most willingely. Wherfore I shall desire yowre Lordship not to take aduantage of my promes till yow haue giuen me sum honorable assurance by letter or word, of yowre performance of the condition which beinge obserued, I caud [=could?] y[i]eld, as it is my dutie to her Magesties request, and beare withe yowre fatherly desire, towards her. otherwise, all that is done can stand to non effect.

Oxford had taken rooms at Charing Cross, as the Court had convened for the brief period 10–22 July at St James's Palace.[24] Acceding to the Queen's request, Oxford would permit Anne to attend the Court, but only when he himself was not there, and on the understanding that Anne would not attempt to speak with him. Oxford further stipulated that Burghley must agree 'by letter or word' not to make further appeals. Burghley swallowed his pride and grief, and for the next five months kept silence.

28 Orazio Coquo

As Burghley's memoranda constitute first-person reports of his agony following Oxford's return from the Continent in April 1576, so Orazio Coquo's testimony to the Venetian Inquisition on his return in August 1577 constitutes an eyewitness report of Oxford's life in Venice and London in 1576 and early 1577. Orazio's interrogation was conducted by Pasquale Ciconia on Tuesday 27 August 1577.[1]

> [Inquisition of] Horatius [=Orazio], son of a certain Francesco Coquo, clerk of the Church of Santa Marina; and he was asked his age: Orazio: I am seventeen years old.
>
> He was asked: Have you been out of this country? Orazio: Sirs, yes.
>
> He was asked: In what place? Orazio: In England. He said further (being asked): It was a year and a half ago, as I recall, that I left this city for England. He said further (being asked): I went with a count related to the Queen of England named My Lord of Oxford ('Millort d'Voxfor').
>
> He was asked: How long did you reside in England? Orazio: Eleven months. He said further (being asked): I lived the whole time in the house of this count.
>
> He was asked: What office did you hold in his house? Orazio: I was a page.
>
> He was asked: Did you live with anyone else? Orazio: Sirs, not while I was in England.
>
> He was asked: How long has it been since you left England? Orazio: Seven or eight months.
>
> He was asked: How long has it been since you arrived back here? Orazio: (I arrived) on the Assumption of the Virgin last (=15 August 1577)
>
> He was asked: With whom did you leave England? Orazio: Only with [certain] gentlemen [Signori].
>
> He was asked: Where were you and with whom in these [past] seven or eight months? Orazio: I lived in Flanders for four months with Captain Signore Juan Battista da Monte, and then I left Antwerp where I lived with the same Captain and I lived in Borgogne for a time, from Borgogne to Lorenzo, and in Lorenzo for a time, and then from Savoia to Cremona, from Cremona to Mantua, from Mantua to Padua, from Padua to Venice.
>
> He was asked: Where did you depart from the Captain? Orazio: At Fontanelle above Cremona.
>
> He was asked: With whom did you come from Fontanelle to here [=Venice]? Orazio: I was alone.
>
> He was asked: Who sent you to join the English earl? Orazio: No one.

He was asked: By what means did it happen that you went with him? Orazio: He heard me singing in the choir at [the church of] Santa Maria Formosa and asked me if I wished to go with him to England; and I came to this count.

He was asked: Did you seek advice from anyone as to whether you should go or not? Orazio: I asked my father and mother, who advised me that I should go; and they died [since] of the plague.

He was asked: Where is this count now? Orazio: In England.

He was asked: Does he live as a Catholic? Orazio: Sirs, no.

He was asked: At the time he invited you to go with him into this country [=England], how long thereafter did he actually depart? Orazio: On 'Fat Thursday' [=1 March 1576] I went to stay in his house, and he departed on Monday of Carnival next following [=5 March 1576]

He was asked: On the Friday and Saturday following Fat Thursday, what did you eat in his house? Orazio: Fish.

He was asked: In England and on the journey to England, what did you eat during Lent and the vigil? Orazio: Fish on the journey because there was no meat available.

He was asked: And in England during Thursday in the vigil and on Saturday what was eaten? Orazio: Meat and fish.

He was asked: On this occasion was there meat during the fasting-period? Orazio: Sirs, no.

He was asked: Were you made to eat meat on days of prohibition? Orazio: Sirs, no. In his house were also a 'romanier' and a gentleman who were Catholic.

He was asked: Were you made to attend the heretics' church services? Orazio: Sirs, no.

He was asked: Did you attend the heretics' church services on your own volition? Orazio: Sirs, no. I went to mass in the house of the ambassadors of France and Portugal.

He was asked: And was there anyone in England who urged you to read prohibited books and to study the doctrine of the heretics? Orazio: Sirs, yes.

He was asked: And who were those people? Orazio: A man called Master Alexandro [Margin: Alexandro Forlan/Furlan]. I think he was banished from Venice on religious grounds. (There was also) another man, one Ambrose Venetiano [=Ambrose of Venice], a musician of the Queen of England, who has two children and has taken a wife there, even though as I understand he has a wife still living in Venice and, they say, he used to send her financial support. And there are also five Venetian brothers who are musicians of the Queen and play flute and viola; and there is a Venetian gentlewoman from Ca' Malipiero who keeps a school and teaches reading and Italian language. And I know of no more.

He was asked: Did you ever speak to the Queen? Orazio: Sirs, yes. And I sang in her presence. He said further (being asked): She wished me to convert to her faith. He said further (being asked): A certain merchant, that is, Signor Christopholo da Monte, a Milanese, told me that I would be corrupted if I remained, and he didn't want me to stay there any longer, and I left for Belgium in the company of other merchants, and he gave me 25 ducats for the journey.

He was asked: Did you receive permission from the count? Orazio: Sirs, no, because he would not have allowed me to leave.

He was asked: During the journey, in Antwerp and in other places where you lived, did you always live as a Catholic? Orazio: Sirs, yes. I came with Italian Catholic soldiers.

He was asked: Since you came back here, did anyone inquire about the Earl with whom you went? Orazio: Sirs, no.

He was asked: What did the Earl do when he was in this city? Orazio: He saw something of the country; he attended mass at the Greek Church [=S. Giorgio]; and he was a person who spoke Latin and Italian well.

He was asked: Whether the Earl had ever wanted him to convert to his faith. Orazio: Sirs, no. He let each person live in his own way.

These things done, [Orazio Coquo] was granted his licence

An event noted in *Coryates Crudities* (1611, p. 225), suggests that Orazio's willingness to join Oxford saved his life:

> In the yeare of our Lord M.D.Lxxvj [=1576], there hapned a most grieuous pestilence in Venice which destroyed at least a hundred thousand persons, but at last God looked downe from heauen with the eyes of mercy, and sodainly stayed the infection.

Orazio's mother and father would both fall victim to the plague. As for Oxford, Orazio reports that he was a great lover of music, and attended churches including the Greek Church – notorious for attracting religious dissidents, with services in Latin (not Greek). Orazio testifies further that Oxford was a fluent speaker of both Italian and Latin.

29 Oxford's Poetry (1)

We have already noted Oxford's first known poem, ostensibly composed on 1 January 1572 and printed in 1573 and 1576 as 'The Earle of Oxenforde to the Reader'. Eight new poems (2–9) appeared in *The Paradyse of Daynty Deuises*, first published in 1576. The title page explains that within the volume are dainty devices, or poems, aptly furnished, with sundry pithie and learned inuentions: deuised and written for the most part, by Master [Richard] Edwards, sometimes of her Maiesties Chappel: the rest by sundry learned Gentlemen, both of honor, and woorshippe. viz.

S. Barnarde.	Jasper Heyvvood.
E. O.	F. K.
L. Vaux.	M. Bevve.
D. S.	R. Hill.

M. Yloop, vvith others.

Oxford is identified both here and in 'signatures' appended to seven poems within the volume as 'E. O.'

Through numerous subsequent editions of *Paradyse*, certain attributions became even more explicit: as early as 1577, 'L. Vaux' sometimes became 'Lord Vaux', 'F. K.', 'F. Kindlemarsh', and 'E. O.', 'E. Ox.' or 'E. Oxf.'.[1]

The nine Oxford poems published by 1576 cover a range of iambic metrical forms:[2]

1: The labouring man that tills the fertile soil (pentameter: alternating rhyme, closing couplet)
2: Even as the wax doth melt (poulter's measure: couplets; possibly stanzaic)
3: A crown of bays shall that man wear (complex format; stanzaic)
4: Framed in the front of forlorne hope (fourteeners: couplets; stanzaic)
5: I am not as I seem to be (tetrameter: ababccdd, stanzaic)
6: If care or skill could conquer vain desire (pentameter: ababcc; stanzaic)
7: My meaning is to work what wonders love hath wrought (poulter's measure: couplets; possibly stanzaic)
8: The lively lark stretcht forth her wing (tetrameter: ababcc; stanzaic)
9: The trickling tears that falls along my cheeks (abab pentameter; cc tetrameter; stanzaic)

Eight poems follow established metrical conventions, including three in pentameter, two in tetrameter, one in fourteeners, and two in poulter's measure. All eight in *Paradyse* are either certainly or probably stanzaic: (2) is printed as three stanzas of six lines each, (4) contains a refrain which recurs every sixth line, (5) is printed as four stanzas of eight lines each, while (7) is printed as two stanzas of four lines, each followed by a closing couplet.

The metrically complex 'A crown of bays shall that man wear' (3) is structured as three stanzas of eight lines or four couplets each, as in the first stanza:

A Croune of Bayes shall that man weare, That triumphs over me:
For blacke and Tawnie will I weare, Which mornyng colours be.

The more I folowed on, the more she fled awaie,
As Daphne did full long agone, Apollo's wishfull praie.

The more my plaints resounde, the lesse she pities me,
The more I saught the lesse I founde, that myne she ment to be.

> *Melpomeney*, alas with doleful tunes helpe than
> And sing *bis* wo worthe on me forsaken man

The first couplet, a kind of opening refrain, is fourteeners with internal rhyme, while the two medial couplets are poulter's measure with internal rhyme. The fourth couplet, a closing refrain, begins (like poulter's measure) with a line of six feet or twelve syllables, but ends with an unmetrical eleven-syllable line:[3]

> And sing *bis* wo worthe on me forsaken man

Here *bis* is Latin for 'twice', while 'wo worth on me' means 'woe be to me' (*OED* worth (v.I.B.I.c)) – all monosyllables except 'forsaken'.

Only slightly less problematic is the thirteen-syllable opening line of (2):

> Even as the wax doth melt, or dew consume away

This would be fine for a poem of fourteeners, but as the balance of the poem is poulter's measure the line must be reduced to twelve syllables, perhaps 'E'en as the wax doth melt, or dew consume away'. Though the line now scans, a stress falls unnaturally on 'as'.

Unnatural stresses occur not infrequently in Oxford's poems, as in these two examples:

> u / u / u / u / u/u /
> For my best luck leads me to such sinister state (2)

The otherwise natural rhythm of the line produces 'leads ME' for 'LEADS me' ('sin-IS-ter', however, is probably correct: see *OED*).

> u / u / u / u / u / u /
> Drown me you trickling tears, you wailful wights of woe (3)

Here the unnatural 'drown ME' struggles with 'DROWN me' – and so forth.

Heavy, throbbing alliteration is characteristic of Oxford's verse, as in these extreme examples:

> Thus like a woefull wight, I wove my web of woe (1)

> My life through lingring long is lodged, in lare of lothsome wayes (2)

> Help fish, help foul, that flocks and feeds upon the salte sea soil (4)

In the last, f galumphs through the four opening feet of the heptameter line, s through the three closing syllables.

Other faults in Oxford's verse include inverted word order, and line-fillers in rhyme positions, shown here with two instances of each:

> With due desert reward will never be (1) (for 'reward will never be with [=follow] due desert')

And helpe for thee there is none sure (9) (for 'there is none sure help for thee')

The greyhound thereby doth miss his game we know (1)

And others yet do gather them, that took less pain I know (2)

Faults are legion in Oxford's earliest known poem (1), composed well past his twenty-first birthday. It begins awkwardly:

> The labouring man, that tills the fertile soil,
> And reaps the harvest fruit, hath not indeed
> The gain but paine, and if for all his toile
> He gets the straw, the Lord will haue the seed.

Here 'indeed', a line-filler supplying a rhyme for 'seed', increases the distance between the verb in line 2 and its objects in line 3 ('gain' / 'pain'). Even worse is the closing couplet:

> For he that beats the bush the bird not gets,
> But who sits still, and holdeth fast the nets.

The dog-trot iambs, heavy alliteration on 'beats', 'bush' and 'bird', and the inverted 'bird not gets' are so atrocious that we might hope the poem was written by Thomas Bedingfield and merely given out for Oxford's. Such a hope is dashed, however, by Oxford's use of the same conceit in (2):

> And he that beats the bush, the wished bird not gets,
> But such I see as sitteth still, and holds the fowling nets.

Here 'wished', 'I see', and 'fowling' merely stretch pentameters into fourteeners, while normal word order is sacrificed to make 'gets' rhyme with 'nets'. Oxford's clumsiness may be contrasted with Edmund Spenser's disposition of the same conceit in *Shepheardes Calendar* (1579), 'October' (l. 17):

> I beate the bush, the byrds to them doe flye

Oxford would use the conceit two decades later in a private letter to Burghley:[4]

> Thus I was to have beaten the bushe, whylst other howldinge the nett, had taken the bwyrd.

Here, as elsewhere, Oxford's prose is better than his verse. The numbing repetition that burdens his verse can nevertheless burden his prose, as in his letter to Bedingfield:

> What doth auaile the tree vnlesse it yeld fruite vnto an other, what doth auaile the Vyne vnlesse an other delighteth in the Grape? What doth auaile the Rose vnlesse an other toke pleasure in the smell? Whye should this tree be accompted better then that tree, but for the goodnes of his fruite? Whye should this Vyne be better then that Vyne, vnlesse it brought forth a better Grape than the other? Whye

should this Rose be better esteemed then that Rose, vnlesse in pleasantnes of smel it farre surpassed the other Rose? And so is it in al other thinges as well as in man. Whye should this man, be more esteemed then that man, but for his vertue, throughe which euerye man desireth to be accompted of.

Not that Oxford is entirely without talent. The refrain of (2), '[I] never am lesse idle loe, then when I am alone', for example, is memorable – only the filler 'loe' offends.

We have noted how odd it is for a man who was himself a lord, a landlord, a resident of 'Lordlye halles', to decry inequality. The same egocentric, cry-baby attitude runs throughout Oxford's poems. 'Even as the wax doth melt' (2) recapitulates 'The labouring man' (1); 'A crown of bays' (3) grudgingly compliments a rival in love, but complains against the woman who has rejected the poet, making him want to 'hide myself from shame'; 'Framed in the front of forlorne hope' (4) repeats the theme of shame without disclosing a specific cause; 'I am not as I seem to be' (5, a variant on Petrarch's Sonnet 102), laments the misfortune 'That forceth me to love my foe'; while 'If care or skill could conquer vain desire' (6) browbeats a beloved who alone among her sex disdains gifts of Venus, Juno, and Pallas. 'My meaning is to work what wonders love hath wrought' (7) muses 'why men of wit have love so dearly bought' – observing that 'love is worse than hate, and eke more harm hath done': but there is no escape, so that the poet is like a cruel judge who embraces the very crime he punishes in others. The last of these early poems, 'The trickling tears that falls along my cheeks' (9), ends with a prayer that the tables may be turned: 'And let her mourn, and none lament her need':

> And let all those that shall her see,
> Despise her state, and pity me.

Not for Oxford Sir Thomas Wyatt's gentle recognition that unrequited love is the lot of all: no, this poet hates the woman who has dared to reject him, and hopes the rest of the world will hate her too.

'The lively lark stretcht forth her wing' (8), the best of Oxford's nine early poems, is apparently original; it nevertheless anticipates (11), which is translated from the Italian. 'The lively lark' is the only early poem known to have been copied into a manuscript anthology.[5] It is written in tetrameter, which seems to have kept Oxford from faults of wordiness. In the version selected by May as superior to all others the poem allows – if it does not positively invite – a homoerotic interpretation:[6]

> The Lyvely Larke stretcht forth her wynge,
>   The messenger of morninge bright;
> And with her Chearfull voyce did Singe
>   The dayes approache discharginge Nyght,
> When that Aurora blushinge Redd
>   Dyscride the guylt of Thetis Bedd.

I went abroad to take the Ayre,
   And in the meades I mette a knyght
Clad in Carnation Colour fayre.
   I did salute this gentle wyght,
Of him I did his name enquyre;
   He sighed, and sayd he was Desyre.

Desire I did desire to stay;
   Awhile with him I cravde to talke.
The Courteous knyght said me no nay,
   But hand in hand with me did walke.
Then of Desyre I askde agayne:
   What thinge did please and what did payne?

He smylde, and thus he answerd than:
   Desire can have no greater payne,
Then for to see an other man
   That he desirethe to obtayne;
Nor greater joy Can be than this,
   Than to enjoy that others mysse.

Though 'Desire' is clearly allegorical, the poem seems to recall a chance meeting between two men 'in the meades' early one morning. Inclined to talk, they walk hand-in-hand. The poet asks: What gives pleasure; and what brings pain? He is answered: Nothing gives greater pain than to see another man enjoy that which he himself desires; nothing gives greater pleasure than to enjoy what others miss out on.

The potentially homoerotic meaning that I have extracted from 'The lively lark' may misrepresent the author's 'intended' meaning, for the final stanza is more or less defective in all surviving versions. The printed version, for example, suffers from an obviously corrupt fifth line:[7]

He smild and thus he answered me,
Desire can haue no greater paine:
Then for to see an other man,
The thyng desired to obtaine,
No ioye no greater to then this,
Then to inioye what others misse

The stanza is less obviously corrupt in a manuscript version:[8]

He smylde, and thus he answerd than:
   Desire can have no greater payne
Then for to see an other man
   The thinge desyred to obtayne;
Nor greater joy can be than this,
   That to enjoy that others mysse.
          Finis. Earle of Oxforde

Even rationalized, or perhaps merely corrected, 'The Lyvely Larke' perversely insists that the greatest joy of love is to have one's beloved at the expense of another. True pleasure comes not from winning the beloved, but from besting a (male) rival. The disappearance of the poem from print after the first edition, along with its survival in three manuscripts, supports – but does not prove – the supposition that it was considered scandalous.

PART V

Alienation
1576–1579

30 The Lure of Rome

On 21 August 1576 the Privy Council issued a directive concerning 'lewde wordes':[1]

> A letter to Sir William Walgrave, Sir Thomas Lucas, knightes, Henrye Golding and John Tornour, esquiers, for thexamininge of a Dutche man touchinge lewde wordes by him used against the Earle of Oxford, &c., acording to the minute, &c.

Walgrave was an Essex magnate, as were the now-familiar Lucas, Golding, and Turner.[2] The Dutchman and a companion were imprisoned until 15 February 1577:[3]

> A letter to the Bailiffes of Colchester to set at libertie Walter De Fourde and Basirie Linghoer, Duchemen, committed to the goale for having spoken lewde wordes of the Earle of Oxford, which they are sory for, alleadging that they mistoke him for the Earle of Westmerland; wherefore thinking that this their imprysonment is sufficient, upon some good lesson and submyssion to be taken of them in the presence of sum witnesses of both nations, they shold sett them at libertie.

Deflecting their charge of treason from Oxford to Westmorland, the two were released.

On 8 September 1576 William Lewin wrote to Sturmius in Zurich, who was seeking financial support from Burghley:[4]

> ... I perceive that you inquire respecting the earl of Oxford, whether he did not recommend your case to [Sir Amias] Paulet. But you must know that I diligently interested myself with the earl, who replied, that he would not only recommend his friend Sturmius to Paulet, but would also request the earl of Leicester to recommend him in every possible way. He added also, that unless you are relieved from France, he will take care that assistance shall be obtained for you in England; lastly, that he had a most high opinion of you, and had made most honourable mention of you; which things afforded me the greatest pleasure when I heard them, and certainly ought to delight you on being informed of them. But do you, as an old man, both make much of our archbishop [=Matthew Parker], who is also advanced in years, and who is so firm and stedfast in friendship; and do not disparage this young earl, who has so favourable an opinion of you: from both I

dare hope every thing, while from the one I dare promise every thing.

But now, my Sturmius, you will perhaps expect me to state what I advise or recommend to yourself. First of all, you should write as soon as possible to sir Amias Paulet, knight, and who will be our ambassador in France before this letter reaches you. You may state what you have heard from me from England, especially respecting the good-will and interest on your behalf manifested by the lord archbishop; and you may, if you please, add that of the lord treasurer [=Burghley] and sir Francis Walsingham. I hope also that the earls of Leicester and Oxford will commend you to Paulet, but this is not yet ascertained by me: I heard from the earl of Oxford that they would do so, but do not yet understand that they have done it.

We will discover that Lewin was quite wrong to assume that Oxford's interests abroad lay with the Protestants rather than the Catholic opposition.

On 5 December the wife of Sir John Petre of Essex paid off a 'bargain' (or wager) of £2:[5]

Deliuered to my ladye the vth daie to geve to Mr Lychefelde one of the erle of Oxfordes men, lost to him vpon a bergayne made with him when she was a mayde, to be paid when she shoulde be a ladye xls

The recipient was Henry Lichfild, author of *The First Set of Madrigals of 5. Parts*, published in 1613 when he was in the employ of Lady Cheyney of Toddington, near Luton, hired as her steward and only secondarily a domestic musician (*New Grove*). Presumably Lichfild rendered similar services to Oxford.

On 1 January 1577 the Queen gave Countess Anne a gilt plate weighing 27¾ ounces; Anne reciprocated with 'a Iuell being an agathed [=agate] garnesshed with golde and a lawrell garlonde garnesshed abought with Sperkes of Rubyes and a pendant with viij Sparkes of rubys & a hophall [=opal] in the mydes [=midst]'. No gift is recorded this year either to or from Oxford.[6]

On the same day Burghley broke the silence that Oxford had enjoined on him the previous July:[7]

My Lord: My scilence and forebearing of speech to your Lordship (nowe a good time) in a cause of that waight [=weight, heaviness] to me as concerneth soe nearely my dearest beloued daughter your Lordships wife – hath hitherto proceeded partly in hope that after some space of monethes some change to the better might followe, partly to avoid the offending of you in whome I haue seene some changes from your old wonted Countenance, but considering with my selfe & that seriously, how long both I as a father to your afflicted wife (and be it spoken without offence of Comparison) for my part as loveing and as well deserving a freind towardes you since I first knew you as anie whosoeuer of anie degree, And alsoe your loveing, faithfull and dutifull wife hath suffered the lack of your love, Conversacion and Company – though in seuerall respectes desired, yea in some sort due by seueral desertes to vs. I cannot my Lord see this old yeare passed with such disgraces, and a new entered meete to record a concourse of graces, nor feele the burthen of the griefes to growe as they dayly doe without apparance of amendment, but assay by reasonable meanes to seeke reliefe, specially for my daughter whose griefe is the greater & shall alwaies bee inasmuch as her love is most fervent and addicted to you and because she cannot or may not without offence be suffered to Come to your presence as she desireth to offer the sacrifice of her heart, nor can I find oppertunitie in open places where wee sometymes meete to reveale my griefes, both for myselfe, but especially to relieve them for my daughter. I doe heartily by this my instant lettre beseech your Lordship (and by Contestacion of your honour I require you[)] to assent that I may haue some time convenient to speake with your Lordship in your owne Chamber or in some other meete place meaning not to move anie thing to your Lordship but that shall proceede from a ground of meere love towardes you, and that shalbe agreeable to your Honour and calling, to your profitt and Comfort and not vnmeete for either of vs both. And if your Lordship shall for anie respect though vnknowne to me like to haue any person of noble or other good degree present I shall not refuse the presence of any such to be named by your Lordships selfe. And to this my request (my Lord) I pray you giue me answer by this bearer as it shall please you by speech or by writing, haveing made noe body privy with this my lettre. ...

No answer has survived, and reconciliation would have to wait nearly five more years.

Anne remained a fixture of the Burghley household, along with little Elizabeth, eighteen months old on 2 January, and still a stranger to her father. Anne's presence is recorded in the Theobalds' kitchen-book; also present was Robert Devereux, 2nd Earl of Essex, Burghley's ward since September of the previous year, whose name first appears on 28 March, in the middle of his tenth year.[8] A particularly extensive entry appears under Thursday, Friday, and Saturday, 16–18 May:[9]

This weke the Queens Maiestie with herre Lordes, Ladies, & Ientellmen was at my Lorddes house at Thebaldes. there [=three] dayes, viz. Thursdaye, ffrydaye & sattardaye ...

Two subsequent entries record Anne's movements:

June 18: The Covntes of Oxford & My Ladye at my Lorde Maiors house in Hackney
August 28: My Lorde & the Ladies came from Burlle [=Burghley House]

Not once in these records are Oxford and Anne on record as being in the same place at the same time, nor is Oxford ever recorded in the company of 'the children'.

Having arrived at Dover with Oxford on or about 20 April 1576, Orazio Coquo took his French leave on or about 20 March 1577: we will discover that he was replaced by other boys and other pages. About this time Oxford became deeply involved in pro-Catholic conspiracies, as recalled in the French ambassador Mauvissière's dispatch of 11 January 1581:[10]

... about four and a half years ago on his return from Italy[, Oxford] made
profession of the Catholic faith together with some of his relatives among the
nobility and his best friends, and had sworn, as he says, and signed with them a
declaration that they would do all they could for the advancement of the Catholic
religion ...

Henry Howard and Charles Arundel both recall Oxford's miraculous vision of
Christ crucified, as the priest Stevens held the consecrated eucharist between his
hands (LIB-3.1/3@51; 4.2/2.13). But Oxford accused his accusers, in a scene
described by Mauvissière:

The Earl of Oxford, finding himself alone and unsupported [in December 1580],
threw himself on his knees several times before the Queen, and begged her to hear
from my lips whether it was not true that I knew of a Jesuit who had celebrated the
Mass about four years ago at which they [=Howard, Arundel, and Southwell] were
reconciled to the Roman Church.

Howard and Arundel admitted attending a mass celebrated by one Stevens in
Southwell's chamber six years earlier; Southwell also acknowledged the mass in a
private note to Howard.[11] Howard and Arundel date the mass impossibly early,
doubtless to persuade the authorities that it had occurred prior to the Privy
Council's act of 20 October 1573 declaring the celebration of and attendance on
masses outside the precincts of approved churches illegal (*TRP*, No. 599). Both
Arundel and Southwell adamantly denied that this was a mass of reconciliation
(LIB-2.1.5/2; 2.2.3/5; 2.3.1/2; 3.6.2@148). If we take Mauvissière literally, Oxford
reconciled about July 1576, while Stevens celebrated the mass of reconciliation
about January 1577. Mauvissière may be taken as the more credible witness
because his personal involvement was less.

Though Arundel confessed that 'Oxford was never at mass in our company'
(LIB-2.3.1/1), he testified that Oxford was involved with the priest Stevens for
two reasons. First, Oxford wished to please 'his reconciled schoolmaster' (LIB-
2.3.1@109). Oxford's only known schoolmasters, however, were Thomas Fowle
and Laurence Nowell, both Protestants. Even admitting the coincidence that
Nowell died in late 1576,[12] it would be a stretch to imagine that he reconciled on
his deathbed. Perhaps Arundel had yet another schoolmaster in mind of whose
identity we remain ignorant.

Second, Arundel reported that Oxford, 'being greveid in conscience about the
killing of (*blank*) as it semed, abowte a five year since desired conference with
some learnid man whervppon I brought him vnto (*blank*)' (LIB-4.1.1). The learned
man was almost certainly the priest Stevens. If by 'abowte a five year since' Arundel
meant about five years prior to the date of the conference, we may guess that the
murder on Oxford's conscience was that of George Saunders, killed by George
Brown in 1573. If, however, he meant about five years prior to the declaration, the
victim may have been William Sankey, whose story we are about to learn.

Mauvissière attributed to Oxford yet another act of sedition:

> [Oxford] reminded me that he had sent me a message begging me to assist the said
> Jesuit to return in safety to France and Italy, and that when I had done so he gave
> me his thanks.

Mauvissière seems to concede he had rendered assistance; as we shall see, however, it was evidently Oxford above all who expedited Stevens's return to France.

Details concerning 'the said Jesuit' closely match the story of Richard Stevens,
a native of Salisbury and student at New College, Oxford, where he had been
considered a Catholic; thereafter he became secretary to John Jewel, Bishop of
Salisbury. Upon Jewel's death in 1571 Stevens took service with Matthew Parker,
Archbishop of Canterbury, whereupon, apparently at the urging of a prisoner
named Boxall, he re-converted, embarking in 1574 for Douai with a dozen other
Catholics. On 19 April 1576 he became STB and was ordained to the priesthood.
Three months later, on 23 July, he left for Paris with Francis Cotton and others.
Returning to Douai, he left for England on 10 November, probably arriving on
the 11th or 12th.[13]

Arundel reports that Stevens kept lodgings in Holborn, just outside the north-
west corner of London's wall (LIB-2.1.5/21). A man of principle, Stevens earned
Oxford's wrath 'for refuseinge to geve him the sacrament, till he promisid to
receave his wife againe' (LIB-4.2.9/8). On 14 July 1577 Stevens returned to Douai,
again in the company of Francis Cotton,[14] having presumably left England on or
about 12 July. Not an active seeker after martyrdom, Stevens continued to study
(evidently at Douai) and attained his doctorate in theology by 19 April 1586.

The means of Stevens's escape from England is suggested by articles of
complaint dated 1577 on independent grounds. The first two articles establish a
general background, and family connections:[15]

> There be divers bold disorders and riotous assemblies of diverse Papistes at
> Colchester and there neare about. Which [contribute] to the greate greife of many
> good men.

> There is one Mistris Awdley, a widowe, basterd daughter of Sir Richard Southwell,
> a verie welthie and dangerous woman. There meete verie often papistes, well
> knowen, by 20 or 30 at a tyme. Shee dwelleth at Beerechurch within Colchester
> iurisdicion. There hath been Masse said commonly; it is like to bee so still.

Mistress Audley of Colchester, born Kate Southwell, was in fact the sole legitimate issue of Sir Richard Southwell of Woodrising, Norfolk. A strong-minded
woman who wore her recusancy as a badge of honour,[16] she was an aunt of Robert
Southwell, the Jesuit poet who would be martyred in 1595. Her manor, Berechurch, lay within Colchester, south of the town centre.[17] Kate's illegitimate half-
sister Mary wed Dr William Drury of Brett's Hill at Tendring, the subject of
another article of the complaint:

Doctor Drewrie dwelleth at Wivenowe neare Colchester vppon the waters syde, and there dw[elle]th one Loue, a mariner whome he mainteineth. This Loue is a Shipmaster and carieth newes and bringeth newes (as it seemeth) ... he caried awaye Mistris Awdleys sonne and a masse priest from her howse over the Sea to Doway.

Love is probably the yeoman of Colchester indicted on 3 March 1575 for dealing in engrossed agricultural products: 'which John Love carried overseas, contrary to statute'.[18] On 10 November 1576, the very day Richard Stevens embarked for England, a 'Mr Sowtwellus' and an 'Audleius' departed with others from Douai. On 15 June 1577 Mr Thomas Smith STB returned from Paris with 'three splendid young disciples' – one Southwell and two Audleys[19] – probably all close kin of the Southwell–Audley clan. We have seen that Wivenhoe was one of Oxford's three principal residences in Essex, that it contained a 'lading place', and that when Oxford himself fled abroad in 1574, 'He toke shipping by his howse in Essex'.

A letter from Leicester to Burghley dated 13 June 1577 suggests that Oxford was again restless:[20]

I am sorry my Lord of Oxford shuld for any respect think any more of going over sea. I can but wyshe and advyse him to take such a[d]vyce in all thinges as were best & most honorable for him & spetyally in his considercion toward her maiestie & his contrey.

Secret correspondence between Mauvissière and the French King Henri III gives substance to Leicester's anxiety, for on 12 July and again on 5 September the King consulted the ambassador concerning 'le jeune Comte d'Oxford' – alternatively '[le]dit jeune Seigneur Comte d'Oxford'.[21] Given that 'jeune' serves as a constant epithet, there can be no question of the reference in a letter from Mauvissière to the King on 23 September, concerning *the five ships* which have been offered to me and are offered daily on behalf *of a jeune seigneur* whom I have previously named'.[22] Both the selected encoding (here italicized) and the suppression of the proper name underline the secrecy of the offer. Also on 23 September, the King wrote from Poitiers concerning 'English vessels' commanded and led by 'un Milord d'Angleterre'.[23] Oxford seems indeed to have agreed that he and his associates would lead a revolt of the 'Catholic Party' on the condition that they would receive support from France.[24]

Meanwhile, certain of Oxford's men were active in Catholic affairs abroad. On 10 July Amias Paulet wrote to Walsingham from Poitiers:[25]

This bearrer intendeth nothing lesse then to remayne here with me, ... haueing resoluid to follow the Duke of Guyse into Champaigne, as the twoe yonge Veares, Denny, seruant to the Erle of Oxford, and Walter Williams (whoe are now here) doe the like. ...

On 24 September Paulet wrote again to Walsingham:[26]

Whereas your Honor desirethe to be advertised yf I did give a horse to the yonge Vere, I begine to doubt herein if my doinges haue ben brought in question, and shall not be quiet vntill I heare from you of the trew cause of this your motion, wherof I shall most humbly pray you, not doubtinge but the truethe of the matter will defend me against the malice of the envious. The two yonge Veres came to this towne accompanied with Denny and Williams, and after two or three dayes the elder Vere and Williams came vnto to me (the yonge Vere and Denny I did not see,) and after some wordes of courtesie this Vere told me that he came into this contrye with intent to serve in the warres, and findinge the armye of Monsieur broken, and thereby frustrat of his expectation, was constrained to retorne to Parys, and being vnprovided of money to hire post-horses, should be constrained to make this voyage on his fete onleast [=unless] I did provide him of some remedye, and therefor desired mee to doe him the pleasure to bestow a horse vppon him, sayinge that he doubted not but that the Earle of Oxford would be thankefull vnto me for yt. I answered I had not so many horses as I had servants, that I was subiect to dayly removes, that I was farre from any meane to recouer new horses, and therfore might not well spare the horses which I had alreadye. He confessed me he was very bold with me vppon so small acquaintance (as in deed I had never seen him before), but was constrained therevnto by necessytie, wherof he prayed me to haue soche consyderac[i]on as I might. I told him that I would be ashamed for the honor of my countreye and for the reputacion of the Earle of Oxford that he should goe to Paris on fete, and therefore would provide him of an amblinge nagge which would be good ynnoughe and great ynoughe to carye him to Paris, trustinge that he did not loke for a horse of service at my handes, which I could not spare in theise dangerous tymes. I caused the horse to be deliuered to this gentleman accordinge to my promis, whoe sold him the next daye and prayd Mr Locke (whoe was then here and hathe said this moche to some of my servants) to say nothinge of this horse to my Lord of Oxford.

'Mr Locke' was evidently Oxford's servant Henry Lok. Paulet continued:

The askinge of the horse so earnestlye, the sellinge of him so sodainelye, and his vnwillingnes that my Lord of Oxford shoulde knowe that he had ben anye way behouldinge vnto me, doe decipher the disposition of the gentleman. God send him better companye to make him a better man! Thus haue I deliuered vnto you truly and faithefullye how and in what manner this horse was given, and now yt may please you to give me leave to answere an obiection, which perchaunce is not ment or intendede. Yt may be said that, knowinge his intencion to serve the Kinge's partie, vnder the leadinge of the Duke of Guys [Guise], I ought not to haue given him anye aid or succoure. Surelye yf he had been my kinsman or familiar frind, I wold not haue fayled to haue diswaded the voyage, but others had been recommended not longe before by great personages of England, to serve here in like sorte, and Mr Locke had told mee that those only had the reputation amonge the nobilitye of the court that sought to serve the King's side, and therefore, in my symple opinion, I had playd the foole yf I hade made a quarell of this matter, which did nether touch me nor ymport the cause to any purpose, and yet you may be assured no man might perswade me to geve to any man anye matter mete for service in this case. And to be plaine with you, I was not sorye to see some yonge felowes, especiallie soche as were of no great countenaunce or service, to ioyne themselues with the King's partie, which might serve to have excused the yonge (*blank*) and soche others as Mr Locke said to be then readie to goe to Rochell, and haue ben affirmed that yonge felowes sought there as best liked them, and that soche as served the Frenche King were not misliked by her Maiestie, and, indeed, I did help my selfe with this argument yn my speache with Queene Mother about that tyme, as may appere by my lettres, I am jalous of my poore creditt, which maketh me to be so troblesome vnto you, not doubtinge but that your Honor will pardon me in a greater fault.

Still later, on 19 November, Paulet wrote to Walsingham yet again from Poitiers:[27]

There is a badd nest of theise felowes in this towne, and there are dayly meetinges and consultacions betweene them. Denny and Williams are recomended to Don John by the Duke of Guise, and serve in the Castle of Namure; where are also Wiseman, Blomfield, Owen, Digby, and diuers others Englishe men. ...

Wiseman may have been William Wyseman, a Catholic recusant from Broadoaks, Essex.[28]

Years later, on 17 November 1605, Francis Vere recalled a youthful indiscretion:[29]

Most honorable, I receyued the enclosead from Thomas Morgan this mornyng by on[e] Wylmer a stranger to me butt as he saythe weall knowen to Syr Wyllyam Waad itt was delyuered hym by Syr Roberte Dormer, the contents ar strange to me for I neuer borrowead mony of hym nor to my remembrance spake with hym butt suche a man I sawe when I was verrye yonge at Paris by reason of the companye I keapt with Syr Roger Wyllyames and on[e] Denys a frencheman followers of my Lord of Oxfordes to whom he sometymes resortead. It is trew I was for a tyme with the Duke of Guise as your Lordship may haue heard: [I] was callead thence by her Maiesties commandment and made to knowe the error of thatt course which hathe seruead me for a warnyng euer synce. The man is knowne to be no weallwisher to this state, and I cannott guease [=guess] what his purpos is in challendgyng a supposead debt of 30 yeers owld in this conjuncture of troublesume and traiterous practyses; butt his meaning I take hathe some further scoape, and therefor I thought itt my deewty to acquaynt your Lordship with his lette[r] and theas feaw cyrcumstances, being ready if need requyre to attend your Lordship for your further satisfactyon reastyng euer your Lordships.

Vere, together with his youthful companions, Oxford's men one and all, was thus indeed 'with the Duke of Guise'.

Back in England on the domestic front, R. Brakinbury wrote to Rutland on 15 February:[30]

This will be a long Lent to Lady Mary Vere and Mrs. Sydney, for at Easter consummatum est. ... Lord Pembroke is much made of, and lodged in the house; Lord Oxford is in the old sort. Lord Howard is great with Sir William.

Henry Herbert, 2nd Earl of Pembroke, would take Mary Sidney (Philip's sister) as his third wife on 21 April (*Peerage*), Mary Vere evidently having been Mary Sidney's rival in the match. On 16 February Thomas Screven reported still other prospects in a letter to Rutland:[31]

> Most think that a marriage will take effect between the Earl of Hertford and Mrs. Frances Howard, and also between Lord Garrat and Lady Mary Vere.

Gerald Fitzgerald, commonly styled Lord Garrat, was a known acquaintance of Oxford's – he was to meet a premature death in June 1580.

On Monday 8 April, as we have noticed, when Burghley was with Anne, Oxford was at Court, along with Burghley's wife:[32]

> Thearle & my Lady at the Courte

Though Oxford received seven of eight possible votes for the Garter this year (G-BL), Burghley abstained, nor did Elizabeth make the appointment. Now twenty-seven, Oxford must have felt more than ever like an outsider among insiders.

Lady Mary did not in fact marry Lord Garrat, but became engaged instead to Peregrine Bertie. On 2 July the Countess of Suffolk, Peregrine's mother, wrote to Burghley, objecting to both Mary and Oxford:[33]

> It is very true that my wise son has gone very far with my Lady Mary Vere, I fear too far to turn. I must say to you in counsel what I have said to her plainly, that I had rather he had matched in any other place; and I told her the causes. Her friends made small account of me; her brother did what in him lay to deface my husband and son; besides, our religions agree not, and I cannot tell what more. If she [=Mary Vere] should prove like her brother, if an empire follows her I should be sorry to match so. She said that she could not rule her brother's tongue, nor help the rest of his faults, but for herself she trusted so to use her as I should have no cause to mislike her. And seeing that it was so far forth between my son and her, she deserved my good will and asked no more. 'That is a seemly thing', quoth I, 'for you to live on; for I fear that Master Bertie will so much mislike of these dealings that he will give little more than his good will, if he give that. Besides, if Her Majesty shall mislike of it, sure we turn him to the wide world.' She told me how Lord Sussex and Master Hatton had promised to speak for her to the Queen, and that I would require you to do the like. I told her her brother used you and your daughter so evil that I could not require you to deal in it. Well, if I would write, she knew you would do it for my sake; and since there was no undoing it, she trusted I could, for my son's sake, help now.
>
> But God knows I did it not so but for fear of this marriage and quarrels. Within this fortnight there was one spoke to me for one Mistress Gaymege, an heir of a thousand marks land, which had been a meeter match for my son.

The Countess's husband – Peregrine's father – was Richard Bertie. The Countess felt she had been injured by Oxford's 'tongue', and by the fact that he 'did what in him lay to deface my husband and son'. Her objections recall Edward Bacon's letter of 13 May 1574, reporting 'a most vile libell fownd in court'.

On 14 July the Countess wrote to Burghley once more, from Willoughby House:[34]

> My good Lord, I received this letter here enclosed yesterday from my husband wherein your Lordship may perceive his head is troubled, as I not blame him. But if he knew as much as I of my good Lord of Oxford's dealings it would trouble him more. But the case standing as it doth I mean to keep it from him. ... I cannot express how much this grieveth me, that my son, in the weightiest matter, hath so forgotten himself to the trouble and disquiet of his friends, and like enough to be his own undoing and the young lady's too. For if my Lord of Oxford's wilfulness come to my husband's ears I believe he would make his son but small marriage.
>
> I wot not what to do therein. If I should stay for Her Majesty's good will in it, and my husband far off from it, you know he cannot take that well at my hand, that I should seek to bestow his son as it were against his will ... and so I am dead at my wit's end. And yet I think if Her Majesty could be won to like it, I am sure my husband would be the easier won to it, if my Lord of Oxford's great uncourteousness do not too much trouble him.
>
> My good Lord, I cannot tell what to do or say in this; but as my good Lord and very friend I commit myself and the case to your good advice and counsel and help.

The Countess knows – and her husband does not – of 'my good Lord of Oxford's dealings', of 'my Lord of Oxford's wilfulness'.

Meanwhile, Oxford had not overlooked the need to repair his finances. On 25 July John Stanhope added a postscript to a letter to Burghley:[35]

> Yt maye further plese your lordship to be advertysed that my Lord of Oxforde gyveth hys diligente attendance on her Majestye and earnestly laboreth his sute, the which he was once perswaded and had yelded to leve, but now renewinge it with intente to procede therin for his owne good, sum unkyndnes and strangnes ensueth betwixt my Lord of Surrey, my Lord Harrye, and his Lordship. Yt is saide her Majestye hathe promysed to gyve him the fesymple [=fee simple, outright owner-ship] of Rysinge and as much more of those landes in fee farme as shall make up the sum of two hundred and fifty pounds.

Castle Rysing was a Howard property forfeited to the crown by the attainder of Norfolk five years earlier. Philip Howard, styled Earl of Surrey, and Henry, his uncle, were prepared to resent its loss to their clan, a sentiment which had given rise to 'sum unkyndnes and strangnes' between the two parties.

31 Murder by Hire

The closing days of July 1577 witnessed a murder recalled by Henry Howard in December 1580:[1]

> ... Wekes was comaundid to kill Sankie my Lords man, and so he did after he was turned away because he wold not geue the stabbe to York, when he mette him in Holborne. Wekes confessed with what violence he had bene sette [on] by my lord [=Oxford] after he [=Weekes] had woundid him [=Sankey] to the death without eyther cause ore courage; [Weekes told it on] his death, both to the minester, his wife, and diuerse others. Thus laid he suche straight wayte for Rowland York that George Whitney had lyke to be slayne for him one night at the Horse Heade in Cheape.

Charles Arundel tells the same story but with other details. He characterizes Sankey as 'beinge sometime a speciall favorite to this Monster' – meaning Oxford; specifies that Weekes confessed to the minister 'at the gallous'; and reports that Oxford 'gave him a hundrid powndes in gold after the murder committid to shifte him a waye, and so muche was fownd abowte [him] when he was apprehendid'.[2]

Sankey's murder occupied the Privy Council on 27 November:[3]

> A letter to the Bishop of Durham that where their Lordships are geven to understand that there is one William Weekes latelie apprehended within the Bushopricke of Durham upon suspicion of a murder by him to be committed in London about July last past; for that the frinds of the partie slaine have ben humble suiters unto their Lordships that the said Weekes might be brought to London, where the facte was comitted, the rather for that there be manie circumstances depending on the said facte which cannot be so convenientlie dealt in wher he now remaineth, he being so farr from London, his Lordship is therfore required accordingly to cause the person of the said Weekes forthwith to be delivered to Hamblet Holcraft, the bearer herof, taking sufficient bands [=bonds] of him to her Majesties use for the safe delivering of the said Weekes here at London.

Thus William Weekes had been apprehended at Durham, suspected of a murder committed in London, while Hamlet Holcraft *alias* Holcroft had been engaged to escort him back to London.

The murder, and the identity of the primary suspect, are verified by a damaged but partly legible memorandum issued by the Middlesex coroner Richard Vale on 30 July.[4] William Weekes, yeoman of London, was to be examined concerning a certain 'felonia & murdro', while John Tomlynson of the parish of St Andrews, Holborn, agreed to appear as a witness under pain of forfeiture of ten pounds. (Tomlynson was the father of the legitimately born Dorithe Tomlynson, baptized on 17 September 1576, hence already a married man; his wife – first name unknown – and he both died in 1593, probably of the plague, on 30 July and 16 August respectively.)[5] The suspect was evidently William Wilkes of the parish of

St Clement Danes, buried on 6 March 1578,[6] whose widow Joan was buried on 22 September following. A son, William, had been born on 5 November 1575, a daughter, Susan, on 27 October 1577 (after the murder). Susan was buried on 21 February 1578, which means that father, mother, and daughter all died within a year, leaving the son an orphan.

On 24 April 1578 William Sankey's nuncupative will (spoken aloud to witnesses) was proved in the Prerogatory Court of Canterbury:[7]

> Memorandum that William Sankye late of East barnet in the Countie of Middlesex gentleman lying on his death bedd about the latter end of Iuly or the beginning of August Anno Domini 1577 being required by Gilbert Sherington of Grayes Inne in the Countie of Middlesex gentleman to dispose his goodes and all thinges in order to the end he might wholly bequeath him self to God answered cherefully then being in perfecte memory I giue all my goodes and all that I haue to my wief Mary Then being present, and sayd this was is and shalbe his will And at the time of these his woordes or sone after he required his sayd wief to stand good mother to his children being present at that same time William Sherington Citezen and (*blank*) of the Citie of London Hamlett Holcrofte and Gilbert Sherington gentleman with others. By me Wyllyam Sherington per me Gilbertum Sherington.

William and Gilbert Sherington may have been called in as lawyers, but Hamlet Holcroft seems to have maintained his personal interest in the case. Sankey suffered a lingering death, doubtless as a result of a wound inflicted by William Weekes.

William Sankey had married Mary Walgrave at the parish church of St James, Clerkenwell, on 13 January 1572. Though he is described in his will as being a resident of East Barnet, the Sankey name is otherwise associated with Clerkenwell.[8] Mary Walgrave began life as the daughter of George Foster and his wife Alice. When Foster died, Alice married Henry Golding, who thereby became step-father to Mary and her sister Joan. By 2 December 1559 Mary Foster had married Robert Walgrave, Esquire, of Thornedon, Essex.[9] When that marriage did not work out to her satisfaction, she wed William Sankey.[10] Though bigamous, the marriage lasted the five years until Sankey's death. Mary Foster-Walgrave-Sankey subsequently married Robert Cryspe, persuading her mother and step-father Alice and Henry Golding to grant Cryspe a lease on their property of Little Birch in Essex.[11] Thus Sankey's initial attachment to Oxford was grounded in family allegiances: Sankey was the (bigamous) husband of Henry Golding's step-daughter.

Both Arundel's report that Weekes was convicted of Sankey's murder and subsequently hanged, and Howard's report that £100 had been found on Weekes's person at the time of his arrest at Durham, deserve full credit, since neither man could have lied about matters judicial. Their joint claim that Weekes confessed both to 'the Minister' and to his wife that Weekes had been paid exactly that amount by Oxford to kill Sankey was open to verification by calling the wife and minister as witnesses. More speculative are their assertions that the real target of Oxford's animosity had been Rowland York, and that Sankey had erred in attacking George Whitney instead of York at the Horse's Head in Cheap, nearly killing him. Of the principals, Weekes and Sankey were now dead, George Whitney had been wounded, while Oxford and Rowland York roamed free – much to the annoyance of Howard and Arundel.

On 8 September Robert Beale wrote to Walsingham of the 1576 piracy:[12]

> ... I look for little good, no more than was in the matter of My Lord of Oxford; for the three ships and parties being known that misused him, during Sir William Winter's and my abode there, one Cantillon was imprisoned, and after without any other form released, so as he is now far [=far away], is reported again upon the seas to do the like. ...

Despite the Prince of Orange's promises, Channel piracy continued, and for the most part went unpunished.

On 28 October Oxford attended the marriage of William Howard to Elizabeth Dacre (3.1/2.2@25). On 11 November Thomas Screven wrote to Rutland:[13]

> The marriage of the Lady Mary Vere is deferred until after Christmas, for as yet neither has Her Majesty given licence, nor has the Earl of Oxford wholly assented thereto.

Peregrine Bertie wrote to Lady Mary:[14]

> [I] let [you] understand how uncurteously I am delte with by my Lord your brother, who, as I heare, bandeth against me and sweareth my death, which I feare nor force not, but lest his displeasure should withdraw your affectionn towards me, otherwise I thinke no way to be so offended as I can not deffend.

Oxford was as hot-headed and threatening as ever, perhaps hoping to put off the date on which he must provide his sister's dowry from their father's estate.

On 4 December Sturmius wrote to Burghley:[15]

> As I write this I think of the Earl of Oxford, for I believe his lady speaks Latin also. But these are my wishes; dreams and senile meditations, not counsels.

The letter provides unique evidence of Anne's competence in Latin.

As Burghley began the year, so the Countess of Suffolk ended the year with an attempt at reconciliation. On 15 December she wrote to Burghley from Willoughby House:[16]

> My very good Lord, Upon Tuesday last Harry Cook being here and my daughter entering in to talk with him of my Lord of Oxford, of his sister, of my Lady his wife, and the young Lady his daughter, at the last he uttered these speeches: that he thought my Lord would very gladly see the child if he could devise how to see her and not to go to her. My daughter said she thought if it might so like him my Lady your wife would send the child to him; but to that he answered my Lord would not

be known [MS: aknowen] of it that he so much desired to see it. So because it was but a young man's words I took no great hold [=heed?] of it.

On Thursday I went to see my Lady Mary Vere. After other talks she asked me what I would say to it if my Lord her brother would take his wife again. 'Truly', quoth I, 'nothing could comfort me more, for now I wish to your brother as much good as to my own son.' 'Indeed', quoth she, 'he would very fain see the child, and is loth to send for her.' 'Then', quoth I, 'and [=if] you will keep my counsel we will have some sport with him. I will see if I can get the child hither to me, when you shall come hither; and whilst my Lord your brother is with you I will bring in the child as though it were some other child of my friend's, and we shall see how nature will work in him to like it, and tell him it is his own after.' 'Very well', quoth she; so we agreed hereon. Notwithstanding, I mean not to deal in it otherwise than it shall seem good to your Lordship, and in that sort that may best like you. I will do what I can either in that or anything else what may anyway lie in me. If it be clear [=free of sickness] about your house here in London I think if it may so please you it were good that both my Lady of Oxford and the child were there, and so the child might be quickly brought hither at my Lord's being here. I would wish speed that he might be taken in his good mood. I thank God I am at this present in his good favour. For one other besides his sister and Harry Cook told me that my Lord would fain have the child a while in my house with his sister, and no doubt of it if he be not crossed in this his liking he will sure have me laid to, and then I trust all things will follow to your desire. I hear he is about to buy a house here in London about Watling Street, and not to continue a Courtier as he hath done; but I pray you keep all these things secret or else you may undo those that now take pains to bring it to pass if my Lord's counsel should be bewrayed [=betrayed] before he list himself. And above all others my credit should be lost with him if he should know I dealt in anything without his commission; and therefore my good Lord I pray you keep it very secret, and write me two or three words what you would have me do in it. ...

The Countess supplied a postscript on a separate scrap of paper:

After I had sealed my letter I began to remember what grief it would be to my Lady your wife to part with the child, but let her not fear that; for after he hath seen it it can not tarry here and though [=even if] he would, for here is no apt lodging for her, and I doubt not after the first sight but he will be well enough content to come see her at her own home. But if I may counsel, in no wise let him not be crossed in his dysser [=desire].

This letter from the Countess of Suffolk is perhaps the most deeply human document from the entire Oxford 'archive'. She confirms that Anne lived with her parents, doubtless at Burghley House and at Theobalds, which for little Elizabeth was 'home'. We further learn that Harry Cook functioned as go-between, and that in December 1577 Oxford considered withdrawing from Court, and purchasing a house in Watling Street – just to the East of St Paul's Cathedral. As for reconciliation, that would not materialize for another four years.

32 Put Away your Feeble Pen

On 15 January 1578 Oxford received the hugely valuable Manor of Rysing, Norfolk, as a grant from the Queen:[1]

> We, as well in consideration of the good, true and faithful service done and given to Us before this time by Our most dear cousin Edward Earl of Oxford, Great Chamberlain of England, as for divers other causes and considerations moving Us by Our special grace, and out of Our certain knowledge and mere motion, We gave and granted, and by these presents for Us, Our heirs and successors do give and grant to the above named Edward Earl of Oxford, all that Our Lordship or Manor of Rysing ...

The justifications given for the grant, including 'good, true and faithful service', and 'divers other causes and considerations', are standard legal formulas: no special construction can be placed on them.

Details of the grant reveal what a prize was now Oxford's:

> ... the manor of Rysinge ad Castrum, the castle of Rysinge alias Rysinge Castell, the site of the said castle and a close (named) in Rysinge aforesaid, late of Thomas, late duke of Norfolk, attainted of treason, and all the Crown's lands in Rysinge aforesaid, late of the said duke; a chase and free warren called Rysinge Chase, late of the said duke; the advowsons of the rectories of Rysinge and Rydon; the manor of Geywood and the lands etc (named) in Geywood, late of the said duke; the advowson of the rectory of Geywood; the manor of Easte Rudham and manors of Easte Rudham and Houghton, late of the said duke, and all the Crown's lands in Eastrudham, Westrudham, Gestwicke, Folsham, Woodnorton, Sydersterne, Oxwiche, Houghton, Harpley, Thorpe Markett and Burneham late of the said duke; the site and 'lez demeane landes' of Coxforde priory; the rectory of Easterudham, late of the said duke, the advowson of the vicarage of Estrudham, a water mill in Estrudham and all the Crown's lands in Estrudham, Westrudham, Lynne, Houghton, Hillington and Bromisthrope late of the said duke; the rectory of Westrudham, late of the said duke; the advowson of the vicarage of Westrudham; all tithes in Bradfild late of the said duke; lands (named) in Westrudham and all the Crown's lands in Hawtboys Magna, Coteshall and Harstead late of the said duke; and 7½ quarters of barley yearly in Estrudham and Westrudham. To hold the manor and castle of Rysinge and the rest of the premises in Rysinge, the manor of Geywood, the manor of Estrudham and Houghton and the site of Coxford priory by service of the fortieth part of a knight's fee and by yearly rents of £60 11s 3¼d and 1 lb of pepper for the manor and castle of Rysinge and the rest of the premises appertaining to the said manor of Rysinge ad Castrum, £58 13s 3⅞d for the manor of Geywood and the rest of the premises appertaining therto, £34 5s 10d for the site and demesne lands of Coxford priory, the rectory of Estrudham and the water mill belonging to the said priory, £10 for the rectory of Westrudham and £52 16s 9¼d for the manor of Estrudham and Houghton and the rest of the premises belonging thereto; and to hold the rest as of the manor of Estgrenewiche in socage. Issues from Michaelmas last. The grantee to pay yearly £9 2s 6d to the keeper of the castle

and chase and the bailiff of the manor of Rysinge ad Castrum, £3 10d to the bailiff of the manor of Geywood, £4 to the bailiff of the manor of Estrudham and Houghton, 15s 3d for the proxies and synodals of Estrudham and Westrudham churches and 13s 4d for a pension to the vicar of Estrudham. For his service.

Again the closing words are merely formulaic: no particular service is implied.

Lady Mary Vere and Peregrine Bertie were married on an unknown day between Christmas 1577 and 12 March 1578, when the Countess of Suffolk wrote to Burghley concerning her 'daughter' Mary and 'her husband'.[2] According to the terms of the 16th Earl's will, Mary was to receive £1333–13–4 on the day of her marriage – money that now had to be provided from Oxford's estates. On 22 April Oxford received votes from five of the thirteen electors for the Order of the Garter, including Burghley, down from the nearly unanimous support the previous year (G-BL).

On 8 June William Lewin wrote from London to William Davison, then resident in Antwerp:[3]

> The bearer having been born in those parts and having occasion to resort thither from 'My Lord of Oxenford', whom he serves in very good place and credit, being 'well furnished with the languages and other good qualities', has requested my letters of commendation to you. Please yield him, as occasion shall serve, such favour and countenance as the goodness of your nature easily yields to gentlemen so qualified, and your office makes available to such as receive the same. He has the rather required this of me because he understands your special friendship towards me, and I do so the rather because he has special good 'guyftes' and wishes.

The identity of the 'bearer' – evidently a Belgian servant of Oxford's fluent in languages – is unknown.

On 3 July Edward Fytton wrote to Burghley from his 'pore cotage' in Aldford, Cheshire:[4]

> After sending letters by John Passe, importing the inheritance of the Earl of Oxford and Burghley's daughter, the Countess, for lands in Roode within this county, was, upon occasion, enforced to send [the] bearer, partly with these letters from his father, but chiefly for a cause of his own, which toucheth him near and comes commanded from the Earl of Leicester. If Burghley grants his petition it will be worth £100 a year, and a denial will force him to break with his father-in-law, Sir John Holcroft. ...

As we shall learn, John Passe, evidently Burghley's servant, was a notorious drunk. Countess Anne was remembered by still other correspondents, including Walsingham, who wrote to Burghley from Antwerp on 18 July:[5]

> So thanking you for your letter of the 12th I take my leave, beseeching that I may be remembered to my lady [=Lady Burghley] and the poor solitary Countess.

On 29 July Lord Cobham also wrote to Burghley from Antwerp:[6]

> I send you with this packet two new books in Latin, done by 'D'Aloogondye' [=Aldegone?]. Commend me to the Countess of Oxford and to my Lady, and so to all my little friends.

Cobham's 'little friends' doubtless included three-year-old Elizabeth, the daughter whom Oxford had not yet deigned to meet. On 20 October Warwick wrote to Burghley from Court:[7]

> My most hearty commendations not forgotten to my good lady your wife, as likewise to the sweet little Countess of Oxford. My 'amys' hath the like to your good lordship and to both the ladies.

'Amys' was Ambrose Dudley's third wife, Anne Russell (*Peerage*, under Warwick). On 24 October the Countess of Shrewsbury wrote to Burghley from Richmond:[8]

> ... With my most hearty commendations to your lordship, my good lady your wife, and good Lady Oxford, with her little sweet lady ...

Again, the 'little sweet lady' was Elizabeth Vere.

While Oxford's wife and daughter elicited wide-ranging affection (Oxford only excepted), his sister became the target of gossip. On 25 September Thomas Cecil wrote to Burghley from Grantham:[9]

> because of an unkindness, the Lady Mary 'will be beaten with that rod which heretofore she prepared for others'.

We have seen that Mary, like her brother, had a sharp tongue: she was now receiving a dose of her own medicine.

In high summer, Oxford attended the Queen on her progress through East Anglia. On 15 July Burghley wrote to Dr Richard Howland, Vice-chancellor of Cambridge University, from Havering, anticipating a royal visit:[10]

> ... they should do well to provide for the Earl of Leicester, the Lord Chamberlain, and the Earl of Oxford, some gloves, with a few verses in a paper joined to them, proper to every of their degrees; so that in number they exceeded not above eight verses.

The Queen's entourage did not make it to Cambridge, but rested at Audley End near Saffron Waldon, where members of the University were gathered. On 26 July Burghley's advice was followed to the letter:[11]

> Item, unto the Erle of Oxford a paire of Cambridge gloves were given with verses.

Also present were Burghley and 13 other guests: the Earl of Sussex, Lord Hunsdon, Sir Christopher Hatton, Sir Francis Knollis, Sir Thomas Heneage, Mr Thomas Wilson (Secretary), Sir James Croft, the Master Comptroller of the Queen's household, Lord Charles Howard, Lord Henry Howard, Lord Ormond, the Earl of Surrey, and the Earl of Leicester. Listed as not present were the Lord Keeper, the Earl of Warwick, and Lord North.

Among the witnesses to the Queen's progress was Gabriel Harvey, whose *Gratulationum Valdensis* (1578), in four parts, is dedicated first to Elizabeth, second to Leicester, third to Burghley, and fourth to Oxford, Hatton, and Sidney. The dedication to Oxford includes the following words of praise:[12]

> England will discover in you its hereditary Achilles. Go, Mars will see you in safety and Hermes attend you; aegis-sounding Pallas will be by and will instruct your heart and spirit, while long since did Phoebus Apollo cultivate your mind with the arts. Your British numbers have been widely sung, while your Epistle testifies how much you excel in letters, being more courtly than Castiglione himself, more polished.[13] I have seen your many Latin things, and more English are extant; of French and Italian muses, the manners of many peoples, their arts and laws you have drunk deeply. Not in vain was Sturmius himself known to you, nor so many Frenchmen and polished Italians, nor Germans. But, O celebrated one, put away your feeble pen, your bloodless books, your impractical writings! Now is need of swords! Steel must be sharpened! Everywhere men talk of camps, everywhere of dire arms! You must even deal in missiles! Now war is everywhere, everywhere are the Furies, and everywhere reigns Enyo. Take no thought of Peace; all the equipage of Mars comes at your bidding. Suppose Hannibal to be standing at the British gates; suppose even now, now, Don John of Austria is about to come over, guarded by a huge phalanx! Fated events are not known to man, for the Thunderer's counsels are not plain: what if suddenly a powerful enemy should invade our borders? if the Turk should arm his immense cohorts against us? What if the terrible trumpet should now resound the 'Taratantara'? You are being observed as to whether you would care to fight boldly. I feel it; our whole country believes it: your blood boils in your breast, virtue dwells in your brow, Mars keeps your mouth, Minerva is in your right hand, Bellona reigns in your body, and Martial ardor, your eyes flash, your glance shoots arrows:[14] who wouldn't swear you Achilles reborn?

Harvey bears witness to Oxford's literary reputation, but denigrates it, urging that true glory lies in military action.

Oxford remained with the Queen during her progress through Suffolk in early August.[15] On 14 August Mendoza wrote to Zayas, the King of Spain's secretary:[16]

> ... the Queen sent twice to tell the earl of Oxford, who is a very gallant lad, to dance before the [French] ambassadors, whereupon he replied that he hoped her Majesty would not order him to do so as he did not want to entertain Frenchmen. When the Lord Steward took him the message the second time, he replied that he would not give pleasure to Frenchmen, nor listen to such a message, and with that he left the room. He is a lad who has a great following in the country, and has requested permission to go and serve his Highness, which the Queen refused, and asked him why he did not go and serve the Archduke Mathias; to which he replied that he would not serve another sovereign than his own, unless it were a very great one, such as the king of Spain.

So Oxford hoped to serve Don John of Austria, half-brother to the King of Spain, or even the King himself, deprecating the Queen's proposal that he take service with Archduke Mathias, the 22-year-old brother of the Hapsburg Emperor.[17] Mendoza hoped indeed that Oxford could eventually be brought to serve the King his master.

Oxford's months of travel with the peripatetic Court finally ended. On 4 September the Privy Council issued a commission 'for viij cartes to carry my Lord of Oxfordes stuff from the Courte to London'.[18] Clearly, Oxford had not gone on progress without the comforts of home. He probably settled into rooms he had taken on Broad Street near Bishopsgate.

33   In the Chiefest of his Royalty

Oxford evidently participated in Accession Day tilts from 1578 to 1580.[1] Indications of his expenditures on the tilts, held on 17 November, come from a formal complaint made on 21 May 1598 by Judith Ruswell, widow of William Ruswell (or Russell), tailor, seeking to recover monies never repaid by Oxford.[2] Denying the claim, Oxford conceded that Ruswell was indeed his 'sometime servant and taylor', and that about 1580 he had provided Ruswell with a stock of cloth worth £700 or £800. The lawsuit reveals the identities of 13 deponents who confessed to having known Judith and William Ruswell, and Oxford, the defendant.

Five of the deponents were Oxford's servants (ages adjusted to 1578): 1) Nicholas Bleake, yeoman, 36 years, Oxford's servant and bookkeeper: admits having created a book of accounts for transactions between Oxford and Ruswell, and having signed the book; Oxford's final obligation to Ruswell was £809–3–2, of which he paid £300–6–0 by William Walter, leaving a debt of £508–17–2; 2) William Walter, gentleman, 29 years, Oxford's purse-keeper: admits knowledge of little or nothing; 3) Edward Hubbard, Esq., 37 years, then Oxford's officer; later one of the Six Clerks of Chancery:

> longe before that tyme spoken of in the Interrogatory viz when thearle had licence to travell beyond the seas this defendant made a collection of all thearles dettes amongst which there was a debt of l or lx li [=£50–60] then sett downe to be due to the sayd William Russell

4) Israel Amyce, 35 years, Oxford's servant subsequent to 1578:

> [Ruswell] did often very earnestly speake vnto this deponent to move the defendant for the payment of his debt (but admits knowledge of little or nothing).

5) John Lyly (or 'Lilly') Esq., 23 years:

> when he, this deponent, at the plainantes request hath spoken to the defendant for money claymed by her to be by him due, he, the defendant, hath denyed that he ought [=owed] her anythinge

This was of course John Lyly the Elizabethan man of letters. Born of a Kent family in 1554, Lyly matriculated at Oxford from Magdalen College in 1571. He received his BA on 27 April 1573 and his MA on 1 June 1575.[3] He admits that he had known Ruswell, but nothing of consequence about Ruswell's finances. (Lyly's statements are consistent with other evidence that he began working for Oxford about 1578, and that he lived at the Savoy.)[4]

At least four and possibly five of the deponents were servants of William Ruswell: 1) Bennett Salter, hosier, 18 years, servant and apprentice, dwelling with Ruswell about 1576 to 1579: kept a 'booke of reckenynges ... so simply as he co[u]ld'; identifies Ruswell as Oxford's tailor and Master of his Wardrobe, Oxford 'being at what tyme the defendant was as this deponent termeth yt in the cheiffest of his Royaltye'. Further, Ruswell

> did vppon his owne creditt take vpp silkes & silver and gould lace & other wares and stuffes as broadcloth & holland & canvas for lynynges & such thinges for the sayd defendant & to his the defendantes vse by his order & appoyntment which wollen or broadecloth was taken vp for the moost parte of one Peter Hardcastle a wollendraper then dwelling in Fleet Streete & sometymes of one Mr Dunche-combe a wollendraper then dwelling in Watling streete at the signe of the Bottle and the lynnen lynynges were taken vp of one Maynerde [=Maynard Buckwaye] a lynnen draper then dwelling in the Strond ...

> this deponent did fetche moost of the sayd stuffes himself & had order therevnto & for thinges of much more value at that tyme from & vnder the said William Ruswell ... and saith that in the latter tyme of this deponentes being servaunt to the said William Ruswell he the said William Ruswell attending on the defendant at her Maiesties Court this deponent was ymployed the more vnder him for fetching & taking vpp of wares & stuffes such as aforesaid for the defendantes vse here in London ...

> thies thinges ... were not a quarter nor half quarter of the value of those garmentes which the sayd William Ruswell made for the said defendantes vse ... for garmentes of greattest place the wares & stuffes that went therevnto were taken vpp by direccion of Mr Walters the defendantes pursebearer & the said William Ruswell together by whose direccions this deponent did fetche moost of those thinges ...

> and for such wares so taken vp this deponent had an accompt of three thosand & odd poundes to make for Alderman Skynner then but Mr Skynner of whome those wares were taken vpp and for xvij hundred & odd poundes more then due by the defendant & vppon the defendantes accompt to one Mr Phipps of St Martyns for wares fetcht & taken vpp by this deponent by direccion as aforesaid ...

> Walters was then all in all for & vnder the defendant to take charge of those accomptes & reckenynges

2) Humphry Stile, St Martins in the Field, near London, 15 years; servant to Ruswell about one year (c. 1582); lived in the same street as Ruswell before coming to dwell with him as his servant; Ruswell (who 'could not write himselfe')

did make apparell for the defendant and Liveryes and other apparrell for some of his servantes

3) Anthony Brown, tailor, 29 years; served as a journeyman under Ruswell:

for his silkes he [=Ruswell] went for the most part to Mr Skinners and to one Mr Phipps and one Anthony Bates hard by St Martins ...

for gold lace and buttons and such thinges and for linninges and linnen clothe he fetcht them for the most part att one Maynardes ...

and his wollen Cloth at Mr Peter Legattes by St Dunstanes churche in ffleetstreete ...

[Oxford] did some tymes paye the sayd William Ruswell an hundred poundes att a tyme, and some tymes more and some tymes lesse, in dischardge of part of the debt which he had in such sort as is aforesayde taken vp for his Lordshipp, and he remembreth well that the defendant was indebted vnto the sayd William Ruswell for the makinge of some of his owne apparell and for the makinge of very much apparell and livery for divers of the defendantes servantes especially his boyes and pages and some others, both att Tiltinges and other tymes

4) William Milles, tailor, 27 years, Ruswell's servant: Ruswell

beinge servant and Taylor vnto the defendant, might in those dayes, and did very often take up divers thinges vpon Credite, as gold lace, silkes, lininges, and other stuffes, from tyme, to tyme to the vse of the defendant ... of Mr Skynner, Mr Stone, Mr Legate, Mr Minars, and others

5) Michael Grigg, St Gregory in Paul's Churchyard, tailor, 25 years, presumably Ruswell's servant:

he verily thinketh in his conscience that in the book of the said William Ruswelles accountes and reckoninges now shewed to him att the tyme of this his examinacion ther are many debtes which are due to the Complainant in equity to be allowed, and do yet remayne vndischardged for any thinge he knoweth or can coniecture

One of the deponents was a businessmen, one his servant, and one the wife of a businessman: 1) Peter Legate, gentleman, 25 years, supplier of goods and credit: Ruswell

kept touche and payde him honestly and truly till att the last, he became some threescore poundes [=£60] or an hundred markes [=£66–13–4] in this deponentes debt and left it vnsatisfied. ...

Legate had Oxford's debt to Ruswell 'sett over vnto him' as a good debt, which he discussed with Oxford at Burghley House. Oxford

did acknowledge the debt, and tolde this deponent that he should be payde it by his offecers and withall willed this deponent to be good to Ruswell, and promised that this deponent should not lose a groat by him ...

[Legate] remembreth the same by a very good token, for this deponent havinge a litle before provided white clothe for his lordshippes Liveries by his owne appoynt-ment which his Lordshipp afterwardes fancied not, he caused Mr Byshopp one of his servantes to give this deponent att the same tyme six pounes for a reward, to take the white clothes agayne and to lett him have some other sort of clothe ...

the bookes remayned many yeares in his custody to the ende that if he should receave any mony vpon them, which he never could ... he hath redelivered the same bookes vnto her [=Judith Ruswell] beinge executor or administrator to her husband, to see if she might recover the sayd debtes towardes her releaffe

Legate claims that he did not attempt to recover the debt

by any violent or chardgeable course in sutes of Lawe, more then this that vpon peticion made by the now Complainant to the right honorable Sir Christopher Hatton late Lord Chancelour of England this deponentes lord and Maister, it was dealt & proceeded in, to some good poyntes of forwardnes, that the defendant should sell a lease of the Mannor of Avelye aforesayd, and should have accepted the sayd debtes to the valewe of seven hundred and odd poundes as he remembreth in part of payment, and the rest to be payde him in mony, and therupon an hundred poundes was lent vnto him for a longe tyme without allowance for it, yet afterward that bargayne brake of[f] and never tooke effect ...

2) Morgan Allen, 14 years, subsequently a draper, then servant to Peter Legate:

he did then take vp clothe and silke lace and such other Commodityes of Peter Legate this deponentes master

he thinketh that the defendant hath not dischardged any parte of it [=Oxford's debt to Ruswell], for the sayd Peter Legate was an earnest sutor vnto his Lordshipp to have the sayde debt satisfyede in some reasonable sort, and had the bookes left with him for that purpose, but cold never gett any payment by that meanes

3) Mary Buckway, wife of Maynard Buckway, linen draper, 35 years; subse-quently married to James Howson: Ruswell

was of very good creditt and accounte for a tyme and kept a dosen or 16 men at worke ... Maynard Buckwaye this deponentes former husband, beinge then the sayd William Ruswelles neighbour, and keepinge a linnen drapers shopp, did give him creditt dyvers tymes for such wares as he sold, as all kindes of Linnen clothe, holland, and canvas, and as she taketh it the same was all taken vp for the defendant and for his vse, and the sayd William Ruswell payde this deponentes husband very truly and honestly from tyme to tyme till att the last, he brake [=broke, went bankrupt], and left himselfe 64*li* [=£64] in this deponentes husbandes debt for such wares so taken vp as is aforesaid

The lawsuit reveals the identities of one otherwise unknown servant of Oxford's, a Mr Bishop, along with eight Londoners who supplied goods, credit, or both, for Oxford's clothing and livery:

Anthony Bates, hard by St Martins: supplied silks
Maynard Buckway, linnendraper, the Strand: supplied gold lace, buttons, linings, and linnen cloth; also credit
Mr Dunchecombe, woolendraper, Watling Street at the sign of the Bottle: supplied woolen or broadcloth and credit
Peter Hardcastle, woolendraper, Fleet Street: supplied woolen or broadcloth
Mr Minars: supplied goods and credit
Mr Phipps of St. Martins: supplied silks and credit of £1700 and more
Mr Alderman Skynner: supplied silks and credit of £3000 and more
Mr Stone: supplied goods and credit

Of these eight men, Thomas Skinner was the most prominent: a clothworker, citizen, Alderman, and eventually Lord Mayor, he would become a major purchaser of Oxford's lands.

34 The Lure of Gold

In 1576 Humphrey Gilbert published *A Discourse of a Discovery for a New Pasage to Cataia*. Like Michael Lok and John Dee, Gilbert believed in the existence of a north-west passage around (or through) North America to the trading ports and thence the spices and other luxury commodities of China (Cataia or Cathay), Japan, and the East Indies.

We know today that the North American land-mass is so broad and extends so far to the north that a north-west passage is a practical impossibility. By 1575, informed Europeans knew the lie of the Atlantic coast up to Hudson's Bay, and of the Pacific coast for at least half the length of what is now California. A navigable passage could have been possible only if the Pacific coast north of San Francisco Bay sheared obliquely to the east. Ortelius's map of 1572, which shows the east coast of North America with remarkable accuracy, shows the Pacific coast lying even further west than it does in fact, with nothing remotely suggesting a waterway through or around. European cartography did not stop the English from claiming to know better than their Spanish and Continental rivals.

David B. Quinn notes the connection between English exploration and magic:[1]

> ... Dee was busy constructing maps (he gave one to Gilbert in 1582) which confidently showed passages through and round America both in Arctic and temperate latitudes, and was also engaged in conducting seances to summon up supernatural guidance on the discovery of a passage.

Quinn elaborates on the nature of the resulting maps:[2]

> John Dee's maps of 1580 and 1583, the latter of which he compiled for Gilbert, and Lok's map published by Hakluyt in 1582 [Fig. 8] are a mass of unproved assumptions,

the coastlines only very broadly correct and revealing all kinds of theories about water passages around and through the landmass of North America. They were quite inadequate as charts for sailors or maps for settlers.

Martin Frobisher, the leader of the first expedition, set out on 12 June 1576 from Gravesend to 'Meta Incognita' (unknown land) in three vessels, returning on 2 October empty-handed. Oxford got into the game with a £25 investment in a second expedition, which lasted from May to September 1577, and quite neglected the north-west passage for iron pyrite – fool's gold. Of three resulting assays, one estimated the return at 10 ounces of gold per ton of ore; one concluded that the ore contained no precious metals at all; while John Dee estimated over his signature a prospective yield of 7 ounces of silver per hundredweight. On the basis of the two optimistic estimates, which even disagreed over the identity of the precious metal, a third expedition was organized to recover 500 tons of ore at an estimated cost of £15,000. Frobisher's ships were to sail on 25 May 1578. On 21 May Oxford wrote to the commissioners from Court (LL-12):

> To my very loving fryndes William Pellham & Thomas Randolphe esquiers, Mr Yonge, Mr Lok, Mr Hogan, Mr Fyeld, & others the Commyssyoners for the voyage to Meta Incognita/.

> After my very harty Commendacions / vnderstandinge of the wyse proceding & orderlie deallinge for the contynewynge of the voyage for the dyscourye [=discovery] of Cathay by the Northwest, which this bearar my frynd Mr Froobusher hathe alreadye very honorablye attempted, and is now eftsones to be employed for the better atchyvyng therof / and the rather induced aswell for the great lykynge her Maiestie hathe to haue the same passage dyscoured, as also for the speciall good favour I beare to Mr Frobusher, to offer vnto you to be an adventurar therin for the summ of one thousand pounds or more, yf you lyke to admytt therof, which summ or summes vppon your certifficat of admyttance, I wyll enter into bond shalbe paid for that vse vnto you, vppon Michaelmas day next comyng / ...

Not only was Oxford's offer of £1000 accepted, but he bought up £2000 of Michael Lok's investment of £5000. Unable to raise cash, Oxford raised credit in the form of a bond. His reference to 'the contynewynge of the voyage for the dyscourye [=discovery] of Cathay by the Northwest' suggests either that he had bought into the fictional cover for Frobisher's third expedition, or that he allowed himself to be deceived as to its true purpose.

On 25 September, exactly four months from the day of their setting out, Frobisher's ships made landfall in Cornwall; Frobisher himself brought samples overland to Richmond and thence to London, where an assay found them worthless. Oxford had not a penny to show for his £3000 investment, and 29 September, the due-date of his bond, was at hand. Suspicion of fraud lighted upon Michael Lok, who had so readily (or so it seemed in retrospect) allowed Oxford to purchase £2000 of his investment – though indeed, both had suffered losses.

On 20 November Frobisher and a gang of 40 men approached Lok's house in riotous assembly, calling him[3]

> a false accountant to the Company, a cozener to my Lord of Oxford, no venturer at all in the voyages, a bankrupt knave.

We may suspect that the men acted on Oxford's orders, for a massed attack on the residence of a personal enemy was, as we shall learn, Oxford's *modus operandi*. Oxford made a partial escape from his indebtedness by the simple expedient of not producing his £3000 in full: on 30 November he was listed as still owing £450.[4] Fortunately for himself, it was not possible to arrest an earl for debt. Lok, who still owed £460, became a prisoner in the Fleet. Oxford still owed the debt on 14 January 1579, as Lok indicated in a letter to Walsingham, written from London:[5]

> Right honorable / I haue receued your letter, wherin I am charged to pay ixC xli [=£910] to Mr Allyn, for my part of the ffraight of the ships retorned home with Mr Furbusher, in the third voyage / for answere wherof that it may please your Honor to be advertysed / my part of that ffraight came to iiijC xvjli vs [=£316-5-0] / which I haue paid, as by myne accountes dothe appere, which accountes the awditoures are now in hand withall / and by them your Honor shalbe advertised very shortlye / bothe of thatt, and of all the rest of my doinges in the Companies busynes. And for more part of the said ixC xli [=£910] / it is sett downe that the right honorable Therle of Oxford, ys to paye iiijC Lli [=£450] / accordinge to the order & rate of all the rest of the venturars / wherfore it may please your Honor to call on his Honor; for the same Somm [=sum] / And yf that his Honor be not satisfied of this matter, I am to be ruled by your Honor & others, vppon vew of the bargayne which I made with his honor, which he hathe vnder my hand & sealle / for I wyll not doo any wronge wyllingly to any man Lyving especially to his Honor, to whome I doo owe bothe duetye & reverence. ...

It is not known whether Oxford ever settled this debt.

While Frobisher was squandering his investors' wealth in a vain search for the north-west passage, or for gold, Sir Francis Drake brought a huge return to his investors when, after a three years' circumnavigation via the south-west passage around South America, he returned to England in 1580. Oxford was not one of those who had the foresight or good luck to invest in Drake's plunder of Spanish gold. He would, however, invest in a venture similar to Drake's, this time to the tune of £500. The expedition, in which Frobisher had been replaced by Edward Fenton, set out at the very end of May 1581, returning in May 1582 – another fiasco.

On 1 October 1581 Frobisher wrote to Leicester:[6]

> ... I have not moved Sir Francis Walsingham nor any of the rest but my Lord of Oxford, who bears me in hand he would buy the Edward Bonaventure, and Mr. Bowland & I have offered 1500 pounds for her, but they hold her at 1800.

Apparently Frobisher and Bowland offered the £1500 as Oxford's agents, but their offer was rejected by the ship's owner, Henry Ughtrede, of Netly, Hampshire.[7] Instead, the *Edward Bonaventure* (named after Edward VI) came under the control of Fenton, along with a galleon called the *Leicester* (formerly the Ughtrede) and the *Talbot*.[8]

Undiscouraged after losses of some £3525, in 1584 Oxford became a shareholder in 'The Colleagues of the Fellowship for the Discovery of the North West Passage', along with Adrian Gilbert, John Dee, and Walter Ralegh. In 1585 the Fellowship's expedition under captain John Davis probed as far as the eponymous Davis Straits in Canada. Oxford's losses from this voyage are unknown, but were presumably substantial.

The essential difference between Drake's voyage on the one hand, and Frobisher's and Gilbert's on the other, is that Drake knew where to find gold – in Spanish ships and ports. By contrast, Frobisher and his successors went on speculative expeditions where the spiritualist John Dee told him he would find a north-west passage, or gold, or both. Oxford staked a fortune on the spiritualists, and lost.

35 Superlative in the Prince's Favour

Fulke Greville, Lord Brooke, describes Oxford in early 1579 as 'Superlative in the Princes favour',[1] where by 'the Prince' Greville means 'the Queen'. But rather than conform his character to his auspicious public image, Oxford pursued a course that led by March 1581 to nearly total self-destruction.

Henry Howard paints a detailed, heart-rending picture of an attack by Oxford and his 'cutters' on the London residence of the 63-year-old William Somerset, Earl of Worcester, after his return from Paris on 27 February (LIB-3.1/4):

> Who euer delte more frendlie with him [=Oxford] then my Lord of Worcester? And yet nowe since his laste comminge ouer, without offence or any quarrell in the world, he rushed into the said Lordes howse in Warwick Lane, and all his cutters with him, hauinge their swordes drawen, and theare had murdered my lord and all his people if the doores had not bene spedily shutte vppe against [them]; and my lord constraynid as if he had bene in a forte in tyme of warre to parley out of his owne windowes.

Charles Arundel similarly reports that Oxford 'brake into my Lord of Wosters howse with an intent to murther him and all his men, as he often times protested afterward' (LIB-4.2/4.11).

In March seditious talk was reported between Gregory Clover of Colchester and Thomas Wixsted of Dedham, saltpetreman.[2] Clover spoke first:

> My Lord of Warwick and my Lord of Leicester [=Ambrose and Robert Dudley] are
> traitors and come of a traitor's blood, and if they had right they had lost their heads
> so well as others for making away of King Edward.

Wixsted replied:

> he would go to the Lord of Oxford's town [=Castle Hedingham?] in spite of the
> Lord of Oxford, who was not worthy to wipe my Lord of Warwick's shoes, and the
> Earl of Oxford was confederate with the Duke of Norfolk and was well worthy to
> lose his head as he, meaning the duke.

According to Emmison, 'The saltpetreman's taunt doubtless refers to the claim
by the de Veres, Earls of Oxford, of Hedingham Castle, for exemption of their
manors from searches for saltpetre, essential to the making of gunpowder. Wixsted
was evidently in the service of the Earl of Warwick, Master of the Ordnance,
which explains the insulting comparison of the two earls.'[3]

On 5 March 1579 Gilbert Talbot described for his father the recent Shrovetide
shows at court (this year Shrovetide ran from 1 to 3 March). Talbot was not
impressed:[4]

> ... It is but vayne to troble your Lordship with suche shewes as was shewed before
> her Maiestie this Shroftyde at nyghte. The chefest was a devyse presented by the
> persons of th'Erle of Oxforde, th'Erle of Surrye, the Lords Thomas Haworthe
> [=Howard] & Wynsoure. The devyse was prettyer then it had happe to be per-
> formed, but the beste of it (& I thynk the beste lyked) was twoe ryche jewells which
> was presented to her Maiestie by the ii Erles.

In Nichols's words (ii, p. 278), 'The young Noblemen, it seems, did not so well
acquit their parts'. Oxford, now nearly thirty, was the oldest of the presenters: his
younger companions were Philip Howard, Earl of Surrey, twenty-one; Philip's
younger brother Thomas, seventeen; and Frederick Windsor, Oxford's nephew
(son of his half-sister Katherine), twenty. Though Talbot does not name the
author of the failed device, Oxford is an obvious candidate. Evidently the text
was superior to its performance.

On 8 April Mendoza wrote to his master, the King of Spain:[5]

> With respect to giving hostages for the coming of Alençon, it is proposed that the
> earls of Surrey and Oxford and Lord Windsor should be chosen, because, although
> they are only youths, their houses are very ancient and of high rank.

Marriage was under consideration between Alençon (Anjou) and the ageing
Queen Elizabeth. Hostages offered for Alençon's safe return included three of the
four participants in the abortive Shrovetide shows. Mendoza classes Oxford as a
youth – at any rate he held no office of responsibility, and so might be dispensed
with during the time of the visit. Later this same month Oxford received votes
from all seven electors who cast votes for the Order of the Garter, a considerable
improvement over the previous year (G-BL).

On 1 May Oxford alienated Great Hormead, Hertfordshire, to Anthony Cage. To this property was thought to attach the right to serve as the Queen's Chamberlain. Since Elizabeth was not the consort of a king, the claim was currently moot. As we will see, however, in 1603 Oxford would assert his claim even though he had sold the property – as if he had merely sold its use while retaining its dignities. Indeed, throughout his life Oxford had a tendency to think of alienation as a temporary loss of use – though in fact alienation was normally forever.

36 Alienations

Writing in 1599 or 1600, when Oxford was still very much alive, Thomas Wilson declared that in 1575 the Earl had been worth £12,000 per annum, but that within two years he was worth nothing, having dispersed all his properties, 'even to the selling of the stones, timber and lead of his castles and howses'.[1] Wilson doubtless exaggerated the speed of the earldom's decline, but his general point is accurate enough. Thus, for example, the 16th Earl's 1562 *inquisition post mortem* for Essex, a survey of his properties in that county, takes up ten large sheets of parchment, while the 17th Earl's 1604 *inquisition post mortem* for the same county takes up one.[2] Of the numerous estates attributed to the earldom in the wardship survey of 1562, not a single one remained to the earldom in 1604.[3] Properties sold or otherwise lost by Oxford include several which virtually defined his title: Castle Hedingham (which went to Oxford's three daughters), Earls Colne, Wivenhoe, and Oxford House (*alias* Vere House) in London at London Stone.

The 1562 wardship survey must serve as the principal document for evaluating the economic foundations of the earldom. One inheritance listed there, the Great Chamberlainship, though nominally attached to the county of Middlesex, was not a landed estate but an office with a token income. The remaining 77 inheritances consisted, for the most part, of complex properties. Oxford's Cornish inheritance, for example, consisted of Roseworrey, Tregenow, Goswyn, Dennybrock, Tregenowe Worthy, Tresthney, and Tregorick.[4] The 77 landed inheritances included one each in Berkshire, Cornwall, Kent, Leicestershire, London, Norfolk, Staffordshire, Warwickshire, and Wiltshire; two each in Buckinghamshire, Devon, and Northamptonshire; three each in Cambridgeshire and Hertfordshire; five in Suffolk; six in Cheshire; and 45 in Essex. Thus well over half of the landed estates lay in the home county, nine lay in nearby Kent, Suffolk, and Cambridgeshire, while the rest were widely scattered.

Upon the 16th Earl's death, eight estates went to his brothers for the terms of their lives: two to Geoffrey, five to Aubrey, and one to Robert. Leicester, the Queen's favourite, was granted control of ten for the duration of Oxford's minority, while Countess Margery controlled 20,[5] the 16th Earl's executors controlled nine (to finance the payment of his obligations and debts until the expiration of twenty – or twenty-one – years after his death), while 31 remained in the hands of Oxford himself, or rather, during his minority, under the control of his guardians, including Burghley.

Though temporarily deprived of land by the ancient system of wardship, Oxford eventually recovered all his father's estates, as dictated by events: the death of his mother in 1568; the expiration of his minority in 1571 and the suing of his livery in 1572; the deaths of his several uncles;[6] and the recovery in 1582 (or 1583) of estates set aside for the discharge of his father's debts. Additionally, as we have seen, Oxford received the Duke of Norfolk's immensely valuable Castle Rysing in 1577. As Pearson has demonstrated in rich detail (p. 3), Oxford's inherited properties were sufficient to have sustained him not only during his minority, when his expenses should have been minimal, but during his entire life.

Elizabethan property-owners could hope to live directly off their lands, whether from crops, livestock, timber, game, or other 'in-kind' benefits. They might also live indirectly, for example by securing income through rents. It was generally understood that land should be rented for one-twentieth of its absolute value per annum, or, conversely, that land should be sold for twenty times its annual rental value. In effect, then, lands returned to their owners approximately 5 per cent of their absolute value per annum. If a landowner and his heirs were content with such a modest return, they might live on the income forever.[7] But since land which would yield £100 per annum in rent might be sold for £2000 in cash, the temptation to liquidate might be difficult to resist. Though future income would be lost to both the seller and his heirs, the loss might seem to be justified, in theory at least, by a shrewd investment in land, by a streak of luck at a gambling table, or by a return on an overseas venture.

To follow the disposition of property in Elizabethan England requires an elementary understanding of sales, alienations, leases, and mortgages. A sale is the irrevocable transfer of property to another, usually for a monetary consideration or its equivalent. An alienation is the sale of property in which the Crown has an interest (technically defined as 'knight's service').[8] Since the Crown often had an interest in lands acquired over time by an earldom, the sale (and occasionally the purchase) of such lands is usually well documented. Alienations fall into two categories: a 'licence to alienate', granted for a fee, results from permission secured in advance; a 'pardon of alienation', accompanied by a fine, occurs when the seller has not secured a licence. No opprobrium seems to have attached to a pardon to alienate: rather, the fine seems to have been regarded as a routine business expense by the seller and welcome extra income by the Crown.

A lease is 'a contract between parties, by which the one conveys lands or tenements to the other for life, for years, or at will, usually in consideration of rent or other periodical compensation' (*OED*). A mortgage is a loan, generally at interest, with property being offered as a pledge or guarantee.[9] Since failure to repay the mortgage by a specified day resulted in forfeiture of the pledge, a mortgage could offer an easy means to acquire quick cash, though at great risk.

Elizabethans, like their predecessors, were endlessly creative with property law. Land might be leased for such an enormous length of time as to constitute a virtual sale. Thus, for example, on 11 January 1577 Oxford leased Hayredge in the parish of Thorncombe, Devon, to Robert Peers *alias* James for two thousand years.[10] A lease might entail an 'entry fine' under which the rent would be reduced in exchange for a large initial payment – so the lessee might enrich himself at the expense of his heirs. An individual of speculative bent might purchase the 'reversion' of a property, in effect the right to succeed on another's death: but enforcing a reversion might easily involve a suit against a rival claimant. Pearson describes still other ingenious legal devices, including 'feet of fines' (p. 39) and secret trusts (p. 43).

Much too complex a matter to be covered in a brief chapter, Oxford's dispersal of his inheritance has been studied at length by Pearson, and needs only to be summarized here. Pearson has noted (p. 18) that Leicester received an annual income of £859 on Oxford properties which he held from 1563 to 1571, but owed the Queen £803 on the same properties, resulting in a net income of £56 per annum. Though Pearson concludes that Leicester was satisfied with personal prestige in lieu of significant financial benefit, an effective administrator might conceal income from the crown, pocketing far more than the official rent through private deals and offers of patronage. Concealed incomes may account for Sir Thomas Wilson's estimation of the earldom's true worth in 1562 at more than £12,000 per annum, as against the £3000–4000 which Pearson has traced through official documents.

Given that fiscal restraint was a trait remote from Oxford's character, the story of his life becomes in large part the story of the loss of his lands. Oxford's first documented alienation occurred on 1 January 1575, about a month before he embarked on his first licenced visit to the Continent.[12] By 20 December 1578 he had alienated 12 more properties, and by the end of 1580, another 22. By 1584–85 his alienations approached and possibly surpassed a further 20.[13] By about 1592 Oxford had alienated every landed estate inherited from his father, all the estates received at the hands of the Queen, and a London estate he would purchase in 1580, Fisher's Folly. The very roof over his deathbed was secure only because ownership was retained by his second wife's family.

Pearson has calculated (p. 40) that at their peak Oxford's estates in Essex, Suffolk, Cambridgeshire, Hertfordshire, Warwickshire, and Buckinghamshire alone yielded a total of 857 separate annual rents. Even by Pearson's conservative reckoning (p. 162), income from the earldom's estates fell from £3500 in 1562 to

£20 in 1604. With a declining income, Oxford fell increasingly into debt, as calculated by Pearson (p. 25): in 1571, £3500; in 1573, £6000; in 1575, £9000; in 1576, £12,000; in the mid-1580s, £11,000 to the Queen alone; by the 1590s, £21,000 to the Queen alone.

'By 1592', in the words of Pearson (p. 24), 'the Oxford estates were no more.' Not only would Oxford make no will at the time of his death in 1604, but his widow would refuse to take out the normal letters of administration – for who would bequeath non-existent property, or who would willingly accept an inheritance whose debts vastly outweighed its assets?

PART VI

Intrigue
1579–1580

37 Oxford vs. Sidney

From 17 to 27 August 1579 Elizabeth entertained Alençon and his French 'Commissioners', having arrived without the contemplated exchange of hostages. While Oxford seems to have been sympathetic to a possible marriage, the determined opposition of Sir Philip Sidney and his uncle Leicester may have triggered an incident between Oxford and Sidney known to history as the 'tennis-court quarrel'.[1]

Sidney, born in 1554 and thus four years younger than his rival, had been formally pledged to Anne Cecil before she married Oxford instead (Ward, p. 61). Sidney had accompanied Lincoln to Paris in 1572, along with Henry Burrough and Charles Arundel: there Sidney witnessed the St Bartholomew's Day massacre. Sidney was returning from his three-year Continental tour when he ran into Oxford's entourage at Strasbourg in April 1575, Ralph Hopton leaving Sidney for Oxford. In August 1578 Oxford and Sidney had accompanied Elizabeth to Saffron Walden, whence both men became dedicatees of Harvey's *Gratulationes Valdenenses*.

The most elaborate description of the 'tennis-court quarrel' occurs in Fulke Greville's 'Life of Sidney', in manuscript until 1652. Born in 1554, Greville was Sidney's exact contemporary, indeed his schoolmate. He characterizes Sidney as one who enjoyed 'the freedome of his thoughts'; rather than naming Oxford, he calls him simply 'a Peer of this Realm':[2]

> And in this freedome of heart [Sir Philip] being one day at Tennis, a Peer of this Realm, born great, greater by alliance [i.e., to Burghley], and superlative in the Princes [=the Queen's] favour, abruptly came into the Tennis-Court; and speaking out of these three paramount authorities, he forgot to entreat that, which he could not legally command. When by the encounter of a steady object, finding unrespectiveness in himself (though a great Lord) not respected by this Princely spirit, he grew to expostulate more roughly. The returns of which stile comming still from an understanding heart, that knew what was due to it self, and what it ought [=owed] to others, seemed (through the mists of my Lords passions, swoln with the winde of his faction then reigning) to provoke in yeelding. Whereby, the lesse amazement, or confusion of thoughts he stirred up in Sir Philip, the more shadowes this

great Lords own mind was possessed with: till at last with rage (which is ever ill-disciplin'd) he commands them to depart the Court. To this Sir Philip temperately answers; that if his Lordship had been pleased to express desire in milder Characters, perchance he might have led out those, that he should now find would not be driven out with any scourge of fury. This answer (like a Bellows) blowing up the sparks of excess already kindled, made my Lord scornfully call Sir Philip by the name of Puppy. In which progress of heat, as the tempest grew more and more vehement within, so did their hearts breath[e] out their perturbations in a more loud and shrill accent. The French Commissioners unfortunately had that day audience, in those private Galleries, whose windows looked into the Tennis-Court. They instantly drew all to this tumult: every sort of quarrels sorting well with their humors, especially this. Which Sir Philip perceiving, and rising with inward strength, by the prospect of a mighty faction against him; asked my Lord, with a loud voice, that which he heard clearly enough before. Who (like an Echo, that still multiplies by reflexions) repeated this Epithet of Puppy the second time. Sir Philip resolving in one answer to conclude [=confute, 'shut up' (*OED*4a)] both the attentive hearers, and passionate actor, gave my Lord a Lie, impossible (as he averred) to be retorted; in respect all the world knows, Puppies are gotten by Dogs, and Children by men.

In effect, Sidney accused Oxford point-blank of lying. Both Sidney and Oxford were poets, of course, and both understood that a word like 'Puppy' may be taken in a metaphorical as well as in a literal sense. But insults, however colourful, are not dismissable as lies. Perhaps Sidney was also saying: 'I may be a dog (metaphorically speaking), but you are not a man (in any sense of the word)'; or worse: 'Men beget children, but as you live not only apart from your wife, but with boys, you are no man and will beget no male heirs'.[3] Greville continues:

Hereupon those glorious inequalities of Fortune in his Lordship were put to a kinde of pause, by a precious inequality of nature in this Gentleman. So that they both stood silent a while, like a dumb shew in a Tragedy; till Sir Philip sensible of his own wrong, the forrain, and factious spirits that attended [=watched]; and yet, even in this question between him, and his superior, tender to his Countries honour; with some words of sharp accent, led the way abruptly out of the Tennis-Court; as if so unexpected an accident were not fit to be decided any farther in that place. Whereof the great Lord making another sense, continues his play, without any advantage of reputation; as by the standard of humours in those times it was conceived.

A day Sir Philip remains in suspense, when hearing nothing of, or from the Lord, he sends a Gentleman of worth to awake him out of his trance; wherein the French would assuredly think any pause, if not death, yet a lethargy of true honour in both. This stirred a resolution in his Lordship to send Sir Philip a Challenge. Notwithstanding, these thoughts in the great Lord wandred so long between glory, anger, and inequality of state, as the Lords of her Majesties Counsell took notice of the differences, commanded peace, and laboured a reconciliation between them. But needlessly in one respect, and bootlessly in another. The great Lord being (as it should seem) either not hasty to adventure many inequalities against one, or inwardly satisfied with the progress of his own Acts: Sir Philip on the other side confident, he neither had nor would lose, or let fall any thing of his right. Which her Majesties Counsell quickly perceiving, recommended this work to her self.

The Queen, who saw that by the loss, or disgrace of either, she could gain nothing, presently undertakes Sir Philip; and (like an excellent Monarch) lays before him the difference in degree between Earls, and Gentlemen; the respect inferiors ought [=owed] to their superiors; and the necessity in Princes to maintain their own creations, as degrees descending between the peoples licentiousness, and the anoynted Soveraignty of Crowns: how the Gentlemans neglect of the Nobility taught the Peasant to insult upon both.

Whereunto Sir Philip, with such reverence as became him, replyed: First, that place was never intended for privilege to wrong: witness her self, who how Soveraign soever she were by Throne, Birth, Education, and Nature; yet was she content to cast her own affections into the same moulds her Subjects did, and govern all her rights by their Laws. Again, he besought her Majesty to consider, that although he [=Oxford] were a great Lord by birth, alliance, and grace; yet hee was no Lord over him: and therefore the difference of degrees between free men, could not challenge any other homage than precedency. And by her Fathers Act (to make a Princely wisdom become the more familiar) he did instance the Government of King Henry the eighth, who gave the Gentry free, and safe appeal to his own feet, against the oppression of the Grandees; and found it wisdome, by the stronger corporation in number, to keep down the greater in power: inferring else, that if they should unite, the over-grown might be tempted, by still coveting more, to fall (as the Angels did) by affecting equality with their Maker.

This constant tenor of truth he took upon him; which as a chief duty in all creatures, both to themselves, & the soveraignty above them, protected this Gentleman (though he obeyed not) from the displeasure of his Soveraign. Wherein he left an authentical president [=precedent] to after ages, that howsoever tyrants allow of no scope, stamp, or standard, but their own will; yet with Princes there is a latitude for subjects to reserve native, & legall freedom, by paying humble tribute in manner, though not in matter, to them.

Vague about dates and the duration of the quarrel, Greville leaves the denouement uncertain: did Elizabeth take kindly to being lectured by Sidney? and did Sidney let the matter drop?

We may conclude that after withdrawing from the tennis court, Sidney waited 'A day'; then, 'hearing nothing of, or from the Lord', though the French would deem it a disgrace to wait any time at all, Sidney 'sends a Gentleman of worth to awake him out of his trance', presumably with a verbal reminder. Thus awakened, Oxford finally sent Sidney a challenge in writing.

Arundel supports Greville's accounts, and supplies names (4.3/4@120):

At what time the quarell fell owte betwene this monsterous villayne and Mr Sidneye, he [=Oxford] imployes Rawlie and my selfe, with a message to this effect, that the question myght be honorablie endid.

Arundel identifies himself and Walter Ralegh as Oxford's messengers, requesting a duel.[4] He continues:

> Mr Sidnie acceptid gladlie therof, and desireid muche it might not be deferrid ...

So Sidney gave a verbal response to Oxford's challenge.

Sidney himself makes up for Greville's failure to supply dates. Christopher Hatton had already spoken or written to Sidney on behalf of the Privy Council (this confirms Greville's reference to 'her Majesties Counsell'); now, on 28 August, Sidney replied to Hatton:[5]

> Sir, the greate advauntage which I have, by the singuler goodnes and frendshippe, it pleaseth you to shewe me, which in trewthe I doo, and have a good while, reputed amongest the chief[es]t ornamentes of my lief and fortune, makes me fynde my self at as muche disadvantage when my hart, longinge to shewe my self gratefull can present nothing which maye be servisable unto you. Butt as I knowe, and have well founde, that you doo esteeme a trewe good will, of some valewe, in that kynde only, can I shewe my self, and assure yowe, that the litell that I am, is and shalbe in all tymes and fortunes, so to be disposed by you, as one, that hath promysed love, and is bounde by deserte to performe it. That is all therefore I can saye, though you loose me, you have me. As for the matter dependinge betwene the Earle of Oxford and me, certaynly, Sir, howe soever I might have forgeven hym, I should never have forgeven my self, yf I had layne under so proude an injurye, as he would have laide uppon me, neither can any thinge under the sunne make me repente yt, nor any miserye make me goo one half worde back frome yt; lett him therefore, as hee will, digest itt; for my parte I thincke, tyinge upp, makes some thinges seeme fercer, then they would bee. ...

Since Sidney rejects the advice of the Privy Council conveyed through Hatton, only the Queen could now put a stop to the quarrel.

No duel had yet taken place when Sidney's friend Hubert Languet wrote on 14 October from Antwerp ('Clusius' in the letter being an unidentified mutual acquaintance):

> ... On my arrival here, I found our friend Clusius prepared for a journey, which I delayed for a day or two, that I might hear from him all about your affairs. From your letter as well as from his mouth, I was informed of the dispute between you and the Earl of Oxford, which gave me great pain. I am aware that by a habit inveterate in all Christendom, a nobleman is disgraced if he does not resent such an insult: still I think you were unfortunate to be drawn into this contention, although I see that no blame is to be attached to you for it. You can derive no true honour from it, even if it gave you occasion to display to the world your constancy and courage. You want another stage for your character, and I wish you had chosen it in this part of the world.

> On the other hand be careful lest under the influence of swashbucklers you should overstep the bounds of your native modesty. In this very quarrel, sound as your

position was, you have gone further than you ought to have done, for when you
had flung back the insult thrown at you, you ought to have said no more; as a
matter of fact, carried away by your quick temper, you supplemented it with a
provocation,[6] and thus you have deprived yourself of the choice of weapons if at
any time this controversy should have to be decided by a duel; for it is the people
who want to teach us how we should go mad by rule who have applied their own
laws to duels, which of all things are the most unjust. If you had stood fast after you
had given your adversary the lie, it would have been his business to challenge you.
In our time not a few jurists have written about dueling. William of Neuburg, an
English writer, quotes the decrees of a certain Synod by which duels are altogether
condemned, and Christians forbidden to take part in them.

Since your adversarius has attached himself to Anjou's party, if your procus[7] shall
return to you with a crowd of French noblemen about him, you must be on your
guard, for you know the fiery nature of my countrymen. ...

Languet wrote again on 14 November:[8]

From the letter which I gave Henry White for you, you will have learnt that I
received yours, in which you mention the dispute between yourself and the Earl of
Oxford. Someone has written on the same subject to his Excellency Prince John
Casimir, for he wrote to me the other day that it had given him great pain. He begs
you to consider whether he can do anything to assist you, for he assures you that
you shall not want his good offices. ...

Now I will treat you frankly, as I am accustomed to do, for I am sure our friendship
has reached a mark at which neither of us can be offended at any freedom of the
other. It was a delight to me last winter to see you high in favour and enjoying the
esteem of all your countrymen; but to speak plainly, the habits of your court seemed
to me somewhat less manly than I could have wished, and most of your noblemen
appeared to me to seek for a reputation more by a kind of affected courtesy than by
those virtues which are wholesome to the state, and which are most becoming to
generous spirits and to men of high birth. I was sorry, therefore, and so were other
friends of yours, to see you wasting the flower of your life on such things, and I
feared lest that noble nature of yours should be dulled, and lest from habit you
should be brought to take pleasure in pursuits which only enervate the mind.

If the arrogance and insolence of Oxford has roused you from your trance, he has
done you less wrong than they who have hitherto been more indulgent to you. ...

Languet hoped that Sidney would become more involved in public life, perhaps
on the Continent, rather than retiring to his family's estates.

Languet's two letters, the first written six weeks and the second more than ten
weeks after Sidney's reply to Hatton, suggest that the quarrel was not quickly
resolved. This supposition is reinforced by Arundel:[9]

Mr Sidnie acceptid gladlie therof [i.e., of Oxford's challenge], and desireid muche
it might not be deferrid; whiche when he [=Oxford] h[e]ard, never meaninge any
thinge lesse as after it appereid, told vs playnelie he was not to hazard him selfe,

> haveinge receaveid suche an iniurie, and therfore he had a nother cowrse, and that
> was to have him [=Sidney] murtherid in his lo[d]geinge. The manner howe he
> wold have done it, and what wordes I gave him, and howe I withstode it, lett my
> Lord Harrye, who dothe verye honorablie, and Rawlie, as honestlie, report.

Considering himself the injured party, Oxford thus resolved not to face Sidney in
a duel, but rather to have him murdered. Howard supports Arundel's account:[10]

> Thus but for me, as I will proue by witnesse, Mr Philip Sidney, proffering his
> person to the combat like a gallant gentilman, had notwithstandinge beine most
> beastly murderid by twelue caliuers in his bedd at Grenwich, and a barge with 12
> caliuers more should haue carried them away to Graues Ende, whear a littell higher
> [=upriver] a barke of Baker, brother to his sourgion, should have wayted for them.

Howard, claiming credit for deflecting Oxford's murderous plot, here supplies
details: having murdered Sidney in his bed at Greenwich with muskets, Oxford's
twelve henchmen were to escape by a barge manned by another dozen caliver-
men to Gravesend; there a bark, or small ship, would have been waiting, owned
(and perhaps commanded) by Christopher Baker, brother of George Baker, Oxford's surgeon. (This is another example of shipping controlled by Oxford.) As
we shall learn, Oxford and Sidney were at it again – or still at it – in January 1580.

38 Oxford vs. Leicester

In the course of 1579, Oxford precipitated a quarrel with Sidney's uncle Leicester,
who remained in Elizabeth's bad books over his unauthorized marriage on 21
September 1578 to Lettice Knollys, widow of the 1st Earl of Essex and mother of
Robert Devereux, now 2nd Earl of Essex and Burghley's ward. Henry Howard
reveals that Oxford, citing Rowland York as witness, complained to Walsingham
that Leicester had been engaged in sedition if not treason. Howard situates the
event after Oxford's attack on Worcester (LIB-3.1/4):

> This owtrage could not be forgotten when he [=Oxford] falles to Mr Secretary
> Walsingham, his constante and approuid frend, aduertising [=accusing] my Lord
> of Lester of a certayne practise which himselfe forsoth had founde out against him
> by Roland York, wherin the said Mr Secretary, my Lords of Huntingdon, and
> Essex, wear consorted; but when uppon the deniall of Roland Yorke my Lord of
> Oxford was put to bed for wante of proufe, he wold haue wrestid me by flattery ore
> any meane to iustifie the knowledge of suche practisis from Rowland York, of
> whom I neuer h[e]ard any suche word nor syllable.

An independent memorandum, headed 'Articles wherof Oxford wold have
accusid Lester' (LIB-1/1), contains two major accusations: first, that Leicester had
stockpiled weapons, powder, and food at Kenilworth Castle, as well as a large

cache of money, in preparation for a rebellion; second, that Leicester had been complicit in the death of Walter Devereux, the 'old' Earl of Essex, on 22 September 1576. Oxford's principal informant is named as Edward York.

Charles Arundel, under the heading 'Mercenarye faythe', declared of Oxford (LIB-4.2/3):

> He willed me to saye to one in Ingeland [?] that what soever he wold have him affirme as sayd to him by my Lord of Lester he wold affirme it to his face at Greenwich he proferrid my Lord Harrye and my selfe five hundrid powndes to affirme vppon owre one [=own] knoledge the wordes vtterid by Rowland Yorke of Mr secretorie Walsingham.

Again, under the charge of 'Dangerous practice' (LIB-4.2/5.1):

> A device fatherid vppon Rowland Yorke, that Mr Walsinggam shuld packe [=conspire] with my Lords of Essex and Huntingeton, first to begine with my Lord of Lester abowte his wife makeinge all the strengthe he could vnder culler of pretending request of iustice, and when that shuld ether be denied or abridgeid to attempte the reformation of the goverment. the practice with my Lord Harrye, and my self, to avowe the knoledge of the sayd practice from Rowland Yorke his mouthe which we refuseid ...

Arundel even reported Oxford's 'sekeinge for poyson of Ceasare¹ that was with my Lord of Lester' (LIB-4.2.5/10).

Howard and Arundel declare further that Oxford planned a physical attack on Leicester at the 'garden stayre' – doubtless at Whitehall – 'as he landid from my Lord of Essex' – evidently returning from a visit to his step-son at Burghley House. Oxford planned a second attack near Wanstead, Leicester's estate across the river from Greenwich. Finally, Oxford inscribed Italianate grafitti 'vppon the garden wall vndir [Leicester's] windowes [at Whitehall]', with the sneering text, *Palazzo de Castiti* [sic] (LIB-3.6.1/2@126; 4.2/5.3). Howard claims personal responsibility for having warned Leicester of the impending assaults: further, Oxford's 'practises were neither one nor two, as not my voice alone but nine ore ten both can and will depose if they may be callid' (LIB-3.8; 4.4/7).

Arundel reports that 'my Lord of Oxford' was 'commaundid to kepe his chamber abowte the libellinge betwene him and my Lord of Lester' (LIB-2.3.1/3), while Howard identifies the place of confinement as 'Greenwich[,] whear [Oxford] was restrayned to his chamber' (LIB-3.2). Though Oxford could not roam abroad, he could receive visitors. Thus, writing in early 1581, Arundel recalls a meeting with Oxford 'a year and a half since, walking in the garden at Greenwich'.² Oxford's confinement probably ended when the court decamped from Greenwich after 21 December 1579.³

Oxford's house at Greenwich had doubtless been taken on short let, for wherever the court moved, courtiers must follow. Howard and Arundel supply architectural detail, Howard recalling a conversation 'at Grenwich in [Oxford's] gallery', Arundel one conversation with Oxford 'in his chamber', and another 'walking in the garden' (LIB-3.2; 4.3/2; 4.4/1; 2.1.5/24). Southwell is even more descriptive: 'Oxford shewed me [a book of prophecies] in his gret chamber, and maed me the onli exposition of yt. Mr Charles Arundel was than in the bottome of the chamber very ernestli writing a letter and never to my knowleg saw the said boke' (LIB-3.4/2). Arundel declares of the same book: 'suche a toye Oxford layd vpp in his deske' (LIB-2.3.1/3). It was here that Oxford was 'drunk as a beggar' (LIB-4.3/2), and here that he held forth 'at his table' (LIB-3.2@95).

Burghley's retrospective Diary entry for September 1579 may shed further light on some of Oxford's activities while under house arrest (ii, p. 780):

> Mons. the D. of Alanson, came to Greenwych secretly, and lodged at Mr. Light's House.

Alençon's visit at the end of August was a matter of public knowledge, but his return in September was secret. That Oxford and Arundel not only knew about Alençon's presence but were in active contact with him through his agent Simier may be inferred from questions later put to Arundel (LIB-2.1.4/6):

> Item who they were that did geve Monsieur de Simiers secret intelligence of the Quenes dealinges and whether you kno not when that by makeinge a marke on a stone in Lightes garden did geve knoledge for the sayd Simiers that he had advertisment to geve him of importance and therfore he shuld by that marke kno howe to kepe atyme [=a time] and howre of meteinge

> [Arundel:] ... I protest before God I was never acquaynetid with any man, that gave Monsieur Simiers intelligence of her Maiesties dealinge, nor with any suche marke in Lightes garden. Onelie I sawe as I conceavid Simiers toke vpp a paper which he re[a]d longe of, but whether it fell owte of his hand or whether he fownd it ther I do not knoe, but not longe after, du Burge tolde me that Simiers had advertysment that he should have stabbe with a dagger gewen him, yf he [looked] not well to it.

Someone – by implication Oxford – communicated with Simier (and Alençon) by making a mark in the garden of Alençon's Greenwich residence. The next question points to more sinister eventualities:

> Item who it was that told Monsieur de Simiers that he should have a stabb with a dagger[?] and likewise who it was that vppon this cause wold have borrowid a privie dubblet of the Earl of Oxford

> [Arundel:] ... it is most trewe I never h[e]ard by whome or whose procurement it shuld have bin don, nor where he lernt it, but herevppon he sent to me to borrowe him a privie dubblett.

Beginning by denying knowledge of intelligence-gathering activities, Arundel ends by stating that he had learned through one du Burge that a threat on Simier's life had been conveyed through a note which Simier either had received earlier and dropped, or had found lying on the ground near Light's garden. Du Burge, other-wise Captain Bourg, a messenger-factotum of Alençon and Simier,[4] informed Arundel that Simier had received a threat that he should be stabbed with a dagger – presumably from an opponent of the proposed marriage. Arundel admits supplying Simier with a 'privie dubblett' borrowed from Oxford. (A privy doub-let, or coat, was 'a coat of mail worn under the ordinary dress': *OED*.)

Meanwhile, on 16 November, apparently while still under house arrest in Greenwich, Oxford pursued a life-long attempt to recover his ancestral rights:[5]

> The title of Edward Earl of Oxford to the offices of steward, bailiff and keeper of the Forest of Waltham and the House and Park of Havering. Traces his descent from Thomas de Clere, who received the offices from Richard Munfichet.

Fulfilment of this dream would have to wait until after the Queen's death in 1603.

39 Table, Gallery, Garden

On the testimony of Henry Howard, Charles Arundel, and Francis Southwell, Oxford railed against Leicester and the Queen all the time he was confined to residence at Greenwich in the latter months of 1579. Here Oxford strikes what was perhaps his most characteristic pose: presiding at a well-furnished table, flanked by male companions, high in his cups, firing satirical salvos and witticisms, en-listing his guests in his conspiratorial fantasies. Nothing and nobody was off limits.

Evidence that Oxford allowed scandalous talk at his table, whether at Green-wich, Westminster, or elsewhere, comes from his own pen, among charges against Arundel in January 1581 (LIB-2.2.1/4):

> a littell before Christmas at my lo[d]ginge in Westmester [=Westminster] Swift [=Thomas or Hugh Swift] beinge present and George Gyfford talkinge of the order of liuinge by mony and [the] dyfference betwien that and revenu by land, he [=Arundel] sayd at the last if George Gyfford could make [=assemble] thre thousand pound he wowld set him in to a course whear he ne[e]d not care for all England and theare he showld liue more to his content and wythe more reputatione then ever he dyd or myght hope for in England and they wowld make all the cowrt wonder to heare of them. Wythe diuers other braue and glorious speches whearat George Gyfford replyd Gods blud Char[l]es whear is this. he answerd yf yow haue thre thousand pound or can make it he could tell the other saying as he thought he could find the means to make thre thousand pound. that speache finished withe the cominge in of supper ...

Dangerous conversation ceased when servants entered with food. Arundel recalled the same discussion:

> ... I remember well beinge at the Earl of Oxfords lodgeinge in Westminster we fell
> in talke, of travell and travellers how a Ientill man [=gentleman] that wold travell
> myght live and after what sorte that had three thowsan powndes in his purse and
> my opinion was, that beinge but a private man no man leveid [=lived] more
> gallantlie in the cort, and for this matter I referre my spechees to report of Mr
> Gifford and Mr Swifte

Arundel softens the topic of conversation into a discussion of travel rather than
voluntary exile. He ends with a cut against Oxford, for living 'more gallantly'
than any other.

Arundel further portrays Oxford at table as a garrulous inebriate (LIB-4.3/2):

> The second vice, wherwith I meane to towche him ... is that he is a most notorious
> drunkerd, and verye seldome sober ... I require no more for my acquitall but that
> my Lord Harrye, Sowthewell and Rawlie, may be askeid, whoe it was that beinge as
> druncke as a begger, in his chamber at Grenewidg added further vnto those speches
> that he fownd it trewe, that Ceasar had writen of the Frenche in his commentaries,
> and howe Godd was fallen in to a strange vayne of crowneinge none but cockes-
> comes. ...
>
> in his drunken fittes, he is no man but a beast disposest of all temperance, modestie,
> and reason and rvnes [=runs] as one posest with a wicked spright in to all actes of
> cruelltie, inyurye, and villonye and yf I accownetid otherwise of him then of Iohn
> Passe to whome I have most aptelie often comparde him I culd not with dewtye
> have concealeid what hathe past him but so livelie dothe the one resemble, the other,
> in all condicions, as settinge aside ther degree, ther is smale difference in bestlie
> drunckeennesse this Monster excedes the other, and in raylinge of all estates he over
> runnes him spareinge no woman be she never so vertuous nor any man be he never
> so honorable, and this beast beinge never restrayned from this libertie of raylinge ...

Arundel compares Oxford to John Passe, Burghley's servant, evidently a notorious drunkard.

Confirmation of Oxford's characteristic inebriation comes from an unexpected
source. Whereas Howard and Arundel accuse Oxford of many vices, Southwell is
comparatively restrained. When Howard attributes to Oxford the complaint
'that the Catholices wear good aue mary Cockescombes for yeldinge their heades
which might be sauid by rebellion', Southwell agrees: *Audivi* [=I heard it myself].
Southwell similarly concedes that Oxford railed against the Duke of Norfolk 'for
comminge vppe when he was sent for': *Audivi*. Southwell adds his own charge
that Oxford had 'promised to sack London, and geve me Day Aldermans house ...'
But to the more serious report of Oxford's 'daily railinge of the quene', Southwell
responds, in mitigation of Oxford's fault: *Audivi in poculis* – I heard it – but he
was in his cups.

Arundel and Howard similarly proclaim Oxford's untruthfulness at table, his
'ordenarye vse to lie for the whetstone in the worst degree' – the whetstone being
a traditional prize in a lying contest.[1] 'Lett these examples plede', writes Arundel:

– that the cobblers wyves of Millaine, are more richlie dressid everie workeinge daye then the Qwene on Christmas daye

– that but for the comminge of Beningefeld [=Thomas Bedingfield] and the Duke of Alvaes [=Ferdinand de Toledo's] perswation rather to omitte the service then forsake his cuntrie he had surpriseid Bommle[2] wittnesse my Lord Howard of Effinggam, Lord Henry Francis Southwell Walter Ralegh and my self.

– that yf my Lord [Charles? Henry?] Howard had not in the Quenes name callid him a waye by letter, he had bin governer of Millayne [=Milan], Henry Howard Walter Ralegh Francis Southwell Harrye Burroughe[3] Robinson.

– that he was in the waye to genoa with 3000 horsees a 10000 fotemen to take it for the Kinge of Spayne by Don Iones [=John's] direction when the Cardinall Moron toke vpp the matter[4]

– that he was profferid ten thousan powndes a yere by the Pope and more by Kinge Phillipp at Napales.

– that the cownetesse of Mirondola came fiftie miles to lie with him for loves

– that the Qwene of Navare sent a messenger to desire him to speke with him in her chamber

– that St Markes churche is paveid at Venice with diamowntes and rubies

– that a marchant in Geane [=Genoa] hathe a Mantell of a chimnye of more price then all the treasure of the Towre

– that he red the reathoricke lecter publikelie in sermies [?sermons] preached at Strosbreke [=Strasbourg]

Here is a potpourri: denigrations of the Queen and her wealth; boasts of military prowess thwarted by the Queen; travellers' tales; sexual braggadoccio; and boasts of intellectual prowess.

Many of Oxford's fabrications are recited at length, as for example by Arundel (LIB-4.3/1.1):

And first will I detecte him of the most impudent, and sencelesse lies, that ever past the mowthe of any man, Whiche as heretofore they have made muche sporte to the hereers, so are they nowe turnyd to the preiudice of divers [persons]. of a Million at the least that hathe past his tonge, I will onelie speke of three in affirmacion of whiche lies being voyde of sence, and withowte coullor of truthe, to have them beleveid he hathe periurde him selfe a hundrid times, and damnyd him selfe to the pitt of hell. a vice not inferior to manye that him ateneid [=attend] and leveinge all his circumstances this is the first lie. at his beinge in Flawnders [i.e., in 1574] the Duke of Alva, as he will constantlie affirme, grewe so muche to affecte him for those rare partes he sawe in him, as he made him his lifetenant generall over all the armye then in the lowe cuntrye. and imployd him ferther in a notable pece of service, wher according to his place he commawnedid and directed, the ambassador of spaine that is nowe here, Mountdragon, Sansoe Davela[5] and the rest of the captaines, but these, whom I have namid, as he will saye, of all others were most glad to be commaundid by him, and so valiantlie he behaveid him selfe as he gayned great love of all the soldiers, and no lesse admiracion of his vallure[6] of all sortes: and in this iornye he passid manye straytes and divers bridgees kepte by the enemye whiche he bett [=beat] them from with the losse of many a mans life, but still he forseid [=forced] them to retire, till at the last he approcheid the place that he went to besege [=Leiden?], and vseinge no delaye the Canon was plantid, and the batterie continuyd the space of ten dayes by whiche time he had made suche a breche, as by a generall consent of all his captaynes he gave an assaulte, and to encourrage his soldiers this valiant prince ledd them therto and throughe the forse of his murtheringe arme, many were sore wondid, but more killed[.] notwithstand-inge beinge not well followid bye the royters [=ritters, knights] he was repulseid but determaninge to geve a freshe and generall assalte the next day Mr Beningefeld [see 4.2/2.1], as the devell wold have it, came in vppon his post horse, and callid him from this service by her Maiesties letters beinge the gretist disgrace, that ever eny suche generall receaveid and nowe the question is, whether this noble generall were more troblid with his callinge home, or Beningefeld more moveid with pittye and compassion to behold this slaugheter, or his horse more aferd when he past the bridges at sight of the ded bodies, wherat he startid and flunge in suche sort as Beninfeld cold hardlie kepe his backe. Whether this hathe paste him I leve it to the report of my Lord Charles howard, my Lord Winser, my Lord Compton, my Lord Harrye Howard, and my Lord Thomas Howard. Rawlie, Gorge, Gifford, Waldose, Noell, and Sowthewell with divers other Ientillmen that hathe accompanid him, and yf in his soberist modes [=moods], he wold owne this, it maye easalie be gatherid what will pas him in his cuppes.

Oxford similarly claimed to have settled Italian disputes at Genoa and elsewhere (LIB-1/2), and to have made 'certayne excellent oracions' at Venice, Padua, and Bologna, so that he was 'reputed for his eloquence another Cicero and for his conducke [=conduct, accomplishments] a Ceaser' (LIB-1/3).

Arundel incidentally supplies a list of Oxford's dinner-guests: not only Howard, Arundel, and Southwell, but Charles, Lord Howard of Effingham, Edward, Lord Windsor (son of Oxford's half-sister Katherine), Henry Compton,[7] Thomas, Lord Howard (younger brother of Philip Howard), Walter Ralegh, Arthur Gorge, George Gifford, and Henry Noell (a well-known courtier).

Most nearly verging on sedition was Oxford's 'Vnduetifull dealinge to the Quene' (LIB-4.2/9):

[1] his contynuall raylinge against hir Maiestie and fle[e]inge the companye of my Lord Harrye Sowthewell and my selfe with ill wordes of vs all to his men for perswadinge him to applie him selfe to content and serverve [=serve] her Maiestie (see LIB-3.1/2.2@36).

2 that the Quene sayd he was a bastard for whiche cause he wold never love hir and leve her in the lurche one daye. one Mistris for love another for the pownd.

3 diswation, to my Lord Harrye for settinge furthe a treatise callid Encomia Elizabethii and the reasons whiche he vsed profferinge my [=me] monnye to diswade my Lord Harrye from printinge of it

4 the Catholickes good Avemarye Cock[sc]omes that wold not rebell against the Qwene ...

6 raylinge at Francis Sowthwell for commendinge the Qwenes singeinge one night at Hamton Cort protestinge by the blud of God, that she had the worst voyce, and did everye thinge with the worst grace, that ever any woman did, and that he was never, non plus [=at a loss for words], but when he came to speke well of hir ...

11 his continuall raylinge of my Lord of Arundell,[8] for puttinge his trust in the Qwene ...

13 no companion but the vicecownt of Baltingglas [=James Eustace] for he sayd that the Qwene wold challenge the primacye which Christ wold never geve vnto his one [=own] Mother ...

In his third item, Arundel refers to Howard's *Encomia Elizabethii*, now among Howard's unpublished papers in the British Library (MS Egerton 944). In his fourth, Arundel cites Oxford's characterization of English Catholics as 'Ave-Maria Cockscombs' unwilling to rebel against the Queen. In his sixth, Arundel reports Oxford's denigration of the Queen's singing voice. In his thirteenth, he refers to Oxford's cherishing of a copy of a letter that James Eustace, the Irish Viscount Baltinglas, sent to the Queen in the summer of 1580.

Howard confessed to similar knowledge of Oxford's reproaches in a letter written about 29 December 1580 (LIB-3.1/2.1).

Concerninge wante of duty to your Maiesty which I destested most in him and so did all that kept him company I am to witnesse and avowe ane vtter condemnatione of thos princelye vertewes and good giftes whiche the worst disposed can not but admire and wonder at And least [=lest] I may be thought to speak of splene I craue that Charles Arundell Francis Sowthwell William Cornwallys may be chargid one [=on] their othe to tell whither he could euer broke [=brook] the prayses of your witte or of your persone I will not speak in this respecte so fullie as I may but I can proue by witnessis inowe [=enough] that when I scaped best I was reproued to my face of seruile flattery and so weare diuerse other as I can declare by setting downe bothe tymes and places of this bitter dealinge Howe often hathe he sworne to me perswadinge him with all the reasons I could possibly deuise to be directed by your Maiestis aduise alone and prosequte your fauor, that he neuer was non plus but when he delte with youe and the reason was bycause he was enforcid still to speake against his harte and lyking This is but a taste your Maiesty shall here of better stuffe if euer I be called face to face for proufe of thease particulers Neither will I runne forth with a single voice as my Lord is faine to doo but vouch more honest then himselfe for warrantise

Howard now moves to a more particular charge:

> I speak not of his strange digesting of your slight disgracis when they came vppon
> his owne defaulte and made both me and others pensiue for his sake bicause I wold
> not gladlie wound him furder then the tearinge of[f] this painted maske and visard
> of hypocrisy

Having mentioned the Queen's 'slight disgraces' as if they were not merely a
figment of Oxford's (or Howard's) imagination, Howard addresses the matter of
his own failure to report so serious an offence:

> It was a faulte I graunt to couer this but still me thought it was but frothe and
> wantonesse of youthe which eyther tyme wold alter ore correction wold amende
> the scourge wherof althoughe I held to be the fittest instrumente of calling home
> this wandering and wastfull child yet could I neuer yeld to be the meane ore author
> of his trouble At the last I found this mallice was engraffed in his nature
> wheruppon I laborid with all my frendes to kepe aloofe from him that had no
> playefellowes but kinges and quenes to sporte withall ...

Thus Howard claims that he had accepted Oxford's own argument that his indis-
cretions were 'frothe and wantonesse of youthe', until he finally discovered that
'mallice' was engrafted into his nature. In naming kings and queens as Oxford's
playfellows, Howard seems to take Oxford's boasts (sarcastically) at face value.

Howard's reference to the Queen's 'slight disgraces' provoked a demand for
clarification. His undated response must have been submitted on or about 31
December 1580 (LIB-3.2). Howard confessed that Oxford

> hath vauntid [=boasted] of some fauores from your Maiesty which I dare take myne
> othe vppon the sacrid testament wear neuer yet imparted vnto any man that liued
> one [=on] this earth

Clearly the favours which Oxford claimed to have received from the Queen are
here imagined as sexual.

The Queen's presumptive 'slight disgraces' are more pointedly hinted at in the
aphoristic statement reported by Arundel in Item 2 above, and by Howard in
slightly different words:

> your Maiesty must be [caressed] for the pownde and another for his pleasure

Thus Oxford boasted that he had caressed Queen Elizabeth for financial reward
but looked elsewhere for pleasure – or love. Oxford's braggadoccio is of course no
more than a high-class version of the low-class slanders against the Queen reported
by Oxford's father in June 1560.

Following his dinners, and sometimes independently, Oxford often took a con-
fidant aside for more secretive chat. Howard tells of one such occasion (LIB-2.2):

> Walkinge one the tarris [=on the terrace] at Howard Howse ... he said he wolde
> deale plainly with me ...

Arundel attributes to 25 December 1580 a similar incident (LIB-4.1.1):

> On Svndaye last beinge Christmas day, the Earell of Oxenford desirid secrett conference with me as he had don the night before whervnto I assenteinge, we mett in the eveninge at the Maydes chamber doore, and after longe spechees in secret ... we departid thense to have gon to the garden but the dore beinge dubble locked or boltid we colde not gett in then we returnid to the Tarris [=terrace] and ther in the farther part of the lowe gallerie the sayde Earell vsid this speche vnto me ...

Thus Arundel describes their search for a place sufficiently remote and unobserved for them to exchange or disclose secrets.

Again, Arundel (LIB-2.1.5/24) admitted that he had heard

> of a rime, by one Edeward Heywod a yere and a halfe since, at whiche time I told it the Earl of Oxford walkeinge in the garden at Grenwidge alone with him vppon what occasion him selfe knoes & will remember his Lordship when time serves and never thinkeinge to have h[e]ard more of it but a little after her Maiesties comminge last to this towne,[9] beinge with him private in his chamber, he put me in mynd of suche a thinge I told him, and desirid me to repeat the wordes. whiche after some studye, callinge them to my remembrance, havinge almost forgotten them, and least mistrustinge wherabowte he went, with his helpe, rehearste them to him ...

As we now move to an investigation of Oxford's most intimate beliefs and practices, we must constantly keep in mind his penchant both for hush-hush conspiracy and for open boasting to close companions, particularly in the presence of food and drink.

40 Atheist

Oxford's erstwhile friends accused him of atheism, Henry Howard, for one, distilling his thoughts into five propositions (LIB-3.6.1; also 3.1/1):

> The Trinity a fable / Iosephe a wittollde [=wittol, knowing cuckold] / Nothinge so defensible by scripture as bawdry / Scriptures for pollicye / The Turke only wise who made his owne Alchoran

To this list Francis Southwell adds two more (LIB-3.6.1/1):

> what a blessing Salamon hadd for his 3C [=300] cuncubinnes / the Bible only to be to hold men in obedience, and mans devis[e]

Charles Arundel presents a list of his own (LIB-4.2/1):

> the glorious Trinitie was an old wives tale and voyde of reason / that he [=Oxford] cold make a better and more orderlie scripture in [six] dayes warninge / that Christ

was a simple man / that Iosephe was bothe a cuckckold and a wittold / that
nothinge was so defensible by the scripture as bawderie / that he cold never beleve
in suche a God as delte well with those that deserveid evell and evell with those that
deserved well / that he wuld prove by scripture that after this life we shuld be as yf
we had never ben and that the rest was deviseid but to make vs afrayd – like babes
and childerne – of owr shadowes.

In yet another list Arundel reports of Oxford (LIB-4.3/5, also 4.4/3):

his most horrible and detestable blasphemy in deniall of the devinitie of Christ,
owre Saviour / terminge the Trinitie as a fable / that Iosephe was a wittold, and the
Blessid Virgin a [w]hore

Arundel adds that Oxford said these things in Richmond, 'in the presence of a
number as my Lord Winsor, Mr Russell, and Rawlie'.

Such atheism is not so much a principled belief as mere sacrilege – dragging in
the mud the most cherished beliefs of the Christian faith.[1] First comes a rejection
of the Trinity, whose very incomprehensibility is a test of faith.[2] Next Oxford
attacks the historical foundation of Christianity, asserting that Jesus was a mere
mortal, his purported miraculous birth a fable, since Joseph was a cuckold and
Mary 'made a fault'. As for her purported virginity, 'To the first of Mathewe,
when I vouchid it against this beastly paradox, wherin she is affirmed to conceyue
by the Holy Ghost, he [=Oxford] sayd the Iewes of Italy wold tell another tale
and put both Mathewe, Marke, and Ihon to sylenc[e]'. Scripture itself is 'mans
device', so full of bawdry as to incite lechery rather than holy contemplation. The
Turks were right to compose their own 'Alcoran', and Oxford himself could write
an improved scripture on six days' notice. On presumably ethical grounds,
Oxford 'co[u]ld never believe in suche a God as delte well with those that deserveid evell, and evell with those that deserved well'. As to an afterlife, 'he wuld
prove by scripture that after this life we shuld be as yf we had never ben'. Religion
'was deviseid but to make vs afrayd – like babes and childerne – of owr
shadowes': so religion is merely a device of sovereigns and governments.

Oxford's putative atheism derived from widely available sources, most obviously
John Proctor's *The Fal of the Late Arrian* (1549), which lists and then answers
some two dozen articles of the Arian heresy. Reading against the grain, it is a
simple matter to extract the articles of disbelief, exactly what was done by the
author of the 'vile hereticall Conceiptes Denying the Deity of Ihesus Christ our
Savior fownd emongest the papers of Thomas Kydd prisoner / Which he
affirmeth that he had ffrom [Christopher] Marlowe' in the early 1590s.[3]

Closer to the date of the accusations, Arian heresy was charged against Matthew
Hamont in 1579, as told in 1592 by William Burton in *Dauid's Euidence* (sigs.
K6–6v):

I haue knowen some Arrian heretiques, whose life hath bene most strickt amongest
men, whose tounges haue bene tired with Scripture vpon Scripture, their knees

euen hardned in prayer, and their faces wedded to sadnesse, and their mouthes full of prayses to God, while in the meane time, they haue stoutly denied the diuinitie of the sonne of God, and haue not sticked to teare out of the Bible, all such places as made against them, such were Hamond, Lewes and Cole heretikes of wretched memorie lately executed and cut off in Norwich.

Earlier, in his 1580 *Chronicles*, John Stow had reported that Hamont 'had published these Heresies followyng' (sig. FFff2):

That the newe Testament and Gospell of Christe are but mere foolishnesse, a story of menne, or rather a mere fable.

Item, that man is restored to grace by the meere mercy of God, wythout the meane of Christs bloud, death, and passion.

Item, that Christe is not God, nor the Sauiour of the world, but a meere man, a sinfull man, and an abhominable Idoll.

Item, that al they that worshippe him are abhominable Idolaters: And, that Christe didde not rise agayne from death to life by the power of his Godhead, neither, that hee did ascend into Heauen.

Item, that the holy Ghoste is not God, neither, that there is any suche holy Ghoste.

Item, that Baptisme is not necessarie in the Churche of God, neither the vse of the sacrament of the body & bloude of Christ.

Hamont had his ears cropped on 13 May 1579, and was burnt at Castle Hill, Norwich, on the 20th.[4] A heretic in the eyes of Bishop Edmund Freake (*DNB*) and secular authorities, Hamont was probably a religious dissenter, possibly an adherent of the Family of Love. He was followed into the fire at Norwich by John Lewis (18 September 1583), Peter Cole (1587), and Francis Kett (14 January 1589).[5] Articles against Kett very similar to those against Hamont survive in manuscript.[6]

Fine distinctions which may have mattered to Hamont, Lewis, Cole, and Kett would probably not have mattered to a scoffer like Oxford.[7] Though we may observe a similarity between Hamont's rejection of the Gospel and Oxford's scorn of scripture; between their mutual understanding of Christ as a 'simple' (mere) man; and their rejection of the doctrine of the Trinity; nevertheless, Hamont was ready to give his life for his beliefs, whereas Oxford was not.

Articles of atheism brought against Walter Ralegh in 1594 may date back to his association with Oxford in 1579:[8]

2. Item, whome doe you knowe, or have h[e]arde, that have argued, or spoken againste, or as doubtinge, the beinge of anye God? ...

4. Item, whome doe you knowe, or have h[e]arde, that hath spoken againste the truth of God his holye worde revealed to vs in the scriptures of the Oulde & Newe Testament? or of some places therof? or have sayde those scriptures ar not to be

beleived & defended by her Maiestie for doctrine, & faith, and salvacion, but onlye of policye, or Civell gouernment …?

6. Item, whome do you knowe, or have h[e]arde, … that hath otherwise spoken againste the beinge; or immortallitye of the soule of man? or that a mans soule shoulde dye & become like the soule of a beaste, or such like …?

John Jessop reported that 'he hath h[e]arde that one Herryott of Sir Walter Rawleigh his howse hath brought the godhedd in question, and the whole course of the scriptures'; and John Davis affirmed that 'he hath h[e]arde Sir Walter Rawleigh by generall reporte hath had some reasoninge against the dietye of God, and his omnipotencye'. Also caught up in the charges were Thomas Allan, lieutenant of Portland Castle, and his servant Oliver, quoted to the effect that Moses was not to be commended, for he kept 52 whores: this he had declared

> … as they came togeither from the said Mr Tyllies sermon from Lillington. At which time he deliuered vnto them manye other thinges in derogacion of God & the scriptures, and of the immortallitye of the soule.

Robert Hyde of Sherborne, shoemaker, is similarly quoted to the effect that Allen told him, among other things, 'that we dye like beastes, and when we are gonne there is noe more rememberance of vs'. The atheism attributed to Christopher Marlowe in the early 1590s similarly accused Moses and Paul of being jugglers, or magicians, and Christ of having had illicit sexual relations with the woman of Samaria and her sister, and even with His disciple John.[9]

For his part, Oxford may have learned his atheism in Italy – we have noted Sir Stephen Powle's complaint that Italians account 'religion but pollicie to keepe men within the compas of sum honest limittes; preachinge to be but pratlinge of fryers and moncks: all inordinate pleasures to be but solaces of nature'. Narrowing our focus to Venice, in 1577 Alvise Capuano was denounced to the Inquisition for his heterodox beliefs:[10]

> … that the world was created by chance … that when the body dies the soul dies also … that during the time that you were an atheist – that is, when you believed that the world was created by chance – you believed that Christ was the adopted son of the Madonna, born as other men are … At times you have believed that the world has neither beginning nor end, and that when you were an atheist you did not believe that God existed, or, indeed, any supernatural beings. And that Christ's miracles were not true miracles but natural acts … and that the only law that must be obeyed is the law of nature … and that the entire Old Testament is a superstition.

Sentenced on 7 May 1580, Alvise was condemned to perpetual imprisonment – but was soon released. Other beliefs expressed by Alvise, 'that there are no true witches', and 'that belief in witchcraft arises from melancholic humours', sound more like Henry Howard or Reginald Scot (whom we shall meet in the next chapter but one) than like Oxford.

Oxford's assertion (cited by Howard) that 'the Iewes of Italy wold tell another tale, and put both Mathewe, Marke, and Ihon to sylenc[e]' (LIB-3.1/1) suggests that he had met with Jews in the Venetian Ghetto. Many years later Thomas Coryate reported the opinions of Venetian Jews:[11]

> ... that Christ forsooth was a great Prophet, and in that respect as highly to be esteemed as any Prophet amongst the Iewes that euer liued before him; but derogated altogether from his diuinitie, and would not acknowledge him for the Messias and Sauiour of the world, because he came so contemptibly, and not with that pompe and maiestie that beseemed the redeemer of mankind.

> ... they cannot endure to heare any termes of reconciliation to the Church of Christ, in regard they esteeme him but for a carpenters sonne, and a silly poore wretch that once rode vpon an Asse, and most vnworthy to be the Messias whom they expect to come with most pompous magnificence and imperiall royalty, like a peerelesse Monarch, garded with many legions of the gallantest Worthies, and most eminent personages of the whole world, to conquer not onely their old country Iudæa and all those opulent and flowrishing Kingdomes, which heretofore belonged to the foure auncient Monarchies ...

The precise details are not Oxford's, but Venice may well have provided fodder for his dissatisfaction with the established church, both of England and of Rome.

41 Sodomite

Charles Arundel accused Oxford of sexual crimes under the heading 'Dishonestye of life':[1]

> – [Oxford] confessid buggerie to William Cornwallis.

> – The cooke, wepeinge to my Lord Harry and my selfe at Hampton Corte, confessid how my Lord had almost spoyleid him, and yet he durst not open his grefe to Baker.

> – Rafe Hopton, beinge commawnedid by my Lord to staye Mackwilliam in his bed chamber till he came downe, wept to my Lord Harry and me, fearinge least yf my Lord shuld deale with him as he delte with Rocco in Brodstrete, the matter comminge owte he might be callid to accownte for an instrument; declaringe further that his harte akeid to consider what he knewe and what the worel[d] vnderstode at this time, sayinge that once when he was my Lordes page he was abowte to have stabbid him [=Oxford] with his [=Oxford's] dagger for profferinge so great a villonye. ...

> – Auracio [=Orazio] that came with him owte of Italie made it the quarrell of his departure, as Henrye Locke can testefie.

– He wold often tell my Lord Harrye, my selfe, and Sowthewell that he had abusid a mare.

– That the Ingelishe men were doltes and idiots for ther was better sporte in *passa pecora* – which they knewe not – then in all ther occupiynge.

– That when wemen were vnswete, fine (yonge) boyes were in season.

– He hathe a yerelie celebracion of the Neapolitan malaldye.

The *passa pecora* that surpasses all sexual habits practised by the English is an unorthodox position, recorded by Aretino and translatable as the 'grazing sheep'.[2] Henry Howard's charges echo Arundel's, with greater circumspection. Francis Southwell, even more circumspect, confesses the hearing of scandalous reports, but will not accuse Oxford of 'pedication'.[3]

Arundel and Howard drew upon both the broad and the narrow range of significations attached to buggery or sodomy. On the one hand, Oxford was a 'compleat' sodomite, guilty of the triple crime of atheism, pederasty, and necromancy, and their correlatives: prevarication, murder, and *lèse majesté*. Arundel characterizes Oxford as a 'monster' capable of any crime: 'my monstrus adversarye Oxford, who wold drinke my blud rather than wine, as well as he loves it' (LIB-5.12).

Many of the sodomitical multiple sins laid against Christopher Marlowe in the Baines–Marlowe libels of 1593 were identical to those laid against Oxford in 1580–81. In both cases, we have supporting evidence: for Marlowe, witnesses in Richard Cholomley and Thomas Kyd; for Oxford, active witnesses in the figures of Henry Howard, Charles Arundel, and Francis Southwell (before he got cold feet); and potential witnesses in William Cornwallis, Ralph Hopton, Henry Lok, and the alleged victims. Charges were laid against Marlowe so near the time of his death that they could not be adjudicated; Oxford, by contrast, remained very much alive, and his accusers hoped to bring him to the dock.

Supporting evidence is available in passages from Corinthians 6, marked in Oxford's own copy of the Geneva Bible – if indeed the notating hand is his:[4]

9 Knowe ye not that the vnrighteous shal not inherite the kingdome of God? Be not deceiued: nether fornicatours, nor idolaters, nor adulterers, nor wantons, nor bouggerers, 10 Nor theues, nor couetous, nor drunkards, nor railers nor extorcioners shal inherite the kingdome of God. 11 And suche were some of you: but ye are washed, but ye are sanctified, but ye are iustified in the Name of the Lord Iesus, and by the Spirit of our God. ... 15 Knowe ye not, that your bodies are the membres of Christ? shal I then take the membres of Christ, and make them the membres of an harlot? God forbid. 16 Do ye not knowe, that he which coupleth him self with an harlot, is one bodie? for two, saith he, shalbe one flesh. 17 But he that is ioyned vnto the Lord, is one spirit. 18 Flee fornication: euerie sinne that a man doeth, is without the bodie: but he that committeth fornication, sinneth

against his owne bodie. 19 Knowe ye not, that your bodie is the temple of the Holie Gost, which is in you, whome ye haue of God? and ye are not your owne. 20 For ye are bought for a price: therefore glorifie God in your bodie, and in your spirit: for they are Gods.

Was the marking of these verses prompted by a guilty conscience?

At the same time as they were accusing Oxford of all possible sins, Howard and Arundel were bent on having Oxford tried for the specific crime of pederasty. To this end they offered testimony from nearly a dozen victims, near-victims, and non-victim witnesses. They charged Oxford with the sexual abuse of 'so many boyes that it must nedes come out', especially of pages (LIB-3.6.1/3). Names are supplied, along with specific times and places: Ralph Hopton (who claims to have been approached by Oxford, evidently in Venice); the Italian boy Orazio, who 'complayned howe horribly my Lord had abusid him, and yet wold not giue him any thinge'; Tom Cook; Power the cook at Hampton Court (1577–78), at Whitehall and at Oxford's house in Broad Street; another Italian boy named Rocco at Oxford's residence in Broad Street; and young MacWilliam in Oxford's bedchamber – a liaison foiled by the intervention of Ralph Hopton.

Arundel's most detailed report concerns the cook Power (LIB-4.3/3):

> Thirdlie, I will prove him a bowgerer of a boye that is his coke, aswell by that I have bin an yeye [=eye] wittness of, as also by his confession to[o] often to my selfe, and others who will not lie. It is most trewe that I have sene this boye many a time in his chamber t[w]o [h]ours close lockeid together with him, namlie at Whitehall, and at his howse in Brodestrete. And findinge it so, I have gone to the backe dore to satisfie my selfe; at the whiche the boye hathe come owte all in a swete, and I have gone in and fownd the beast in the same plight. But to make it more apparant, my Lord Harrye sawe more, and the boye confest it vnto Southewell, and him selfe confirmid it to Mr William Cornewallis. Thus muche for profe of his sodomye, who is a be[a]st stayned with all impudicitie.

Arundel anticipates subsequent testimony against Anthony Bacon and his page, who 'remained together in Monsieur Bacon's room for hours at a time, in broad daylight and at night'.[5] In an adultery case at Cambridge Elizabeth Atkin testified thus on 28 August 1595:[6]

> Aboute Lente last paste, she beinge in the kitchin of her saide Master (*videlicet* of Iohn Edmunds the yonger) did here a noyse in the hall, and h[e]arde Mr Covill and her saide Mistris (*videlicet* Brigitt Edmunds) struglinge togither there, wherevpon she (the said Elizabethe Atkin) came forthe of the saide Kitchin into the entre that leadethe into the saide Hall; and she beinge there, did looke into the saide Hall at the dore there, it beinge open, and did then see the said Mr Covyll and hir said Mistris (Brigitt Edmunds predictam) naughte [=naughty] togither in the said hall in a chayre at the tables ende there by the fyre, her said Mistris then sittinge in the said chayre, and Mr Covill haveinge his gowne one, and she sawe hir Mistris hir heade then hange over the saide chayre, and hir hands aboute Mr Covills middle,

and did then and there he[a]re the said Mr Covill blusteringe and bloweinge verie muche, and afterwards did see him in the yarde there (he beinge gone out thether as it should seeme to cowle [=cool] him selfe), verie redd in his face and with a highe color.

Changes in Covell's physiognomy were thus introduced as evidence of an immediately prior orgasm.

Arundel reports that the same boy Power, 'wepeinge to my Lord Harry and my selfe at Hampton Corte, confessid how my Lord had almost spoyleid him, and yet he durst not open his grefe to Baker'. Power's injury was evidently sustained between 21 December 1577 and 23 February 1578, when the Queen last resided at Hampton Court;[7] 'Baker' was George Baker, Oxford's surgeon. So also Howard (LIB-3.6.1/3): 'Power hurte at Hampton Courte, and wold haue reuealed the matter to Baker – as with wepinge teares he told some, if my lord had not forbidden him – geuinge the boye salue, which serued his owne leggs at the same present.' The unheeded complaints to individuals whom the youths Cook, Power, and MacWilliam would have regarded as authority figures are strikingly similar those of twentieth-century children whose appeals for protection from wardens or priests went so long unheeded.

Also of account is Oxford's own statement in his letter to Burghley of July 1581 (LL-13/LIB-7.4):

> I have vnderstood ... certeyne of my men hathe resorted vnto yowre lordship, and sought by fals reportes of other of ther fellowes bothe to abuse yowre lordship and me. But [because] this bearer semes most herin to be touched, I have sent him vnto youre lordship, as is his ernest desire, that yowre lordship myght so know him, as yowre evill opinion, being conceyved amis by thes lewd fellowes, may be removed. And truly, my lord, I heare of those thinges wherwithe he is charged, and I can assure yow wrongfully and slaunderously. But the world is so conninge, as of a shadow they can make a substance, and of a leklihode a trothe. And thes fellowes, yf they be those, whiche I suppos, I do not dought but so to decyfer them to the world, as easly yowre lordship shall loke into ther lewdnes and vnfaythfulnes. Whiche tyll my liberte I mean to defer, as more mindfull of that importinge me most at this time, then yet sekinge to revenge my self of suche peruers[e] and [impudent] dealinge of servants – whiche I know have not wanted incoragment and setting on.

The bearer of the letter (could it have been Power himself?) has himself been a target of accusations. Anxious to regain his liberty, Oxford will defer revenge.

Oxford's letter meshes perfectly with Howard–Arundel libels: servants are prepared to testify against fellow servants and against their master Oxford; Oxford is prepared to back one set of servants, and to revenge himself on the others when time is ripe. The matter of controversy is not named (no surprise!); Oxford confesses a shadow and a likelihood, but denies substance or truth. Perhaps the accusing servants were indeed suborned by Howard and Arundel, but they could not have made their accusations lightly: it is evident from Oxford's letter that the 'unfaithful' servants were willing to put their jobs on the line. It is evident as well that Ralph Hopton took the matter seriously: he was afraid of being 'callid to accownte for [being] an instrument'.

Evidence for Oxford's bestiality is entirely hearsay: 'he wold often tell my Lord Harrye, my selfe, and Southewell that he had abusid a mare; [and] that the Ingelishe men were doltes and idiotes, for ther was better sporte in *passa pecora*, which they knewe not, then in all ther occupiynge.' As far as Arundel was concerned, these were mere words, and he makes no pretence of being able to verify them. Also hearsay is the statement attributed to Oxford, 'that when wemen were vnswete, fine (young) boyes were in season', which anticipates Marlowe's subsequent and subsequently more famous quip, 'That all they that loue not Tobacco & Boies were fooles'.[8]

Arundel concludes with a declaration that Oxford 'hathe a yerelie celebracion of the Neapolitan malaldye' – syphilis. Presumably a doctor (George Baker?) could have verified this claim, and we can point to Baxter's report concerning the infection Oxford incurred at Venice; but of course syphilis is more commonly associated with heterosexual than with homosexual activity in the English Renaissance.

Oxford has a contemporary literary counterpart in the 'character' of the highborn, flashy homosexual, of which Bray (1988) locates some dozen instances, most of them rather late for our purposes. One of Bray's earliest examples comes from John Marston's *Satyre 3* (1598, sigs. D6v, D7v):

Behold at length in London streets he showes. ...
His clothes perfum'd, his fustie mouth is ayred,
His chinne new swept, his very cheekes are glazed.
        But ho, what Ganimede is that doth grace
The gallants heeles. One, who for two daies space
Is closely hyred.

In *Scourge of Villanie* (1598, sigs. C6v, C6), Marston similarly alludes to 'male steews' and to a 'Ganimede, / His perfum'd shee-goate'. Bray worries that such 'characters' may have been purely literary in origin: 'the danger is that what we are seeing is not Renaissance London but second-century Rome at one remove' (p. 35). Bray adds (p. 37): 'certainly there is no sign whatsoever of the figure to be met with so frequently in the pages of the satirists'. But indeed there is sign of such a figure, and Oxford is he!

Of Oxford's three accusers, only Arundel seems to be entirely free from the suspicion of homosexuality himself: letters to his 'sweet lady' (LIB-6.1–9) seem to convey genuine (if self-serving) passion, and the delightful female 'bedmate' of the lady (LIB-6.5) even more than the lady herself approves the match. As for Howard, his only known approach to marriage was with Mary Queen of Scots – an impossible dream, of course, clearly inspired by dynastic ambitions rather than heterosexual passion. Only after 1603, as a declared 'favourite' of the bisexual King James I, was Howard finally elevated to the title of Earl of Northampton.

Nor was Oxford exclusively homosexual, but rather a bisexual adventurer. He was clearly attracted by the nubile Anne Cecil when he was twenty-one and she was fourteen. He boasted of heterosexual conquests while abroad (LIB-4.2/2.5–6):

– that the cownetesse of Mirondola came fiftie miles to lie with him for loves

– that the Qwene of Navare sent a messenger to desire him to speke with him in her chamber

Mirandola lay approximately 60 miles S.W. of Venice: its most famous son was the Renaissance philosopher Pico della Mirandola (long since dead). Oxford also refers to Marguerite of Valois, spouse of Henri of Navarre, 'a spoilt, talented, amorous young woman who flitted from lover to lover despite the watchful eye of her mother Catherine de Medici'.[9] We have also noted Oxford's liaison with the Venetian courtesan Virginia Padoana, and are about to discover a heterosexual adventure conducted under the very nose of the English Queen.

Although Arundel and Howard hoped that the Queen would be scandalized by their charges of pederasty, her greatest concern lay rather with Oxford's boast that his heterosexual conquests included herself. As for charges of homosexuality, the Queen's suggestion that his erstwhile friends accuse Oxford openly in Court smacks more of royal entertainment than of royal justice.

42 Prophet

Still under house arrest in late July or August 1581, Charles Arundel recalled Oxford's charge 'That my Lord Harrye shuld be present when I presentid a certayne boke of pictures, after the manner of a prophesie and by interpretacion resemblid a crowned sone [=son] to the Quene &c' (LIB-2.3.1/5). The book evidently prophesied the date of the Queen's death and the identity of her male successor.

Arundel, denying that Henry Howard ever saw the book of prophecies, attempted to turn the tables on Oxford:

O[f] all other, this pointe is most childishe, vayne, and most ridiculus, for as my Lord Harrye never sawe this payntid boke, I protest – much lesse expowndid it or playd the paraphrast – so in my knoledge dyd he never of any suche, till my Lord of Oxford, beinge commaundid to kepe his chamber abowte the libellinge betwene him and my Lord of Lester, I declarid to my Lord Harrye that suche a toye Oxford layd vpp in his deske, which some man of his (as I conceavid) thrust vppon him vnder cullor of a prophesye, to [cozen] him of crownes [i.e., money] – as indede it

was not rare to picke his purse with pretence of novelties and future accidentes –
addinge further that I fearid lest Sir Thomas Henedge, who had the kepeinge of the
fole [=the Queen's fool] at that time, lightinge on the same, might wilfullie pervert
it to his [=Oxford's] hurt, and geve a greter oportunitie to those that had a mind to
temper or to worke against him. This was mye sincere and honest care of my
ingratefull and accurseid fri[e]nd, and this was all that ever my Lord Harrye h[e]ard
of the payntyd gewegawes, so farr his iudgment and discretion was from geseinge
or interpretinge. And for his further clereinge in this cawse, I will depose on my
othe, he was never privie to the boke, and that Oxford shewinge it to me coniurid
me by soleme othe never to impart the thinge to my Lord Harry, bycause he
[=Howard] wold not hide it from my Lord Treaserer [=Burghley]. Nowe iudge
whether it be likelie, that he wold make his eies wittnessis of that, wherof he was so
lothe his eares sold receave the sownd by report of another. And suche vnkindnesse was at that time wherof he speakeithe betwene them, that not so muche as
ordenarye speche, muche lesse private secretes, were currant on ether syde.

Given that one picture dangerously 'resemblid a crowned sone to the Quene',
Arundel denigrates the entire book as 'payntyd gewegawes': but Oxford, who
valued the book, kept it 'layd vpp in his deske' and took pains to ensure that
Howard did not see it, lest he should disclose its existence to Burghley. Arundel
claims that Oxford compiled the book with his own hand (he was of course a fine
calligrapher) under the illusion of demonic inspiration (LIB-4.2/2.12): 'he had
often sene the devell by coniuringe with Parsones of the chappell that died, and
by his direction paynetid owte a bok of prophesies; the coniuringe was in the
little howse in the tilte[ya]rd at Grenewidge'.

   That the book of prophecies became a matter for serious inquiry is evident
from Howard's letter to Walsingham, apparently written on 14 September 1581
(LIB-3.6), in which he acknowledges 'the sight, concealement, and construction
of a prophecie' as the 'thing which hir maiestie was wonte to vrge against me
cheflie'. Howard declares to Walsingham: 'I will take mie othe vppon the Bible
that I neuer sawe [the book]'; 'Beside, theie that wear acquaintid with that book
of babies in my Lord of Oxford his hande will clere me both from sight and
knowledge by ther othe'.

   Howard is somewhat uncomfortable describing in detail a book he insists that
he never saw. For his part, Arundel backs Howard's claim of ignorance, as does
Francis Southwell, writing to Howard in a state of some anxiety (LIB-3.6.2):

   My most honorable good Lord and deareste frende (if yow will voutcsaf), I may so
   trouble your Lord, I never said yow saw the book of pictures, nor that ever yow
   gave eny comente of thos figures. This I only saide of the said book: my lord
   Oxford only shewed me yt in his gret chamber, and maed me the onli exposition of
   yt. Mr Charles Arundel was than in the bottome of the chamber very ernestli
   writing a letter and never to my knowleg saw the said Boke. // I never h[e]ard yow
   spek the profesy of England ...

Here Southwell contradicts Arundel, for each swears that he himself and not the other saw the book. Doubtless all four principals had perused the book, and Arundel, Howard, and Southwell were all willing to lie in the interest of protecting Howard from what had become a very serious charge.

Howard's release from house arrest not long after the date of this letter was evidently contingent on his agreement to publish an attack on the very kinds of prophecy contained in the 'book of babies in my Lord of Oxford his hande'. The result, published in 1583, carried the elaborate title,

> A defensatiue against the poyson of supposed Prophesies: Not hitherto confuted by the penne of any man, which being grounded, eyther vppon the warrant and authority of old paynted bookes, expositions of Dreames, Oracles, Reuelations, Inuocations of damned spirites, Iudicalles of Astrologie, or any other kinde of pretended knowledge whatsoeuer, De futuris contingentibus: haue beene causes of great disorder in the common wealth, and cheefely amonge the simple and vnlearned people: very needefull to be published at this time, considering the late offence which grew by most palpable and grosse errours in Astrology.

The very title names 'old paynted bookes'. The only book printed with Howard's name attached during his lifetime, *A Defensative* was registered on 13 June 1583 (Arber, ii, p. 424) and printed the same year by the Londoner John Charlewood, 'Printer to the right Honourable Earle of Arundell', with a dedication 'To the Right Honorable, Sir Frauncis Walsingham, principall Secretarie to the Queenes Maiestie, and one of her most honourable priuie Counsayle'. It was thus all a kind of family matter. Though the title indicates that prophecies were a danger 'cheefely amonge the simple and vnlearned people', it is clear from the full record that the real danger lay with the highest levels of the social order, most particularly with Oxford.

The connection between Howard's printed book and Oxford's painted book appears in a lengthy passage well into Howard's treatise (sigs. Kki–iv):

> It was once my happe to be examined, vpon the sight of a certayne paynted Treatise of this kinde, garnished with sundry beastes & byrds, and fitter (as I gather) by some freendes of mine, who made good sport thereat, for a childishe game, then a sober iudgement. It is certayne that I neuer was admitted to this Sibillas Oracle, although I could haue beene as well content to feede mine eyes without offence for any thing I knowe, as others were to content theyr humours, in a wyldernesse of follie. But whether it be probable that eyther I did euer see the same, or make account thereof, or would afford expence and waste of time which is most precious, to fancies of this kinde which are most friuolous: let them conceyue that eyther are acquainted with my selfe, or wyll vouchsafe to reade, and scanne the reasons of this booke, which hauing beene collected in a booke of notes, out of the full course of all my reading, from the fifteenth yeere of mine age vntyll this daye, vppon a mortall mallice against prophecies, in respect of some progenitours, and auncestors of mine which smarted, for presuming ouer much vpon their hopes, should neuer

haue beene recommended to the printe, if meere necessitie, and care to satisfie the
world heerein, had not preuayled at the length, against my bashfull and retrayte
humor. For mine owne parte, I always conceyued them to be the froth of follie,
the scumme of pride, the shipwracke of honour, and the poyson of nobilitie. But
notwithstanding, forsomuch as I can gather by report of some deere freendes of
mine, who sawe the gewgawe in the keeping of another (that esteemend it too
much) it should appeare eyther to haue beene ouer flourished in a paynters shoppe,
with matter correspondent to theyr humors, which delyght in newes, or else to
haue beene drawne vpon the gesse of one, Verdungus[?]: who during the tyme of
king Henrie the eight, seeking according to the guise of such badde persons, to
content and please the moodes of certayne Princes, which were then in warre and
deepe vnkindnesse with the King: gaue out in writing that the Realme should be
giuen vppe, In praedam diuersis animantibus, for a praye or spoyle to sundery
beastes: The certaintie he durst not lymitte, nor set downe as it seemes, for feare of
beeing taken with a grosse and shamefull lye: neyther durst hee publishe or reueale
the pointes and reasons, wherevpon the iudgement stoode, because the man himselfe beeing posted foreward with a wrekefull humour of reuenge, sought rather by
this meane, to make his voice a trumpet of encoragement, then a messenger of
tribulation. For proofe wherof we are to note the ende, & cheefely that the King
was layde to rest with his Fathers, in conuenient time when Verdungus hauing
made a shamefull wrack, both of conscience and credite, was scorned and deryded
for his vaine presumption without ground, and mallice without moderation. This
may suffice to shaddowes of pretence, and to descrie the groundes of prophecies,
eyther written in olde bookes, or paynted with freshe colours: nowe let vs proceede
as we haue begunne, to the substaunce of aucthoritie.

Two manuscripts in the Folger Shakespeare Library may hint at the nature of
Oxford's 'Book of Prophecies'. The first is the pictorial commonplace-book of
Thomas Trevelyon, compiled circa 1608, replete with pictures of the labours of
the months, scenes and characters from the Old Testament, kings and queens of
England and Scotland, vices and virtues, Roman emperors, the Worthies, the
Muses, the twelve apostles, embroidery patterns, decorated alphabets, and much
else.[1] The second and more important for our purposes is a 'Book of Magic' of
circa 1580, variously illustrated with circles, charts, and images, and with recipes
for raising and communicating with spirits (Fig. 9).[2]

The connection between Howard's *Defensatiue* and Oxford's 'Book of Pro-
phecies' suggests a necessary revision of the received history of Howard's treatise.
The *Dictionary of National Biography* proposes that behind *A Defensatiue* lay
Richard Harvey's *An Astrological discourse vpon the Coniunction of Saturne &
Iupiter*, registered on 22 January 1583 and published that year in numerous editions.
Harvey's *Astrological discourse* attracted ridicule for its confident prediction of
disasters that never materialized, in particular a great wind and civil unrest.[3] Harvey
built his predictions not only on the forthcoming planetary conjunction, but on a
spectacular comet of October 1577 and a great earthquake felt throughout south-

east England and across the English Channel about six o'clock in the evening on 6 April 1580.[4] Linda Levy Peck argues that Howard also had in view ideas popularized by Gabriel Harvey and John Dee.[5] The *DNB* asserts in addition that Henry Howard spent the year 1582–83 ensconced at St Alban's composing his *Defensatiue*.

The retreat to St Alban's is perfectly compatible with the composition of a work that required a good deal of consultation of sources, but it is difficult to agree that Howard's *Defensatiue* could have been completed within six months of the publication of Harvey's *Discourse*. In fact Howard was reacting not to the brothers Harvey or to John Dee,[6] but to his hostile interrogation over Oxford's 'Book of Prophecies'. His dedication of the book to Walsingham was doubtless intended to disarm his most dangerous critic.

However duplicitous his pronouncements regarding his personal involvement with the 'paynted Treatise ... garnished with sundry beastes & byrds', Howard's *Defensatiue* is a significant rejection of prophecy and prognostication of any and all kinds, for he represents all prophetic astrology as rubbish. Howard's treatise antedates three better-known publications which laid the intellectual groundwork for England's escape from the witchcraft horrors that swept Scotland and much of Europe: Reginald Scot's *Discovery of Witchcraft* (1584: STC 21864), and Samuel Harsnett's *Discovery of the fraudulent practices ...* (1599: STC 12883), and *Declaration of egregious Popish impostures* (1603: STC 12880). If Howard's book lacks the bite of the others it is because its documentation is too learned and its rhetoric too antique, so that it is difficult (as with all Howard's compositions, including his personal letters) to see the forest for the trees.

Arundel was also interrogated on the book of prophecies. Pointedly asked 'What prophesies have you latelie sene or h[e]ard, whiche might concerne the contemp[t], reproche, and overthrowe of owre most gracious soveragne whome owr Lord God blesse forever?', Arundel characteristically turns the tables on Oxford, as we have noted (LIB-2.1.5/24):

> As I never sawe eny prophesie writen, so can I not deny but that I heard of a rime by one Edeward Heywod a yere and a halfe since ...

Neither the prophetic verse nor the identity of Edward Heywood has been established, but like many such prophecies the poem probably foretold the death or overthrow of the reigning monarch. Though such poems were strictly forbidden, they were popular among Puritans and extreme Catholics.[7]

But if Howard and Arundel exempt themselves from superstition, both characterize Oxford as wallowing in it. They separately report Oxford's claim 'that he sawe the reall bodie of Christ visablelie betwene the handes of Stevens at masse',[8] while Arundel expresses contempt for Oxford's appeal to his 'nativity' – or horoscope – as an excuse for avoiding imprisonment: 'Indede it was not rare to picke his purse with pretence of novelties and future accidentes' (LIB-2.3.1/3@112).

Contemporary evidence supports the claims of Howard, Arundel, and South-well that Oxford was more than ordinarily superstitious. A river of books and pamphlets that issued from the London presses in the immediate aftermath of the earthquake of Wednesday 6 April 1580 were largely the work of Oxford's servants and protégés, including Thomas Churchyard, Abraham Fleming, Arthur Golding, Anthony Munday, and Thomas Twyne.[9] The only two people killed as a direct result of the tremor, Thomas Grey and Mabel Everitt, were both sitting piously in the church at Christ's Hospital when stones from the ceiling fell upon them. Oxford's protégés nevertheless read the quake as a warning not against church-going, but against play-going, bear-baiting, cross-dressing, and other social sins. As we shall see, both Fleming and Munday, himself a playwright, called for the demolition of the Theatre and the Curtain as a protection against divine punishment.[10] Munday, in his typically crude and grossly supersitious *A View of Sundry Examples ... Also a short discourse of the late Earthquake the sixt of Aprill* (1580), openly signed himself 'A. Munday, Seruaunt to the right Honorable, the Earle of Oxenford', and dedicated the volume 'To the Worshipfull Maister William Waters, and Maister George Baker, Gentlemen, attendaunt on the Right Honourable, his singuler good Lord and Maister, the Earle of Oxenford'.

William Waters may have been a servant of the Burghley household, since a man of that name appeared on the jury that acquitted Oxford of the murder of Thomas Brincknell in 1567. George Baker dedicated three of his four published books either to Oxford or to Anne. In his *The Composition or making of the ... Oil called Oleum Magistrale* (1574), Baker calls Oxford 'his singuler good Lord and maister'. Similarly, Baker's translation of Conrad Gesner, *The newe jewell of health* (1576), is dedicated 'To the Right Honourable, Vertuous, and his singular good Lady, the Noble Countesse of Oxeforde, &c.' by 'your humble seruaunt ... George Baker, Chirurgian.' (In his letter of late December 1580 (LIB-3.1/4@68) Henry Howard confirms that Baker was Oxford's surgeon.) In the course of his book Baker gives his address as 'my house in Bartholomewe lane beside the Royall exchaunge in London', and the date as 'this xxj day of February 1576'. The second edition of the same book, published in 1599 as *The practice of the new and old phisicke*, was dedicated to Oxford (Anne died in 1588). At this late date Baker identified himself as 'one of the Queenes Maiesties chiefe chirurgions in ordinary'.

Baker's translation of Gesner, which he calls 'this worke of Distillation', is richly illustrated with furnaces, retorts, and other instruments of the profession. His introduction to the first edition recommends four current practioners of the art in addition to himself: 'One mayster Kemech an Englishe man dwelling in Lothburie'; 'mayster Geffray, a French man dwelling in the Crouched friers'; 'Iohn Hester dwelling on Powles wharfe'; and 'Thomas Hyll' – the latter supposed to have been the initial translator of *The newe jewell*.

Thomas Hill, who apparently outlived the century (*DNB*), was under various hats a distiller, physiognomist, herbalist, astrologer, cosmologist, prognosticator, interpreter of dreams, and author of numerous books in multiple editions, including *A Contemplation of Mysteries: Contayning the rare effects of certayne comets* (printed circa 1574 but entered in 1570 or 1571 as 'Rayre wonders and feyrefull syghts in earth as in heaven' – Arber, i, p. 441). Master Geffray, 'a French man dwelling in the Crouched friers', was Geffray (or Godfrey) Le Brumin, a Huguenot immigrant doctor.[11]

John Hester, author or translator of some dozen books,[12] dedicated his translation of Leonardo Fioravanti, *A Short Discours ... vppon Chirurgerie* (1580), to 'the Right Honourable his singuler good Lorde and Patrone, Edwarde de Vere, Earle of Oxenforde', using Oxford's wood-cut coat of arms. Hester describes himself as 'Practicioner in the arte of Distillation', and adds:

> ... I most humbly craue your Honorable patronage, that according to your name and poesie [=Vero nihil verius] your name and propertie may be to protect the truth ... The most affectioned of all those, which owe your Lordship dutifull seruice, Iohn Hester.

Hester signs his preface 'to the gentle Reader' with his address: 'From my house at Paules Wharfe, the 23 of Iannuary 1579 [=1580]', and to the end of the book he appends an advertisement repeating his name and address, and specifying the sign by which his shop could be identified:

> If any be disposed to haue any of these afore-sayd compositions redy made, for the most part he may haue them at Paules Wharfe, by one Iohn Hester practisioner in the Arte of distilliations, at the signe of the Furnaises.

Remarkably, another of Hester's imprints that has survived is a broadsheet advertisement, apparently from the mid-1580s, bearing the title: 'These oiles, waters, extractions, or essences, saltes, and other compositions, are at Paules Wharfe ready made to be solde'. The only surviving copy (STC 13254) was preserved by Gabriel Harvey, who marked it up, signed his name and the date 1588, and added a significant note: 'Now M. Keymis, the great Alchymist of London'.

Eccles insightfully identifies Master Keymis with the Laurence Keymis from Wiltshire who matriculated from Balliol College, Oxford, on 2 May 1581.[13] This university student was evidently born in 1562, and would have been no more than fourteen years of age in 1576 when George Baker saw fit to recommend the services of 'One mayster Kemech an Englishe man dwelling in Lothburie': perhaps Laurence was the son or nephew of this older Keymis. I have not been able to discover much more about Keymis the alchemist: his name does not appear in the 'Vestry Minute Book of the Parish of St Margaret Lothbury in the City of London', though a William Kemishe lodged in the parish in 1625.[14]

For us, the important point is not so much the identity of Master Keymis as the fact that Gabriel Harvey identified him, and thus by association George Baker,

John Hester, and the rest, as alchemists in addition to being mere distillers, just as Churchyard, Fleming, Golding, Munday, and Twyne all prove on closer inspection to be superstitious alarmists. The patron of this whole clutch of alchemists and prognosticators – this credulous crew – was Oxford.

Finally, it seems possible that John Lyly also became entangled in the web of prophecy. In 1582, in an incident we shall examine at length (pp. 288–89), Lyly directed a letter to Burghley, ending with an expression that has mystified his biographers:

> Loth I am to be a prophett, and to be a wi[t]che I loath.

One biographer has noted accusations on other grounds of his 'dabbling in magic'.[15] If Lyly stood accused of being a prophet and a witch, it may have been because he practised within the circle created by Oxford and his 'book of babies'.

43 A Passing Singular Odd Man

In the summer months of 1580 the same Gabriel Harvey who complimented Oxford in Latin prose back in August 1578 found himself in trouble for satirizing Oxford in English verse. Under the title of *Speculum Tuscanismi*, that is, 'Mirror of Tuscanism' or 'Italian Mirrour', Harvey's poem appeared without his permission in *Three Proper, and Wittie, Familiar Letters* (sigs. E2–2v), evidently edited by Edmund Spenser, with a preface to the reader dated 19 June 1580. Harvey's poem is introduced as a 'bolde Satyriall Libell lately deuised at the instaunce of a certayne worshipfull Hartefordshyre Gentleman, of myne olde acquayntaunce'[1] – a give-away description of Harvey. The proper name Galateo assigned to the mock hero derives from Robert Peterson's 1576 translation of Giovanni della Casa's *Galateo* (STC 4738, sig. B1), a treatise 'of fashions and maners'.

Though Harvey's experiments with 'quantitative verse' are obscured by tortured grammar and limited comprehensibility, the target of the satire was openly recognizable – and recognized – as Oxford:

> Since Galateo came in, and Tuscanisme gan vsurpe,
> Vanitie aboue all: Villanie next her, Statelynes Empresse.
> No man, but Minion, Stowte, Lowte, Plaine, swayne quoth a Lording:
> No wordes but valorous, no workes but woomanish onely.
> For life Magnificoes, not a beck but glorious in shew,
> In deede most friuolous, not a looke but Tuscanish alwayes.
> His cringing side necke, Eyes glauncing, Fisnamie smirking,
> With forefinger kisse, and braue embrace to the footewarde.
> Largebelled Kodpeasd Dublet, vnkodpeased halfe hose,

Straite to the dock, like a shirte, and close to the britch, like a diueling. [diueling =
A little Apish Hatte, cowched fast to the pate, like an Oyster,   little devil]
French Camarick Ruffes, deepe with a w[h]it[e]nesse, starched to the purpose.
Euery one A per se A, his termes, and braueries in Print,
Delicate in speach, queynte in araye: conceited in all poyntes:
In Courtly guyles, a passing singular odde man,
For Gallantes a braue Myrrour, a Primerose of Honour,
A Diamond for nonce, a fellowe perelesse in England.
Not the like Discourser for Tongue, and head to be found out:
Not the like resolute Man, for great and serious affayres,
Not the like Lynx, to spie out secretes, and priuities of States.
Eyed, like to Argus, Earde, like to Midas, Nosd, like to Naso,
Wingd, like to Mercury, fittst of a Thousand for to be employde,
This, nay more than this doth practise of Italy in one yeare.

None doe I name, but some doe I know, that a peece of a tweluemonth
Hath so perfited [=perfected] outly, and inly, both body, both soule,
That none for sense, and senses, halfe matchable with them.
A Vulturs smelling, Apes tasting, sight of an Eagle,
A spiders touching, Hartes hearing, might of a Lyon.
Compoundes of wisedome, witte, prowes[s], bountie, behauiour,
All gallant Vertues, all qualities of body and soule:
O thrice tenne hundreth thousand times blessed and happy,
Blessed and happy Trauaile, Trauailer most blessed and happy.

Any number of lines might be excerpted for comment, but the poem points
above all to foppishness as Oxford's most characteristic trait:

No wordes but valorous, no workes but woomanish onely.
For life Magnificoes, not a beck but glorious in shew,
In deede most friuolous, not a looke but Tuscanish alwayes.

His braggadoccio is unmatched by manly deeds. Glorious in show, his actions are
frivolous, his appearance Italianate. He wears 'A little Apish Hatte, cowched fast
to the pate, like an Oyster', with French cambric ruffs, bleached white and
starched; 'queynte in araye: conceited in all poyntes'; 'a passing singular odde
man'. An odd man indeed!

Also a man sensitive to a slight. That Oxford took offence at Harvey's 'fleeting'
is known from the fact that in Spenser's 1592 *Four Letters* (p. 21), Harvey
defended himself from this very imputation. He begins by boasting that at the
1578 royal visit, Dr Andrew Perne of Cambridge

... wished me to proceede louingly with the Vniuersity ... And that was all the
Fleeting, that euer I felt: sauinge that an other company of speciall good fellowes,
(whereof hee was none of the meanest, that brauely threatned to coniure-vpp one,
which should massacre Martins witt, or should bee lambacked himselfe with ten
yeares prouision) would needs forsooth verye courtly perswade the Earle of

Oxforde, that some thing in those Letters, and namely the Mirrour of Tuscanismo, was palpably intended against him: whose noble Lordeship I protest, I neuer meante to dishonour with the least preiudiciall word of my Tounge, or pen: but euer kepte a mindeful reckoning of many bounden duties toward The-same: ... But the noble Earle, not disposed to trouble his Iouiall [=Jovial, god-like] mind with such Saturnine paltery, stil continued, like his magnificent selfe: and that Fleeting also proued, like the other: a silly bullbeare, a sorry puffe of winde, a thinge of nothinge.

As we shall see, the person who 'would needs forsooth verye courtly perswade the Earle of Oxforde' that the poem was an attack on him was John Lyly.

Thomas Nash celebrated Harvey's discomfiture twice in *Strange Newes* of 1592 under the running-head, 'Four Letters Confuted'. First (sig. G1):

... needes hee must cast vp certayne crude humours of English Hexameter Verses that lay vppon his stomacke, a Noble-man stoode in his way as he was vomiting, and from top to toe he all to bewrayed him with *Tuscanisme*.

Nash subsequently denies (sig. G1) that Spenser had any part in the publication of the 1580 *Letters*, insisting (sig. G2) that 'The sharpest part of them were read ouer at Counsell Table, and he refered ouer to the Fleet ...' Nash then confirms that it was Lyly, author of *Pap with a Hatchet* (1589), who persuaded Oxford that 'the Mirrour of Tuscanismo, was palpably intended against him' (sig. G4):[2]

He that threatned to conjure vp Martins wit, hath written some thing too in your praise in Pap-hatchet, for all you accuse him to haue courtlie incenst the Earle of Oxford against you. Marke him well, hee is but a little fellow, but hee hath one of the best wits in England.

The 'little fellow' is clearly Lyly, not Oxford as is sometimes argued.[3]

Nash twisted the knife thrice more in his 1596 *Have With You to Saffron-Walden*. Nash first refers to Harvey (sigs. F3v–4) ...

... as he was when he libeld against my Lord of Oxford, but in the single-soald pumpes of his aduersitie, with his gowne cast off, vntrussing, and readie to beray himselfe ...

Perhaps conflating *Four Letters* of 1592 and *Three ... Letters* of 1580, Nash next refers (sig. L2v) to ...

... foure notable famous Letters: in one of which hee enterlaced his short but yet sharpe iudiciall of Earth-quakes, & came verie short and sharpe vppon my Lord of Oxford, in a ratling bundle of English Hexameters.

Finally, Nash hints at even greater consequences (sig. M3v):

I had forgot to obserue vnto you out of his first foure familiar Epistles, his ambicious stratagem to aspire, that whereas two great Pieres [=peers] beeing at iarre, and their quarrell continued to bloudshed, he would needs[,] vncald and when it lay not in his way[,] steppe in on the one side[,] which indeede was the safer side (as the foole is crafty inough to sleepe in a whole skin) and hewe and slash with his Hexameters, but hewd and slasht he had beene as small as chippings, if he had not playd ducke Fryer and hid himselfe eight weeks in that Noblemans house, for whome with his pen hee thus bladed.

Reference seems to be to the hostility between Oxford and Leicester during the latter months of 1579. Nash as much as affirms that Harvey spent some eight weeks under Leicester's protection.

Yet another satire, from Barnaby Rich's 1581 *Farewell to Militarie Profession* (sigs. B1v–2v), may conceivably point at Oxford, as argued by his apologists:[4]

... many now adaies goe aboute by as great deuise as maie bee, how thei might become women theimselues. How many Gentlemen shall you see at this present daie, that I dare vndertake, in the wearyng of their apparell, in the settyng of their Ruffes, and the freselyng of their heire, are more new fangeled and foolishe, then any curtisan of Venice.

And I beseche you (Gentlemen) giue me leaue to tell you a tale, that comes euen now in my mynde: the matter is not worthe the hearyng, but yet very straunge vnto me at the first.

It was my fortune at my last beyng at London, to walke through the Strande towardes Westminster, where I mett one came ridyng towardes me, on a foote-clothe Nagge, apparailed in a Frenche Ruffe, a Frenche Cloake, a Frenche Hose, and in his hande a greate fanne of Feathers, bearyng them vp (verie womanly) against the side of his face: And for that I had neuer seen any man weare theim before that daie, I beganne to thinke it vnpossible, that there might a manne bee founde so foolishe, as to make hym self a scorne to the worlde, to weare so womanish a toye. But rather thought it had been some shamelesse woman, that had disguised her self like a manne, in our Hose, and our Cloakes: for our Dublettes, Gounes, Cappes, and Hattes thei had got long agoe.

But by this tyme he was come some thyng nire [=nigher, nearer] me, and I might see he had a bearde, whereby I was assured that he should haue been a manne, whereat I beganne to muse with my self, whether his simplicitie were more to be pitied, or his follie more to be laughed at. For in myne opinion it is as fonde a sight to see a manne with suche a bable in his hande, as to see a woman ride through the streate with a launce in hers.

And as he passed by me, I sawe three followyng that were his menne, and taking the hindermoste by the arme, I asked hym what Gentlewoman his master was: but the fellowe not vnderstandyng my meanyng, told me his masters name, and so departed.

I beganne then to muse with my self, to what ende that fanne of Feathers serued, for it could not bee to defende [=guard against] the Sunne from the burnyng of his beautie, for it was in the beginnyng of Februarie, when the heate of the Sunne maie bee very well indured.

> Now if it were to defende the winde, or the coldnesse of the aire, my thinke [=methinks] a French hoode had been a great deale better, for that had been bothe gentlewoman like, and beyng close pinde doune aboute his eares, would haue kepte his hedde a great deal warmer. And then a Frenche hoode on his hedde, a Frenche Ruffe aboute his necke, a French Cloake on his backe, and a paire of Frenche Hose on his legges had been right *a la mode de Fraunce*:[5] & this had bin somethyng sutable to his witte.
>
> But I thinke he did it rather to please Gentlewomen, and the better to shewe what honor he bare theim, would weare one of the greatest vanities that long to their sexe. ...

Rich evidently attacked the man by attacking the stereotype.

The 1615 edition of Stow's *Annales* reported (for the first time in print) that on his return from Italy, Oxford affected a new stylishness of dress (p. 868):

> Milloners, or Haberdashers had not then any gloues Imbroydered, or trimmed with Gold, or Silke, neither Gold nor Imbroydered Girdles and Hangers, neyther could they make any costly wash or perfume, vntil about the fourteenth or fifteenth yeare of the Queene the right honourable Edward de Vere, Earle of Oxford: came from Italy, and brought with him Gloues: sweete bagges, a perfumed leather Ierkin, and other pleasant thinges, and that yeere the Queene had a payre of perfumed Gloues trimmed onely with foure Tuftes or Roses, of cullered Silke, the Queene tooke such pleasure in those Gloues, that shee was pictured with those Gloues vppon her hands, and for many yeeres after it was called the Earle of Oxfords perfume.

Oxford's contemporaries believed that Italy had effeminized him.

44 Oxford's Folly

On 1 January 1580 Oxford presented to the Queen, as a New Year's gift, 'a fair juell of golde, being a shippe garnished fully with dyamonds and a meane perle pendant'; similarly, the still-estranged Anne presented 'a payre of braceletts of gold, conteyneing 24 peeces, whereof in seven of them are two perles in a peece, and six stones being lapis lazareus, and six clowde stones or shelles of the sea'.[1]

On 27 January Sir Edward Seymour, styled Earl of Hertford, noted in his diary following a visit to Burghley at Whitehall:[2]

> At 11 the same morning I went into the orchard where her Majesty was walking with my Lord of Oxford.

Seymour does not reveal the conversation that may have passed between Queen and Earl. The apparent tranquility of the meeting belies the mayhem and scandal that were to touch Oxford in the ensuing months.

From the diary of Arthur Throckmorton we learn that on this very day the quarrel between Oxford and Sidney flared anew:

> Wednesday, 27 January: my lord Oxford wrytte [i.e., wrote] a challenge to Sir Philip Sidney.

Rowse, who first noted this entry in print, thought he had caught Oxford dispatching the formal challenge of the 'tennis-court quarrel'.[3] If so, Oxford delayed far longer than is usually supposed. Possibly Oxford was renewing the quarrel, using Throckmorton (rather than Charles Arundel and Walter Ralegh) to convey the challenge. The entry at any rate cuts the ground from under Ward's thesis that Oxford played a passive rather than an active role in the dispute between himself and Sidney. Throckmorton wrote further in his diary:

> Thursday, 28th: I supte with my lord Oxford.
>
> Friday, 29th: my lord Oxford comanded to kyppe [=keep] hys chamebere by the Queen.
>
> Thursday, 4 February: I wryte to my lord of Lestere.
>
> Friday, 5 February: I was commaunded to my chamber by my lord Chamberlyne [=Sussex].
>
> Saturday, 6 February: I writ a letter to my Lord Chamberlyne.
>
> Monday, 8 February: I came from Londone to the courte.
>
> Wednesday, 10 February: I spake with my Lord Chameberlyne. I resceauid a letter from my mother. I came from courte to Londone.
>
> Thursday, 11 February: my Lord of Oxford relleassed.

Thus Oxford remained under house arrest from 29 January to 11 February, about a fortnight. The facts are tantalizingly similar to those of the 'tennis-court quarrel', but by now the Court had moved from Greenwich to Westminster, and Oxford had evidently moved also.[4]

Sidney now withdrew from court life, not returning until 20 October (Ward, p. 177). Though he kept his honour intact, he incurred the Queen's wrath by composing a treatise – doubtless at Leicester's behest – advising her against marriage with Anjou.[5]

On some occasion between Ash Wednesday and death of Henry Fitzalan (the 'old' Earl of Arundel), that is, between 16 and 24 February, Henry Howard and Oxford chatted on the terrace at Howard House (LIB-3.1/2.2). The first topic of conversation was Fisher's Folly, which Oxford had recently acquired as his London residence. Oxford complained about the extraordinary cost of 'trymming vppe' the property, while Howard thought the purchase 'no great portion of his Lordships wisdome considering the price he told me that he was in hand with it' (LIB-3.2/2.2).

Fisher's Folly is described by Stow in his *Survey of London* of 1598.[6] Just outside Bishopsgate is 'a faire house of late builded by John Powlet':

> Next to that, a farre more large and beautifull house with Gardens of pleasure, bowling Alleys, and such like, builded by Jasper Fisher, free of the Goldsmiths, late one of the six Clarks of the Chauncerie, and a Justice of peace. It hath since for a time beene the Earle of Oxfords place. The Queenes Maiestie Elizabeth hath lodged there. It now belongeth to Sir Roger Manars. This house being so large and sumptuously builded by a man of no greater calling, possessions or wealth, (for he was indebted to many) was mockingly called Fishers folly, and a Rithme was made of it, and other the like, in this manner.

> Kirkebyes Castell, and Fishers Follie,
> Spinilas pleasure, and Megses glorie.

> And so of other like buildings about the Cittie, by Citizens, men haue not letted to speake their pleasure.

The house soon proved too much even for Oxford, who would sell it to his friend William Cornwallis in 1588. By 1598 the house belonged to Sir Roger Manners, but by 1607 it was back in the Cornwallis family.[7] It is unclear whether the Queen lodged at Fisher's Folly before, during, or after Oxford's approximately eight-year tenure.

Continuing his late-February conversation with Howard, 'Thear is a cause', said Oxford, 'that dryues me to depart from hence'. If Howard did not immediately comprehend Oxford's 'cause', he soon learned that Oxford had impregnated Anne Vavasor, a 19-year old Yorkshire girl whom Arundel called cousin, a maid of the Queen's bedchamber.[8] Anne – or Nan – was not quite a classic beauty, but still a woman to die for – or at least to risk a great deal for.

A similar affair conducted two decades earlier gives us a good idea of how such a tryst might have been managed. In March 1563 Edward Seymour, Earl of Hertford, and Lady Katherine Grey were separately interrogated to determine the legitimacy of their clandestine marriage. Thomas confessed that 'he did first make suit for marriage to the said Lady Katherine in a closet of his sister's which she had privately to herself within the maidens' chamber of honour, his sister and no other being then and there present with them'; Katherine admitted that she had met her lover 'after the Queen's grace was come to Westminster, in the closet within the maiden's chamber'.[9] Presumably Oxford had similar access to a closet within the maids' chamber.

A year later Howard charged Oxford with having evolved a scheme 'to cary away Nan Vaviser at Easther was a 12 monthe when he thought hir first to haue bene with child' (LIB-3.6.1/2@128). Easter in 1580 fell on 3 April, but since Oxford knew of Anne's pregnancy by late February, we may infer that sexual congress had occurred in December, perhaps soon after Oxford's release from house arrest in Greenwich. Howard reports that Oxford had thought 'to haue married [Anne

Vavasor,] disposinge his [bank] of monny to the purpose'. Marriage would have made Oxford a bigamist – like his father before him! He had a cache of £15,000 in Spain, and hoped to persuade Howard to join him in exile, or at least to keep the Queen and court in the dark until he could make his escape. Howard refused to do anything that might erode the Queen's confidence in his nephew Philip, the family's heir presumptive. In vain Oxford railed against Howard and against the Queen, who, he claimed, despised and mistrusted everyone in the Howard line. Howard did, however, agree to keep Oxford's secret.

Anne Vavasor's pregnancy evidently ended in a miscarriage. Almost certainly she had not attempted an abortion, for when she conceived again in July, under virtually identical circumstances, she carried her child to term. Oxford remained in London over the summer, while Howard remained with the Court at Oatlands from about mid-July to mid-September.[10] Returning to London, Howard sardonically bade Oxford 'welcome out of Spain'. 'The lyke occasion', replied Oxford – knowing that Anne was pregnant again – 'might renew the lyke aduenture'. At least one other person knew of the affair and tried to persuade her to break off. When Oxford learned of this interference, he swore an oath 'to kill Sir Harrye Knevett at the privie chamber dore for spekeinge evell of him to his ne[i]ce' (LIB-4.2/5.4).

Knyvet was by no means the only target of Oxford's wrath. Arundel reports Oxford's 'layinge wayte for Rawlies life before his goinge into Ireland' (LIB-4.2/5.8). Howard is more specific (LIB-3.1/4@70):

> Thus for a recompence of Rawleys seruice, his life should haue bene latched betwene both the walles before his goinge ouer, and sutes of apparell geuen to those that should haue killed him for seking my Lord of Lesters fauor.

A violent confrontation 'betwene both the walles' occupied the Privy Council on 17 March:[11]

> Walter Ralley and (*blank*) Wingfield committed to the Marshaelsea for a fray besides the Tennis Courte in Westminster.

A subsequent entry identifies the second party as Edward Wingfield.[12] Similarly, on 18 March Ralegh's cousin, 'Arthur Gorge, one of the Gentlemen Pensioners', was 'committed to the Mareshalsea for giving the lye and other speaches passed betwen him and the Lord Windesour in the Chamber of Presence'. Windsor was Oxford's nephew, the son of his half-sister Katherine.[13]

The site of the quarrel on 17 March between Walter Ralegh and Edward Wingfield lay literally 'betwene both the walles' of a narrow path through White-hall known as 'The Street', at either end of which stood a gatehouse 'thwart the high streete to saint Iames Parke, &c' (Fig. 10). Stow imagines the layout as seen by a pedestrian heading south: 'On the right hand be diuers fayre Tennis courtes, bowling allies, and a Cocke pit, all built by king Henry the eight'.[14] The narrow 'Street' was the perfect spot for an ambush.

On or about 28 June Wingfield, aged about eighteen,[15] was summoned before the Privy Council for 'outrages' at his residence of Kimbolton.[16] On 1 July Sir Francis Knollys, Treasurer of the Household, wrote to Walsingham:[17]

> ... I wrote vnto youe three or fowre dayes paste, desiring youe to move my Lords of the previe cownsayle, attendyng at the cowrte, to send theyre letters to Edward Wynkfeld nowe playing revell Rex,[18] at Kymbolton, commandyng hym to make his parsonall appearance forthewith at the cowrte to answr to soche owtrage as I had to charge him with. And my desyre is to knoe theyre or youre answr therein, yf theye and youe shall thynk good to wryte for hym accordynglye. I wold be gladd to have the convayance of those letters vnto hym; in the mean tyme, bycawse I herd not from youe, I have this daye sent a couple of my servyng men to Kymbolton with my letters directing them bothe to the father Thomas Wynkfeld, and to the sonne Edward Wynkfeld whoe is accvmpanyed with Vere my Lord of Oxfords man his fellowe. And I have gyven to my sayd servantes none other commyssyon, but to see and to vnderstand of theyre vnlawfull doyngs, in breykyng of mr Chancyllor of the exchequers [=Sir Walter Mildmay's] orders and myne, and to gyve theym and all others good cownsayle to deale lawfullye, and to defend theymselffes lawfully yf any vyolence shal be offerd theym.

Knollys confirms the connection between Wingfield and Oxford in his declaration that 'Vere my Lord of Oxfords man' was Wingfield's fellow.

That the event that triggered the Privy Council's intervention at Kimbolton was a riot, and not merely the cutting of timber or other depredation, is confirmed by references to violence in both the Walsingham letter and its contemporary endorsement:

> From Sir Francis Knollys. He desirethe lettres from my Master to represse the ryotous dealynge of the Winkfelds at Kimbolton contrary to his & Mr Chancellors order. He hathe sent twoe of his men to Kimbolton.

We are left with some puzzles, but in no doubt that the Edward Wingfield who attacked Ralegh on 'The Street' was Oxford's man.

A similar provincial riot occurred some time during this same year in Essex. At Stock Common and at Pressons Common an armed assembly 'riotously assaulted a male servant of Edward Atslowe, doctor of physic, and "divers other tenants" of Edward Earl of Oxford, the common being in his manor of Downham Hall'.[19]

On 22 April Oxford received votes from five of the fourteen electors for the Order of the Garter, a considerable fall-off from the previous year. Burghley cast one of the five votes.

Howard and Arundel report Oxford's private approval of a letter from the Irish rebel James Eustace, viscount Baltinglas of Munster, to the Earl of Ormond, arguing that Christ himself refused to make his mother an empress on earth – proof that a woman could not be head of the Church, or of the kingdom (LIB-3.6.1/2@137; 4.2/9.13, 15; 4.4/10). This was the letter:[20]

My lord I haue received your letter wherin, yow profese goodwill, and frendshipp towardes me, for which I thanke your honour, and beseche almightie God to make yow his frende, and servaunte, and give yow the Grace to knowe his will, and followe the same. Wheras yow he[a]re, that I assemble great companis of men to gethere, yow knowe I ame not of suche powre, but what so euer I can make, it shalbe to maintaine truthe, and not for eny vndutifulnes towardes my prince. Iniuris indeed thoughe I haue received, and that very greatt, yet I forgett them for eny conceipt I haue of my selfe, as to truste, vnto myne owne strenght or powre, I leave that to men that knowe not God. As for Counsellors I haue, the one is he that said feare not those that kill the bodie onlie, and haue no powre ouer the soule, Another he that bides vs obaie the hier powre, for he that resisteth the hier powre, doth resiste God, the which although he do for a tyme, yet at lenght he shalbe confounded and brought lowe. Seinge that the hieste powre on earth dothe Commaunde vs to take the sworde, And (seinge it can not better be) to fight and defend our selves, againste traitours & rebelles, which do seeke onlie the Murderinge of soules, he is no Christian man, that will not obaie. questionles it is great want of knowledge, and more of grace to thinke and beleve, that a Woman vncapax of all hollie orders should be the supreme governour of Christes Churche, a thinge that Christe did not graunte vnto his owne Mothere. Yf the Quenes pleasure be as yow alleadge to minister iustice, it weare tyme to begine, for in this xxti yeares paste of her Raigne, we haue sene more damnable doctrine maintained, more oppressinge of poore subiectes, vnder pretence of Iustice within this land, then euer we reed, or hearde (since Englande firste received the faithe) Done by Christian princes. Yow counsaill me to remaine quiett, and yow wilbe occupied in persequting the powre [=poor], members of Christe, I would yow should learne, and consider, by what meanes your predecessours cam vpp to be Earls of Ormound Trulie yow should finde, that yf Thomas Beckett Bishopp of Caunterburie, had never suffered deth in the defence of the Churche, Thomas Butlere alias Beccett had never bine Earl of Ormonde I knowe not what Counsell yow haue but I darre bouldlie affirme, that emonges them all that gives yow counsell to maintaine heresie, ther is not one but loves him selfe more then God, the Earthe more then heaven, the pleasure of the bodie more then the health of the soule. I would be verie loth yow should loose throughe maintaigninge of false doctrine, that your aunsitours [=ancestors] wanne by maintaigninge of the truthe. Beware in tyme for it is harde to striue againste God. *Et sapentia huius mundi stultitia est apud Deum.*

How a copy of this letter came into Oxford's hands is unclear. It seems fairly certain that Howard did not hear Oxford's diatribe until after 11 September, the date of Howard's return from Oatlands.

Howard and Arundel accused Oxford of involvement in another contemporary incident (LIB-3.1/4@71; 4.2/5.6; 4.3/4@123):

[Howard]: Thus at her Maiestys last being at Richemond should Gerard and Wingfeld haue slayne Arthur Gorge as he crossed ouer the grene to get to his lodginge.

[Arundel]: His settinge Iarre and Winkefeld to kill Arthur Gorge as he shuld walke over the grene at Richemond.

[Arundel]: ... not longe since, as my Cosine Arthur Gorge well knowes (by the discoverye of a gentillman that serves this monster and wold not consent to suche a villonie), he had warninge geven him to loke to him selfe, and howe it was intendid he shuld be murtherid on Richemon[d] Grene, goinge home to his lodgeinge at twelve a clocke at night. And a nother ientillman of his reveleid it to me, with whome likewise he delte in the matter, and this ientillman, refuseinge to be commaundid bye him to so fowle a facte, was shakeen of[f], and for no other cause.

Elizabeth's term at Richmond extended from 11 September to 1 December. The attack on Gorge was planned for midnight on Richmond Green, but averted when one of Oxford's servants, subsequently dismissed for disloyalty, warned Gorge to look after himself.

Among Wingfield's (or Oxford's) putative associates in crime, 'Vere' may have been one of Oxford's numerous male cousins, while 'Jarre' or 'Gerard' may have been Oxford's servant Gerret, destined to be killed by Sir Thomas Knyvet in a fray of 3 March 1582.

In his draft interrogatories submitted on 18 January 1581, Oxford would accuse Arundel of having sent his servant Pike to the French representative La Mote and to the king of Spain, rewarding Pike by financing his marriage. Arundel would protest: 'as I kno[w] not his wife so I made not the marriage'; he then proposes that Pike himself, who dwells 'not farr hense', and who 'can remove this dowte', be interrogated. Arundel observes, with reference to Oxford: 'Yf my accuser be as free from such practyce it is the better for him'. Arundel then charges Oxford with a 'practice with the Spanish ambassador [Mendoza] for goinge into Spayne, and committinge his monye to his kepeinge to be conveyed over'; further, 'sendinge away Curtese, that was his instrument and meane to the Spanish ambassador, for the preparinge of thingis on the tother side' (LIB-4.2/9.9–10). 'Curtese' was perhaps Philip Curtoise, a merchant known to the spy Henry Fagot as a Mendoza henchman.[21]

The identity of another Spanish agent is revealed in an anonymous report:[22]

One William Wyseman, servant to the Earl of Oxford, left London for Spain on May 20 and arrived in Laredo on the 31st. I spoke with him in Valladolid. He brought two letters from the Spanish ambassador, one for the Duke of Alva and the other for Don Rodrigo Sapato, which letters he said, were hidden under the ballast at Gravesend, and if they had been found about him, he would have been hanged. He had a passport signed and sealed by the ambassador.

Wyseman, who may have served Oxford in 1577, along with Denny and Williams, is known independently (along with Mistress Audley) as an Essex recusant.[23]

Recalling Oxford's words from Christmas 1580, Arundel provides incidental evidence of Oxford's smuggling operation (LIB-4.1.1):

Southwell hathe bewrayd all; therfor yf you wilbe gon, which I wishe for your safetie, Litchefild my man shall shifte you a way wher you shall remayne for a time at a house of myne in Norfolke ...

Arundel adds: 'or Suffowke – I do not well remember whethir, but nere the sea'. What Oxford said – or meant to say – was doubtless 'Essex'. 'Litchefild my man' was Henry Lichfild the madrigalist. The fact that the Spanish ambassador Mendoza knew nothing of Howard, Arundel, and Southwell before Christmas 1580 supports the conclusion that Arundel himself was innocent of contacts with Spain.

On 4 November, in a calm before a storm, Oxford wrote 'To Edward Hubbert esquier my Receyver generall' from Vere House, with instructions for property in Lavenham, Suffolk:[24]

> Where the rent of Lavenham Parke hath heretofore ben payed to my Lady and wiffe by appoyntment by [Robert] Christynmas the fermer [=farmer, rent collector] thereof, which parke beinge nowe in my handes and Christynmas clerely dischardged therof, my will and pleasure is that you do from hensforth pay vnto my said Lady twoo hundreth poundes yerely owte of your Receipt of my Revenewe, to be payed to hir half yerely And that yow do also pay vnto Mynors my Solicitor one hundreth poundes of the first money by yow to be Received at my next Audit, by hym to be payed over to my said Lady for the half yere dewe to hir at Michaelmas Last. And these shalbe your suffycient warraunt and dischardg in that behalf. ...

Oxford's solicitor was almost certainly 'Iohn Mynours gentleman dwellinge in Aldersgatestreete in London beinge the next howse vnto the signe of the Cock at Longe Lande ende', a member of the legal establishment who would be examined on 11 January 1584 regarding Thomas Alfielde, a West Country seminary priest.[25] The fact that Oxford made separate financial arrangements for Anne is here confirmed. This is the only surviving evidence placing Oxford at Vere House, his property at London Stone. Perhaps he had not yet removed to Fisher's Folly, which needed refurbishment.

45 Literary Patronage (1)[1]

Like other members of his class, Oxford was the frequent dedicatee of printed books. Most of the dedications attracted by Oxford were for translations, including the first four: three of ancient histories, one of Calvin's commentary on the Psalms:

Arthur Golding (tr.), *Thabridgment of the Histories of Trogus Pompeius* (1564: STC 24290).

Thomas 'Vnderdoune' (tr.), *An Æthiopian Historie, by Heliodorus* (1569?: STC 13041).

Edmund Elviden (tr.), *The most pleasant metaphoricall historie of Pesistratis and Catanea* (?1570: STC 7624).

Arthur Golding (tr.), *The Psalms of David and others, with J. Caluins Commentaries, by Jean Calvin* (1571: STC 4395): dedication signed 20 October, from London.

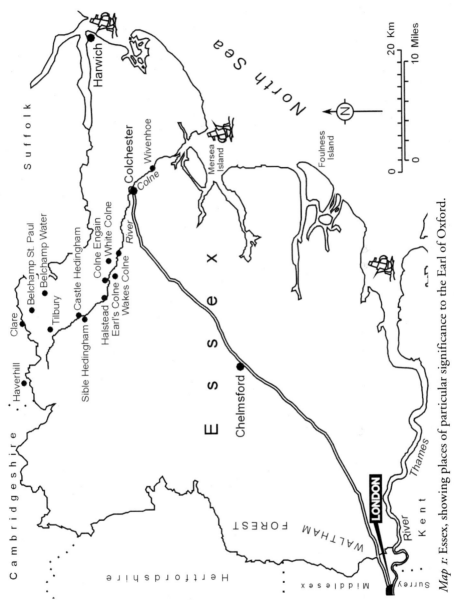

Map 1: Essex, showing places of particular significance to the Earl of Oxford.

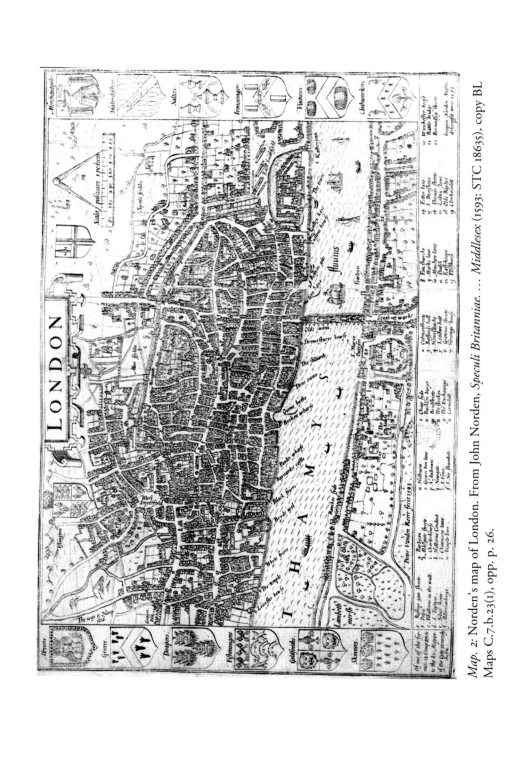

Map. 2: Norden's map of London. From John Norden, *Speculi Britanniae. … Middlesex* (1593: STC 18635), copy BL Maps C.7.b.23(1), opp. p. 26.

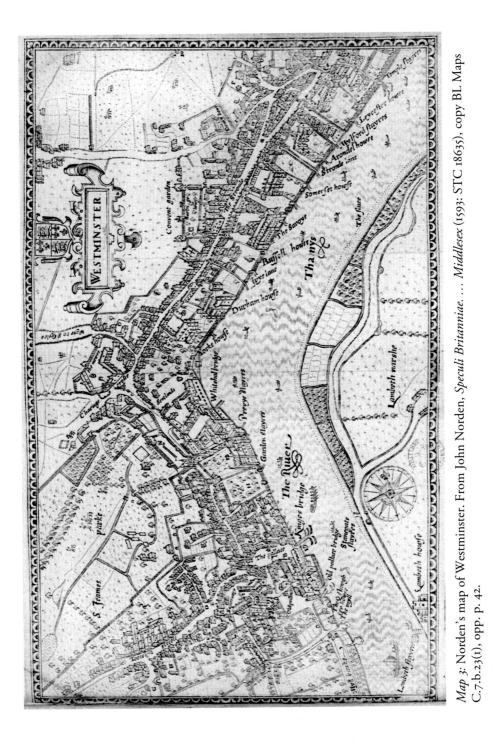

Map 3: Norden's map of Westminster. From John Norden, *Speculi Britanniae. … Middlesex* (1593: STC 18635), copy BL Maps C.7.b.23(1), opp. p. 42.

Map 4: Norden's map of Middlesex. From John Norden, *Speculi Britanniae. … Middlesex* (1593: STC 8635), copy BL Maps C.7.b.23(1593).

Fig. 1: A sixteenth-century childbirth, with astrologers. From Jacob Rueff, *De Conceptu* (1587), copy BL 1173.1.4.

Fig. 2: A suit of armour from the 'Almain Armourer's Album', Victoria and Albert Museum, London

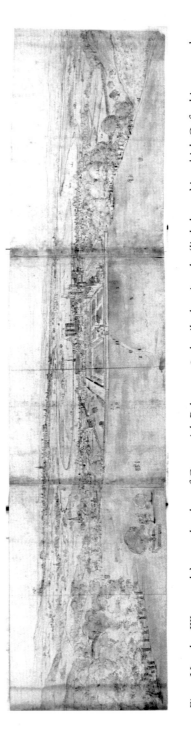

Fig. 3: Van den Wyngaerde's two sketches of Greenwich Palace, 1558, details showing the 'little house' in which Oxford is reported to have conjured: see lower map near right hand crease. Ashmolean Museum, Oxford.

Fig. 4: 'Ser George Howarde Knight Master of the Quenes Maiesties Armory Anno Domini 1561'. From Sir George Howard MS on long-term loan from the Earl of Dartmouth to the Royal Armouries, H.M. Tower of London.

Fig. 5: Satan. From Folger Shakespeare library MS V.b.26, p. 172.

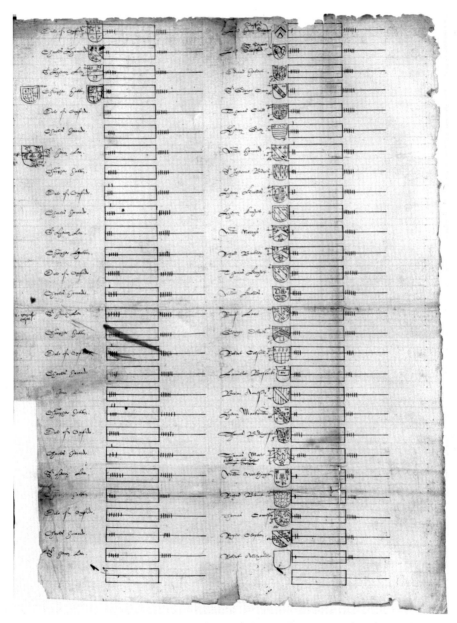

Fig. 6: 'Tilting table', 1571. From Oxford, Bodleian Library MS Ashmole 845, f. 164.

Il Signior Tomaso Odcombiano   *Margarita Emiliana bella Cortesana di Venetia*

Gu: Hole sculp

Fig. 7: Venetian courtesan. From Thomas Coryate, *Coryates Crudities* (1611), copy Folger Shakespeare library STC 5808 (Copy 2), opp. p. 261.

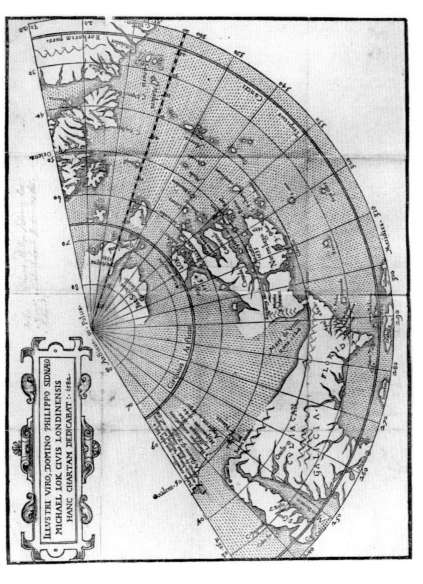

Fig. 8: Michael Lok's map, 1582, showing North-west passage. From Richard Hakluyt, *Divers Voyages* (1582: STC 12624), copy John Carter Brown Library at Brown University.

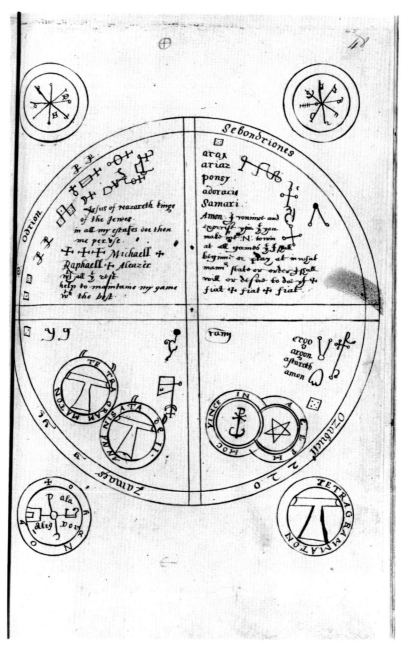

Fig. 9: 'Book of Magic' c. 1580, showing magic circles, magic figures; MS also contains recipes for raising and communicating with spirits. From Folger Shakespeare Library MS V.b.26, f. 48.

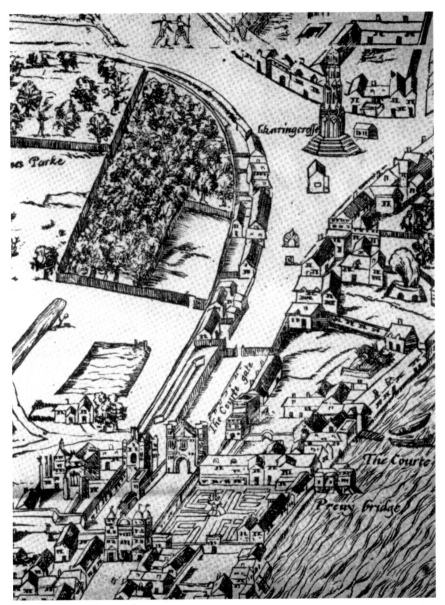

Fig. 10: 'The Street', Whitehall, between gatehouses lower left. Detail from Agas map. From Colvin, iii, Plate 4.

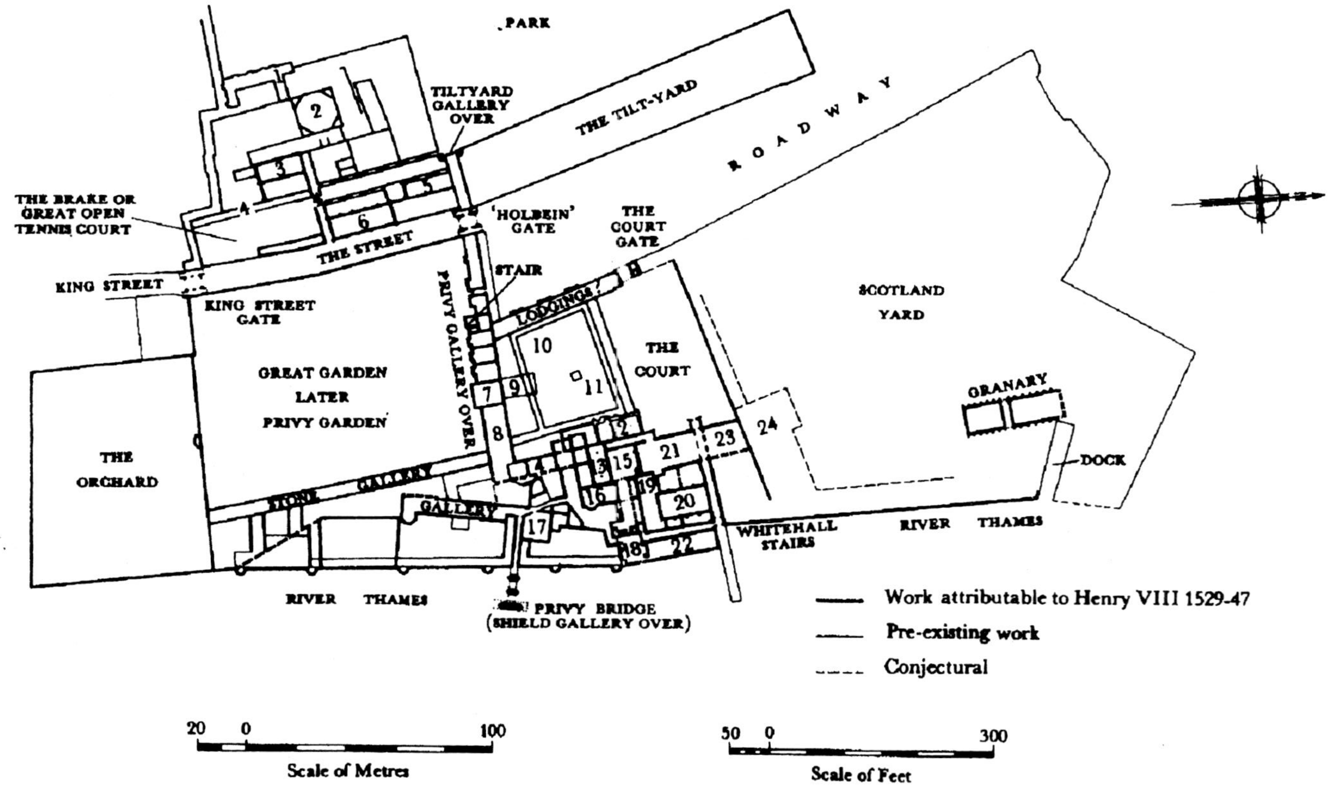
PARK
TILTYARD GALLERY OVER
THE TILT-YARD
ROADWAY
THE BRAKE OR GREAT OPEN TENNIS COURT
'HOLBEIN' GATE
THE COURT GATE
THE STREET
KING STREET
KING STREET GATE
STAIR
LODGINGS
SCOTLAND YARD
GREAT GARDEN LATER PRIVY GARDEN
PRIVY GALLERY OVER
THE COURT
GRANARY
THE ORCHARD
DOCK
STONE GALLERY
GALLERY
WHITEHALL STAIRS
RIVER THAMES
RIVER THAMES
PRIVY BRIDGE (SHIELD GALLERY OVER)
Work attributable to Henry VIII 1529-47
Pre-existing work
Conjectural
Scale of Metres
Scale of Feet

Fig. 11: Low gallery along the terrace, known as 'the Stone Gallery'. From Colvin, iv, Fig. 24 (p. 309).

TO THE RIGHT
honourable *Edward de Vere*
Earle of Oxford, Vicount Bulbeck, Lord of Escales and Badlesmere and Lord great Chamberlaine of England, his singuler good Lord and maister, George Baker wvisheth helth, long life wvith much increace of vertue & honor.

IT IS NOT
vnknovvne to any (right honorable) which haue beene but meanly conuersant in good learning, how far the Gretiãs did surmount all the nations of the world in renown of vertue, learning, politique gouernmēt and noble victoryes. For what nation dooth not reuerēce their sages? what people dooth nat

A.ij. imbrace

VERO NIHIL VERIVS

Fig. 12: Earlier of two Oxford wood-block coats of arms. From George Baker, *The Composition or Making of the … Oil called Oleum Magistrale* (1574: STC 1209), copy Huntington Library 59192.

¶ To the right Honourable Lord, *EDWARD de VERE, Earle of* Oxenford, Viscount Bulbeck, Lord Sandford *and of Badelesmere, and Lord great Camberlaine of England,* all Honour and happinesse, correspondent to his most Noble deserts, and in the commutation of this earthlie being, endlesse ioyes and an euerlasting habitation.

*EVXES endeauou-*ring to paint excellent lie, made Grapes in sheme so naturall, that presenting thē to view men were deceaued with their shapes and the birdes with their culours.

When Apelles drew Venus (though the shew of bewtie seemed woonderful) be daunted not in bis workmanship, becaufe be knew bis cunning excellent.

If

Fig. 13: Later of two Oxford wood-block coats of arms. From Angel Day, *The English Secretorie* (1586: STC 6401), copy BL C.116.bb.33.

Oxford's uncle Arthur Golding dedicated two of these four. Underdowne's dedication in *Æthiopian Historie* embodies an oddly characteristic message discour-
aging the young Earl from intellectual pursuits:

> ... I doo not denie, but that in many matters, I meane matters of learninge, a Noble
> man ought to haue a sight; but to be to[o] muche addicted that waye, I think is not
> good.

An imprint from 1571, Bartholomew Clerke's *De Curiali*, translated into Latin
from Baldassare Castiglione's original Italian (STC 4782), is dedicated to Queen
Elizabeth, but contains a kind of secondary dedication to Thomas Sackville, and
letters of compliment to the author from, among others, Sackville and Oxford.
The latter, as we have seen, is taken by Gabriel Harvey to have been Oxford's
original composition. It is replete with predictable and characteristically repetitive
literary observations.

A fifth translation, published in 1573, has also been noted already: *Cardanus
Comforte*, Englished by Thomas Bedingfield (STC 4608). In the same year
appeared a sixth translation, Humphrey Llwyd's *The Breuiary of Britayne* (STC
16636), rendered from the Latin by 'Thomas Twyne, Gentleman', with a dedication to Oxford on the grounds that 'your honour taketh singular delight' in
'bookes of Geographie, Histories, and other good learnynge'. (Twyne was among
the hysterics who would compose pamphlets on the earthquake of 6 April 1580.)

In 1574 appeared the first book dedicated to Oxford which is not merely a
translation: his surgeon George Baker's *The Composition or Making of the ... Oil
called Oleum Magistrale* (STC 1209). Presumably Baker composed his dedication
prior to Oxford's flight in July of the same year. Baker's was also the first book to
bear Oxford's coat of arms (Fig. 12). On 4 February 1576, with Oxford still in
Italy, (Sir) Geoffrey Fenton dedicated his *Golden Epistles* (STC 10794) to Anne,
not as Oxford's countess but as Burghley's daughter, signing off: 'At my chamber
in the Blacke Friers in London the fourth of February'. A year later George Baker
followed suit by dedicating his translation of Conrad Gesner's *The newe jewell of
health* (STC 11798) to Anne: his Epistle to the Reader is signed 'From my house
in Bartholomewe Lane beside the Royall Exchaunge in London, this xxj day of
February [1577]'; this too bore the Oxford coat of arms. Also in 1577, 'Iohn
Brooke of Ashe next Sandwiche' dedicated his translation of Guido's *The Staffe of
Christian Faith* (1577: STC 12476) to Oxford, followed in 1578 by his translation
of *A Christian Discourse vpon Certeine Poynts of Religion* (STC 5158), dedicated to
Anne. Also in 1578, Gabriel Harvey's *Gratulationum Valdensis* (STC 12901),
already noted, contained dedications to Queen Elizabeth, Leicester, and Burghley
in the first three parts, and to Oxford, Hatton, and Sidney in part four, with
coats of arms for all but Sidney. In 1579, Geoffrey Gates dedicated *The Defense of
Militarie Profession* (STC 11683) to Oxford, with the same coat of arms, and

dating his epistle 23 December 1578.

In 1579 Anthony Munday published *The Mirrour of Mutabilitie ... Selected out of the sacred Scriptures by Antony Munday, and dedicated to the Right Honorable the Earle of Oxenford* (STC 18276), once again with the coat of arms. Munday described Oxford as 'his singuler good Lord & Patron', and recalled an earlier composition:

> After that I had deliuered (Right Honorable) vnto your courteous and gentle perusing, my book intituled Galien of Fraunce, wherein, hauing not so fully comprised such pithiness of stile, as one of a more riper Inuention could cunningly haue carued: I rest Right Honorable on your Clemency, to amend my errors committed so vnskilfully. ...

Munday's 'Galien of France' has not survived, and may not have been printed. (Did Oxford bother to return the manuscript?) In his *Mirrour of Mutabilitie* Munday printed two verse acronyms, the first on 'EDWARD DE VERE EARLE OF OXENFORD', the second being 'Verses written by the Author vpon his Lords Posey. VERO NIHIL VERIVS', translatable as 'Nothing truer than truth'.

In 1580, again using the coat of arms, Munday dedicated his *Zelauto, the Fountaine of Fame* (STC 18283) to Oxford, claiming a connection on the title-page: 'By A. M. Seruaunt to the Right Honourable the Earle of Oxenforde'; in the dedication: 'To the Right Honorable my very good Lord Edward de Vere, Earle of Oxenford'; and at the sign-off: 'Your Honors moste dutifull seruaunt'.

Also in 1580, Thomas Churchyard pledged in *A Light Bondell of liuly Discourses called Churchyardes Charge* (STC 5240), dedicated to Surrey, a future dedication to Oxford (sig. *4):

> ... Prouidyng that my nexte booke maie shewe somewhat among the rest that goeth before: for that it shall be dedicated to the moste worthiest (and towards noble man), the Erle of Oxford, as my laisure maie serve, and yet with great expedition.

Similarly, in *A Pleasaunte Laborinth called Churchyardes Chance* (STC 5250), Churchyard promised to dedicate future books, including his 'Challenge', to Oxford (sig. K4v).

Still in 1580, John Lyly made Oxford the dedicatee of *Euphues his England* (STC 17068), a sequel to his enormously successful *Euphues the Anatomy of Wit* (1578: STC 17064). Lyly followed Munday's lead in dedicating the work openly to 'my very good Lorde and Maister, Edward de Vere, Earle of Oxenforde', and incorporating the Oxford coat of arms. We have noted that John Hester, who called himself 'Practicioner in the arte of Distillaton', dedicated his translation of Leonardo Fioravanti, *A Short Discours ... vppon Chirurgerie* (STC 10881), to Oxford, using the coat of arms. Hester personalized his epistles:

> I most humbly craue your Honorable patronage, that according to your name and poesie, your name and propertie may be to protect the truth ... The most

affectioned of all those, which owe your Lordship dutifull seruice, Iohn Hester. ...
From my house at Paules Wharfe, the 23 of Iannuary.

Hester added a piece of advertising: 'If any be disposed to haue any of these aforesayd compositions redy made, for the most part he may haue them at Paules
Wharfe, by one Iohn Hester practisioner in the Arte of distillations, at the signe
of the Furnaises.'

Finally, in 1580 Abraham Fleming dedicated his translation of Niels Hem-
mingsen's *The Epistle of ... Saint Paul ... to the Ephesians* (STC 13058 [13058+]) to
Anne. (Fleming was another of the hysterics who would compose pamphlets on
the earthquake of 6 April 1580.)

Between 1564 and 1580, then, some 12 imprints were dedicated directly to
Oxford, 13 counting Munday's lost 'Galien of France'. To this number we may
add four imprints dedicated to Countess Anne. Most of the dedicated texts were
of small consequence, failing to make second editions. Notably successful, by
contrast, were Arthur Golding; Antony Munday, who dedicated more books to
Oxford than any other; and John Lyly, whose *Euphues his England* became a repeat
bestseller. All three were Oxford's servants, while George Baker was his surgeon.

London publishers who commissioned a wood-block of Oxford's coat of arms
(as they had done for other noblemen) passed the block from hand to hand
between 1574 and 1580. The block was used not only for books dedicated to
Oxford himself, but for at least one book dedicated to Countess Anne.

46 Oxford's Players (1)

The 16th Earl's players survived their master's death by two years, playing at
Ludlow (Shropshire) as late as 1564–65.[1] Then, following a fifteen-year hiatus, the
17th Earl took over another company altogether, the Earl of Warwick's men.
Warwick was still patron on 1 January 1580,[2] but by April the company's transfer to
Oxford was complete. The transfer was also controversial, as revealed in a 12 April
letter from Sir Nicholas Woodrofe, Lord Mayor of London, to Sir Thomas
Bromley, Lord Chancellor:[3]

> My dutie humblie done to your Lordship. Where it happened on Sundaie last that
> some great disorder was committed at the Theatre, I sent for the vnder shireue of
> Middlesex to vnderstand the cercumstances, to the intent that by my self or by him
> I might haue caused such redresse to be had as in dutie and discretion I might, and
> therefore did also send for the plaiers to haue apered afore me, and the rather
> because those playes doe make assembles of Cittizens and their familes of whome I
> haue charge. But forasmuchas I vnderstand that your Lordship with other of hir
> Maiesties most honorable Counsell haue entered into examination of that matter, I
> haue surceassed to procede further, and do humbly refer the whole to your

wisdomes and graue considerations. Howbeit I haue further thought it my dutie to informe your Lordship, and therewith also to beseche to haue in your honorable remembrance, that the players of playes, which are vsed at the Theatre, and other such places, and tumbleres and such like are a very superfluous sort of men, and of suche facultie as the lawes haue disalowed, and their exersise of those playes is a great hinderaunce of the seruice of God, who hath with his mighty hand so lately admonished vs of oure earnest repentance. It is also great corruption of youthe with vnchast and wicked matters, occasion of much incontinence, practises of many ffrayes, querrells, and other disorders and inconueniences, bisid [=besides] that the assemble of terme and parliament being at hand, against which time the most honorable Lordes haue given vs earnest charge to haue care to auoide vncleanenesse and pestering of the Citty, the said playes are matter of great daunger. Therefore I humble [=humbly] beceche your Lordship, for those and other graue considerations that your Lordship can better call to mind, it will please you that some order be taken by commaundement from your Lordship and the rest of the most honorable Lordes that the said playes and toumbelers be wholy stayed and forbidden as vngodlye and perilous, as well at those places nere our liberties as within the iurisdicsion of this Cittie.

The 'great disorder' had occurred at the Theatre 'on Sundaie last' – that is, on 10 April. The Privy Council acted on three separate occasions, beginning the day after the Mayor's letter:[4]

[13 April] Robert Leveson and Larrance Dutton, servantes unto the Erle of Oxford, were committed to the Mareshalsea for committing of disorders and frayes appon the gentlemen of the Innes of the Courte.

[26 May] A letter to the Lord Chiefe Justice, Master of the Rolles and Mr. Justice Southcote, to examine a matter of a certaine fraye betwene the servauntes of th'erle of Oxforde and the gentlemen of the Innes of the Courtes.

[18 July] A letter to the Master of the Rooles and the Recorder of London to take bondes of Thomas Chesson (sometime servant to therle of Oxford) for his good behaviour for one yere next following, and to release him out of the prison of the Gatehowse.

With Thomas Chesson's release the controversy was effectively at an end.

Lawrence Dutton, one of Oxford's 'servants', was a well-known actor who had served under Sir Robert Lane (1571), Lincoln (1572), Warwick (1575), and now Oxford; indeed, transfer of loyalty was a *modus operandi* of both Lawrence and his brother John.[5] A contemporary poem confirms that the transfer itself was a *cause célèbre*:[6]

The Duttons and theyr fellow-players forsakyng the Erle of Warwycke, theyr mayster, became followers of the Erle of Oxford, and wrot themselues his Comoedians; which certayne gentlemen altered and made Camoelions [=Chameleons]. The Duttons angry with that compared themselues to any Gentleman[;] therfore these Armes were devysed for them.

The fyeld, a Fart durty, a Gybbet crosse corded,
A dauncing Dame flurty of all men abhorred.
A lyther Lad stampant, a Roge in hys Ragges,
A whore that is rampant, a stryde wyth her legges.
A woodcocke displayed, a Calfe, and a Sheepe,
A Bitche that is splayed a Dormouse a sleepe.
A vyper in stynche la part de la Drut,   [stynche='stink' or 'stench']
Spell backwarde this Frenche, and cracke me that Nut. [i.e., 'Drut'='turd' (reversed)]

Party per pillery, perced with a Rope,
To slyde the more lytherly anoynted with Sope.
A Coxcombe crospate in token of witte,
Two Eares perforate, a Nose wythe a slytte.
Three Nettles resplendent three Owles, three Swallowes,
Three Mynstrell men pendent, on three payre of Gallowes.
Further Sufficiently placed in them,
A knaves head for a difference from alle honest men.

The wreathe is a Chayne of chaungeable red,
To shew they are vayne, and fickle of head.
The Creste is a lastrylle whose feathers ar Blew,
In signe that these Fydlers will neuer be trew.
Wheron is placed the Horne of a Gote,
Because they ar chast lo this is theyr lotte.
For their bravery, indented and parted,
And for their knavery innebulated.

Mantled lowsy, wythe doubled drynke
Their ancient house is called the Clynke.
Thys Posy they beare over the whole Earthe,
Wylt please you to have a fyt of our mirthe?
But Reason it is, & Heraultes allowe welle,
That Fidlers should beare, their Armes in a Towelle.

Clearly, the 'gentlemen of the Innes of the Courte' upon whom the Duttons and
their company had committed 'disorders and frayes' were the very 'Gentlemen'
who had denounced them as 'Camoelions'.

Four members of Oxford's new company are identifiable from these records:
Lawrence and John Dutton, Robert Leveson, and Thomas Chesson. It is prob-
able that others who are known to have served under Warwick, including Jerome
Savage, also became Oxford's men.[7]

If Oxford's servants were playing at the Theatre on Sunday 10 April, it is likely
that they were already playing there on Wednesday 6 April, when the famous
earthquake struck between five and six in the evening.[8] This is the event alluded
to in the Mayor's reference to God, 'who hath with his mighty hand so lately
admonished vs of oure earnest repentance'. We have already noted the books and

pamphlets connecting the earthquake to the theatres. As early as Friday 8 April, a 'ballet' was registered by Henry Carre, of which only the title survives (Arber, ii, p. 368): 'Comme from the plaie, comme from the playe; / The house will fall, so people saye; / The earth quakes: lett vs hast[e] awaye'. Registered simultaneously were 'A true report of this earthquake in London' by Richard Tarleton, and 'A warnyng toe [=to] wise' by Thomas Churchyard, two pamphlets subsequently issued in one volume (STC 5259: Churchyard's text runs to sig. B8, Tarleton's to C7). Tarleton was almost certainly the subsequently famous clown, known to have joined the Queen's Men along with the Duttons in 1583 (Nungezer) – possibly he was a member of Oxford's company from its inception. Churchyard refers to Mabell Everitt as merely wounded, while Stow reports in his 1580 *Chronicles* that she 'liued but foure dayes after' (p. 1210); we may infer that the Churchyard–Tarleton pamphlet appeared within a few days of the earthquake.

Churchyard gives the clearest surviving description of audience reactions (sig. B2):

> ... A number being at the Theatre and the Curtaine at Hollywell, beholding the playes, were so shaken, especially those that stoode in the hyghest roomthes and standings, that they were not a little dismayed, considering, that they coulde no waye shifte for themselues, vnlesse they woulde, by leaping, hazarde their liues or limmes, as some did in deede, leaping from the lowest standings. ...

The highest and lowest 'roomthes' or 'standings' were the top and the bottom galleries. Churchyard's versified observations provide a less distinct image (sig. B3):

> The Theatre, for (some great regarde) that open world shoulde note,
> Was shakte so sore, that Sundrye there, a feareful frighting goett.

Three years later Philip Stubbes cribbed from Churchyard in his *The Anatomie of Abuses* (1583sigs. P3v–4), under the sub-title 'A fearfull Iudgement of God, shewed at the Theaters', and with the marginal note, 'A wofull spectacle':

> The like Iudgement (almost) did the Lord shew vnto them a litle befor, being assembled at their Theaters, to see their bawdie enterluds, and other trumperies practised: For, he caused the earth mightely to shak[e] and quauer, as though all would haue fallen down, wherat the People sore amazed, some leapt down (from the top of the turrets, pinacles, and towers, wher they stood) to the ground, wherof some had their legs broke, some their arms, some their backs, some hurt one where, some another, & many sore crusht and brused: but not any, but they went away store [=sore] affraid, & wounded in conscience. And yet can neither the one, nor the other, fray them from these diuelish exercyses, vntill the Lorde consume them all in his wrath: which God forbid. The Lord of his mercie, open the eyes of the maiestrats, to pluck down these places of abuse, that God may be honored, and their consciences disburthened.

Any statement in Stubbes's description which goes beyond Churchyard may be simple hyperbole.[9]

Arthur Golding's *A Discourse vpon the Earthquake that hapned the sixt of Aprill 1580* (1580), registered on 27 June (Arber, ii, p. 372), includes a brief complaint (sig. C2v) against 'Beare-baytings and stageplays'. Far more expansive is a passage in Abraham Fleming's *A Bright Burning Beacon* (1580), apparently registered at the same time as 'A thinge of thearthequake'. The bulk of the treatise was probably written before the earthquake, but Fleming appended a *Commemoration of our late Earthquake, the 6 of April, about 6 of the clocke in the euening 1580* (sigs. D3v–4):

> *Margin*: The sound of a watchword, or Alarum bell, to all prophaners of Gods sacred Sabbaoth, and specially to players, plaiemakers, and all such as fauour that damnable facultie.
>
> Tremble and quake therefore O yee shameles breakers of Gods Sabbaoth, which display your banners of vanitie, selling wind for monie, infecting the tender mindes of youth with the poison of your prophanations, & kindling in them the fire of inordinate lust, to the wounding both of bodie and soule. Doth not God see your filthines, or thinke you that your trade of life depending wholy vpon those your Heathenish exercises, are not offensiue to his Maiestie? Will he winke at such wickednes, & keepe silence at such filthines as is continually concluded vpon and committed in your Theatre, Curtaine, and accursed courtes of spectacles?
>
> *Margin*: As much is God glorified in the pulling downe of polluted places, as in the building vp of holie temples.
>
> O how glorious a worke shoulde that be! how happie a day! how blessed an howre! wherein the people of God might see all such abhominable places dedicated to Gentilisme, or rather Atheisme, (for who can directly say, that either God or the diuell, heauen or hell, is once thought vpon in the prosequuting of such shamefull shewes?) vtterly torne vp from the foundations, rent in peeces the timber from the stone, wasted with fire, laid euen with the ground, and no appearaunce thereof remaining. And thus much touching Comoedies and Comoedians, by way of digression, an enormitie often cried out against of Gods ministers, and in a Christian Commonwealth altogether vnsufferable.

Finally, Anthony Munday, in *A View of sundry Examples ... Also a short discourse of the late Earthquake the sixt of Aprill* (1580), includes a report on London theatres (sig. D4):

> ... At the play houses the people came running foorth supprised with great astonishment.
>
> Many places for sinne haue been greeuously punished, as Sodom and Gomorra, Ierusalem, Niniuie, and many other places. Let vs remember that it shalbe better for Corazaine & Bethzaida at the dredful day of Iudgement then for Tire and Sidon. [=Matthew 11.21]

Munday may also have been responsible for a lost versified admonition registered on 10 November by Edward White:[10]

> A Ringinge Retraite Couragiouslie sounded,
> Wherein Plaies and Players are fytlie Confounded.

In the anonymous *A True Report of … M. Campion* of 1582, Munday is said to have been at first 'a stage player' who 'did play extempore', perhaps as a clown:[11]

> those gentlemen and others whiche were present, can best giue witnes of his dexterity, who being wery of his folly, hissed him from his stage. Then being thereby discouraged, he set forth a balet against plays, but yet (o constant youth) he now beginnes againe to ruffle upon the stage.

Evidently the earthquake scared the hell out of Anthony Munday – temporarily.

Despite anti-theatrical fulminations from his own protégés, Oxford backed his acting company, even soliciting help from his father-in-law. On 9 June the ever-supportive Burghley wrote to John Hatcher, Vice-chancellor of the University of Cambridge:[12]

> After my very hartie commendacions. Where the bearers hereof servauntes to the Right honorable my very good Lord the Erle of Oxford are desierous to repaire to that vniuersitie and there to make shewe of such playes and enterludes as have bene heretofore played by them publykely, aswell before the Queens majestie as in the Citie of London, and intend to spend iiij or v. daies there in Cambridg as heretofore they haue accustomed to do with other matters and argumentes of late yeres, and because they might the rather be permitted so to do without empechment or lett of yow the vicechauncelor or other the heades of howses, have desired my lettre vnto yow in their favor. I haue thought good in respect they belong to a noble man a peere of the realm, and seek this permission by favor and lycence, to recommend them vnto yow by these fewe lynes. trusting that, as their discretion hath served them to make their entrie thether among yow by these meanes, so they will haue lyke care and consideracion in all their behaviors and actions, to observe that modestie and comlines, which the gravitie of that place, and the iudgment of such an auditorie doth require. And so yow see the occasion and scope of this my lettre, which I referre to your consideracion, and the parties to your direction as shall seme good vnto yow. …

This very letter, carried by the actors from London to Cambridge, survives as a rare theatrical artefact. On 21 June Hatcher sent Burghley his reply:[13]

> My bownden dewtye remembred with moste humble and hartye recommendacions whear it hath pleased your honor to commende vnto me and the headdes of the vniuersitye my Lorde of Oxenforde his players that they might shew their cunninge in certayne playes allready practysed by them before the Queens Majestie, I dyd speadely covncell with the heddes and others viz. Doctor Styll. Doctor Howland. Doctor Binge. Doctor Legge &c: and consydering & ponderinge, that the seede, the cause and the feare of the pestilence is not yet vanished & gone, this hote tyme of the yeare; this mydsommer fayre tyme having confluence oute of all

countries as well of infected as not, the commencment tyme at hande, which requireth rather dilligence in stodie then dissolutenesse in playes; and also that of late wee denyed the lyke to the right Honorable the Lord of Leiceter his servantes, and speciallie for that all assemblies in open places be expresslye forbidden in this vniuersitie and towne or within fyue myles compasse by her Majesties covncelles letters to the Vicechancler 30° Octobris 1575 our truste is that your honor our most deare lovinge chaunceler will take our aunswere made vnto them in good parte: and being willinge to impart somthinge from the liberalitie of the vniuersitie to them I could not obtayne sufficient assent therto, and therfore I delivered them but xxs towardes their charges. Also they brovght letters from the right honorable the Lord chavncler and the right Honorable the Lord of Sussex to the vicechauncelers of Cambridge and Oxford: I trust their honors will accepte our avnswere. ...

Hatcher's letter reveals the extensive network of support – ineffective in this case – that Oxford had taken the pains to marshal on behalf of his theatrical enterprise.

Despite their initial setback, Oxford's Men had good success, as we learn from records of provincial touring:[14]

1580–81 (4)
Kent: Dover and Hythe
Norfolk: Norwich
Warwickshire: Coventry
1581–2 (3)
Norfolk: Norwich
Suffolk: Ipswich
Warwickshire: Coventry

1582–83 (9)
Derbyshire: Ticknall (26 August)
Devonshire: Exeter
Gloucestershire: Gloucester (26 May)
Hampshire: Southampton
Lancashire: Liverpool
Somersetshire: Bath and Bristol
Suffolk: Ipswich
Warwickshire: Coventry

Recorded performances must of course represent only a small fraction of the whole.

In 1583 John Dutton was drafted into the newly created Queen's Men[15] – a compliment to the company that lost him. Oxford's Men carried on, initially perhaps under the leadership of John's erratic brother Lawrence:

1583–84 (10)
Devonshire: Exeter (13 May)
Dorset: Lyme Regis (4 May)
Gloucestershire: Gloucester
Kent: Dover (30 March) and Fordwich

Norfolk: Norwich
Shropshire: Ludlow (5 August)
Somersetshire: Bridgewater
Warwickshire: Coventry and Stratford

1584–85 (10 towns; 11 entries)
Devonshire: Totnes
Dorset: Lyme Regis (25 May)
Gloucestershire: Gloucester
Kent: Dover (3 April), Faversham and Maidstone
Somersetshire: Bath (between 16 June and August; again between May and 16 June)
Suffolk: Ipswich, Sudbury (17 April)
Warwickshire: Coventry
Yorkshire: York (30 June)

1585–86 (1)
Norfolk: Norwich (two payments, distinguished as 1585–6 and 1585/6)

1586–87 (1)
Suffolk: Ipswich

The appearance of a collapse after 1584–85 is contradicted in a letter of 25 January 1587 from Maliverny Catlyn to Walsingham:[16]

> ... The daylie abuse of Stage playes is such an offence to the godly, and so great a hinderance to the gospell, as the papistes do exceedingly reioyce at the blemyshe theareof, and not without cause: for every day in the weeke, the playeres billes are sett up in sondry places of the Cittie, some in the name of her Maiesties menne, some the Earle of Leicesters, some the Earl of Oxfordes, the Lord Admyralles, & dyvers others, so that when the belles tole to the Lectores, the Trumpettes sounde to the Stages, wheareat the wicked faction of Rome lawgheth [=laugheth] for ioy, while the godly weepe for sorrowe. Woe is me, the play howses are pestered [=filled to overflowing], when the churches are naked, at the one, it is not possible to gett a place, at the other voyde seates are plentie. the profaning of the Sabaoth is redressed, but as badde a custome entertayned, and yet still our longe suffering God forbayrith to punisshe. Yt is a wofull sight to see two hundred proude players iett [=jet, strut] in theire silkes, wheare fyve hundred pore people sterve in the Streetes: but yf needes this mischif must be tollerated, whereat (no doubt) the highest frownith: yet for Godes sake (sir) lett every Stage in London pay a weekely pention to the pore, that *ex hoc malo, proueniat aliquod bonum* ['from this evil may come some good']: but yt weare rather to be wisshed, that playes might be vsed as Apollo did his lawghing, *semel in anno* ['once a year']. ... the spoyle and overthrowe of Nineue is feared, and dayly looked for, thearefore more tyme to pray then to play. nowe mee thinkes I see your honor smyle, and saye to your self, theise thinges are fitter for the Pullpitt, then a Souldiers penne: but God (who searchith the hart and Reynes [=kidneys, bowels]) knoweth that I write not hipocritically: but from the veary sorrowe of my soule. ...

Oxford's was thus one of four principal companies of London, along with the Queen's, Leicester's, and the Lord Admiral's. All four habitually set up 'players billes ... in sondry places of the cittie', and summoned audiences with trumpets. Performances occurred every day of the week, including Sundays – as on the occasion of the riot of 10 April 1580. Players (200 seems an exaggeration) paraded in silk through the London streets, Oxford's among them.

Oxford also patronized boy actors, tumblers, and musicians. His boys' company is named in a 1580–81 entry from Bristol:

> Item paid to my Lord of Oxfordes players at thend of their play in the yeld hall [=guild hall] before master mayer & master mayer Elect and the Aldremen being j man and ix boyes at ij s. per piece, the sume of xxs.

Thus one man led a troupe of nine boys. For court performances on 1 January and 3 March 1584, 'the Erle of Oxforde his seruauntes' received the standard payment plus gratuity of £20, or £10 per play, paid to 'Johon Lilie'. The following Christmas season, on 27 December 1584, Henry Evans received the standard payment (minus gratuity) of £6–13–4 'for one play ... by the children of Therle of Oxforde'. This was the lost 'History of Agamemnon and Ulisses presented and enacted before her majesty by the Earl of Oxford his boys on St John's Day at night at Greenwich'.[17]

John Lyly was certainly attached to Oxford, whether as servant, literary protégé, or both, from at least as early as 1580.[18] Testimony relative to Blackfriars dates from about 1584, in a document headed 'Touching the matter in variance between me and Anne Farrant, widow, for an house in Blackfriars':[19]

> 1. First I let the said house to Sir Henry Neville for a term of one-and-twenty years, and took of him no fine for the same. Sir Henry Neville added a new kitchen and set up ... partitions in the house.

> 2. Afterward Sir Henry Neville desired me by his letter to let the said house to Farrant, which I did upon condition that he should not let nor set the same, nor any part thereof, to any person without my consent had and obtained in writing ...

> 3. Farrant pretended unto me to use the house only for the teaching of the Children of the Chapel, but made it a continual house for plays, to the offence of the precinct, and pulled down partitions to make that place apt for that purpose, which Sir Henry Neville had set up; and contrary to the condition let out part of the said house for the which I charged him with the forfeiture of his lease, whereunto he yielded and offered composition; but before I could take remedy against him he died.

> 4. After whose death I entered upon the said house, and refused to receive any rent but conditionally, nevertheless offering Farrant's widow that if she would commit the cause to two lawyers indifferently chosen, or to any two judges, I would yield to whatsoever they should determine therein; which she utterly refused.

> 5. Immediately after, she let the house to one Hunnis, and afterward to one New-
> man or Sutton, as far as I remember, and then to Evans,[20] who sold his interest next
> to the Earl of Oxford (who made a gift of his interest to Lyly); and the title thus was
> posted over from one to another from me, contrary to the said condition ...

(Henry) Evans, Oxford, and (John) Lyly appear as successive owners of the lease
on the theatre in Blackfriars. Oxford's 'gift' of the lease to Lyly may well have
been part of a legal shell-game intended to keep Widow Farrant from recovering
her property and closing it down as a theatre.

E. K. Chambers, summing up the evidence, reasonably concludes: 'I do not
feel much doubt that the companies under Lyly and Evans were the same, or that
in 1583–4 they in fact consisted of a combination of Oxford's boys, Paul's and the
Chapel, working under Lyly and Evans at the Blackfriars theatre'. Oxford's company of boys, unlike his company of men, was short-lived, for in the spring of
1584 Sir William More regained possession of Blackfriars, nor are Oxford's boys
known after the 1584–85 Christmas season except once: in his *Ironicall Letter* of
1585, Jack Roberts admonishes Sir Roger Williams to 'take heed and beware of
My Lord of Oxenfordes man called Lyllie, for if he sees this letter, he will put it in
print, or make the boyes in Paules play it uppon a stage'.[21] This theme was
parroted by Gabriel Harvey in his 1593 *Pierces Supererogation* (sig. R4v):

> ... all you, that tender the preseruation of your good names, were best to please
> Pap-hatchet, and see Euphues betimes: for feare lesse he be mooued, or some One
> of his Apes hired, to make a Playe of you; and then is your credit quite-vndone for
> euer and euer; Such is the publique reputation of their Playes.

'Pap-Hatchet' was the anonymous pamphlet of 1589, then and now attributed to
Lyly.

On 1 January 1585 a troupe appeared at court under the name of 'John Symons
and other his fellowes Servauntes to Therle of Oxford': Symons was paid 'for ...
feates of actiuitye and vawtinge [=vaulting]'. The same event is elsewhere described as 'Dyuers feates of Actyuytie ... shewed and presented ... on newe yeares
daye ... by Symons and his fellowes'.[22] In 1581–82 and 1582–83 this troupe had
been patronized by Lord Strange, and by 1596 it had returned into the service of
the Stanley family.[23] On 12 March 1583 Burghley wrote to Hatton that one of the
few servants kept by his son-in-law Oxford was 'a kind of tumbling-boy' –
doubtless from the same company of acrobats.[24] Evidently Oxford's patronage of
Symons's tumblers extended from 1583 to at least 1586.

Oxford also patronized a company of musicians: in 1584–85 the city of Oxford
made a payment to the Earl of Oxford's 'musytions';[25] in the same year Barn-
staple paid 5s 'to the earle of Oxfordes musicions'.[26] During the 1590s Oxford's
Men – his adult players – seem to have practised a kind of disappearing trick.
They persevered nevertheless until 1602, as we shall learn in due course.

PART VII

Sedition
1580–1581

47 Denunciations

On a Friday before Christmas 1580, apparently on 16 December, in the Presence Chamber at Greenwich, Oxford publicly accused his three erstwhile friends of sedition – indeed, of treason.[1] Oxford named Henry Howard as the most villainous person on earth, and the entire Howard clan as the worst noble family on earth.[2] Throwing himself on his knees before the Queen, he confessed to a pro-Catholic conspiracy over the past four years involving himself, Howard, Charles Arundel (who was present), and Francis Southwell. More particularly, he accused Howard of having reconciled to Rome through the offices of the mass-priest Stevens; and he confessed that he himself had spirited Stevens out of the country with the help of the French ambassador Mauvissière, to whom he appealed as a witness. Mauvissière denied the imputation.[3]

> On hearing [my denial,] the Earl of Oxford once again threw himself on his knees before [the Queen], and implored her to urge me to tell her the truth. At the same time he begged me to do him the favour to recall a circumstance which touched him very closely. He reminded me that he had sent me a message begging me to assist the said Jesuit to return in safety to France and Italy, and that when I had done so he gave me his thanks. I replied clearly and unequivocally to the Queen that I had no recollection whatever of this incident. The effect of my reply was that the Earl was fairly put to confusion in the presence of his Mistress [=the Queen].

Desperate, Oxford implored Mauvissière to report what it was that he did remember. Mauvissière continues, referring to the proposed Elizabeth–Alençon marriage as 'the match':

> I bade him speak no more. He is evidently trying to sicken those who were earnest on the side of the match. Perhaps he is jealous of others, or is of the Spanish faction.

Without Mauvissière's backing, Oxford's petition looked merely ridiculous.

Arundel seconds Mauvissière's testimony. Having denied one charge, he now denies the other (LIB-2.2.3/2):

> ... but this is as trewe, as that the Frenche Ambassader conveyed awaye the Iesuite, in deniall wherof Oxford put vpp a lie in presence of the Qwene and with shame inoughe was put to silence.

Oxford's charges were belittled not only by Mauvissière, but, according to the latter, by fellow courtiers and even by the ladies of the court. Oxford had confessed his own subversion, but had not succeeded in implicating anyone else. He stood alone.

Several explanations have been offered for Oxford's confession and denunciations. Ward, more hagiographer than historian, argues that Oxford, having dabbled in pro-Spanish activities, and having learnt that the Jesuits Persons and Campion were returned from the Continent, experienced an access of patriotism, and single-handedly alerted Queen and Privy Council to the country's danger: 'Lord Oxford had opened their eyes'.[4]

Bossy, dismissing the idea that Oxford acted as an independent agent, traces the incident back to Mauvissière's disclosure of Leicester's September 1578 marriage:[5]

> Leicester got in a smart riposte to Mauvissière's coup of the previous year. He dislodged Oxford from the pro-French group and elicited from him the story of his intrigue with Mauvissière in 1577. He then persuaded him [=Oxford] to make a public confession to the Queen in the ambassador's presence, accusing his former friends of becoming reconciled to Rome and conspiring against the State.

Peck, who believes that Oxford had converted to Catholicism 'through [Charles] Arundell's agency', elaborates on Bossy's scenario:[6]

> During the Christmas season of 1580, Leicester unveiled his answer to Simier's revelation of his marital status. Intent upon rendering Sussex's allies politically useless, he successfully weaned the unstable Oxford away from his friends. The young nobleman confessed to the Queen his intrigues of 1577 with the French ambassador and accused his coreligionists of conspiracy against the state. When his confession and accusations were not immediately believed, he allegedly offered Arundell a thousand pounds to verify his charges and focus the blame upon Howard and Southwell; Arundell, according to his own testimony, refused the offer. Elizabeth told Mauvissière that she had known of the religious persuasions of Howard, Arundell, and Southwell all along but esteemed the men highly anyway, especially in light of their support for her marriage; 'she would close her eyes to it: as long as it was not found to go deeper'.

Bossy and Peck are doubtless correct, but perhaps exaggerate the seriousness of revelations concerning Leicester's marriage, and mis-date Arundel's earliest surviving letter to his lady, written not in late December 1580, but in late March or early April 1581.[7]

I myself suspect that Oxford was motivated by the recent exposure of 'William Wyseman, servant to the Earl of Oxford'. Learning that his Spanish intrigues had been detected, Oxford acted to save not the throne, but himself. (The first conspirator to turn state's evidence has the best chance of saving his own skin.) No doubt Oxford was also still smarting from Howard's expressed intent to withdraw his companionship, as reported by Arundel (LIB-2.3.2/6):

> Ten dayes before this brabble was begone [=begun,] he [=Oxford] sent him [=Howard] a message that ether by meanes direct or indirect, by right or wronge, he wold make him repent his leaveinge of his companye.

Arundel's charge is compatible with evidence that Oxford nursed an unremitting hatred of the Howard clan, whose functioning head was Henry, but whose symbolic head was Philip, just now in the process of being created Earl of Arundel (LIB-2.3.2/3, 5–6).

The Spanish ambassador Mendoza, writing on 9 January 1581 of the imprisoned trio, reports Leicester's intervention, which suggests that Oxford had at least partly overcome the animosity that had landed him in trouble in the latter months of 1579:[8]

> What adds to the mystery of the matter is ... Leicester's having spread the rumour that they were plotting a massacre of the Protestants, beginning with the Queen. His object in this is to inflame the people against them and against the French, as well as against the earl of Sussex who was their close friend.

In a letter to his lady, Arundel gives independent witness to Leicester's role (LIB-6.3):

> ... the formall cause of my staye was a supplicacion presentid to the Quene by Lester from Oxford

Elsewhere Arundel is more circumstantial (LIB-2.3.2/7):

> Nowe the truthe is, that this noble cownt, findinge him selfe forsaken for his horrible enormities rather to be buried in the dunge hill of forgettfullnesse then reportyd by any modest tonge, obtayned my Lord of Lesters favor by the mediation of his man Milles, vppon condition that he shuld spede vs three, and thus the bargaine was concludid.

Oxford's 'man Milles' was Arthur Milles, with whom we will become better acquainted. According to Arundel, then, Oxford secured Leicester's protection at the price of his friends' freedom.

Oxford had only recently expressed his antipathy to the Howards upon the hearth (LIB-3.1/2.2) or at table at Howard House, with a dubious pun on the pet name 'Chick' (LIB-3.2/4 – the italics are mine):

> This was *chick*, and he detested all his *kinne*, which made chicken: thus hathe he pretily begonne his solemne vowe to be reuengid of all the Howardes in England one after another, though he could not paye them all at once; for it was the most

villanouse and treacherouse race vnder heaven, and my lord Howard of all other
the most arrant villaine that liued.

In the background of the dispute lay not only Howard's sardonic remark at his
return from Oatlands, but Oxford's acquisition of Castle Rysing in 1578.

The Privy Council decided that Oxford's charges against Howard, Arundel,
and Southwell were sufficiently serious to warrant further investigation, and so
ordered their arrest. Knowing that his own best hope was to deprive Howard of
support, Oxford met secretly with Arundel, both on Christmas Eve and on
Christmas Day (LIB-4.1.1):

> On Svndaye last beinge Christmas day, the Earell of Oxenford desirid secrett
> conference with me as he had don the night before; whervnto I assenteinge, we
> mett in the eveninge at the Maydes chamber doore, and after longe spechees in
> secret betwene him and my cosine Vaviser, who was the meane of owre meteinge,
> we departid thense to have gon to the garden.

Thus Oxford and Arundel approached the maid's chamber at Westminster, where
Arundel roused Anne Vavasor. After an exchange of cousinly greetings, Arundel
retired while Oxford and Anne conversed *tête-à-tête*. Six months into her second
pregnancy, she and Oxford faced the same dilemma as the previous Lent.

Oxford's need for an ally must have seemed overwhelming. He and Arundel
must now talk – but where? The garden on the up-river side of Whitehall Palace,
of course! But there the gate was bolted and double-locked. Where else? The
bottom of the low gallery along the terrace, known as 'the Stone Gallery' (Fig. 11).[9]
Here Oxford exercised all his arts of persuasion (LIB-2.3.2/7):

> [Oxford] proferid me a pardon from the Qwene, and a thowsan[d] pownd in
> mony, [and] a hundryd pownd land, in case [=on condition] I wold concurr with
> him in pointes wherof he had accusid the Lord Harrye and Southwell; whiche I
> refuseinge, and professinge to doe against him that wold charge me with the small-
> est thought against my prince, he wold have geven me as muche to flie, that bye the
> flight of one, he might have wreakeid his depe mallice on a nother. But this
> succedeinge as evell as the rest, with menacis that I shuld be toren in pecees with
> the racke, he left me.

Arundel's second version of the same event is even more colourful, containing
lively quotations from Oxford (LIB-4.1.1):

> Ther in the farther part of the lowe gallerie, the sayde Earell vsid this speche vnto me:
>
> – Charles, I have ever loveid the[e] and as you have alredie geven yowr word to my
> Mistris, so nowe I crave it to my selfe.
>
> And after some assurance geven, he vnfoldeid to me all his trecherie, vsinge many
> cunnynge perswasions to make me an instrument of dishonist practice against my
> Lord Harrye and Francis Soothewell, with the proffer of one thowsan powndes to
> affirme that they were reconcileid by one Stevans a pr[i]est. I so muche mislikeid of

this mocion as I perswadeid the sayde Earl from so dishonorable a purpose, protestinge before God – which is most trewe – I nether knowe nor h[e]ard of any sutche thinge.

– Well Charles (sayde the Earl), Stevans is takeen and racked, and hathe confessid, and therfore I wishe you, as a frind, to be gon and depart the realme yf you have fawlted as farr as others.

– (Whervnto I answerid) God I take to witnis, suche offence I my selfe am free of, and so am I perswadeid of others.

– You are deceaveid (sayde the Earl): Sowthwell hathe bewrayd all Therfore, yf you wilbe gon, which I wishe for your safetie, Litchefild my man shall shifte you away wher you shall remayne for a time at a house of myne in Norfolke

or Suffowke: I do not well remember whethir, but nere the sea.

– You shall have a thowsan powndes, ether with you or billes for so muche – the ambassador of Spayne [=Mendoza] hathe of myne more then that. And when you are gon, I will find the meane to send vnto you. And yf the sale of a hundrid pownd land will do you good, it shalbe the rather then you shall want.

I likeeid so ill of this vnsownd cownesell as I vtterlie refusid it Then my Lord fell to a playnenesse and told me what he had confessid to the Quene: that he was reconcillid; … that he had his pardon to appech; and if I wolde be ruleid by him, he wolde save me. I thanke[d] him much, but refusid. His conclusion was that no man coulde do him harme but my selfe (and that my Lord will I never [do]). His driafte [=drift] – as I colde Iudge of it – was to this end: that by my flight he might be freed of his monsterous dealinge, and others browght to more suspicion. And not refusinge vtterle to yeld to his reqwest, I prayed him I might thinke vppon it, and thervppon wrat [=wrote] vnto the Earell a letter by Pore [=Power] his page, the copye wherof I exhibityd to your Lordships [=members of the Privy Council].

When Arundel states that Oxford 'had his pardon to appech' he means that a pardon had been offered on the condition that Oxford would name names – then as now a standard gambit in a criminal investigation. The racking of Stevens was clearly Oxford's invention, since the real Stevens was living in safety on the continent; also, Arundel was right to insist that Stevens was not a Jesuit.[10] On the other hand, Southwell may indeed have been arrested and made his confession – he was not with Howard and Arundel while they were on the run.

Arundel, by his own report, refused either to turn against Howard and Southwell, or to flee England with Oxford's assistance. The story is now taken up by the Spanish ambassador Mendoza:[11]

On hearing that the earl of Oxford had accused him and Francis [error for Charles] Arundel of submitting to the Roman Church, and that the Queen had ordered them both secretly to be arrested, they came to my house at midnight, although I had never spoken to them, and told me that they had been warned of their danger by a Councillor, a friend of Lord Harry's. They had been in close communication with the French ambassador, but they did not dare to trust him at this juncture, and feared that they would be taken to the Tower and their lives be sacrificed. They therefore came to me in their peril, and asked me to hide them and save their lives. As they were Catholics, I detained them without anyone in the house knowing of it, excepting one servant, until their friend the Councillor informed them that they would only be placed under arrest in a gentleman's house, whereupon they immediately showed themselves in public.

The friendly 'Councillor' may well have been Sussex, a kinsman of both Howard and Arundel; 'sone after one of vs, and within towe dayes bothe the rest, were committed' (LIB-2.3.2/7).

The conspirators' incarceration is noted in a Fugger letter of 1 April 1581:[12]

The English … declare that a plot has been formed by the Jesuits, Catholic nobles and other persons, whom the Queen has imprisoned. One important gentleman has fallen away, abjured the Roman faith and been set at liberty. The others are still in prison. In a word the English have a horror of the King of Spain and do not trust us here overmuch either.

The 'important gentleman' eventually set at liberty upon abjuring his faith was almost certainly Oxford.

Oxford not only abjured his allegiance to Catholicism, but put his erstwhile friends in danger to the extent of his powers. Of the 26 questions put to Howard and Arundel in their first formal interrogation, about 12 January, 11 (numbers 10 to 20) came from the Catholic-hunter Thomas Norton; most of the rest can only have come from Oxford (LIB-2.1.1–4; see also 3.3; 4.3; 6.8):

Imprimis what conference was had betwene you the Lord Harry Francis Southwell and in what sort did you combine in consent for the answeringe of such accusations as you supposid shuld be layed against you

2 Item whether have you bin reconciled to the churche of Rome and at what time and place and who were reconcileid with you and howe many others do you kno so reconcileid

3 Item howe often have you h[e]ard mas[s]e and bin confessid within thes v yeres last past and in whose howse and in what companye

4 Item what intelligence have you had in Ireland with any of the nobilytie ienteillmen or others of that cuntrye, what letters have you writen thither or receavid thense, what confereince have you had with any of that cuntrye, here in the realme or with any other of this realme toucheinge causees of Ireland

5 Item what conference have you had with certayn obstinate and dysobedient persons of Cornewall and Wales

6 Item who they were that did geve Monsieur de Simiers secret intelligence of the Quenes dealinges and whether you kno not when that by makeinge a marke on a stone in Lightes garden did geve knoledge for the sayd Simiers that he had adver-

tisment to geve him of importance and therfore he shuld by that marke kno howe to kepe atyme [=a time] and howre of meteinge

7 Item who it was that told Monsieur de Simiers that he should have a stabb with a dagger and likewise who it was that vppon this cause wold have borrowid a privie dubblet of the Earl of Oxford

8 Item who they were that vsid to take her Maiesties letters and other private advertismentes oute of her pocket when her Maiestie was gone to bed.[13] then who had the pervsinge of the same and howe often you have bin at the sight and hearinge of suche letters and advertisments and in what presence and companye

9 Item whether do you kno of eny offer made to the Earl of Oxford from Monsieur (=Anjou) that yf he wold forsake the realme and live in Frawnce Monsieur with the helpe of the Kinge his brother wold better howse him and furnishe him with better abilytie and revennewe the[n] ever he had in Ingeland, and whether vppon this offer was there any Iuell [=jewel] or other thinge geven the sayd Earell[14] ...

21 Item whether dothe any Iesuite say mas[s] for any man before reconcilement to the churche, and whether did not Stevans and other so declare vnto you before they wold suffer you to here there mas[s].[15]

22 Whether have you at any time spokeen or h[e]ard it spokeen that for the great mislyke the people have of this religion Wales and Ireland wold revolt

23 What dealinges have you had with Thomas [*for* Edward?] Somersett and Charles Paget[16] or ether of them, and with whome of her Maiesties have they intelligence and to what end.

24 What prophesies have you latelie sene or h[e]ard whiche might concerne the contemp[t], repro[a]che and overthrowe of owre most gracious soverange whome owr Lord God blesse forever.[17]

25 What papers and priteinges [=printings] did you and the Lord Henrie burne to gether. what did you at sir Thomas Kitsons[18] and whether did you here any masse ther and whether did you burne any writeinges ther or what did you at the Lord Dacres house[19] and lastlie what in yowr one [=own] lodgeinge or the Lord Harrys did you burne or other wise convaye.

26 At what places in London be those Iesuites entertayned wher be they lodgeid howe many kno you of them and what be ther names what parsons [=persons] haunte to them

Not only does Oxford himself figure in many of these 15 articles, but the articles are virtually identical to subsequent charges that are even more clearly his.

Those subsequent charges, in Oxford's hand, survive in two sheets of paper endorsed '18 Ianuary 158<.> Notes deliuerd by the Earl of Oxeford'. Their tone and format afford direct access to Oxford's mind (LIB-2.2.2):

[1] Item to be demanded of Charles Arundell, and Henry Howard ... what combination, for that is ther terme, was made at certeine suppers, on[e] in

Fishstreat as I take it an other at my Lord of Northumberlands.[20] for they haue often spoken hearof and glanced in ther speaches.

[2] further for Henry Howard ... Yf he never spake or h[e]ard thes speaches spoken that the kinge of Scots began now to put on spures on his heales, and so sone as the matter of Monsieur wear assured to be at an end, that then wythe in six monthes we showld se[e] the Queens Magestie to be the most trobled and discontented parson [=person] liuinge.

[3] further the same ... Hathe sayd the Duc of Guise who was a rare and gallant gentleman showld be the man to come into Scotland, who wowld briche [=breech, whip] her Magestie for all her wantonnes. and it wear good to let her take her humor for a while for she had not longe to play.

[4] Item to Charles Arundell ... a littell before Christmas at my lo[d]ginge in Westmester [=Westminster] Swift[21] beinge present and George Gyfford talkinge of the order of liuinge by mony and dyfference betwien that and revenu by land, he sayd at the last if George Gyfford could make [=assemble] thre thousand pound he wowld set him in to a course whear he ne[e]d not care for all England and theare he showld liue more to his content and wythe more reputatione then ever he dyd or myght hope for in England and they wowld make all the cowrt wonder to heare of them. Wythe diuers other braue and glorious speches whearat George Gyfford replyd Gods blud Char[l]es whear is this. he answerd yf yow haue thre thousand pound or can make it he could tell the other saying as he thought he could find the means to make thre thousand pound. that speache finished withe the cominge in of supper

[5] Item ... Whither [=Whether] Charles Arundell dyd not steale ouer into Irland withein thes fiue yeres, wytheought [=without] leaue of her Magestie and whether that yeare [=1576–77?] he was not reconciled or not to the churche lekwise, or how long after.

[6] Item ... When he was in Cornwale at Sir Ihon Arundels what Ihesuit or Ihesuits he met thear and what compagnie he caried withe him of gentelmen.

[7] Item ... Not longe before this sayd Christmas entringe into the speache of Monsieur, he passed into great tearmes against him, in so muche he sayd thear was nether personage religion, witt or constancie, and that for his part he had longe since giuen over that course and taken an other way. which was to Spaine, for he never had opinion therof since my lord chamberlan [=Sussex] playd the cokescome, so he termd my lord at that time as when he had his enymy [=Duke of Norfolk] so lowe as he myght haue troden him quight vnderfotte, [8] that then he wowld of his owne obstinacie followinge no mans aduise but his owne, whiche he sayd was his fault, bringe all thinges to an equalitie whearin he was greatly abused in his owne conceit and so discoraged Semier as never after he had mind to Spaine any lenger [=longer] reputinge the whole cause then to be ouerthrowne. [9] And further for Monsieur a man now well inought [=enough] knowen vnto him and he wowld be no more abusd in him, and it was for nothinge that Semiers saud [=saved] himself, for he knew his vnconstancy, and Busse d'Ambois[22] had ben a sufficient warninge vnto him, whom Monsieurs trecherie had caused to be slaine,

and wowld by practise bringe Semier into the slander therof that his vilanie myght not be found but it was plaine Inought [=enough]. [10] and he had made an end and quight done withe the cause and leket [=liked] of it no more, and so withe a great praising (*sideways*) of the Kinges [*sic*] of Spaines greatnes, piete, welthe, and how God prosperd him thearfore in all his actions, not doughtinge but to se him Monarch of all the world and all showld come to on[e] faythe he made an end and thus muche consideringe his practise withe Gerningham,²³ and the (*upside-down, top of page*) other articles whearwithe he is charged import a further knowlege and giues sume lyght to his dealinges wythe thes persones of religion and Irishe causes whearin the kinge of Spayn semes vnderhand to deale.

So far the first sheet. The second sheet is similar:

Item to my Lord Henry

[11] How he cam to the inteligence, that ther showld come imbassadoures of France Spaine and others whiche showld assist the kinge of Scots imbassadoure in the demand of his mother [=Mary Queen of Scots], and this showld be determined among them on the other sid[e] [=abroad] as he sayd and shall shortly com to pas

Lekwise bothe Charles and Henry

[12] Lekwise they haue bene great serchers in her Magesties welthe, hauinge intelligences ought [=out] of all her receyts, [13] from her Magesties courtes in laue [=law], customes as well of them that goo ought as are brought in, what subsides priui seales and fiftenes [=fifteenths, taxes] she hathe made since her cominge to the croune, [14] what helpes, as they say by the gatheringes made as for the buildinge of Paules steple,²⁴ the loteries,²⁵ and other deuises from the clergie and what forfits by attainder or other wise, and what pensions, when other ought [=either out] of bishops liuinges to sume of her counselers what giftes she hat[h] bestoued, what charges she was at in her houshould reperations of her houses and castels fees and a number of thinges whiche now I cannot call to remembrance whearof they ordinaryly wowld speake and of her Nauie the charge she was at what the wares of Lethe Newhauen²⁶ and other peti iornyes²⁷ in Irland and Scotland and in the time of the rebellion whiche ar to[o] longe²⁸ as well what she receiued as what she spended [=spent, expended] in all offices places &c.

lekwise to the sayd Charles

(*sideways*) [15] Item for what cause he sent Pike to La Mote,²⁹ and who he was [who] went into Spaine and whether Pike went or no, but he assuredly remayned the others returne [16] whoo caried letters from La Mote and brought bake [=back] againe letters from the kinge and recompence whearvpon Pike returned withe answer to Charles Arundell. [17] who help[ed] the man as I h[e]ard to a mariage and whether the fellow brought his master sume assurance and reward from the kinge to his Master I know not but ever since he liues of himself and giues no more attendance to color as I coniectur[e] the cause better,³⁰ and the course (*upside down in top margin*) as I g[u]es[s] and haue great reason to coniectur put in to sum others hands, a thinge whiche yf it be well loked into, cannot be void of great and sume notable practise yf it will pleas her Magestie but to loke in to [the] zelous mind whiche the sayd Charles hathe since caried more then couertly to the masse. Lekwise bothe Charles Arundell and Henry Howard are priuie as often times they haue declared by theare speaches thes last yeares past for 4 or 5.

[18] what increas hathe bene made of soules to theare churche in euery sheare [=shire, county] throught [=through] the realme

[19] who be of theares, and whoo be not who be assured and who be inclined for this difference they make betwien them that are reconciled, and suche as ar affected to thear opinion and are to be brought in. and in every shere throught the realme whear they be stronge and wheare they be weake, and this is knowen by certeyne secret gatheringes [=collections of money] for the relefe of them beyond the seas [=exiled Catholics]: whear in therbe notes of very houshowlds.[31]

Even apart from the willingness of Oxford to betray his erstwhile friends, his questions are endued with a hypocrisy, a pettiness of mind, and a lack of mental control that reveal far more about the accuser than the accused. The fourth article is both hypocritical and petty in the extreme, for Oxford was himself given to imagining how much better he would be treated abroad than in England.

Though each sheet starts off with succinct questions neatly formatted, each ends in rambling, disjointed paragraphs which had to be broken up into separate questions by the interrogators.[32] On each sheet, moreover, Oxford's accusations are written first to the bottom of the page, then in the left margin (the paper having been turned 90 degrees), and finally upside-down in the top margin (the paper having been turned another 90 degrees). The document recalls the French Princess's observation on Navarre's poetical maunderings in *Love's Labour's Lost*: 'as much love / As would be cramm'd up in a sheet of paper, / Writ a' both sides the leaf, margent and all' (LIB-5.2/6–8). Rather than love, however, Oxford crammed his paper with what a later observer would call 'emulation' – in this case, hatred and resentment of the whole Howard clan.

48 Tables Turned

Writing of Howard and Arundel on 8 January 1581, Mendoza noted 'their having been taken to the Tower',[1] but Mauvissière, writing on the 9th, reveals that they were soon transferred:[2]

It was to her great regret, as the Queen herself told me, that she was obliged to place them under restraint in the custody of some her Councillors: Lord Henry under the charge of Sir Christopher Hatton, Captain of the Guard; and Francis Southwell under the charge of Sir Francis Walsingham.

Arundel too was placed in Hatton's care, which may explain the ease with which he and Howard mounted a coordinated counter-attack (LIB-2.2.1/1, 3.1, 4.2). Howard may also have been kept for some time by Sir Thomas Bromley (LIB-3.3).

Howard and Arundel issued a stream of letters, whether directly to their keepers, or indirectly to the Queen. Their strategy was threefold: they would admit to minor crimes; 'disabel' Oxford's charges by proving him a liar; and demonstrate that he posed the real danger to the Crown. No mere summary can do justice to the letters' vituperation and salacious detail. A paragraph from Howard's letter of 12 January is typical of his cool, convoluted style (LIB-3.3):

> Touching mine accuser if the botchis and deformites of his mishapen life suffice not to discredit and disgrace the warrant of his wreckfull worde yet let his practise with some gentilmen to seke my lif his message by Charles Arundell one [=on] Fridaie next shall be a monthe [=16 December?] that either indirectelie or directelie by right or wronge he wold be reuengid and his seking once againe since that [time] to corrupte Charles Arundell with a thowsand pownde declare what truthe or plainesse restith in his dealinges

Arundel's charges tend to be more rumbustious and therefore more quotable (LIB-4.2):

> The strenthe of this monsters evidence against my Lord Henrye Mr Sowthewell and my selfe we[a]kend and takeen downe by the sufficient profe of the mans insufficiensie to beare wittnesse against any man of reputacion. for these respectes no lesse warrantid by lawes of honor and of armes then by the cevyle lawes and the lawes of owre one [=own] cuntrie

> Atheisme 1
> ordenarye vse to lie for the whetstone in the worst degree 2
> mercenarie faythe 3
> bowcherlie bluddiness 4
> dangerowse practice 5
> notable dishonestie of life skant to be nameid 6
> drunkeennesse 7
> particuler grudge to vs all three 8
> vndutifull dealinge to the Quene 9

Thus Arundel accuses Oxford of (1) atheism, (2) pathological lying, (3) suborna-tion, (4) murder by hire, (5) sedition, (6) sexual perversion including pederasty, (7) chronic inebriation, (8) nursing of private grudges (especially against mem-bers of the Howard family), and (9) *lèse majesté*. Arundel follows up with one or more paragraphs on each accusation in turn.

We have already considered both the form and substance of most of these charges, but now others arise, such as this from Arundel (LIB-4.2/4.2):

> [Oxford] wrought the deathe of Davie the fenser by Locker and often vawntid of his deade [=deed]

Evidently a master of defence named Davie was killed by another named 'Locker' – perhaps David Locher.[3] Though the event is otherwise unrecorded, the death of the fencer must have been known at the time: in any case, Oxford's share in the event cannot be independently verified. A second new charge comes from Howard (LIB-3.1/2.2):

> I askid howe he wold doe when this stock was spent he said befor that tyme he wold find a better trade then the bearinge of a white waster

The white 'waster' – or staff – signified the empty office of Lord Great Chamberlain.

On 9 January Mauvissière reported that the first part of the prisoners' strategy seemed to be working:[4]

> Having been questioned regarding the accusations preferred against them by the Earl of Oxford, namely that they had conspired against the State, they were able to clear themselves very satisfactorily; and as concerns Catholicism, they are known to be well affected to it, as indeed is the case with most of the nobility of this kingdom. The Queen knew this perfectly well; and Lord Henry Howard, Arundel, and Southwell, although Catholics at heart, are nevertheless much esteemed and favoured by her, seeing that both they and their friends have always been in favour of the marriage and of the French alliance. …

Mauvissière took up this same theme on 11 January:

> The Queen earnestly begged me to tell her the facts not so much to injure them in any way, but to satisfy her as to the truth. She said that I knew quite well her favourable attitude towards Catholics who did not place their consciences in antagonism to the State, and entreated me to let her know about it.
>
> I denied all knowledge of the business; saying that I not only knew nothing about it, but that I had never even heard it talked about.

While the French ambassador's first purpose of course was to protect himself and the interests of his country, his bland denial contains an assertion of the Queen's goodwill towards non-rebellious Catholics, including the three prisoners.

Despite deposing to 26 articles on or about 11 January, and 19 articles extracted from Oxford's questions dated 18 January, under pressure from Oxford and probably Burghley, Howard remained under house arrest into August, Arundel into October or November. In vain did Howard try to persuade the Queen that Oxford himself was the real trouble-maker (LIB-3.2):

> My lord of Oxford telles me that your Maiesty desirith nothinge more then to take me in a trippe that youe may trice [=ensnare] me, and to Charles Arundell he said your Maiestye desired no mannes head in England halfe so much as myne

Similarly, both Howard and Arundel begged for a trial to accuse their accuser. Thus Arundel about 15 January (LIB-5.2):

My case requiringe indifferencie, will a byde any tryall

But neither indictment nor trial was forthcoming for any of the three accused, nor for Oxford their accuser.

49 Knight of the Tree of the Sun

On 1 January 1581, perhaps while under arrest, Oxford gave the Queen 'a fayre juell of goulde, being a beast of ophalls with a fayre lozanged dyamonde, three great pearles pendante. fully garnished with small rubies, dyamondes, and small pearles, one horne lackinge'; for her part, Anne presented the Queen with '24 buttons of goulde, enameled with one pearle in everie button'.

Elizabeth's Fifth Parliament sat from 16 January to 18 March. Evidence of Oxford's release from confinement occurs in records of his presence on January 20 and 26, February 23 and 27, March 2 (first session) and 18 (second session); his absence is noted on January 16, 18–19, 23–24, 28, 30–31, February 1, 4, 6–9, 11 (two sessions), 13, 15–16, 18, 20–22, 25, 28, March 1, 2 (second session), 3 (two sessions), 4, 6, 7 (two sessions), 8 (two sessions), 9–11, 13–17, 18 (first session).[1] Thus of 44 sessions, Oxford attended six, including the closing but not the opening session. On 21 February[2]

> ... The bill concerning the ratifying of the particion betweene the heires of the Lord Latimer was brought in by the commyttees with two provisoes, the one for the Earle of Oxforde, the other for Sir Thomass Tindall; agreed to be ingrossed.

Oxford insisted on the inclusion of a clause to his own advantage (as did Sir Thomas Tindall); but he did not attend when agreement concerning the bill was achieved.

On 22 January, four days after submitting his handwritten questions for Henry Howard and Charles Arundel, Oxford participated in a tournament at Westminster celebrating Philip Howard's elevation to the Earldom of Arundel. A related expense appears in the royal accounts:[3]

> Repairinge of an old bridge ouer against the Tiltyeard, grauelling of the same and all the hye way betwixt the Masgaite and Whitehall gaite to bringe ouer the Erle of Arundelles Pagin [=Pageant] and other noblie menns pagins. ... makinge a new Timber bridge againste the Tryvmphe, for the brinenge ouer soundrie noblie menns Pagins iiijli x s ... Makinge redie soundrie tymes for plaies and dauncinge xlixli sviijs ixd ob

Some of the recorded expenditures may have been for subsequent accession-day pageants (17 November) and the Alençon marriage embassy, but the bridge that served 'noblie menns pagins' may have been rebuilt for this occasion.

Burghley noted the event thus in his current almanac:[4]

> the Iustes at Westminster wher the Erl of Arundel was challanger as[s]isted with Sir William Drury. Erl of Oxford Lord Wyndsor and 14 more defended.

The three named challengers were Oxford; Sir William Drury, a member of what had been the Oxford–Howard set;[5] and Oxford's nephew, Frederick Windsor. Participation in a tournament to elevate a Howard may have been easier for Oxford because his party opposed.

The joust was proclaimed by a broadsheet entered in the Stationers Register on 16 January as 'the challenge of the Justes'. The unique copy of the broadsheet surviving in the Folger Shakespeare Library (STC 13868.5) announces: 'Callophisus, being brought by the greatest perfection … wilbe at the tilts ende vpon the two and twentie day of Ianuarie next. …' 'Callophisus' himself was almost certainly Philip Howard.

Speeches from Oxford's pageant in the tournament found their way into print in a 1592 pamphlet entitled *Plato, Axiochus. A most excellent dialogue, written in Greeke by Plato. Tr. by Edw. [sic] Spenser. Heereto is annexed a speech spoken at the tryumphe at White-hall by the page to the earle of Oxenforde.* The unique copy, surviving in the Pforzheimer Library, now at the University of Texas (STC 19974.6), contains, as announced, 'A speech spoken at the Tryumph before the Queenes most excellent Maiestie, by the Page to the right noble Champion, the Earle of Oxenford' (sig. D1).[6] The full speech (sigs. D1–4) sheds abundant light on Oxford's thoughts and actions:

> By the Tilt stoode a statelie Tent of Orenge tawny Taffata, curiously imbroydered with Siluer, & pendents on the Pinacles very sightly to behold. From forth this Tent came the noble Earle of Oxenford in right gilt Armour, and sate down vnder a great high Bay-tree, the whole stocke, branches and leaues whereof, were all gilded ouer, that nothing but Gold could be discerned. By the Tree stoode twelue tilting staues, all which likewise were gilded cleane ouer. After a solemne sound of most sweet Musique, he mounted on his Courser, verie richly caparasond, when his page ascending the staires where her Highnesse stood in the window, deliuered to her by speech this Oration following.

> This Knight (most fayre and fortunate Princesse) liuing of a long time in a Groue, where euery graft beeing greene, hee thought euery roote to be precious, found at the last as great diuersity of troubles as of Trees: the Oake to be so stubborne that nothing could cause it to bend; the Reede so shaking, that eury blast made it to bow; the Iuniper sweete, but too lowe for succour; the Cipresse faire, but without fruite; the Walnut tree to be as vnholsome to lye vnder, as the bud of the Figge-tree vnpleasant to taste; the Tree that bore the best fruite, to be fullest of Caterpillers, and all to be infected with wormes; the Ashe for Rauens to breede; the Elme to build; the Elder to be full of pith & no perfection, and all Trees that were not fertill, to be fit for fuell, and they that were fruitfull, but for the tyme to please the

fancy. Which trying, he forsooke the wood, and liued a while in the plaine Champion [=open field]: where, how he was tormented, it were too long to tell, but let this suffice, that hee was troubled, when euery Moate fell in his eye in the day, and euery Ant disquieted him in the night: where, if the wind blew, he had nothing to shielde him but heade and shoulders, if the Sunne blazed, he could find the shadow of nothing but himselfe, when seeing himselfe so destitute of helpe, he becam desperate of hope.

Thus wandeirng a wearie way, hee espyed at the last a Tree so beautiful, that his eyes were daseled with the brightnesse, which as hee was going vnto, he met by good fortune a Pilgrime or Hermit, he knew not well, who being apparelled as though hee were to trauaile into all Countries, but so aged as though hee were to liue continually in a Caue. Of this olde Syre he demaunded what Tree it was, who taking this Knight by the hand, began in these words both to vtter the name and nature of the Tree.

This Tree fayre Knight is called the Tree of the Sunne, whose nature is alwaies to stand alone, not suffering a companion, beeing it selfe without comparison: of which kind, there are no more in the earth then Sunnes in the Element. The worlde can holde but one Phenix, one Alexander, one Sun-Tree, in top contrarie to all Trees: it is strongest, & so statelie to behold, that the more other shrubs shrinke for duetie, the higher it exalteth it selfe in Maiestie.

For as the cleere beames of the Sunne, cause all the starres to lose theyr light, so the brightnesse of thys golden Tree, eclipseth the commendation of all other Plants. The leaues of pure Golde, the barke no worse, the buddes pearles, the body Chriso-colla, the sap Nectar, the roote so noble as it springeth from two Turkeies [=turquoises] , both so perfect, as neither can staine the other, each contending once for superioritie, and now both constrained to be equals. Vestas bird sitteth in the midst, whereat Cupid is euer drawing, but dares not shoote, beeing amazed at that princely and perfect Maiestie.

The shaddowes hath as strange properties as contrarieties, cooling those that be hoat with a temperate calme, and heating those that be colde with a moderate warmth, not vnlike that Sunne whereof it taketh the name, which melteth Waxe, and hardeneth Clay, or pure fyre, which causeth the gold to shine, and the straw to smother, or sweete perfumes, which feedeth the Bee, and kylleth the Betell.

No poyson commeth neere it, nor any vermine that hath a sting. Who so goeth about to loppe it, launceth himselfe, and the Sunne wyll not shyne on that creature that casteth a false eye on that Tree, no wind can so much as wagge a leafe, it springeth in spite of Autumnus, and continueth all the yeere as it were Ver.

If Syr Knight you demaunde what fruite it beareth, I answere, such, as the elder it is, the younger it seemeth, alway rype, yet euer greene. Vertue Syr Knight, more nourishing to honest thoughts, then the beauty delightfull to amorous eyes; Where the Graces are as thicke in vertue, as the Grapes are on the Vine.

Thys fruite fatteth, but neuer feedes, wherwith thys Tree is so loaden, as you cannot touch that place which vertue hath not tempered. If you enquire whether any grafts may be gotten, it were as much as to craue slyppes of the Sunne, or a Moulde to cast a new Moone. To conclude, such a Tree it is, as he that hath longest knowne it, can sooner meruaile at it, then discribe it, for the further hee wadeth in the prayse, the shorter he commeth of the perfection.

Thys olde man hauing ended, seeming to want wordes to expresse such worthinesse, he went to hys home, and the Knight to his Sunne Tree, where kissing the grounde wyth humilitie, the princely tree seemed with joy[?] to bidde him welcome. But the more he gazed on her beautie, the lesse able he was to endure the brightnesse, like vnto those that looking with a stedfast eye to beholde the sun, bring a darke dazeling ouer theyr sight.

At the last, resting vnder the shaddowe, he felt such content, as nothing coulde bee more comfortable. The dayes he spent in vertuous delights, the night slypped away in golden Dreames, hee was neuer annoyed with venemous enemies, nor disquieted with idle cogitations.

In so much, that finding all felicity in that shade, and all security in that Sunne: hee made a sollemne vowe, to incorporate hys harte into that Tree, and ingraft hys thoughts upon those vertues, Swearing, that as there is but one Sunne to shine ouer it, one roote to giue life vnto it, one toppe to maintaine Maiestie: so there should be but one Knight, eyther to lyue or die for the defence thereof.

Where-vppon, he swore himselfe onely to be the Knight of the Tree of the Sunne, whose life should end before his loyaltie.

Thus cloyed with content, hee fell into a sweete slumber, whose smyling countenaunce shewed him voyde of all care. But hys eyes were scarce closed, when hee seemed to see dyggers undermining the Tree behind him, that Sun-Tree suspecting the Knight to gyue the dyggers aid, myght haue punished him in her prison, but fayling of theyr pretence, and seeing every blowe they strooke to light vppon their owne braines, they threatned him by violence, whom they could not match in vertue.

But he clasping the Tree, as the onely Anchor of hys trust, they could not so much as mooue him from hys cause, whom they determined to martyr without colour. Whereuppon, they made a challenge to winne the Tree by right, and to make it good by Armes. At which saying, the Knight beeing glad to haue his trueth tryed wyth hys valoure, for ioy awaked.

And nowe (most vertuous and excellent Princesse) seeing such tumults towards for his Tree, such an Honourable presence to iudge, such worthy Knights to Iuste: I cannot tel whether his perplexitie or his pleasure be the greater. But this hee will auouch at all assayes, himselfe to be the most loyall Knight of the Sun-tree, which who so gaine-sayeth, hee is heere prest, eyther to make him recant it before hee rune, or repent it after. Offering rather to die vppon the poynts of a thousande Launces, then to yeeld a iote [jot] in constant loyaltie.

FINIS

The speech beeing ended, with great honour hee ran, and valiently brake all the twelue staues. And after the finishing of the sports: both the rich Bay-tree, and the beautifull Tent, were by the standers by, torne and rent in more peeces then can be numbred.

Every detail bespeaks Oxford. Tawny – here designed as 'Orenge tawny' – was Oxford's personal colour (SWM3):

A Croune of Bayes shall that man weare
That triumphs over me:
For blacke and Tawnie will I weare,
Whiche mornyng colours be.

Tawny's complement in the tournament was not black, but the more precious silver and gold. The 'solemne sound of most sweet Musique' was perhaps supplied by Oxford's servant Henry Lichfild. Though Oxford must often have appeared in public 'mounted on his Courser, verie richly caparasond', it is rare that we find him so directly described.

The title-page attribution of the Axiochus translation to 'Edward' Spenser compounds doubts over the authorship of the pageant text.[7] At least four candidates spring immediately to mind. Edmund Spenser's *Faerie Queene*, first published in 1590, celebrates knighthood and contains near its opening a long list of trees (I.i.8–9). Anthony Munday has been proposed as the author of both pieces (STC 19974.6, note), while their lexical doubling and balanced grammatical structures may suggest John Lyly the Euphuist. Both Munday and Lyly were now Oxford's men. Finally, the aphorisms and the redundancies may suggest Oxford himself.

The allegory of the pageant is easily deciphered. Oxford is 'the Knight of the Tree of the Sun', while the 'dyggers undermining the Tree' are Howard, Arundel, and Southwell. The Queen is 'the Tree of the Sun', who, 'suspecting the Knight to gyue the dyggers aid, myght haue punished him in her prison, but fayling of theyr pretence, and seeing every blowe they strooke to light vppon their owne braines, they threatned him by violence, whom they could not match in vertue'.

No longer the novice of 1571, Oxford was now the victor, a verdict which must have given him enormous satisfaction. He was not only free, but lionized, the object of such popular acclaim that his Sun-Tree and tent were torn to shreds by souvenir-hunters. Charles Arundel, hearing of the event in his close confinement, grudgingly describes Oxford, perhaps with a deliberate pun on 'ox', as wandering freely 'vp and downe the towne, graseinge in the pastures' (LIB-5.7). Arundel believed Oxford was now confident enough to allow his case to come before a court: 'he was most ernest bothe with the Queen and him selfe for triall' (LIB-6.8@42). The same sentiment was publicly proclaimed in the tournament speech: 'the Knight beeing glad to haue his trueth tryed wyth hys valoure, for ioy awaked'.

50 Anne Vavasor

On 23 March 1581 (Holy Thursday) Walsingham sent news to Hastings:[1]

> On Twesdaye at nyght Anne Vavysor was browght to bed of a sonne in the maydens chambre. The Earl of Oxeforde is avowed to be the father, whoo hathe withdrawen him selfe with intent as yt is thought to passe the seas. The ports are layd for him and therfor yf he have any sooche determynation yt is not lykely that he wyll escape. The gentlewoman the selfe same nyght she was delyvered was conveyed owt of the howse & the next daye commytted to the Towar. Others that have ben fownde any wayes partyes to the cavse have ben also commytted. Her maiestye is greatly greeved with the accydent, and therfor I hope there wyll be some sooche order taken as the lyke inconvenyence wyll be avoyded [i.e., in the future].

The child was born Tuesday 21 March. Assuming a gestation period of 38 weeks, we may infer that Anne Vavasor's son – and Oxford's – was conceived on or about 28 June 1580.

As ever, Oxford's instinct was for flight, his route the sea. He was captured, however, by the 29 April date of a Fugger newsletter:[2]

> Since amongst other things you ask for information about what has been done to the prisoners arrested four months ago, you should know that the brother of the last Duke of Norfolk and two knights are still in prison. This because they have again become reconciled to the Roman Church, having been led thereto by certain agents instigated for the purpose by the Pope. This is taken very ill in the country. There is a suspicion too that they have been plotting against the crown and realm of England. But, as hitherto nothing has been brought home to them, they remain in prison, simply because they are in bad odour. The Earl of Oxford, also arrested but soon set at liberty, is in the Tower for forgetting himself with one of the Queen's Maids of Honour, who is in the Tower likewise. This in spite of his having a pretty wife, daughter of the Treasurer. But he will not live with her.

It is doubtful that Oxford eluded his pursuers more than a day or two past 23 March. Charles Arundel reports that Oxford was given the very room that the Lieutenant of the Tower – Owen Hopton – had prepared for Henry Howard (LIB-6.7@27):

> I he[a]re he hathe the lodgeinge that the Lifetenant had of speciall favour appointed for my Lord Harrye …

It is unclear how long Oxford's 'grasse widdowe', as Arundel calls Anne Vavasor (LIB-6.8), remained in the Tower. Though her child, baptized Edward Vere, would survive to manhood, Oxford took no responsibility for his upbringing or education. Rather, the boy was raised by his mother, who despite a besmirched reputation was a woman of courage and character. In later years her son became a protégé of Oxford's inestimable cousin, Sir Francis Vere.[3]

Sir John Harington's epigram *Lelia* must surely have found its inspiration in Oxford's affair:[4]

> When louely Lelia was a tender girle,
> She hapt to be deflowred by an Earle;
> Alas poore wench, she was to be excused,
> Such kindnesse oft is offered, seeld refused.
> But be not proud; for she that is no Countesse,
> And yet lies with a Count, must make account this,
> All Countesses in honour her surmount,
> They haue, she had, an honourable Count.

A more sympathetic response took the form of an 'echo-poem' – innovative for English literature – in which the last syllable of each line (here lines 11–20 only) is repeated as implied dialogue (SWM–1):

> Sittinge alone upon my thought in melancholye moode,
> In sighte of sea and at my backe an aunceyent, horye woode,
> I sawe a fayre yonge ladye come her secreate teares to wayle,
> Clad all in colour of a vowe and covered with a vayle.   [vowe=votary, nun]
> Yet for the daye was clere and calme, I might discerne her face,
> As one mighte see a damaske rose thoughe hid with cristall glasse.
> Three tymes with her softe hande full harde upon her heart she knockes,
> And sighte soe sore as mighte have moved some mercy in the rocks;   [sighte
> From sighes and sheadinge amber teares into swete songe she brake,   =sighed]
> And thus the eccho answered her to every woorde she spake.

> O heavenes (quothe she) who was the firste that bred in me this fevere?   Vere.
> Who was the firste that gave the wounde whose scarre I we[a]re forever?   Vere.
> What tyrant, Cupid, to my harmes usurpes thy golden quivere?   Vere.
> What wighte first caughte this hearte and can from bondage it delivere?   Vere.

> Yet who dothe most adore this wighte? O hollowe caves tell true?   You.
> What nimphe deserves his likinge beste, yet dothe in sorrowe rue?   You.

> What makes him not regarde good will with some remorse or ruthe?   Youth.
> What makes him shewe besides his birthe suche pride and such untruthe?   Youth.

> May I his beautye matche with love if he my love will trye?   Aye.
> May I requite his birthe with faythe (then faythfull will I dye)?   Aye.

> And I that knewe this ladye well said, 'Lorde, how great a myracle,
> To heare the eccho tell her truthe as 'twere Apollo's oracle!'

In case anyone missed the point, the poem is marked 'Vavaser' in some of its manuscript sources.

Sir John Harington, who copied this poem into his personal manuscript anthology, added: 'The best verse that ever th'author made … ffinis quod E. Veer.

count d'Oxford'. Though Harington's note might seem to settle the matter of authorship, the observations of Oxford's editor must be considered:[5]

> [This poem] was written by someone partial, at least, to the Earl, for it flatters him with references to his beauty and birth, while suggesting that Anne might be worthy of his favors. If she wrote the poem she went far out of her way to debase herself and glorify her lover. At best, the authorship is disputed and, in its tone and point of view, quite inappropriate for either of its principals. It seems more likely that neither of them wrote the piece, but since their names were connected with it the manuscript anthologists simply attributed it to one or both of them.

The poem was composed, if not by Oxford, by someone acquainted with his habit of attributing his troubles to his youth. This despite the fact that at the time Oxford got Anne Vavasor pregnant the first time he was twenty-nine.

Oxford was granted at least one interview with the Queen soon after his arrest. Having taken pains to learn of the meeting, Arundel conveyed his intelligence to his 'sweet lady' (LIB-6.1). Burghley, acting as attorney for the defence, argued that his client's mind 'was nowe as zealous and as dewtifull to hir as any mans alive'. Doubtless on his knees, Oxford insisted that he had fled not to escape the Queen's authority, but for more defensible reasons: first, 'a judgement of his nativitie', which is to say his horoscope; and second, misgivings over the prospect that he would be held in 'durance'. The Queen's reported response deserves to be enshrined among her 'sayings':

> Wold you not mervell … that this purgacione shuld be used by some of yowre owne place!

Which is to say: What an example for a nobleman to set for his inferiors!

Sir Thomas Bromley, now Howard's jailor, protested the Queen's inclination to let Oxford off the hook:

> My Lord Chamberlain longe debateid against this favore, as to seem alleginge that a crime co[u]ld not be satisfied with wordes & owre [=our] libertye suspended.

In Oxford's case, however, words alone could suffice. A barely legible sentence suggests that a message to this effect had been conveyed to Oxford through 'instruccions by Milles', that is, through Oxford's servant Arthur Milles. Finally, even Oxford's flight was discounted as evidence against him …

> as thoughe in fliinge [=flying] he co[u]ld say more then at his abidinge here. But this must be because the Grete Devell will have it so.

The 'Grete Devell' is Burghley, Oxford's shield even under these extreme circumstances. Arundel continued:

> Milles hathe reporteid that ther is a grete p[e]rson who, not semeinge to have any conference with the villaine his master since his flight, takeithe a certayne message

from his mowthe pretendid to be sent him from the villaine at his goinge owte, to this intent: that her Maiestie should not so farr show her self with chollor for this facte.

Oxford seems to have dictated his own terms for his release: the Queen must not show too much anger towards him. Arundel concludes:

… thus hathe he delte ever and this is his stinkeinge and mallicious nature.

In his next surviving letter (LIB-6.3) Arundel reports his belief that the Queen had intended to free him, probably around Easter (26 March), but that Oxford had persuaded Leicester to supplicate the Queen to keep his erstwhile friends under arrest, for if his friends prevailed, he would have no option but to flee for shame. Thus, unless the Queen was prepared to banish him from her sight forever, she must exonerate him to deprive his enemies of the 'excedeinge trivmphe which they wold make vppon this disgrace'; she was all the more obliged to grant Oxford his wish, 'consideringe that for her sake he had gotten the name of a promoter' – that is, of an agent provocateur.

Remarkably, according to Arundel, not even his staunchest supporter alleged virtue or honour in Oxford, or even negligence ('oversight'); instead, the best arguments made on his behalf stemmed from the gorgeousness of his retainers' suits of apparel 'against this time of triumph', and the 'strange device' of his servants' livery (LIB-6.7@30). The man is son of the 'White Hen' (read Burghley), and must be exonerated. Even Oxford's friends are beginning to faint (LIB-6.8) because they understand that freedom for Oxford would make the Court no better than a brothel.

In the meantime, Oxford received no votes at all from the 11 electors for the Order of the Garter, representing a total collapse of support (G-BL). Not until 1585 would he receive a single vote from any quarter.

On 9 June the Privy Council wrote to Sir William Gorges, yeoman porter of the Tower:[6]

… that where their Lordships understand that the Earl of Oxford, being yesterday by Her Majesty's commandment released of his imprisonment in the Tower, at his Lordship's departure he did demand his upper garment and other things as fees due unto him by his office; and hath thereupon caused certain of his Lordship's stuff to be stayed: giving him to understand that for as much as his Lordship was not committed thither upon any cause of treason or any criminal cause, it is thought that he cannot challenge any such fees; and therefore do hereby require him to forebear to demand the same and to suffer the stuff stayed by him to pass; whereof he is to have regard also for that the Earl supposeth he may not a little be touched in honour if he shall be brought to yield unto a custom only upon persons committed to that place for treason, and for that respect especially neither may the Earl well yield thereunto, nor he demand it.

Released on 8 June, and unwilling to seem guilty, Oxford refused to give garments to the yeoman porter, since this might be construed as an admission of guilt.

That Oxford, though no longer in the Tower, remained under house arrest may be inferred from Burghley's chronology for 2 July:[7]

> about this tyme the Erl of Oxford sett to full liberty by Mr Walsyngham.

A letter from Walsingham to Burghley dated 12 July from Court suggests that Burghley's date is too early (LIB-7.2):

> My verry good Lord I had thowght to have taken some tyme this afternoone to have seen your Lordship and to have acquaynted you with my proceadynge with the Earl of Oxeforde: but by reason of a quarrell favlen owt betwene the Earl of Svssex and the Earl of Leycester which her Maiestye seekethe to take vp in respecte of the inconvenience that may favle owt therbye I am stayed by her Highness commavndement The cavse of the quarrell grewe abowte Haveringe …

Oxford was scarcely in a position to press a suit, though perhaps Sussex had taken his part in the argument. Walsingham continued:

> Her maiesty is resolved (vppon some perswatyon vsed) not to restore the Earl of Oxeford to his full lybertye before he hathe ben dealt withall for his wyfe. Mr Vycechamberlyn [=Christopher Hatton] the daye he retvrned from your Lordship dyd verry honorably acqvyte him selfe towardes yow in that way …

Against Walsingham's reference to Oxford's wife, Burghley penned a marginal ·note: 'This is more [*for* less?] easyer to be doone, than Courtyers do thynk'. Nevertheless, Oxford seems to have communicated with his wife, for in December she would concede 'your favor that yow began to shew me this sommar'.[8]

On or about 13 July Oxford wrote to Burghley from 'my howse [=Fisher's Folly?] this morning' (LL-13/LIB-7.4):

> My lord, Robine Christmas dyd yester day, tell me, how honorably yow had delt withe her magestie as touchinge my Lybertye, and that as this day she had made promes to yowre lordship that it showld bee. vnles yowre Lordship shall make sume to put her magesty in mynd therof, I feare, in thes other causes of the too [=two] Lords, she will forget me. for she is nothinge of her owne disposition, as I find, so ready to deliuer, as spedie to commit. and every littell trifell, giues her matter for a longe delay. …

Robin Christmas was still Oxford's servant, or at least his go-between with Burghley. Oxford is fairly open in his criticism of the Queen. He continues:

> I willed E. Hamond[9] to report vnto yowre Lordship, her magestys message vnto me by mr secretarie Walsingham whiche was to this effect, first that she wowld have h[e]ard the matter agayne touchinge Henry Howard, Southwell and Arundell. then that she vnderstood I ment to cut doune all my woods, especially abought my housse; whiche she dyd not so well leke of, as yf I showld sell sume land els other wheare. and last that she h[e]ard I had bene hardly vsed by sum of my servants,

duringe this time of my committe [=commitment, incarceration]. whearin she
promised her ayd so far as she could withe iustice, to redres the loss I had susteyned
therby. to whiche I made answear, as I willed Hamond to relat[e] vnto yowre
Lordship …

Oxford's reconciliation with his wife seems no longer to have been a precondition
of reconciliation with the Queen. The latter agreed that Howard, Arundel, and
Southwell should have their case against Oxford heard; and required Oxford to
spare his woods. Evidently he was in negotiations with Nicholas Northen of
Alsford and William Morley of Wivenhoe, who on 7 December would secure a
charter allowing them to fell 536 small trees in Wivenhoe Park for £50.[10]
    We have already noted the passage from this letter in which Oxford expresses
his unhappiness that 'certeyne of my men' had accused him of unnamed crimes:
of a shadow they had made a substance, and of a mere likelihood, a truth.[11]
Oxford closes by expressing his willingness to overlook the issue (for a while), and
thanking his mentor for his intervention:

> but lettinge thes thinges pas for a whyle, I must not forget to giue yowre lordship
> those thankes, whiche ar[e] due to yow, for this yowre honorable dealinge to her
> magesty in my behalf. which I hope shall not be wythought effect. the whiche
> attendinge from the court, I will take my leaue of yowre lordship …

At a minimum Oxford's letter constitutes proof that certain of his servants had
expressed a willingness to testify against him.[12]
    On 13 July Burghley wrote to Walsingham to thank him for his intervention
on Oxford's behalf:[13]

> Sir, though I can not alwayes paye my debtes, yet I vse to acknowledg them many
> tymes, to moue my creditors to accept my goodwill, in towardnes of payement:
> and so at this tyme, though I knowe my self many wayes indebted vnto you for
> your good will, except you will accept for acquytall my reciproque goodwill, I shall
> not be able to pay you, that I owe you. Yet, yesterdaie, beeing aduertised of your
> good & honorable dealing with her maiestie, in the case of my dawghter of Oxford
> [=Countess Anne], I could not suffer my thanckes, to growe above one daye olde,
> and therefore in these fewe lynes, I doo presentlie thank you, and doo pray you in
> anye proceeding therin, not to haue the Earle dealt withall straynably, but only by
> waye of advise, as good for him self: for otherwise, hee maye suspecte, that I regard
> my self, more for my dawghter, then hee is regarded for his libertie. I knowe only
> the Quenes maiesties motions, shall further the cause [i.e., of reconciliation with
> Anne], and more then her motions, I wishe nott. you see, beeinge a debter, I
> prescribe my manner to increase the debt / butt yf I can not acquite it, I knowe it
> belongeth to Almightie God to doo itt. I am most sorry to here of the disaster fallen
> oute yesterdaye, betwixte two greate planettes [=Sussex and Leicester], but I hope
> they knowe their Iupiter, and will obey her maiestie, rather to content her, then to
> followe their owne humors/. It is far oute of season, to haue these breaches: our
> adversaries ar ever ready to make them greater, and to leape in also, to our common

harme. I am not yet fully recouuered: this north west wynde keepethe me back from my porte of health …

Walsingham wrote to Burghley, again from court, on 14 July, confirming an intention on the Queen's part to stage a direct confrontation between Oxford and his three accusers:[14]

> My verry good Lord I have ben all this daye by her maiestys expresse commavnde-ment set a woorke about the examynatyon of certeyn persons charged to have conspyred to have attempted somewhat ageynst her owne person. But as far as I can gather by thos examynatyons that I have alreadye taken I thinke yt will prove nothinge. And yet it is happye that the partyes charged are taken for that they be Rvnnegat prestes sooche as have ben bredd vp at Rome and Dovey [=Douai] and seeke to corrvpt her maiestys good subiectes within this realme …

> I dealt verry earnestly with her towching the Earl of Oxefordes lybertye pvttyng her in mynde of her promyse made bothe vnto your Lordship and the Ladye his wyfe [=Anne]. The only staye growethe thorrowghe the importenat svte that is made for the delyverye of the Lord Henry and Mr Charles Arvndel whom before there delyverye her maiesty thinkethe meet they shoold be confronted by the Earl. Whoo hathe made hvmble request to be sett at lybertye befor he be browght to charge them, as he was at the tyme he geve [=gave] fyrst informatyon ageynst them. Her maiesty notwithstandyng the reasonablenes of his request and the promyse made vnto yowre Lordship that he shoold be fyrst sett at lybartye before he be browght to confronte them, can not as yet be browght to yelde.

> I hope yet this evenyng to prevayle so farefoorthe as to procvre that he may be inlarged to morrowe ffor my owne opynyon I doe vtterly myslyke the confrontyng, and as I svppose they are awthors of that advyce[?] [and] doe yt to that ende that the Earl may be charged by them. And so being sent for by her maiesty I am dryven to ende.

Thus Walsingham promises Burghley he will do everything in his power to forestall a confrontation, which would almost certainly have provoked a challenge.

Walsingham and Burghley persuaded the Queen to let Oxford walk free without the precondition of reconciliation with his wife and without bringing the case of Howard, Arundel, and Southwell to trial. On some occasion in July she made Oxford the gift of a hat:[15]

> delivered to the Erle of Oxford by the Queenes majesties commaundement j hat of the du[t]ch fation [=fashion] of black taffeta with band enbrodered with A sheepe [=ship?] of pearle and golde

Since she had already given him the standard New Year's gift on 1 January, this mid-year gift may have served as recognition that Oxford was not only free, but wholly back in the Queen's good graces.

A Diary entry of 23 July suggests that Burghley may have consulted with Oxford in person:[16]

23 July: I cam from my houss to Grenwych. E.O.

The Mr Rich/Richards/Richardson in an entry dated 31 July, 'Mr. Rich. went to the Erle of Oxford', remains unidentified. Whatever the specific details, it is clear that Burghley was moving behind the scenes for a reconciliation between Oxford and Countess Anne.

51 Prisoners

While Burghley helped extricate Oxford from royal wrath, Henry Howard, Charles Arundel, and Francis Southwell remained under arrest. About Easter 1581, which fell on 26 March, Arundel was removed to the 'wilderness' (LIB-5.3) of Sutton in West Sussex. From here, in a letter dated 1 May, he enlisted his 'Sweet Lady' as his London intelligencer (LIB-6.4):

> yf you cold drawe your selfe to a certayne place of contynuance [i.e., residence] in London or theraboutes and so able your selfe to be corespondent to my letters from time to time as I will be with you by God his grace we shall drawe some good cowrse amonge vs profitable to souche as we tender and honorable for you to take in hand.

Like the rest of Arundel's letters, this was read by Walsingham's agents, so Arundel's 'Lady' was soon caught. News got back to Arundel, who wrote to her again (LIB-6.9), still unaware that he was being spied upon: 'I vnderstand by common report of yowr disgrace and banishement'.[1]

On 20 July Arundel again requested official adjudication (LIB-5.5):

> cravinge of charite and iustice, that my tryall, which hath ben longe promised, maye not be any longer deferred, for then [i.e., if not deferred] shall my ennemyes, syncke with shame, & I departe, out of the feilde with honor: and what soever, either malice hath vniustly buylt, or a foole devised, vppon a false ground, must playe castell cum downe, and dissolue to nothinge.

Later in the month, when news of Oxford's full freedom had filtered down to Sutton, Arundel wrote to Hatton with particular bitterness (LIB-5.7):

> I trust her Maiestie will not denye you as muche favoure in the behalfe of me lightlie suspected of nothinge, and never offendinge in thought I take God to wittnesse, as she hathe latelie grawntyd vnto some others, in the behalfe of my monsterous adversarye Oxford, a parson [=person] convicted [i.e., accused] of great bestlynesse, as you knowe. yf her Maiestie vppon yowr motion pretend a pawse [=postponement], or promis to take a time as she hathe done all this while, withowte any frute, yow may wekeen that excuse by alleging my 7 monthes imprisonment, withowte ether <...> of my defence or regarde of my credit or callinge

> me to answere yf she limite [i.e., determine] my restraint by Oxfords punishement first remember that owre causees are not one then that I was kept close in yowr howse fowre monthes togither when Oxford went vp and downe the towne graseinge in the pastures ...

Rather than show mercy as he had been shown mercy, Oxford gave his former friends another twist of the knife. In late July or August Arundel drafted 'A breife answer to my Lord of Oxfords slawnderous accusations' (LIB-2.3.1). Of five new articles, 1 and 2 concern hearing of mass, which Arundel replies he had already partly confessed. Article 3, 'That my Lord Harrye shuld be present when I presentid a certayne boke of pictures, after the manner of a prophesie and by interpretacion resemblid a crowned sone to the Qwene &c' was the one that Arundel took most seriously and, as we have seen, was answered at greatest length. Article 4 reveals both accuser and accused at their most absurd:

> That I shuld once bringe in a Iesuite to see the Qwene dawnce in her privie chamber // Christ never receave me to his mercye nor forgeve me my sinnes yf ever I spake with Iesuite muche lesse browght then to the sight of suche an exercise ...

Answering Article 5, 'that I bothe sent letters and messengers to Monsieur', Arundel (or Walsingham's amanuensis) invokes a code-name: 'yf hir Maiestie obiect [=put] it to X as I thinke she will not he maye best acquite me of all others as beinge best acquaynetid with his Masters intelligence'.

Mendoza's report of 10–11 September reveals that Howard had now been granted his freedom (doubtless with conditions). Mendoza writes of Don Antonio, the Portuguese pretender:[2]

> [The Queen] sent a gentleman of her chamber to tell Lord Howard and Philip Sidney to accompany Don Antonio. The four ships were ready to leave to-day by the midday tide, but a message from the Queen came at 10 o'clock, which further delayed them, and it is expected they will sail tomorrow. The Earl of Oxford has been ordered to accompany him, but I do not venture to assert that they will go, as it depends upon these fickle people, and I fear he may still be detained here. I do not know whether he [=Don Antonio] will go to France or to the Prince of Orange, to whom he has sent two Portuguese, but I will let your Majesty know as soon as I can learn. I have advised Tassis some days ago of his intention of leaving. Four Portuguese came for him recently, having come in a poor boat from St. Ules in 18 days. They landed at Dover, and wore false beards.

> Alençon has sent back to the Queen her gentleman of the chamber, Sterling [Somers?], who went over with Lord Harry [Howard].

Howard, Sidney, and Oxford were all variously instructed to see Don Antonio safely put to sea, but Mendoza is not certain he can count on the promises of these 'fickle people'.

Southwell may also have been released by now, but Arundel made an unauthorized journey to Petworth, ten miles distant from Sutton, to hunt – perhaps at

Philip Howard's invitation – and was ordered back to Sutton. Arundel appealed to Sussex, whose letter of 19 October (LIB-5.11) tells us all we know about the episode. Thanks probably to Sussex, Arundel seems to have been released in November. He had been confined for more than ten months without a formal charge, thanks to accusations by Oxford that never proceeded to trial. Arundel's bitterness over his long incarceration and another twist of Oxford's knife is almost incandescent in a letter to Hatton apparently written in December (LIB-5.12):

> my Monsterus adversarye Oxford (who wold drinke my blud rather then wine as well as he loves it) as I am credablie enformyd hathe saide in open speche and in maner of avant [=boast] since his comynge owte of troble that wheras I builte my onelie trust on the frindshipp of yowr honor he had spedd me to the purpose in bringeinge me in condemmnation of a libel that shuld be writen against you, whervnto a frind of myne [=Howard?] beinge present doubting whether I had writen this indede Oxford answerid with an othe that he cold not tell but he was verye sure that it had geven Charles his full payment. …

> triall is all that I require and triall shall acquite me, and hange the villayne for sodomye that hathe no profe of anythinge but the slawneder of his one [=own] blasphemowse tonge &c of this last practice against my selfe, and others more monsterous, whiche speke the fownedacion wheron I bwilte all hope, I shall one daye tell you more and make you to wonder, at that is come to light

Thus Arundel complains that Oxford had named him in public as the author of a satire against Hatton then circulating among London wits. Though the attribution may have been accurate – Arundel had a penchant for satire[3] – it was scarcely the place of Oxford, a libeller since at least 1574, so to accuse another.

Fresh trouble threatened not only Arundel, but Howard, who on 3 December wrote to Walsingham from Ivy Bridge, Howard's official London residence (LIB-3.9):[4]

> God shall be my witnesse that I am not guiltie of the leaste offence, as theie that haue most strictely ciftid [=sifted, examined] me can tell, and yet I he[a]re by common voice of a freshe attempte to shake and vndermine my libertie Since my laste waytinge on youe, I haue bene often menacid, that roddes wear in preparinge for me, notwithstanding all the labor of my frendes

Howard's accuser and threatener, like Arundel's, was doubtless Oxford. A presumably contemporary letter from Howard to Hatton, also from Ivy Bridge, seems to continue the complaint (LIB-3.10):

> God I take to witnes, and as manye as were present, that in this matter, I gaue no more cause of iust offence to any man, then hee that was as farr from Grenewich at that instant, as my self was from London:

Evidently Howard had been charged with misconduct at Greenwich by Oxford, who had been in London at the time, and who was thus a mere retailer of hearsay.

PART VIII

Release
1581–1585

52 Starting Over

On 11 November 1581 Oxford sued for the guardianship of four-year-old Henry Bullocke of Much Wigbrowe, Essex, made a ward by the death of his father. In a will signed on 19 January 1579, Henry Bullocke the elder named his wife Agnes, daughter Marie, son Henry, and an unborn child as his beneficiaries. Four days earlier, on 15 January, Bullocke had sold his estate of Dawes *alias* Bacons in West Mersea to his brother-in-law Richard Wiseman for £160. He appointed Wiseman one of two executors, holding him responsible for the £160 (along with the rest of his assets), and requiring both executors to take out bonds of £500 to insure faithful performance.[1]

As complainant, Oxford, who held knight's service on the estate, claimed that Dawes *alias* Bacons had been sold fraudulently:[2]

> [Henry Bullocke the elder] about twoo yeres past lieng very sicke vppon his deathes bed, and not above six daies before the daie of his death did by the advice of one Richard Wiseman his brother in lawe and of divers other very craftie personnes make a feoffement in ffee to the said Richard Wiseman to the ende to defeate and defraude your oratour of the wardeshippe of the said infant his sonne and heire, expressing no other vse vppon the said fe[o]fment apparantly then [=than] to the vse of the said Richard Wiseman and his heires but in secret trust to be to the vse of the said infant his sonne and heire

Wiseman answered that he had purchased the property 'in the presens of diuerse persons of good abilitee and credite':

> which said estate and feoffement so made and taken was in truth pleynely and absolutely to the only vse of the said defendant and his heires and not to eny other vse intent and purpose Sithens the makeinge of which said feoffement he the said defendant hath bene seazed therof accordingly and hath from tyme to tyme euer sithens taken and receyved the yssues and profittes of the same to his owne vse as well and lawfull was for him to doo without that the said feoffement was made of eny covenous intent to defeate or defraude the said Complainant of the wardshipp of the said infant as in the said bill of Complaint ys surmised.

Wiseman was determined to keep Oxford from taking physical custody of the child:

> And forasmuch as by the truth of the matter it ys very manifest and apparant that the said Complainant hath no iust cause or good title as gardeine [=guardian] in Chevalry or otherwise to haue the custody or wardshipp of the said Henry Bullocke the infant And for that his custody edvcacion and bringinge vpp during his mynoritee was specially ment and appointed by his father vppon his death bedd vnto the said defendant so that the said Complainant hath neyther by lawe or conscience eny cause or authoritee to deale either with his body or with eny other thinge belonginge or apperteyninge to him the said infant

In his will Henry Bullocke the elder had insisted that his wife was to retain custody of all their chlidren:

> That the said Agnes my wife ... shall well and honestlie bringe vpp all my saide children with sufficiente meate drinke apparell and learninge and all other necessaries convenient for theire callinge and degree vntill theire seuerall ages aforenamed ...

Bullocke's intention would clearly have been defeated if Oxford were to win his suit.

In reply Oxford denied that the actions by Henry Bullocke the elder and Wiseman ...

> were made done or executed to any other ende effect or purpose, than to defeate defraude and avoid this Complainant of the wardeshippe of the said Henry Bullocke the soonne. And without that that the said somme of Eight score poundes [=£160] was agreed vppon betwene the said defendant and the said Henry Bullocke the father to be paid to him the said Henry Bullocke for and in consideracion of the purchase of the said landes absolutely truly and bona fide, but fraudulently to cover and shadowe the covine and deceipt aforsaid purposed and practized against this complainant in this matter vnder pretence and showe of this bargaine.

Whatever Oxford thought about his upbringing by Burghley, he was ready, like his father before him, to profit from wardship. As with most Chancery suits of the period, the outcome of this suit is unknown. Other suits were to follow, mostly over property, for Oxford was not merely a litigious man in a litigious age, but the cause of litigation in others.

On 17 November a Swiss visitor, Lupold von Wedel, witnessed an Accession Day tournament at Whitehall:[3]

> The 17th of November (the anniversary of the day on which Elizabeth was proclaimed Queen), the date on which the tournament is annually held having arrived, the Queen at twelve o'clock seated herself with her ladies at the windows of a long room facing Whitehall near Westminster. A broad staircase before the tilt-yard leads up to this room. Round the yard are erected wooden stands. Every one who wishes to look on and have a seat on the stands must pay eighteen pence. As however one penny is of pure silver, it is worth as much as in our country a

groschen. On the stand were very many thousands of men, women, and girls, to say nothing of those who were in the tilt-yard and had nothing to pay. The tournament began with two knights, who were desirous of contending with one another, riding simultaneously into the lists to the loud blare of trumpets and other music. And this mode of procedure was observed throughout the tournament. Every knight taking part in the tournament had dressed himself and his attendants in particular colours, although none of the underlings rode into the lists with the knights, but walked beside them on either side. Some of the knights had bedizened themselves and their train like savages; some like natives of Ireland with their hair streaming like a woman's down to their girdles. Some had crescent moons upon their heads; some came into the lists with their horses caparisoned like elephants; some came driving, their carriages drawn by people most oddly attired. Some of the carriages seemed to be drawn along without traction. All of these carriages were oddly and peculiarly fitted up, but all the knights had their horses with them, and being ready accoutred for the fight mounted their steeds. Some of them however were dressed like horsemen and bravely decked out. If any failed to take part in the tournament it cost him some thousands of crowns, willynilly.

Now when a knight entered the lists with his following, he rode or drove up to the staircase that led up to the room in which the Queen was. Then one of his followers ascended the staircase into the Queen's presence. This servant wore a very fine livery in the colours of his master. He then addressed the Queen at length in rhymes that he had learnt by rote and at the same time quaintly and decorously cut merry capers. This evoked laughter from the Queen and those around her. When the man had finished his speech, he in the name of his master handed the Queen a beautiful present which she accepted and then gave the donor permission to take part in the tournament. Now the knights jousted and broke lances in the lists two at a time. On this day there were to be seen many fine horses and beautiful women, not only amongst the ladies of the Queen, but also amongst those of the gentry, nobility, and burghers. This tournament lasted until five o'clock. Then my Lord Lester, the Queen's Master of the Horse, bade the knights cease from combat. The Queen then presented the prizes to the Earl of Oxenfort and to the Earl of Arrendel, the eldest son of the Duke of Norfolk whom the Queen had beheaded on Catharine Place where the scaffold still stands. Although the Duke's son had for his father's sake been so long in disfavour, he is now again in the Queen's good graces, and she permitted him to take part in the tournament. Lastly each knight who had acquitted himself well and nobly received a gift, and so this tourney closed.

Oxford thus repeated his success of 22 January. Presumably his page was again one of those who 'addressed the Queen at length in rhymes that he had learnt by rote and at the same time quaintly and decorously cut merry capers', but no text has survived from this occasion.

On 7 December Anne addressed her husband in a letter now lost. A draft in Burghley's hand suggests that he was the true author:[4]

My Lord. In what Misery may I accompt my self to be, that nether can se any end therof, nor yet any hope how to deminish it. And now of late havyng had some hope in my own concept [=conceit, thought], that your Lordship wold haue renewed some part of your favor that yow began to shew me this sommar, whan yow made me assurance of your good meaning though yow semed fearefull how to shew it by oppen actions. Now after long silence of hearyng any thyng from yow, at the length, I am informed but how truly I know not, and yet how vncomfortably, I do fele it, that your Lordship is entered into some mislykyng of me without any cause in dede or thought. and therfor my good Lord, I beseche yow in the name of that God, that knoweth all my thoughtes and my love towardes you notwithstand-yng your evill usadg of me, lett me know the truth of your meaning towardes me, vppon what cause yow ar[e] moved to contynew me in this misery, and what yow wold have me do in my power to recover your constant favor, so as your Lordship may not be ledd still to deteyne me in calamyte, without some probable cause, wherof I appeale to God, I am vtterly innocent. from my fathers houss in Westminster …

Oxford had showed Anne favour during the past summer, making her 'assurance of your good meaning though yow semed fearefull how to shew it by oppen actions'. The letter affirms that any cause for 'mislyking' of Burghley had been 'without any cause in dede or thought'. Anne asks 'what yow wold have me do in my power to recover your constant favor'.

Oxford's reply is lost, but its content can be inferred from Anne's reply of 12 December, again in Burghley's draft:[5]

My very good Lord, I most hartely thank yow for your lettre, and am most sorry, to perceave how yow ar vnquieted with the vncertenty of the world wherof I my self am not without some tast[e]. but seing yow will me to assure my self of any thyng that I may as your wiff challendg of yow, I will the more paciently abyde the adversety which otherwise I feale. and if God wold so permitt it and that it might be good for yow I wold beare the greatar part of your adverss fortune and mak it my comfort to beare part with yow.

as for my father I do assure yow, what so ever hath bene reported of hym, I know no man can wish better to yow than he doth, and yet the practices in Court I feare do seke to mak contrary shews.

for my lady Drury, I deale as lytle with hir as any can, and care no more for hir than yow will have me. but I have bene dryven sometymes for avoydyng of mallyce and envy, to do that both with hir and others which I wold not with my will do. Good my Lord assure your self, it is yow whom only I love and feare, and so am desyrooss above all the world to please you, wishyng that I might heare oftenar from yow vntil bettar fortune will have us mete to gither.

Oxford seems to have objected to Anne's inquiry into his behaviour; to Burghley's failure to do 'better to yow'; and to interference from Lady Drury. Anne (using Burghley's words) assures Oxford that she will abide his rejection in patience; that Burghley wishes him well, any setbacks coming from the practices of the court; and that she is willing to have as little to do with Lady Drury as she can, though she cannot avoid her (or others) entirely without incurring their malice and envy. Whether in response to Anne's appeals or for reasons of his own, Oxford finally agreed to a reconciliation.

Burghley's second daughter, Elizabeth, now entered into marriage negotiations with William Wentworth, eldest son of Lord Wentworth of Nettlested. They would marry on 26 February 1582, which was Shrove Monday,[6] Burghley himself probably helping to organize Shrovetide plays at Greenwich.[7] The 'Cowrt newes' survives in the diary of Richard Madox of Oxford University, under 3 February 1582:[8]

> I heard … that my Lord of Oxford had taken his wyfe agayn and that my Lord Treasurer shold mary a second daughter to my Lord Wentworth desyring rather a man than money. God send them al to do for the best.

53   Quarrels and Killings

The same Richard Madox who hoped on 3 February 1582 that Oxford would 'do for the best' reports under 3 March a lethal quarrel between Oxford and Thomas Knyvet:[1]

> My Lord of Oxford fowght with Mr Knevet abowt the quarel of Besse Bavisar and was hurt and Gerret his man slayn, which greeved the Lord Treasurer so muche the more for that the yerl hath cumpanie with his wyfe syth Christmas and taken hir to favowr but throe this mishap and throe the payns he took at the mariage of an other dawghter to my Lord Wentworth on Shrovemunday my Lord Treasurer was syck. God send hym health for he is the health of the whole land.

The slain 'Gerret' – Oxford's man – was probably the Gerard who, along with Edward Wingfield, attacked Arthur Gorge at Richmond in 1580. 'Besse Bavisar' is clearly a misreported Anne Vavasor. Thomas Knyvet, born circa 1545, was the younger brother of the Sir Henry Knyvet whom Oxford swore to kill in 1580 'for spekeinge evell of him to his nece'. A man of parts, Knyvet had been a member of parliament from Westmorland in 1572, 'of the privy chamber' by the same year, and a Groom of the Bedchamber by 1579.[2]

Oxford's quarrel was reported on 17 March by Nicholas Faunt in a letter to Anthony Bacon:[3]

> In England of late there hath bene a fraye betwene my Lord of Oxford and Mr Thomas Knevett of the Priuy Chamber, who are both hurt, but my lord of Oxford more dangerously: you knowe Mr Knevet is not meanely beloued in Court, and therfore he is not like to speed ill whatsoeuer the quarrell bee.

Faunt knew his man: in 1584 Knyvet would become a member of parliament from Westminster, sponsored by Burghley.

A second, less lethal, quarrel ensued on Monday, 18 June. Witnesses deposed on 22 and 24 June (LIB-7.7) 'that ther should be a freye betwene my Lord of Oxford & Mr Knevit & that they should fyght on thother syde [=across the Thames] in the marshe'; in fact, the fray occurred at the river-stairs at Blackfriars. Two of Oxford's men, one Gastrell and Horsley or (Harsley) the glasier, fought many of Knyvet's men, while servants, watermen, and others either watched or joined in with weapons of their own. One observer was Roger Daobye, servant to Mistress Brekeley of St Nicholas Shambles:

> Shortly after, Mr Knevet came, & then the freye begonne. And, se[e]inge that they were but ij of my Lords [=Oxford's] men, & many men on thother syde, he [=Daobye] went in emongest them to kepe the peace. He sawe besydes iiij with staues, besydes watermen with ther hookes & staves which they occupye in ther botes.

Thus watermen fought with boat-hooks. Turboughe Magrice, usher to Francis Caverley or Calvert, master of the fencing school at Blackfriars, added more touches:

> [He] sayth that he was in the house of one Andrewe Berrye, not knowinge nor he[a]ringe of any entent of a freye, but beinge ther by chaunce & seinge swordes drawne, & havinge onlye aboute him a single sworde, he went in emongest them only to kepe the peace, & did nothinge ells, & none otherwyse did meddle in the matter. He taketh ther were aboute v or vj men with staves, & diuerse of the water men with ther hookes. He knewe Gasterill & Horsley, but nether they nor any other mayd him acquaynted with any suche thinge, nor desyered him to take parte therin.

Remarkably, no injuries were reported.

Another witness was Roger Townshend, a wealthy lawyer who would purchase Wivenhoe from Oxford two years later (LIB-7.9).[4] Townshend had been at Arundel House in the company of Philip Howard, now Earl of Arundel, Thomas Howard (the Earl's younger brother), and Knyvet. The four set off to Mrs Arundel's, a victualling and gaming house in St Lawrence (Jewry) Lane off Cheapside, whither Lord Ormond came also. As the party of five dined and gamed they received reports that Oxford and Peregrine Bertie intended to intercept Knyvet's party on its return to Arundel House. After more delays occasioned by more reports, the five departed for Blackfriars Steps, hoping for a boat which would take them back to Arundel House:

> And so we went to the Blacke Fryers, whare Mr Knevet (going before vs) was sett vppon; but who they were that did it I knowe not, for I was so farre behynde as I colde not discearne what they weare.

> And so I tooke boate with my Lord of Arrundell, & went to Arrundell House. Being in the boate with hym, he asked me why I did not tell hym of that I had tolde my Lord of Ormonde? I answered hym ageyne, I was very vnwilling to tell any body of yt, but that I was desirous of all the quiet that might be aslonge as he &

theirs weare in the company; and therfore I made choice of my Lord of Ormonde, as a man best experienced to advise in the cause, yf there had bene any such action in hand. He answered me ageyne, you might very well haue made me privie, for you maye be sure, I wolde not ioyne with any man willingly to be partye in any quarrell.

In the evening, fynding my Lord Wylloughbie walking in his garden, I desired to speake with hym. So, going talking with hym, I told hym that I thought my Lord of Oxforth & he wolde not thincke me so idely occupied, as that I wold ioyne in any quarrell ageynst them. Then he sayed to me that he did perceive there had flying tales [come] to vs, aswell as to them, for saieth he, yt was told my Lord of Oxforth, that Mr Knevett, with others, came braving hard by the dore here. Thervppon my Lord of Oxforth hym self (and also his men) was somwhat greived at yt. I answered my Lord I thought that was very vntrue, for Mr Knevet was not out of my company all the afternoone, & before dynner we came altogither, & went no farther then Aldersgate, and that truly I did thincke in my conscience there was no such intent, for there was none in the company prepared to any such purpose. Truly Cosyn Townishend (sayd my Lord Willoughbie), yf the matter had growen to any further extremytie, I wolde have sent both to the Mayor, & to the Recorder. But whither he sayd he did send or no, I doe not very well remember.

In effect Townshend represents himself as an innocent suspected by both sides.

Oxford's men and one of Knyvet's men quarrelled a third time on Friday 22 June, possibly in Fleet Street, the residence or workplace of two witnesses. These were Danyell Bothame, churgeon, and William Crowche, mercer, who deposed on Monday 25 June (LIB-7.8) that Oxford's man Harvey urged Gastrell to put up his sword, but that taunts from Knyvet's men were more than Gastrell could endure. Harvey 'was hurte by chaunce by Gastrill for he did not see any of mr Knevetes men strycke at him or he att any of them',

> & then one of mr Knevetes men said, Gastrill, an other tyme vse thy discretion. Whervppon Gastrill drewe againe & rane vppon one of Mr Knevetes men furyouslye, & they stroke v or vj blowes, & Mr Knevetes man hurte Gastrill. The other of Mr Knevetes men & Harvye stroke not at all that he did marke.

Thus Gastrell was wounded by Knyvet's men, and Knyvet was among those arrested.

On 27 July Christopher Hatton asked Lord Chancellor Sir Thomas Bromley to release Knyvet.[5] A marginal note explains:

> Mr. Knyvett had slayne a man of the Earle of Oxfords in fight. / He was a suiter to the Lord Chaunceler that his cause of *se defendendo* myght be determined by a pryuy sessions in the vacatione tyme, which at his bare request, beeing the party, my Lord thought not fitt to graunt hym without farther commaundement.

Since Gastrell was apparently still alive (as we shall learn), the issue may have been the death of Gerret in March. Hatton reports that a coroner's inquest had found Knyvet responsible for the death, but with the mitigation of self-defence (*se defendendo*). Unless Knyvet's case were heard in vacation-time, he could not be set free until the next legal term. The Queen pressured Bromley to accede. Hatton seconded the Queen:

> You knowe ... who he [=Knyvet] is, and where he serueth, and therefore in a cause, so littell ymportant as this, you might haue restreyned the mallyce of his enemyes well ynough: happely [=perhaps] she thinketh, they would have his tryall at New-gate, amongst common theeves, or in the benche in like sorte, of purpose to make hym suffer, asmuch publike reproche, as they could lay on hym.

Thus Hatton argues that Knyvet lay under restraint merely through the malice of 'his enemyes' – clearly meaning Oxford and his associates.

Hatton's campaign validates Nicholas Faunt's opinion: 'You knowe Mr Knevet is not meanely beloued in Court, and therfore he is not like to speed ill what-soeuer the quarrell bee'. Bromley stood his ground, however, with a magnificent reply to Hatton, and through him to the Queen, on 28 July, from Weld Hall, Essex:[6]

> I never knew, nor I never heard, that any party supposed to be an offender might of ordinary course have a special commission at his proper [=own] suit; neither is it reason it should be so, for that were to open a gap to let offenders pass through without due punishment ... [Mr Knyvet] standeth subject to the appeal which the brother of him that was slain may bring at any time within the year and day after the fact, notwithstanding any trial that might have ensued upon that special commission.

Bromley answers Hatton's blood-chilling characterization of the manslaughter as 'a cause so little important as this' with a reminder that death could be not only a tragedy for the victim, but a matter of concern for his family – in this case his brother.

For the next seven or eight months all was quiet, but in February 1583 fresh quarrels arose. On Thursday 21 February a burial was recorded in the parish register of St Botolph near Bishopsgate:[7]

> Robart Breninges the Lord Oxfordes man slayne the 21 ffebruary

The burial is also noticed, though anonymously, in the churchwardens' accounts of the same parish for 1582–83:[8]

> Receaued for the graue for my Lord of Oxfordes man vjs viijd ...
> Paied for pauinge my Lord of Oxfordes mans graue xijd
> Paied for makinge the same graue iiijd

Though the circumstances of Brenings's death are unknown, a connection to Oxford's feud with Knyvet may be inferred from a letter from Burghley to Hatton dated 12 March, noting that the quarrel had continued:[9]

Good Master Vice Chamberlain. ... I perceived yesterday by my Lord of Leicester that you had very friendly delivered speeches to Her Majesty tending to bring some good end to these troublesome matters betwixt my Lord of Oxford and Mr. Thomas Knyvet; for the which your doings I do heartily thank you, and beseech you to continue your former good meaning, though the event expected and desired hath not followed. And now perceiving by my Lord of Leicester some increase of Her Majesty's offence towards my Lord of Oxford, and finding by Mr. Thomas Knyvet that he only being called and demanded of Her Majesty what he would say herein, he did, as served his turn, declare to Her Majesty that his men were evil used by my Lord of Oxford's men, and namely that one of his men was killed by a man of my Lord of Oxford's, and no redress had, I cannot but think that Her Majesty had just occasion given by such an information to be offended towards my Lord of Oxford, or his man, and did therefore, like a Prince of justice and God's minister, command the matter to be examined, which was done yesterday at great length by my Lord of Leicester, to his trouble and my grief; and I doubt not but my Lord of Leicester will honourably declare to Her Majesty how my Lord of Oxford resteth untouched, or at least unblotted, in any kind of matter objected by Mr. Knyvet, whom we heard at great length, and his men also.

Having reported that the 'troublesome matters' had been investigated, Burghley now reports on specific findings:

But because Mr. Knyvet's man, called Long Tom, that once served and was maintained by my Lord of Oxford, a bad fellow to serve any honest man, came to his death, I am bold to send to you the inquisition before the Coroner of London, with the verdict of the jury and the depositions of the ocular witnesses; by all which, and by a new acquittal at Newgate, Gastrell, the party named my Lord of Oxford's man, and yet was not then his man, nor yet is, though Mr. Knyvet report him so to be, was and standeth acquitted of the death of the said Long Thomas; so as, where her Majesty had just cause to conceive somewhat hardly of my Lord of Oxford, I doubt not but when her Majesty shall be informed by my Lord of Leicester of the truth which he hath seen and not disproved, her Majesty will diminish her offensive opinion: and I trust also, after you shall have read these writings, which I will on my credit avow to be true, you will be of the same mind, and, as opportunity may serve, will also move her Majesty in this case to think otherwise hereof than the informer meant to induce her to think.

Here Burghley discloses the otherwise unreported killing of Knyvet's man Long Tom by Oxford's man Gastrell, who had been hurt in the quarrel of 22 June 1582. Burghley continues:

As to the rest of the brabbles and frays, my Lord of Leicester can also declare upon what small occasions of reports and light carriages of tales, whereof my Lord of Oxford is nowise touched, these brabbles are risen. And for the quarrel of one Roper, of the Guards, against Gastrell, my Lord of Oxford's man, it is confessed that Roper challenged Gastrell that he had complained of him; whereas in truth yourself knoweth it was my Lord of Oxford that did complain to you of Roper and of one Hall, so as Roper was therein too [=also] busy. And hereupon he wrote a long epistle to Gastrell to challenge him to fight, and so also Costock made the like challenge, whereby appeareth that these frays grow by challenges made to my Lord of Oxford's men: and yet it must be informed that my Lord of Oxford's men do offer these frays. Good Master Vice Chamberlain, these things are hardly carried, and these advantages are easily gotten where some may say what they will against my Lord of Oxford, and have presence to utter their humours, and my Lord of Oxford is neither heard nor hath presence either to complain or defend himself: and so long as he shall be subject to the disgrace of her Majesty (from which God deliver him), I see it apparently, that, how innocent soever he shall be, the advantages will fall out for his adversaries; and so I hear they do prognosticate.

Having characterized Oxford as innocent – or virtually so – in the year-long frays with Knyvet, Burghley defends Oxford against charges of extravagance:

It hath been also informed her Majesty that he hath had fifteen or sixteen pages in a livery going before him in Cheapside; but, if their tongues that uttered this were so much lessened by measure in their mouths as they have enlarged in their number, they would never be touched after with making any verbal lie. Indeed I would he had less than he hath, and yet in all his house are, nor were at any time, but four: one of them waiteth upon his wife, my daughter; another in my house, upon his daughter Bess [=Elizabeth] Vere; a third is a kind of tumbling-boy; and the fourth is a son of a brother of Sir John Cutts, lately put to him.

On Burghley's evidence Oxford had two servants: 'a kind of tumbling-boy', presumably from John Symons' company, an odd choice unless Oxford kept the boy for sexual purposes; and an unnamed nephew of Sir John Cutts. Burghley's explicit denial of the charge that Oxford 'had fifteen or sixteen pages in a livery going before him in Cheapside' may or may not be credible. Extravagance had certainly been Oxford's habit for years, as turning a blind eye had been Burghley's. From Burghley we learn that Anne now lived in the same household as Oxford, while their daughter Elizabeth – nicknamed Bess – remained at Burghley House on the Strand. Burghley continues:

By this false, large, lying report, if her Majesty would cause it to be tried, she should find upon what roots these blasphemous branches do grow. But I submit all these things to God's will, who knoweth best why it pleaseth Him to afflict my Lord of Oxford in this sort, who hath, I confess, forgotten his duty to God, and yet I hope he may be made a good servant to her Majesty, if it please her of her clemency to remit her displeasure; for his fall in her Court, which is now twice yeared [=two years in duration], and he punished as far or farther than any like crime hath been, first by her Majesty, and then by the drab's friend in revenge to the peril of his life. And if his own punishment past, and his humble seeking of forgiveness, cannot recover her Majesty's favour, yet some, yea many, may think that the intercession of me and my poor wife, so long and importunately continued, might have obtained some spark of favour of her Majesty; but hereof I will in nowise complain of too much hardness, but to myself. I would I could not, in *amaritudine animae* ['bitterness of spirit'], lament my wife's oppressing of her heart for the opinion she imprinteth therein of her misfortune, a matter not to be expressed without mistaking: and therefore both I and she are determined to suffer and lament our misfortune, that, when our son-in-law was in prosperity he was the cause of our adversity by his unkind usage of us and ours; and now that he is ruined and in adversity, we only are made partakers thereof, and by no means, no, not by bitter tears of my wife, can obtain a spark of favour for him, that hath satisfied his offence with punishment, and seeketh mercy by submission; but contrariwise, whilst we seek for favour, all crosses are laid against him, and by untruths sought to be kept in disgrace. ...

On 18 March Burghley wrote to Hatton from Burghley House:[10]

... A last matter whereof my Lord spake was a divers answer to my expectation for my Lord of Oxford, whose infortunes increase my wife's griefs and mine more than I will mention, because I see not the way to remedy them, otherwise than by continuing in the beaten heavy ways of forced patience. ...

Hatton replied the next day from Richmond, at Court:[11]

... My Lord of Oxford's cause standeth but in slow course of proceeding to his satisfaction; but yet, for my own part, I have some better hope than heretofore, wherein as a preservative you must all use patience for a while. His Lordship wrote me a very wise letter in this case of his, the report whereof her Majesty took in reasonable good gracious part. By the next messenger I will briefly write ... the answer. ...

Oxford's 'very wise letter' to Hatton, which so mollified the Queen, has unfortunately not survived.

As we anticipate Oxford's return to the Queen's favour and so to Court, we may take a parting glance at the havoc wreaked by his year-long quarrel with Thomas Knyvet. Oxford's man Gerret (or Gerard) was killed, perhaps by Knyvet himself. Knyvet and Oxford were both wounded, Oxford the more seriously. Oxford's man Gastrell was hurt by one of Knyvet's men, while Oxford's man Harvey was wounded accidentally by Gastrell. Oxford's man Gastrell killed Long Tom, who served Knyvet but had once served Oxford, 'a bad fellow to serve any honest man'. Roper of the Guards challenged Gastrell, as did Costock; Oxford complained to Hatton of both Roper and Hall. Oxford's man Robert Brenings was 'slayne' in undisclosed circumstances. The principal challenges seem to have come (logically enough) from Knyvet's side, 'and yet it must be informed that my Lord of Oxford's men do offer these frays'. Little wonder the Queen was upset!

Lawrence Stone concludes a twelve-page survey of violence in Tudor society by recalling the Oxford–Knyvet feud:[12]

Thanks to the studied neutrality of the Queen, two great courtiers were allowed to commit murder after murder with complete impunity. Both in the brutality of their tactics and in their immunity from the law, the nearest parallels to the Earl of

Oxford and Sir Thomas Knyvett in the London of Queen Elizabeth are Al Capone and Dion O'Banion, Bugs Moran and Johnny Torrio in the Chicago of the 1920's. It is against this sinister background of rival court factions with their hired killers and 'cutters', of sporadic murder and violence in the streets of London, and of occasional pitched battles in the countryside, that the wisdom of Elizabeth's tactics must be judged.

54 Oxford's Literary Circle

While mortal quarrel raged between Oxford and Thomas Knyvet, on 31 March 1582 Oxford's fellow parishioner Thomas Watson registered a collection of verse, called 'passions manifestinge the true frenzy of love', with the Stationers Company (Arber, ii, p. 409). Published within the year as *The Hekatompathia or Passionate Centurie of Loue*, the collection carried a dedication claiming Oxford's patronal approbation (sig. A3):[1]

> ... For since the world hath vnderstood, (I know not how) that your Honor had willinglie voutchsafed the acceptance of this worke, and at conuenient leisures fauourablie perused it, being as yet but in written hand, many haue oftentimes and earnestly called vpon mee, to put it to the presse, that for their money they might but see, what your Lordship with some liking had alreadie perused. ...

Other preliminaries include a stylized letter from 'Iohn Lyly to the Author his friend', and commendatory poems signed 'G. Bucke', 'T. Ascheley', 'C. Downhalus', 'M. Roydon', and 'G. Peele'. Thus *Hekatompathia* implies a literary 'circle' with Oxford as patron. The fact that most of of his protégés are regarded by posterity as second- or third-rank befits Oxford's own modest talent.

On 16 April, in a letter to Walsingham, Mauvissière sought protection for Rocco Bonetti:[2]

> Signor Rocco, the present bearer, having addressed himself to me on his return from Scotland, where he has been staying for some time, has requested me to write to you, begging you to give him your aid and favour in any recourse he might have to you to recover the goods of his wife, who died last year, and a trunk with some clothing and leather articles, which have been taken from his boy. Further he tells me that he is threatened by the people of the Earl of Oxford, which puts him in great trouble and despair of ever being able to live securely in this realm, if you do not kindly help him, according to the courtesy which you are wont to use to every one, and especially to those of his nation. Please help him so far as you deem just and reasonable.

The French ambassador confirms the fear that ordinary people might have of Oxford's henchmen, even apart from the Oxford–Knyvet affair.

On 23 April Walsingham's informant Henry Brooke, writing under the code-name Cobham, sent word from Paris:[3]

> … I have lately been intreated by letter from the Abate del Bene to recommend Bartolomeo Spatafora the Sicilian, who has, as he says, some time served the Earl of Oxford. I have given him a letter to yourself only, being since informed he has spoken with the Pope's nuncio.

Spatafora, otherwise unidentified, may have served Oxford in Italy.

In July, John Lyly, having fallen out with Oxford, asked Burghley to intercede on his behalf:[4]

> It hath plesed my Lord vpon what colour I cannot tell, certaine I am vpon no cause, to be displesed with me, the grief wherof is more then the losse can be. But seeing I am to liue in the world, I must also be iudged by the world, for that an honest seruaunt must be such as Cæsar wold haue his wif, not only free from synne, but from suspicion. And for that I wish nothing more then to commit all my waies to your wisdome, and the deuises of others to your iudgment, I heere yeld both my self and my soule, the one to be tried by your honnor, the other by the iustic[e] of God. and I doubt not but my dealings being sifted, the world shall find whit[e] meale, wher others thought to shew cours [=coarse] branne. It may [be] manie things wilbe obiected, but that any thing can be proued I doubt. I know your Lordship will soone smell deuises from simplicity, trueth from trecherie, factions from iust seruic[e]. And God is my witnes, before whome I speak, and before whome for my speach I shall aunswer, that all my thoughtes concerning my Lord haue byn[e] ever reuerent, and almost relligious. how I haue dealt, God knoweth and my Lady can coniecture, so faithfullie, as I am as vnspotted for dishonnestie, as a suckling from theft. This consci[e]nc[e] of myne maketh me presume to stand to all trialls, ether of accomptes, or counsell, in the one I neuer vsed falshood, nor in the other dissembling. my most humble suit therfore vnto your Lordship is, that my accusations be not smothered and I choake in the smoak, but that they maie be tried in the fire, and I will stand to the heat. And my only comfort is, that he that is wis[e] shall iudg[e] trueth, whos nakednes shall manifest her noblenes.
>
> But I will not troble your honorable eares, with so manie idle wordes only this vpon my knees I ask, that your Lordship will vousalf [=vouchsafe] to talk with me, and in all things will I shew my self so honest, that my disgrac[e] shall bring to your Lordship as great meruell, as it hath done to me grief, and so thoroughly will I satisfie everie obiection, that your Lordship shall think me faithfull, though infortunat.
>
> That your honnor rest persuaded of myne honest mynd, and my Lady of my true seruic[e], that all things may be tried to the vttermost, is my desire, and the only reward I craue for my iust, (if iust I dare tearme it) seruic[e]. And thus in all humility submitting my caus[e] to your wisdome, and my conscinc[e] to your triall.

Lyly added, by way of footnote:

for that I am for some few daies going into the countrie, yf your Lordship be not at leasure to admitt me to your speach, at my returne I will giue my most dutifull attendaunc[e], at which time, it may be my honesty may ioyne with your Lordships wisdome and both preuent, that ne[i]ther, wold allow. In the meane season what color soever be alledged, if I be not honest to my Lord and so meane to be during his plesure, I desire but your Lordships secret opinion, for I hold my Lord to be most honorable, so I besech God in time he be not abused. Loth I am to be a prophett, and to be a wi[t]che I loath[e].

Lyly seems not to have been told the grounds for Oxford's dissatisfaction. His declaration of willingness 'to stand to all trialls, ether of accomptes, or counsell', suggests that he both kept financial accounts for Oxford, and served as his private secretary. Supporting the inference that Lyly served Oxford as an accountant is his testimony in the 'Ruswell' lawsuit; supporting the inference that he had access to closely kept secrets is a passage on Lyly in Gabriel Harvey's 1593 *Pierces Supererogation* (sigs. S1–1v): 'a whole sinke of such arrant phrases, sauour wholty of the same Lucianicall breath, & discoouer the minion Secretarie aloofe'. Since Lyly continued to serve as Oxford's 'minion Secretarie' until 1584 and probably beyond, his dispute with Oxford must have been resolved, perhaps with Burghley's help.

The twenty-year sequestration of lands for the payment of the 16th Earl's debts finally expired on 2 August. A document of 2 October 1582 preserves rare evidence of Oxford's exercising his duties as lord of the manor of Castle Hedingham, or principal peer of Essex:[5]

> Copy of Court Roll of the Manor of Hedingham Castle, held before Edward Vere Earl of Oxford, for the admission of Matthew Ellyston to a butcher's shop and other premises in the village of Hedingham, on surrender of William Mosse.

About this same time Chelmsford churchwardens noted 'mustering horsemen before Earl of Oxford'.[6]

55 To Give the Earl Warning

On 6 May 1583 Nicholas Faunt wrote to Anthony Bacon from Greenwich:[1]

> ... Yt is long since you heard of the death of Mr Wentworth and his wyfe my Lord Thresurers daughter th'one not long after th'other ...

The loss of his son-in-law Wentworth and his daughter Elizabeth within a month left Burghley prostrate.[2] Faunt's letter conveyed news even more devastating:

> God had sent my Lord of Oxford a Sonne but hath taken it awaie from him ... so it pleaseth the Lord to afflict the best and mightiest ones ...

An entry in the parish register at Castle Hedingham confirms the report:[3]

> The Earle of Oxenfords first sonne was buried the 9th of May 1583.

Circumstances imply that the birth had occurred in London, the child dying before it could be baptized and given a name. A poem in John Soowthern's 1584 *Pandora* (sig. C3v), in Anne's voice, suggests that the child lived two days:

> And *Destins*, and Gods, you might rather haue tanne,   [tanne = taken]
> My twentie yeers: then the two daies of my sonne.

Anne was in fact twenty-six. This and a second lament were translations by Soowthern from the French verse of Desportes.[4] The event confirms that Oxford and Anne had resumed conjugal relations.

On 12 May, after an attempt by Burghley to get Oxford restored to the Queen's grace, Walter Ralegh wrote to Burghley from Greenwich:[5]

> The eueninge aftre the recept of your Lordship[s] letter, I spake with her Maiesty, and ministringe sum occasion touchinge the Earle of Oxford I told her Maiesty how greuously your Lordship receiud her late discumfortable awnswere. her Maiesty as your Lordship had written (I know not by whom latley, and strangly perswaded) purposed to haue new repetition betweene the Lord [Henry] Haward, Arundle, and others, and the Earle, and said it was a matter not so slightly to be passed ouer. I awnswered that beinge asured her Maiesty would never permit anything to 'be procecuted to the Earles dangre, if any such possibility were, and therfore it were to small purpose aftre so longe absence, and so many disgraces, to call his honor, and name, agayne in question, wherby he might apeare the less fitt ether for her favor or presence, in conclusion her Maiesty confessed that she ment it only therby to geue the Earle warninge, and that as it semed to mee beinge acquaynted with his offences, hir grace might seme the more in remittinge the revenge, or punishment, of the same. I deliuered her your Lordships lettre and what I sayd farther how honorable, and profittable it weare for [her] Maiesty to haue regard to your Lordship[s] healthe and quiett, I referr to the wittnes of God, and good reporte of her highness, and the more to witness how desirous I am of your Lordships favor, and good opinion, I am content for your sake to lay the serpente before the fier, as muche as in mee lieth, that hauinge recouered strenght my sealf may be moste in danger of his poyson and sting. for awnswere her Maiesty would geue me none other, but that she would satisfy your Lordship, of whom she euer had, and would euer haue special regard.

Some unnamed person – perhaps Henry Howard – had requested a hearing of charges against Oxford more than two years previously. In response to Elizabeth's insistence that the charges were 'not slightly to be passed over', Ralegh begged her to face a truth: she would never allow Oxford to be put in legal jeopardy, never subject him to public accusations of sedition and pederasty. Ralegh's logic is clear if not commendable: after such long absences from court, and after so many disgraces, if Oxford's honour and name were called into question (as they had been once already), he would be forever unfit to receive the Queen's favour or even come into her presence. The Queen agreed to bestow her grace on Oxford – but only on a guarantee of good behaviour.

Ralegh explains that he let the Queen know how highly Burghley regards Oxford, and has even shown her Burghley's letter; Ralegh moreover is content, for Burghley's sake, 'to lay the serpente before the fier'. In this breath-taking image, inverting the proverb, 'When the serpent is dead the poison will not hurt',[6] Ralegh imagines Oxford as a poisonous serpent apparently lifeless, but in truth only chilled. Ralegh will do what he can to restore Oxford to the warmth of the Queen's presence – though he knows he himself may be at mortal risk from 'poyson and stinge' when the serpent regains its vigour.

On 27 May Roger Manners wrote to Rutland from Greenwich:[7]

> I will make myself ready to wait on her Majesty at Theobalds ('Tybolles'), where, it is thought, Lord Oxford will work some grace. ...

On 31 May Faunt wrote to Bacon, also from Greenwich:[8]

> ... Her majesty hath spent this last week at Theobald's, where my lord of Oxford was reconciled and received to her majesty's favour, and now is here at court.

On 2 June Manners wrote again to Rutland, this time from the Savoy:[9]

> Her Majestie cam yesterday to Grenwich from my Lord Tresurer's. She was never in any place better plesed, and sure the howse, garden and walks may compare with any delicat place in Italy. The day she cam away, which was yesterday, the Earl of Oxford cam to her presence, and after some bitter words and speches, in the end all sins ar[e] forgiven and he may repayre to the court at his plesure. Mr. Ralley [=Ralegh] whas a great mean herin, whereat Pondus is angry for that he could not doe so moch.

By 'Pondus', Manners probably means Burghley.

On 9 June Oxford's friend and father-figure Thomas Radcliffe, 3rd earl of Sussex, died. About 20 June Oxford wrote to Burghley (LL-14):

> I have bene an ernest suter vnto yowre Lordship, for my Lord Lumley, that it wowld pleas yow for my sake to stand his good lord and friend whiche as I perceyve yowre Lordship hathe alreadie very honorablye <done ... for> the which I am in a number of thinges more then I can reken bound vnto yowre lordship so am I in this lekwise especially. for he hathe ma[t]ched [=married] withe a near kinswoman of myne, to whose father I allwayes was behouldinge vnto, for his assured and kind disposition vnto me. further amonge all the rest of my blud, this only remaynes in account ether of me or els of them, as yowre lordship dothe knowe very well, the rest havinge imbraced further alliances, to leaue thear nearer consanguinite. and as I hope yowre lordship dothe account me now on whome yow have so muche bound as I am to be yowrs before any els in the world, bothe through ma[t]che, whearby I count my greatest stay, and by yowre lordshipes friendly vsage and stiken

[=sticking] by me in this time whearin I am he[d]ged in withe so many enemyes, so lekwise I hope yowre lordship will take all them for yowre followers and most at Command whiche are inclyned and affected to me. Whearfore I shall once agayne be thus bould withe yowre lordship to be <…> importunat in this matter for yowre lordships fauour in case my lord Lumleys payment to her magestie whearin we do all giue yowre lordship thankes, and yow shall do me as great an honor hearin, as a profit yf it had ben to my self. in this throught [=through] yowre lordships fauour I shalbe able to plesure my friend, and stand nedles of others, that have forsaken me. thus for that yowre lordship is trobled withe many matters whear yow ar I crave pardon for troblinge yow. …

In 1582 John, 1st Lord Lumley, took as his second wife Elizabeth Darcy, daughter of John, 2nd Lord Darcy of Chiche; her grandmother was Elizabeth de Vere, Oxford's aunt.[10] John Darcy had died on 3 March 1581. Just why Lumley needed Oxford's or Burghley's support is not explained.

In Essex a case of slander was brought before the archdeacon's court:[11]

From Pontisbright (the parish now called Chapel) in 1583 Thomas Baker senior brought a case against a man named Crowche, who had related how Baker 'reported and affirmed that Mistress Turner whilst she dwelt at Thomas Boteslye played the whore with my Lord of Oxford's men, that Mistress Beriffe had played the whore with that short-legged knave Lawrence her man, and that Mistress Hawkin had played the whore with Browninge a physician late of Peldon'. Crowche's answer was that Baker was 'not thereby defamed, for he spake the words in deed, and Baker is the same Crowche his father (i.e. Crowche's father-in-law), for Crowche married with the daughter of Baker, which is yet alive'. (The will of a James Browninge of Peldon, proved in 1591, does not term him a physician.)

A Thomas Baker of Kelvedon was also charged this year with keeping idols – perhaps as a Catholic recusant.[12] Though Oxford now walked the straight-and-narrow, his men retained their reputation of old.

56   I Am that I Am

On 15 March 1584 Sturmius wrote to Queen Elizabeth from Strasbourg:[1]

If the German discipline were set up by someone in single companies, the explanation and undertaking of this art and faculty would be easy. And if all the horsemen would obey some one faithful and zealous personage, such as the Earl of Oxford, the Earl of Leicester or Philip Sidney, it might be more convenient, speedy and fitting to entrust this matter to him.

Doubtless Sturmius's proposals represent the good wishes of an elderly philosopher and theologian towards Oxford, Leicester, and Sidney, rather than any realistic way ahead in the Protestant battle against Catholicism.

On 6 April Anne gave birth to a second daughter, Bridget.[2] The fact that conception must have occurred in August 1583, within months of the burial of a child the preceding May, testifies to the practical success of the marital reconciliation reported in 1582 and 1583. In July 1584, a memorandum, 'An estimate of my Lady Oxfords Charges for one whole yere in the Courte', was prepared on Anne's behalf.[3] Here we learn that Anne attended Court with a personal retinue of two gentlewomen, one chambermaid, one gentleman, and two yeoman. As a follower of the Court, she accepted the obligation to bestow a New Year's gift on the Queen and (this year) on Leicester, as well as gratuities on royal servants down to the 'Children of the Kitchen'. Anne had to pay for wood, coal, torches, candles, soap, and rushes, and incurred an expense whenever the Court moved from one location to another, whether by land or by water.

Anne maintained separate facilities for her daughters Bridget, now three months, and Elizabeth, who turned nine on 2 July. Anne herself was served by two gentlewomen, one laundress, and one gentleman. Bridget required a nurse, a 'rocker', and a laundress, while Lady Elizabeth had a female attendant in the person of Margaret Browne, as well as a laundress. She was also served by three servants, a man, a boy, and a schoolmaster, whose wages and liveries were provided by Oxford. A male servant named Brooke carried wood and coal to the ladies' chamber. Lady Elizabeth received a supplementary allowance of £30, while £10 was set aside for Bridget. Not counting the servants funded by Oxford, the total annual charge for Anne and her two daughters was a relatively modest £232–17–8.

On 14 July Mary Queen of Scots, imprisoned at Sheffield, wrote to Queen Elizabeth (as cited by Nicholas):[4]

> ... the Earl of Oxford dared not cohabit with his wife '[out of fear of losing the favour which he hoped to receive from making love to you]' ...

Nicolas admits: 'The admirers of Mary affect to doubt the authenticity of this letter'; but he gives reasons to believe that it is indeed authentic. The gist of Mary's statement is that the Queen was so jealous of Oxford that he dared not live with his wife for fear of losing the Queen's favour. This is close in sentiment to the statement, noted in Gilbert Talbot's letter of May 1573, that Lady Burghley was jealous of Oxford's attachment to the Queen. By 1584, however, Mary's information may have been seriously out of date.

On 30 October Oxford wrote to Burghley, for once dictating his letter to an amanuensis (LL-15):

> It is not vnknowne to your Lordship that I haue entred into a greate nomber of bondes to suche, as haue purchasyd landes of me, to discharge them of all Incombraunces: And bycause I stande indebtid vnto her Maiestie (as your Lordship knowythe) many of the said purchasers do greatly feare somme troble likely to fall vppon them, by reason of her Maiestyes said debt, & espesialy if the Bondes [or

Londes?] of the Lord Darcy and Sir William Walgraue should be extendyd for the
same, who haue two seuerall statutes of great sommes for their discharge
Wheruppon many of the said purchasers haue ben suters vnto me to procuer the
discharginge of her Maiestyes said Debt, and do seme very willinge to beare the
burden therof, yf by my meanes the same might be stalled paiable at some
convenyent dayes / I haue therfore thought good to acquaynte your Lordship with
this their suyte, requierynge moste earnestly your Lordships furtheraunce in this
behalfe, wherby I shalbe vnburdened of a greate care, which I haue for the savynge
of my honor, And shall by this meanes also vnburden my wyves Ioincture of that
charge which might happen herafter to be ymposyd vppon the same, yf God
should call your Lordship and me away before her. /

Because Oxford had not paid his debts to the Crown, any properties he sold were
encumbered with liens; if the Queen were to call in her debt, the obligations
would fall on those who had purchased the lands. Those to whom he had sold
land expressed a willingness to assist in the repayment of the debt and the clearing
of the liens. (This problem would be addressed again in 1587.) Oxford incidentally concedes that Burghley had made a significant and continuing contribution
to Anne's financial support.

   Oxford added a postscript in his own hand which sorts oddly with his attempt
to gain Burghley's cooperation:

   My lord, this other day yowre man Stainner towld me that yow sent for Amis my
   man, and yf he wear absent that Lylle showld come vnto yow. I sent Amis for he
   was in the way. And I thinke very strange that yowre Lordship showld enter into
   that course towards me, wherby I must lerne that I knev [=knew] not before, bothe
   of yowre opinion and good will towards me. but I pray, my lord, leaue that course,
   for I mean not to be yowre ward nor yowre chyld, I serve her magestie, and I am
   that I am, and by allyance neare to yowre lordship, but fre, and scorne to be offred
   that iniurie, to thinke I am so weake of gouernment as to be ruled by servants, or
   not able to gouerne my self. Yf yowre Lordship take and follow this courcse, yow
   deceyve yowre self, and make me take an other course then yet I have not thought
   of. whearfore thes shalbe to desyre yowre Lordship yf that I may make account of
   yowre friendship, that yow will leave that cours as hurtfull to vs bothe.

'Stainner' was Burghley's servant, otherwise unidentified. 'Amis' was Israel Amyce,
Esquire, who had also been a servant of Oxford's father.[5] 'Lylle' was almost
certainly John Lyly, still with Oxford despite their July 1582 contretemps. Oxford
objects to Burghley's practice of treating Oxford's servants as if they were his own,
and threatens to adopt a new course of action if Burghley does not change his
ways.

   On 23 November began Elizabeth's Sixth Parliament, which would sit until 29
March following, the first session running until 21 December (*TE*). In the
opening procession, 'the Earle of Oxford, then great Chamberlaine of England'
went on the right hand of the Earl of Kent, who carried the sword of state.[6]

Oxford's presence is recorded on November 23, 26, February 4, and March 29; his absence is recorded on November 24–25, 28, 30, and December 1, 3–5, 7–10, 12, 14–17, 19, 21, February 5, 8–11, 15–16, 17 (two sessions), 18, 20, 22 (two sessions), 23–25, 27, March 1, 3–6, 8, 10, 11 (two sessions), 13, 15 (two sessions), 16 (two sessions), 17, 18 (two sessions), 19–20, 22–24, 26–27, 29 (first sessions).[7] Thus of 64 sessions Oxford attended only four, of which one opened and one closed this Parliament; Oxford was one of ten lords appointed as 'triers of petitions from Gascony and other lands beyond the seas and from the islands'. The fact that he could hold this same post during parliaments he attended only once (1597) or not at all (1601, 1604) suggests it required no effort. Indeed, since England had long since lost Gascony, the post can scarcely have been as significant as that of the 'triers of petitions from England, Ireland, France, and Scotland', to which he had been appointed for the Parliament of 1572 only.

On 1 September Oxford sold his manor in Earls Colne, with numerous attendant properties, to Roger Harlackenden.[8] Oxford retained Fisher's Folly, commissioning a pew at St Botolph's Bishopsgate:[9]

> Paied for making my Lord of Oxfordes gentell mens pew and for waynskote for the sam[e] ixs

Only this once are we permitted to visualize Oxford's men in church.

57 Use not thy Birth for an Excuse

On 19 January 1585 Anne Vavasor's brother (?)Thomas sent a written challenge to Oxford, evidently in response to provocation by Oxford's men:[1]

> If thy body had bene as deformed as thy mind is dishonorable my house had bene yet vnspotted and thy self remayned with thy cowardise vnknowne. I speake this that I feare thow art so much wedded to that shadow of thine that nothing canne haue force to awake thy base and sleapye spyrytes. Is not the reveng[e] alredy taken of thy vildnes [=vileness] sufficyent but wylt thou yet vse vnworthy instrumentes to provoke my vnwytting mynd? or dost thow feare thy self and therfore hast sent thy forlorne kindred whom as thow hast left nothing to inheryte so thow dost thrust them vyolently into thy shamefull quarelles? If yt be so (as I too much doubt) then stay at home thy self and send my abusers. but yf ther be yet left any sparke of honour in the[e], or iott [=jot] of regard of thy decayed reputation, vse not thy byrth for an excuse for I am a gentleman but meete me thy self alone and thy lacky to hould thy horse for the weapons I leaue them to thy choyse for that I challendge, and the place to be apoynted by vs both at our meeting which I think may convenyently be at Nuington or els where thy self shalt send me word by this bearer. by whom I expect an answere

Vavasor refers to an unnamed male relative of Oxford's – perhaps one of his many Vere cousins – as 'that shadow of thine', 'thy forlorne kindred whom … thow hast left nothing to inheryte', and 'thy lacky': perhaps this was the un-identified 'Vere' named by Sir Francis Knollys back in 1580. Oxford turned the challenge over to Burghley, who endorsed it as 'a lewd lettre from Vavaser to the Erl of Oxford'. That Oxford would overlook such a torrent of abuse shows how thoroughly the Queen had tamed him.

On 4 March Mendoza wrote to the King of Spain:[2]

> It is understood that they are going to discuss with the king of Scotland the release of the Queen, his mother, if they can come to terms on the matter. To this end they say the king of Scotland will go to England; and rumour still runs that the earls of Bedford, Arundel, and Oxford, will be sent to Scotland as hostages for his safety.

The same news was conveyed by Barnaby Penethorne to Edward Seymour, Earl of Hertford:[3]

> It is said that my Lords of Arundell and of Oxfforde go to Scotland as pledges to the King.

No formal negotiations ensued, and Oxford remained in London.

In April Oxford received votes from five of thirteen electors for the Order of the Garter, including Burghley, the first time since 1580 that he had received any votes at all (G-BL). He was firmly back in the Queen's good graces – though she did not choose to make the appointment.

On 11 August Burghley wrote to Leicester from Nonesuch:[4]

> … Now when your Lordship's self doth not use me evil to my understanding, as to knowledge of myself, and that my children are so well used; yea, I judge hitherto my daughter of Oxford, who always affirmeth the like of you; it may seem strange, that I should not so settle mine opinion constantly to make sure account of your Lordship's favour upon these short proofs …

Evidently Leicester had complimented Burghley because his children were so well 'used' or taken care of, and Anne (through Burghley) returned the compliment. Although Leicester had no children of his own, he was step-father to Robert Devereux, Earl of Essex, Burghley's ward. Indeed, we caught a glimpse (p. 201) of Leicester paying a visit to his step-son at Burghley House.

At the age of thirty-five Oxford was trusted with a position of official respon-sibility for the first time in his life: in late summer he was commissioned to travel to the Low Countries at the head of a company of horse. We may recall that in 1582, Oxford witnessed a muster of horsemen at Chelmsford, and that in 1584, Sturmius imagined Oxford, Leicester, and Sidney in command of horsemen. Now, on 27 August 1585, Oxford's company landed at Flushing.[5] On 1 September Mendoza wrote to the King of Spain:[6]

About 2,000 Englishmen had gone to Zeeland under Colonel Norris, and 4,000 more were to follow. The latter force was being raised and it was said that the leader of it would be the earl of Oxford. … I have received a letter from England, dated 30th ultimo [=20 August O.S.], whilst writing this, but it gives no fresh news, except that the earl of Oxford had left on the previous night for Zeeland by the Queen's orders.

On 3 September 'instructions were issued regarding the inspection of the English troops at the Hague, and also for the victualling of the Earl of Oxford and his retinue, Colonel Norris, and the Captains and superior officers assembled there'.[7] Further 'Advices from England' followed on 9 September (O.S.):[8]

… Five or six thousand English soldiers have arrived in Flanders with the earl of Oxford and Colonel Norris, and it is said that Philip Sidney will follow them shortly to take possession of Flushing, whilst other gentlemen will go to assure the governorships of other towns, and the earl of Leicester will then follow as chief of the expedition.

Burghley reports in his retrospective Diary for October (ii, p. 783):

A Commission to the Erle of Leycester to be Generall of the Forces in the Lowe Countryes, with Authority to levy 500 of his owne Seruants and Tennaunts.

And again for November:

The Erle of Lecester appoynted Generall of the Succors of 5000 Foot and 1000 Horss.

As of mid-October, Oxford's loyalties were put to the test. Would he cooperate with Leicester and Sidney to advance the Queen's interests in the Low Countries?

He would not. On 21 October William Davison, the Queen's political agent in the Low Countries, wrote to Captain Henry Norris, concerned that the companies at Flushing were below strength:[9]

… My lord of Axenforde is returned this night into England, upon what humour I know not.

Davison's report suggests that Oxford quit his post in a fit of pique. Perhaps he could not abide the thought of cooperating with Leicester, who outranked him, or with Sidney, his ancient rival.

On 14 October several of Oxford's men and his personal effects were captured off Dunkirk, as described in a letter from the imprisoned Thomas Doyley to Walsingham dated 12 November (2 November O.S.):[10]

Six of our company have not been able to take order for their ransom, Skarborow, a merchant, set at 600 guilders; Hyham, of my lord of Oxford's chamber, set at 150; Terry, his man, and other three poor passengers. There are also Mr. Shelton, two Tracys and Mr. Whithed, who were there before us, and are rated at two thousand apiece, besides their charges.

Perhaps unknown to Doyley, Thomas Whithead was also Oxford's man. (Whithead may have concealed his full identity for his own safety.) On the same day Doyley also wrote to Leicester, giving a more vivid account:[11]

> Hauing by manie difficulties ridd my self out of the hands of the helhounds of Dunkerk & arriued at Calleys, wher I may boldly write vnto your Honour the vnluckie euent of our iourney. These are to aduertise your Honour that puttinge out from Grauelinge the 13 of October[,] the 14 of the same we weare taken not farr from Dunkerk our Pylot saylinge of[f] his course bendinge to[o] much southward, at the takinge of vs ther wear too [=two] men of warr the one called the Lour haane the other the Skeur Water. hauinge too pricis [=prizes, captured ships] in his companie. our ship beinge heauie & full frayted both the vpper & nether deck so that we could make no fight so that we yelded & wear rifled of al our goods & apparrel vnto our doubletts & hose, with ther daggers at our throts, & brought to the common iayle [=jail] & after our beinge ther an hower, cam the vnderbaylife & sargeant maior of the toune with ther poignards to our brests strippinge vs stark naked searched vs againe. & took awaye such monie as the mariners fayled of. ther we remayned from Thursdaye vntil Mondaye hauinge nothinge sayed vnto vs. that daye we wear examined before the Gouuernor, the Baylife, the Bourghemester, pensionar, and others, of our owne estate[,] of her Maiesties actions in Flanders, of your Honours comminge ouer &c this examination signed with our hands was too dayes after sent to the Prince of Parma to Antwerp whose resolution we must attend, the same daye fortnight he went[,] he retourned after fower dayes consultation vppon the Princis Letters we wear called to the Toone Howse, & ther told by the Baylif that the Prince had declared our goods confiscat & our boddies to be sett to ransomm, we demanded if he had declared vs enemis; they answered no, but we wear therefor put to our ransom because enemies goods wear found in our ship namly the Earl of Oxfords, which they proued by letters of my Lord treasurars to him whearin he wrote of her Maiesties grante of the commanding of Horsmen which letter one of the Earl of Oxfords chamber brought ouer in our bote, with his monnie apparrel wine & venison, etc. then wear we seuerally put to our ransom & rated at ther plesurs, marchants, mariners ship & all, my ranson with my chargis in prison was 500 gulders which by the means of Mr Hudson & Mr Beal marchants I dischardged[.] Mr Stephens [=Stephen Le Sieur] was excepted from this puttinge to ransom because by the letters he had, they pretended him to be an agent of matters of estate, and an especial instrument in matters of Flusshinge. & sett him doune articles wher vnto they commaunded him to answere peremptoriely vppon payne of the torture, the coppie wherof with his answer to them he hath sent to Mr Secretarie, the answerr to the articles is sent to the Prince. so that I dout his [for it], wil be a longe & a difficult matter, I escaped wel because they found nothinge in my chest but physick & astronomie books al letters & notes for your Honours busines I drouned out of a porthole when they entred the ship which Mr stephens by no means could doe his tronk beinge ouerwhelmed with sondrie packs. Ther camm awaye in my companie t[w]o Marchants & your seruant Iohn Potter for whose ransom I haue giuen my wourd, we left behinde vs, som marchants too [=two] of the Earle of Oxfords men [=Hyham and Terry] besides the fower [=four]

gentilmen which wear ther befor vs namly Mr Shelton too [=two] Traceys & Mr Whithed for whom they nowe demaund 2000 gulders a peece. & as yet growe no lower. ...

Ther remaynith in Dunkerk Mr Staynhurst the Lord of Tunsans brother, & Mr Copley surnamed Lord, whose sister Mr Staynhurst maried, also Mr Kemp called Don Gulihelmo. ...

Mr Stephens humbly requestith your Honours assistance in the procuring his libertie he hath wrote to Mr. Rowland York for his retourne, & to St. Aldegonde to that effect as he hath conferred with your Honour. ...

Hyham and Terry apparently gained their freedom in 1586, Thomas Whithead only in 1587.

Doyley reveals that among Oxford's captured effects was his commission from Burghley, along with money, clothing, wine, and venison. Oxford's 'tronk' had been so 'ouerwhelmed with sondrie packs' that Le Sieur could not throw the commission out of the porthole as the ship was attacked.

PART IX

Reiteration
1586–1591

58 Maintenance for his Nobility

On 21 June 1586 Burghley wrote to Walsingham:[1]

> I pray yow send me word if yow had any commoditie to spek with hir Maiesty to spek for my Lord of Oxford, and what hope ther is, and if yow have any to lett Robert Cecill vnderstand it, to releve his sistar, who is more troubled for hir husbandes lack, then he hym self.

Oxford had petitioned the Queen, with Burghley's support, for an annuity to repair his damaged finances, incidentally bringing relief to Anne. On the morning of 25 June Oxford wrote to Burghley from court (LL-16):[2]

> My very good lord as I have bene behowldinge vnto yow diuers tymes & of late, by my brother [=brother-in-law] R. Cecill, wherby I have bene the better able to follow my sute, wherin I have sume comfort at this tyme from Mr Secretarie Wallsingham, so am I now bowld, to crave yowre lordships help at this present. for beinge now almost at a point to tast[e] that good whiche her Magestie shall determine[,] yet am I [as] on[e] that hathe longe besieged a fort and not able to compas the end or reap the frut of his travel [=travail], beinge forst to leuie [=raise] his si[e]ge for want of munition. Beinge therfore thus disfurnished and vnprouided to follow her Magestie as I perceyve she will loke for, I most ernestly desyre yowre lordship that yow will lend me 200 pounds tyll her Magestie performethe her promes. out of which I shall make my payment yf it pleas yow with the rest that yowre lordship hathe at sundrie tymes to my great furtherance and help in my causes sent me by yowre seruant and stuard [=steward] Billet.[3] I wowld be lothe to have trobled yowre lordship with so muche yf I were not kept here bake [=back] with this tedious sut, from London, where I wowld have found means to have taken vp so muche to have serued my turne tyll her magestie had dispached me, but for that I dare not, hauinge bene here so longe, and the matter growinge to sume conclusion, be absent. I pray yowre lordship beare with me, that at this time wherin I am to set my self in order I doo become so troblesume

Burghley's response, noted in his endorsement, was to lend Oxford half of the requested £200. As Oxford himself reports, this was only one of a succession of such loans.

Finally, on 26 June, Elizabeth granted Oxford £1000 per annum under a Privy Seal Warrant, to be paid in quarterly instalments:[4]

> Elizabeth etc., to the Treasurer and Chamberlains of our Exchequer, Greeting. We will and command you of Our treasure being and remaining from time to time within the receipt of Our Exchequer, to deliver and pay, or cause to be delivered and paid, unto Our right trusty and well beloved Cousin the Earl of Oxford, or to his assigns sufficiently authorised by him, the sum of One Thousand Pounds good and lawful money of England The same to be yearly delivered and paid unto Our said Cousin at four terms of the year by even portions [beginning at the Feast of the Annunciation last past]: and so to be continued unto him during Our pleasure, or until such time as he shall be by Us otherwise provided for to be in some manner relieved; at what time Our pleasure is that this payment of One Thousand Pounds yearly to Our said Cousin in manner above specified shall cease. And for the same or any part thereof, Our further will and commandment is that neither the said Earl nor his assigns nor his or their executors nor any of them shall by way of account, imprest, or any other way whatsoever be charged towards Us, Our heirs or successors. And these Our letters shall be your sufficient warrant and discharge in that behalf. Given under Our Privy Seal at Our Manor of Greenwich, the six and twentieth day of June in the eight and twentieth year of Our reign.

Because the grant was made retroactive to 25 March 1586, Oxford received an initial payment of £500 on 26 June, £250 per quarter thereafter. The annuity was not a payment for services, but an exemplification of 'the necessity in Princes to maintain their own creations'.[5] Though the grant was to remain in effect 'until such time as he shall be by Us otherwise provided for to be in some manner relieved', it was continued to Oxford's dying day – and beyond.

That the purpose of the annuity was to keep the wolf from Oxford's door is expressed in a manuscript composed by Thomas Wilson near the end of Oxford's life:[6]

> haveing ... prodigally spent and consumed all even to the selling of the stones timber and lead of his castles and howses, ... yett he liveth and hath the first place amongst Earles, but the Queen is his gracious Mistress and gives him maintaynance for his nobilty sake, but (to say the truth) out of the Bishoprick of Ely, which since his decay co[u]ld never see other Bishope.

Thomas Thirlby, nominated to Ely under Mary on 10 July 1554, and formally provided on 21 June 1555, was deprived under Elizabeth on 5 July 1559, and died on 26 August 1570. The Protestant Richard Cox was nominated to the see on 15 July 1559, and consecrated on 21 December of the same year. After Cox's death on 22 July 1581 the see remained vacant. Christopher Hatton was granted control of the Bishop of Ely's magnificent residence in Holborn, while Oxford was now granted £1000 per year. (Since a new bishop – Martin Heton – was nominated to the see of Ely in December 1599,[7] we may safely infer that Wilson's paragraph on Oxford was composed in November 1599 at the latest.)

A similar understanding of Oxford's annuity is advanced in a letter of 20 August 1604, written soon after Oxford's death by his dowager Countess (Elizabeth Trentham) to Robert Cecil, who from this point forward I will identify simply as 'Cecil':[8]

> Your Lordship may truly inform his highness that the pension of a thousand pounds was not given by the late Queen to my Lord for his life, and then to determine, but to continue until she might raise his decay by some better provision.

In 1604 King James wrote to Cecil concerning an appeal for an annuity by Baron Sheffield:[9]

> … and as I had already told him, never greater gift of that nature was given in England. Great Oxford when his state was whole [=wholly] ruined got no more of the late Queen …

Thus James, on the understanding that the annuity was to repair Oxford's estate, would continue the grant into the next generation, though at a reduced rate.

On 30 June the prisoner Stephen Le Sieur wrote to Walsingham from Dunkirk:[10]

> What exclamations there are here upon such Englishmen as have been here prisoners and now gone, specially my lord of Oxford's gentlemen, (this bearer can tell you, and all other things of these parts, for he hath thoroughly tasted both of the sweet and sour).

Oxford's men seem to have been particularly troublesome cell-mates. Though Hyham and Terry had gained their freedom, Thomas Whithead remained a prisoner.

On 27 September the commission for the trial of Mary Queen of Scots assembled at Westminster. Details appear in 'The Conference or Commyssone between the Quene of Scottes and the Lordes, concerninge her examinacion'.[11]

> Upon Wednesdaie, the 12 of October, the Lordes Commissioners for hearinge the Scottishe Quene came to the Castle of Fotheringhey, in the County of Northampton, about nyne of the clocke in the morninge …

> Upon Thursdaie there wente unto her, in her lodginge, the Lord Chauncellor, the Lord Treasourer, the Earles of Oxforde, Shresburie, Kente, Worcester, Viscount Montague, the Lordes Zouche, Graye, Lumley, Sir Raphe Sadler, Sir James Crofte, Mr. Vicechamberlaine, Sir Amias Pawlette, the two Chief Justices of England, Doctor Dale, and Doctor Forde, Barker, and Wheler, notaries, who remained with her allmost the space of two houres, signifyinge unto her that yf shee woulde not come furthe before the Commissioners they woulde proceede againste her accordinge to ther Commissione. That whole daie was spente in Councell and sendinge unto her.

Yet another contemporary account specifically identifies Oxford as 'Lord great Chamberlaine'.[12] Among the 42 participants, Oxford was outranked only by the Marquess of Winchester.

Elizabeth's Seventh Parliament sat from 29 October until 2 December (*TE*). Oxford's presence is recorded on October 29, 31, and November 10, 19; his absence is recorded on November 4–5, 7–9, 15, 22, 25, 29, December 2, 15, February 22–23, 25, 27, March 2, 4, 6–9, 10, 13–18, 20–23.[13] In all, of 35 sessions Oxford attended four: on 10 November Oxford was appointed to a committee that was to address Elizabeth on the sentencing of Mary Queen of Scots.

59 No Enemy can Envy this Match

On 8 February 1587 Mary of Scotland was executed at Fotheringhay Castle. Whatever Oxford thought about the proceedings, he would gather at the trough with the rest, petitioning the English Queen for lands forfeited by Edward Jones, one of the Scottish Queen's attainted partisans.

On 12 March Stephen Le Sieur wrote to Walsingham from his prison in Dunkirk:[1]

> … However it fall out, I must beseech you for more money, that I may not have to stay here for want of it. If I had not been forced to pay 230fl for Captain Brackenbury; 112fl for Thomas Whithead, a gentleman of my lord of Oxford; and 50fl for one Robert Galeys, the fifty pounds your honour sent me of late would suffice. If those bound had care of their credit and thought upon God, they would long since have sent me the moneys with which I assisted them in their necessity.

Thomas Whithead, now openly identified as Oxford's man, had been ransomed, Le Sieur having put up the required 112fl. Brackenbury, Whithead, and Galeys had promised to secure Le Sieur's freedom once they made it back to England, but had reneged.

In April Oxford received four votes from eight Garter electors: Burghley, as usual, supported him; as usual, Oxford was passed over (G-BL). On 30 April Cecil wrote to Burghley:[2]

> … My Lady of Oxford hath willed me to desire your Lordship, if in your wisdom you think it may do any good, to impart her letter to your Lordship to the Queen, otherwise, according to your pleasure, to let it alone.

Apparently Anne hoped the Queen would persuade Oxford to provide adequately for their children. Burghley's letter of 5 May to Walsingham, which chiefly concerns Oxford's acquisition of attainted lands, touches incidentally and pathetically on Oxford's treatment of Anne in the sixteenth year of their marriage:[3]

> Sir although I am sure that yow will not omitt any convenient tyme to move hir Maiesty, to assent that hir Maiesties gift to my Lord of Oxford of Edward Iones landes and goodes might be perfected yet I was so vexed yesternight very late by some grevous sight of my poore daughters affliction, whom hir husband had in the

afternoone, so troubled, with wordes of reproch of me to hir, as though I had no care of hym, as I had to please others, naming Sir Walter Ralegh and my Lord of Cumberland whose bookes, I had spedely sollicited to pass, as she spent all the evening in dollor and weapyng. and though I did as much as I co[u]ld [to] comfort her with hope, yet she, being as she is great with child, and Contynvally afflicted, to behold the misery of hir husband, and of his children, to whom he will not leave, on[e] farthyng of land, for this purpose I can not forbeare, to renew this pitefull case, prayeng you to tak[e] some tyme, to have hir Maiesties resolvt[e] answer.

and for your Instruction to inform hir Maiesty of the vallev [=value] of the gift, I do send yow a bill conteaining the trew state therof, and I am prive [=privy] that ther hath bene layd ovt aboue 1C [=£100] by the Earles sollicitor at my request, above 1C xxL [=£120] for the charges of sondry inquisitions and Commisionars to serch out the truth of the thynges sovght with great labor to be concealed, with monny I feare must fall to my lott to paye.

No enemy I have can envy this match, for therby nether honour nor land nor goodes shall come to their children for whom being 3 already to be kept, and a 4th lyk to follow, I am only at chardg even with sondry famylyes in sondry places, for ther sustentation / but if ther father war of that good natur, as to be thankfull for the same, I wold be less greved with the burden / and so I will end an vncomfortable matter …

Burghley added a postscript:

If hir Maiesty will have Iones wiff considered, it may be provyded that she shall have an anuite of xxxli per annum

Enclosed with Burghley's letter was 'The Queen's Majesty's title to the lands called Penley in the county of Flint, late part of the possessions of Edward Jones, attainted'.

In this private letter to Walsingham, Burghley laments Oxford's behaviour at its most inhumane. Burghley's daughter, who had borne Oxford three daughters, as well as a son who had died in infancy, was now eight months pregnant with another child who, so far as Oxford knew, might be a son and heir. Nevertheless, he showered her with such verbal abuse that she spent the entire evening wracked with sobs. Thinking as usual only of himself, Oxford complained that Burghley had not supplied him with attainted lands as he had others, including Sir Walter Ralegh and George Clifford, 3rd Earl of Cumberland.

The three Vere daughters mentioned by Burghley were Elizabeth, Bridget, and the infant Frances (of whom more shortly); on 26 May Anne would give birth to yet another daughter, Susan.[4] Since Oxford had not made financial provision for his daughters, Burghley himself had borne the cost of their lodging and nurture. He tells Walsingham that he would have been satisfied if his son-in-law had at least expressed gratitude; but this was an emotion as foreign to Oxford's character as care for the mother of his children. By contrast, Burghley's deep humanity is revealed not only in his natural sympathy for his own flesh and blood, but in his sympathy for a stranger, the widow of Edward Jones, the Welshman who had been involved in the 'Babington Plot' and whose lands Oxford now coveted. Burghley ensured that despite the confiscation of her husband's estate, the woman would receive £30 per annum.

On 13 May Walsingham wrote to Burghley from Nonesuch to report success in obtaining the Queen's consent to Oxford's petition for Jones's lands:[5]

> I haue acquainted her Maiesty with the contentes of my Lord of Oxfordes late lettre, whom I found willing to passe his suyte vppon condicion that he shall assure vnto Iones his wydow an annuity of thirty poundes during her lyfe, to go out ether of thes landes or of some other landes of his Lordship that she shall lyke of, and that where her maiesty meant the graunte should haue past only to my Lord and to theires [=the heirs] of him and my Lady your daughter onlye / his Lordship desyring to haue the same to his heires generall in respect of his advauntag in the sale, shall assure to the Crowne in remaynder so much of some other of his landes wherfore yt maye please your Lordship to cause the book to be drawen accordinglye.

The Queen had proposed – perhaps at Burghley's suggestion – that the attainted lands should be inheritable by none but Oxford's issue by Anne. Oxford successfully objected that the restriction would inhibit any future sale of the land – evidence of his intention to liquidate the grant.

On the same day Burghley replied to Walsingham:[6]

> I hartely thank yow for yowr care had of my Lord of Oxfordes cause, wishyng his own care war the lyke to convert hir Maiesties goodnes, to his own benefitt, and in some part for his children, being thre doughters to be sene and pitted [=pitied], and a 4° [=fourth] / in his wyves body at hand shortly also with lyk pite to be sene. I fynd, that he hath a meaning to mak part sale of these landes to be gyven wherin sometyme he sayth he will follow my advise which was to convert the monny to the redemption of some of his own landes sold, which I know may be done, to be left amongst his poore children, with whom duryng my liff, he nether is nor shall be charged/.

> He hym self wold have these lands to be graunted from hir Maiesty in the name of ij others, for otherwise they will be lyable to his debtes at all tymes/ ...

> Concerning this latter clause, I mynd to send for on[e] Beston [=Beeston] whom my Lord vseth at this daye, and to cause hym to wayt vppon you for to determyn of the procedyng therin

> When the form is agreed on, I must pray yow, that my Lord of Oxford may perceave, that the makyng of the bookes may be directed from yow as by hir Maiesties order to Master attorney. for any thyng directed by me is subiect to his lewd servantes, who still vndo hym with flatteryes. ...

Oxford wanted Jones's lands held by agents, secure from his creditors.

On 17 May Oxford applied to the Queen for the post of gauger of vessels for beer and ale, a request he would pursue in vain for the next five years, until 9 January

1592.[7] On 1 July Oxford finally received the grant of the attainted lands. His two 'serjeants', or agents, were Cecil and Hugh Beeston:[8]

> Grant in fee simple to Robert Cecyll and Hugh Beeston the younger, serjeants of Edward, earl of Oxford, of lands ... all late of Edward Johnes attainted of treason ... At the suit of Edward, earl of Oxford.

Cecil would become increasingly important to Oxford over the years. Hugh Beeston's name will occur in various records to 1599.[9]

The favourable treatment Oxford received from the Queen on this and other occasions since 1583 may account for a piece of gossip retailed by John Poole, in Newgate Prison on suspicion of coining, to the agent John Gunstone on 25 July 'betwene x & xj of the clocke at nighte':[10]

> The Earle of Oxford he said the Quene did woe [=woo] him but he would not fall in at that tyme

The statement recalls (and confirms) boasts attributed to Oxford by Henry Howard and Charles Arundel in the 1570s.

On 12 September a baby girl was buried at the church of All Saints, Edmonton, just north of London:[11]

> Frauncis Vere filia Comittis Oxfordie

Though the date of birth of 'Frances Vere daughter of the Earl of Oxford' is unknown, she must have been between twelve and thirty-two months old at the time of her death.[12] Perhaps Anne had been dwelling near Edmonton at Pimms, one of Burghley's country residences.[13] Anne's three remaining daughers, Elizabeth, Bridget, and Susan, would all survive to womanhood.

On 15 December Burghley replied to a letter (since lost) in which Oxford complained (as he had complained to Anne) about his lack of advancement:[14]

> I receaued your lettre late yesternight when I was in such payne of my head as I scarsly co[u]ld read it much less answer it. I perceaue by it an opinion of your Lordships that yow think it hath bene and may be in my power, considering, as yow write, that the mannaging of all causes passeth throwgh my hands, to strengthen your estate: and therfore yow seeme to Inferr that the lack of your preferrment cometh of me for that yow co[u]ld neuer heare of any way prepared for yowr preferrment.
>
> My Lord for a direct answer I affirme for a trewth, and that to be well proued, that your Lordship mistaketh my power, how so euer yow say that I manage th'affayres: the troble wherof is laied vppon me, but no power to do my self, or any kin or freend any good: but rather Impeached, yea crossed; which I am tawght these many yeares paciently to Indure, yea to conceale.
>
> Secondly, that ther hath bene no waies prepared for your preferment I do vtterly deny, and can particulerly make it manifest by testimony of Counsailours, how

often I haue propownded wayes to preferr yow to seruices. but why these co[u]ld not take place I must not particulerly sett them downe in writing, lest either I discouer the hindrers, or offend your self in shewing th'allegations to impeach your Lordship from such preferrments.

And therfore if your Lordship please not to admitt my defence, by avouing to yowr Lordship on my faith afore God, that I haue at all tymes when occasion serued had your Lordship in remembrance to be vsed in honorable seruice; then I must content my self with the wrong yow do me in noting me as yow do very rowndly, that yow find yowr self by me little strenghthened in estate and nothing in frendship.

And so I conclude, my lord, that finding yow thus affected I mind not to dispute of this matter with yow by any writing, but wish yow such other freends as yow may be better perswaded of then yow ar[e] of me.

As for the matter of Iohn Wottons report of my speaches of your Lordship, wherwith all the Cowrt was full, that yow war offended with me I haue chardged Iohn Wotton therwith, who doth in a sort deny it; but if he sayd to your Lordship that I vsed any woord to yowr disgrace in counsaile I affirme to your Lordship that he lieth; and so with me do all the Counsailours that heard my speach, affirme him therin to haue belyed me. but I leaue him to his owne defence, and sory I am that your Lordship wold put him in a balance of Creditt against me, afore yow had heard of [from] me. yowr Lordship must take in good part my hasty writing for neyther my health nor my leisure doth permitt me to write so aduisedly, as otherwise the cawse requireth. and yet, my Lord, I hope I write nothing but that I may auowe howsoeuer yow may in your doubtfull mind of me otherwise Interprete it.

Burghley insists that some things are beyond his control, whatever Oxford may think. Particularly revealing is Burghley's explanation for not disclosing the identities of those who object to Oxford, or the nature of their objections: doing either might 'offend your self in shewing th'allegations'. Burghley reintroduces John Wotton from the 1573 Gravesend incident. Wotton 'doth in a sort deny' leaking Privy Council secrets, but Burghley calls him a liar, expressing sorrow that Oxford would take Wotton's word over his own.

During this same year, perhaps as the obverse of Elizabeth's willingness to enrich Oxford with royal annuities and attainted lands, a comprehensive plan was set in train to settle Oxford's debt to the Crown. On 30 April '[t]he rate for the purchasers of the Earles Landes was made', while on 29 November '[t]he decree was made whereby the Earles whole dette of MMMCCCvjli xviijs ixd qr [=£3306–18–9¼] was appoynted to be paide by the purchasers'. The debt was to be paid off over five years, finishing in 1592. Among the incumbered purchasers were Thomas Skinner, Sir Roger Townshend, John Glascock, Israel Amyce, Edward Hubbard, William Stebbing, John Mabbe, and Robert Plumbe.

Skinner, who had purchased Oxford's lands in Lavenham (Suffolk), the Camps (Cambridgeshire and Essex), and Fulmer (Buckinghamshire), would lease his interest in Lavenham to Arthur Milles on 13 April 1590, and his lands in Fulmer to Nicholas Minne on the following 3 August. He and Minne were to become defendants in a suit over Castle Camps brought by Christopher Marshall, executor of William Marshall, in the same year:[15]

> The castle of Campes, with the lands thereto belonging, being the demesnes of the manor of Campes, the inheritance of Edward de Vere earl of Oxford, and by him demised to Henry Goldinge and John Turner, and by them assigned to William Marshall the testator; the reversion of which premises being afterwards seised into the Queen's hands, under an extent, became vested in the defendants.

Skinner would die in 1596 possessed of his three Oxford properties.

60 Another Grissel for her Patience

Burghley notes in his retrospective Diary (ii, p. 787) that in January 1588, 'The Earl of Derby, Lord Cobham, Sir James Crofts, and Dr. Dale sent to Ostend to treat with Commissioners of the King of Spayne':

> And Robert Cecill, my Son, did attend upon them, and went to the Duke of Parma and to Antwerp.

This entry explains Cecil's presence in Ostend on 27 February, whence he wrote to Burghley:[1]

> If my lady of Oxford were here her beauty would quickly be marred, for when we sit in our poor lodging by the fire, we look all as pale and wan as ashes by the smoke of our turfs, which makes me envy your lordship's porter, that sits all day by a sweet fire of sea coal in your lodge. *Sed ferre quamsortem patiuntur omnes nemo recuset* [='But we must each bear the fate which is appointed us'].

Two days later Cecil sent another letter, with a separate message (now lost) for Oxford:[2]

> I have written to the Earl of Oxford and pray that my lady his wife may send it to him.

Cecil assumes that Anne is in touch with her (absent) husband. From Cecil's compliment to his sister's beauty and because he takes for granted that she will forward his letter, we may infer that she was in good health. Doubtless she was preoccupied with her three daughters, Elizabeth fourteen (the age at which Anne was engaged to Oxford), Bridget nearly four, and Susan not yet out of her first year.

In April, Oxford received votes from three of the seven electors for the Order of the Garter; as usual, Burghley was one of his backers (G-BL). As usual, Oxford was not appointed to the Order. In May, as Burghley noted in his retrospective Diary (ii, p. 788), Elizabeth re-granted Oxford two ancient properties:

A Graunt of the Priory of Earles Colne, and the Mannor of Colne in Essex, to the Earl of Oxford, and the Heyres of his Body, yelding the Rent of 66*l*.

Oxford had of course already sold these lands to Roger Harlackenden.

On 5 June, quite unexpectedly, Anne died at Greenwich, in her thirty-second year.[3] Her funeral is described by Sir William Dethicke, Garter King at Arms:[4]

She was interred in Wesminster Abbey on June 25th, attended by many persons of great quality and honour. The chief mourner was the Countess of Lincoln, supported by the Lords Windsor and Darcy, and her train borne by the Lady Stafford; and among other mourners at her funeral were the Ladies Russel, Elizabeth Vere, Willoughby, sister to the Earl of Oxford, Cobham, Lumley[,] Hunsdon, Cecil, wife to Sir Thomas Cecil. Six bannerets were borne by Michael Stanhope, Edward Wotton, Anthony Cooke, William Cecil, John Vere and Richard Cecil.

Conyers Read observes: 'It is not recorded that her husband was among those present'.[5]

The essential details of Anne's life and death are emblazoned on the Westminster Abbey tomb which Burghley erected in her memory:[6]

Anna Countess of Oxford, daughter of William Cecil baron of Burghley, was born 5 December 1556. She became the wife of Edward Vere, illustrious Earl of Oxford, in the 15th year of year of her life. From this union she became the mother of several sons, but left behind three surviving virgin daughters: Lady Elizabeth Vere aged 14; Lady Brigit Vere aged 5; and, third, an infant girl, Lady Susan. This Anna lived ever a modest maiden and a chaste wife, faithful in her love, a daughter wonderfully devoted to her parents in all exigencies, exceedingly diligent and devout in her devotion to God. Debilitated by a burning fever, in the hope of the power of heaven, she gave up her soul along with her spirit with most earnest prayers to God as her creator and redeemer, on 5 June 1588 in the palace of Queen Elizabeth at Greenwich.

Burghley's inscription provides the only evidence that Anne had given birth to more than one son. Her death seems to have affected Burghley more deeply than any other event in his life, leaving him '*in Crepusculo* ... a dark nyght afor[e] a black morning for me and myn'.[7]

A contemporary biographer records Burghley's attitude towards his children: 'to whom there was never man more loving nor tender hearted, and yet with so wise moderation and temper as he was inwardly more kind than outwardly fond of them'.[8] Of all his offspring, he was fondest of Anne, nor was grief over her death merely private. Burghley received notes of condolence on 7 June from P. Ortell, writing from London; on 18 June from Sir James Croft, writing from Bourborough in the Low Countries; and on 20 June from Peregrine Bertie, Lord Willoughby de Eresby, Oxford's brother-in-law.[9] On 17 June Henry Stanley, Earl of Derby, wrote from Bourborough:[10]

I take it as a special favour that notwithstanding your head is fully fraught with the affairs of the realm … [and the] late accident by God's order (which I do also mourn for) you have been pleased to send some few lines in your own hand. …

On 30 June Morgan Colman wrote to Burghley from The Hague:[11]

The cause of your lordship's sorrow has been very grievous to me, and has also fallen out unfortunately for my lord and his business, as I could not see you before my departure. I send the enclosed notes [not now with the letter], which, to prevent further danger I beseech you to consider. 'I find that my Lord [Willoughby] resolveth, and therefore have discharged my duty in declaring humbly how I find it.'

Thus word of Anne's death and Burghley's grief spread to the Continent.

Third-party correspondence similarly touched on Anne's death. On 13 June Philip Gawdy wrote his brother from London:[12]

… Brother I forgott to wryte to yow of the deathe of a great lady vppon Thursday last in the for[e]no[o]ne. My Lady of Oxforde dyed at the court, and is interred at Westminster. Ther is a great funerall a preparing and I neade not to wryte to you of the heauines and morning of her best frends. …

In an undated letter from the same period, Walsingham wrote to Lord Willoughby:[13]

… This should have been done from the court by reason of the death of the Lady Oxford; and the Lord Steward being also absent, her Majesty had desired me to write in her name that her pleasure is that you conform yourself thereto.

Evidently Anne's death temporarily interrupted life at court.

More than 40 memorial poems composed by admirers of Countess Anne survive among Burghley's papers,[14] one from the pen of Wilfred Samonde, 'written upon the death of the right honourable Lady Anne Countess of Oxford':[15]

For modesty a chaste Penelope,
Another Grissel for her patience,
Such patience as few but she can use,
Her Christian zeal unto the highest God,
Her humble duty to her worthy Queen,
Her reverence unto her aged Sire,
Her faithful love unto her noble Lord,
Her friendliness to those of equal state,
Her readiness to help the needy soul,
His worthy volume had been altered,
And filled with the praises of our Anne,
Who as she liv'd an Angel on the earth,
So like an Angel she doth sit on high,
On his right hand who gave her angel's shape.
Thrice happy womb wherein such seed was bred,

And happy father of so good a child,
And happy husband of so true a wife,
And happy earth for such a virtuous wight,
But happy she thus happily to die.
And now fair Dames cast off your mourning weeds,
Lament no more as though that she were dead,
For like a star she shineth in the skies,
And lends you light to follow her in life.

Much of the poem is conventional, but a notable sentiment, startling in a memorial poem, is the characterization of Anne as 'Another Grissel for her patience'. The story 'Patient Griselda' was one of the most popular of the European Renaissance, told by Boccaccio, Petrarch, and Chaucer (Clerk's Tale), and dramatized as *Patient Grissel* (1603: STC 6518). Griselda's husband, Walter, puts her to every manner of mental torment, taking her children from her, divorcing her, taking a younger woman as his second wife, requiring Griselda to serve as his new wife's handmaiden; but Griselda never protests in thought, word, or deed. If Anne is Griselda, Oxford is Walter, the abusive husband. As recently as May 1587, Oxford had abused Anne openly in the eighth month of her fifth pregnancy.

Whatever relief Oxford may have felt at being freed from a marriage that had been a drag on his liberty from its inception, he now faced a new crisis: at the age of thirty-seven he had not yet produced a male heir, and could not do so without acquiring a new wife.

61 Rid of my Lord Oxford

Even as Anne was laid to rest, a great Armada threatened England from across the Bay of Biscay. On 19 July 1588, about four weeks after Anne's interment, Spanish ships appeared off the coast of Cornwall and Devon.

The saga of the Spanish Armada is immense, surviving documentation vast. For our purposes it is enough to appreciate that the huge Spanish fleet was constantly harried by the English as it made its way along the south coast, prevented from landing at Portsmouth; it was then driven towards the sandbanks off Gravelines (near Calais) as it made a fruitless attempt to rendezvous with Parma, commander of Spanish land troops. A plan to tow barges full of Parma's men into the mouth of the Thames near Tilbury was thwarted not only by Parma's reluctance, but by the inherent difficulty of the enterprise, and by English fireships launched into the anchored Spanish fleet. By 29 July the Armada broke to the north, facing open seas, enormous distances, starvation, capture, and shipwreck, limping around Scotland and through the Irish Sea before finding safety in Spanish ports.

Evidence for Oxford's role in the battle of the Armada takes two separate forms: literary-historical reports and contemporary letters from Leicester. A modern recapitulation of the literary-historical thesis is given by Duff Hart-Davis, writing in 1988, the 'Armada Year':[1]

> ... a huge wave of patriotism had sent volunteers pouring into the ports along the south coast, many of them physically alerted by the thunder of the day's engagement, which had been audible for miles inland. Just as the Spanish noblemen now drifting helplessly up the Channel had been drawn to join the Armada by dreams of loot and glory, so now young English bloods came flocking (in Hakluyt's description) 'as unto a set field, where immortal fame and glory was to be attained, and faithful service performed unto their prince and country'.
>
> Chief among them were the Earls of Oxford, Northumberland and Cumberland, Sir Thomas and Sir Robert Cecil, Sir Walter Raleigh and Sir William Hatton, besides many other knights and gentlemen. With Lord Cumberland came young Robert Carey, later the 1st Earl of Monmouth, who described in his memoirs how, when 'the King of Spain's great Armado came upon our coast, thinking to devour us all', he and Cumberland took post horse and rode straight to Portsmouth, where they found a frigate which carried them to sea. For a whole day they sailed in search of the fleets, and, when they eventually sighted some ships, discovered they were in the middle of the enemy. 'Finding ourselves in the wrong, we tacked about, and in some short time got to our own fleet, which was not far from the other'. At first they went on board the *Ark*, but 'finding the ship much pestered [with people] and scant of cabins', they transferred to Captain Reyman's ship, where they were 'verry welcome, and much made of'.

Richard Hakluyt, cited briefly by Hart-Davis, provides even more detail in the second issue of the second edition of his *Principal Navigations* (1598–1600: STC 12626a, p. 599):

> In which number [of English men] there were many great and honourable personages, as namely, the Erles of Oxford, of Northumberland, of Cumberland, &c., with many Knights and Gentlemen: to wit, Sir Thomas Cecill, Sir Robert Cecill, Sir Walter Raleigh, Sir William Hatton, Sir Horatio Palauicini, Sir Henry Brooke, Sir Robert Carew, Sir Charles Blunt, Master Ambrose Willoughbie, Master Henry Nowell, Master Thomas Gerard, Master Henry Dudley, Master Edward Darcie, Master Arthur Gorge, Master Thomas Woodhouse, Master William Haruie, &c. And so it came to passe that the number of the English shippes amounted vnto an hundreth ...

Hakluyt's source, and the source of the literary-historical tradition, including Stow (1615) and Camden (1625),[2] and even a pack of Restoration playing cards,[3] is a 1589 propaganda pamphlet entitled *An Answer to the vntruthes, pvblished and printed in Spaine*, by I. L., purportedly a translation of *Respvesta y Desengano contra las falsedades pvblicadas e impresas en Espana enbituperio de la Armada Inglesa* ..., attributed to D. F. R. de M., a Spaniard said to have sought refuge in

England after the collapse of the Armada. Both *Respvesta y Desengano* and *An Answer* were published by Thomas Cadman, and entered in the Stationer's Register on 1 February 1589 under the hand of Walsingham himself, with the notation, 'Written in the Spanish tonge by a Spaniard' (Arber, ii, p. 515).

The Spanish tract features a poem, 'Romanze en loor de la Nobleza Anglicana' ('A "romance" in praise of the English nobility'), with the following verses:

> Yllevan en la memoria,
> los hechos de sus pasados,
> para nose acobardar,
> mas mostrarse mas osados,
> Son los que ban de esta suerte,
> Caballeros muy Gallardos,
> el Conde de Cumberland,
> con valor y efuerzo estrano,
> Y el Conde de Oxford le sigue,
> Robusto mozo y osado ...

These and similar verses celebrate heroes whose names appear in the margins: Conde de Cumberland; Conde de Oxford; Conde de Nortumberland; Sir Horatio Palavicino; Sir Thomas Cecil; Sir Guillelmo Hatton; Sir Carlos Blunt; Sir Walter Ralegh; M. Henrique Brook; M. Artur Gorge; Lord Dudley; M. Thomas Gerardo; M. Roberto Cecil; M. Guillem Cecil; M. Roberto Carie; M. Roberto Harvy; M. Edwardo Darcey.

An Answer contains two purported translations of the Spanish verse. The first, 'A song in praise of the English Nobilitie', follows the Spanish closely but without any attempt at rhyme (p. 49):

> They print in their memorie, the facts of their forefathers,
> to shew themselves no cowards, but bold, fierce, and stout,
> And they, who thus do go are Gentles passing brave,
> the Earles of Oxford, Northumberland, & Cumberland ...

The second purported translation, 'The translator to the same effect', supplies rhyme and epic touches (p. 52 – 'Earle of Oxford' in left margin):

> De-Vere whose fame, and loyaltie hath pearst,
> The Tuscan clime, and through the Belgike lands,
> By winged Fame, for valor is rehearst:
> Like warlike Mars upon the hatches stands,
> His tusked Bore gan fome for inwarde ire,
> While Pallas fild his breast, with warlike fire.

... and so forth.

How seriously are we to take the poems by D. F. R. de M. and I. L.? They have, unsurprisingly, been taken very seriously indeed, particularly by Ward (p. 291, n 1):

The graphic description of the Earl 'standing on the hatches' with the Boar on his helmet 'foaming for inward ire' conveys the impression that the ballad was written by someone who actually saw Oxford standing in full armour on the deck of his ship. There could hardly have been a more likely eye-witness than John Lyly, Oxford's private secretary. Lyly always signed his name 'Ihon Lyllie', whence no doubt the initials 'I. L.' of the author of the ballad.

The most recent edition of the *Short Title Catalogue* identifies I. L. not as John Lyly but as James Lea; the description of Oxford, furthermore, is entirely conventional.

John Knox Laughton, the nineteenth-century scholar who assembled more Armada documents than anyone before or since, considered the list of noble warriors in the literary-historical tradition, especially in Camden:[4]

> Of these, only three are mentioned in these papers as having joined the fleet: – the Earl of Cumberland, Charles Blount, and Thomas Gerard. Robert Cecill was at Dover, writing to his father, and, on the 30th of July, neither was nor had been on board any of the ships. That Oxford, Burghley's son-in-law, or Thomas Cecill, Burghley's son; that Northumberland, Seymour's first cousin; Robert Carey, Howard's brother-in-law, and Sir Walter Ralegh, a man of high repute and official rank, could be in the fleet and not be once mentioned by Howard, by Robert Cecill, by Seymour, or by any of the correspondents of Burghley and Walsyngham, or by these, would seem incredible if we had not Robert Carey's own statement to the effect that, at the battle of Gravelines, he was on board the E[lizabeth] Bonaventure. It must therefore be admitted as possible that the others were also in the fleet, though – without corroborative testimony – it remains extremely improbable. That Ralegh had a command in the fleet and 'led a squadron as rear-admiral'[5] is virtually contradicted by the evidence now before us.

Even Hart-Davis concedes:

> … In fact the last thing that the Lord Admiral needed was a rush of enthusiastic amateurs, who could only get in the way, whether they came aboard the ships already with the fleet or put out to join it in small vessels of their own. What he did need, desperately, was powder and shot …

Even earlier than *An Answer* or *Respvesta y Desengano*, and the source of their lists of Armada heroes, is *The Copy of a Letter sent out of England to Don Bernardino de Mendoza, Ambassador in France for the King of Spain, declaring the State of England*, carrying the publication date 1588 and thus published before 25 March 1589. The first edition (STC 15412) was quickly followed by two more in English (15413, 15413.5); by a French translation (15414.2) with another issue (15414.3) and second edition (15414.4); by at least two more French editions without imprints (15414.4, note); and by an Italian translation (15414.6), purportedly from the French but in fact from the English. All these imprints are dated 1588; all except the Italian translation were printed in London by J. Vautrollier for Richard Field. A near-contemporary of Shakespeare and like him an import from Stratford-on-

Avon, Field served under the Huguenot printer Thomas Vautrollier, and married his widow Jaklin (Jacqueline).[6] With his knowledge of printing and her knowledge of French, Richard and Jaklin Field were the ideal couple to handle pamphlets aimed at both an English and a French readership.

Conyers Read notes that 'A large part of the pamphlet was devoted to the demonstrated loyalty of the English Catholics'.[7] Thus the earls of Northumberland and Cumberland, both suspected of harbouring Catholic sympathies (*Peerage*), are praised for their eager opposition to the Armada. Oxford is named separately (the 'voice' is that of a presumed Spaniard):

> And yet to make it more manifest, how earnest all sorts of Noblemen and Gentlemen, were to aduenture their liues in this seruice, it is reported, that the Earle of Oxford, who is one of the most auncient Earles of this land, went also to the Sea, to serue in the Queenes Armie. There went also for the same purpose, a second sonne of the Lord Treasurer called as I can remember, Robert Cecil: there went also about that time to the Seas, the Lord Dudley an auncient Baron of the Realm, and Sir Walter Ralegh a Gentleman of the Queenes Priuy Chamber, and in his company a great number of young Gentlemen, amongst whom I remember the names of the heire of Sir Thomas Cecil, called William Cecil, of Edward Darcy, Arthure Gorge, and such others: with the rehearsall of whom I doe not comfort my selfe, but only to shew you, how farre we haue bene deceiued, to thinke that wee should haue had a partie here for vs, when as you see both by lande and by Sea, all sorts of men were so readie of their owne charges, without either commanndement, or entertainement, to aduenture their liues in defence of the Queene and the Realme.

The Spanish are thus berated, apparently by their own countryman, for thinking that the English nobility was ready to rise against the Queen and her Protestant advisers.

That the author of this pamphlet was not in fact a Spaniard but the quintessential Englishman Burghley is demonstrated by manuscript drafts among the Lansdowne papers in the British Library.[8] The pamphlet went through at least four stages of composition:

1) first draft, entirely in Burghley's own distinctive hand

2) fair copy of 1) in the hand of an amanuensis

3) corrections and insertions in 2) in Burghley's own hand

4) printed copy, dated 1588, with internal dates of August and September, probably printed in October

Oxford's name appears first at stage (3), in an interlineation in Burghley's hand (f. 161):

> the Erle of Oxford also in this tyme repayared to the sea co[a]st, for seruice of the Queen in the navy.

On the same page Thomas Cecil's name is added in much the same way, though by an even more tortured interlineation (italicized):

> amongst many others of the Lord tresorer ... *ther went the sonn and heyr* called Thomas Cecill ...

The text must have undergone at least one more revision at Burghley's hands, since the credit given to Oxford 'for seruice of the Queen in the navy' appears in print as service 'in the Queenes Armie', and Burghley's son Robert now appears for the first time. The qualification 'as I can remember' attached to both Robert and Thomas Cecil is clearly meant to disguise the fact that Burghley himself wrote the pamphlet.

Even more startling is an addition by Burghley at stage (3) which broadens his claim that the participants included 'the substance of all the Great lordes' of England (f. 161):

> ... saving the Erle of Arundell [=Philip Howard] who is in the towre for attemp-tyng to have fled owt of the realm, by provocation of hym that now is Cardinall Allyn [=William Allen] who howso ever he may be affected to the Catholique rellygion, yet I here [=hear] most certenly, that he offreth his liff, in defence of the Quene, ageynst all the world.

Here Burghley is caught in a flat lie, since several months later, in early 1589, the House of Lords, Burghley and Oxford among them, found Arundel guilty of high treason for praying for the success of the Armada while imprisoned in the Tower. In short, Burghley added the names of Oxford and others not in the interest of historical accuracy, but as part of a deliberate disinformation campaign meant to persuade England's enemies that the Queen received unanimous support from her nobles during the battle of the Armada.

Oxford's actual movements are disclosed in two letters, the first on 28 July from Leicester at Tilbury to Walsingham in London:[9]

> Your other lettre concerned my lord of Oxford who was with me as he went, and returnyd ageyn yesterday by me with Captain Huntley in his company. he semed only his voyag was to have gonn, to my lord Admyrall, & at his retourn semed also to retorn ageyn hether to me this day from London whether [=whither] he went yesternight for his armour & furnyture. yf he come I wold know from you what I shall doe. I trust he be fre to goe to the enymy for he semes most wylling to hazard his lyfe in this quarrell.

Since Oxford had 'returned again' to Tilbury on the 27th, he must have been there previously, perhaps on the 25th or 26th, having sought out the Lord Admiral in London in the interim. Returning to Tilbury on the 27th, he left again to fetch his 'armour and furniture'. Oxford struck Leicester as 'most willing to hazard his life in this quarrel' and Leicester sought Walsingham's advice on how best to use him.

In the same letter Leicester reported that the Spanish fleet was off Boulogne, visible from English shores. Further, of 5000 fresh soldiers who had recently come under his command he intended to send 500 Essex men to Harwich. Among Leicester's papers from this time is a chart of the Thames estuary, with Harwich the most northerly point shown on the coastline.[10] Harwich was the last deep-water port available to the Spanish as they broke out toward the North Sea. Lord Admiral Howard later wrote to Burghley:[11]

> On Wednesday last I went to Harwich which I had not seen this 27 years. My Lord, it is a place to make much of for the haven hath not its fellow in all respects not in this realm and especially as long as we have such enemies so near in the Low Countries ... My Lord, we can bring all the ships that her Majesty hath around there ... I know not that we can do so in any place elswhere but here in Chatham.

Frobisher had embarked from Harwich; an investigation of its readiness for defence had been undertaken in 1585, while in August 1587

> the Earl of Warwick asked for 19 guns for defence, and in November it was estimated that £1,288 was needed to repair the old walls, construct a palisade to defend the quays, and a stone bulwark which would defend the port and scour the haven. ... when old Harbottle Grimston was writing from Bradfield in 1643 asking for £100 to fortify Harwich, he recalled that in 1588, the year of the Armada, new defences were constructed 'with not less than 46 great guns upon them', and there were 17,000 soldiers. Sir Harbottle was on the *Ark Royal* which lay at Harwich, and which, he believed, 'would have done more good service than all the land forces'.

Indeed, the *Ark Royal*, commanded by Thomas Grey, took up its last defensive position of the Armada battle at Harwich. As the battle drew to a close, Harwich required an able governor.

On 1 August Leicester wrote again to Walsingham:[12]

> I did as hir maiestie lyked well of deleuer to my Lord of Oxford hir gratious concent of his willingnnes to serve her. And for that he was content to serve here [=her] amonge the formost as he semed, she was pleased that he shuld have the gouerment of Harwich & all those that ar[e] apointed to attend that place which should be ijM [=2000] men. A place of trust & of great daunger. My Lord semed at the first to lyke well of yt, afterward he cam to me & told me he thought that place of no servyce nor credytt, and therefore he wold to the court and vnderstand hir maiesties further pleasur to which I wold not be ageinst / but I must desier you as I know hir maiestie wyll also mak[e] him know that yt was of good grace to apoint that place to him having no more experience than he hath. and then to vse the matter as you shall think good. for my none [=my own] part being gladder to be rydd of him than to haue him but only to have him, contented. which now I finde wyll be harder than I tooke yt & denyeth all his former offers he made to serve rather than not to be sene to be Imployed at this tyme & I pray you Inform her maiestie hereof that she may gyve him such answer as ys fytt ...

Leicester finished off his letter with a postscript:

> I am gladd I am rydd of my Lord Oxford, seing he refuseth this & I pray you lett
> me not be pressed any more for him what sute so euer he mak[e]

Thus Oxford positively refused a post in the Armada campaign – an ironic develop-
ment in the light of his declaration to Burghley in his letter of 22 September 1572
that he hoped to be 'imploide on the sea costes, to be in a redines withe my
contrie man against any invasione'.

Clearly Oxford's motivation was pique – as in the 1585 campaign in the Low
Countries – rather than cowardice or subversion; but pique cannot excuse a
refusal to obey a superior officer in time of war. Supervision of the coastal defences
of Essex was a hereditary obligation, accepted by Oxford's father over virtually
the whole of his tenure as 16th Earl.[13] The 17th Earl, by contrast, was so indifferent to his military responsibilities that the defence of Essex had long been left to
others.[14]

William Segar's 1602 *Honor Military, and Civil* specifies the military penalty
for disobedience (p. 15):

> Touching contumacie, or disobedience, the law determineth, that whosoeuer
> refuseth or omitteth to execute that which the General commandeth, or doth what
> he forbiddeth, ought to be punished by passinge the pikes; yea though he hath
> effected what he would ...

Oxford should have been made to run the gauntlet for refusing to obey
Leicester's order.

Oxford was not only excused his dereliction, but lionized, as revealed in a
ballad celebrating a service of Thanksgiving at St Paul's Cathedral: 'A joyful
ballad of the Royal entrance of Queen Elizabeth into the City of London, the
24th of November in the thirty-first year of Her Majesty's reign, to give God
praise for the overthrow of the Spaniards':[15]

> An hundreth knights and gentlemen did first before her ride,
> On gallant fair and stately steeds their servants by their side;
> The Aldermen in scarlet gowns did after take their place;
> Then rode her Highness trumpeters sounding before her Grace ...

> The noble Lord High Chancellor nigh gravely rode in place;
> The Archbishop of Canterbury before her Royal Grace.
> The Lord Ambassador of France and all his gentlemen
> In velvet black among the Lords did take his place as then. ...

> The Lord Marquess of Winchester bare-headed there was seen,
> Who bare the sword in comely sort before our noble Queen;
> The noble Earl of Oxford then High Chamberlain of England
> Rode right before Her Majesty his bonnet in his hand. ...

And afterwards unto Paul's Cross she did directly pass,
There by the Bishop of Salisbury a sermon preached was.
The Earl of Oxford opening then the windows for her Grace,
The Children of the Hospital she saw before her face. ...

A contemporary plan confirms the seating arrangements in St Paul's:[16]

Lord Great Chamberlain of England (left) || Earle Marshall of England (right)

In private the Queen did not forget the truth: while she lived, Oxford never
received another vote for the Order of the Garter.

62 City House, Country House

On 20 December 1588, the danger from the Armada past, Sir Thomas Cornwallis
replied to a letter from Burghley on the infinitely more mundane subject of his
son William's purchase of Fisher's Folly:[1]

> I have lyved to[o] longe to se[e] nothyng but new trubles & greaves [=griefs] to
> dysquiet my oulde yeres, beyng latlye made tunderstande yow ar dyspleasyd with
> my Sonne for the bargen made with my Lord of Oxforde, wherein yf he do not
> satysfye yowr Lordship when he may aweyght [=await] vpon yow, he hathe
> deceyvyd me, but most hymselfe. but for my parte I meane not to enter the defence
> of my Sonnes action, as wone [=one] not pryvye what hathe passyd in the mater:
> And therfor hope yowr Lordship wyll not Impute hys rasheness & wante of
> regarde, to me, who in all my lyfe dyd never adventure vpon a mater of lesse weyght
> then thys, wythout muche longer tyme to loke in to yt. I dyd dysswade boathe my
> Sonne & dawghter [=daughter-in-law] for dealyng with the purchase: but when
> ther will & fancye preveyled agenst my advyce, I kept my purse frome the loone or
> gyfte of eny penny towardes yt. besides thys to shew my indysposytion to the
> bargeyn, I protest that I never sawe nor herde eny parte of thassurance which hathe
> passyd betwene Therle & my Sonne, thowghe summe of the same were offeryd me
> to vew. Thys ys the playne & symple truthe of my knowlege, assent, or advyse in
> the mater: If yt be otherwyse, let me feele as muche of yowr dyspleasure, as I have
> done ease & comfort of yowr favor. And good my Lord have yowr wontyd opinion
> & concept [=conceit, estimation] of me, & thynk me not so dotyng & folyshe in
> my age, that for thatteynyng of Fysheres Follye, I woulde once but put in adventure
> to loose the goode wyll & favor which I have ever fownde towardes me sithe owr
> fyrst acquayntance, but especyally in the change of tyme when I most neadyd yt.
>
> I humblye beseache Ihesu delyuer yowr Lordship of the greate peynes which I here
> [=hear] yowr [sic] ar[e] vexid with at this tyme, & sende yow longe & happye lyfe

Apparently the sale of Fisher's Folly had been concealed from Burghley, who had
been keeping his eye on Oxford's assets for the sake both of his grand-daughters

and of the Queen. On 31 December Sir Thomas wrote to Burghley once more:[2]

> I received yowr lettres with more comfort to my selfe then now I can answer them: for I fynde my Sonne & hys wyffe so addyctyd to lyve aboute thys Cytye, as I have cawse to thynke the coste done vpon my howse in the cuntrey to be evell bestowyd.
>
> If after meny ernest perswasyones, & profytable offeres made by me, they coulde have framyd ther fancyes agreable to my dysposytion to leade a cuntrey lyfe, they had avoyed some perylles in courte, & bene better in value in lande & goodes by 6000li at the leaste. I acquayntyd my Sonne with the partes of yowr lettres, but he wyll not confesse eny entent or knowlege to defeate eny purpose of yowr lordship ffor the secresye he vsyd, he alleggythe some reasones: but for the hastye con-clusyon, he layethe yt wholly vpon my Lord of Oxenforde. but my Lord yf he do not content yow better in thys mater, wherby he may recover yowr wontyd favor I have ernestly assuryd hym he shall mysse of myne.
>
> And so prayng almyghtye God for the recovery of yowr helthe, & to sende yow a goode new yere, in token wheroff I present a poore rememberance by my servant the berer, & humbly take my leave.

Conceding that William was not without blame, Sir Thomas insisted that Oxford alone was responsible for the unusual haste of the transaction.

The transfer of Fisher's Folly from Oxford to Cornwallis is confirmed by the disappearance of Oxford's name from St Botolph's churchwarden's accounts, and the first appearance of Cornwallis's name in 1589–90:[3]

> Receaued of Mr Cornewallis for the charges of the Churche iiijs …
>
> Given among the poore of the parishe the monney received of Mr Cornwallis iiijs

For at least a year before his sale of Fisher's Folly, Oxford had kept a team of joiners busy there under the direction of Edward Johnson, whose 'servants' included John Bennett of the parish of Allhallowes Staninge in Marke Lane, London, and Thomas Harvey of the parish of 'Stebinheath' or Stepney, east of London.[4] The same team refurbished Oxford's new residence, Plaistow House (or Plaiston House) in the remote Essex village of the same name, about a mile and a half south of Halstead, not far from Earls Colne. Altogether the joiners worked some eight years (1588 to 1596), undertaking

> such worke as were appointed vnto them as in sawing wainscottes into leaues and in sawing wainscottes for Crestes & making dores of wainscott wainscotting of other places & <…> about Playstow howse and in much other such kind of worke

A witness to the works at Plaistow House was Robert Mefflin of the parishe of St Ethelburga within Bishopsgate, a leatherseller about twenty-seven years of age in 1589. In 1612 he deposed that he had known Edward Johnson 'verry well' and 'did knowe Edward the late Earle of Oxenforde deceassed for he was with him somtymes when the plainant was with him'. Further, 'he knoweth that the Late

Earle of Oxenforde was possessed of a house within the Countye of Essex called and knowne by the name of Playstowe house, and also of a house in Bishopsgate Streete called Fishers Follye. ... he knoweth [Johnson and his men] did woorke Ioyners woorke for the said Earle in the said houses for he was privie to the same'. Mefflin himself was probably one of 'Oxford's men'.

Queen Elizabeth's Eighth Parliament opened on 4 February 1589 and sat until 29 March (*TE*). Oxford's presence is recorded on February 4, 6(?), 10, 14, March 22; his absence is recorded on February 8, 15, 17–18, 20, 22, 24–25, 27, March 1, 3–6, 8, 10–11, 13–15, 17–21, 24–29.[5] Oxford was thus present for perhaps five of 35 sessions. He was present on 10 February when a bill concerning captains and soldiers, of which he himself was one of the commissioners, was read for the first time; he was present again at its second reading on the 14th, but absent on 22 February, the day of its third and final reading.

In his retrospective Diary, Burghley notes that in March the Crown turned its attentions to Philip Howard, Earl of Arundel (ii, p. 789):

> Erle of Arundel examyned at the Tower by the Lord Charles [Howard,] Lord Tresorer, &c.

On 7 April, by Burghley's dating in his retrospective Diary, the Earl was indicted for high treason (ii, p. 746):

> Philippus Comes Arundel condemnatur Westmonasterio per pares suos.

Oxford sat as one of the peers on 14 April when the formal charge was read in open court:[6]

> At the approach of the Spanish fleet, [Arundel] caused mass to be sung for its prosperity, and had prayers of 24 hours made for the success of the conflict expected at Calais. Whereupon, and by the contents of the bull which the Pope says he has caused to be executed at the solicitation of many principal noblemen, they concluded that he had conspired the invasion of the realm, and deprivation of the Queen, which is treason, and he was found guilty by his peers, Lord Derby, the Lord Treasurer, Marquis of Winchester, Earls of Oxford, Kent, Pembroke, Sussex, Lincoln, &c.

Though found guilty, Arundel was not executed, but lingered in the Tower until he died of natural causes – no doubt aggravated by his close confinement – in 1595.

Whatever satisfaction Burghley experienced with the successful prosecution, these were difficult days, for on 4 April his wife died:[7]

> Die Veneris inter horis 3 et 4 mane obdormit in Domino Mildreda, Domina Burgley.

'On Friday between 3 and 4 o'clock in the morning Mildred, Lady Burghley, fell asleep in the Lord.' She was buried at Westminster Abbey on the 21st:[8]

> Funeralia Mildredae Dominae Burghley: beata mortua, quae in Domino mortua est.

'The funeral ceremonies of Mildred, Lady Burghley: blessed is the dead who has died in the Lord.' Burghley erected a joint tomb for Mildred and Anne, announcing the present circumstances of his three grand-daughters:[9]

> Lady Elizabeth Vere, daughter of the most noble Edward Earl of Oxford and Anne his wife, daughter of Lord Burghley, born 2nd July 1575. She is 14 years old and grieves bitterly and not without cause for the loss of her grandmother and mother, but she feels happier because her most gracious Majesty has taken her into service as a Maid of Honour.

This is our first evidence of Lady Elizabeth's participation in court life.

> Lady Bridget Vere, born 6th April 1584, scarcely four years old … yet it was not without tears that she recognized that her mother had been taken away from her and shortly afterward her grandmother as well. It is not true to say that she was left an orphan seeing that her father is living and a most affectionate grandfather, who acts as her painstaking guardian.

> Lady Susan, born 26th May 1587, who was too young to recognize either her mother or her grandmother, but is beginning to recognize her most loving grandfather, who has the care of all these children, so that they may not be deprived either of a pious education or of a suitable upbringing.

Burghley, his household stripped by death of female leadership, assumed responsibility for raising Oxford's three daughters himself.

63 I Have not Had my Health

By 1590, the year he turned forty, Oxford's life had narrowed down to an agonizing pursuit of financial security. Having squandered his lands, his letters reflect an ever-increasing desperation, and – finally – resignation. William Segar's *Booke of Honor and Arms* of this year contains a chart (sig. Q1v) listing 'The names of those that are presentlie of the same most noble Order [of the Garter]'. Among the 20 members listed are 'Sir Christopher Hatton, Lord Chauncelor of England', and 'The Earle of Essex', twenty-two years of age and the Queen's new favourite – but not Oxford.

On 2 June Thomas Launcelott complained to Cecil that he had 'received the tithe of Duddleston, upon the report of his adversaries, at harder terms than he deserved':[1]

> … your worship must not thinke that I was so symple but I could haue gone too [=to] Typper my self to haue the thing passed / but that I respected your frendship

/ & Countenaunce / & specially for Duddleston / by cause yt concerned my Lord of Oxenford / nowe George Leigh for whom Hugh Beiston pleaded so earnestly / careth not ijd [='tuppence'] for the matter / Sir Ruland Haward in like sort / ...

While the exact issues are unclear, it is clear that Launcelott was concerned not to cross Oxford's interests, and that Oxford's sergeant Hugh Beeston was somehow involved.

On 16 June Burghley wrote to Attorney General Popham from Court:[2]

ffor that her Maiestie would be assured that the points conteined in the paper inclosed showld be duelie performed by the patentees for my Lord of Oxfordes landes, that such purchasers as by due Corse purchased anie of his Lordships Landes might not be trowbled thearebie: hir Maiestie therefore before the signing of the Booke would haue yt soe to be provided, either by the grawnt it self, or by sufficient Bond to that effect to be entred by the said Patentees: wherefore I praie yowe to Considre howe such assurance maie be best had for hir Maiesties satisfaccion, to be inserted in the Book, if the same be not alreadie sufficientlie expressed thearein, which if yt be than would yt more amplie be conteined in the dockett of the Booke, or by Bond of the Patentees, or by anie meanes yowe cann devise: vntill which assurance had I find hir Maiestie maketh difficultye, and will not be induced to signe the Bill. ...

The Crown was now attempting to enforce the 1587 agreement under which Oxford's debts to the Queen were to be paid by the purchasers of his lands.

On 15 July Sir Thomas Stanhope wrote to Burghley, denying rumours that he wished to marry his daughter Elizabeth – now fifteen – to Henry Wriothesley, 3rd Earl of Southampton, now Burghley's ward. In any case the match had been refused, as revealed by Southampton's mother: 'I doo not fynde a disposition in my sonne to be tyed as yet'.[3] According to the Jesuit Henry Garnet, writing in 1594:[4]

... the young Earl of Southampton refusing the Lady Vere payeth £5,000 of present money.

Elizabeth's feelings are not recorded, but as Southampton was famously good-looking, she may well have been disappointed.

On 5 August Oxford sought Burghley's help with several leases (LL-17):

... where I morgaged my lease of Auely to Mr Herdsone, and not as yet redemed, and now aswell for the supplye of my present wantes, as allso to haue sume thre hundred powndes of redye monye, to redeme certeyne leases at Henyngham [=Hedingham], whiche were gotten from me very vnresonablye, for diuers yeares yet induringe, and are of as good clere yerely walue, as my sayd leasse of Auely is, I therfore most earnestlye desyre yowre Lordship, to signefie yowre lickinge [=liking, approval] to me in wrightinge, to dispose of the sayd leas, at my plesure; otherwise ther is not any will deale wythe me for the same, nor for any part therofe, wherin I shall be greatlye behowldinge to yowre Lordship, as I am in all the rest of my whole estate.

He added a postscript:

> The lesse [=lease] dependethe vpon diuers casuallties, whiche lease I howld chieflye by yowre lordships fauoure, and the casualties, & defectes are as followe.
>
> First the lease is made by the name of the master and chapleynes callede the Hospitall of the Sauoye, where the corporatione is, the master & the chapleynes of the hospitall of the Sauoy, & not called the Sauoye, & therfore the lease supposed voyde.
>
> Secondlye Mr Paynes clayme, and pretendinge interest to the sayde leasse, dothe cost me on[e] hundred pownd by the yere to defende.
>
> Thirdly any creditoure of myne, to whome I am indetted, may by wryte of *elegit*, or *fyre facias*, or *leuare facias*,⁵ extend and sell the sayd leasse for a tryffell, and vtterly defait me therof. And I intend for 300l [=£300] in monye, to redeme leases of myne owne Lande, of a greater yerlye value.

In the more or less distant past Oxford had put out to mortgage his leases both on Avely and on certain properties at Hedingham. He now proposes to re-mortgage his lease on Avely, and to use the proceeds to clear his Hedingham mortgage. But the speculators to whom he had offered the Avely lease would not proceed until it was freed from three incumbrances: an irregularity in the wording of the legal title; a rival claim by a Mr Payne; and a threat that the current lease might be sold on the open market at less than its presumed value. Oxford assumes that Burghley has it in his power to resolve all three incumbrances; in addition, he seems to have been under a requirement to obtain Burghley's approval before disposing of any lease.

In return for renewing the Avely lease, speculators had promised Oxford ready cash to supply his present needs, plus the £300 required to buy back his leases at Hedingham. He explains to Burghley that in his youth he had sold his interests in the Hedingham properties for less than their value; now, by making a single payment of £300, he could recover leases worth more than £300 per annum. Burghley's response is unknown, but he doubtless realized that this was yet one more ploy by Oxford to milk his properties for ready cash.

On 8 September Oxford wrote again to Burghley from London, reporting optimistically on efforts undertaken by his servant Thomas Hampton (LL-18):

> I wowld haue bene wythe yowre Lordship before this, but that I have not had my helthe, Neuerthe lesse Hamptone beinge returned from the Contrie, I have sent him to yowre Lordship, that he may aduertis[e] [=inform] yow of his procedinges there. At Otlandes I thinke yowre Lordship remembers a complaynte, of (*blank*) Bellingiame sune [=Bellingham's son], of his mothers puttinge forthe of the castell, whiche was before any thinge done, whervpon yowre Lordship directed a letter vnto the sherife, <......> wherofe, as yt semes, Thomas Hamptone, hade delt wythe more fauoure towards her, then the letters vnto the Sherife imported. Notwythstandinge I

vnderstand Bellinggiame is gone to the Court, incoraged I know not by what friendes, to complayne, as he dyd report here in towne not to yowre Lordship, but to her Magesties self. My lord yt was ever ment that he showld have consideratione, as reason and conscience myght afford him. But sythence he taketh a violent course, and refusethe resonable offers, I have sent Hamptone to informe yowre Lordship, the state of the mane [=man], whoo hathe receyved hertofore a pardone for thre burglaries, and standes bownde to the good behavioure. whiche behavioure for sundrie and manyfest breches therof, whiche I cane prove, he hathe lost the benyfite of his pardone, wherby as Lord of the manner by eschete, I am to dele wythe him, as he hathe giuen me occasione, and herin I hope her Magestie will have consideratione, sythe the same case hathe bene sene once in Henry the seventhes tyme, and on[e] example in this her Magesties. for those thinges whiche fales [=falls] to me by eschet I do not dowt that her magestie will [not] agaynst her lave [=law] giue any eare, or harken to suche wrongfull complaynt.

Skinner hathe bene often wythe me, for a compositione: vpon what poynte of lav [=law] Hampton is to informe yowre Lordshipe, referringe my self wholly to yowre lordship who In all my causes I find myn honorable good Lord, and to dele more fatherly then friendly wythe me. for the whiche I doo acknowlege and ever will my self in most especiall wyse bownde. And wheras ther is a lease in Arthure Myles hande of the manner and Landes of Lauenhame, I desyre yowre Lordship to cause him to make ouer his truste vnto my seruant Minn, to whome the other lease is made. Yf therbe complayntes made vnto yowre Lordship as I dout not but that ther will, agaynst the procedinges of myne officers; I most ernestly desyre, that there may be sume resonable tyme appoynted for the answeringe of them, because my cowncel is not in towne, but shalbe before, or at the beginninge of the terme, to satisfies [=satisfy] yowre lordship and answer there particuler complayntes.

The lease on Castle Hedingham having been acquired by the deceased Henry Bellingham by indenture from Oxford, Bellingham's son is now in dispute with Bellingham's widow. Evidently young Bellingham had expelled his mother from the property. Oxford characterizes the young man as having taken 'a violent course', and having been responsible for three burglaries. Oxford's report that Bellingham 'refusethe resonable offers' suggests that he himself was trying to recover the property. Oxford had also attempted to recover Lavenham from Arthur Milles, using his servant Minn as an intermediary. Oxford is quite aware that his own officers have used threats of violence, and that complaints will be forthcoming: he asks Burghley not to react before he has had a chance to explain.

Oxford began his letter with an excuse for not coming to Burghley in person: 'I have not had my helthe'. Problems with his health were to be a constant refrain in Oxford's letters to the end of his life.

On 6 November Oxford's former servant Henry Lok penned a letter of appeal to Burghley from Edinburgh. The letter is long and not entirely comprehensible, but represents the confessions and complaints of a servant of long standing:[6]

Althowgh the coors [=course] of my life haue not bin so happy as to make me
known to yowr Lordship in that measure of desert which the duty I haue caried to
yowr person, and the reuerens [=reverence] I owe to yowr vertues, wold gladly haue
aforded: Yet the manifold experiens I haue of yowr honors beningne eare lent to
the petitions of many of meane woorth: maketh me bold by theas my Letters to
preuent the report of the caws [=cause] of this my abode in Scotland (which
comming by others might hap sownd the les fauorable) by deliuering to yowr
Lordship a trueth perticularly of my intent herein.

The rather for that it is not vnknown to yowr honor howe from my first enterans
into the world (now almost twenty years sins) I haue bent my self wholy to folowe
the seruis of the honorable Earl of Oxford. whos fauor shewn [=shone] sumtims so
gratiusly vppon me that my yong years weare easely drawn therby to accownpt it, as
impossible that the bewty therof shold be eclipsed; or bownty fr<...>les: wherof yet
(to make dowptful the first) I had the true president [=precedent] of many faln
before therfrom: But of the other am myself becum the onely example: as one who
may Iustifie by o[a]th to yowr honor (before whos gracius presens a falshud weare
very vnfitly vttered) that of all that euer folowed him I alone, neuer tasted of his
liberality by gift or any procurment of land, leas, or permanent gift of his own
<estates?> by his procurment nor in cloths, money, or any waye to the extent of one
hundred markes (for towhiching [=touching, concerning] the los of his Lordships
2000li ke<pt?> with Michael Lok, (which I haue herd my credit inc
ressed in for as
I repute the man far from purpos to desauie [=deceive]: so to acquit my self from
any intelligens with the practis vsed thairin saue in being a conducter of the mony
at time of paiment: I must be redy by o[a]th and otherwis to proue what I affirm,
(and his honor knoweth for true that Sir Martin Furbisher perswaded it, Edward
Fenton writ Letters and William Walters caried thaim betwen my Lord and my
vncle, til al was concluded during my absens in Lincolnshire with my Lord
Willowghby.)

Hauing therfore re[a]ped so litel benefit by his seruis wherin throwgh my own
indiscretion I haue vainly spent & browght to nothing aboue one hundred pownds
a yeare which I had to liue on and consumed al my yowth vnprofitably, neglecting
such better coorses as my best frendes thowght me more fit for: I of late (indede
to[o] late) resolued to stop the opinion of many, which thowght me among the
number of the ouermany gredy hors[e]le[a]ches which had sucked to[o] rauenusly
on his swete liberality (as indede his fauor and my acses [=access] had giuen me also
suffisient means to imitat thair example in, had I held it honest, or had it ben
agreable to my nature, & purpos in seruing him.)

And therfore I craue, of his honor, this fauor to be commanded by his lordship to
sum plase of seruis, or preferred otherwise to soom coors of life: by trauail in which
I might supply the necessitis of my life. Or els that it wold pleas his Lordship to
Infrancis[e] me of my former profession. And with my discharge to examen my
actions past, and such accownts as I had bin interessed in, aswell to discouer the
truth of things conserning my own delings; as to preuent any falshod which during
my absens might be by others vsed in thair accownts. And withall I made likwise
knowne a dept [=debt] of aboue fowrscore pownds, which is yet vnpaied vnto me

(throwgh the indirect deling of Aimes) sins his Lordships and his Ladies of good memories first being at owldfoord [=Old Ford] and Hiningam [=Hedingham] Park. which was forsed for howshold prouision to disbors [=disburse].

for in al the time from my first coomming to waight at yowr honors hows in Strand, til my withdrawing my self from daily attendans which was at Aimises: I neuer resaiued aboue 360li or nere thereabowts from any his Lordships officers. But was continually forsed, either to borow mony for his occasions, or by sutes (which yowr honor fauored him in) or by selling of chenis & niels⁷ of my own soomtims to furnish him. & I dare affirm to yowr honor that in all that time I neuer suffered one peny of dept to growe, for anithing spent abowt him or his, but kept I hope his proporsion of expens (considering the honorable coors he then tooke) within more resonable bownds then any my predesessor or sucsessor. And for the mony I borowed, I neuer intangled his lands or surtis [=sureties] any way. which considerations made me the more boldly to craue the restitution of this smale sum of mony due to me: which was the only remainder of al his depts grown in my time, and the best part of the stock of my decayed estate. which when I cowld not procure: neither yet (as a requital of my seruis, which I wold haue reputed it) I cowld haue my accownts examined, for which I had by Letters to his honor and by sute to Aimes, Lily, Mils, and al of credit with him often bin a sutor. I at length (being destitute of means for longar attendans on the sute) and seing that ther was no difference made from those which had most spoiled [=ruined] him, & theim who with silens had (as the prouerb saieth) faithfully serued: And considering how vnlikly it was for me in cort or contry to be preferred being by him discownteanced but that I lived to haue al the world behold dayly the losse of my former <...>nities: I chose therfore (as the les[ser] euel) to withdraw my self for a space, til that it showld pleas God, throwgh the reuolution of times, to minister means, and to towch the hart of soom honorable person with wil to procure my good: which wold to God might grow, by the seruis of my coontry in any honest caling for which I weare accownted fit, euen as I wold with al faith & diligens indeuor with any hasard or trauail to deserue the same: the rather to redeme the los of my former time. This right honorable is the truth of my estate & purpose, wherin if yowr Lordships gratius respect to a poore conuertite may induce yow to try the sinserity of my purpose, I hope yowr Lordship shal not repente yowr fauor altogether euel plased [=placed] on me, who wold continually (in supply of my defectiue desert) craue of God for yowr Lordships requital, the dayly increas of honor, & perpetuity of al happines.

Henry Lok, nephew of Michael Lok the mariner, must have begun his twenty-year career as Oxford's servant about 1570, when Oxford was still Burghley's ward. Henry's fellow servants over the years included Israel Amyce, John Lyly, and Arthur Milles. He seems to have left Oxford recently, taking temporary refuge with Amyce before escaping to Edinburgh. Though his service under Oxford had its moments of beauty, in retrospect it has led to financial disaster, as he has been forced over the years to assume personal debt in the discharge of Oxford's affairs. He has fled, perhaps not so much to escape his creditors as to avoid accumulating further indebtedness in Oxford's employ. But having taken refuge in Edinburgh, he fears the wrath Oxford habitually directs against servants who have left his employ without permission. Lok seeks repayment of 'aboue fowrscore pownds' (£80), unpaid for almost twenty years, and employment with Burghley or re-employment with Oxford.

64 Weary of an Unsettled Life

On 6 January 1591 Thomas Churchyard, now in his seventies, wrote to Julian (or Julia) Penn, mother of Baptist Hickes and of Michael Hickes, Burghley's private secretary. Mrs Penn was both a money-lender and the owner of a house on St Peter's Hill in London described thus by Stow:[1]

> a large House of antient Building, sometime belonging to the Abbot of St. Mary in York, and was his abiding House when he came to London.

Churchyard's letter concerns rooms he had taken on behalf of Oxford and his men:[2]

> good Mrs Pen I haue lovyngly & truelly dealtt with youe ffor the earll off Oxfford, a noble man off sutch worth, as I wyll employe all I haue to honor hys worthynes, So towtchyng whatt bargayn I maed & order taken ffrom hys own mowth ffor takyng som rowlms in your howse by quartter, affither the raett [=rate] off a hondreth pownds a yeer, (wyth sutch nessesaryes as I can naem) I stand to thatt bargayn, knowyng my good lord so noble (& off sutch greatt consytheracyon) thatt he wyll perfform whatt I promesed, in the hyghest degre off hys bowntty & becawse I allways syckly & reddy to partt ffrom thys vayn lyeff, wold neyther quyck nor dead se youe a lozar [=loser] by any off my dryfftts bargayns or doyngs, I absoluettly heer ffor the love & honor I owe to my lord, bynd mye selff & all I haue in the world vnto youe, ffor the satyesffyeng off youe ffor the ffyrst quartters rentt off the rowlms my lord dyd taek, & ffurther ffor the coells [=coals], bylletts, ffagotts, beer, wyen, & any other thyng spentt by hys honorable means, I bynd my selff to answer, yet conffessyng thatt napery & lynnen was nott in any bargayn I maed wyth youe ffor my lord, whych indeed I knoe my lords nobullnes wyll consyther, so Mrs Pen to sho[w] my selff honest in all my accyons, I yeld my bodye goods & lyberte ffreely vnto youe whyells [=whiles] youe do lyve, to vse by lawe & ryght as reason is tyl my good lord do satyesffye youe in all resonable poyntts & demands heer in in wyttnes off thys my true meanyng I putt to my hand & seall, to this myen own wryttyng, The syxtt off Ianuarye ensuyng The enttry & commmyng off my lord off Oxfford in to your howse/

The letter bears Churchyard's annotation: 'Maed & wrytten the syxtt off Ianuarye & delyvred as my deed in the presens off Mr Somnar off the Temple, Mr Harry Russell off London & Mr Babtyst Hycks off Cheap Syed'.

Because Oxford could not or would not produce the quarterly rent of £25, his aged servant Churchyard was compelled to assume the debt by taking a bond for £50 (double the amount of the obligation) on 24 December.³ The condition of the bond bears the same date:

> The condicion of this obligation ys suche that yf the abouebounden Thomas Churcheyard his heires executours or assignees or anie of them doe well and trulie content and paye or cause to bee contented and payde to the Withinnamed Iulian Penn her executors and assignees the somme of twentie and five pounds laufull money of Englande in or vpon the feast daye of Thannuncyacion of our Ladie the Virgin next ensuinge the date of these presents, at the nowe dwellinge house of the sayd Iulian one St Peters Hill in London aforsayde without fraude or further delaye that then this present obligacion to bee voide and of none effect, otherwise to stande in full force strengthe and vertue.

Churchyard promised the first quarter's rent of £25 by Lady Day, that is, by 25 March 1591.

As the required £25 was not forthcoming from Oxford, Churchyard took sanctuary, as he explains in an undated letter:⁴

> Good Mrs Pen I never dezarvd your dyspleasuer, & haue maed her maiestie vnderstand off my band towtchyng the earll, & ffor ffear off restyng [=of arrest] I lye in the senttuary, ffor albeit youe may ffavour me yett I kno I am in your danger / & am honest & true in all myen accyons, I ffynd in cowrtt cawses to fforsaek it, & the realm to[o], yett wold ear [=ere, before] I goe se youe & all my ffrynds well pleased, as knoeth God who bles & prezarve youe to his pleasuer

Since Mrs Penn understood that Oxford had left Churchyard in the lurch, she directed her reply to the Earl. Her orthography renders her message so obscure that I have 'translated' her letter into modern English:⁵

> My Lord of Oxford: The great grief and sorrow I have taken for your unkind dealing with me, which no man could make me believe (till I saw the deed) but all honour and virtue to be in your speech and dealing, you know I never sought assurance at your Lordship's hands, but Mr. Churchyard's bond (which I would be loth to trouble him for for your honour's sake). You know, my Lord, you had anything in my house whatsoever you or your men would demand, if it were in my house; if it had been a thousand times more I would have been glad to pleasure your Lordship withall. Therefore, good my Lord, deal with me in courtesy, for that you and I shall come at that dreadful day and give account for all your doing. My Lord, I thought to have been a suitor to that virtuous gentle-woman Mrs. Trentham, but I thought it not good (so to do) because I know not your Lordship's pleasure – I would be loth to offend your honour in anything. I trust I have not been burdensome to your honour, that I do know in anything [sic]; but, my Lord, if it please your Lordship to show me your favour in this suit, I shall be much bound to your honour, and you shall command me and my house or anything that is in it whensoever it shall please you. By one that prayeth for your Lordship's long life here and in time to come …

Oxford's purpose in renting rooms in Mrs Penn's house is unknown, but as he had been a bachelor since Anne's death in 1588, sold Fisher's Folly the same year, and maintained a remote residence in Plaistow, Essex, he probably required a London *pied à terre*. Mrs Penn's coy assertion that she had thought of approaching 'that virtuous gentle-woman Mrs. Trentham' – but decided against it – can only be understood in the light of what was to develop during the course of the year. Her statement that 'you had anything in my house whatsoever you or your men would demand, if it were in my house' may be sufficient cause for a raised eyebrow. In any case, Churchyard would survive another dozen years, outliving his younger master.

On 18 May 1591 Oxford wrote to Burghley inveighing against Thomas Hampton and Israel Amyce – for he had now fallen out with two more of his servants. He first thanks Burghley for having punished Hampton (LL-19):

> My Lord I doo thanke yowre Lordship for the punishment of Hamptone whose evill delinges towards me, beinge put in trust with my causes in Lave [=law], I hope yowre Lordship will thinke them sufficient to deserue yowre disgrace [=displeasure], especially knowinge his corruptiones, which for the more assured knowlege of yowre lordship, I have sent vnto the parties them selues, from whome he hathe dravne monye to his owne behofe. whose confirmationes so sone as they canbe brought out of the contrie, they shalbe deliuerd to yowre lordship. In the meane seasone I shall most hartely pray yowre lordship to perseuer in yowre good fauour towards me, wherby I may procure redres agaynst this which Amis hathe passed vnder the greate seale, by the practise of Hamptones fraudilent deuise, as shall appere, yf I may have lesure to manifest the same every day more and more. The changinge of the name of my seruant without my priuoyte [=knowledge], and putting in an other in trust for himself, as badd as I vnderstand as himself, yf yowre Lordship will, may giue yowre Lordship certeyne knowlege of the deceyt. The coseninge of so many tenantes of there monye, and the forfetinge of my lease of Skinners land, do wittnes inoughe his corruptione. I know yf yowre lordship will stand myne honorable good lord and friend herin, by handlinge this Hamptone ruflye, and this Amise so that he be but put in feare, that yow may bringe them to that order which is reasone, that I may enioy myne owne lands, as from the beginninge was ment by her magestie. And as for this letter of Amises which I have returned to yowre lordshipe, bothe concerninge my messages to him and the dealinge of my seruant, as he reportes is most fals.

Hampton had been Oxford's trusted agent as recently as September 1590. Israel Amyce had been lord of the manor at Tilbury Hall outside Tilbury-juxta-Clare since 1585. Here Oxford accuses Hampton of converting moneys – evidently rents – to his own use; testimony to this effect has been solicited from tenants of Oxford's lands and will be sent on to Burghley. Oxford further alleges that Thomas Skinner's lands remain unjustly in Amyce's possession – perhaps by collusion. Oxford continues:

> wherfore I will refer all to yowre lordship whoo knowes the intent of her Magesties first meninge to me, was far otherwise in the beginninge, when with this sut of myne, she thought to recompence me in sume sort, for forberinge my sute for the forest, and cane iuge how vnfaythfully I am delt wythall by thes parties.

Here Oxford reminds Burghley, and through him the Queen, of his claim to Waltham Forest in Essex (part of which survives today as Epping Forest). Although he had pressed his suit in the past, he now claims that the Queen had promised some particular reward if he would back off for the time being.

> Whiche fauoure yf yowre lordship shall doo for mee, then wowld I gladly breake vnto yowre Lordship an other matter which I wowld have done ere this, had I not bene intercepted by thes vnlokedfore [=un-looked-for] trobles. And this yt ys.

> Wheras I have h[e]ard, her magestie ment to sell vnto one Mideltone a marchent, and one Carmarden the demaines of Denbyghe, which as I ame informed is 230l by yerly rent, now as yt ys, I wowld be an humble suter to her magestie, that I myght have had this bargen payinge the 8000l, as they showld have done acceptinge for 5000l therofe the pencione which she hathe giuen me in the exchechore and the other 3000l the next terme, or vpon suche resonable dayes as her magestie wowld graunt me by her fauoure.

Now Oxford proposes to acquire Denbeigh, worth £230 per annum and currently for sale at £8000. He has not a penny of liquid capital, but proposes to relinquish his £1000 annuity for a one-time payment of £5000, and by taking a loan from the Queen for the remaining £3000. Oxford seems unfazed either by the fact that capitalization of a £1000 annuity at £5000 assumes an interest rate of 20%, or by the fact that he is asking for an interest-free loan from the Queen for the balance. Oxford continues in a kind of blackmail tactic:

> and further yf her magestie wowld not except the pencione for 5000l that then she wowld yet take vnto yt, to make yt vp that value, the tytell of the forest which by all counsell of lave [=law], and conscience is as good ryght vnto me as any other land in England. And I thinke her magestie makes no evil bargen, and I wowld be glad to be sure of sumthinge that were myne owne and that I myght poses [=possess]. Yf her magestie thinkethe it showld offend the tenantes, and for that she hathe graunted them a lease, yf they complayne or be agaynst yt, I will cease my sute. but yf I can get there goodwils, and that they shall lett there lease fall which her magestie hathe graunted, whervpon I dare presume to yowre lordship, then that her magestie will lett me have yt on those former conditiones. This is a thinge that I have bene desirous to impart vnto yowre lordship, but that I have ether found yow trobled with other busines, or I myself have ben incombred with thes trecheries of Hamptone.

Assuming the Queen will not capitalize his annuity, Oxford offers to relinquish his claim on Waltham Forest for the same £5000. If the Queen would agree, he would own one property – Denbeigh – outright.

Oxford now turns to the subject of his three daughters living under Burghley's guardianship:

> The effect herof is I wowld be glad to have an equall care with yowre Lordship ouer my children, and yf I may obteyne this resonable su[i]t of her magestie, grantinge me nothinge, but what she hathe done to others and mean persones, and nothinge but that I shall pay for yt, then, those lands which are in Essexe as Hedingeham, Brets and the rest what soever, which will come to sume 5 or 600*l* by yeare, vpon yowre Lordships frendly help towards my purchases, in Denbighe, shalbe presently deliverd in posessione to yow, for there vse. And so muche I am sure to make of thes demaynes for my self.

If Burghley will cooperate over Denbeigh, then Oxford will release his interests in Hedingham and Brets, which will produce £5–600 per annum to the use of his daughters.

> So shall my children be prouided for, my self atlenghe [=at length] setled in quiet, and I hope yowre lordship contented, remayninge no cause for yow to thinke me an evil father, nor any dout in me, but that I may enioy that friendship from yowre Lordship, that so nere a ma[t]che [=marriage], and not frutles, may laufully expect. good my Lord, thinke of this, and let me have bothe yowre furtherance, and councel, in this cause. for to tell trothe I am wery, of an vnsetled lyfe, which is the very pestilence that happens vnto courtiers, that propound to them selues no end of there tyme, therin bestowed. …

Oxford reveals in a subsequent letter of 25 October 1593 that, after subjecting him to a preliminary browbeating, the Queen heard him sympathetically at Somerset House, turning the Denbeigh proposal over to Sir Christopher Hatton for formal consideration. Hatton had apparently decided to support Oxford's request, but in the end the Queen would not give him audience. The Queen was not about to capitalize a grant whose distribution by quarterly increments was intended to force Oxford to conform to the pattern of a well-behaved earl.

On 30 June Oxford wrote to Burghley again on the subject of Thomas Hampton and land (LL-20):

> My very good Lord. I doo vnderstand by Mr Foscue [=Sir John Fortescue], yowre Lordshipes good dispositione, and willingnes to plesure me, in this my cause, wherin beinge deceyved by Hamptone, whome I dyd put in trust to followe the matter, forsomuche as he was the deuisor of the sute I sought remedie to her magestie that I myght have a neve [=new] lease to performe the first intentione of her graunte. In this I dyd not dout but to have had yowre Lordships fauoure, for that I was borne in hand by Hamptone that I showld haue a better lease. But I do finde his report was vntrue, and yowre Lordship not aduertised of myne estate. Now therfore I have sent vnto yowre Lordship a remembrance, wherby yowre Lordship may vnderstand how I have ben delt wythe. And I hope ther is no occasione giuen, but that yowre Lordship may bothe fauoure, and further, my matter as yow have ever done, being ryghtly informed. whiche beinge once ended

as I dout not by yowre Lordshipes good meanes, and her Magesties dispositione to succore me at this tyme. As I desyred of yowre Lordship by my letters when fyrst this troble began to breake out, whilst her Magestie was at Thebaldes so I remayne in every poynt to satisfies [=satisfy] yowre Lordship, to yowre content and my quiet. whiche I hope by thes feve [=few] lynes yow will conceyve. and I have included herin thes notes as briefly as I may. whiche also I have sent vnto her magestie for the better vnderstandinge how to giue me remide [=remedy]. Thus desyringe yowre Lordship to fauoure me at this present as yow have done in this sute and in others hertofore I will take my leave, remayninge yowre Lordshipes to Command.

Oxford's 'remembrance', written in his own hand, still accompanies his letter (LL-47).

It may please yowre Lordship to remember … At what tyme the Lord Chanceler was to giue vp his opinione to her Magestie concerninge my clayme to Walthame Forest, and Haueringe Parke, by her commandment I dyd let fall my sute, wythe promes of sume consideratione. Whervpon se[e]kinge for sume fytt sute, I craved this of Skinners whiche for thre causes her Magestie graunted.

fyrst in consideratione of her promes, then for the forberinge of Skynners felonie, whiche was proued by wittnesses examined, confessed by his fellowe Cacher and yet restinge in the hands of her Magesties Atturney. Last of all to disburden me of the 20000*l* bonds and statute which the same Skinner hade caused me to forfet, by procuringe his owne land to be extended for the 400*l* whiche he dyd agree wythe the rest of the purchasers to pay for his portione into the Cowrt of wardes mindinge to benifite himself by the same.

Now that yt may appeare to yowre Lordship that her magesties me[a]ninge [=intent] was to graunt me leases duringe the forfeture of a xjM [i.e., £11,000 – inserted in Burghley's hand] whiche my selfe had forfited in the Cowrt of wardes as apperethe of record, part of them for the rate of my Land whyle I was vnderage, and part of them for the fine of my mariage and suinge of my liuerie as they appeare by 12 seuerall obligationes, yowre Lordship must vnderstand, that I had no other meanes to saue my self agaynst the 20000*l* but by her magesties graunt <…….> foeffes of trust to my vse, to leuie that 11000*l* bands [=bonds], vpon Skiners Landes. And so to hold yt in lease tyll It were exspired. And to showe that her plesure was that my lord Chanceler and none of the other purchasers showld be trobled but those that were nominated, the names of suche as showld have there landes extended, were sett downe, of which number Skynner was the fyrst. And so gaue order to yowre Lordship to make me suche leases as yow myght doo by the vertue of yowre office her maiesties particuler fauoure and meninge beinge declared vnto yow.

Now my Lord at the first takinge of this land in lease, Thomas Hamptone beinge put in trust to followe the cause, after her Magesties graunt obteyned havinge an intentione bothe to gayne by me and Skinner, toke my leas out of the Court of Wardes for 400*l* whearas he showld have taken it for a 11000 and kept the lease from the lesse [=lessee] beringe me in hand that yt was a perfit lease duringe [*sic*] the sume of the 11000*l* At leng[t]he when yt showld come to the re[a]dinge in open

Court his falshodd apperinge, he made excuse that yowre Lordship wowld make no better tyll yow save [=saw] how this was vsed. Now findinge that he was not lekly [=likely] to make further commodite by thes extentes, havinge taken mony of all those with whome he delt And knowinge that the lease was to be ended when 400*l* were payed, went vnto Skynner and offerd him for the moyetie of his extentes and 13 hanginges [=tapestries?] to help him to his land agayne.

Now yowre Lordship may perceyve how this 11000*l* comes to be leuide [=levied] on his land whiche I desyre to have in lease, whiche I hope yowre Lordship will further, consideringe her magesties willingenes whiche she hathe vpon my motion signified vnto yowre Lordship.

Accompanying documents, and notes made by Burghley on both the letter and the memorandum, help to clarify this complex case. In round sums, Oxford owed the Crown £3000 for his wardship, £4000 for his livery (apparently including a relatively negligible 'fine' for his marriage), a pittance for rents still unpaid from the time of his minority, and £4445 in penalties – in effect, accumulated interest, for a total of £11,000 (rounded down to the nearest £1000). Against these Oxford had apparently signed bonds for £20,000 – approximately double his actual debt (following the normal rule for bonds).

In 1587, as we have seen, arrangements were made whereby Oxford's debt was to be discharged by those who had purchased his lands, including Skinner and Hampton. According to Burghley's figures, the original debt of over £7000 by June 1591 had been whittled down to £3100–18–0 plus penalties. On 23 July 1590 Oxford had signed a warrant to 'extend' eight new properties through the agency of Thomas Hampton, who acted or failed to act as follows (the date references are to 29 September 1590):

1) Extent returned Michaelis 32 Elizabethe Regine
2) Thextent delivered to Hampton, but by hym returned vnexequted
3) Extent returned Michaelis 32 Elizabethe Regine
4) Extent returned Michaelis 32 Elizabethe Regine
5) The extent staide
6) returned by Hampton vnexequted
7) Taken out by Hampton but not returned.
8) Thextente taken out by Hampton but not returned

Oxford felt that the irregular handling of the extents had put his finances in jeopardy. Moreover, Hampton had purchased from the Court of Wards for £400 leases (or extents) that jeopardized Oxford to the extent of £11,000. As we shall discover, Hampton would be punished – but lightly. Skinner, a London alderman resident in the parish of St Mary Magdalene, Milk Street, elected Lord Mayor in 1596, died in office, bequeathing lands that he had acquired from Oxford to his three sons.[6]

On 4 July Oxford sold ten acres of land in London, including a garden; his right to have purchased the garden in the first place was disputed long after his death:[7]

> Case of the Master and Fellows of Magdalen College, Cambridge, with reference to a tenement and 10 acres of land in the city of London, belonging to the said university. The college, by its foundation charter, has power to purchase only, and plead and be impleaded in any of the King's Courts, and to do all things according to the Statutes of Lord Audley their founder, of which one of the principal is, that all grants made by them for more than 10 years shall be void. Queen Elizabeth, by patent 29 January 1575, granted the said messuage and garden to Benedict Spinola and his heirs for ever, and the Statute of confirmation of grants made by and to Her Majesty was made in 1575. The premisses, by bargain and sale, came from Spinola to Edward Earl of Oxford, father of His Majesty's ward [i.e., of Henry de Vere, Oxford's son]; and Earl Edward, 4 July 1591, sold the same to John Wolley and Francis Trentham, to have the same assured to Trentham for life, and in default of such assurance, receive the rents for life, the reversion and remainder, and the entire fee simple, to be disposed of for the advantage of Elizabeth, sister of the said Francis Trentham.

Thus Spinola acquired the garden on 29 January 1575, subsequently selling it to Oxford. Since the property is described as 'the garden of Christes Church in the parish of St Buttolph London', we may suspect that it was acquired as part of the Fisher's Folly adventure, but not sold to Cornwallis in 1588. The receivers of the property sold on 4 July were John Wooley and Francis Trentham, 'to be disposed of for the advantage of Elizabeth, sister of the said Francis Trentham'. This Elizabeth Trentham – whom Mrs Penn described as 'that virtuous gentle-woman' – would soon become Oxford's second wife.

On 2 December Oxford alienated Castle Hedingham to Burghley in trust for Ladies Elizabeth, Bridget, and Susan Vere.[8] Before Burghley could take possession on behalf of his grand-daughters, however, the castle, its appendages, and many outbuildings were stripped or razed at Oxford's direction and on his warrant.[9] In 1599 Thomas Wilson recalled Oxford's recklessness, 'even to the selling of the stones timber and lead of his castles and howses'.[10] With the property finally under his control, Burghley engaged Oxford's estranged servant Israel Amyce to draw up an expert survey of the castle and its environs.[11]

PART X

Renewal
1592–1595

65 Mistress Elizabeth Trentham

On 5 April 1582 J. Farnham had written to Roger Manners:[1]

> … Mistress Trentham is as fair, Mistress Edgcumbe as modest, Mistress Radcliff as comely and Mistress Garrat as jolly as ever …

Now, almost ten years later, Elizabeth Trentham was no doubt still a beauty – but more importantly an heiress. Listed as a Maid of Honour on the subsidy roll of 10 November 1590, she had exchanged New Year's gifts with the Queen in 1584, 1588, 1589, and doubtless in intermediate years.[2] Elizabeth was the daughter of Thomas and Jane Trentham of Rocester, Staffordshire, whose offspring included at least three sons – Thomas (the heir), Francis, and Godfrey; and three daughters – Katherine (who married Sir John Stanhope), another (who married Mr William Cooper of Thurgarton), and Elizabeth. Jane had been a Snead (or Sneyd), from whom also came cousins William, Ralph, and Thomas, and perhaps Marie, now Mrs Marie Mynors.[3] On the marriage market for at least ten years, Elizabeth was not only far older than Anne Cecil had been at the time of her marriage, but far more independent. If Anne had been a dove, Elizabeth was a hawk. Oxford had met his match.

Evidence for the new marriage appears in a property transaction dated 2 March 1592:[4]

> A licence of alienacion to be graunted to Edwarde Erle of Oxford and Elizabeth his wief to aliene the Priorie of Water Belchampe alias Belchampe Water with thappurtenaunces and the tithes of corne haye wolle lambe wood and all other tithes oblacions obvercions and emolumentes whatsoever … to Frauncys Trentham Esqr and Raffe Sneade Esqr … The value by yere – viijli

Despite the alienation, Belchamp Water continued to provide current revenue.[5] Doubtless the sale of the London garden and of Water Belchamp rectory were legal manoeuvres to secure the properties from Oxford's creditors.

Oxford's wedding received royal recognition in an entry dated 23 November 1592 recording the Queen's gift of a gilt bowl with a cover at Oxford's marriage to

Mrs Elizabeth Trentham.[6] The wedding itself may be dated to 27 December 1591 (at the latest) from a record of the Queen's gift to the new Countess:[7]

geuen the Countess of Oxforde at her marridge the xxvij of December Anno 34°.

On 5 May 1592 Sir Henry Unton wrote to Burghley, using his French secretary Reziers as his bearer:[8]

For want of posts he had to send his letter of May 5 by his secretary, who once in Burghley's house instructed Lady Vere in French.

Rezier's pupil was doubtless Elizabeth Vere, still living under Burghley's guardian-ship. About June, Mary Harding sent marriage gossip to the Countess of Rutland from Court at Greenwich:[9]

I have h[e]ard of another motion, which is my Lord of Northumberland. Ther was ernest sute maide by my Lord Treaserer for my Lady Vear, but my Lady Veare hath answered her grandfather that she can not fancye him, and it is thought by dyvers [i.e., divers persons] that the matther weare very easy to be had for my Lady. It must be procured by your honour's meanes or some by your honour's procure-ment, for your honour doth know that such great matters must have meanes. Yf it happen, I hope your honour shall have great comfort, yf not, it can be noe dishonour unto her Ladyship, for ther must eyther of[f]ers be mayd, or else I fear me her Ladyship shall stay to[o] longe in this place. But she is in very great favoure with Her Majestie and is employed with the nearest service about her; for she carves at all tymes and is no way at commaundement but by her Majestie. All the rest of the ladyes and others doth like very well of her disposition. So I trust in God your Ladyship shall have much comfort, for she groweth every day better to be liked of.

Mary Harding added a postscript: 'I durst not make Mr. Roger Manners ac-quainted in thes matters because I thinke him so slowe'. The rejected suitor was Henry Percy, 3rd Earl of Northumberland, who two years later would marry the widow Dorothy Perrott, sister of Robert Devereux, Earl of Essex (*Peerage*).

Two years previously, on 17 July 1590, as noted in his retrospective Diary (ii, p. 794), Burghley had given 'the Custody of the Office of Controller of Wool in London to Doctor Foster, at the Request of the Lady Regine [=the Queen]'. This grant did not stop Oxford from applying in July 1592 for a licence to control the import of oils, fruits, and wools (LL-48):

My desire is to haue lycense from her Maiestie, for the bringing into the Realme of theis comodities followinge; and I will geive her Maiestie a yearly increase / as appeareth over and above her vsuall custome, viz. for

Oylles	CCli per Annum
ffrutes	lli
Woolles	CCli

notwithstanding ther are fyve years in D Actors [=Dr. Foster's?] grant yet to come. /

So that I do geive her a yearly increase of CCCCll [£450]

(*Oxford's hand takes over from an amanuensis*) The reasons of this sute.

Whearas after longe sute for the titell whiche I lay to the forest, yt was committed to the arbitrament of the Lord Chanceler, whoo hauinge h[e]ard the cause was redie to have made his report to her magestie. yt pleased her I showld lett falle the sute determininge to dispose therof at her plesure. in the mean seasone she promised to doo sumthinge for me in sume other matter. whervpon I preferred to her magestie the sute I hadd agaynst Skinner wherto she dyd graunt, and to that purpose I hadd diuers bookes dravne [=drawn (up)], but her maiestie dyd reiect them all. puttinge me over to my Lord Thresorer. whoo thowghe he dyd so muche as in him lay in my fauoure, yet it succeded not, wherby I lost all my charge, and ame to pay areareges to her magestie for the tyme that Skinners land was in myne handes. so that the consideratione which her magestie promised remaynes yet to be performede.

Ther is no sute, wherin I may lesse charge her magestie then in this, where I increase her magesties sume 450*l*

Thus I most humbly besche her magestie to have a fauorable consideratione also of my attendance here vpon her magestie, which I am not able to continue, yf by this meanes my charges bothe for the tyme past [=passed, spent] in followinge thatt matter of Skinners whiche succeded contrarie to myne expectatione, and other crosses of fortune, be not helped sythe I have ben so vnhappie that her magestie lekes [=likes] not that I showld seke the forest which by all councell in laue [=law], that I can gett, I ame made to beleve I have good interest vnto, and I am put by the same by her plesure, and not by course of lave [=law]. Whervpon I hope her magestie will thinke this sute as fitt for me as any other, and also for thes con-siderationes bestowe the same on me, wherby I may ease myne dettes, and charges I have ben at as is a foore sayde.

As we shall see, more than a year later, on 25 October 1593, Oxford had still not received a decision from the Queen.

On 1 September Ralph Bowes wrote to Burghley:[10]

May yt please your good Lordship I am informed by a ferend [=friend] of myne of a matter wherin your Lordship (yf so yt please yow) may do me a favoure / a matter preiudicial to none nor vnfytt to be graunted. a thing as yet vnsought for by any, but wilbe I knowe presently vndertaken by som other of as lyttle desart as my self / ether to your Lordships or hir Maiestes; but the thing I take to be within your Lordships grauntinge, or at the least I am suer so. if your Lordship graunt a lease of yt no other will then seek yt at hir Maiestes handes / And as in this svte If I happily prevayle by your Lordships good favoure, he that hath informed me of yt is to tast somwhat; so shall I most gladly agre in respect of my good affection towardes my Mistres my Lady Veere, and my most bound dewtye towardes your Lordship for your favour therin, that she have a thyrd parte of the beneffyt therof towardes the supply of som parte of hir extraordynary charges as occasion shall sarve. to whom in the execution of the svte I will vowe vnto your Lordship vpon my poore Credit to be a trewe sarvant and Iust Steward to bring vnto hir such benefytt as from tyme to tyme shall growe dewe vnto hir / if your Lordship shall allow yt reasonable that she geve me so much Creddytt. if not I shall then well like that she appoynt some other for hir self

> in that behalf. I forbere (vnder your Lordships favoure) in thes to sett doune the manner of the svte, least my letter might by chaunce com to som others sight / but will attend your Lordship withall when yt hath pleased youe to have redd thies.

Bowes is deliberately mysterious, having information but no money. Nevertheless, as a servant of Lady Elizabeth Vere ('my Mistres'), and perhaps as steward of her purse, he knows of a ready supply of cash. Thus he proposes, with Burghley's permission, to purchase property with a loan from Lady Elizabeth's account. In return he offers to provide one-third of his new annual revenues to Lady Elizabeth, retaining two-thirds for himself. Out of his two-thirds he will reward his informant and (it is to be assumed) repay the principal. Whether Burghley went along with this dubious proposal is unknown.

On 14 September Lord Keeper Puckering, Lord Buckhurst, and Sir John Fortescue interrogated George Dingley on matters of sedition.[11] Dingley reported

> … that manye of the nobillitye being dyscontentyd for that they were not aduanced nor preferyd as they happelye expected wold easelye be movyd to folow the Spanish king who wold promes largelye & put them in places of authoritye if so be he should possesse this land, the names which I haue h[e]ard them talke of were the erle of Oxford the erle of Cumberland the Lord Strange & my Lord Percye whom they thoughte to be men not so dignifyed as they deservyd, & that descontentment would muche alyenate ther mynd the hope which most the rebels to my knowledge relye vpon ys the deathe of her maiestie whom almightie God long preserve to raigne over all true Englishe subiects in despyte of her foes, wherto the Spanish king hathe an eye gyvinge yt for a reason of his lingering in reattempting a newe assaulte …

Any hope that Oxford would lead a revolt against the Queen was wishful thinking by Catholics wearing out their years in Continental exile. The document nevertheless shows that Oxford was identified as chief among those lords who felt themselves 'not so dignifyed as they deservyd'.

66 Oxford's Grammar School

In 1519–20, the wealthy Cambridge graduate Christopher Swallow, vicar of Messing, Essex, founded a grammar school at Earls Colne and Coggishall, stipulating that the school should alternate between villages every three years.[1] Though this remarkably impractical scheme may have been attempted, subsequent documents place the school uniquely at Earls Colne. The appointed schoolmaster was to

> teache and instructe in grammer there the number of thirtie children whose parentes shoulde be dwellinge and abydinge in the said townes and parishes where the said landes tenementes and hereditamentes are sett lyinge and beinge and others whose parentes shoulde be poore withoute any ffee or reward to be demaunded for the same

The catchment area of the school included Ardley, Coggishall, Mark's Tey, Messing, and Stilsted. Before his death on 22 August 1539 Swallow secured an agreement that each successive Earl of Oxford would serve as guardian.

Some time after attaining his majority in 1571, but 'a longe tyme before' 1592, Oxford appointed William Adams schoolmaster. A student at St John's College, Cambridge, Adams had taken his BA in 1568, and became vicar of Earls Colne about 1575 without taking an MA (Venn). Complaints against Adams were upheld by a commission of inquiry on 13 March 1592, whereupon Oxford ceded governance to 'William Lewyn doctor of lawe and Iudge of the Prerogatyve Courte of Canterburie and Roger Harlakenden of Earles Colne aforesaid and William Tyffyn of Colne Wake in the said County of Essex Esquier'. The triumvirate exercised

> full power and aucthorytie by all good and lawfull meanes to increase and advaunce the yearly revenue of the said land and tenementes assigned for the mayntanaunce of the said Schoole and therewithe to provide a sufficiente and able Schoolemaister suche as may from tyme to tyme supply that roome and to demyse and lett to ffarme the said landes or tenementes or everie of them for terme of one and twenty yeares or three lyves to suche parson or parsons as should offer vnto the said William Lewyn Roger Harlakenden and William Tyffyn sufficiente and Competente Rente for the same to be frome tyme to tyme imployed to the vse and for the mayntenaunce of the said Schoole and of the Schoolemaster teachinge therein

The choice of schoolmaster fell on George Harlackenden – neither the first nor the last time Roger Harlackenden would look out for the interests of a male relative. This George, who has been identified as the son of John Harlackenden, Esq., of Warehorn, Kent, was a graduate of Cambridge University, having matriculated sizar from Magdalene College in 1580, received his BA in 1584, and his MA in 1587. He remained only one year, becoming instead rector of Great Yeldham in 1593. About March 1593 the triumvirate appointed John Stockbridge, also of Essex, who had matriculated from Hart Hall, Cambridge (a non-collegiate 'hostel') on 22 January 1585: Stockbridge subsequently received his BA on 12 February 1588, his MA on 7 July 1592 (Venn).

Refusing to recognize Stockbridge, on 3 December 1593 Oxford unilaterally voided the commission's appointment:[2]

> To all People, to whom this present writinge shall come, I Edward de Veer, Earle of Oxenford, Lord great Chamberleyn of England, Vicount Bulbeck and lord of Badlesmere & Scales, send greetings, whereas here tofore at the request, of William Lewen doctor of the Civill lawes, promysing me, that he would for the better mayntenance of the free schole vsuallie heretofore kept at Erlescolne in the Countye of Essex, inlarge the lyvinge therto belonginge by such good ordre, that he would take in lettinge the landes therto belonginge, as also in allowinge of his owne free will, some exhibition therevnto, and that he would place a sufficient Schole-

> master there, for the teachinge & instructinge of youth in good literature To which
> intent & purpose I graunted vnto him, and Roger Herlakenden & William Tiffyn
> a Commission vnder my hande & seale Now forasmuch, as the same neyther is nor
> hath ben performed accordinglie Knowe ye that I the said Edward de Vere Earle of
> Oxenford doe by these presentes, Revoke adnihillate & make voide the said Com-
> mission, and all power, and authoritie to them or to any of them thereby geven for,
> touchinge, or concerninge the lettinge, or sellinge, the landes & Tenementes, to
> the said schole belonging, or nominatinge or appointinge any Scholemaster there
> or touchinge, or concernynge any other matter, or thinge, therein, by them, or any
> of them to be donne And doe by these presentes, nominate, present & appoint
> William Adams Master of Art & vicar of Erlescolne afore said, to be Scholemaster
> there, & to vse & exercise the same place, during his life, in such sort, as he hath
> heretofore vsed

Oxford not only re-appointed the incompetent Adams, who was not in fact MA,
but approved new leases of school properties to a new set of tenants at rents far
below prevailing rates, and allowed the lands to be stripped of timber for the
private benefit of Adams and of Simon Ive, a 'dishonest servant' of Oxford's who
had connived with Adams to milk the school lands for their joint personal benefit.

Accused of conversion and depredation, Adams proposed to take the rent for
one of the properties for a whole year, while Stockbridge could have all the rest.
Stockbridge agreed, but over the next decade Adams persuaded tenants to pay
rents to himself or to Ive rather than to Stockbridge. That Stockbridge nevertheless remained at his post is demonstrated by his own subsequent suit and by the
fact that when Bartholomew Church, 16-year-old son of John Church of Earls
Colne, entered Caius College, Cambridge, on 6 April 1601, the college's admissions register identified him as a pupil of Mr Stockbridge of Earls Colne.[3]

In this latter year Stockbridge complained so bitterly of the school's irregular-
ities that the Court of Chancery ordered the Bishop of London, Richard Bancroft,
to hear the dispute. Following a mediation session on 12 November 1601, Bancroft submitted his report, along with articles signed by both Stockbridge and
Adams, on 6 February 1602. Adams declared himself satisfied with back rents on
various properties; agreed to pay Stockbridge a cash sum and to take no further
monies from the school properties, and, finally, that he would

> never hereafter challendge nor clayme any thinge in the same Schoole nor landes
> but that all the tenauntes and ffermors of any of the landes and tenementes
> aforesaid shall forever hereafter pay all their Rentes vnto the said Iohn Stockebridge
> soe longe as he shalbe Schoolmaster there.

Though the articles were ratified by the Court of Chancery on 2 July 1602, Adams
broke his word almost as soon as the ink was dry. Nine years later, on 4 March
1611, a new inquisition was convened at the White Lion in Kelvedon, Essex, and a
new decree issued on 12 March. The Commissioners' report noted that Stock-

bridge – the only Earls Colne schoolmaster known to have succeeded in preparing a pupil for admission to a university – had abandoned the school for a less troubled life in Navestock, Essex. Adams had meanwhile recovered the office of schoolmaster, teaching through a deputy – an arrangement forbidden by the school's statutes. Meanwhile, the houses and other buildings on the school's lands

> are much spoiled wasted and decayed, and the tymber thereof sold awaye, And ... since the saide lease soe made to the saide Symon Ive as aforesaide the saide Addams & Ive have made sale of as much wood & Tymber as came to the value of thirty powndes and vpwardes, and Converted the same to theire private vse and benefite.

The new Commissioners reported that Ive had again assigned his interests in the school's leases,

> [and] that vppon the lease made to the saide Ive as afore said there is reserved a farre lesser rent then the said landes are annually worthe, and that the said lease was gotten by fraud & covin from the said Earle, and by practise & misinformacion geven by the said Ive vnto the saide Earle (as by thafforesayd decree aperethe[)] and that the said Ive paide noe valuable consideracion for the saide lease ...

The Commissioners further declared that Adams had obtained the original grant of the schoolmastership by simony,

> [and] that the said Addams is an vnfitte man either for learninge or manners to be a school maister ther and noe waies capable of the saide schoolmaistershippe.

Finally the 1611 Commissioners discovered

> that there was not anie power or Clause to theire knowledge lymited by the saide Conveyaunce made by the saide Swallowe wherebie the saide Earle or anie other of the ffeoffees should have the nominacion of the saide schoolemaister

Thus Oxford had exceeded his authority in presenting Adams to the schoolmastership in the first place.

The Earls Colne grammar school survived Oxford's interference and neglect, and survives today. But its only known 'graduate' between 1519–20 and 1619 was the aforementioned Bartholomew Church, subsequently of Caius College, Cambridge, where his uncle, Robert Church, held a fellowship.[4] Robert, born in Earls Colne about 1544, had attended school in Colchester prior to his own admission to Caius in 1560.[5] Its financial base milked by an unworthy schoolmaster and a dishonest servant, the grammar school at Earls Colne did not under Oxford's supervision attain the distinction of a Harrow or Eton, or even the distinction of a King's New School at Stratford-upon-Avon.

67 A New Lord Bolbec

Queen Elizabeth's Ninth Parliament sat from 19 February to 10 April 1593 (*TE*). Oxford attended the opening session on 19 February and the next two sessions on 22 and 24 February, but missed the next 30 sessions, returning for the final session on 10 April.[1] Thus of 34 sessions, he attended four, including the ceremonial first and last. During the remaining eleven years of his life, he would attend only one more day of Parliament (in 1597).

Reporting on Stoke Newington, which lay just to the north of Shoreditch, John Norden reported as current news in his *Speculi Britanniae ... Middlesex* (1592, p. 37): 'there, the Earle of Oxforde is sometime resident, in a very proper house'. Here Countess Elizabeth gave birth to her first and only child:[2]

> Henrye Vicount Bulbecke sonne to the right honourable Edward Vere Earle of Oxford was borne the xxiiijth of February 1592 [=24 February 1593] and christened the xxxjth day of March [=31 March] in the yere – 1593

Oxford finally had his son and heir.

Oxford wrote to Burghley on 25 October, renewing his effort to recover Waltham Forest (LL-21). He opens with a reference back to his letter of 18 May 1591.

> My very good lord, I hope yt ys not out of yowre remembrance, how longe sythence I hawe [=have] bene a suter to her maiestie, that she wowld giue me leaue to try my tytell to the forest at the laue [=law]. But I found that so displesinge wnto her, that in place of receyvinge, that ordinarie fauoure, which is of course graunted to the meanest subiect, I was browbeaten, and hade many bitter speches giuen me. Neuertheles at lenghe by meanes of sume of the lords of the councel, amonge whiche yowre lordship especiallye, her maiestie was persuaded to giue me eare. At that tyme which was at Summerset house, yf yowre lordship please to call to mynde, her maiestie wowlde nedes haue yt committed vnto arbitrers, pretendinge therin, to doo me espetiall fauoure, in cuttinge of[f] the longe circumstances of the lave [=law], and charges perteyninge therto. But after I hadd consented thervnto, for me, cowld be no other arbiter permitted, then the lord Chanceler, whome she had chosen for her self. this I am assured yowre lordshipe hathe good cause to remember, by her maiesties exceptione agaynst yow, in that she thowght yow partiall, to yowre sune in lave.

The Lord Chancellor was Sir Christopher Hatton – who had died on 20 November 1591, within six months of the interview.

> But thes thinges I call only to myned for yowre lordships better remembrance, which throwghe so many affayres otherwise, in so longe a tyme, yt ys no merveile, yf perhapes yow have easly forgotten. therfore I will to purpose only further call to remembrance the succes of this arbitement. which was thus. After muche a doo, and a goode yere spent, by delayes frome her maiestie, my lord Chanceler then Sir Christopher Hattone beinge ernestly called vpone, appointed a tyme of he[a]ringe

bothe for her maiesties lerned councell at the lave, and myne. Whervpone what he conceyved therby of my tytell, he was redie to have made his report vnto her maiestie. But suche was my misfortune, (I doo not thinke her minde to do me any wronge,) that she flattly refused, therin to here my lord Chanceler, and for a finall answer commanded me no more to followe the sute, for whether yt was hers or myne, she was resolued to dispose therof at her plesure. A strange sentance my thowght [=methought]: which beinge iustly considered, I may say, she had done me more fauoure, yf she hadd sufferd me to trye my tytell at lave, then this arbitrement vnder pretence of expeditione, and grace. the extremite had bene fare more safe, then the remedie, whiche I was persuaded to accepte. But after I hade made sume complainte of this harde determinatione, yet in so desperat a state, she promised this relyefe to my cause, that in sume other matter, that showlde be as commodious as that vnto me, she wowlde recompence me in the meane whyle. Hence rysethe the cause, my lord, wherfore I have preferred many sutes to her maiestie, but have found in them all, the same delayes, and difficulties, that I dyd in the other before. But now the ground wherone I lay my sut beinge so iust and resonable, that ether I showlde expect sume satisfactione, by way of recompence, or restoratione of myne owne, as I ame yet persuaded, tyll lave [=law] hathe convinced me:

Oxford now renews his request for the monopoly on wools, fruits, and oils:

thes are most ernestly to desire a continuance of yowre lordships fauoure and furtherance in my sute, which I made at Grenwiche, to her maiestie at her last beinge there, about thre commodites, to witt the oyles, wolles, and frutes, in giuinge therfore, as then my profer was. I doo the rather now reneve [=renew] the same for that I doo not he[a]re as yet they are disposed otherwise, and that the tyme, is fittest, aswell for her maiesties commodite, as his that shall take yt. and consideringe, yf her maiestie will have a iust consideratione of the premisses, I ame to chalenge and expect sumwhat. yowre lordship knowes the whole proces of the matter, and can better iuge then any other, as to whome my estate is best knowne, & how hardly I may forbeare so great an interrest, without any recompence. And therfore as to the me[e]test, (for that my state and cause, bothe in right, and conscience is best vnderstood,) to conceyve of the iust desyre I make of this sute, I doo adres my selfe to yowre lordshipe, most ernestly to crave bothe yowre opinione, and councell, yowre fauoure, and furtherance, whether I were best to followe this sute, which I have commenced, or yt standinge soo, that ther is no good ore hope to be done, or conceyved therin, to seeke agayne her maiesties fauoure, that I myght procede, in lave, to trye my titell to the forest. And thus desiringe yowre lordshipe to howlde me excused, for that I am so longe, in a matter that concernethe me so muche, I will make an ende …

Oxford would pursue his appeal for Waltham Forest for another ten years.

Documents that survive from the Queen's visit to Theobalds on 20 October reveal Burghley's determination to raise Elizabeth Vere to a prominent place in Court:[3]

In the Earle of Rutlandes Chamber vnder my Lord Vooke [=Vaux's] Chamber: Lady Warwick // Next to that chamber: lady Elizabeth Vere …

Inventory of all such Lynnen as is to be vsed at such tyme as the Queens maiestie is at Thebaldes

... a portion of lynnen for my lady Vere

A Maid of Honour, Elizabeth was now eighteen – and still unmarried.

68 A Husband for Lady Elizabeth

Ferdinando Stanley, 5th Earl of Derby, died on 16 April 1594. On 9 May Alice, Dowager Countess, wrote to Cecil from Latham:[1]

> I must entreat the continuance of your kind favours towards me in a cause wherein I have written to the Lords and others of the Privy Council, and for that it will come to your view, I must desire you to effect what I have entreated their Honours unto, the matter being so just as you shall find it is, and I hope my lord your father's wonted favour will not be drawn from me by any means or persuasions, albeit I hear of a motion of marriage between the Earl, my brother, and my lady Vere, your niece, but how true the news is I know not, only I wish her a better husband.

The marriage under consideration was between William Stanley and Elizabeth Vere. As Ferdinando's younger brother, William had the potential to deprive Alice of the Derby inheritance. About this same time George Carey wrote to his wife about Ferdinando's death:[2]

> in the time of his sickness, finding himself at the first stricken with death ... [Ferdinando] hath by good advice in law given Lathom, Knowsley, Colham, the Isle of Man and whatsoever he hath in England [i.e., his principal estates] (besides what Henry the 7th gave to his ancestors) from the nidicock his brother, to your sister and her daughters, whereby we yet hold that both she and they will be exceeding great marriages.

Thus Carey too was ready to disparage William, calling him in effect a ninny – but then Carey's wife was one of the sisters who would now inherit.

Rowland York, in the company of Sir William Stanley, who together had betrayed Deventer to the Spanish, weighed in from Continental exile:[3]

> ... Yorke spake being at dynner with Stanley Williams being present and my self about the death of the yonge Erle of Derby they musinge how he came by his end Yorke said It is no maruell when Machiuilian policies gouerne Englande, I durst pawne my life said he that the Lord Treasurer [=Burghley] caused him to be poysoned that he [=Ferdinando] being dead he [=Burghley] might marry the yonge Lady Vere vnto the Brother of the said Erle of Derby. It is tyme said he to cut them of[f] that go about to be Kingis

Not even murder by poisoning for the sake of a favourable marriage alliance is put past Burghley by York – himself such a Machiavellian that he is said to have died by Spanish poison.

William agreed to give Alice £5000 plus a third of the earldom's revenues, with additional monies for her daughters.[4] Still unsatisfied, Alice now claimed to be carrying Ferdinando's child, who, if male, would become the 6th Earl of Derby in William's place. This odd circumstance explains a letter, endorsed 19 November but written earlier, in which Father Garnet the Jesuit reported:[5]

> The marriage of the Lady Vere to the new Earl of Derby is deferred, by reason that he standeth in hazard to be unearled again, his brother's wife being with child, until it is seen whether it be a boy or no.

The world waited, and Elizabeth and William waited to be married, until the following January.

By early May Oxford had initiated a suit against Roger Harlackenden, in which Barnaby Worthye had deposed on 3 May. Two weeks later Worthye changed his testimony in a most peculiar pair of documents, the first headed '15 May 1594: between Edward Earl of Oxford complainant and Roger Harlackenden defendant':[6]

> fforasmucche as the Right honorable the Lord Keeper of the greate Seale of England was now informed That one Barnabye Worthy havinge ben examyned as a wytnesse in this Cawse on the parties behaulf before Mr Nicholson one of the Examyners of this Court And being afterwardes very carefull, that his Examynacion should not be set downe otherwise than he meant, yet, (which he distrusted it was)
>
> The same Barnaby Worthy did repayre to the said Examyner, and desyred him before publicacion he avouched, That becawse he was vnlearned he might heare his Examynacion read / And havinge yt read vnto him, And fyndinge therby that it was set down Contrary to his meaninge, desyred the Examyner to haue yt reformed according as he meant yt which the said Examyner would not do: Becawse as he then sayd, That Reformacion which the said Worthy desyred wold alter the whole matter / And now publicacion ys he avented [=prevented?] The said Worthy fyndeth the said Examynacion to be cleane contrary to his meaninge And therfore desyreth yt may be reformed as he meant the same
>
> His Lordship dothe therfore referre thexamynacion therof to the Right worshipfull the Master of the Rowles requyrynge him to take such order theron, as he shall thinke meete.

The second document:[7]

> Barnabye Worthye deposeth that about a ffourtenight after his examynacion taken by Mr Nicolson thexamyner, In the cause betwene the right honorable the Earle of Oxfford, and Roger Harlackenden & al. he repayred to the said Nicholson, & desyred to heare his Examynacion readde agayne vnto hym, because he had affyrmed some thinges, which, callinge hym selfe better to remembrance, were vntrewe, and therfore he desysred to haue the same amended. Whervpon after some spech, passed betwene Mr Nicolson & hym, the same Mr Nicholson dyd readde

his said former Examynacion to the seconde Interrogatory, vnto hym, and in his deposicion to the said seconde Interrogatory, where yt was sette downe that he had hearde that amongest others, Edmunde Felton, named in the Interrogatory, was a meane vnto the said Earle, on the said deffendantes behalfe, for the better affecting of his said sute, he desyred the said Mr Nicolson that the same might be stryken out, because he did not knowe yt nor had euer hearde yt. And thervpon the said Mr Nicolson, dyd stryke out the same clause accordinge to this Examinantes request, he further sayeth, that vpon the hearinge of his former deposicion to the viijth Interrogatory, beinge lykewyse readde vnto hym by the same Mr Nicolson, perceyvinge that yt was sette downe, as herafter foloweth, viz., Savinge that he hath crediblye hearde that the said Felton had of the said Roger Harlackenden aboue CCli [=£200] more in money, for effectinge of the said bargayne. He dyd lykewyse desyre the said Mr Nicolson to stryke out that clause because in truth he dyd never heare any such credyble report, and besydes vpon calling hym selfe to better remembrance, he dyd well knowe & remember that the same CCli was payed at Westminster, to the said Earles owne vse. and thervpon Mr Nicholson, at this deponentes request, dyd stryke out the same clause lykewyse.

And touchinge the contentes of all the resydue of his deposicion to the said viijth Interrogatory as yt is sette downe by the said Nicholson, this deponent sayeth that in truthe he knoweth not any thinge, nor can saye any thinge by credible report or otherwyse, savinge that the 52li [=£52] was payed to Mr Felton. But for what cause or to what vse he knoweth not, and thervpon moued Mr Nicholson to altere & reforme yt. Whervnto Mr Nicholson answered he coulde not so doe, for he might aswell stryke out the whoale examinacion. And he further sayeth that (as he remembreth) he dyd not affyrme vpon his former examinacion before Mr Nicholson, that the 52li was payed for any such cause, as is sette downe in his deposicion to the said 8th Interrogatory, Neither dyd he vse any such words of combynynge betwene Harlackenden and Felton to decceyue the Earle, as is sette downe in the said deposicion, for he knoweth not what the worde Combyned meanes, neyther dyd he then speake any wordes of lyke effecte, viz., that they conspyred, or confederated or practysed or agreed to deceyue the said Earle, or any lyke wordes to his now remembrance.

he sayeth that the same daye that he was examyned by Mr Nicholson, & before his said examynacion, Mr Ivye Solycyter to the Earle of Oxfford, dyd reade to this Examinant the Interrogatory whervpon he was afterwarde Examyned, and before that tyme he dyd not knowe nor had hearde whervpon he shoulde be examyned nor dyd euer declare or telle to any person, what he coulde testyfye or depose in that matter, saving that he dyd declare to the same Mr Ivye, that he did knowe that the 52li was payed to Edward Felton by Mr Harlackenden, but he dyd not tell hym for what cause yt was payed, for he sayeth he dyd not know for what cause yt was payed.

he sayeth that about a weke after he was examyned by Mr Nicolson, he toulde one (*blank*) Prynce of Kyng Weston in Somersette shyre, that he had bene examyned as a wytnesse for the Earle of Oxfford, in a cause betwene the said Earle & Mr Harlackenden and thervpon (*blank*) Prynce sayed vnto hym, yt was good for hym to take hede what he had done, and yf he had sayed any thinge vntrulye, to cause yt to be amended, leste trouble might growe of yt, And thervpon callinge to remembrance, the thinges before mencioned he repayred to Mr Nicholson to haue his Examynacion altered & amended, But he denyeth that he was moued or persuaded by Mr Harlackenden, or by any for hym, or by his promyse vnto hym, for doinge so. And he denyeth also that he dyd vtter or declare eyther to Mr Harlackenden, or any of his Counsell, or to any of his solycyters or servantes what he had deposed, beinge examyned by Mr Nicholson as aforesaid.

he sayeth that when Mr Nicolson refused to altere the said deposicion to the 8. Interrogatory, he the said Mr Nicolson offered to goe with this Examinant to the Master of the Rolles, touchinge the same, but this Examinant vnderstode not what yt meant, and made no answere to yt.

The 'Mr Ivye Solycyter to the Earle of Oxfford' was probably the Simon Ive connected to the Earls Colne grammar school.[8]

Barnabye Worthye was initially deposed as a witness for Oxford's cause. His extraordinary reversal, so complete that Nicholson declared that it amounted to a cancellation of his entire testimony, admits of two explanations. Either he was threatened by Harlackenden's side into withdrawing evidence unfavourable to their cause; or the testimony which he gave in the first deposition was doctored by partisans of Oxford's cause. Either way, Worthye seems to have become caught up in a dispute that threatened to overwhelm him.

On 7 July Oxford wrote to Burghley (LL-22):

My very good Lord. yf yt pleas yow to remember, that about halfe a yere or there about past, I was a sutor to yowre lordshipe, for yowre favoure. that wheras I found sundrie abuses, wherby bothe her maiestie, & my selfe, were in myne office greatly hyndred, that yt wowlde please yowre Lordship, that I myght fynde suche fauoure from yowe, that I myght have the same redressed. At which tyme I found so good forwardnes in yowre Lordship, that I thowght my self greatly behowldinge for the same; yet by reason at that tyme myne Atturnye was departed the towne, I could not then send him to attend vpon yowre Lordship, accordinge to yowre appoyntment. But hopinge that the same dispositione styll remaynethe, towards the iustnes of my cause, and that yowre Lordship to whome my estate is so well knowne & how muche yt standethe me on, not to neglect as hertofore, suche occasions as to amend the same may aryse, frome myne office, I most hartely desyre yowre Lordship, that yt will please yow to giue eare to the state of my cause, and at yowre best lesure, admit ether myne Atturnie, or other of my councell in lave [=law] to informe yowre Lordship that the same beinge perfectly layd open to yowre Lordship, I may inyoy the fauoure from yow which I most ernestly desyre. In whiche doinge I shall thinke my self singulerlye behowldinge in this, as I have ben in other respects.

The specific favour requested by Oxford is not spelled out; perhaps he is referring to his claim to Waltham Forest, or perhaps he was still hoping for the monopoly on wools, fruits, and oils.

Alice Stanley's pregnancy seems to have been merely fictional – or if she was pregnant, then she was not quick to report a miscarriage. On 13 September William Stanley, now confident that he was indeed the 6th Earl of Derby, wrote to Burghley, his prospective (grand)father-in-law, from his house in Canon Row:[9]

> My very honourable good Lord I vnderstand, by my seruants Ireland and Doughtye that according to your Lordships last speeche they haue tho[ro]ughly acquaynted your Lordship with my estate and that nowe it pleasethe your Lordship to partly refer the further procedinge to my liking eyther nowe or the next terme to be consummated: how grat[e]full the message was vnto me I leaue [to] your Lordships censure. In which cause I pray your Lordship to consyder my affectyon to that honourable Lady The dawntinge of my vnfrendes, the gladdinge of my wel wisshers, and the inuestinge me, in this estat [i.e., earldom]; whervnto Almyghty God hath called me. In which by so honourable a patrone with my Lady and Mystris to both owre contentments and your Lordships comfort God the worker of all goodnes may send me a sone, wherfor I wish your Lordship allowance of a present dispatche Neuertheless I must and wilbe wholly dyrected by your Lordship in this and all other respects and soe humbly take my leaue …

William was evidently asking Burghley to agree to a date for the wedding – finally set for January 1595.

Later in the year the French ambassador delivered a note addressed to Oxford from the French King Henri IV, written on 25 September (O. S.):[10]

> Lord Great Chamberlain, I am having this note brought to you by Loménie whom I send before the Queen my good sister with respect to the matters which concern the well being of her affairs and mine, in order to inform you of the satisfaction I feel for the good offices you have performed on my behalf in her presence, which I beg you to continue and believe that I will always consider it a great pleasure to reciprocate in whatever might bring about your personal satisfaction, as I have charged the said Loménie to tell you, whom I pray you to believe as myself, who prays God to keep you, Lord Great Chamberlain, in his care.

Similar letters sent on the same day to Burghley and the Lord Admiral, and an even longer letter to Essex, suggest that Oxford's letter had no personal significance.

69 Some Say my Lord of Oxford is Dead

In early 1595 Lady Elizabeth Vere, then nineteen, married William Stanley, 6th Earl of Derby:[1]

> The 26 of Ianuarye beinge Fridaye [in fact, Sunday] in the yere of [Christ] 1594 and the 37 of the reigne of Quene Elizabethe at Grenewiche with great solempnitie and triumphe was William erle of Darbye (brother and heyre male to Ferdinando erle

of Derbye and the sonne of Henry erle of Darbye & of his wyfe Margaret daughter
to the erle of Cumberlande) maried to (blank) one of the daughters of Edwarde erle
of Oxeforde by his first wyfe Anne the daughter of William Cecill lorde Burgh-
leighe tresurer of England.

On the same day an unknown play was acted at Greenwich by the Lord Chamberlain's (Shakespeare's) company, doubtless as part of the festivities.[2]

On 31 January John Carey wrote to Burghley from Berwick:[3]

> Touching the latter part of your lettre wherin your honour writes of the mariadge
> of your daughter the Ladye Vere, I am gladde as a feeling member of your Lord-
> ships Ioye and reioice at her ladyships good fortune in preserving your honours life
> so longe wherby thimperfections of her father shall be no blemishe to her honour
> whome I pray God make as happye a couple as ever were of that name. Being also
> very gladd that her maiestie will vouchsafe so honorablye to solempnise the matter,
> with her Royall presence which will be I dare saye a great comfort to your lordship
> and a great honour to the yonge couple.

The writer was the second son of Henry, 1st Lord Hunsdon, Lord Chamberlain
from 1585 to 1596. Upon Henry's death his eldest son George Carey would became
2nd Lord Hunsdon, also succeeding his father (after a year's hiatus) as Lord
Chamberlain. John, the writer of the letter, would succeed as 3rd Lord Hunsdon
on George's death in 1603. At the time of the letter John was deeply involved in
Scottish affairs.[4] Elizabeth was Burghley's grand-daughter, but like her sisters she
thought of Burghley as her father. Carey attributes to Oxford 'imperfections'
which 'shall be no blemishe to her honour'. Nevertheless – as we will discover –
Oxford's 'imperfections' would follow Elizabeth Vere into her marriage.

On 28 March Oxford addressed one of his numerous 'tin-mining' letters to
Michael Hickes at Burghley House 'frome Bishopesgate this present morninge'.[5]
If Fisher's Folly was still in the hands of Cornwallis, Oxford may have stayed
there as a guest, but he may of course have stayed elsewhere, whether with an
acquaintance or in rented rooms.

In a letter to Cecil dated 24 April, Oxford insisted that his newly married
daughter receive an agreed-upon £1000 per annum from her husband (LL-23):

> … wheras I have delt with the Earle of Darbye, about my dowghters allowance,
> and that he hathe promised me to assure her to that intent a thowsand pound a
> yeare, for so muche as I now vnderstand vpon sume discontentment that he hathe
> not attayned to that honor which yt semethe he dyd at thys tyme expect, he
> determines to morrow to depart into Lancashiere, and that he hathe neyther in his
> house, or for herself, sett downe any stey [=stay, prop], wherby ether in her owne
> lo[d]ginge, or yf she shall follow her attendance vpon her Maiestie, she is prouided
> as his wyfe. I doo therfore most hartely desyre yow as her vncle, and good friend to
> deale ernestly with my Lord Thresorer, vnto whome I have also wrytten, that he
> wowld send vnto him, or els speake with him, to the end that eyther he showld
> fulfyll his promes, or vntyll suche tyme as he shall, to take that order which is fytt

for her place wherin she serues her Magestie and for his wyfe. I doo vnderstand by my dowghter how good an vncle she findes yow, and how redie to friend her, wherin I allso take my self behowldinge vnto yowe. of whatt fancies his humors are compounded, yow know well inowghe, and therfore I pray yow to be ernest with my lord, that he may deale effectually vpone so good a ground as his woord and honor, which he hathe giuen.

Oxford seems to share doubts of Derby expressed by the Dowager Countess and by George Carey, and assumes that Burghley harbours them also: 'of whatt fancies his humors are compounded, yow know well inowghe'. In Oxford's continuation we discover that his misgivings extend to his daughter:

Also I vnderstand that my Ladie Russell for sume offence conceyved of my doughter hathe lat[e]ly written to my Lord Thresorer to discorage and diswade him to vrge the Earle of Darby. But for that she was her self the fyrst that moved this allowance, and hathe sythence altred her mynde vpon sume conceyt, I hope my lord wyll not be carried away vpon suche vnconstant ballence. Yet yf yow finde any suche hinderance, I pray yow never the lesse styke to yowre nece, and further her in what yow can, sythe her desyre is iust [=just], in that yt ys his promise, & resonable in that she ys his wyfe. Thus what yow shall doo for her, esteminge yt myne owne bond, I refer her whoole cause to yowre kindnes.

We may wonder whether Oxford did not have his own designs on his daughter's prospective £1000 per annum, an amount equal to his own pension from the royal treasury.

Oxford's letter constitutes an implicit acknowledgement that Robert Cecil had now become a means of access to royal power comparable to his father Burghley: increasingly from now on, Oxford's letters were addressed to the son rather than to the father. On 20 October, writing from an unnamed location, Oxford pressed his suit via Cecil not only for Waltham Forest but also (as mooted in his memorandum of 16 November 1579) for Havering Park (LL-24):

Good Sir Robert Cecil. I have often receyved from yow manye wordes of curtesies, & fauours, when I showld have occasions to vse ye, all which I have beleued, & doo styll, imagininge those promises to procede of a free & lyberall dispositione. wherfore havinge at thys tyme an espetiall opportunite to trye my friendes In a cause which I doo not dowt but iust, I make thus far bowlde wythe yow, that wheareas a fewe yeares sythence I was a swter [=suitor, petitioner] to her Magesty, for her fauour thus farr, that my ryght which I dyd not dowt, to the Forest of Waltham & Parke of Haveringe concerninge the kepinge therof, myght have tryall at lave [=law], which is a common course to every subiect, & that then vnder pretense to doo me a fauour her Magesty to avoyd charge, and delay of the lave [=law], greatly to myne ease and for better expeditione, her plesure was that the matter showld be referred to arbitriment, which was so done as her Magesty takinge exception to my arbitror, had her owne Sir Christopher Hatton then Lord Chanceler, appoynted as indifferent for vs bothe, as she dyd measure yt. He havinge h[e]ard the matter and her Magesty['s] councell with myne, was resolued, and hervpon wished me to vrge her Magestie to call for his report, which accordinglie I dyd and the Lord Chancelor present. In short she refusd to heare him. She flattly sayd whether yt weare myne or hears [=hers] she wowld bestowe yt at her plesure, and so vnder pretence of kepinge the same from spoyle tyll the matter weare decyded betwiene her Magesty and my self, she put yt into the handes of Sir Thomas Henige [=Heneage], and thys after a yeares travell [=travail], I had for my short expeditione. Now my lord yowre father is a full wittnes of all thes thinges, beinge present when the matter was committed, and the intentiones and all are sufficiently knowne to him with all the course obserued. I have written also to him and also to her Maiestie. I only desyre my friendes that may speake theare myndes to her Magesty & have oportunite that they will be meanes, that eyther she will lett me inyoy that which my ryght dothe cast vpon me and the lave [=law] with her fauoure, or that she will protect me with her lave [=law] as her subiect, and that yf yt be none of myne she will rather take yt away by order, then oppressions. ...

Oxford is filling in the background for Cecil by referring back to events before Hatton's death in 1591. He finishes by challenging the Queen to deny his rights to Waltham Forest and Havering Park by royal order rather than by mere tyranny.

Oxford's double postscript is of greater immediate interest than the principal text:

As I was fooldinge vp this letter I receyved a very honorable answer from my Lord Thresorer. my whole truste in this cause ys in yow twoo, my lord for that he ys pryvie to the whole cause and handlinge therof from tyme to tyme, and in yow for that I assure myself in so iust [=just] a matter yow will not abandone me.

He semethe to dowt [=doubt, anticipate] yet of his dethe, & wishethe me to make meanes to the Earle of Essex that he wowld forbeare to deale for yt. A thinge I cannot do in honor, sythe I have alredie receyved diuerse iniuries and wronges from him, which bare [=bar] me of all suche basse [=base] courses. Yf her maiesties affectiones be forfets of mens estates we must indure yt.

So Burghley was already anticipating his death, though he had three more years to live. Evidently his purpose was tactical, attempting to create a peaceful understanding between Oxford and the Queen's new favourite, Essex. Oxford, however, would have none of it: for reasons unknown, he felt he had received injuries and wrongs so great that reconciliation would bring dishonour.

The next day, 21 October, Oxford tried again on the same subject, with a similar opening (LL-25):

Theare are tymes, whearin the vse of friendes, are so necessarie, that althoughe we be lothe to be combersone [sic], yet are we compelled, to thrust into theare handes, the trust of owre troblesume causes. Suche ys my state at this present, whoo in myne owne conceyte have no mistrust of yowre good dispositione towardes me, yet am I forced by what vnloked for occasione I can not tell, at thys tyme to turne my thowght vpon yow, as the only friend, wythe whome, I thinke I may be bowldest.

Whearfore for that I vnderstoode, the great danger of lyfe, whearin Mr vicecham-berlane lay,[6] consideringe the vaynes & humors of thys worlde, I doo not mistrust, but many thinges hearby, fallinge into her Magestyes handes to bestowe, that theare wowld be many suters. And for that to the kepinge of the Forest of Walthame, & the Parke of Haueringe, myne evidences show me a certeyne ryght to the same, from whiche I cannot be perswaded tyll I know better to the contrarie. I haue most humbly wrytten to her Magesty that after so many bestowinges of yt vpon others voyd of any pretence [=claim], she will now atlenghe [=at length] giue eare, to the iustnes of my cause, & as she hathe often disposed yt vpon others vpon fauoure, that now not only vpon iustice, but also vpon grace she will deygne yt to the ryghtfull keper.

And thys I do not notice to yow, as yf I thowgh [=thought] yt in yowre powre to doo more then yt shall please to come of her maiesties owne dispositione, but for that yow are the only person that I dare relye vpon in the Courte, and at this present to implore as an instrument, to make my desyre knowne vnto her Magestye.

And thus hauinge opened to yow my cause, what I haue wrytten in effect to her Magestye and what I crave of yowre curtesie, I commit yow to God. ...

Oxford's characterization of Cecil as his only friend at Court contains more than a touch of flattery. While it is true that Oxford was desperately short of friends who had the Queen's ear, it was Burghley rather than Cecil who rose to his defence time after time, year after year. By contrast, virtually all of Oxford's numerous appeals to Cecil were to end in bitterness.

By 7 August Oxford betook himself to Byfleet, a village in West Surrey some 22 miles south-west of London, whence he wrote to Burghley (LL-64):

I most hartely thanke yowre Lordship for yowre desyre to knowe of my helthe which is not so good, yet as I wishe yt, I find comfort in thys ayre, but no fortune at the Cowrt.

Oxford's problems did not, however, prevent him from harping on about the matter of his daughter's promised £1000 per annum during a visit with the newly-weds at Derby House in Canon Row:

I hope yowre Lordship hathe yowre helthe and I shalbe glade to heare therofe, and thys one thinge I have to informe yowre Lordship before I make an ende, and that ys at my comminge hether frome Chaninge Roo, the Earle of Darbye, was very ernest that he myght assure a thowsand pound a yeare for my daughters findinge [=financial support] addinge farther that he merveled that Sir Robert Cecill her vncle & I her father weare so slake [=slack, slow] to call vpon yt. wherfore I shall desyre yowre Lordship as yow shall chuse best tyme, that sumthinge may be done therin, my daughter, hathe put her trust in me, bothe to remember yowre Lordship and her husband wherfore I wowld be gladd, that sume certeynte were effected to her mynde.

Evidently Derby, who may have been cleverer than he had been given credit for, attributed any delay in the establishment of his wife's annuity to the failure of Oxford and Cecil to urge the matter to a conclusion.

On 9 November Rowland Whyte wrote to Sir Robert Sidney:[7]

> Some say my lord of Oxford is dead.

The report that Oxford's health 'is not so good' must have circulated widely: in fact, he had another nine years of life left in him.

At an unknown date, evidently toward the end of this year, Dr William Paddy, physician, wrote to Cecil concerning a niece, probably Bridget, now eleven:[8]

> Right honorable: I can send you no more or less comfort, then that your Lady Niece is as much better, as so litle tyme can worke and effect. Her stooles (sit honos auribus ['may it not offend the ears']) haue ben somewhatt less, her sleepe this daie somewhatt better, and she hath fedd a litle. Her weakness (as I haue euer foretold) is like to be much and long, for it is nowe att the highest which can be in a lyuing creature: And for the conception we must hope that out of her owne storehouse she that can overcome such a sickness maye supplie nourishment. Ther shalbe nothinge omitted in care (I beeseech you be assured) for her farder and perfect recouerye, whervpon we mynde to consult att fiue of the clock this evening when all the rest of my fellowe phisitions will be present.

Since Paddy had called fellow physicians to the girl's bedside, the danger was real. Bridget's 'owne storehouse' would prove sufficient, however, to win the day.

PART XI

Re-engagement
1595–1599

70 The Lure of Tin

On 20 March 1595 Oxford addressed a letter to Burghley which opened with a reflection on a subject that, in his own word, had 'consumed' the earlier years of the 1590s (LL-51):

> My very good Lord vpone yowre message vnto me by yowre servant [Michael] Hykes, I receyued no small comfort, that God puttinge into yowre hart to fauoure and assist me in my swtes to her Magestie after a longe travell [=travail], and doutfull labor, I myght obteyne sume ende to my contentment. Wherfore I most ernestly, and hartely desyre yowre Lordship to have a feelinge of myne infortunat estate, which althowghe yt be far vnfitt to indure delayes, yett have consumed fowre or fyve yeares, in a flatteringe hope of idell wordes. But now havinge receyued this comfortable message of furtherance & fauoure frome yowre Lordship althowghe her maiestie, be forgettfull of her selfe, yet by suche a good meane, I doo not dout, yf yow lyst but that I may receyve sume frute of all my travell [=travail].

By four or five years of 'flatteringe hope of idell wordes' Oxford signifies his so far vain attempts to acquire a monopoly on the gauging of beer (1587–92); to license the import of oils, fruits, and wools (1592–93); and to recover Waltham Forest. Now he feels he has received encouragement, since 1594, in another quarter:

> This last yeare past I have bene a swter [=suitor] to her Magestie that I myght ferme her Tynes …

Oxford's reference is to the famous tin-mines, or 'stannaries', of Cornwall and Devon.

Oxford hoped to 'farm' the Queen's tins by securing the 'preemption' of this humble but wealth-producing metal. Preemption was a monopolistic practice intended to forestall competitive underbidding by suppliers: instead, one person or corporation would buy up the whole annual production and offer it for sale at a controlled price. In the case of tin, this was an ancient practice dating back to the twelfth century:[1]

the stannaries were turned over in return for an annual rent to a succession of petty wardens who, besides the right of granting licenses for exporting tin, perhaps exercised the right of preemption as well. When the mines came under the power of the earls of Cornwall, the preemption was doubtless habitually exercised, and probably formed an important source of Richard of Cornwall's great wealth. ...

For two centuries the preemption was apparently never exercised, and when in the sixteenth and seventeenth centuries it was again put into operation, its revival was actuated not entirely by the fiscal motive in the mine predominant in the earlier exercise of the claim. ... [A] second and weighty argument for the revived use of the preemption was that in this way only could the tinners, ground down by the merchant dealers, find a permanent and equitable price for their metal.

Indeed, controversy raged over much of the sixteenth century as to how tin production should be financed: in 1591 an anonymous adviser suggested that the Queen take the preemption to herself, but in fact Ralegh seems to have secured the office until he withdrew in anticipation of his 1594–95 voyage to Guiana, leaving the field to other contenders, including Oxford and his chief rival Lord Treasurer Buckhurst.[2] Oxford's offer, already clarified in his opening salvo (LL-51), is that in exchange for the preemption he would guarantee the Queen £10,000 per annum, or £3000 more than her current income from the mines. Neither the Queen nor Oxford would invest money of their own; in particular, 'I only bearinge but the name of the su[i]te, lay owt never a pennye but have as ys sede [=said] a fyft part' of the endeavour and thus of the profits. If, however, the Queen's income were to fall short, 'I ... will what I can strayne my self to make yt vp full 10 thowsand...'

   Approximately one-third of Oxford's surviving letters and memoranda derive from his tin-mining campaign. These missives fall into two groups: first, 15 letters (LL-51–65) and some three memoranda (LL-69–71), 20 March 1595 to 14 March 1596; second, three letters (LL-66–68) and some six memoranda (LL-72–77), in or about June 1599. For the most part these missives make for dreary reading, except perhaps to aficionados of Elizabethan finance: the argumentation is dense and redundant, the style inward and crabbed. Occasionally the prose is relieved by a literary conceit: in his letter of 20 March 1595 (LL-51) Oxford deploys the conceit of the bird beaten from the bush which we have noted in Chapter 29; in a subsequent memorandum (LL-74) Oxford writes: 'But where the serpent lay hyde [=hid] in the herbe, they never thought [it] showld be perceived'. But such relief occurs only twice in some 10,000 words. Nothing reveals more than these utilitarian letters and memoranda the essentially prosaic character of this peculiar – and perhaps uncharacteristic – Elizabethan mind.

   Occasionally, to the reader's relief, a ray of light escapes to illuminate some corner of Oxford's life or character: here, his despair at having 'consumed fowre or fyve yeares, in a flatteringe hope of idell wordes', and his plan for financial recovery which requires that he himself 'lay owt never a pennye'; his offer on 25 March (LL-53) to attend Burghley 'at yowre house' ('as well as a lame man may'); his regret on 28 March (LL-54) concerning 'the shortnes of the tyme this day which I hadd with yowre Lordship'; his regret the same day in a letter addressed from Bishopsgate to Michael Hickes (LL-55) 'that I am not able nor fytt' to attend court, 'beinge yete no better recovered' from an illness, and a concomitant request that Burghley 'loke into my doughter Darbies house or myne'. On 9 April (LL-57) Oxford complained that he had 'labored so muche as I cowlde possible' to advance the Queen's cause – and his own – and that he would have brought it off 'yf myne vndertakers hadd kept promise with me', but of course his undertakers had not, but rather reneged 'throwghe the cunninge dealinge' of unnamed opponents. On 4 June (LL-71) Oxford begged Burghley to 'pardon my scrybled hand' as 'I have be[e]n this day lett bloode, that I cowld not wright so playne as else I wowld have done for yowre better eas[e]'.

On 16 June Burghley wrote to Oxford from court at Greenwich:[3]

> My Lord – I am sorie that my last lettres doth not so satisfy yow, as I ment, ffor my mistaking of your writing, I may Confesse it possible, but I do not knowe it, if I did I would Confesse it. If my speaches with Catcher have not bene agreable to your mynd therein I Confess myne error, for I tooke Catcher from the beinninge to have bene your informer, for by some yow must have bene informed. And I see now by your lettre it was not Catcher but rather one Robartes whom I knowe not, otherwise then that I heare that one Robarts is Catchers sonne in Lawe. But whether he be the partie, whom yow Commend I knowe not. But to the body of the matter, my Lord besides my writing yesterday, I did this daye verie earnestlie move hir maiestie to Commande a steye of the deliuerye to the entent the same might be boughte for hir maiesties proffett. But I assure yow my Lord I was sharply rebuked for the reiteratinge of this matter, so as I meane to deale no more therein, without hir maiestie shall Commande me. And wheare your Lordship hath Conceaved that (to your misfortune) it semeth to your Lordship that I am wonne from yow, therein who soever hath moved yow so to thinke they do me manifest wronge, and if I might knowe any that so give cause to slaunder me, I would both reprove & disprove them; adding that (as god shall save me) I have furdred your motions to the offence of others, and so I mynd not to deale any furder herein.

No doubt it had been Oxford himself who complained that Burghley had been 'won' by Oxford's rivals: so that it is Oxford whom Burghley accuses of slander. By 7 August, as we have noted, Oxford was writing from Byfleet in Surrey, where he had gone for the sake of his health.

Since Burghley would die between the first spate of tin-mining letters and the second, the latter are addressed rather to Robert Cecil. In his first of the second group, written on a Saturday in June 1599 (LL-66), Oxford reveals that he had 'wrott [sic] to her Magestye, hopinge she will not suffer me imployinge my selfe in her seruice to be rewarded for my labor with a moke' – but of course she did allow him to be recompensed with a mock, by virtue of a countermand 'which stoppethe the Preemptione'. In a letter endorsed June 1599 addressed directly to the Queen (LL-67), Oxford points out that he 'had nott of longe h[e]ard from yowre Majestye', but instead, 'my wyfe comminge from the courte, towld me that yowre Majestye sayd to her yow h[e]ard not that there wass any monye gotten' – so the Queen was not even bothering to reply to Oxford except by word-of-mouth through his wife. In a memorandum of approximately the same date (LL-75), Oxford in effect apologizes to Cecil for his 'rude hande', having compiled a 'rufe [=rough] account as short as I could deuise to contract a matter, so Intricat[e]'.

Oxford's five-year effort resulted in no benefit whatsoever to himself, doubt-less because it was impossible for him to persuade the Queen that he had the financial acumen or the personal capital to sustain the enterprise. The Queen did evidently send an agent, one Middleton, into the West to discover the real con-ditions prevailing among the tinners, and perhaps even exercised the preemption herself in 1599 and 1600; but the monopoly escaped Oxford altogether, and was rather held in succession by Sir Bevis Bulmer, Ralegh, and finally Brigham and Wemmes.[4] On 31 October 1599 Sir John Popham wrote to Cecil from West-minster:[5]

> Upon Sunday was se'nnight, when her Majesty had speech of the tin cause, she directed that my Lord of Oxford should be made acquainted with Bulmer's offer. If you have not already written to his Lordship in it, and understood his opinion therein, for that I hear her Majesty will have some speech of that cause to-morrow, I have thought good to put you in mind thereof

When it became clear to everyone, including himself, that he was simply incapa-ble of matching Bulmer's offer, Oxford's five-year obsession with Cornish tin came to a bitter end.

71 Oxford not to be Touched

Perhaps it was his alliance with the Countess of Cumberland through his daugh-ter's marriage to her son that brought Oxford a gift from the town Chamberlain of Bath between October 1595 and October 1596:[1]

> Paid for two couple of capon and two dozen of chickens and two dozen of pigeons and 15lb and 10oz of sugar given to my Lord of Oxon' and to the Countess of Cumberland   xliiijs

Perhaps, on the other hand, Oxford went to Bath for the sake of his health.

On 7 March 1596 Sir Francis Vere wrote to Essex:[2]

Ingengers [=Engineers] ar[e] very scant in Englande butt some thear [=there] ar[e] Theoricians, and suche a on[e] wear very fytt; in the army some wilbe founde nott altogeather voyead [=void] of practyse. Thear is Edward Hamnun, in London, sometymes belongyng to my Lorde of Oxforde who is nott ignorant in architecture and myght searve to good purpos...

Conceivably Edward Hamnun is to be identified with the E. Hamond mentioned in Oxford's letter of July 1581 (LL-13).

On 10 July the Archbishop and Council at York wrote to the Privy Council concerning Richard Atkinson of Ripon:[3]

May yt please your good Lordships to be advertised. That, whereas both the authoritie of this Counsell, and the procedinges of certaine Iustices of Peace, within the Countie of Yorke, hath bene latelie attempted to be brought into greate question & disgrace, by the contempteous & willfull prosedinges, of one Richard Atkinson of Rippon, whoe se[e]keth to call into examinacion, the Iurisdicion of this Counsell, by pursewinge of divers accions of false imprisonment, bycause the keeper of Yorke Castle, the Typstaffe here attendinge, and one Rounder gailer of Rippon; the same Atkinson being iustlie imprisoned, for his contempteous & Lewde behaviour, as by a declaracion hereinclosed, the whole cause & the procedinges thereof will apeare vnto your good Lordships. yt pleased you, to directe your Lettres, beringe date the xxth of Iune, to me the Archbishop, to convente Atkinson before me, and to take order for his apparaunce, before your Lordships, which is don accordinglie. he is to appeare at the Courte before you the xviijth daie of this moneth, moste humblie praieng your good Lordships, that the presumpteous & bold attemptes of this Atkinson to the derogacion of the authoritie here established, maie receave such punishment, as your honours wisedomes shall thinke moste fitt, for thadvancement of the credit and authoritie of this Councell; & of the Iustices in the Liberte of Rippon, to the example, of anie such busie contempteous person, that shall attempte the like hereafter. ...

Members of the Privy Council gave the case their attention on 16 and 20 June, and again on 18 July.[4] Oxford's name is brought in not by any official statement, but by an endorsement to the original letter in Cecil's hand:

Corn / wyne / stirr sedition / Promoter / Caterpiller / 90000li / Erl of Oxford not, to be touched

Atkinson submitteth / accuseth Elson and Cawley

Oxford clearly stood in danger of being touched by the scandal. Anthony Atkinson and Michael Cawley were both agents of Oxford's Countess.[5] Richard Atkinson, apparently stirring sedition, was considered both a promoter and a 'Caterpiller' ('rapacious person; an extortioner; one who preys upon society' – *OED*).

On 6 September Oxford wrote from Canon Row – Derby's residence – to Cecil. Oxford owned a portable desk – which on this occasion he had left behind (LL-26):

The wrightinge which I have ys in the contrye, for I hadd suche care thearofe as I carried yt with me in a lyttell deske, to morow or the next day I ame to goo thether, and so sone as I come home by the grace of God I will send yt yow.

By now Oxford had lost virtually all his country estates, but perhaps he had visited Plaistow, where joiners were completing their lengthy refurbishment. Oxford turns to his daughter Elizabeth's promised annuity:

The Earle of Darby showld have sett his hand and seale to thys copie, as he hadd done to yowres, but his promises, beinge but delayes and shiftes, in the meane seasone, I caused his officer Irland and an other to sett theare handes vnto yt, to wittnes that yt was a trwe copie. I named to yow in hast in my last letter, Mr Hykes. But I hadd forgott my self, yt was Mr Barnarddeux whome my lord imployed in that cause. and therfore I think him able to satisfise [=satisfy] all suche doutes as my lord may cast. I doo not dowte, but yf my lord hadd then any care therof, or Mr Barnarddeux but that this assurance ys as fyrme as the lave [=law] can make yt theare was imployed in yt the Master of the Rooles then and now lord keper, and others of my lords lerned councell in lave [=law], whoo I hope are sufficient to passe greater matters then ytt.

The £1000 was not yet settled on Elizabeth. On 17 September Oxford wrote to Cecil regarding her 'pension' (LL-27):

I have sent yow by this bearer the Copie which was in my hands but pervsinge the same, yt semethe to be not as I toke ytt, but rather a counterpane of her ioynture, then [=than] of her pensione. How my daughters occasiones are to vse the same I am ignorant, beinge made rather aquaynted thearwythe by common report, then [=than] frome her selfe, or any of her friendes. But I dout not, but that my lord and yow, dyd so well loke to the same, when yt was to be performed, that whatt assurance was to be made, was done wythe good aduise. I know that Barnardeux was the man who was imployed, and that the intent was for a pentione [=pension] of one thowsand poundes by yeares to be assured her so longe as my Lord of Darby liued, and to that end a lease to her vse was to be made over vnto yow and myself. How yt was followed yf this be not yt I know not. Wherfore I pray yow good Sir Robert Cecill, pervs[e] this, and yf yt be not as I take yt yet have that care of yowre Niece, that yf yt be in the handes of Barnarddeux, yt may be sought owt.

Now Oxford turns to the surprising topic of his daughter's personal reputation:

Also I am most ernestly to desyre yow that as yow are her vncle and nerest to her next my self, that yow will friendly [=as a friend] assist her with yowre good aduise, yow know her yowthe, and the place wherin she lyves, and how muche to bothe owre houses, yt importes that she carrie her self, according to her honor. Enemies are apt to make the worst of every thinge, flatterers will doo evill offices, and trwe and faythfull aduise, will seme harshe to tender eares. But sythe my fortune hathe sett me so far of[f] as I cannot be at hand in this her troblesume occasiones, I hope yow will doo the good office of an vncle, and I commit vnto yow the authorite of a parent in myne absence. Thus confounded with the smalle vnderstandinge of her

estate, and the care of her welldoinge, I leaue to troble yow any farther, most
ernestly desyringe yow as yow can gett leysure, to aduertise me how her causes stand,
and vpon whatt termes. whearof I assure yow I cannot yett tell whatt to thinke.

Suspicions that Elizabeth was unfaithful to her husband were to grow over the
following year.

The Court lay at Greenwich this year from 4 April to 25 September.[6] It was
apparently during this term that Robert Mefflin, leatherseller, and Edward Johnson, joiner, met with Oxford; Johnson asked for his money:[7]

> att his Lordshipps lodginge in Greenwich the plainant moved his lordshipp in this
> deponentes hereinge for monney but howe much he rememberith not. but as the
> plainant reported for about Syxe and thirtye poundes which his Lordshipp then
> owed the plainant for Ioyners woorke and Stuffe, vnto which his Lordshipp
> answeared sayinge,

> be Content Ioyner, I haue no monney to paye thee, take vpp soe much monney att
> Intereste to serve thy turne, and I will paye for yt, and paye yt againe, thou shalt be
> no Looser by me.

> with which answeare the plainant Rested Satisfied and lefte his Lordshipp ...

Johnson now addresses the intervening years:

> but what with the delay of the Earle of Oxford himself, his said Lady, & with delay
> of his officers your sayd Subiect was from tyme to tyme putt of[f] from the receipt
> of such money as was due vnto him by meanes of which delayes your sayd Subiect
> being without his money and being indebted in diuers places for himself & for his
> men was arrested three or fower seuerall tymes and was enforced to take vp money
> at interest & to lay most of his goods to pawne to his great losse and hinderance to
> pay those debts which he was arrested for

Eight years later, as Oxford lay on his deathbed, Johnson the joiner had still not
recovered his debt.

72 I Have not an Able Body

On 11 January 1597[1] Oxford wrote to Cecil concerning a suit brought against his
wife (LL-28):

> Good Sir Robert Cecill, wheras my wyfe hathe showed me, a supplicatione
> exhibited to the lordes of the Councell, agaynst her, I have longed bothe to yelde
> yow thankes for yowre curtesie, to her and my self in makinge her aquainted
> therwythe, and also to aduertise yow, how levdly [=lewdly, ignorantly] thearin he
> behaves himself. For as for my wyfe he chargethe, wythe a matter wherto she was
> never acknowleginge, as yf yow consider the datte [=date] of his supplicatione,

> which signefieth a fyve yeares agone, at whatt tyme I thinke she never knew the
> man, and muche lesse had any dealinges wyth him, as he cannot denye, and If I
> then weere maried vnto her yt was all.

Oxford complains that the suit is stale, concerning events five years earlier, when
Oxford had only recently married. He continues:

> Whearas he pretendethe I made over to her my pensione with a conditione to pay
> all former warrantes graunted by me, yt is mearly fals, neyther hathe he any ground
> to say yt. wherfore how presumptuously he dothe abuse her, yow may easly iuge, as
> that [he] dares to make so impodently [=impudently] his complaynte of her, beinge
> as she ys: and to suche personages of qualite and statte, as are the pryvie Councell.

Oxford denies that he had transferred his £1000 annuity to his wife, though he
had transferred property titles to her, her brother, and her uncle Ralph Snead.
Oxford insists it is impudent for a mere commoner to bring a suit against a countess, or to disturb men of such quality and estate as Privy Councillors. Oxford
wishes an appropriate punishment upon his tormentor:

> I doo not dowt therfore, but as yow have begune wythe so honorable a procedinge,
> but yow will lett him have his desertes accordinge to his presumptione.

> And in the meane seasone for that a longe letter may be troblesume vnto yow,
> which have matters in hand of more importance, I thowght yt fytt, thus shortly to
> show the wronge don to her, and to refer the very ground and culler of his
> complaynt vnto an other s[ch]edule [=memorandum] which I shall send yow.

> Whearin yf he hath hadd any cause to have complayned, it showld then have bene
> agaynst my self, as the same will explayne. But his shyftes and knaveries are so grosse
> and palpable, that doutinge to bringe his partes [=parts? parties?] and iuglinges
> [=jugglings, deceptions] to light, he dothe adresse his petitione agaynst her that ys
> vtterly ignorant of the cause. Thus desyringe yow to conceyve how thankfuly I take
> thys honorable dealinge with my wyfe and friendly care to me, I will the lesse sett
> forthe in woordes whatt I the more desyre in deeds to show, if I weare so happie as
> to fynd oportunite.

Oxford is of course perfectly aware that he himself is a virtual bankrupt, that it
would therefore be pointless to sue him, and that the only logical move is to sue
his wife, who holds his assets.

The explanatory 'sedule', entitled 'The Ground whearone Thomas Gurley
playntyfe to the Councel makethe his petitione', is also in Oxford's hand (LL-49):

> In Flushinge and in the lowe contries thearabout, weare certeyne poore men
> whiche hadd a longe tyme serued her Magestye in place of Gunners, whiche beinge
> behynd hand for want of theare pay, and not able to susteyne the longe delaye,
> which then hapned at that tyme (vpon what occasione I know not) and for want of
> friends dispayringe to recover the same, to supplie theare poore estate in tyme,
> sowld theare interest to this Thomas Gurley, whoo to compas the commodite of

this bargayne, came vnto me, offringe 300*l* yf I cowld gett my lord Thresorers allowance therofe and his letter to Sir Thomas Sherley vnder thresorer then for the lowe Contries.

The affair thus transpired within a month of Oxford's landing in the Low Countries on 27 August 1585. Since the salary promised to English gunners was not forthcoming, Thomas Gurlyn agreed to pay them from his own funds if he could eventually collect their pay from the Treasury. Gurlyn promised Oxford £300 if he would secure a letter from Burghley authorizing Sir Thomas Sherley, under-treasurer, to release the gunners' salaries. Oxford accepted the proposal, but soon despaired of receiving the £300 from Gurlyn:

> Vpon this offer, I becam suter to my lord [=Burghley], and pretendinge [=professing] that this Gurley owed me 300*l*, I cowld not by reasone of his bare estate, hope otherwise how to come by this monye.

Gurlyn protests that he had not paid Oxford because he had not yet received his money from Sherley. Since release of the funds by Sherley was not a condition in his agreement with Gurlyn, however, Oxford thought that Gurlyn owed him £300 regardless. Oxford took his case to Burghley:

> After sume proces of tyme my lord [=Burghley] examininge the testimonialls of this dett, found it dwe [=due], and therfore in favoure of me, after he had often spoken with Gurle, who dyd also acknowlege his dett to me, dyd not only giue allowance therto, but also wroot his letter to Sir Thomas Sherley for to see yt payed.

Though Burghley ordered Gurlyn to pay Oxford and Sherley to pay Gurlyn, nothing happened:

> But for that Sir Thomas Sherley was yet vnfurnished, sythe he was to attende my lord Thresores [sic] dispaches in those matters, theare grew an Interim, wherin for that I had occasione at this tyme to vse monye, Gurle offerd me yf I wowld make him my receyver of the anuite in the Exchecker, he wowld find the meanes to take vp so muche monye as showld serue my turne, tyll the other mony showld be payed by Sir Thomas.

Thus, as Oxford was desperate for money, Gurlyn offered to pay the £300 on a new condition: that Oxford would appoint him receiver of his £1000 annuity. (Since Oxford was granted his annuity on 26 June 1586, these negotiations were undertaken long after Oxford's return from Flushing in October 1585.)

> to this I consented and he browght me 200*l* which he was to pay of the 300*l* as he sayde, and at the quarters end he hoped to bringe in the other 100*l*. but at this quarters end, Sir Thomas Sherle was not yett dispache[d] by my lord Thresorer. Wherfore I sendinge to the Excheker cowld theare receyve no more then 50*l*, for that Gurley had receyved therof before hand by vertue of my warrant, 200*l*.

Gurlyn thus paid Oxford £200 of the £300 agreed, and promised another £100.

But Oxford soon discovered that the £200 had been drawn from the Exchequer on Oxford's blanket authorization, so that in effect Gurlyn paid Oxford with Oxford's own money. Rather than receiving £300 from Gurlyn and £250 from the Exchequer, Oxford received £200 from Gurlyn and £50 from the Exchequer. Thus Gurlyn still owed Oxford £200 in real (not borrowed) money, not to mention the final £100 of the promised £300:

> So heare yt may appeare playnly inowghe that the monye which Gurle pretendethe to be parcel of the 300*l*, was only but myne owne, and that aquighted [=acquitted] to the receyvers at the quarters end, so that this so allowed (as yt was) he was stille behind hand with me for the 300*l*.

Gurlyn begged Oxford to understand that so long as Sir Thomas Sherley was not forthcoming with the gunners' salaries, he himself was not in a position to reimburse Oxford:

> But for that tyme he satisfised me, with excuse that yet Sir Thomas Sherle, could not helpe him to his monye, and therfore he wowld take vp agayne afore hand 200*l*, for the meane seasone, and by the next quarter he douted not but to have his monye to my full satisfactione.

Gurlyn now repeated his charade, paying Oxford with £200 drawn from Oxford's Exchequer account:

> This quarter beinge rune out as the other, as I did before, I receyved frome the Excheker but 50*l*, by the former reasone. So the 200*l* also beinge theare discharged, now Gurley yet was to bringe in his thre hundred poundes.

Thus everything was back to the beginning.

When Sir Thomas Sherley finally paid out the gunners' salaries, Gurlyn took the money and made himself scarce:

> In This quarter he had receyved his mony, but cam not at me as he wont to doo but sildommer [=seldom?], and then put me of[f] frome day to day. Tyll at the last beinge assured he was payed by Sir Thomas Sherlye I pressed him for his monye.

No longer dependent on Oxford's influence with Burghley to spring the money from Sir Thomas Sherley, Gurlyn denied that there ever had been an agreement with Oxford of any kind:

> Wythe a notorious impodentie [=impudency] he denyed his promes, and sayd he had only promised to lend me so muche, whiche he hadd all redie performed and a hundred pound more for whiche I was in his dett, and for this he alleaged the 400l which he hadd at twoo seuerall tymes payed vnto me, at every tyme 200l.

Gurlyn thus claimed that he had merely promised Oxford £300 as a loan; since he had delivered £400 (in two £200 increments), Oxford now owed him £100. Gurlyn now also denied that Burghley had performed a service at all, since

Gurlyn had a legal right to the gunners' salaries:

> And as for my lord Thresorer [=Burghley], he [=Gurlyn] denyed that ever he receyved any other fauour then that whiche he was to doo him by Iustice

Moreover, as the agreement with Oxford was merely verbal, Oxford had no proof in writing:

> for me he hadd but my good word, whiche the longe delayes considered eare [=ere, before] he dyd effect his sute, yt stood him in lyttell steed [=stead].

> Thus he replied I showld have fyrst sett downe vpon my positione, for that I had obiected vnto him, how he hadd made me both speake, and wright often tymes ernestly to my lord, and the principall cullor I hadd, was for that his estate was so bare as I cowld not els tell how to come by 300l, which he owed me as himself also vnder that shadowe hadd often come to the speache of my lord, and hadd acknowlegd yt to him.

> Heare ys the very state of the cause playnlye set downe, and the very grownde of his pretended dett by me to him, which for that he knowes I can remember, and that my wyfe ys not aquainted with the cause; yt semethe he framethe his petitione the bowldlier agaynst her.

Oxford finally complains that Gurlyn directs his suit against the Countess, who knows nothing, rather than against himself, who remembers everything. We may add that Gurlyn doubtless sued the Countess rather than the Earl because she had deeper pockets.

Oxford now introduces a new player, a Mr Taylor, evidently a clerk in the Exchequer:

> But sythence that tyme, by those former warrantes how he hathe preuented me by takinge vp a fore hand [=beforehand] diuers sumes throwghe the frendship of Taylor, whoo notwythstandinge I vpon this aforsayd dealinge, calld for my warrantes in agayne as none knowes better then yowre self, what the patent ys and how yt runes [=runs], yett wowld aver them to be good, and flatly wroote vnto me, he had my hand and warrant, which was sufficient for his discharge in lave [=law].

In brief, Oxford attempted to cancel the warrant that allowed Gurlyn to draw funds from his Exchequer account, but Taylor continued to recognize the old warrant as still valid.

> But after he hadd payed this Gurley diuers sumes in this manner and that he better hade loked into my pattent, besydes hering I ment to call him before my Lord Thresorer, then he submitted himself by a letter, sent in my warrants, and surseased [=surceased, ceased] his further payments to Gurley ...

By threatening to call him before Burghley, Oxford finally persuaded Taylor to surrender the old warrants. But this did not discourage Gurlyn,

> … who nowe clayminge of a 140*l* from my wyfe, as bound by conditione to se[e] those his warrantes discharged, showes that all which he acknowlegethe to be payed allredye, so muche he hathe robbed me of by this meanes, which ys a 260*l* for he sayes of the 300*l* he lent me yet ys dwe to him a 140*l* by my wyfe …

Up to now Gurlyn's claim, as reported by Oxford, had been £100: he does not thoroughly explain why the suit is now for £140, but perhaps Gurlyn was also asking for interest. Oxford concludes by reminding Cecil of the basic facts:

> … and that 400 which he browght me as the premisses show was all myne owne mony discharged and allowed vnto Taylor and the officer then in the Excheker.

> Many prankes besydes he hathe played me, which at this tyme I forbeare tyll yt shalbe my hap to speake with yow at one tyme or other for that in suche a trifell, my thinkes [=methinks] I have bene alreadie to[o] long yet I cowld not chouse, to make it playne vnto yow.

In short, Gurlyn had been playing a kind of shell-game.

No doubt Gurlyn used every trick in the book, but what about Oxford? The leader of a troop of horse in wartime conditions, he agreed (by his own admission) to sell access and influence for £300. Since his agreement with Gurlyn was not legally enforceable – indeed, it was unethical even by standards of the time – he had put nothing in writing. Moreover, it should have been clear to him from the beginning that until Sir Thomas Sherley surrendered the gunners' salaries, Gurlyn could claim that Oxford hadn't kept his side of the bargain; but after Sherley surrendered the funds, Gurlyn had no need of Oxford.

Oxford's letter had its effect: that Cecil called Gurlyn on the carpet is evident from a counter-petition of 30 January (where the author's signature – 'Tho: Gurlyn' – resolves the question of pronunciation):[2]

> Right Honorable Maye it please yow, vnderstandinge of your harde opinion conceived against me, by reason that I preferred a petition concerninge the right honorable the Counties [=Countess] of Oxeforde, fforasmuch as your honor doth Censor euery mans cawse in one equall Ballance; and I knowinge my cawse honest and iust, ame the rather imbowldened to presume to intreate your honor by waitinge[?] to permite me into your honorable presentes, and to geive me leave aswell to answer her honors obiections, as to shewe the Cawse I did preferr the same. And if I shall shewe the parte of an honest man towardes her Ladyship, then that I may crave your honorable favour, (otherwise) to falle into your honors conceipt, and willingly endure such punnishment as your honor shall please to impose one me. …

Doubtless Gurlyn would argue that since Oxford made his Countess or her agent the receiver of his annuity, she was responsible for his debts. Nevertheless, Gurlyn did not prevail. In 1610 Countess Elizabeth (who clearly had a better ear for names than her husband) would refer back to this case as that of 'Thomas Gurling whoe sueinge for a debte pretended to be due vnto him from the said late

Earle was at the triall thereof overthrowne vppon manifest proofe made of the satisfaction of that debte'.[3]

On 16 March 1597 Rowland Whyte wrote to Robert Sidney:[4]

> I am credibly informed that the Lord Cobham, who shall marry my Lord Oxford's daughter, hearing how disdainfully my Lord of Essex speaks of him in public, doth likewise protest to hate the Earl as much.

Reference is to Bridget, now thirteen, and to Henry Brooke, who would become 8th Lord Cobham less than a month later (William, Lord Cobham, was buried on 5 April). The rumoured marriage, which did not come off, is merely an aside in Whyte's report on the quarrel raging between Cobham and Essex.

On 31 July Sir Edward Fitton wrote to Cecil:[5]

> Now Sir for the Lease mad[e] to my Lord of Oxford and you: ther is noe other lease nor assurance. But the lease made for my Ladyes Ioynture, which lease is warranted by syne [=sign]: and the deed dothe Remayn as Mr Irland assurethe me vnder my Lord Treasurers Hand the yerle of Oxfordes and yours with my Lord and my Lord Treasurer Hathe the deed vnder the erle of derbyes Handes. whereby the very interest of the possessyon is in your Honour instantly. it weer good you caused my Lord your father to seek it vppe and peruse it. But this is most trew yf Ireland say trew: But I beseeche your Honour keep this to your self vntill I see you for itt is Better for me to speak all I know then wrytt [=write]. I haue apoynted all the names of the Gentlemen that mett my Lord to be sett downe for your Lordship to see. my Lady was Honorably entertayned at Sir Thomas Gerrerdes. But his mothers sicknes did keep thens [=from thence] bothe ther daughters and son in lawes. ...

The first lease mentioned by Fitton was made jointly to Oxford and Cecil: its terms are unknown. The second was part of the jointure meant to protect the lands that Elizabeth Vere brought to her marriage, as distinct from the £1000 annuity pledged by her husband. When Fitton assures Cecil that the 'very interest of the possession' of the lease is 'in your Lordship instantly', he means that on Elizabeth's death the lease would revert to Cecil and not to Oxford. The lands in question are named in an undated but contemporary memorandum:[6]

> Note of the lands assured to Lady Elizabeth Vere, afterwards Countess of Derby, and Ladies Bridget and Susan Vere, daughters of Edward Earl of Oxford, in reversion after Lord Burghley; viz., Heningham castle, manor, and priory, assigned to them by Edward Earl of Oxford, with reversion to his heirs; and Boothby and Bichfield manors, co. Lincoln, and Clawson, co. Leicester, by Wm. Lord Burghley, with reversion to his heirs.

While Castle Hedingham would revert to Oxford or his heirs in the event of the deaths of all three daughters, the estate was otherwise beyond his reach.

On 20 August, at Greenwich, the Earl of Derby issued an open challenge in writing:[7]

> Yf any on[e] can say that I knowe my wyff to be dishonest of her body or that I can
> Iustly proue ytt by my self or any on[e] els I chalenge him the combatt of lyff. Yf
> any on[e] suppose any speeches of myn to haue proceded out of that doubt he doth
> me wronge.

The challenge was countersigned by Burghley, Lord Charles Howard, and Cecil.
Rumours had been flying about Elizabeth, who was suspected of a sexual relationship with Essex.[8] Was this merely wild gossip? or was Elizabeth a chip off the old
block?

   In the course of 1597 Oxford and his Countess removed from Stoke Newington
to an even more remote estate in Hackney known as 'King's House' or 'King's
Place', later 'Brooke House' or 'Hackney House'.[9] The licence of alienation,
dated 2 September, traces the recent history of the site:

> Alienation on payment of ten pounds, granted to Anthony Radcliff Esquire,
> Nicholas Moseley Citizen and Alderman of London, Alexander King Esquire,
> Edward Pilsworth Citizen and Clothworker of London, and William Cotton
> Citizen and Draper of London, of The King's Place in Hackney, Middlesex,
> formerly the property of Sir Roland Hayward, to 'our dear cousin' Elizabeth
> Countess of Oxford wife of Edward Earl of Oxford, Francis Trentham Esquire,
> Ralph Snead Esquire, and Giles (Egidio) Young gentleman.

Acquisition by the Trentham–Snead–Young consortium meant that the property
lay beyond the reach of Oxford's creditors.

   According to the 1618 revision of Stow's *Survey of London*, edited by Oxford's
former servant Anthony Munday, the house, known as 'King's Manor', was also
called 'Shore-ditch Place … But how it tooke that name, I know not' (p. 800).
An early document describes it as[10]

> a ffayre house all of bricke havinge a ffayre hall and a parlour, a ffaire ketchyn, a
> pastory, a drye larder with Buttry, Pantery and all other houses of office necessary
> and many ffayre chambers, a ffaire long Gallerye, a proper Chappell and a closet
> commynge out of the great Chamber over the Chappell, a proper lybrarye to laye
> bokes [and] many other proper Rowmes wythyn the same place.

An inventory, undated but perhaps compiled on the death of Countess Elizabeth
in 1612, provides a detailed enumeration of rooms and their contents.[11] Though
the moveables may have changed since Oxford lived there, the rooms must have
remained more or less the same:

> the Staircase, my Ladies chamber, the Study, the Maydes Chamber, the Entry to
> the Office house, Rowland Beresfourdes Chamber, Mistres Norris her Chamber,
> the Entry to the great Chamber, the great Chamber, the foure vpper Loftes of the
> new frame, the little Chamber, the Presse chamber, the Study in the great
> Chamber, the washe house, the Chamber over it, the washe yarde, the Stable, the
> Hen house, the olde storehouse, the great Corne loft, the next Lofte, the mens
> chamber, the next Chamber, the well yarde, the milke house, the little Parlor, the

greate Parlor, the buttery, the Hall, the kitchin, the Lardery, the Styll house, my
Ladys Chamber, the little chamber.

Oxford and his wife were now parishioners of St John, Hackney, *alias* St Augus-
tine. The church, except for its tower, was demolished in 1798.[12]

On 8 September Oxford wrote to Burghley concerning yet another prospective marriage for Bridget, this time to William Herbert, son of Lord and Lady
Pembroke, who were promoting the match (LL-29):

> My very good lord I have pervsed thes letters, which according to yowre Lordships
> desyre I have returned. I do perceyve how bothe my Lord and Ladie doo perseuer,
> whiche dothe greatly content me, for Brigets sake, whome alwayes I have wished a
> good husband suche as yowre Lordship and my selfe may take comfort by. And as
> for the articles which I perceyve have bene moved betwiene yowre Lordship and
> them, (referringe all to yowre Lordships wisdome and good lekinge) I will frely sett
> downe myn opinione, according to yowre lordships desyre.

Thus the negotiations had gone as far as the drafting of a pre-nuptial agreement.

> My Lord of Pembroke ys a man syklye [=sickly] and therfore yt ys to be gathered he
> desyrethe in hys lyfte tyme [=lifetime] to se his sune bestowed to his lekinge
> [=liking]. to compas which my thinkes [=me thinks] his offers very honorable, hys
> desyres very resonable. Agayne beinge a thinge agreable to yowre lordships fatherly
> care and loue to my dowghter. A thinge which for the honor, friendship, and
> lekinge I have to the ma[t]che [=marriage] very agreable to me so that all part[i]es
> desyre but the same thynge. I know no reasone to delay yt, but according to there
> desyres, to accomplishe yt with convenient speede. and I do not dowt, but yowre
> lordship and my self shall receyve great comfort therby. for the ionge [=young]
> gentelman, as I vnderstand hathe bene well browght vp, fayre conditioned, and
> hathe many good partes in hym. Thus to satisfise [=satisfy] yowre Lordship I have
> as shortly as I can set downe my opinion to my Lords desyres, notwythestandinge I
> refer thers, and myne owne which ys all on[e] with theres, to yowre lordships
> wisdome. I am sorye that I have not an able bodie, which myght have serued to
> attend on her Magestye in the place where she ys, beinge espetially there, whyther
> without any other occasione, then to see yowre Lordship I wowld alwayes
> willingelye goo. …

Once again Oxford discloses a physical infirmity: 'I have not an able bodie'. The
proposed marriage to William Herbert did not come off.

Queen Elizabeth's Ninth Parliament sat from 24 October to 20 December,
and again from 11 January to 9 February 1598 (*TE*). Oxford attended once only,
missing 39 sessions (*Journals*). The fact that he missed both the opening and closing
sessions may suggest that he was now, if not an invalid, at least chronically ill. His
attendance on 14 December 1597 was to be his last at any Parliament.

73 The Death of Father Burghley

Some time in the late 1590s, Cecil endorsed a list of 'Noblemen we are sure of to be here':[1]

> Earls of Oxford, Shrewsbury, Derby, Worcester, Cumberland, Hertford, Lincoln, Nottingham; Viscount Bindon; Lords Delaware, Morley, Cobham, Stafford, Gray of Wilton, Lumley, Winsor, Rich, Darcy of Chiche, Chandos, Hunsdon, St. John of Bletsoe, Buckhurst, Burghley, Compton, Howard of Walden.

The exact import of this list is unclear, but it suggests that Oxford was counted among the loyal.

Burghley died on 4 August 1598, aged 78. The greatest Englishman of his age, in his domestic life he was father to Thomas, Anne, Elizabeth, and Robert Cecil, to a host of wards including Oxford, and to Oxford's children, especially Elizabeth, Bridget and Susan. He had supported these 'daughters' all along,[2] but in his will dated 1 March he remembered them again, in many successive clauses.[3] Burghley requests burial at Burghley House in Northamptonshire, but if that is not possible, at Westminster, 'neare where the bodies of my wiefe and my daughter of Oxford are buried'. He then makes his bequests, which are worth noting at length:

> … I giue to my saide sonne Sir Robert Cecill and to the Ladie Bridgett & Ladie Suzan Veare the daughters of my deceased daughter the Ladie Anne Countesse of Oxforde all my goodes monie plate, and stuffe that are or shalbe remayneinge at my deathe within my bedchamber at Westminster and in my two Closettes and anie chambers therto adioyneinge and extendinge to the lodginge of the saide Robert Cecill at my dwellinge howse called Cecill or Burley Howse in Westminster. All which stuffe plate and monie I will shalbe devided by my servante Thomas Bellott and the Deane of Westminster equallie into three partes betwixt my saide sonne Robert Cecill and the saide two Ladies. And that the same be deliuered for the saide two younge Ladies by the order of my daughter Countesse of Darbie [=Elizabeth Vere] the Lady Dennie & my sister White and my Steward Thomas Bellott or by anie two of them. saveinge I will that the value of one thowsande poundes shalbe deliuered to the countesse of Derbie …

Thus Elizabeth received only £1000, doubtless because she had already received a marriage portion from Burghley. Instructions are then given concerning the distribution of certain plate:

> And further I will and my meaneinge is that the other moitie not giuen to my sonne Thomas Cecill nor chardged with the particuler Legacies aboue mentioned shall be deuided into fouer equall partes whereof I giue to my sonne Sir Robert Cecill one fourth parte. And to the Ladie Elizabeth Veare nowe Countess of Derbie one other fourth parte. And to the Ladie Bridget Veare one other fouerth parte. And to the Ladie Suzan Veare one other fouerth parte. … [with provision for

the equitable division into parts for distribution to Sir Robert Cecill] and the two younge Ladies …

Item I giue vnto the Ladie Bridgett Veare and the Ladie Suzan Veare all manner of plate stuffe and furniture of houshold in the chambers Schoolehouses and Nurseries where they doe vsuallie lodge or lie both in my house at Westminster and at Theobaldes with all such plate as pottes boulles plates salt, lynnen, spoones and beddinge and other vtensells commonlie occupied for their lodginges dynners and suppers in the places commonlie vsed by them privatlie for their dynners suppers or diette in my absence to be enioyed by them for their vse wheresoeuer they shall remaine the same to be chosen out for them by my sister White and Thomas Bellotte.

Mention of 'the chambers Schoolehouses and Nurseries' where Bridget and Susan normally lived, whether at Burghley House or at Theobalds, allows us visualize the girls' domestic arrangements. The will continues:

Item I will and giue to my saide sonne Sir Robert Cecill all my houshold stuffe and furniture of houshold vsuallie occupied at and about my house at Theobaldes … saveinge such stuffe as the younge Ladies haue had and vsed to haue in their lodginges … All which plate besides the lynnen soe chested I doe giue to my two daughters the Ladie Bridgett and Ladie Suzan Veare …

Item I do giue to the two Ladies Bridgett and Suzan all manner of houshold stuffe as shalbe in my lodge at Chesthunt Parke. And if the same shall not be furnished with houshold stuffe at my death Then I giue to them all such houshold stuffe or the like as was ocupied by them at Pimmes or asmuch to be taken oute of my stuffe at Theobaldes and for increase thereof to furnishe the saide Lodge for them I haue caused my Stewarde Thomas Bellotte to make an Inventorie of all stuffe necessarie to be vsed for them in the lodge which I doe giue to them to be by him chosen out of my stuffe before bequeathed to my sonne Sir Robert Cecill.

Item I doe also giue to the two younge Ladies Ladie Bridgett and Ladie Suzan the choise by them to be made with the advise of the Ladie of Derbie their sister or my sister White theire Aunte of anie two beddes or stuffe for the same bedding with Pallett thereto belonginge[,] Cupboarde, Carpett, stooles and chaires that shalbe in anie chamber within my houses at Theobaldes, savinge and exceptinge such two chambers as my sonne Sir Robert Cecill shall requier to be excepted, soe as either of the saide two Ladies maie haue a bedde & Bedstedd fullie furnished with a Pallett and pillowes and sheetes thereto belonginge besides their owne private beddinges vsed by them in anie of my houses. …

[Provision for] the Mannour and Castell of Esenden in the Countie of Rutlande [to Robert Cecil (and his heirs)] because it maie remaine as a place for him and the heires of his bodie or the heires of the bodie of his sister the Countesse of Oxforde to resorte vnto … [More granted to Robert and his heirs,] the remainder to the heires of the bodie of my daughter the Ladie Anne Countesse of Oxforde [Moreover, that part of Essenden Park lying in Lincolnshire, like that lying in Rutland, to Robert Cecil and his heirs,] the remainder to the children of the saide Countesse of Oxford and the heires of their bodies …

[All lands not bequeathed to Robert] and such other landes as I haue purchased for the three younge Ladies daughters of the Countesse of Oxforde [to remain to Sir Thomas Cecill] …

Item I doe giue to the two Ladies Bridgett and Suzanne the choise of anie of my Coaches and of anie two of my Coache horses with all furniture thereto belonginge and the choise of anie fouer horses or geldinges either in my Stable or in anie Parke or Pasture … [Thomas Bellott to have his choice of horses] next after the choise made for two for euerie of the Ladies Bridget amd Susan. …

[All servants to have their wages continued for two years.] And if anie of them shall vppon request of anie my sonnes or of the two younge Ladies continue in service with anie of them I will that they shall so longe continue in their service …

Item I will that my sonne Thomas Cecill shall not take full possession of my house here in Westminster dureinge the space of six weekes after my decease dureinge which tyme I will that Thomas Bellotte as my Executor shall keepe my houshold there with meate drincke and lodginge for the Ladies as hath bene vsed in my absence within which tyme there maie be order taken where the two Ladies shall remaine whoe shall haue a revenue parte in Essex and parte in Lincoln and Leicester shere to mainetaine for theire apparrell and diett. And the two Pawlettes [=pallets] to be deliuered to their grandfather Sir Thomas Cecill. …

Item where Thomas Bellotte hath in his charge in my plate house certaine portions of monie and some bondes for monie to be paide to me I doe committee soe much trust to him as I requier him to make Doctor Goodman Deane of Westminster privey thereto And I doe make them two Executors of this my will and to dispose the same monie to the advancement of the Ladie Bridget and Ladie Susan for their marriages with these condicions that which of them shalbe married with an Earle or the heire apparant of an Earle shall haue fouer thowsande poundes parte of the monie left with the saide Thomas Bellotte. And if they shall marrie with a Baron or the heire apparante of a Baron then but three thowsand poundes. And if vnder that degree then but two thowsand poundes. But my meaning is the saide Thomas Bellotte shall oute of the saide monie nowe in his Custodie take allowance for all the charges laide oute by him for my housholde charges and for my Legacies to my servantes: And the remainder beinge devided into two partes I will that the one halfe [be given] to the Ladie Elizabeth Countesse of Darbie and her two sisters and the other moitie to be giuen to such godlie vses as my Executors shall thincke good.

I will that all my gold Plate be duelie wayed by order of Thomas Bellotte and the Deane of Westminster. And that my two sonnes Sir Thomas and Sir Robert Cecill shall haue the one halfe thereof and the other halfe to be giuen to my three daughters the Countesse of Derbie the Ladie Bridget and the Ladie Suzan so as there be giuen to my sister White one peece of thirtie or fortie ounzes. …

Burghley's graduated provisions for the girls' marriages may suggest that he had the same social ambition for Bridget and Susan that he had had for Anne and Elizabeth. It is also true that he knew that it cost more, for example, to support the life of an earl (and an earl's wife) than a baron (or a baron's wife).

Burghley's provisions were so generous that they became the subject of gossip: on 30 August, three weeks after Burghley's death, John Chamberlain wrote to Dudley Carleton:[4]

> Of his [=Burghley's] private wealth there is but 11000li [=£ 11,000] come to light and that all in silver; whereof 6000li [=£ 6000] (with eight or nine hundred pound land) he bequeathed to his two neeces of Oxford, the rest in other legacies.

Thus rumour had it that more than half of Burghley's moveables went to his two unmarried grand-daughters.

In 1604 Cecil calculated Lady Susan's inheritance:[5]

in Plate	1500*l*
in Iewells	400*l*
in Money	5537*l*
a Divydend of	500*l*
Lands	230*l*

This amounted to £7767 plus £230 per annum in rents. Bridget would already have received a similar bequest in 1599. Elizabeth of course had already received her portion, presumably including £4000 for her marriage to an earl.

Cecil directed an undated but contemporary letter to Michael Hickes, acknowledging dissatisfaction with Burghley's will on the side of the 'Doctors' – probably the legal institution known as Doctors' Commons – and from Sir Thomas Cecil. Robert Cecil, however, stood firm, though his inheritance was diminished by Burghley's generosity to his grand-daughters. He was also alert to a prospective custody battle with their biological father:[6]

> Mr Hyckes I thank you for your lettre and for your Care. As for my Lord of Oxfords claime If Mr Bellot do but towrne [=turn] him to vs we shall do well inowgh and above all things we desire that he do say, thogh not sweare, that swch [=such] chardg was given him by Paroll [=parole, word of mouth] which Mr Maynard shall witness

> For the Doctors Cavill to defeate them of their portion God knowes I never intend it, but be yow swre [=sure] my brother thinks so hardly to have none of the Iewells as I feare me he will stand now vppon all Advantages but I will never consent in such a kind / to breake my Fathers Testament /

> For any privat things at Theobalds good Mr Hyckes, end them for I am weary of the Noyse of such beggarly things as they ar[e] and wilbe when they are at best / I comitt all to you /

> Tell Mr Bellot, If the Erl of Oxford shold desire the custody he can not haue them of any body, for If he look vppon the Deeds, wherby my Lord hath conveied them their Lands, he shall find that for default of Isswe, their Land comes to the Heires of his body, nor whyther he that never gaue them groat, hath a second wyfe, and a nother Child be a fitt Gardien consider you / If once my Lady Bedford were come to Towne we wold quickly conclude / I wish Mr Bellott to haue good care they be

not stollen away by his meanes, I wold they had some honest Man there while Mr Bellots Ey [=eye] is absent from them. When you are there I pray you take order with my wardrope that any stuff they want or any thing els may be given them /

On Monday night I shalbe at London but I pray you do not come from Theobalds without some end [=purpose]. I haue written out mine ey[e]s to day and therfore Fare well /

Cecil clearly thought that Oxford might even stoop to kidnapping to get control of his daughters – and their inherited wealth.

On 12 October 1598 Bridget Vere wrote to Cecil from Theobalds in her fine italic hand:[7]

Good Vncle my duetie remembred vnto yow giueing yow thankes for your kind receiueinge of my letter better then it deserued by a greate deale: and more for your good and fatherlyke councell in your letter: which I pray God giue me the grace to followe as I trust he will. as for the workinge of slypes[?] it is some part of our dayly exercise and the drawinge of them I trust with exercise to frame in some sorte to it. my Aunte White hath her duetie remembred vnto yow giueinge yow greate thankes for your kind remembrance. / I ende with thes fewe lynes being loufth [=lothe] to trouble you any further from your house at Theoboulds …

'White', Burghley's sister, was evidently looking after Bridget, and had doubtless helped look after both Bridget and Susan since Anne's death in 1588.

74 A Husband for Lady Bridget

On New Year's Day 1599 the Countess of Oxford exchanged gifts with Queen Elizabeth.[1] On 28 January Derby wrote to Cecil from Thistleworth:[2]

My very good vncle. I was wished by my wyff, to moue youe for a letter to repryue [=reprieve] a poor yonge man for where yow haue alredy wrytten once befor, att her request, to morow the man dyes vnles he be repryvd: itt semes, by his petytyon his offence was for stealinge a lyttle silwer skellett owtt of her chamber which being the first falt she was loth to haue him dy, yett nearless [=nevertheless] he was condemnedd befor he cowld make any means thus desyringe yow to bear with thess hasty lynes in regard I am to waytt on the Countess of Oxford home to her howse who lodged here att my howse att Thislworth:

Oxford's eldest daughter seems to have had a tender heart. The letter also contains a rare indication of friendly relation between Oxford's second Countess and her step-daughters. Derby planned to accompany the Countess back to her house in Hackney.

On 3 March Robert Bertie, eldest son of Peregrine Bertie and Oxford's sister Mary, wrote to his uncle Oxford from the Continent:[3]

Monseigneur, Je désire infiniement de vous faire paroistre par quelque effect l'honneur que je vous porte, ayant esté tousjours bien veu de vous; mais d'autant que je n'ay trouvé encores aucun subject assez digne de vous divertier de vos plus serieux affaires, je n'osoy pas prendre la hardiesse de vous escrire, de peur d'estre trop mal advisé de vous importuner de lettres qui ne mériteroyent pas d'estre seulement ouvertes, si non en ce qu'elles vous asseureroyent de l'éternelle service que je vous ay voué et à toute vostre maison: vous suppliant très humblement, Monsieur, de l'avoir pour agréable et de me tenir pour celuy qui est prest de rec'evoir vos commandemens de telle devotion que je seray toute ma vie vostre très humble serviteur et neveu.

For the most part this is merely a demonstration of young Robert's command of French – but perhaps it doubles as testimony of happy relations between Oxford on the one hand and his younger sister and her family on the other.

Two days earlier, on 1 March, John Chamberlain in London wrote to Dudley Carleton in Venice:[4]

> … the match is made vp twixt younge Norris and the Lady Briget second daughter to the erle of Oxford …

The prospective bridegroom was Francis Norris, whose father William had died in 1579, but whose grandfather, Baron Henry, Lord Norris (or Norreys) of Rycote, was yet living. On 7 April Bridget wrote to Cecil again from Chenies in Buckinghamshire, where she and Susan had been taken under the wing of Lucy (née Harington), Countess of Bedford. Bridget refers to Burghley's recent death:[5]

> Good Vnckle, hauinge no buisnes wherewith to trouble you at this time, but onely in this slender measure of thankefullnes, to acknowledge the manyfoulde kindnesses which I haue always founde in yow towardes mee, the which as far as in mee, lyeth I will endeuour to deserue, and nowe that he is gone that was so deare vnto yow and mee, yow are vnto mee, as a father in his steede, and in hauinge you, I shall thinke the want of him to be the lesse, soe with my kinde remembraunce vnto yow, I leaue to trouble you any further, / I commit you to the protectione of the Almightie …

Guardianship had been resolved in favour of Cecil, doubtless in accordance with Bridget's desire.

On 16 April Bridget dictated a letter (now severely damaged) to Mr Henry Maynard at Westminster, again from Chenies:[6]

> Mr Mainard whereas it <hath pleased my Lady Bedford> to geue leave to this berer M<r Arnold her Chaplayne> to be at libertie frome her, for <some little time,> (he havinge nowe a present opp<ortunity …> offered him in London, yf he <can obtain one> or two of a certaine company <I am so bold as> to request youe in his behalfe <for> a man<date or …> letters as effectually as youe can: where<by you shall> gratifie me, and pleasure a frend that will in <all things be> very thankfull vnto youe. …

Bridget seems to have been acting as a kind of personal secretary to the Countess. On 21 April the Countess of Bedford wrote to Cecil from Chenies:[7]

> Sir this presente morninge I haue receaved your lettres, and have concydered of your good advice concerninge the solemnizynge of your neeces maryadge; and wheras yow write that yow thincke it not decente to make a publicke matter thereof, so was it fardeste from my mynde, onlye desyringe suche a course as might be bothe answerable to the expectation of summ of there honorable friendes, & in sum sorte pleasynge to your neece. Which I have this morninge also certefyed by a lettre vnto Francis Norreys, with which I have purposelye sente a messenger to retourne a perfecte resolucion thereof./ Yet notwithstandinge if the countrye be beste pleasynge vnto yow, althoughe the wantes be greate, as I have alredye wrytten, and besydes, havinge loste my deare sonne verye neare me, who should have bin my greateste comforte and assistance in all advices, I must crave to have Mr Bellott & sum people from yow which maye be helpfull in the managinge thereof. ...

The marriage was to be a private and quiet affair, in view of Burghley's death the previous August. On 28 April the Countess of Bedford at Chenies wrote once again to Cecil:[8]

> Sir, I haue nowe fullie resolved to take such course for effecting of this marriage, as your selfe have appoynted, and to haue it kept in this place, onelye desiringe that (consideringe yow wishe it private which well agrees with my owne di[s]pposicion) yf any offence be taken by frendes of either parte, yow will take vpon yow the excuse, as better able to vndertake that burden then I am. and for my owne parte I will not loke for any guestes but such as yow shalbe pleased to invite, and bringe with yow to kepe yow companie, as I haue acquainted my Lady Brigett whome I finde so plyant to your will, as she semes best pleased with whatsoeuer yow shall think good to prescribe: and in all other her accions & Carriage so honorablye and vertuouslie inclined, as I doe (I assure yow) receave excedinge comforte in her companie/. ...

On an unknown date in May or June, Bridget Vere, aged fifteen, married Francis Norris, who would turn twenty on 6 July.

Meanwhile, on 28 April Oxford was sued in Chancery by Judith Ruswell for some £500 in reference to her husband's service to Oxford twenty years previously as 'Master of his Wardropp'. Like Julian Penn and so many others, Judith Ruswell claimed that Oxford had failed to pay his debt. Oxford answered that the events had occurred very long ago, and that he was

> verye suer that the said William Ruswell hathe not made anye garment for him this defendant nor for anye of his Servantes by this defendant his appointment at anye tyme within the space of Eighteene or nynetene yeares nowe last past ... that he this defendant hathe paide and satisfied vnto the said William Ruswell for all suche worke as the said William Ruswell did for this defendant or anye of his servantes by the direccion or appointment of this defendant nether did the said William Ruswell at anye tyme take vp by this defendant his appointment or to his vse vppon the creditt of the said Ruswell anye silke silver or gould lace, silkes, or other Stuffe

for anye the garmentes of this defendant or anye of this defendantes servantes by the appointment of this defendant, nether was the said William Ruswell at anye tyme of suche creditt as he could soe doe ...

Now Oxford turned the tables against his sometime servant:

the said William Ruswell aboute seventene or eightene yeres sythence, havinge receaved certen cloth of gould and sylver, and other Stuffe of this defendant to the valewe of eight hundred poundes or theraboutes to this defendantes vse did runne awaye (*long blank*) with the same sythence which tyme this defendant albeit he this defendant hath manye tymes caused dilligent enquirey to be made for him the said Ruswell [he] hathe not seene him nor never receaved nor had the said cloth of goulde and sylver and Stuffe nor anye satisfaccion or recompence for the same.

Thus Oxford claims that Ruswell was in his debt and skipped town with his goods.

Of the 13 depositions taken in the case, by far the most circumstantial was submitted by Peter Legate, gentleman, of Avaley, Essex, forty-six at the time of the deposition and thus about twenty-six at the time of the original events. Legate like the rest confessed that he knew all the parties including Oxford and that William Ruswell had been 'servant and Taylor to the defendant'. Further:

3 That ther is no doubt but that the defendant was very much in the sayd William Ruswelles debt both for makinge of apparell, for his lordshipp and some of his servantes, and for the stuffes them selves which many tymes the sayd William Ruswell tooke vpp on his Creditte

4 That he remembreth that the sayd William Ruswell did cause to be sett downe in bookes of accountes all such thinges for the most part as the defendant stood indebted to him for, and he sayeth that after the booke of accounte now shewed vnto him att the tyme of his examinacion was by his Lordshippes appoyntment audited by one Nicholas Bleake one of his lordships officers and therupon a Remaynder of a debt allowed to the summe of five hundred and eight poundes, seventene shillinges and two pence [=£508–17–2], as may appeare vpon the foote of the same accounte in the sayd booke firmed with the handwritinge of the sayde Nicholas Bleake ...

Legate now explains that Ruswell, being also in debt to himself, turned his book of accounts receivable over to Legate in lieu of payment, so that it was Legate's turn to try to collect from Oxford:

this deponent was dealt with all to have had the sayd debt of 508li and odd mony sett over vnto him, and therupon when he vnderstood by the sayd Nicholas Bleake, and Mr Walters and other of his Lordshippes servantes that the same was a very good debt, this deponent att my Late Lord Treasurers house in the Stronde, had some speeche with the defendant touchinge the sayd debt, wher his lordshipp did acknowledge the debt, and tolde this deponent that he should be payde it by his offecers and withall willed this deponent to be good to Ruswell, and promised that this deponent should not lose a groat by him ...

So, as we have noted (p. 185), Legate recalls a meeting with Oxford at Burghley House in which Oxford assured him that the debt would be paid …

> … and he remembreth the same by a very good token, for this deponent havinge a litle before provided white clothe for his lordshippes Liveries by his owne appoyntment which his Lordshipp afterwardes fancied not, he caused Mr Byshopp one of his servantes to give this deponent att the same tyme six pounes for a reward, to take the white clothes agayne and to lett him have some other sort of clothe …

This transaction did not put a stop to Ruswell's dealing with Oxford:

> 5 That after the Auditinge and allowinge of the sayd debt of 500 and od poundes his Lordshipp grew further into the sayd William Ruswelles debt, and the same as he verily thinketh are Duly sett downe in these other bookes of the sayd Ruswelles accountes now shewed to him att this his examinacion, for this deponent was privy to a great part of them how they did grow, as for silke, lace, and clothe which are therin sett downe and which he sold to Ruswell, and he hath heard the defendant acknowledge a great part of them And he is perswaded in his conscience that nether the sayd debt of the sayd five hundred odd poundes nor the other debtes remayninge in those bookes of accountes are in any part dischardged, for they were shortly after they grew due sett over to this deponent, and the bookes remayned many yeares in his custody to the ende that if he should receave any mony vpon them, which he never could, he might satisfye himselfe and other the sayd William Ruswelles Creditors as farr as the monyes so receaved would extend vnto …

Failing to collect anything from Oxford over a period of many years, Legate returned the books to Ruswell's widow as an act of prospective charity:

> … and since att the earnest request of the Complainant he hath redelivered the same bookes vnto her beinge executor or administrator to her husband, to see if she might recover the sayd debtes towardes her releaffe, which this deponent did not, nor went about to do, by any violent or chardgeable course in sutes of Lawe, more then this that vpon peticion made by the now Complainant to the right honorable Sir Christopher Hatton late Lord Chancelour of England this deponentes lord and Maister, it was dealt & proceeded in, to some good poyntes of forwardnes, that the defendant should sell a lease of the Mannor of Avelye aforesayd, and should have accepted the sayd debtes to the valewe of seven hundred and odd poundes as he remembreth in part of payment, and the rest to be payde him in mony, and therupon an hundred poundes was lent vnto him for a longe tyme without allowance for it, yet afterward that bargayne brake of[f] and never tooke effect

Thus Legate did not bring a suit against Oxford, but secured an understanding (through the mediation of Hatton, his master) that Oxford would sell Legate the lease of the manor of Aveley for a certain sum, from which £700 would be deducted as payment on Ruswell's debt. Evidently Legate gave Oxford £100 as earnest money, but this was merely returned after 'a long time' as if it had been a loan. Since the land transaction 'never tooke effect' as far as Legate was concerned – and he was closer to the matter than anyone else except Ruswell – the original debt was never paid. Whether it was paid in response to Judith Ruswell's suit must be doubted. Though Peter Legate had his principal residence in Aveley, he did not secure the lease on the manor.

On 23 June the Countess of Bedford wrote to Henry Maynard from Chenies, including a mention of Susan Vere, now eight:[9]

> … My Lady Susan hath complayned these three or fower dayes, but what it will prove vnto whether the worms or measells I cannot perceave …

The Countess of Bedford wrote to Cecil again in August:[10]

> … My Lady Susan I thanke God is very well, and I hope you will remember to deliuer her from this solitary imprisonment. I assure you there are very many good thinges in her, and I find her very tractable to my vnderstanding. I nothing doubt but you shall reape both many and great Comfortes by her. Francis Norris is gone this iourney without my Consent or Lyking, yet my hope is the same God that presarued him at land will also defend him at sea. …

Thus Francis Norris went abroad within a month or two of his marriage to Bridget. About this same time Thomas Raynton described himself in a petition to Cecil as 'sometyme seruant vnto your right honourable father & now attendaunt seruant vnto thonourable lady Suzan Veere'.[11] Evidently he was one of the servants kept on after Burghley's death.

Also in August, Oxford's Countess stood deputy godmother for the Queen at the christening of the daughter of Lady Elizabeth Hatton, widow of Sir William Hatton.[12] On 30 November Derby and Elizabeth were staying at King's Place with Oxford and his Countess:[13]

> My verie good vncle [Cecil], I geue yow harty thanks for your kind paynes, taken in my Cause, wherof I pray your Contynuaunce, and whatsoeuer yow shall think fitt to be done by me for the further effectinge and Conclusion of the agreement and peace betwene me and my Neeces, I wilbe ready to Confirme. I wold haue ben there my self, but for seeinge my wife at Hackney, and therefore do eftsones pray yow vndertak for me.

Some time before December 1599, when the Queen nominated Martin Heton to the bishopric of Ely, vacant since 1581, Thomas Wilson composed his 'State of England Anno Dom. 1600', including a passage that we will now examine in its entirety:[14]

> … I find great alteracions almost every yeare, so mutable are worldly thinges and worldly mens affaires; as namely the Earl of Oxford, who in the yeare 1575 was rated at 12,000 a yeare sterlinge, within 2 following was vanished and no name of him found, haveing in that time prodigally spent and consumed all even to the selling of the stones timber and lead of his castles and howses, and yett he liveth and hath the first place amongst Earles, but the Queen is his gracious Mistress and gives him

maintaynance for his nobilty sake, but (to say the truth) out of the Bishoprick of Ely, which since his decay co[u]ld never see other Bishope. And other, the Earl of Arrundell, about the same time was reckoned not much inferior to him in state, and before him in dignity, and in one 6 months all was confiscate to the Queen for Treason. The other Earls some daily decay, some encrease accordinge to the corse of the world, but that which I have noted by perusinge many of the said bookes, and of the later sort, is that still the totall sume groweth much to one reckoninge and that is to 100,000 rent yearely, accounting them all in gross to avoyde prolixity. If a man would proportion this amongst 19 Earles and a Marquis it would be no great matter, to every one 5,000 rent, but as some exceed that much, so many come short of it.

Oxford had sold, or given long leases on, virtually all his properties. Additionally, he had failed to commute his £1000 annuity; failed to secure the post of gauger of vessels for beer and ale, of the monopoly on wools, fruits, and oils, or the monopoly on Cornish tin, and so far failed to recover Waltham Forest.

75 Literary Patronage (II)

On 6 May 1581, while Oxford lay under arrest for his affair with Anne Vavasor, Thomas Stocker, who was 'brought vp in your Lordships fathers house', chose him as dedicatee for a translation of Calvin's *Diuerse sermons* (STC 4437):

> … And I haue the rather dedicated this my rude translation vnto your Lordship, partly, for that I would shew some peece of my humble dutie vnto your honour, as a publike testimony therof, in respect of being sometimes, as then verie young, brought vp in your Lordships fathers house: but especially & chiefly, because (Syr) you seeke by al means possible, (the Lord bee thanked for it, & continue you in the same minde all your life long to his glorie) to vse conference with a certeine godly learned man, for the better reforming of your self and your whole family, to the obedience of the word. … In the meane while, I shall beseech the Lord our God, the Father of all mercy and consolation, to strengthen you in that good course, which he of his meere loue and singular goodnesse, hath so lately begun in you, that you may bee like vnto a confortable bright shining light in his Church, to shewe your selfe a constant mainteiner of the trueth of the glorious Gospell of his deare Sonne Christ Iesus our Lorde, for the stirring vp of many thereto. …

The 'certeine godly learned man' with whom Oxford used 'conference' is unnamed: perhaps Stocker means Burghley, then serving as the dedicatee's counsellor. The transformation 'so lately begun in you' is more likely a recent rejection of Catholicism than moral reform or marital reconciliation.

On 21 November 1581 Thomas Nicholas wrote to Burghley from the Marshalsea Prison:[1]

The be[a]rer hereof is the prynter that prynted the litle Treatise of Cesar and Pompeyus which I presentid to the right honorable Lady Anne Countes of Oxenford and he it is that hath spent some money to printe that litle pamphlet which I sent to your honour at Wyndsor tochyng the Monasaticall liffe in the abbay of Marshalse[a] The thyng will terrifye all the Papistes in Ingland. if it seme convenyent to your honour yt may please yow to permyt hym to have the pryntyng thereof.

'An Abstracte of the Historie of Cesar and Pompeyus' was licensed to John Charlewood on 6 September 1581 (Arber, ii, p. 401), but no copy is known to have survived. Also in 1581, or early in 1582, appeared Chrysostom's *An Exposition vpon the Epistle to the Ephesians* (STC 14632a), by an unknown translator, with a dedication to Anne dated 24 December 1581, and registered 4 January 1582 (Arber, ii, p. 404).

In 1582 appeared Watson's *Hekatompathia* (STC 25118a: see Chapter 54). In 1584 John Soowthern, a household servant, dedicated his *Pandora* (STC 22928) to Oxford, with thoughts as well for Countess Anne (see p. 290). Also in 1584, Robert Greene dedicated his *Gwydonius. The Carde of Fancie* (STC 12262) to Oxford:

> Your Honour being a worthy favourer and fosterer of learning hath forced many through your excellent virtue to offer the first-fruits of their study at the shrine of your Lordship's courtesy.

In this volume appears also a prefatory poem in Latin, by one 'Richardus Portingtonus', complimenting Oxford on his 'truth' – with the usual pun on 'Vere'.

Two years later, in 1586, Angel Day dedicated his *English Secretarie* (STC 6401) to Oxford, using a new wood-block coat of arms (Fig. 13). Day complimented Oxford on being a man of 'learned view and insight', 'whose infancy from the beginning was euer sacred to the Muses'.

Anthony Munday dedicated his third book to Oxford in 1588, a translation, *Palmerin, The Mirrour of Nobilitie* (STC 19157), with the 'new' coat of arms. Now Munday pronounces himself both 'one of the Messengers of her Maiesties Chamber' and Oxford's 'late seruaunt'. Early in the decade Munday had become a gutter journalist of the worst sort, crowing over the death by hanging and disembowelling of the saintly Edmund Campion on 1 December 1581, and strutting before the mob gathered on 12 February 1584 for the execution of the priest George Haydock, a personal acquaintance from his days in Rome: 'the reporte of them that stood by was that at what time the tormentor was in pulling out of his bowells, Mr Haddock was in life'.[2]

In the 1590s John Farmer dedicated two books of music to Oxford. In *The First Set of Diuers & Sundry Waies of Two Parts in One* (1591: STC 10698) Farmer calls his patron 'my very good lord & master' and 'my singuler good Lord'; he also notes the Earl's love of music: 'I was the rather embouldened for your Lordships great affection to this noble science'. In *The First Set of English*

Madrigals (1599: STC 10697), which carries the 'new' coat of arms, Farmer calls himself 'practicioner in the art of Musicque', acknowledging his service under Oxford, 'my very good Lord and Master':

> I haue presumed to tender these Madrigales onlie as remembrances of my seruice and witnesses of your Lordships liberall hand, by which I haue so long liued … without flattrie be it spoken[,] those that know your Lordship know this, that vsing this science as a recreation, your Lordship haue ouergone most of them that make it a profession.

At mid-decade Anthony Munday dedicated yet another translation to Oxford: *Primaleon, The First Booke* (1595: STC 20366). Though the dedication is lost, as the first edition survives in fragments, a second edition of 1619 (STC 20367) celebrates the memory of the 17th Earl in an address to his son:

> Sir, hauing sometime serued that most noble Earle your Father, of famous and desertful memory; and translating diuers Honourable Histories into English, out of French, Italian, and other Languages, which he graciously pleased to countenance with his Noble acceptance: Among the embrions of my then younger braine, these three seuerall parts of Primaleon of Greece, were the tribute of my duetie and seruice to him: Which Bookes, hauing long time slept in obliuion, and (in a manner) quite out of memory: by fauour of these more friendly times, comming once more to be seene on the worlds publike Theater; in all duety they offer themselues to your Noble patronage; For, you being the true heire to your honourable Fathers matchlesse vertues, and succeeding him in place of degree, and eminency, who should inherit the Fathers Trophies, Monuments and ancient memories, but his truely Noble, hopefull, and vertuous Sonne? In whom, old Lord Edward is still liuing, and cannot die, so long as you breathe.
>
> For his sake then (most honourable Earle) accept of poore Primaleon, newly reuiued, and rising from off your Father[s] Hearse, in all humility commeth to kisse your noble hand; with what further dutifull seruice, wherein you shall please to imploy me.

At decade's end appeared Conrad Gesner's *The Practice of the New and Old Phisicke* (1599: STC 11799), translated by George Baker, now 'one of the Queenes Maiesties chiefe chirurgions in ordinary'. Baker describes Oxford as 'my singular good Lorde,' and calls the volume 'this worke of Distillation' (sig. *2v):

> … I at this time to pleasure my country and friendes, haue published this worke vnder your Honourable protection, that it may more easily bee defended against Sycophants and fault finders, because your wit, learning and authoritie hath great force and strength in repressing the curious cra[c]kes of the enuious and bleating Babes of Momus' charme.

The second and third parts of this same project also contain dedications to Oxford, albeit briefer and less informative.

In addition to dedications, Oxford was the subject of poems written by authors who addressed various members of the nobility, including the Queen. The most significant of these is a sonnet appended by Edmund Spenser to the 1590 first edition of his *Faerie Queene* (STC 23081). The third poem in the sequence, following sonnets to Hatton and Northumberland, is addressed to 'The right honourable the Earl of Oxenforde, Lord High Chamberlain of England':

> Receive, most noble Lord, in gentle gree,   [gree=degree]
> The unripe fruit of an unready wit;
> Which by thy countenance doth crave to be
> Defended from foul Envy's poisonous bit.
> Which so to do may thee right well befit,
> Sith th'antique glory of thine ancestry
> Under a shady veil is therein writ,
> And eke thine own long living memory,
> Succeeding them in true nobility:
> And also for the love which thou dost bear
> To th'Heliconian imps and they to thee,
> They unto thee, and thou to them most dear;
> Dear as thou art unto thyself, so love
> That loves and honours thee, as doth behove.

Thus Spenser celebrates Oxford's long lineage, and his love to 'th'Heliconian imps' – presumably literary protégés such as John Lyly, Anthony Munday, Robert Greene, Thomas Watson, and now, at least prospectively, Spenser himself.

In 1597 Henry Lok published his *Ecclesiastes* (STC 16696), printed by Richard Field. Among many lines addressed to many noblemen, Lok addresses a sonnet to his former master:[3]

> If Endor's widow had had power to raise,
> A perfect body of true temperature,
> I would conjure you by your wonted praise,
> Awhile my song to hear and truth endure:
> Your passed noble proof doth well assure
> Your blood's, your mind's, your body's excellence
> If their due reverence may this pains procure,
> Your patience – with my boldness – will dispense:
> I only crave high wisdom's due defence:
> Not at my suit, but for work's proper sake,
> Which treats of true felicity's essence,
> As wisest King most happiest proof did make:
> Whereof your own experience much might say,
> Would you vouchsafe your knowledge to bewray.

Finally, in 1603 one F. D. published a poem to Oxford (among other noblemen) in his curious broadsheet *Anagrammata in nomina illustrissimorum heroum* (STC 6165). The poem carries the title, 'EDOVARDVS VEIERVS per Anagramma AVRE SVRDVS VIDEO': here a Latinized 'Edward Vere' is anagrammatized as (in English, ridiculously) 'Deaf in my ear, I see'. So incompetent is F. D. as an anagrammatist that he cheats by adjusting his spelling of the original names, changing 'Vere' or 'Veer' to 'Veire' (and 'Talbot' to 'Tailbot') to smuggle in a needed 'i'. The explanatory verse is no less opaque:[4]

> Avribus hisce licet studio, fortuna, susurros
> Perfidiae, & technas efficis esse procul,
> Attamen accipio, quae mens horrescit, & auris,
> Rebus facta malis corpore surda tenus,
> Imo etiam cerno Catilinae fraude propinquos
> Funere soluentes fata aliena suo.

> 'Though by your zeal, Fortune, you keep perfidy's murmurs and schemings at a distance, nonetheless I learn (at which my mind and ear quake) that our bodies have been deafened with respect to evil affairs. Indeed, I perceive men who come close to Catiline in deception, freeing other men's fates by their death.'

In number and kind, books dedicated to Oxford match his character and reputation as these can be ascertained on other grounds. He attracts the attention of theologians, poets, distillers, and a musician, who have translated works from the Continent, or composed original works in English. Many of the dedicators have a previous connection with Oxford, whether as servants of himself or of his father, or, in the case of George Baker, as his physician. Only Lyly and Spenser are read today by other than specialists, while Munday and Greene were regarded in their own time as hacks. The most ambitious literary work dedicated uniquely to Oxford, Thomas Watson's *Hekatompathia* of 1582, comes from a circle of litterateurs who doubtless fancied themselves at the cutting edge, but who were soon overtaken by men of vastly superior genius, including Spenser, Marlowe, Shakespeare, and Jonson.

According to Williams (*Index of Dedications*), Oxford, with about 28 dedications to his name, ranks just above Henry Hastings, 3rd Earl of Huntingdon (24), and Sir Philip Sidney (25), and just below Ambrose Dudley, Earl of Warwick (30). Men of real power, by comparison, were deluged: some 43 for Charles Howard, 46 for Walsingham, 47 for Hatton, 85 for Burghley, and 114 for Leicester – more than four times Oxford's haul.

76 Oxford's Poetry (II)

While *The Paradyse of daynty deuises* (1576) went through many editions, no fresh poem of Oxford's appeared in print until 1591, when Nicholas Breton published *Brittons Bowre of Delights* (STC 3633), including 'When wert thou born Desire', signed 'LO. OX.' ('Lord Oxford').[1] A second edition, with poem and signature unchanged, appeared in 1597 (STC 3634). Around the turn of the century appeared more poems attributed to Oxford, but none actually by him.[2] Meanwhile, contemporary manuscripts assigned six apparently authentic poems to 'the Earle of Oxeforde', 'Earll of Oxenforde', or 'E. O.', making seven beyond the early nine:[3]

> 10: Fain would I sing but fury makes me fret (pentameter: ababcc; stanzaic)
> 11: When wert thou born Desire (poulter's measure: couplets with internal rhyme)
> 12: Wing'd with desire, I seek to mount on high (pentameter: ababcc; stanzaic)
> 13: Whereas the Heart at Tennis plays (poulter's measure: couplets with internal rhyme; stanzaic)
> 14: What cunning can express (trimeter: ababcc; stanzaic)
> 15: Who taught thee first to sigh alas my Heart (pentameter: English sonnet)
> 16: Were I a king I could command content (pentameter: ababcc; single 'stanza')

Four further poems are considered possibly by Oxford:

> I: Sitting alone upon my thought in melancholy mood (fourteeners: couplets ('echo' lines 11–20)
> II: My mind to me a kingdom is (tetrameter: alternating rhyme)
> III: If women could be fair and yet not fond (pentameter: ababcc; stanzaic)
> IVa: In peascod time when hound to horn gives ear (fourteeners: couplets, some with internal rhyme)

May believes that no poem from Oxford's pen is datable later than 1593.[4]

Taking all 20 together, and giving the benefit of the doubt to the four 'possibles', Oxford wrote one poem in trimeter (14), three in tetrameter (5, 8, II); one in pentameter and tetrameter (9), seven in pentameter (1, 6, 10, 12, 15–16, III), four in poulter's measure (2, 7, 11, 13), four in fourteeners (4, I, IVa), and one in a complex variant of poulter's measure and fourteeners (3). The bulk of the poems are stanzaic. Seven rhyme ababcc (6, 8–9, 10, 12, 16, III), while one is a pure English sonnet (15), and one a kind of extended sonnet (1). Of the four poems entirely in poulter's measure and three entirely in fourteeners, all are in couplets, while one, a fourteener (IVa), contains internal rhyme. One complex poem (3), with three stanzas of four couplets each, also contains internal rhyme.

Oxford's poems are remarkable not only for their variety but for their conservatism. Fourteeners were already passé in Oxford's youth, and Oxford's sonnet (15) hearkens back to a form invented by his uncle Surrey, who died by execution in 1547, three years before Oxford's birth. Despite being somewhat antiquated, Oxford's poems and plays were praised in print during his lifetime. As we have noted, in 1578 Gabriel Harvey praised both Oxford's Latin and his English compositions.[5] In 1586 William Webbe, in his *Discourse of English Poetrie* (STC 25172, sig. C3v), proclaimed (in English):

> I may not omitte the deserued commendations of many honourable and noble Lordes, and Gentlemen, in her Maiesties Courte, which in the rare deuises of Poetry,

haue beene and yet are most excellent skylfull, among whom, the right honourable
Earle of Oxford may challenge to him selfe the tytle of the most excellent among
the rest.

By 1586, therefore, readers incapable of cracking the 'E. O.' cypher for themselves
were openly informed of Oxford's 'rare deuises of Poetry'.

In 1589 *The Arte of English Poetrie* (STC 20519, 20519.5), attributed to George
Puttenham, showered manifold praise on Oxford:

> [sig. I1] … And in her Maiesties time that now is are sprong vp an other crew of
> Courtly makers Noble men and Gentlemen of her Maiesties owne seruauntes, who
> haue written excellently well as it would appeare if their doings could be found out
> and made publicke with the rest, of which number is first that noble Gentleman
> Edward Earle of Oxford[,] Thomas Lord of Bukhurst, when he was young, Henry
> Lord Paget, Sir Philip Sydney, Sir Walter Rawleigh, Master Edward Dyar, Maister
> Fulke Greuell, Gascon, Britton, Turberuille[,] and a great many other learned
> Gentlemen, whose names I do not omit for enuie, but to auoyde tediousnesse, and
> who haue deserued no little commendation. But of them all particularly this is
> myne opinion, that Chaucer, with Gower, Lidgat and Harding for their antiquitie
> ought to have the first place …

The poems of Oxford (and others) have been made public; Puttenham laments
the fact that poems by still other courtiers have not entered the public conscious-
ness. This is a point worth making because this very passage has been misread in
support of the argument, now thoroughly discredited, that a 'stigma of print'
discouraged publication by members of the nobility.[6] Oxford was one of many
noblemen whose poems and names were broadcast in print. Thomas Sackville,
later Lord Buckhurst, was openly proclaimed as author of *Gorboduc* on its 1565
title-page (STC 18684), and similarly praised by Puttenham and Meres, while
King James of Scotland shepherded two collections of verse into print, in 1584
(STC 14373; second edition 1585 STC 14374), and again in 1591 (STC 14379).

Puttenham's second mention of Oxford associates him publicly with plays:

> [sig. I2] … Of the later sort I thinke thus. That for Tragedie, the Lord of
> Buckhurst, & Maister Edward Ferrys for such doings as I haue sene of theirs do
> deserue the hyest price: Th'Earle of Oxford and Maister Edwardes of her Maiesties
> Chappell for Comedy and Enterlude. …

We shall examine a third notice from Puttenham below. In 1598 Francis Meres
asserted in *Palladis Tamia* (drawing on Puttenham):[7]

> … so the best for Comedy amongst vs bee, Edward Earle of Oxforde, Doctor
> Gager of Oxforde, Maister Rowley once a rare Scholler of learned Pembrooke Hall
> in Cambridge, Maister Edwardes one of her Maiesties Chappell, eloquent and
> wittie Iohn Lilly, Lodge, Gascoyne, Greene, Shakespeare, Thomas Nash, Thomas
> Heywood, Anthony Mundye our best plotter, Chapman, Porter, Wilson, Hathway,
> and Henry Chettle.

Meres (for one) knew that Oxford and Shakespeare were not the same man.[8]

Contemporary observers such as Harvey, Webbe, Puttenham, and Meres clearly exaggerated Oxford's talent in deference to his rank. By any measure, his poems pale in comparison with those of Sidney, Lyly, Spenser, Shakespeare, Donne, and Jonson. This point was made by a neutral witness, William Buckley, during a *Firing Line* debate between Charlton Ogburn the younger and Professor Maurice Charney. How is it, asked Buckley, that Oxford's known poems are so undistinguished – relatively undistinguished? 'I don't think Bach could have written ugly music.'[9] Though Ogburn begged indulgence in view of Oxford's youth (he was 21 when he composed his first datable poem), great artists tend to be ahead of their contemporaries from the start: consider Chaucer, Spenser, Marlowe, Milton, Mozart, Keats.

Passions generated by the 'authorship debate' have resulted both in unjustified praise and unwarranted denigration of Oxford's verse. For an unbiased estimate it is helpful to reach back before 1920 to the observations of W. J. Courthope (1897):[10]

> ... [Oxford's] own verses are distinguished for their wit, and in their terse ingenuity reflect something of the coxcombry which seems to have been a leading feature in his character. Doubtless he was proud of his illustrious ancestry, and of his own office of Great Chamberlain of England ...; he was, therefore, careful to conform, in his verse at least, to the external requirements of chivalry, as may be seen in his sonnet, 'Love thy Choice' [15], which has something of the old-fashioned air of Surrey, and may have been a youthful composition ...

> But in later years his natural turn for epigram seems to have prevailed over his chivalrous sentiment, as may be seen in the famous lines beginning : 'If women would be fair and yet not fond' [III]. Oxford was a contributor to The Paradise of Dainty Devices, and here his sententiousness takes the shape of devotional poems in Lord Vaux's manner; but on the whole, the epigram, pure and simple, seems to have been his favourite form of composition, and in this his studied concinnity of style is remarkable, as the following examples will show ...

The *Oxford English Dictionary* defines 'concinnity' (2) as 'Beauty of style produced by a skilful connexion of words and clauses; hence, more generally, studied beauty, elegance, neatness of literary or artistic style, etc.'

I myself prefer Courthope's 'studied concinnity' to Buckley's dismissal of Oxford's verse as 'relatively undistinguished', or Rowse's characterization of Oxford as 'the best of a poor lot'.[11] Oxford's poems are, above all, astonishingly uneven. The best, though few, are fine indeed, while the worst, including 'The labouring man, that tilles the fertile soyle,' are execrable.

Of interest to the biographer is the fact that many of Oxford's poems are demonstrably personal. 'A Croune of Bayes shall that man weare, / That triumphs over me' (3) suggests an actual tournament. 'Framd in the front of forlorne hope'

(4) laments the 'losse of my good name', and might have been connected to any of the numerous scandals of Oxford's life, including the Oxford–Arundel libels and the Vavasor affair. The doubtful 'Sittinge alone upon my thought in melancholye moode' (I), openly alludes to the Vavasor affair, even containing an echo on 'Vere' (see p. 267). Finally, 'Love compared to a tennis play' (13) inevitably recalls the Oxford–Sidney 'tennis-court quarrel'.

Also apparently autobiographical are poems on the rejection of women, particularly a doubtfully ascribed poem which survives only in manuscript (III):

> If woemen coulde be fayre and yet not fonde,
> Or that there love were firme, not fickll still,
> I woulde not mervaylle that they make men bonde,
> By servise longe to purchase theyre good will;
>   But when I se how frayll those creatures are,
>   I muse that men forget themselves so farr.
>
> To marcke the choyse they make and how they change,
> How ofte from Phoebus theye do flee to Pann,
> Unsettled still like haggardes willd theye range,   [haggardes willd=wild female
> These gentlle byrdes that flye from man to man;   falcons]
>   Who woulde not scorne and shake them from the fyste,
>   And let them flye, fayre fooles, whiche waye they lyste?
>
> Yet for disporte we fawne and flatter bothe,
> To pass the tyme when nothinge else can please,
> And trayne them to our lure with subtylle othe,
> Till wearye of theyre wiles our selves we easse;
> And than we saye when we theire fancye trye,
>   To playe with fooles, oh what a foole was I.
>   Finis quod Earll of Oxenforde

Oxford's imagined resort to 'woemen' merely 'To pass the tyme when nothinge else can please' is the mirror image of his *bon mot*, 'When wemen were vnswete fine (yonge) boyes were in season'.

Katherine Duncan-Jones makes a specific comparison between a poem by Oxford's uncle Surrey, 'On a lady that refused to dance with him', and yet another misogynistic poem by Oxford:[12]

> [Surrey's] poem is certainly not 'Amatory'; still less is it 'Ethical'. It is a savage hymn of hate against a person of inferior lineage, and a mere woman at that, who has presumed to say 'no' to a descendant of Edward II. It may have served as model to a comparably savage poem by the seventeenth Earl of Oxford, 'Fain would I sing, but fury makes me fret' [10], ... which was perhaps directed toward the 'puppy' Philip Sidney.

We may also recall Oxford's 'jest' of Sir Walter Ralegh (p. 2): 'we all know it savoured more of emulation ... than of truth'.

Three poems on 'desire' are (in my judgment) among Oxford's finest and least personal. The first, 'The Lyvely Larke stretcht forth her wynge' (8), we have already noted (pp. 161–63). The second, 'When wert thou borne desire?' (11), is a more or less straightforward translation of Panfilo Sassi's *Rime* I.221.[13] I cite (and set out as poulter's measure) an excerpt printed in *The Arte of English Poetrie* (1589), with Puttenham's introduction (sig. Z4):

> Edvvard Earle of Oxford a most noble & learned Gentleman made in this figure of responce an emblem of desire otherwise called Cupide[,] which for his excellencie and wit, I set downe some part of the verses, for example.

> When wert thou borne desire? / In pompe and pryme of May,
> By whom sweete boy wert thou begot? / By good conceit men say,
> Tell me who was thy nurse? / Fresh youth in sugred ioy.
> What was thy meate and dayly foode? / Sad sighes with great annoy.
> What hadst thou then to drinke? / Vnfayned louers teares.
> What cradle wert thou rocked in? / In hope deuoyde of feares.

The poem was sufficiently well-known that opening and closing stanzas were added in the seventeenth century:[14]

> Come hither, shepherd's swain. / Sir, what do you require?
> I pray thee shew [to me] thy name? / My name is Fond Desire. ...

> Then, fond Desire, farewel! / Thou art no meat for me;
> I should be lothe [methinkes] to dwell / With such a one as thee.

Thus 'Desire' has become humanized as a 'shepherd's swain'.

The third poem on the topic, 'Wing'de with desyre' (12), is too long to cite here entire, but is well represented by three of its six stanzas:

> [1] Wing'de with desyre, I seeke to mount on hyghe;
> Clogde with myshapp yet am I kept full lowe;
> Whoe seekes to lyve and fyndes the waye to dye,
> Sythe comforte ebbs, and cares do daylye flowe.
>   But sadd despayre would have me to retyre,
>   When smylynge hoape setts forward my desyre. ...

> [4] Lo thus I lyve twyxte feare and comforte toste,
> With least abode where best I feell contente;
> I seelde resorte wher I should setle most,
> My slydinge tymes to[o] so[o]ne with her are spente.
>   I hover hyghe and soare wher Hope doth tower,
>   Yet froward Fate defers my happy hower. ...

> [6] A mall-content yet seeme I pleased styll,
> Braggyng of heaven yet feelynge paynes of hell.
> But Tyme shall frame a tyme unto my will,
> Whenas in sporte thys earnest will I tell;

> Tyll than (sweet frende) abyde these stormes with me,
> Which shall in joys of eyther fortunes be.

A single pronoun in the fourth stanza reveals that this poem is about a 'her'; the closing couplet, not crystal clear as to meaning, appeals to a 'sweet frende' (or beloved) to stick with the speaker, bringing comfort and even 'joys' while the poet awaits his fortune (good or bad). Notable and regrettable are the mechanical caesuras between the second and third foot of each and every line.

Of all Oxford's poems, including the 'possibles', 'In praise of a contented minde', with its memorable opening, 'My mynde to me a kingdome is', is perhaps the most widely recognized today, but the best-recognized poem in his time seems to have been his shortest (16):

> Weare I a kinge I coulde commande content;
> Weare I obscure unknowne shoulde be my cares,
> And weare I de[a]d no thought should me torment,
> Nor wordes, nor wronges, nor loves, nor hopes, nor feares:
>   A dowtefull choyce of these things one to crave,
>   A Kingdom or a cottage or a grave.

The poem is set to music in BL MS Add. 50203, ff. 58v–62v, by John Mundy (c. 1555–1630) (*New Grove*). Several wits took up the implied challenge of choosing between kingdom, cottage, and grave. Two resulting poems are probably from the seventeenth century:[15]

> A King? oh, boon for my aspiring mind!
> A cottage makes a country swa[in] rejoice;
> And as for death, I like him in his kind,
> But God forbid that he should be my choice!
> Nor last, nor next, but first and best I crave;
>   The rest I can whenas I list enjoy,
>   Till then salute me thus,– Vive le Roy!
>
> The greatest kings do least command content;
> The greatest cares do still attend a crown;
> A grave all happy fortunes do[th] prevent,
> Making the noble equal with the clown;
>   A quiet country life to lead I crave;
>   A cottage, then; no kingdom or a grave.

Two more responses derive from a British Library and a Folger Shakespeare Library manuscript respectively:[16]

> To be a king thy care would much augment,
> From Courte to Carte th[y] fortune were but bare.   ['Courte to Carte'
> If death should stricke third wish thou shouldst repent;   =high to low]
> Thus death and lucke thy wandring wish did spare.

Then choyse were hard since better thou mayst have;
Content lives not in cottage, Crowne, nor Grave.

Wearte thou a king, yet not commaund contente;
W[e]r[e] empire none thy mynd could yet suffice.
Wer[t]e thou obscure, still cares would the[e] tormente,
But wearte thou dead all care and sorrowe dyes.
An easye choise of three things the[e] to crave,
No kingdome, nor a cottage, but a grave.

Could this last reply have been composed by one of Oxford's contemporary enemies?

77 Oxford's Players (II)

Maliverny Catlyn's complaint against 'The daylie abuse of Stage playes' reveals that Oxford's Men were one of four leading London companies in 1587. Direct evidence of the survival of his company to the end of the century is limited to a single record from Faversham in Kent for 1594–95:[1]

Item for monye payde to thearle of Oxfords players   iijs iiijd

Nothing more is heard of Oxford's companies of boy actors or tumblers, though in 1597 Coventry paid 5s 'To the Earle of Oxfordes beareward'– evidence that Oxford patronized the brutal sport of bear-baiting.[2]

Oxford's Men resurface, however, in full vigour, as revealed by an anonymous play entered into the Stationers Register on 23 October 1600 (Arber, iii, p. 175) and printed the same year:

The Weakest goeth to the Wall. As it hath bene sundry times plaide by the right honourable Earle of Oxenford, Lord great Chamberlaine of England his seruants.

A second play – whose text is lost – was registered 3 July 1601 (Arber, iii, p. 187):

the true historye of George Scanderbarge as yt was lately playd by the right honorable the Earle of Oxenford his servantes.

The two titles demonstrate the continuity of the company despite the sparsity of recorded performances.

On 31 March 1602 the Privy Council, sitting at Richmond, dispatched 'A lettre to the Lord Maior for the Bores Head to be licensed for the plaiers', wherein members of the Council refer to themselves individually as 'me'; Oxford, by contrast, is referred to in the third person:[3]

We receaued your lettre, signifieinge some amendment of the abuses or disorders

by the immoderate exercise of Stage plays in and about the Cittie, by meanes of our
late order renued for the restraint of them, and with all [=withall] shewinge a
speciall inconvenience yet remayneinge, by reason that the seruants of our verey
good Lord the Earle of Oxford, and of me the Earle of Worcester, beinge ioyned by
agrement togeather in on[e] Companie (to whom, vpon noteice of her Maiesties
pleasure at the suit of the Earle of Oxford, tolleracion hath ben thaught meete to be
graunted, notwithstandinge the restraint of our said former Orders), doe not tye
them selfs to one certaine place and howse, but do chainge there place at there
owne disposition, which is as disorderly and offensiue as the former offence of
many howses. And as the other Companies that are alowed, namely of me the Lord
Admirall and the Lord Chamberlaine, be appointed there certaine howses, and one
and noe more to each Companie. Soe we doe straightly require that this third
Companie be likewise [appointed] to one place. And because we are informed the
house called the Bores Head is the place they haue especially vsed and doe best like
of, we doe pray and require yow that that said howse, namely the Bores head, may
be assigned onto them, and that they be verey straightlie Charged to vse and
exercise there plaies in noe other but that howse, as they will looke to haue that
tolleracion continued and avoid farther displeasure.

With Oxford's Men merged with Worcester's, all sanctioned players now had
patrons on the Privy Council: Worcester (Edward Somerset); the Lord Admiral
(Charles Howard, Earl of Nottingam); and the Lord Chamberlain (Sir George
Carey, Lord Hunsdon, absent, probably through illness, when the decree was
signed). Oxford may well have been shouldered aside precisely because he was
not a Privy Councillor.

The Privy Council decree, passed in response to Oxford's suit, is couched as a
restriction, evidently to please the Lord Mayor and aldermen, but in fact authorized the Boar's Head to continue as a theatre, and Worcester's Men, having
absorbed Oxford's Men, to perform there. And indeed, the company set up at
the Boar's Head in the latter half of 1601, 'probably playing, among other things,
the melodramatic works of Heywood'.[4] About two years later, after the accession
of James, the company would be re-assigned to the new Queen. Among the
prominent players of Worcester's/Queen's Men were Christopher and Robert
Beeston, John Duke, Thomas Greene, Thomas Heywood, James Holt, Will
Kemp, Robert Lee, John Lowin, Robert Pallant, Richard Perkins, and Thomas
Swinnerton/Swetherton (Nungezer). Of these, Greene, Holt, Lowin, Pallant,
Perkins, and Swinnerton cannot be traced to companies active before 1601, and
may have belonged to Oxford's Men – but there is no proof.

Three play titles can be associated with Oxford's Men over the years, in
addition to Lyly's: 'Agamemnon and Ulysses', played at Court by the Earl of
Oxford's boys on 27 December 1584; and *The Weakest Goeth to the Wall* and 'The
True Historye of George Scanderbarge', both evidently performed near the turn
of the century. A text survives only for the anonymous *Weakest Goeth to the Wall*,
whose comic scenes have been attributed to Thomas Dekker.[5]

Oxford is also associated with three quasi-dramatic entertainments, the first occurring at Warwick Castle on Sunday 18 August 1572, an attack on a fort which, as a text, amounted to little but roaring. The Shrovetide entertainment of March 1579, which apparently included a text, was not much to Oxford's credit. A more promising candidate for an Oxfordian 'comedy' occurred on 22 January 1581, as the 'sweet speech or Oration, spoken at the Tryumphe at White-hall before her Maiestie, by the Page to the right noble Earle of Oxenforde': as we have seen, however, that speech has been attributed to several more probable authors.[6]

A contemporary nobleman did evidently write plays for a professional company. This was Oxford's son-in-law, of whom it was reported on 30 June 1599:[7]

> Therle of Darby is busyed only in penning comedies, for the common Players.

Again it was reported on 13 November 1599: 'My Lord Derby hath put up the plays of the children in Pauls to his great pains and charge'.[8] A letter to Cecil in the hand of Elizabeth, Derby's wife and Oxford's daughter, undated but written after her marriage in 1596,[9] constituted a plea on Derby's behalf:

> Good vncle being importuned by my Lord to intreat your fauer that his man Browne with his companye may not be bar[r]ed from ther accoustomed plaing in maintenance wher of the[y] haue consumde the better part of ther substance, if so vaine a matter shall not seame troublesum to you I could desier, that your furderance might be a meane to vphold them for that my Lord taking delite in them it will kepe him from moer prodigall courses and make your credit preuaile withe him in a greater matter for my good ...

An Edward Browne was about this time a member of the Lord Admiral's Men (Nungezer); however, the Browne mentioned in the letter was Derby's servant – perhaps an amateur – not Charles Howard's.

Oxford may well have written comedies prior to 1589, and was of course a well-known poet, but that he wrote comedies for professional players we have no evidence whatever. If he did write for a professional company, it would almost certainly have been for his own, or, at a very great stretch, for the company of his mentor Charles Howard, the Lord Admiral. If, as has been asserted without evidence, his dramatic compositions were known to or encouraged by the Queen, then he might have written for her company, which survived through the 1590s.[10] Not only did Oxford have no demonstrable connection with the Lord Chamberlain's Men – Shakespeare's company – but neither the Carey family – the contemporary Lords Chamberlain – nor their successor patron King James had any particular use for him. Professional players in any case are far more likely to have relied on Oxford's protégés John Lyly and Anthony Munday, or on hack writers such as Thomas Dekker. When all is said and done, the sole candidate for a lost work from Oxford's pen is 'Agamemnon and Ulysses', a play more likely to have been written by John Lyly, or by Henry Evans, who received payment for its performance.

PART XII

Decline
1600–1604

78 Deep Abyss and Bottom of Despair

On New Year's Day 1600 the Countess of Oxford exchanged gifts with Queen Elizabeth.[1] In July Oxford wrote to Cecil from Hackney, entreating his aid in securing the governorship of the Isle of Jersey (LL-30):

> Althoughe my badd succes, in former sutes to her Magestye, haue giuene me cause to burye my hoopes [=hopes], in the diepe Abis and bottome of dispayre, rather then nowe to attempt, after so many tryales made in vayne, & so many oportunites escaped, the effects of fayre woordes, or frutes of gowlden promises. yet for that, I cannot beleue, but that there hathe bene alwayes a trwe correspondencie of woord and intentione in her Magestye. I doo coniecture, that wythe a lyttell helpe, that which of yt selfe hathe brought forthe so fayre blossumes will also yeld frute. Wherfore hauinge moved her Magestye lat[e]lye about the office of the I[s]le whiche by the deathe of Sir Antonie Paulet stands now in her maiesties dispositione to bestowe where yt shall best pleas her, I doo at this præsent most hartely desyre yowre friendship and furtherance fyrst for that I know her Magestye doothe giue yow good eare, then for that owre howses are knyt in alliance, last of all, the matter yt self ys suche, as nothinge chargethe her Magestye sythe yt ys a thynge she must bestowe vpon sume one or other. I know her Magestye hathe swters alredie for yt, yet suche as for many respects her Magestye may call to remembrance ought in equall ballence, to way [=weigh] lyghter then my selfe. And I know not by whatt better meanes, or when her maiestie may have an easier oportunite to discharge the dept [=debt] of so many hopes, as her promises have giuene me cause to imbrace, then by thys, whiche giue she muste & so giue as nothinge extraordinarelye doothe part frome her. yf she shall not dayne [=deign] me this in an oportunitie of tyme so fyttinge, what tyme shall I attend which is vncerteyne to all men, vnles in the graues of men ther were a tyme to receyve benifites, and good turnes frome princes. well I will not vse more woordes, for they may rather argue mistrust then confidence. I will assure my self and not dowt of yowre good office boothe in this but in any honorable friendshipe I shall have cause to vse yow. …

It is true that the Queen was under an obligation to appoint a new Governor: but it is not true that Oxford had a larger claim on her than anyone else in the kingdom. He closes with the histrionic thought that he is now so close to death that if the Queen delays, she may find herself relenting to a dead man.

In the days leading up to 29 July Cecil wrote to old Henry Norris, who was about to dispark his lands, thereby depriving Francis and Bridget of an inheritance:[2]

> My very good Lord. I am sory to wryte vnto your Lordship in any thing that may trouble yow, because I see yow are retyred to your owne pryuate, were it not, that in this case I speake to yow for one of your owne, on whom by lyneall dyscent the tytle of honour must descend which yow receaued by her Maiesties favor, from whom I presume yow would wysh notheng to be taken which might be a blemish to that place wherin he must abyde and kepe the memory of your house in honour and Reputacyon. The matter which I haue to imparte vnto your Lordship is this that there is an intencyon (besydes all that is already done) to cutt downe the woodes about your house, which worke because I assure my selfe it proceedeth no way from your Lordships owne dysposycion, but by the importunyty of those who cannot be contented with the extraordynary goodnesse they receaue from yow But that they must seeke even to tread vppon hym whom God and Nature hath appoynted to be the hedd of your house. I haue thought good to acquaynt your Lordship from whom only he and my selfe (in whose house he is matched) do exspect favour for him hoping thusmuch in your Lordship that howesoever wee know in your power yow are absolute, yet that yow will not execute it in this kynd, which can never be repayred, but that yow wyll be pleased to offer me no such hard measure, as I shall repent me to haue bestowed my Neece in a house where the Grandfather shall so Rygorously deale with her husband, especyally consydering that I had your allowance to the match, and your promyse of favour after, which yf I could have imagyned should have proued no other then it is, [(]although for the gentleman hymselfe I do take comfort in hym) yet the Lord Norreys, and Sir Edward to[o], should haue well perceaued that therle of Oxfordes daughter might have ben aswell bestowed. To conclude [(]my Lord) nether I nor my Nephewe desyre to be beholding to any body but your selfe, and therfore wee do adresse our selfes vnto yow as one who wee doupt [=doubt] not wylbe Ruler of your owne whyles yow lyve. Although yf I woould belyeue what is informed Sir Edward Norreys doth gyve it out that nobody shall ether speake with yow but by his meanes, nor obtayne any thing of yow but by his favour, whereof I desyre by your Lordships aunswere to make tryall, presuming that for so small an advantag as that woodd can be vnto hym, whose Purse soever yow meane to fyll, yow wyll not deface the stat[e] of your Posterytie.

Lord Norris replied curtly on the 29th that the property was his to do with as he wished.[3] The old man was not, however, long for this world, and died on 27 June 1601, whereupon Francis Norris succeeded to the Barony (*Peerage*). In the second year of her marriage Bridget thus became a baroness.

On 20 September Oxford and his men were accused of blocking up 'an ancient footway … leading from Tottenham … to the parish church of Hackney':[4]

> The Queen's jurors declare that Whereas the ancient footpath lying near Stamford Hill and leading from Tottenham (Middlesex) towards the Parish Church of

Hackney (in the same county), by which footpath divers of the Queen's subjects have made a practice of going and coming to the aforesaid parish church and to the city of London since time out of mind, the noble (*blank*) Count of Oxford together with divers servants on 20 September 1600 near Tottenham illicitly blocked up ('hath stopped') that footpath, in such manner that the aforesaid Queen's subjects are not able to come and go as they were wont, to the great injury of all those travelling along the way and against the peace of the aforesaid Queen.

It is unknown whether Oxford, whose first name the Queen's jurors failed to recall, succeeded in this attempt to put his own desire for privacy above the customary interests of his Hackney neighbours.

79 The Weakness of my Lame Hand

Some time before his death in 1598, Burghley made a memorandum of 'Noble men and ladyes that have not paid the subsydy' – concerning the general subsidy assessed throughout England in 1597: 'v Countes 12 barons 12 ladyes'.[1] Exchequer pipe rolls known as the 'Lord Treasurer's Remembrancer' reveal that Oxford was a tax-defaulter in 1600–01, in debt for £20:[2]

> Edwardus Comes Oxon' debet xxli super ibidem assess' & taxat' de primo subsidio ...

The document roll is well-known to Shakespeare scholars – by now the playwright had apparently paid up on his obligation outstanding since 1597, while Oxford remained delinquent.[3] Another defaulter was Ambrose Nicolas, Citizen and Alderman of London, who owed taxes on 'Oxford place or Oxford House', which included 'a longe garden' – this was Vere House, which Oxford had long since alienated.[4]

Queen Elizabeth's Eleventh (and last) Parliament sat from 27 October to 19 December 1601 (*TE*). Oxford missed all 36 sessions, including the ceremonial opening and closing, appointing his old friend Charles Howard (Lord Howard of Effingham) as proxy.[5] The retrospective account compiled by Simonds D'Ewes, who was not born until 1602, errs in supposing that Oxford attended the opening ceremony.[6] He is more accurate as to Essex, returned from his disastrous expedition to Ireland and embarked on his ill-fated rebellion of Sunday 8 February.

Meanwhile, on 2 February Oxford wrote to Cecil seeking support in his bid for the Presidency of Wales (LL-31):

> At thys tyme, I am to trye my friendes: amonge whiche consideringe owre owlde aquayntance, familiarite heertofore, & alliance of houses, (then whiche can be noo streyghter) as of my Broother, I presume especiallye. Whearfore at thys tyme, wheras sume good fortune (yf yt be backed by friendes) doothe in a manner

presente yt selfe. I moost ernestlye crave yowre furtherance soo fare as the place and fauoure yow howlde may admite. And that ys as I conceyve: that yf her Magestie be willinge, to confer the Præcidentcie of Waales to me, that I may assure my selfe of yowre voice in Councell rather then a stranger. Not that I desyre yow showlde bee a mover, but a furtherer. for as the tyme ys yt weare nott reasone. But yf yt shall pleas her Magestie in regard of my yowthe[,] tyme & fortune spent in her Courte, addinge therto her magesties fauours, & promises, whiche drue me one [=on] wythe ought any mistruste, the moore to præsume in myne owne expences, to confer soo good a turne to me. that then wythe yowre good woorde, and brotherlye friend-shipe, yow will incorage her forwarde, and further yt as yow may. for I know her Magestie ys of that princlye dispositione that they shall nott be deceyved whiche put there truste in her. Whiche good office in yow, I will never forgett; and alwayes to my powre acknowlege in loue & kyndnes. hoopinge that as wee bee knytt neare in alliance: so hearafter moore nearer by good and friendly offices. Thus most ernest-lye desyringe yow to haue me in friendlye remembrance, when tyme servethe ...

As usual, Oxford's request came to nothing.

Nine days after Essex's short-lived rebellion, on Tuesday 17 February, the Privy Council distributed a summons for a trial which was to begin on Thursday 19 February at Westminster Hall. Oxford served as 'the senior of the twenty-five noblemen' as Essex and Southampton were tried for treason.[7] Six days later, on the 25th, Essex was executed. Oxford had expressed bitterness against Essex in a postscript to a letter of 20 October 1595.[8] Towards Ralegh, who was sent to the Tower but not executed until years later, Oxford was triumphal, as recorded in Francis Bacon's 1625 *Apophthegemes New and Old* (pp. 7–8):

When Queene Elizabeth had aduanced Ralegh, she was one day playing on the virginalls, and my Lord of Oxford, & another Noble-man, stood by. It fell out so, that the Ledge, before the Iacks, was taken away, so as the Iacks were seene: My Lord of Oxford, and the other Noble-man smiled, and a little whispered: The Queen marked it, and would needes know, *What the matter was?* My Lord of Oxford answered; *That they smiled, to see, that when Iacks went vp, Heads went downe.*

The tale became so popular that Sir Robert Naunton could casually allude to it in subsequent years:[9]

... And as for my Lord of Oxfords iest [=jest] of him [=Ralegh] for a Iack of an vpstart, wee know it sauoured more of æmulacion & of his humour, then of truth ...

Naunton dismisses Oxford's jest as the product of jealousy and caprice.[10]

Apparently in early May Oxford wrote to Cecil, again for the Presidency of Wales; evidently he had reconciled with Henry Lok, who served as his trusted messenger (LL-32):[11]

My very good Broother, I have receyved by Henry Loke yowre moste kynde message, whiche I so effectuallye imbrace, that whatt for the owlde loue [=love] I have borne yow, whiche I assure yow was very greate, what for the alliance which ys betwene vs, whiche ys tyed so fast by my chyldren of yowre owne syster, what for myne owne dispositione to yowre selfe, whiche hathe bene rootede by longe and many familiarites of a moore yowthefull tyme there cowld have beene nothinge soo deerly welcome vnto me. wherfore not as a stranger but in the owld style, I doo assure yow that yow shall have no faster freende & wellwisher vnto yow then my self eyther in kyndnes, which I finde beyond myne expectatione in yow; or in kyndred, wherby none ys nerer allyed then my selfe, sythe of yowre systers, of my wyfe only yow have receyved Nieces. A syster I say not by any venter [=adventure, chance], but borne of the same father, and the same moother of [=as] yowre selfe. I will say no moore, for woordes in faythefull myndes are tedious. only thys I protest, yow shall doo me wronge, and yowre selfe greater, yf eyther throwghe fables whiche are mischeuous, or conceyt, whiche ys dangerous, yow thinke otherwis of me then humanite, & consanguinite requyrethe. I desyred Henry Loke to speake vnto yow, for that I cannot so well, vrge myne owne busines to her Magestye, that yow wowld doo me the fauour, when thes troblesume tymes giue oportunite to her Magesty to thinke of the dispositione of the Præsident of Waales that I may vnderstand yt by yowe, least [=lest] neglectinge throwgh ignorance the tyme, by mishap I may lease [=lose] the sute. for as I have vnderstood, and by good reason conceyved I am not to yowse [=use] any friend to moue yt, so my self hauing movd yt, and receyved good hoops [=hopes], I feare nothinge but throwgh ignorance when to prosecut yt least I showld leas the benifite of her good dispositione one [=on] whiche I only depende.

The Essex rebellion had not diverted Oxford from his personal goal. Cecil replied by 11 May, when Oxford wrote to thank him for his favourable response. In his letter (LL-33), Oxford tells Cecil that he thinks he will attend Court the next day, which was Tuesday 12 May. He uses the excuse of being 'a hater of ceremonies' to explain why he does not intend to thank Cecil more effusively, or in person.

Meanwhile, in the words of Stone (p. 414), 'After the Essex revolt there was a hectic rush for the spoils.' Not least eager among the vulture crew was Oxford, who set his sights on the lands of Sir Charles Danvers, executed on 18 March (*DNB*). Oxford's campaign for Danvers's lands began by 30 June, with a memorandum entitled 'The resolution of my Lord of Oxford's proceedings':[12]

1st. That the parties now brought up should be examined upon interrogatories, and if sufficient light is got for the land or for the evidences, then some order be taken by the Lord Treasurer [=Buckhurst] for bringing in the evidences.

2ndly. That a bill be exhibited in the Exchequer against all those that pretend interest in the land, or are suspected of having any of the evidences.

3rdly. That a commission be issued to inquire what lands, tenements, goods, &c. Sir Chas. Danvers was seized of at his attainder.

(*in another hand*) John Hodgkinson, Richard Atwood, clerk, Richard Danvers, and Jeffrey Bath to be detained for embezzling goods, value 1,000li., and for conveying away evidences, besides many other misdemeanours already delivered in articles to be proved by witnesses, with note of the names of the witnesses, and request that their examinations may be seen before they are discharged.

A note by Buckhurst reveals that the Queen's Counsel 'are to consider and set down what course is best for Her Majesty'.

On 7 August Buckhurst and Sir John Fortescue wrote to Attorney General Coke:[13]

> Master Atturny my lord of Oxford doth desier that he may haue a copie of the case as you haue collected it out of the evidences showed before vs to the intent he may consider therof with his lerned Councell for the benefit of Her maiestie as he affirmeth. the which we think fit he haue & do therfor pray you to deliver the same to him accordingly

Other notes may be dated March 1601 to March 1602.[14] Among these is an articulated memorandum in Oxford's hand denigrating Sir Edmund Carey's rival claims (LL-50):

> The thyrd poynt. – That ther weer thre of Sir Edmund Careys men whiche have continuallye wached Cavlie and that he narrowly escaped them thre tymes, and that they vaunted they wowld take me at my heeles. ...
>
> The foorthe poynt. – That hee termed me a promoter. Arthur Miles myne Author.
>
> The fyft poynt – That there were of the gard in the tumultuous assault at Caules loginge, yt ys trwe but for want of tyme ther names yet cannot be so sone [=soon] lerned yet thus muche ys knowne that he ys a keper I know not whyther in Waltham Forest or where els but yt ys very trwe as shalbe vpon streyghter inquire [=inquiry] and moore respit of tyme found owt. ...
>
> A Contraditiorie in his owne speache. – fyrst as Arthur Miles reported to me thes weere his woords, that I followed yt now with fyre and sword. – That I wass of a strange and vild [=vile] nature that wowld pursue a cause in this sort as a promoter agaynst an other, and yet re[a]pinge noo benifitte to my selfe sythe her Magestye had giuen me nothinge. – yet he yesternyght averred to her Magestye that he arrested Cawlye for his raylinge at him, and sayinge that the tenantes showld returne to my lord of Oxford and not to the Quene. – Her[e] to Arther Miles he sayd I had no benifit therby. – Heer to her Magestye he avouchet the tenantes showld returne to me and nott the Quene

Once again Oxford is accused of being a 'promoter'. Arthur Milles (Oxford's agent) reported Carey's opinion that Oxford, pursuing the desired lands 'with fyre and sword', was 'of a strange and vild nature'; indeed, Carey had arrested Cawley 'for his railing at him'. Oxford would inform Cecil in his letter of 22 November (below): 'I haue vsed [Cawley] and soo doo styll as a follower of my busines, wherin I ... recommend hys diligence.' Arthur Milles would explain in a letter of his own (below) that Cawley was a retainer of Countess Elizabeth. Evidently Cawley's service to Oxford as an informant in the pursuit of Danvers's properties put him at risk from Sir Edmund Carey and his henchmen.

On 7 October Oxford wrote to Cecil from Hackney, opening with a reference to his health (LL-34):

> My very good Brother, yf my helthe hadd beene to my mynde I wowlde have beene before this att the Coorte, aswell to haue giuen yow thankes for yowre presence, at the hearinge of my cause debated as to haue moued her Magestye for her resolutione. As for the matter, how muche I am behouldinge to yow I neede not repeate, but in all thankfulnes acknowlege, for yow haue beene the moover & onlye follower therofe for mee, & by yowre onlye meanes, I have hetherto passed the pykes of so many adversaries. Now my desyre ys, sythe them selues whoo have opposed to her Magestyes ryghte seeme satisfisde [=satisfied], that yow will make the ende ansuerable, to the rest of yowre moste friendlye procedinge, for I am aduised, that I may passe my Booke from her Magestie, yf a warrant may be procured to my cosen [Francis] Bacon and Seriant [=Sergeant] Harris to perfe[c]t yt. Whiche beinge doone, I know to whome formallye to thanke, but reallye they shalbe, and are from me, and myne, to be sealed vp in an æternall remembrance to yowre selfe. And thus wishinge all happines to yow, and sume fortunat meanes to me, wherby I myght recognise soo diepe merites, I take my leaue …

The accompanying memorandum identifies the 'cause' before the Queen as the acquisition of Danvers's lands.

On 22 November Oxford wrote to Cecil, again from Hackney, confessing his poor health, and invoking the Danvers matter (LL-35):

> My good Brother, in that I haue not sent an answer to yowre laste letter, as yow myght expect, I shall desyre yow too [=to] hould me for exscused, sythe ever sythence the receyt therof by reason of my syknes I have not been able to wryght. And wheaeras yow doo conceyve that I haue bene carried to[o] muche by the conceytes of Cauley, I doo asssure yow ther ys no suche thinge. I haue vsed hym and soo doo styll as a follower of my busines, wherin I doo not finde any cause to blame but rather recommend hys diligence. for Councell I haue suche lavers [=lawyers], and the best that I can gett as are to be had in London, whoo have aduised me for my best course, to desyre that her Magestye wowld graunt me her warrant signed, for the dravinge [=drawing] of a booke mentioninge what her plesure ys to graunt me concerninge the Escheete of Sir Charles Davers (*de bene esse, quantum in Regina est*)[15] wherby shall ensue no preiudice vnto any of the pretenders whiche subieste [=suggest, pretend?] to be interessed [=interested] in any of the sayd landes, in regard, that yf the Quiene haue no titell, there passethe nothinge to mee. It ys a common course notwythstandinge any office founde agaynste the Quiene, that her Magestye grauntethe concealed landes in this course, whearof there are many yearly precidentes. So that her Magestye grauntinge this to me, grauntethe but her owne interest, whiche in effect had bene nothinge, consideringe how this cause hathe bene caried, and so lekly to haue bene obscured for ever, yf yt had not bene my hap to have styrred therin.

> for the rest of yowre letter, whatsoever yow have written, although yt be sum discoragment vnto me, yet I cannot alter the opinion whiche I have conceyved of yowre vertu and constancie, neyther can I suffer yt to enter my thought that a

vayne fable can brandel [=disturb] the clearnes of yowre guyltles conscience sythe all the world doothe know that the crymes of Sir Charles Dauers were so byfolde, that Iustice could not dispence any farther; wherfor I cannot leue [=leave, abandon] that hoope and trust whiche I have hadd in yowre promises, but as I have done styll I doo wholy rely my self on yowre only friendship, and thus desyring yow to beare with the weaknes of my lame hand, I take my leaue …

Evidently Cecil was having second thoughts – and even a guilty conscience – over Sir Charles's execution and his family's threatened destitution. Oxford insists that Sir Charles's crimes were so 'byfolde' – manifold – that the full rigour of the law must apply, meaning the Danvers family lands should be entirely forfeited (and Oxford thereby enriched).

For the first time Oxford leaves a clue as to the nature of his infirmity, declaring that 'by reason of my syknes I have not been able to wryght', and apologizing for 'the weaknes of my lame hand'. Perhaps he had suffered a stroke. His handwriting remains clear and confident, but doubtless required more deliberate care.

On 4 December Oxford wrote again to Cecil (LL-36):

I can not conceyve, in so shorte a tyme, & in so smaale an abscence, how so greate a change ys hapned in yow, for in the beginninge of my sute to her Magestie I was doutfull to enter therinto, boothe for the wante I hadd of friendes, and the dowt of the Caries. But I wass incoraged by yow whoo dyd not onlye assurme [=assure me] to be an assured friende vnto me, but further dyd vndertake to moue yt to her. whiche yow so well performed, that after sum dispute, her Magestie was contented. In that good begininge, I was promised fauoure, that I showlde haue assistance of her Magestyes counsel in lave [=law], that I showlde haue expeditione. but for fauoure the other partie, hetherto, hathe found muche moore, and as for assistance of her Magesties councell, whoo hathe bene moore, na[y] only agaynst me, the expeditione hathe bene suche, that what myght haue bene done in one monthe, ys now allmost a yeare differred [=deferred]. At my departure frome Greenwiche, what good woordes yow gaue me, and what assurance, of yowre constancie to me, yf yow have forgotten, yt ys in vayne for me to remember. Now besydes the alteratione whiche I finde in the style of yowre letters, Caulye hathe towlde me that yow ar exempted, and that Carye complaynes as yt weere of yowre partialite. When I tooke my leaue of her Magestie, she vsed me very gratiouslye, & mooreover gaue me thes woordes, that she doughted not for all that was sayed to the contrarie, but that the Escheat of Sir Charles Davers wowld faal owt well and that wythe all her hart she wisht yt and ment yt to me. I was gladd to heare her, and thought my self greatly behowldinge [=beholden] to yow, for I my self had never yet speache wythe her, wherfore I dyd and doo styll imput[e] this her good mynde to yowre friendly and honorable dealinge towards me. Now the cause fallinge owt to be good and by course of laue [=law] her Magesties, yt ys iustice, that her Magestye may bestowe the same at her pleasure, and yf she be willinge to giue yt me, I doo not see in reasone how partiallite showld or canbe imputed to yow, & the matter lyinge thus in the ballence of iustice, I doo not see, but boothe for yowre promise sake even frome the beginninge and for the alliance whiche ys betwien yow and me, wytheout any iust imputatione of partialite, yow may as well and wythe as great honor end as begine yt. And wheras yow assure me that the Lord Thresorer ys now very wyllinge to further me, I am very glad yf yt soo proue, for I have need of as many good friends as I can get, and yf I could I wowld seeke all the adversaries I have in this cause to make them my friendes. Wherof I stand in so muche need, and yet when I hadd done all, I wowlde especiallye thinke my selfe behowldinge to yow, on whome for all thes discoragments past I doo onlye relye. I have written to her Magestie, and receyved a most gratious answer to doo me good in all that she cane [=can],[16] and that she will speake wythe yow, about yt. Now therfore yt ys in yowre poure [=power] alone, I know yt, that yf yow will deale for me, as I have cause to beleue, that yt may have an end accordinge to myne expectatione, for whiche I will esteme and acknowlege only to procede from yow. The Aturnye hathe had a deuice indede, as yow know yf yow lyst, by referringe yt to iugges [=judges] to delay the cause wherby weariynge me with an vnresonable tyme he myght procure an agrement wherto I will never agree, or els an extenuatione, or vtter overthrow of her Magesties lyberalite towards me. But my councell doothe fullye aduise me, that yf yt be her Magesties plesure to have a short end therof, then to graunt yt me (*de benne esse, quantum in nos est,*)[17] wherin yf at any tyme yt shall please yow to heare them, I doo not dowt but they are able to satisfise [=satisfy] yow. In the meane seasone I recommend my selfe and the whoole cause to yow as one hym[?], vpon whome I relye wythe this most ernest desyre, that howsoever, there myght be an end, for as yt hathe hetherto bene handled, yf yt weer to begine agayne I wowld never enter into yt. and yf I cannot obteyne yt, yet an end as yt ys fallne owt ys sumwhat.

Thus Oxford became thoroughly discouraged, and openly recriminatory against Cecil.

A memorandum from Arthur Milles addressed to Cecil and datable to late 1601 or early 1602 reveals that he too had now fallen out with Oxford, more particularly with Countess Elizabeth:[18]

Right honourable I most humbly beeseche yow to pervse theis lynes conteyning the heavy and troblesome wrongs done vnto me by the Lady of Oxforde whoe through her greatnes, and most wicked practises of her agents, Anthonie Atkinson and Michaell Caully 2 of her followers, haue and doe seeke my life (as by the sequell appeareth[)].

It ys so that one Edward Motam my Lady of Oxfords Taylor, that daye her Caskett was miste, was presently accused by my Lord of Oxford (as an eye witnes) for takeing awaie the same, & so he protested vpon his & other deepe protestacions before my lord of Cumberland, Mr Thomas Woodhowse[,] Mr Iohn Parker, Mr George Baker, my selfe & vnto manie others, That hee sawe this Motam take yt awaie, yet my Lady of Oxford did not imprison him, but within some fewe dayes after my servant was taken in the nighte at Greenewich & put close prisoner in the Porters Lodge 3 dayes & 3 nights that noe man might come to him but one Youngs my Ladys trusty servant, whoe in this time offered him rounde somes [=sums] of monie to accuse me, which hee confessed before the Clarcks of the Greenecloth &

before Youngs face, how hee wrought him to accuse mee. Yet my Ladys mallice did not cease there, but some 5 daies after that[,] I was accused for the same vpon theis three seuerall points; ffirst that I was twise that daye with the Lord of Oxford; Secondly, that I did not stey that daye with him so long as I was wont to doe; and the third accusacion was, that I came that daye by his doore with my Cloke [=cloak] caste over my sholders, my Lord at that time stoode firmely to mee, and tould Mr Thomas Woodhouse (as he can testeify) that my Lord protested to him that in truth his man stole yt, and that his wife wold needes in her will accuse me without cause; yet afterwards my Lord was so wrought by my Lady to saye that I mighte receaue some parte. Atkinson & Cauley the twoe onely men that arrested me vpon this felony, so that I was hardlie beseiged with a greate & powerfull mallicious Ladie, & by 2 so counning [=cunning] & crafty persons, to sett the waie for her for my vndoeing in bodie, goods, and life, as I was enforced to apeere at the assises in Kent, where also my Ladies man Motam appeered he being the principall, but was forthwith discharged, having nothing saied to him, and I being but a poore suspected accessary had (contrarie to all law) a Bill of Indictment preferred against mee, from which I was by the Iury acquited, though by Cauley & Younges the Iury were well labored to the contrary, Yet my Innocency cleered me therein. Notwithstanding (as I heare) her Ladiship seaseth [=ceaseth] not her mallice, ffor Cauley tould me my Lady wold arreste me for some threescore thousand pounds [=£60,000] vpon an accompt, for that which the Lord of Oxford spent in the time of my vnfortunate service with him, wherein I spent in Land of my owne which I soulde, 3 hundred Marks [=£200] by yeare, to maintaine my selfe with creditt in his Lordships service.

I was tould also that my Lady meanes to arrest me once againe vpon felonie for stealing certaine hangings & an old hearse cloth and divers other things some xxvtie [=25] yeares since, which weare given me vnder his Lordships owne hand and seale, wherevnto I haue menie good witnesses to testefy the same in particular acquitances, besides his lordshipps generall acquitance for the same & all other things whatsoever; yet this Atkinson & Cauley haue perswaded my Lord (as I heare) to denie his hand & seale. And so what with arrests & trobles my Ladie meanes to vndoe me her Maiesties poore servant, if her gratious Maiesty doe not looke vpon me to defend my inocencey, which hetherto never begged anie other suite. As the Lady gaue greate grace to her servant (being the principall) to be discharged without anie question at all, & I her Maiesties sworne servant openly disgraced with a most shamefull & publicke tryall for felonie, in the same place by the Grand Iury whoe found me most inocent in all my accusacions, Soe I doubte not but if her Maiesty did knowe in howe greate and conning mallice I haue ben prosecuted bothe in body, goods, & name, without anie recompence at all, [(]& noe matter proved) her Maiestie wold looke vpon her inocent servant with her gratious favor (having hetherto protected the inocent only & noe other)./

It may therefore please your good honour to favor & further me in the best course I maie take for my defence in so dangerous a case, prosecuted by so powerfull an adversarie whose mallice I am not able to resist without the favorable Counsell and healpe of some great & honourable person, otherwise, I must needs perish in my

> innocencey vnder the waight of so greate and mallicious an adversarie, to the vtter
> vndoeing of my wife & Children, whereof 2 serve in her Maiesties warrs at this
> present, & haue their maintenance from mee./ …

Milles's letter incidentally reveals Oxford's association with the Earl of Cumberland (George Clifford) and George Baker (presumably the surgeon). Milles himself, who had served Oxford from as early as 1576, when he received the 15th Earl's hearse-cloth by gift, was now accused of theft and charged with a debt to Oxford of £60,000, when (by his own account) he had in fact spent £200 per annum in his master's service.

Milles provides a sharp description of Oxford's Hackney household, supervised by Countess Elizabeth and her 'followers'. On the day of the theft, Milles had been twice with Oxford, remaining for a shorter time than usual, once walking by Oxford's door with his cloak over his shoulders. Oxford initially came to Milles's defence, but was 'so wrought by my Lady' that he turned against him. No wonder Milles characterizes the Countess as 'so greate and mallicious an adversarie'.

80 Nothing more Precious than Gold

In January 1602, still pursuing the Danvers estates, Oxford wrote to Cecil in increasing frustration (LL-37):

> It ys now almoste a yeare sythence by the promises of yowre helpe and assistance,
> when the Escheate of Dauers was found nothinge for her Magestye 26 shyllinges
> excepted, that I dyd vndertake to recover yt. Now Brother I doo nott by thes letters
> make chalenge of yowre woordes, for yf yow lyst to forgett them, my puttinge in
> remembrance wilbe bitter, and to smaale purpose. Only this now ys myne inten-
> tione not to tell any nev [=new] thinge, but that whic[h] ys allredie knowne, vnto
> yow. The matter after yt hade receyved many crosses, many inventiones of delay,
> yet atlenghe [=at length], hathe bene h[e]ard before all the Iugges, Iugges I say
> boothe vnlaufull, and laufull, for so may I affirme sythe Walmsle whoo hadd
> ma[t]ched [=married] in the house of Davers, besydes sum other, weere admitted
> to the decidinge of the cause, notwythstandinge longe sythence I dyd accept
> [=except, protest] agaynst hym, and yt wass then thowght resonable. But now
> tyme, and truthe, have vnmasked all difficulties, and I doo vnderstand, the Iugges
> are, yf they will be indifferent[,] to make a good report to her Magestie. Yet I know
> not by whatt vnfortunat stare [=star], ther arre so many disposed to wythestand yt,
> as the truthe, muche oppressed by the freendes of the contrarie part, ys leklye yf not
> whoolye to be defaced, yet so extenuated, as the vertu therof wilbe of littell effect.
> Now for so muche, as I vnderstand yt ys ment to delay the report to the end, to gett
> a compositione of [=from] her Magestye and so to bringe all my hoope in her
> Magestyes gratious woordes to smoke, I am ernestlye to solicit her, to caale for the

report, whiche I showld not have neded to doo, yf gospell hadd bine in the mouthes of the Lorde chiefe Iustice and the Atturnye, whoo dyd assure me that at the next hearinge, whiche then was appoynted the second day of thys terme[,] yt showld have a full end. Now the matter dependinge in this sort, I fynd my statte weake and destitute of friendes for havinge only relyed allwayes on her Magestye, I have neglected to seeke others, and this trust of myne, many thinges considered, I feare may deceyve me. An other confidence I had in yowre selfe, in whome, wythe-out offence lett me speake yt, I am to cast sume dout, by reasone, as in yowre last letters I founde a waveringe style muche differinge from yowre former assurances, I feare now to be left in medio rerum omnium certamine et discrimine ['In the midst of all, embattled and in danger'] whiche yf yt soo faale owt, I shall beare yt by the grace of God, wythe an equall mynde, sythe tyme and experience have giuen me sufficient vnderstandinge of woorldlye frayelte. But I hoope better, thowghe I cast the woorste, how so ever for finis coronat opus ('The end crowns the work') and then every thynge wilbe layd open, every dout resolued into a playne sence. In the meane seasone, I now at the laste, for now ys the tyme, crave this brotherly freend-ship, that as yow began yt for me wythe all kyndnes, so that yow will continue in the same affectione to end yt. and so I will end, these thinges only desyringe yow to remember, that yow may know I doo not forget, how honorablie yow delt with her Magestye at what tyme yow fyrst moved her, showinge how owt of nothinge to her, for so in manner yt wass founde, yf by myne industrie I could of this nothinge make sumthinge, she showld yet giue a propt [=prop] and stay to my house. Agayne I know and well perceyve how that this Esche[a]t of Davers shalbe made a great matter, to cros[s]e my good happ and to obscure the rest of the lands whiche discend from the mother on Latimer syde, to her Magestye whiche ys as clere her Magestyes as thys. Last of all I shall desyre yow to remember that I craved of this Esche[a]tte only what I cowld recover in Wilshyre and Glocester shyres. Leuinge to her Magestye the lands of Oxford, Lecester, Northamptone and Yorkshyre. whiche ys of muche moore vallue. In the beginninge the whoole was thowght desperat, and yet yow shall se now the lave [=law] to be clere of the Queens syde, notwythstand-inge yt hathe indured all the crosses that can be possible, ye[a] mooreover I will say to yow that I must informe, this case hathe opend her ryght to a far greater Matter, then this of Davers, yf her Magestyes ryght and interrest be not cunningly suppressed, and therfore I hoope her Magesty after so many gratious woordes which she gave me at Grenwiche vpon her departure excedinge this whiche I expect, will not now drave [=draw] in the beames of her princlie grace to my discoragment and her owne detriment. Neyther will I conceyve otherwise of yowre vertu and affec-tione towards me now att the end, then I apprehended all good hoope and kyndnes from yow in the beginninge. thus wythe a lame hand, to wright I take my leue, but wythe a mynde well disposd to hoop [=hope] the best of my friends, tyll otherwis I finde them. which I feare nothinge att all, assuringe my self yowre woords and deeds dwell not asunder.

Oxford claims that he had been promised Danvers's lands in Wiltshire and Gloucestershire; he still hopes to get them, with Cecil's help. Once again he alludes to his lame hand.

On 3 February Lady Dorothy Moryson wrote to Cecil from Caishio, concerning Lady Susan:[1]

> I beseeche your Honour seeing it pleasethe not God to afoard me the happines to
> be able my self to attend your Honour, graunt Leaue to theis lynes, to answere a
> Conceiued errour, that I should Commyit which I intreated my Honourable Lord
> Greye, to deliver the truthe of to your Honour, bothe touching my self and my
> sonne, who forbare to presume to waite on yow then; in respect he h[e]ard yow
> were soe muche insenced against vs bothe, for seeking to take vnfitting Courses,
> towardes my Honourable Lady Susan Veare, to whome neyther of vs will live to be
> soe forgetfull of the Honour we owe to your self, as also the due that we will ever
> acknowledg to her, whome I assured my self would doe nothinge without your
> knowledge and Honourable Consent, which I had no good groundes to presume to
> troble your Honour for, of whose favour, as my sonne and I, haue alreadye tasted,
> and rest most bowned to your Honour for, soe would we further haue presumed,
> to have acquainted your Honour with the Cause, before it had byn laid open to the
> speeche of the world, which I beseeche yow thinke proceeded from neyther of vs,
> nor with our Consentes, but seeing it hathe soe fallen out to be brought in
> question; and that it restes whollie in your Honourable liking and Consent, I
> humblie intreate yow to alowe my sonne the favour, to seeke to deserve the pretty
> Ladies affection (who bothe for the vertues, and kindnes, we have fownd from her:
> will ever Honour, holding it more precious, then what she shalbe woorthe besides)
> which we onlie Leaue to your Honourable favour and direction, and the rest of her
> Honourable ffreendes, and my sonne by yow to be disposed of, who is most deare
> vnto me, and shalbe muche the more, if it will please your Honour to grace him
> with your good Conceight [=conceit, estimation], which I will doe my best to
> make his desertes woorthie of. …

Susan, who would turn fifteen on 26 May, was on the market, and Lady Dorothy
was seeking the pretty young lady for her son. About this time John Manningham
of the Middle Temple recorded an epigram entitled 'LADY SUSAN VERE':[2]

> Nothing's your lott, that's more then can be told
> For nothing is more precious then gold.

Susan's want of a dowry thus made her the target of poetical wits. On 16 December she received a loan from the royal wardrobe for an event at Whitehall:[3]

> Item one rounde gowne of yellowe Satten cut and lined with blacke sarceonet
> wrought allouer [=all over] with short staues billetwise with flate siluer with a like
> passamane.

The loan was acknowledged with a neat signature: 'Susanna Veare'.

On 22 March Oxford wrote to Cecil from Hackney, having heard from Michael
Cawley (LL-38):

> It ys now a yeare sythence by yowre only meanes her Magestye graunted her
> intereste in Danvers escheete. I hade only then her woorde from yowre mouthe I

fynde by thys waste of Tyme, that landes will not be carried wythoute deedes. I
have twice therfore moved her Magestie that yt wowld please her to graunte me
that ordinarie course (*de bene esse quantum in nobis est*) wherof there are moore then
an hundred examples. myne answer ys that I showld receyve her pleasure from yow.
But I vnderstand by Cauley that shee hathe never spoken therof. The matter hathe
beene h[e]ard accordinge to the order with muche a doo twice before the Iugges,
and many also standers by dyd heare the same, ther in open ap[pe]arance, her
Magesties tytell was questionles, The Lord chyef Iustice vpon thys as in forme I was
made beleue [=made (to) believe], was to have taken the opinion of the rest of the
Iugges and conferringe yt wythe his owne to have made vp a report to her Magestie.
As for the Iugges report they weere never caald vnto yt, and the principall poyntes
to confirme her Magesties tytell never opned or moved, but contrarie kept bake
[=back]. So that vnder there hands the Lord chiefe Iustice hathe made no report.
Yet sumthinge he hathe done owt of his owne brest that ys secret and I cannot
lerne, yf he have reported nothinge to Esche[a]te to her Magestie, then ys my sute as
yt was the fyrst day, that ys where her Magestie thowght she hadd nothinge, that she
wowld graunt me her Interest. thys sut I obteyned by yowre espetiall meanes, and
this she promisde me, wherfore Hervpon I chalenge that sumthynge myght be
done, wherby I may vpon grovnde seke and trye her Magesties ryght, whiche
cannot be done wythout this dede a fore spoken of. The course whyche syldome or
never hathe bene vsed before in this cause, to refer yt to the Iugges, how
præiuditiall a præsident I know not to her Magestie, hathe bene obserued, and the
effect hathe showed that whearas yt was pretended to be shortest, yt hathe bene the
furthest way about. and as the beginninge was but sume opinione the end ys but
confusione. Now therfore the matter havinge bene directed by this course for a
whoole yeares space, and come to no better termes, my desyre ys to know her
Magesties plesure touchinge her patent, (*De bene esse*) whyther she will performe yt
or noo. If not then have I bene mocked, yf ye[a], that I myght have answer, wherby
I may vpon reason quiet my selfe, and not vpon wearines. How sooever an answer
shalbe most welcome vnto me, now beinge the best expectatione of my tedious
sute, thinkinge therin, my tyme lost, more pretious then the sute yt selfe. ...

To Oxford's chagrin, the Danvers lands would be restored to Charles's brother,
Henry, following the accession of James in 1603.[4]

Once again Oxford was passed over for the Order of the Garter without
garnering a single vote. William Segar's *Honor Military, and Ciuill*, in a chart
headed 'The names of those Knights that are this present yeere 1602 of the same
most noble Order' (p. 67), lists the earls of Nottingham (Charles Howard),
Cumberland (George Clifford), Worcester (Edward Somerset), Sussex (Robert
Radcliffe), Ormond (Thomas Butler), Shrewsbury (Gilbert Talbot), Northumberland (Henry Percy), and Oxford's 'nidicock' son-in-law Derby. Notably
absent is the name of Oxford himself.

On 29 June the Hackney parish church enacted a special assessment:[5]

A Seassment ffor a Stocke ffor the house of correction: beinge the somme of £70–
13–4 made and rated the 29th of Iune Anno 1602 according to a Recepte to that

effecte directed from the heigh Constable dated the 20 of Iune Anno predicto

The nobilite and knyghts

The right Honorable Earle of Oxenford
The right Honorable Lord Zouche …

While lesser parishioners have amounts listed against their names, neither Oxford nor Zouche paid up.

On 20 November Countess Elizabeth wrote to Dr Julius Caesar from Hackney, kept from an appointment by a coach accident:[6]

> Master Doctor Cæsar, I should haue deliuered a request from my Lord vnto yow, concerning a sute depending in the Court of requests, against an insolent Tenant, that for the space of many yeares, hathe neither payed any rent, nor wyll shewe his lease for my Lords satisfaction. And now being by a late mischaunce in my Coache, preuented from the hope of any present opportunitye to meete yow at the Court, I do earnestly intreate yow, that whensoeuer my Lords counsell shall mooue, against one Thomas Coe, of Walter Belchamp, for the discouerye of his lease, and satisfaction of his rent; that either yourself or Mr Wylbrome, wyll giue the cause that expedition, as in your fauorable iustice, it shall deserue, and preuent, this dilatory pleadings, which the iniustice of Coes cause, wyll offer vnto yow. …

On 1 July 1595 Oxford had sued Thomas, Roger, and Edward Coe for the recovery of rents and the counterpart of a lease for the parsonage at Belchamp Water, Essex.[7] Now, seven years later, his Countess petitioned Cecil on the same matter. The fact that Oxford and Elizabeth were complaining over property they had alienated on 2 March 1592 to her brother and uncle shows that the alienation was a legal fiction. Coe answers that the property was still encumbered with royal liens:

> this defendaunt sayth that the said parsonage for & during so long tyme as the rent hathe not been paid so the said parsonage hath been & yet standeth seised into her maiesties handes for debt due vnto her maiestie by the said Erle, or for want of lycence of alienacion, for the certaynty wherof as also of the tyme how longe the same hath been seized, this defendaunt referreth him self to her maiesties recordes therof in the Exchequer by reason of which seizures, this defendant hath been compelled to paye the said Rent by all that tyme to the Queenes maiesties vse, so that ther is nothing behind or due of the said Rente to the said Playntiffe as he thinketh

Coe thus claims that he had been paying rent into the Elizabethan equivalent of an escrow account established to settle Oxford's debts. By now Countess Elizabeth was serving as Oxford's spokesperson and agent, probably a reflection of his own poor state of health.

81 Missing Person

On New Year's Day 1603 the Countess of Oxford exchanged gifts with Queen Elizabeth.[1]

On 24 March, about two or three o'clock in the morning, the Queen died.[2] No successor having been appointed, the choice of the new monarch was ratified by a 'Great Council' comprised of the Lord Mayor of London, Privy Council members from the previous reign, and non-member peers and bishops.[3] When the Council convened at Whitehall about nine o'clock in the morning, Cecil appeared with a draft proclamation, which 34 worthies signed on the bottom half of the second page. Oxford was not one of the signatories.

About ten o'clock the Council formed into a procession, 'beginning at White hall gates, where Sir Robert Cecile reade the proclamation, which he carried in his hand and after reade againe in Cheapside'. On the way to Cheapside the procession encountered a temporary obstacle:

> The gates at Ludgate and portcullis were shutt and downe, by the Lord maiors command, who was there present, with the aldermen, &c., and untill he had a token [=visual proof] besyde promise, the Lord Treasurers George, that they would proclayme the King of Scots King of England, he would not open.

Lord Mayor Robert Lee thus demonstrated London's privileged status, and his own peculiar authority:

> Upon the death of a king or Queene in England the Lord maior of London is the greatest magistrate in England. All corporacions and their governors continue, [but] most of the other officeres authority is expired with the princes breath.

In fact the Lord Mayor had already signed the proclamation, as his name appears first among the 34. Lord Buckhurst, Elizabeth's last Lord Treasurer, duly produced his 'George' – a token of his membership in the Order of the Garter – and Ludgate was thrown open.

Stow takes the story further:[4]

> On the sayd Thursday the 24. of Marche, the Lordes spirituall and temporall of this Realme, assisted with those of her late Maiesties priuie counsell assembling themselues together, tooke order, that with the publishing of the Queenes departure, should also be declared to the comfort of the whole Realme, her lawfull successor. And about xii. of the clocke at noone of the same day … hauing proclaimed King Iames at the Court gate, entered the Citie of London, by Ludgate, where finding Robert Lee, Lord Maior of that Citie, the Aldermen and Citizens; they all together, with a multitude of other good subiects rode to the Crosse in West-Cheape, and on the West-side thereof, with sounding of Trumpets, caused to be proclaimed, Iames King of Scotland …, now King of this whole Iland … Sir Robert Cicell principall Secretary, re[a]d the Proclamation, William Dethike, alias Garter, principall King at Armes pronounced it with an audible voyce.

> The crowd, listening attentively, cried 'God saue King Iames!'

> From thence they rode into Milke streete, to the house of Iames Pemberton, one of the Shiriffes of London, where they dined, and after sate in Counsell.

From Sheriff Pemberton's house in Milk Street the Council dispatched a 'true copie' of the proclamation – again in manuscript – to Sir John Peyton, Lieutenant of the Tower, with instructions for a public reading at Tower Hill. Thirty-one of the Milk Street signatures are identical to those on the proclamation.[5] Of the three 'missing' signatories, Pembroke (William Herbert) and the mortally ill Hunsdon (George Carey) seem to have left the procession before it reached Milk Street,[6] while Derby (Oxford's son-in-law) apparently missed both venues, but squeezed his signature onto the proclamation, perhaps during the afternoon.

The original proclamation was now carried from Milk Street to Northumberland House on St Martin's Lane within Aldersgate (just north of St Paul's), where Robert Barker, 'Printer to our late Soueraigne Lady Queene Elizabeth', ran off multiple copies for general distribution. Though the printed proclamation is dated 24 March, John Manningham reports that publication occurred on the 25th:

> This day the proclamacions were published in print, with names of many noblemen, and late Counsellors.

Oxford's name did not appear on the printed broadsheet.

When a second impression was run off at the same press, three names were added: 'E. Oxford', 'Scroope', and 'Norreys'. 'Scroope' was Thomas Lord Scrope, while 'Norreys' was Francis Norris, Oxford's son-in-law.[7] The orthographically suspicious 'E. Oxford' (for 'E. Oxenford') suggests that this name was not set from a signature.

If Oxford had merely been late for the nine o'clock meeting at Whitehall, his signature could have been squeezed on to the proclamation like that of 'Wil. Derby'. From the complete absence of his name we may infer that he remained in Hackney as the new king was proclaimed. Indeed, subsequent testimony by Henry, Earl of Lincoln and Sir John Peyton suggests that Oxford had been deliberately shut out of the Great Council for conspiracy.

Henry Clinton *alias* Fiennes, born about 1545, became Earl of Lincoln on his father's death in 1585. Both before and after his elevation, his erratic and violent behaviour had earned him a reputation much like Oxford's own. By his first marriage Clinton became attached to the Hastings clan; by his second, to the Norris clan.[8] Oxford too was related to the Norris clan, through Bridget's marriage to Francis Norris in 1599. Despite these family ties, Oxford and Lincoln were not – as we shall discover – well acquainted.

Peyton had been Lieutenant of the Tower since 1597, but on 30 July 1603 he was in effect sentenced to exile as Governor of Jersey – the very post that Oxford had sought in vain three years earlier. Peyton was on the island by 10 September, when he took his oath before the local court. On 4 October Cecil demanded a response to Lincoln's charge that Peyton had meddled in affairs of state at the time of the Queen's death (*DNB*). In their mutual acrimony Lincoln and Peyton agreed on one point: the most active opponent of James among English noblemen at the time of the Queen's death had been Oxford.

Lincoln's complaint against Peyton, which fills both sides of a sheet of paper, begins with a reference to the French ambassador (Christophe de Harley, Comte de Beaumont) and a Mr Trudgion, apparently a member of the French ambassadorial staff:[9]

> Whylst her maiestie lyved: the French embassador made meanes by dyvers [=diverse persons] to hyre my house at Chelsey among which mr Trudgion did also solycyte me to whom I did ons [=once] in summe sort graunt my consent: but afterwards vnderstandyng that her maiestie was in danger: I refused to lett my sayd house: in respect of my hope of the kyngs maiesties lykehood to reigne over us her maiesties recovery beyng doutfull: in which tyme of her sycknes I had many dyscourses with mr Trudgion touchyng hys maiestie (whom God long preserve) in all which for that I found hym speake doutfully of hym & hys entry to be oure kyng; & seemyd to me rather to leanne to the tytle of the Infanta …

Lincoln, having acquired his Chelsea estate in 1599,[10] considered the French ambassador's request to rent the house, but finally declined. As the Queen's death drew near, and speculation concerning her successor grew, Trudgion informed Lincoln of his preference for the 'Infanta' – a Spanish Catholic descendant of John of Gaunt, the candidate of Robert Persons, Catholic leader in exile.[11] Lincoln now played the role of provocateur:

> I dyd presse hym by the best meanes I coold to delyver hys reasons: which were thes: vydelicet: that he knew that there was a resolution more then iij yeres past by the court of roome [=Rome], the King of Spayn: of France, & other prynces; to keepe hym from cummyng into thys realme & though he dyd [=did]; that he shuld not reygne long after yf he dyd not condyscend [=condescend, agree] to thos artycles in relygion then resolved: & that they all woold make warre agaynst hym, & mayntayn summe other tytle …

Though such talk from an Englishman would have been seditious, Lincoln was merely reporting opinions from within the French embassy. Significantly, he attributes similar opinions to Oxford, and adds important details:

> thes woords beyng delyvered of his knowledg: & those speeches of the Erles of Oxford: that yf any were sent into France (how small soever hys tytle were) showyng the example of one of hys auncestors; & lykewyse namyng the lord Hastings, made me feare: & thynk that thes men myght doo the King good servyce in bewraying their knowledg; which I thought my dyeuty [=duty] to ympart yf I had any possible meanes to enforme hys maiestye …

A man of such impressive ancestry as Oxford would find support and favour in France, where he found none in England; the same would hold for Lord Hastings.

Since Oxford had scarcely a drop of royal blood in his veins, he was not a contender for the throne. But Henry, Lord Hastings, heir to the earldom of Huntingdon, now eighteen years of age, was of the blood royal. Support for Hastings as the Queen lay dying was unquestionably seditious. Lincoln continued:

> but so it pleasyd God, that withyn few days after afore any advertysement culd be sent I saw thys chefest poynt of thys resolution frustrate by Gods goodnes in sendyng hys quyet entry; & yet nevertheles went to the toure [=Tower] afore her maiesties death: told Sir Iohn Peyton therof, who (as one that is hys maiesties faythfull servant,) answered: I hope you will tell the King herof: to whom I sayd: you may be sure of it yf ever I may speake with hym: I told Sir Hew Harrys therof: & sergent Harrys & others: besyde my lettres to hys maiestie sent by Sir H. Brumley & my sonne: & styll remaynyng in hope to ympart it my self to hys maiestie was loth to publysh it to many; in respect of the danger & malyce which I knew shuld be borne agaynst me to my vndoyng: yf hys maiestie doe lyghtly regard my im-mynent danger; which I have great cawse humbly to crave at hys maiesties hand …

Thus Lincoln claims to have reported Trudgion's and Oxford's loose talk to Peyton about 22 March. He reported the same to Sir Hugh Harris and to Thomas Harris, Sergeant-at-Law; and sent letters to James in Scotland by both Sir Henry Bromley and his own son Thomas.[12] Lincoln adds that he did not report more widely for fear of malice – doubtless Oxford's. (Apparently Lincoln had not reported to Cecil.)

Lincoln cites further 'speeches' – Trudgion's rather than Oxford's, but clearly related to Oxford's reported hope of intervention from the Continent:

> thes beyng the poynts materiall & I redy to sett down any cyrcumstances which shall be demanded or thought fytt (yf any be hearafter remembryd;) videlicet: the speeches concernyng the meanes of sendyng an army from Flanders: the hope of a number of Catholyques in England & many such reasons …

Lincoln concludes his initial statement with the plea that men like himself should be allowed to speak freely for the safety of the King:

> thes thyngs that I have for my love & dyeuty [=duty] sett down to thyntent [=the intent] that hys maiestie may know from them theyr further knowledg: I trust by youre wysdoms shall be so vsed; that thos that have a desyre to advaunce hys servyce & safety shall nether be terryfyed with bytter speeches; nor advantages sought to the dyscoragyng of oothers to reveale whatsoever ys lykly, to dyscover hys enemys.

Lincoln now addressed Cecil's demand that he clarify his conversation with the French ambassador in the garden of his Chelsea house:

> the woords of the French Embassador in my garden concernyng the King beyng few, & of no importance are skant woorthy resityng [=reciting]: videlicet when I

spake of the strength by vnytyng the kyngdome he answeryd: in French more men: but lesse mony:

The French ambassador thus agreed that the union of Scotland and England might indeed result in greater manpower to oppose a Catholic invasion from France or the Low Countries, but it would also cause greater demands on the King's limited financial resources.

Peyton's reply to Cecil's letter of 4 October was dispatched from Jersey on 10 October, with a cover letter:[13]

> Right honorable my very good lorde your letters of the 4th of this instant I haue receyued, In the which there is contayned, your noble nature, and honorable care, to contynewe his maiesties gracious good opinion towards me, By the wyche you haue extended my former bands, of affectyon, loue, and seruyse beyonde the bownds of lymytatyon; what therfore I shall want, in externall means or powre, I wyll supply with my prayres to God that he maye multyply, all honors, and blessings, vppon you and your posterytye / Tocheing the Erle of Lyncolnes his imputatyons layed vppon me, his fassion is, to condempe the worlde, if therby he myght excuse him selfe /
>
> I haue therfore sent your lordshippe hereinclosed, a Trewe relatyon of all his discowrses, with there oryginall motyues & cyrcumstances, depending vppon them, haueing with the first wynde dispached this bearer mr Fowles with them, desiring not to lyue, one mynute longer, then I maye reste assured of my deare soueraygne his fauore, whome the Lord presearue with all his Riall progeny in happines and Triumphe, ouer the iniquities of these malytious tymes …

No doubt Peyton meant what he wrote when he stated that his letter was dispatched back to Cecil with the 'first wynd'. His report, entitled 'A trewe relatyon of suche speeches as passed betwen my lord of Lyncolne and me some feawe dayes before her maiesties decesse and within feawe dayes after', fills nearly four pages in manuscript:

> The erle of Lyncoln abowte some syxe dayes before hir maiestyes death (as I remember[)] cvming to visit me at the Towre discowrsed of her Maiestyes weakenes concluding ther was no hoope of hir recouerye The which I well vnderstood from an Immynent parsonne [=eminent person] in the state vnto whom I dayly sent my sonne to courte for that purpose …

Peyton's reliance on his son and namesake was nearly absolute. On the Queen's death, John the younger joined the furious race to Edinburgh to be the first to inform King James. Evidently young Peyton came in second. The elder Peyton defends Lincoln's loyalty to both Elizabeth and James at some length, then takes up his story as the Queen yet lingered:

> Abowte iiijor dayes after as I remember (for at that tyme all the wytts and facultys I had were bothe night and daye kepte wakeing, and so labored, as I myghte bothe

> forgett the tyme and also some materiall cyrcumstances) my lorde of Lyncolne came to me agayne, and as I remember lodged in the Towre that night) being as I take it Twoe dayes before her maiesties decesse / he then towlde me yt was tyme to looke abowte vs for he had discou[e]red an opposytion agaynst his maiestyes Tytle, and that ther was a great nobleman had opennd hym selfe vppon that poynt, and had delte with hym to Ioyne as a partye in the actyon, not nameing vnto me the persone or his purpose / owte of this his generall reporte, for that I cowlde make no certayne Iudgement ether of the danger it selfe, or of means to appoose and preuent it /

Thus Lincoln confessed to Peyton that he had had conversation with a lord who had spoken in opposition to James's title to the English throne. Peyton asked Lincoln to identify the great lord:

> I replyed vnto my lords relation in this sorte / That If the great personne with whome he had this conference were one imminent [=eminent] In Awthorytye in the state, and potent in afyance frends and means, no tyme myght be omitted in Interpoosing agaynste his purpoose, althowygh with some danger, in regarde of the presente tyme, and therfor disired his lordshippe to conceyve what was to be done in that case / praying him to particulerryse [=particularize] the cawse and personne in more open Tearmes, wher vppon his lordshippe towlde me as followeth

> That he had byn inuyted (the daye before as I remember) [=21 March] by a great noble man to Hacney, wher he was extraordinaryly fe[a]sted, at the which he muche maruayled, for that there was no great correspondence betwen them, this noble man haueing precedence of hym in rancke / where by he towlde me I myght knowe hym, there being onely but one of that qualytye dwellyng there /

Though Peyton withholds the name of the 'great personne with whome [Lincoln] had this conference', only two noblemen lived in Hackney, Oxford and Zouche, and of these, only Oxford outranked Lincoln. (Peyton seems to have been un-aware that Lincoln had already identified Oxford by name.)

> This noble man and he, being (after diner) retyred aparte from all companye, began (as the Erle of Lyncolne sayed) to discowrse with hym of the impossibylytie of the Queens lyfe and that the nobylytie being peeres of the realme, were bownde to take care for the Common-good of the state in the cawse of succession / in the which hym selfe, meaning the Erle of Lyncolne, owght to haue more regarde then others, becawse he had a Nephewe of the bludde Riiall, nameing my lorde Hasteings whome he perswaded the Erle of Lyncolne to send for, and that ther showld be meanes vsed, to conuaye hym ouer into France, wher he showlde fynde frends that wolde make hym a partye of the which ther was a presedent [=precedent] in former tymes …

Though reluctant to name Oxford, Peyton names Lord Hastings as a principal object of Oxford's conspiratorial interest.

> he [=Oxford] also as the Erle of Lyncolne sayed inuayed [=inveighed] muche agaynste the natyon of the Scotts, and began to enter into questyon of his maiestyes

Tytle, wher vppon my lorde of Lyncolne (as he Towlde me) Brake of[f] his discowrse, absolutely disalowing all that the great noble man had moued, in suche sorte as he desysted from any further speache in that matter.

My answere vnto this relatyon of my lord of Lyncolne was thus I towlde hym, that I was sorry that he had so soddaynly shewed his dislykeinge of the great noble mans discowrse wyshing that he had contayned hym selfe, vntyll suche tyme as he might haue fully discouered the fowndation of the proiect [=project], and all the parties concurring in that actyon, which at that instant he seemed muche to repent that he had so hastely cutt of[f] the great noble man his discowrse

I also aduysed the erle of Lyncolne to vse all his indeuowre [=endeavour] to vnder-stand what he cowlde, and to be vygyllant, what personns had conferrence or re-cowrse vnto that great noble man, and whether ther were eny messwages or meetyngs betwen the Frenche imbassador and hym, whome I must confesse I suspected

Thus Peyton regrets that Lincoln had not drawn Oxford out further.

Peyton next explains why he had not been more aggressive in raising the alarm against Oxford:

At the firste aprehentyon of my lord of Lyncolnes discovery, I was muche moued and Trobled, but when he had made me vnderstand what great personne it was whome he ment, I knewe hym, to be so weake in boddy, in frends, in habylytie, and all other means, to rayse eny combuystyon in the state, as I neuer feered eny danger to proseed from so feeble a fowndation, but added a more vigillancye and care vnto the saffetie, of the place vndere my Charge [=the Tower], with owte further conference of that cawse, I being also at that instant to geue order for the bringing in of wyne beare bread meate butter fyshe & other prouytyons for the victuallyng of suche extraordinary assistants, as were to be drawne into the Towre, for that it was certaynly informed bothe to my selfe, and to my lord of Sowtham-pton, from whome I did not conceale in discowrse, that her maiestie cowlde not lyue 24 howres.

Oxford, in the days before Elizabeth's death, was so enfeebled in person, so wanting in friends, and so short of money, that he was no conceivable danger to the state. He was a toothless lion.

Now Peyton addresses the death of the Queen, the proclamation of the King, and Lincoln's astonishment at discovering Oxford's name among the signatories on the proclamation as circulated in print:

Within lesse then Two dayes after (as I remember) It plesed God to call hir maiestie to his mercy, and owr deere soueraynge [=James], was proclaymed and the pro-clamatyon shortely after printed and the former spetyfied great noblemans name attested in the sayed proclamatyon, as Ioyneing in the same with the rest of the lords, at the which tyme my lorde of Lyncolne being then with me at the Towre, seemed to wonder and this (according to my remembraunce[)] was 5 or 6 dayes after her maiestyes decesse, at which tyme my lorde of Lyncolne spake not eny more of that matter

Lincoln dates his approach to Peyton in the Tower about 29 or 30 March. Having attended the Great Council on the 24th, and thus aware that Oxford neither attended the meeting nor signed the proclamation, Lincoln was astonished to discover Oxford's name among the signatories on the proclamation as it appeared in print. Clearly Lincoln saw not the first but only the second or some sub-sequent impression of the printed proclamation.

Peyton dates his third conference with Lincoln after the arrival of Lord Kinloss – the Scots nobleman Edward Bruce – who accompanied James on his first entry into London on 7 May, and whom James appointed Master of the Rolls on 18 May (*DNB*):

> The 3d tyme of my conferrence with my lord of Lyncolne was after my lord of gynloosse his ariualle [=arrival], at which tyme he [=Lincoln] being with me in the Towre I towlde hym that nowe we myght discowrse with more freedome and leysure then when hir maiestie lyued, and then I asked hym these questyons
>
> firste whether he had discouered eny other persons to be concenting vnto the purpose of sending his nephewe The lord Hastings into France
>
> secondly whether he knewe of eny second personne vnto whome the great Erle, had partycypated his intentyon …

Clearly, Peyton was attempting to solicit more information about Oxford, in parti-cular, whether he had contacted other conspirators. Peyton cites Lincoln's reply:

> vnto boothe these he answered that he cowlde not vnderstand of eny personne inter-essed in that matter but onely that Erle that had the first conference with hym …

In effect, Oxford nursed his seditious schemes in solitude.

Now Peyton rehearses his patronizing admonition to Lincoln as their meeting in the Tower drew to a close:

> here vppon I advysed hym, to make hym selfe knowne vnto my lord of gynloose and to acquaynt hym with suche aduertysements as mighte eny waye concerne his maiestyes seruyse, and so leafte the discouery of his owne knowleage to hym selfe, conceyueing that if he showlde fayle in the performance therof, he wolde also deny his reporte made vnto me, Rather then to auowche it vppon the other Erle, whoe as hym selfe dowbted, wolde absolutely disauowe the same …

Peyton feared that Lincoln might deny the whole story rather than accuse Oxford, who would deny the accusations in any case. Peyton did not know – as we know – that Lincoln had openly accused Oxford in his own report.

Peyton adds a further ground for apprehension, again based on a misunder-standing that we are in a position to correct:

> vppon this consyderation also, that the noble man whome he accused, was with the cowncell and the other lords, at the proclamacyon of his maiestye, no lykelyhoode

of prouff or other circumstances but onely my lord of Lyncolnes reporte, and the danger in all apparences being passed /

Here Peyton makes the false inference that because Oxford's name appeared on the printed proclamation, he must have been present at the Great Council, and therefore could not have been suspected by higher powers.

Peyton goes on to report that in his first meeting with Lord Kinloss he withheld Oxford's name, merely warning Kinloss that support for James in the days before the Queen's death had not been unanimous among the English nobility. He had named Hastings to Kinloss, but as the target of a conspiracy and not as a conspirator himself. He referred Kinloss to Lincoln for further particulars:

> The which notwythstanding I acquaynted my lord of Ginloose with thus muche, That all the great personns, some fewe dayes before her maiestyes decesse, were not of one mynde, and – I hoope he wyll remember – I spake also to hym of my lorde Hastings and that my lorde of Lyncolne wolde relate the particulers therof when he came vnto hym, and if my memory doe not muche deceyue me I acquaynted Sir Dauyde Fowles and mr Hudsonne also with this speache of my lord of Lyncolnes, before there [=their] goeing to his maiestye /

Thus Peyton brought his account of Oxford's opposition to a close.

By the time Cecil received Peyton's reply, anxieties over James were allayed, and would remain so until the Gunpowder Plot of November 1605 – by which time Oxford was dead. Cecil must have agreed long since that Oxford was not a threat, and that accusations against him should, as ever, have no effect.

The written reports of Lincoln and Peyton reveal that Oxford certainly engaged in oppositional intrigue as the Queen lay on her deathbed. But it remains to ask why Oxford was absent from Whitehall on the morning of 24 March. Since Oxford could have added his signature as late as mid-afternoon on the 24th, tardy receipt of a early morning summons would have been of little or no consequence. We have Lincoln's testimony that Oxford was well enough to receive guests at Hackney up to a few days before the 24th, and we are about to learn that he visited London in April despite his infirmity. From Lincoln's 'wonder' at discovering Oxford's name among the signatories on the printed proclamation, we may infer that he was deliberately excluded from the initial meeting of the Great Council.

But why should Oxford's name have been added to the second impression? As Burghley protected Oxford in 1588 by turning him from a refusenik into a naval hero, Burghley's son seems to have protected him in 1603 by turning him from a scheming opponent into an enthusiastic supporter of King James. If the deception caused Lincoln to wonder, it completely fooled the inquisitive Peyton into thinking that Oxford had actually been present at the Great Council at Whitehall.

This closing brush with power politics was a recapitulation of Oxford's lifelong habit of discontent, entailing (as ever) an invitation to his private residence, a sumptuous feast, secret talk after dinner 'retyred aparte from all companye', and a claim that his title and ancestry would be recognized and rewarded better abroad than at home. But Oxford is now dismissed as a harmless, broken man, sans friends, sans money, sans health, sans everything.

82 This Common Shipwrack

Queen Elizabeth's funeral was conducted on 28 April 1603, just over a month after her death. Depending on his health at the time, Oxford may or may not have been one of six attendant earls noted in a broadside report by Henry Petowe.[1] He certainly did receive a grant of cloth for the occasion:[2]

> To the Earle of Oxford xvj yardes and his seruantes xxiiij yardes [total] xl yardes

Similar grants of cloth and of 'Paris heads' with veils were made to Oxford's Countess and his three daughters;[3] in these same accounts Oxford does not appear among earls designated 'Assistantes for the state', 'Assistantes for the Corpes [=body]', 'The Kings Agent', or 'Bearers for Banners'.

On 3 and 8 April Oxford – with other members of 'The nobilitie & Late Priuie Counsell' – put his signature to letters addressed to Lord Treasurer Buckhurst from Whitehall: notably, his signature had metamorphosed permanently to an italic hand.[4] Though Percival Golding would describe Oxford some years later as 'of the Privy Council to the King's Majesty that now is', he is not named among James's appointees of 3 May.[5]

On 25 and 27 April, just before Elizabeth's funeral, Oxford wrote a more than usually thoughtful letter to Cecil, doubtless from Hackney (LL-39):

> Sir Robert Cecill. I have always founde my selfe behowldinge to yow, for many kyndnesses, and curtesies. Wherfore I am bowlde, at thys presente, whiche gyvethe occasione of many consyderationes, to desyre yow as my verye good friende and kynde brother in Lave [=Law] to impart to me whatt course ys deuised by yow of the Councell, & the reste of the lords, concerninge owre dutyes to the kynges Maiestie Whyther yow doo expect any messenger before hys comminge to lett vs vnderstand hys plesure, or els hys personall arryvall, to be præsently or very shortlye.

Oxford's reference to 'yow of the Councell' proves that Oxford himself was not a member of that august body. He knew that James's arrival in London was imminent.

> And yf yt be so, what order ys resolued one [=on] amongste yow, eyther for the attendinge, or me[e]tinge of hys Magestye, for by reason of myne infyrmite, I cannot come amonge yow so often as I wishe, and by reason my house ys not so nere, that at every occasione I can be præsent, as were fitt, eyther I doo nott heare at

all frome yow, or at leaste wythe the lateste, as thys other day yt hapned to me, receyvinge a letter at nyne of the cloke, not to fayle at eyght of the same mornynge to bee at Whyte Haale. whyche beinge impossible, yet I hasted so muche as I came to followe yow into Luggate, thoughe throwghe presse of people and horses I could not reache yowre compagnie as I desyred, but followed as I myght.

Pleading infirmity and distance from Court, Oxford recalls that 'thys other day' he received at 9:00 a.m. a letter instructing him to be at Whitehall at 8:00. With unusual self-deprecation, he describes his attempt to make his way, presumably by coach,[6] whether to Whitehall and back through Ludgate, or through Ludgate on his way to Whitehall, through a crush of people and horses. Oxford's 'thys other day' seems to suggest a more recent occasion than 24 March.

Oxford next considers the death of the Queen and the accession of the King:

> I cannot but finde a greate gryefe in my selfe, to remember the mistres whiche we have loste, vnder whome boothe yow and my selfe frome owre grenest yeares have bene in a manner brought vp. and althowghe yt hathe pleased God, after an earthlye kyngdome to take her vp into a more permanent and hevenlye state, wherin I doo not dought but she ys crowned wythe glorye, and to gyve vs a prince wyse, lerned, and inryched wythe all vertues, yet the longe tyme whyche we spent in her seruice, we cannot loke for so muche left of owre dayes, as to bestowe vpone an other, neyther the longe aquayntance, and kynd familiarites, wherwythe she dyd vse vs, we are not ever to expect frome an other prince, as denyed by the infermite of age, and common course of reasone. In thys common shypwrake, myne ys aboue all the reste. whoo least regarded, thowghe often comforted, of all her followers, she hathe left to trye my fortune amonge the alterationes of tyme, and chaunce, eyther wythe owt sayle wherby to take the aduantage of any prosperous gale, or wythe [out] anker to ryde tyll the storme be over paste. Ther ys nothinge therfore lefte to my comfort, but the excellent vertues, and diepe wisdome wherwythe God hathe indued owre new master, and soueraygne Lord, whoo doothe not come amongst vs as a stranger but as a naturall prince, succedinge by ryght of bludd, and inhæritance, not as a conqueror, but as the trwe shepperd of Chrystes floke to cherishe and comfort them.

> Wherfore I most ernestlye desyre yow of thys fauowre, as I have wrytten before, that I may be informed frome yow concernynge thes poyntes …

Oxford's letter is notable as his first expression since his letter to Burghley in 1572, following the St Bartholomew's Day massacre, of an interest in something beyond his own personal affairs; nevertheless, as in 1572, private interest remains strongly present.

James, more than a month after he had been proclaimed King of England, was still savouring the acclaim of his new subjects at each stop from Edinburgh to London. On 3 May he arrived at Theobalds, where over four days he received 'most of the Nobilitie of the land and Counsell of Estate'.[7] Oxford was not among the adoring throng. On 7 May, as James made his quiet way into London,

Oxford wrote to Cecil from Hackney, pressing (as ever) for Waltham Forest and
Havering Park (LL-40):

> My very good Lord I vnderstande by Mr Atturnye that he hathe reported the state
> of my Tytell to the keepershipe of Waltham Foreste, and of the housse and parke of
> Haueringe, wherby yt appeares to hys Magestye what ryght and æquite [=equity] ys
> therin. Tyll the 12th of Henry the 8th [=1521–22] myne Auncesters haue posessed
> the same, almost sythence the tyme of William Conqueroure, and at that tyme
> whiche was the 12th yeare of Henrye the 8th the kynge tooke yt for terme of hys lyfe
> from my grandfather, sythence whiche tyme, what by the alterationes of princes,
> and wardshipes, I haue bene kept from my ryghtfull posessione, yet frome tyme to
> tyme, boothe my father and my selfe, we haue as oportunites fell owt not neglected
> owre clayme, twice in my tyme yt had passage by lawe, and iugment was to haue
> passed one [=on] my syde, wherof her Magestie the late Quiene, beinge aduertised
> wythe assured promises and woordes of a Prince to restore yt herself vnto me causd
> me to lett faale the sute. But so yt wass, she wass not so redie to performe her
> woorde as I was to[o] redie to bel[i]eue yt. Whervpon pressinge my tytell farther yt
> was by her Magesties pleasure put to Arbitrement and althoughe yt was an
> vnæquall course, yet not to contradict her will, the Lord Chanceler Sir Chrystopher
> Hattone was sole Arbitrer, whoo after all the delayes, deuised by Sir Thomas
> Hynnage, and the Quienes councell in laue [=law] then beinge, hauinge h[e]arde
> the cause was redie to make hys report for me, but her Magestie refusd the same
> and by no meanes wowlde heare yt, So that by thys and the former meanes, I haue
> bene thus longe disposeste. but I hoope, truthe ys subiect to noo prescriptione, for
> truthe ys truthe thoughe never so owlde, and tyme cannot make that falsse whiche
> was once trwe. and thoughe thys threscore [=60] yeares boothe my father and my
> selfe have bene disposessed therof, yet hathe ther bine claymes made therto many
> tymes wythin those threscore yeares, whiche I take sufficient by laue to avoyd
> præscriptione in thys casse [=case]. Now therfore hys Magestie hauinge h[e]ard the
> report I hoope [=hope] he will in his iustice and fauoure doo me that ryght whiche
> ys to be expected frome so gratious and vertuous a Soverayne. But for that I knowe,
> amonge so many matters of importance, vnles hys Magestie be put in remem-
> brance, he may forget a pryvat cause, therfore I shall moost ernestly desyre yowre
> friendship in thys that yow will ioygne wythe my Lord Admyrall my very good
> Lord and friende to helpe me to hys Magesties resolutione. my Lord Admirall ys
> Lord chiefe Iustice of Oyer and determiner, and to whoose office indeed as I
> vnderstande yt apperteynes to have h[e]ard my cause, but I know not why or wythe
> what aduise yt was referred to Mr Atturnye and his Magesties councell in laue. But
> now howsoever, hys Magestye hathe the report made vnto hym, whiche yf yt be
> forgotten shall lyttell prevayle me. but I hoope in his Iustice, and in yowre twoo
> Lordshipes friendshipes whiche the cause beinge so iust and honorable, I doo fullye
> relye vpone. Hys Magestie departethe [=parteth] wythe nothinge but a keapership,
> and a keeper he must haue. wherfore yt ys muche moore princlye for him to
> restoore yt to me hys laufull keeper, then contrarye [=contrariwise] to bestowe yt
> vpon an intruder. Nothinge adornes a kynge moore thein Iustice, nor in any
> thinge, doothe a kynge moore resemble God then in iustice, whiche ys the He[a]d
> of all vertue, and he that ys indued therwythe, hathe all the reste. So longe as yt was

in the custodie of myne Auncesters the woodes were preserved, the game cherished, and the forest mayntayned in hir full state. but sythence yt was otherwise disposede, all thes thynges have impayred as experience doothe Manifest. ...

Oxford dates his family's loss of the estates back sixty years, perhaps to the 16th Earl's dispute with Somerset in the late 1540s. Perfectly aware of James's passions for the hunt, he characterizes himself as one who, if awarded the keepership, will 'cherish' the game.

Oxford wrote to Cecil again on 12 June, characterizing his suit as an enterprise 'wherin I haue spent so longe a tyme, and passed the greatest part of myne age' (LL-41); and yet again on the 16th, in the face of a new decree that no suit could be presented to the King without the signatures of six members of the Privy Council: 'I most ernestlye therfore desyre yowre Lordship as to the leeke purpose I have written to my Lord Admirall that yow wyll procure me suche a warrant' (LL-42). A fourth letter followed on 19 June, for once in a hopeful mood (LL-43):

My Lord I vnderstand how honorablye yow do perseuer in yowre promised fauoure to me, whiche I takinge in most kynde manner, can at thys tyme acknow-lege yt but by simpel yet hartye thankes, hopinge in God to offer me at sumtyme or other the oportunite wherby I may in moore effectuall manner expresse my gratfull mynde. I further also vnderstande that thys daye Mr Atturnye ys leeke [=like, likely] to be at the Courte. Wherfore I most ernestly desyre yowre Lordshype, to procure and [=an] ende of this my sute in sekinge wherofe I am growne owlde and spent the chiefest tyme of myn age.

Again the recovery of Waltham Forest is Oxford's principal goal, in pursuit of which he has grown old and 'spent the chiefest tyme of myn age'.

The casse as I vnderstand by yowre Lordship, Sir E. Cooke his Magestyes Atturnye hathe reported, the Iustice therof I doo not dout, but [it] doothe appere, there remaynethe only a warrant accordinge to the kinges lat[e] order to be signed by the syx Lordes in Commissione wherby Mr Atturnie generall may procede accordinge to the course vsuall.

The Kynge I he[a]re doothe remoue to morow towards Windsor, wherby yf by yowre Lordships especiall fauour yow doo not procure me a full end thys day or to morrowe, I cannot looke for any thynge moore then a longe delaye. I do well perceyve how yowre Lordship, doothe trauell [=travail] for me in this cause of an espetiall grace and fauoure, notwythstandinge the burden of moore importunat and generall affayres, then thys of my particular. wherfore how muche the expedi-tione of this matter concernes me I leaue to yowre wisdome, that in yowre owne apprehensione, can reede moore then I have wrytten. to conclud I wholye relye vpon yowre Lordships honorable friendeship, for whiche I doo vove [=vow] a most thankfull and gratfull mynde.

Within a month Oxford's hope would be accomplished.
On 1 July Michael Hickes wrote to Cecil:[8]

> May it please your Lordship: I would haue bene glad to haue h[e]ard from my Lord Chamberlayne for the mayne somme: because I haue occasion to vse it, for a payment I am to make very shortly: your Lordship told me at my laste beinge with yow at the Court yow would speak with hym. In the meane tyme may it please yow to giue order to Mr Haughton, or Mr Percevall to discharge the consideration. Mr Billett [=Bellott] desyred me to speake with my Lord Chamberlayne towching the money due to my Lady Susan, which is for half a yeare the second of the last monethe: And whereas, he hath no other assurance for the mayne somme but an assignment from those in whose name the manner of Hadnam [=manor of Hedingham] past [=passed], he saith that he aught to haue the lettre patents of the graunte from the Quene made ouer to hym: without the which the rest is no assurance. As I shall heare from your Lordship herein, so I will returne hym answer: my Apricokes, begyne somewhat to drawe to ripening coulor, as sone as they be worthe the sending, they shalbe sent yow. ...

Survivors from Burghley's household needed their grants reconfirmed. In particular, Lady Susan Vere was now sixteen and marriageable, and thus in need of financial security.

During this same year Susan herself, using a good hand but no punctuation and few majuscules, wrote to Cecil concerning the new queen, Anne of Denmark:[9]

> My honorable good Vnckel nowe at this time I am constrayned to make boulde to trouble you hopeinge of your fauoure which I haue euer founde more then I would deserue the cause of my troubelinge you at this time is conserninge my goinge to meete the Queene which I wrote to Mr billet about and knowinge my charges woulde be more then ordinarie is contented to furnish me with some mony if it may be with your good likinge for otherwise I would not desier it and besides he ses [=says] he dare not without you will doe me the fauoure to send him worde you are contented which if you will you will make me so infinitly bounde to you that amongst the rest of your fauours I shall euer rest readie to doe you any seruise and I hope I shall deserue it and so fearinge least I haue bene to[o] teadious with my rude lines which I hope you will pardon I rest from troublinge you any further ...

It must be a sign of reconciliation that Susan writes from Oxford's residence at Hackney.

James's coronation was deferred to 25 July for fear of the plague. On 7 July Oxford requested dignities and emoluments due to his office of Lord Great Chamberlain:[10]

> ... Edward de Vere, Earl of Oxford, asks that as he is Great Chamberlain of England of the fee of our most dread Lord the King, that it should please the King that he should likewise at the Coronation, as formerly he was permitted, to do the said office and services as he and his ancestors have formerly done. That is to say that the said Earl had freedom and entertainment of the King's Court at all times; and that the said Earl on the day of the said Coronation, on the morning before the King rises, ought to enter into the chamber where the King lies, and bring him his shirt, and stockings, and underclothing. And that the said Earl and the Lord

Chamberlain for the time being together on that day ought to dress the King in all his apparel. And that he may take and have all his fees, profits, and advantages due to this office as he and his ancestors before him have been used to do on the day of Coronation. That is to say, forty yards of crimson velvet for the said Earl's robes for that day. And when the King is apparelled and ready to go out of his chamber, then the Earl should have the bed where the King lay on the night before the Coronation, and all the apparel of the same, with the coverlet, curtains, pillows, and the hangings of the room, with the King's nightgown, in which he was vested the night before the Coronation. He also asks that as his ancestors from time immemorial served the noble progenitors of our Lord the King with water before and after eating the day of the Coronation, and had as their right the basins and towels and a tasting cup, with which the said progenitors were served on the day of their Coronation, as appears in the Records of the Exchequer.

Answer was returned:

My Lord Steward adjudicates to the aforesaid Earl the fees, services, and fees of presenting water to the Lord the King before and after dinner on the day of the Coronation; and to have the basins, tasting cups, and towels. And for the other fees the said Earl is referred to examine the records of the Jewel House and the King's Wardrobe.

Thus Oxford was allowed to carry the basin and ewer with which James would ceremonially wash at dinner, but not to dress the King on the morning.[11] As coronation duties were convertible to cash grants, Oxford would receive a warrant on 22 May 1604 for £200 from the treasury.[12]

Oxford submitted a parallel claim for service as Chamberlain to Queen Anne, along with a request 'that Henry viscont Bulbeck his sonne & heir apparant may bee admitted to doe the sayd office and service for him the sayd Earle his father and to haue & take the sayd fees accordingly'.[13] In this case, however, Oxford encountered both official resistance and a rival. J. Horace Round, authority on the office of Lord Great Chamberlain, describes Oxford's as 'a most impudent proceeding': two of the four manors on which he based his claim 'had never even descended to the earls; Fingrith he had himself parted with many years before, and Hormead was the subject of a counter-petition on behalf of its real owner, Daniel Cage, gentleman. ... It is clear from the silence of the record that this claim was not successful.'[14]

Oxford's far more important claims to Waltham Forest and Havering House were confirmed on 18 July.[15] A major goal of his life had finally been achieved. Yet another piece of good news came on 2 August, when James issued a reconfirmation of Oxford's £1000 annuity.[16]

83 But a Grave

On 30 January 1604 Oxford wrote directly to the King, grateful for Waltham Forest and Havering Park, but venomous against an interim keeper (LL-44):

> Seinge that yt hathe pleasede yowre Magestye of yowre moste gratious inclinatione to Iustice & ryght to restore me to be keper of yowre game aswell in yowre foreste of Waltham, as also in Haueringe Parke. I can doo no lesse in dwtye and love to yowre Magestye, but imploye my selfe in the executione therof. And to the end that yow myght the better knowe in what sorte boothe the forreste, & the parke have ben abused, and yet continued, as well in distroyinge of the Dere, as in spoylinge of yowre demesne woode, by suche as haue pattents, & had lycences hertofore for fellinge of Tymber in the Quiens tyme latlye deceasede, præsuminge therby that they may doo what they lyste. I was bowlde to sende vnto yowre Magestye a man skilfull, lerned & experiencede in foreste causes, who beinge a dweller and ey[e] wytnes therof myght informe yowe of the truthe. And because yowre Maiestye, vpon a bare infomatione, cowlde not be so well satisfyde of every particular, as by laufull testemonye & examinatione of credible wytnes vpon othe, accordinge to yowre Magestyes appoyntmente, by Commissione a course hathe bene taken, In whiche yowre Magestye shalbe fully satisfysde of the truthe. This Commissione together with the depositiones of the witnes I doo sende to yowre Maiestye by this bearer, whoo brieflye can informe yow of the whoole contence [=contents]. So that now, hauinge laufullye provede vnto yowre Magestye that Sir Ihon Graye hathe kylled and destroyede yowre Dere in Haveringe parke wythoute any warrante for the same, hys patent ys voyde in lawe, & therfore I moste humblye besche yowre Magestye to make hym an example for all others that shall in leke [=like] sort abuse there places & to restore me to the posessione therofe, in boothe whiche yowre Maiestye shall doo but Iustice and ryght to the one & other. …

Oxford, as was his wont, demands exemplary punishment – this time, for Sir John Gray.

On 15 March the King rode in triumph through London. While it is uncertain whether Oxford processed with the 'Earls', his wife went second among Queen Anne's retinue of 'Ladyes, according to theire degrees, viz. Dutchesses, Marchionesses, Countesses, Viscountesses, Baronesses, Knights' wives, and Maids of Honour':[1]

> The Lady Arabella.
> The Countess of Oxforde …

Four days later, on 19 March, the King convened his First Parliament, which would sit until 7 July.[2] Among the 78 'Barons' summoned were 'Veare Earle of Oxford'; 'Clynton Earle of Lincolne'; 'Lord Scroope of Bolton'; 'Lord Norris of Ricott'; and Cecil, now 'Lord Cicill of Essendon'.[3] Oxford neither attended, nor named a proxy; he remained, however, a member of the dormant committee to hear petitions from Gascony (*Journals*, ii, p. 264). In April Oxford received his first and only vote for the Garter since before the 1588 Armada year, cast by his brother-in-law Thomas Cecil (G-BL).

Francis Columbell of Hackney, Oxford's servant, describes how the joiner Edward Johnson, hoping for satisfaction of his debt for work on Fisher's Folly and Plaistow House,[4]

> did often tymes before the death of the Earle of Oxenford aforesaid resort to Hackney to the said Earle and offered him Billes of Accomptes and Recconinges for woorke by him and his servantes donne for the Earle but Could not be heard, wherevppon he this deponent hath heard the Earle Calle to his Ladye ... and bidd her gett him [=Johnson] out of the yearde, and soe he weare Satisfied. And somtymes he hath awarded monney there as ffortye shillinges at a tyme but wheather he hath bene satisfied his full due this deponent knoweth not.

The Countess recalled the same visits differently:

> And where the Complaynant in his said Byll suggesteth that the said late Earle ofte acknowledged the said debte to be owinge to the said Complainant, promised him speedy payment & spake to her the said Lady Countesse dowager to pay & satisfie the same for aunswere therevnto the said Countesse vtterly denieth that ever the said late Earle did speake to her to anie such effecte or purpose but contrarywise when the said complaynant dyd sometimes in a frantick manner come & with clamour importune the said Earle for some money he then pretended the said Earle owed him for worke he had done at his said howse without Bishoppesgate London the said Earle hath ofte in her presence or hearinge protested he owed him nothinge at all and that he would cause him to be laid by the heeles yf ever he came more to him about anie such matter. Neyther would the said Earle ever geue him or suffer anie thing to be geven vnto him least [=lest] that should encourage him at other tymes to come & reuiue his clamourous demaundes.

By this account Oxford offered only violence: 'he would cause [Johnson] to be laid by the heeles'.

On 17 May, 'in the dwellinghouse of the ... earl of Oxford', Thomas Skurfell and his wife Jane assaulted and robbed Agnes, wife of John Thomas. For their crime Thomas and Jane were sentenced to death, and hanged.[5] Doubtless the insistence on the death penalty came from the hard-bitten Countess, showing none of Elizabeth Vere's humane concern for the perpetrator of a crime in 1599.

Ward reports (p. 347, without particulars) that on 18 June Oxford 'granted the custody of the Forest of Essex to his son-in-law, Francis Lord Norris, and to his cousin Sir Francis Vere'. Like his father before him, Oxford was settling his affairs in anticipation of death. Long burdened by infirmity, Oxford died on 24 June, and was buried on 6 July in the churchyard of St John-at-Hackney. Of two surviving registers, one notes under burials: 'Edward Veare earl of Oxford'.[6] A second register notes:[7]

> Edward deVeare Erle of Oxenford was buryed the 6th daye of Iulye Anno 1604.

The latter also records the loss of 260 parishioners to 'ye plague' from July to November 1603, with a chilling proviso: 'I haue set downe none but men or weomen of note I haue left out all children and vagrantes.' From December 1603 to June 1604 deaths from all causes fell to nine. These numbers echo circumstances elsewhere, as Stow reports (1605, p. 1425) that 30,578 Londoners died of the plague from 23 December 1602 to 22 December 1603. Since the last Hackney burial attributed to plague occurred on 5 June 1594, Oxford was clearly thought to have died from some other cause.

No acquaintance or stranger is known to have mourned Oxford's passing. As of 27 June his name disappeared from lists of peers eligible to attend the House of Lords (*Journals*, ii, p. 330). The rest was silence.

PART XIII

Aftermath
1604–1613

84 A Husband for Lady Susan

On 1 July 1604, before Oxford's body was in the ground, steps were taken to
secure to Henry de Vere, 18th Earl of Oxford, the hard-won rights to Waltham
Forest and Havering Park:[1]

> Brief of the evidences of Henry de Vere, Earl of Oxford, manifesting his right to
> the custody and stewardship of the King's forest of Waltham, Essex, and to the
> custody of the King's house and Park of Havering at Bower, Essex.

Dowager Countess Elizabeth was doubtless eager to have the property transferred
to her son. Unlike Margery, who in 1562 had released Edward de Vere into William
Cecil's guardianship, Elizabeth in 1604 took the wardship of Henry de Vere herself.
(There was now little property left to protect.)

Before 20 August the Dowager Countess, writing with her own hand, appealed
to Cecil for a continuation of Oxford's £1000 annuity at £500 rather than the
£200 offered by the King:[2]

> My verie good Lord: presuming his Maiestie had referred, the apporcionment of an
> allowaunce, for my owne, and my Childes maintenaunce, vnto yours, and my Lord
> Northamptons consideracyon; I was verie gladde, that the releefe of this ruined
> estate, best knowen to your Lordships, rested in the fauour of such persons, as both
> in honour, nature, and affection woulde regard the desolate estate, of my poore
> Childe and myselfe. But now hearinge from your Lordshipp that the rate was set
> downe by his Maiestis owne determination, and not lefte to your discretion, I
> earnestly entreate your Lordshippe that you would presente my humble petition to
> his gratious Maiestie to enlarge his guifte to fyue hundred pounds rent yearelie.
> Your Lordship may truelie informe his highnes, that the Pencyon of a thousande
> poundes, was not giuen by the late Queene to my Lord for his life, and then to
> determine [=cease], but to continew, vntill she might raise his decay, by some
> better prouision. And as I heare his Maiestie is moste respectiue, in performinge of
> the late Queenes intentions, which makes me the more hopefull, in my great
> distresse, of his Maiestes fauour. It hath beene enioyed but one yeare by his
> Maiestes guifte, and it is all the releefe, I euer looke for, to sustaine my miserable
> estate.

'Lord Northampton' here is the Henry Howard from Oxford's youth, come at last into royal favour and influence.[3]

Though the Dowager Countess was willing to settle for £500, James stuck to his guns, as announced in a royal grant of 26 October, from Westminster:[4]

> Knowe ye that wee of our speciall grace certaine knowledge and meere mocion and for diuerse other good causes and consideracions vs movinge haue geven and graunted and by these presentes for vs our heires and successors wee doe geue and graunte vnto our righte trustie and righte welbeloued cousin henrie Earle of Oxon a certaine annuitie or pencion of twoo hundred poundes of lawfull money of England by the yeare, To haue houlde enioye and yerelie to receave the saide Annunitie or pencion of two hundred poundes by the yere to the saide Henrie Earle of Oxon or his assignes from the feaste of the Nativitie of Sainte Iohn Baptiste laste paste before the date hereof for and during the naturall lyfe of the saide Henrie out of the Treasurie of vs our heires and successors at the Receipte of the Exchequer at Westminster of vs our heires and successors by the handes of the Treasurer and Chamberlaynes of vs our heires and successors there for the tyme beinge at fower vsuall termes of the yeare … by even porcions to be paide …

Though the reduced grant of £200 was made to Henry, it was the Dowager Countess, as guardian, who drew the quarterly payments from the Exchequer.

In 1599 Bridget Vere's marriage to Francis Norris had been kept small and private out of respect for Burghley, who had died less than a year before. No similar respect was accorded to Oxford. On 11 July Philip Gawdy wrote to his brother Sir Bassingborne:[5]

> I writt to you that My Lord of Penbroke had marryed my Lady Mary

Thus William Herbert, who had been a candidate for Bridget's hand in 1597, married Lady Mary Talbot instead. On 16 October Pembroke wrote to his father-in-law the Earl of Shrewsbury from Hampton Court, with news of his younger brother Philip:[6]

> My Lord, Though I had no direct messenger to send unto your Lordship, I rather chose to write by post than leave you unadvertised of that which is as joyful unto me as any thing that ever fell out since my birth; I cannot now write unto you all the circumstances, but at my coming down, your Lordship shall know as much as myself. The matter in brief is that, after long love, and many changes, my brother on Friday last was privately contracted [i.e., engaged] to my Lady Susan, without the knowledge of any of his or her friends. On Saturday she acquainted her uncle [=Cecil] with it, and he me. My Lord of Cranborne [=Cecil] seemed to be much troubled at it at first, but yesterday the King, taking the whole matter on himself, made peace on all sides. It is so pleasing a thing to me that I could not but strive to give your Lordship the first notice of it myself, which now having performed, I beseech your Lordship to pardon my brevity, and impute it to the many businesses this accident hath laid upon me. At my coming down I will make your Lordship a large relation of all that passed in our world, though very little worthy the note …

A modern couple, Philip and Susan agreed to marry without consulting parents or guardian. Cecil's displeasure was overruled by the King. By 24 October, when Philip Gawdy wrote to his brother once more, the news of the impending marriage was out:[7]

> … Sir Phillip Herbert shall marry my Lady Susan Veare …

Did Sir Philip marry the pretty Lady Susan for money as well as for love? In the public mind, as we have seen, Susan's 'lott' was 'Nothing'. Though fathers routinely made provision for daughters in their wills, Oxford did not. Nor was the Dowager Countess about to support her step-daughters at the expense of her son. But Burghley had left £3000 for Susan in case she should marry a baron, £4000 in case she should marry an earl. The faithful Cecil kept accounts of 'Lady Sussans porssions remayninge in my handes':[8]

Money	vijM vC xxxvijli iijs [=£7537–30–0]
Iewells	iiijC iiijxx vijli xvjs [=£487–16–0]
Plate	iijM iiijC liiijli vjs vijd [=£3454–6–7]

Totalis	ixM iiijC lxxixli vs [=£9479–5–7] …	

Rentes per Annum	CCxlli [=£240]

'The Portion of the Lady Susan' thus amounted to £7767 plus £230 annual rent; against this Cecil calculated Susan's expenses since her grandfather's death at £4000. Even assuming that Cecil held back that amount, Susan brought approximately £4000 to the marriage, thanks to Burghley's foresight.

Lady Susan Vere married Sir Philip Herbert on 27 December, six months and three days after her father's death. John Chamberlain described the event to Dudley Carleton in a letter dated 7 January 1605, revealing that the King had expedited the marriage by contributing £500 in land, plus gifts amounting to £2000:[9]

> We began on Saint John's day with the marriage of Sir Philip and the Lady Susan, which was performed with as much ceremony and grace as could be done a favourite. The prince [=Henry] and duke of Holstein led the bride to church, the queen [=Anne] followed her from thence, the king gave her; and she brided and bridled it so handsomely and indeed became herself so well that the king said if he were not married he would not give her but keep her himself. There was none of our accustomed forms omitted, of bride cakes, sops in wine, giving of gloves, laces, and points, which have been ever since the livery of the court; and at night there was sewing into the sheet, casting of the bride's left hose, and twenty other petty sorceries. They were married in the chapel, feasted in the great chamber, and lodged in the council chamber, where the king gave them in the morning before they were up a *reveille-matin* in his shirt and nightgown and spent a good hour with them in the bed or upon, choose which you will believe best. The plate and presents that were given were valued at £2000, but that which the king gave made

it a good marriage, which was a book of 500 land lying in the Isle of Sheppey (whereof Sir Edward Hoby had a lease) passed and delivered that day for the lady's jointure. At night there was a mask performed by my lord of Pembroke ...

The event was also reported by the Venetian ambassador, Nicolo Molin.[10] Although ambassadors from all countries were advised to come incognito, 'so as to avoid all quarrel about precedence', Molin's refusal nearly spoiled the show. His report reveals that after the wedding ceremony and banquet, the hall was prepared for dancing:

But so great was the crowd that dancing was out of the question, and so everybody kept his room till supper. As suppertime approached someone said to me that the crush was so great that he feared they would not be able to serve it. Presently someone said that the bride had taken her place, but such was the confusion that many guests had left. ...

Later,

we reached the hall of the masque. ... We entered a box by five or six steps; in it were two chairs; the King took one, the Queen the other, a stool was prepared for me on the King's right, and another for the Duke [of Holstein] on the Queen's left, but he would not sit down; he preferred to stand uncovered for the three hours the masque and *ballo* lasted. ...

The next day, as we have seen, James appeared 'in his shirt and nightgown and spent a good hour with [the newly-weds] in the bed or upon, choose which you will believe best' – a Pandarus indeed! But James was not done: Philip Herbert was created Earl of Montgomery on 4 May 1605, so Susan became a Countess.

The nearest approximation to a printed eulogy for Susan's father lies obscurely in Nathaniel Baxter's 1606 *Sidneys Ourania*, part of Baxter's tribute to the new Countess of Montgomery. The passage is remarkable for its anxious defence of her father, the 'Paragon' Earl (sigs. B3–3v):

The first was Vera daughter to an Earle,
Whilom a Paragon of mickle might:
And worthily then termed Albions Pearle,
For bountie in expence, and force in fight,
(Mee list to giue so great a prince his right)
In all the Tryumphs held in Albion soyle   .
He neuer yet receiu'd disgrace or foyle.   [foyle=repulse]

Onely some thinke he spent too much in vaine,
That was his fault: but giue his honour due,
Learned he was, iust, affable and plaine;
No traytor, but euer gratious, and true:
Gainst Princes peace, a plot he neuer drewe.
But as they be deceiu'd that too much trust:
So trusted hee some men, that prou'd vnjust.

Weake are the wits that measure Noble-men,
By accidentall things that ebbe and flowe;
His learning made him honourable then,
As trees their goodnesse by their fruites doe showe,
So we doe Princes by their vertues knowe.
For riches, if they make a King; tell then;
What differ poorest Kings, from poorest men?

Baxter concedes that Oxford had faults, but, like Burghley, transfers the blame: those he trusted proved unjust.

85 The Dowager and the Heir

Twelve days after Oxford's burial his Dowager Countess Elizabeth distributed 7s 6d to two Hackney parishioners:[1]

> Money that was given by the Lady of Oxford the 18th daye of Iulye distributed as ffolloweth
>
> Imprimis to Morris Howell   5s
> Item to Iyfferrye [=Geoffrey]   2s 6d

No other largesse is known to have followed upon Oxford's death. Not only did Oxford die intestate, but the Dowager refused administration of his estates.[2] The pitiful remains of Oxford's inheritance are recorded in two *Inquisitions post mortem*, filed for Essex in 1604 and for London in 1608.[3] The first, dated 24 September, reports the Dowager's residence as Hornchurch (Essex), evidently a second home near the forest estates.

In subsequent years Percival Golding wrote, in manuscript, 'The Armes, Honours, Matches and Issues of the Ancient and Illustrious family of Veer', including a memorial of the 17th Earl of Oxford:[4]

> Edward de Veer, only son of John, born the Twelfth day of April Anno 1550, Earle of Oxenforde, high Chamberlain, Lord Bolebec, Sandford and Badelesmere, Steward of the Forest in Essex, and of the Privy Council to the Kings Majesty that now is: Of whom I will only speak what all men's voices confirm; he was a man in mind and body absolutely accomplished with honourable endowments: he died at his house at Hackney in the month of June Anno 1604 and lieth buried at Westminster.

Oxford's half-cousin once removed, Golding errs as to Oxford's membership in the Privy Council, and also his place of burial, for not only do two parish registers record Oxford's interment at Hackney, but we will discover that his body remained there, without a monument.

On 17 September 1604 the 18th Earl of Oxford, signing himself 'Henry Oxenford', wrote to the Lord Admiral Charles Howard.[5] It is necessary to understand that the letter concerns fish called white-herrings (here hyphenated to enhance comprehensibility):

> My good Lorde, the messenger beinge on[e] of the Gromes of the Chamber by whom your Lordship was pleased to send your warrant for wyt-heringes, havinge faythfully delivered your Lordships lettres vnto the partye him selfe, is yesterdaye retourned: reportinge the vtter refusall of wyt-heringes to appeare before your Lordship Sir Iohn Greye vndertakinge in his behalfe to aunswere the matter vnto the Kinge his maiestie, avowinge that what soever hathe bin donne, was donne by his only directions and commaundement, thus much I thought good to signifie vnto your Lordship bothe that you might take knowledge of their disobedience vnto, and neglect of, your Lordships authoritie: as alsoe to praye you that oute of your honorable disposition to releiue the oppresed you woulde take some speedy course in iustice, bothe to chastice this their contempt and alsoe to restore my servaunte to his wife, children, house, and goodes, soe shall they be iustly occasioned to praye to God for the preservation of your honor, and I shall take it as a greate kindenese donne vnto my selfe which in my riper yeares I shall not forgett to acknowledge. …

The text is not in Henry's hand, having evidently been composed by an adult for the entertainment of the child. A party to the 'negotiations' is Sir John Gray, the very man for whom Oxford demanded exemplary punishment in his letter of 30 January to the King. Presumably the new Earl seemed a promising youth: we are about to discover that he was selected almost immediately by King James as a boy-companion for his son and heir Prince Henry.

That the Dowager remained at Hackney, at least for a time, is confirmed by the parish register:[6]

> (p. 63) A true Accounte of such monnye as hath been receaved towardes the reparacions of the Church … the parishe of Hackney 1605 … (p. 68) Claptonn / In primis the Right Honorable the Countesse of Oxen' 20s

'Clapton' is a district within Hackney. Despite this payment of 20s or £1, the Dowager could be as reluctant as her deceased husband to pay her obligations, as revealed in an entry dated about 1606, 'The names of those that have not payde according to the second seassment' (p. 83):

> Clapton – The right Honorable the Countess of Oxen

On 1 April 1609, however, the Dowager alienated King's Place:[7]

> conceditur Elizabeth Comitesse Oxon licenica allienare manerium de Hackney et alios in Comitatu Middlesexie ffulconi Grevill

The Dowager, as we shall see, removed to Canon Row in the parish of St Clement Danes, London. The new owner of the Hackney estate was, by a nice irony,

Fulke Greville, Lord Brooke, Sidney's friend and biographer – whence the subsequent name for the estate, 'Brooke House'. In this same year the Dowager reacquired Castle Hedingham and, on 26 November, the ten acres of garden in Bishopsgate.[8]

On 15 February 1610 John Searle wrote to William Trumbull from Blackfriars:[9]

> The Steward of the Forest is lately dead, and he [='Our Master'] hath made some suit for it, but I fear is like to go without it, seeing it is in the Countess of Oxford's grant, who hath promised it to one Mr. Trevers. It is a place not very gainful, but of good credit. …

On 19 July 1611, when Henry was eighteen, the Privy Council directed a letter to Cecil as Lord Treasurer:[10]

> A Lettre to the Lord Treasurer to pay to the Earle of Oxford an Annuity of 200li formerly graunted to him by his Maiestie & not vnto the Countesse his Mother, although he be vnder yeares & to receive his acquittance for the same.

Henry must have petitioned the Council to be allowed to collect his £200 himself. The directive triggered a petition of 22 July from the Dowager to Cecil and Northampton:[11] she feared that the hereditary canker of moral decay was at work on the 18th Earl. Written entirely in her own hand, the petition and accompanying 'Articles' against John Hunt, Henry's second cousin,[12] display a narrative force, an ease of exposition, and a command of normative syntax, vocabulary, and orthography notably absent from the written communications of her dead husband. She shall therefore tell her own story, in full.

> My very good Lords, the apparant danger of my sonnes ruyne (not to be prevented without present remedy) enforceth me (with noe little greife) once againe to craue your Lordshipps helpe. Being bold to commend my suit to you both ioyntly, for that eyther of you are interested =[interested] in him, one as Master of his Maiesties wardes (whereof he is one) the other by a neare coniunction in bloode: and both of you, as you are principall councellors of State, and he a yong nobleman, neyther of yeares, nor iudgment to advise himselfe, wanting the guidance of a father, and past the gouerment of a mother.

> About a yeare since [=c. July 1610], I acquainted your Lordships with some courses, dangerous, and dishonorable to him, whereinto he had then bene misled by one Hunt[,] a man of noe worth, but extreamely needy, and beggerly in his estate, and noe lesse dissolute and prodygall in his life.

> Wherevppon you then vouchsafed me your honorable assistance, which for the present tooke such good effect, as gaue me much hope, that neyther Hunt durst euer after wards haue presumed to seduce him, nor my sonne haue yeelded to be drawne by him into the like errors.

> But shortely after Hunt agayne attempted by vnderhand messages, and letters to sollicitt my sonne to with drawe himselfe from my government, and to returne to

his former courses, pretending [=promising] to my sonne fayre shewes of liberty, delights, and pleasures (the ordinary baytes for his mis-iudgeing yeares) but intending meerely to compasse to himselfe the absolute commaund, and disposall both of my sonnes person, and estate, as may euidently appeare to your Lordships by the pervsall of the perticulers in this inclosed paper, which i humbly present vnto you. for euer since (hauing noe mennes [=means], or estate of his owne) he [=Hunt] hath liued at a very highe proporcion, more suteable to the estate, and degree of a noble man, then to the meanes, or estate of his father, or himselfe

And least [=lest] my interest in my sonne should (eyther in respecte of his duty to me, or of my loue to him) crosse those his intended purposes, this Hunt hath plotted first to cause my sonne to neglect me, and my directions, afterwardes to distast[e], and contemne them, and now at length openly to oppose himselfe agaynste me, which he hath effected by continuall suggestions, that it is dishonorable for him [=Henry] at these yeares to be guided by me, that it is fitt he shoulde haue the absolute commaund and disposing of all his owne maintenance without my over-sight, that I am a miserable, and vnkinde mother to him, affording him nothing of mine, but reseruing yearely a good part of his proper maintenance to my owne vse.

Whereas (at your lordships pleasure) i am ready to make it appeare vnto you, that (euer since he was put to the Prince, which is nowe about eight yeares [=c. July 1603]) I haue yearely disbursed (besides all his) a greate parte of myne owne little estate for his maintenance And haue allwaies bene well contented to confine my selfe to a priuate Life, and lowe course of expence, that I might in some smalle mesure repaire the decayed fortunes of his howse. And soe shalbe willing to doe hereafter in whatso-euer course your Lordships shall propound, or approue as fitting, and honorable for him: soe as he may by your good meanes be reclaimed to order, duty, and honor: and this Caterppiller, and his confederates be by your power, and authority restrayned from any resort, intercourse, or priuate intelligence with him. for till then i shall neuer hope for, nor expect any comfort from any course, or fortune of his, by trauayle [=travel], mariage, or otherwise: well knowing that all your Lordships, myne, and all other his freindes endeuours for his good, wilbe wholy frustrated by the crosse, and opposite counsells, and disswations of this lewde seducer.

And am therefore absolutely resolued, vnlesse I shall presently obteyne the absolute banishment of him, and his confederates from my sonne (whereof my assurance of your honorable loue, and respect, vnto him geueth me much hope) fourthwith to rennounce, and disclayme any further chardge, or government of him. As being loth (besydes my dayly private obiectes of greife) to drawe vppon my selfe a generall, and publique imputation, that his ruyne hath happened in his nonage, and vnder my chardge and by consequence through my want of care, or respect vnto him. for the world will neuer beleeue (except I make it knowne by a publique renouncing of his further government) but I might with suite vnto his greate, and powerfull allyes, and friends[,] haue easily procured this ivey [=ivy] to be plucked away from this yonge oke, whose grouth is soe much hyndred by it

I therefore humbly beseech your Lordships (in the middest of your many seryous, and weighty affayres of the state) to afford soe much tyme for the redeeming of an vnfortunate yong noble orpahn out of extreme, and imminent ruyne, as to convent [=summon] the sayd Hunt before you, there to answere to such articles as are conteyned in this inclosed paper. and therevppon to inflict vppon him such examplarie punishment, as to your Lordships in your wisedomes shall seeme fitt: soe as he, and others of like disposition may be hereafter discouraged from the like attempts. But especially that your lordships will carefully prouide, that he may be absolutely bannished from my sonnes company, and from all priuate intercourse, and intelligence by sending, or writing to him.

Lastly i beseech your Lordships to make my sonne fully, and playnely to knowe his errors, and to afford him your graue, and iudisious [=judicious] advise, whereby (through Gods blessing vppon it) he may be withdrawen out of these dangerous waies, soe much tending to his dishonor, and vtter overthroughe [=overthrow]. hopeing that when ripenesse of yeares shall discouer to him the true differences betweene good and euill, he will thankfully acknowledge your honorable care herein vouchsafed to him.

In the meane tyme, my selfe for this, and sundry other your honorable favours shall nowe, and ever rest exceedingly bound vnto your Lordships. And thus crauing pardon for this my boldenesse I humbly take my leaue ffrom my howse in Channon Rowe. this 22th of Iuly 1611.

Your Lordships assured freind

(*signed*) Elizabeth Oxenford

Articles preferred by the Lady Elizabeth Countesse dowager of Oxenford agaynst Iohn Hunt for misleading and corrupting the Earle her sonne and for praying vppon his estate:

About this tyme two yeares [=c. July 1609] Hunt (vnder pretence of kyn[d]redd) first insinuated himselfe into my sonnes Aquaintaunce: who till then (both in his attendance on the Prince and exercises of learning at his appointed tymes) had alwayes geven me good satisfaction. Hunt shortly after his first acquaintaunce with him would ofte intrude himselfe into my sonnes Chamber at his appointed tymes for learning, and soe withdrawe him from his booke. whereof being advertised, I caused my dislike thereof to be made knowne vnto him, requiring him to forbeare the same. But not prevayling, and being certeinly informed of his loose, and dissolute disposicion (which could not chuse but make his company very dangerous to my sonne) I did cause him directly to be forbidden both my house, and my sonnes company. Yett would he not cease to resort vnto him sometymes openly, some-tymes priuily (taking opportunityes by lurking secretly about my house) to haue accesse vnto him

In Lent after [=c. March 1610] I sending my sonne from Heningham [=Heding-ham] to London to attend the Prince, Hunt imediatly after his departure from me mett with him, accompanyed him to Chensford [=Chelmsford], procured him greyhounds, and drew him to course in the Forest of Waltham, as he hath ofte done since in his company. whereby his Maiestie hath bene much offended, and my sonnes right, and interest in the saide fforrest much preiudiced.

By these, and other lyke seducements, my sonne (contrary to my direction and knowledge) was kept a good space from repayring to the Prince. And being come thither was presently withdrawne from thence by Hunt to taverns, ordinaryes [=gambling houses],[13] playes, and other places, exercises, and companyes, much to his dishonor and quite contrary to all his former breeding, but agreable in all respects with Hunt his former, and continuall practise, and course of lyfe. My sonne thus misled, hath in effect euer since neglected his attendance on the Prince, delighting wholy in such companyes, exercises, and places as aforesaide, wherein Hunt hath euer bene an vndividuable [=inseparable] companyon with him.

He hath from the very first of his acquaintance with my sonne, laboured by continuall vse of cursing, swearing, filthy and rybaldry talke, and all other leude, and licencious courses to corrupt, and poyson my sonnes tender yeares with the lyke infection.

My sonne wayting on the King in the morning on St. George his day was twelue moneth [=23 April 1610] (according to his place, and duty) was after dynner Drawne away by Hunt who kept him in his company all the day after with neglect of his service to the King in the afternoone, by whome he was missed, called, and sent for, but could not be found.

About Midsommer was twelue moneth [=24 June 1610] Hunt privily, & altogether without my knowledge withdrew my sonne from my house in Cannon Rowe into Essex, where in his company he gott much dishonor by disorderly hunting in diuers parkes, and other like disorderly, and ryotous actions. Hunt in all that iourney taking vppon him to be my sonnes purse bearer, and to commaund the same at his pleasure.

My sonne being recalled home to me by my Lord Treasuorers [=Cecil's] honorable letter, wherein he expressed a great deale of care, and respect vnto him, and being advysed by my Lord of Northampton to be guided by me, Hunt neuer ceased by letters, messengers, and private meetinges to sollicitt and seduce my sonne to the lyke courses. Soe as by his continuall sollicitations (a little before Michaelmasse last [=29 September 1610]) he sodeynly, and without my knowledge withdrew him againe from my house at Henningham to a lodging in Milford Lane [in London],[14] being an ordynary, a greate howse of play [=gambling], and whose host is the tennis Court keeper there. where he kept him from me till sithence Easter last [=24 March 1611]: the place, company, and exercises exceedingly tending to my sonnes dishonor, and preiudice.

During this last absence of my sonne from me, Hunt hath impudently presumed to be his bedfellow, and otherwyse vsed him most vnrespectiuely. In perticuler Hunt haueing drawne my sonne from his olde shoemaker vnto one of his choyce who asked my sonne 15 shillings for a payre of shoes which his olde shoemaker offered to haue made the like for 4 shillinges and six pence, and therevppon my sonne telling Hunt, that he had persuaded him to 3 cosening knaves, viz. a shoemaker, taylor, and bandseller, Hunt openly replyed, that Lords might lye by authoryty.

Item Hunt (in my sonnes name) hath borrowed, and taken vpp diuers somes of money, wares, and commodityes of sondry persons greatly to my sonnes dishonor: soe as my sonne (sithence his last departure from me) is indebted (as themselves report) 700li or 800li besides 150li of his pensyon which they have procured to be receaved out of the Eschequer. And haue pawned and sold all his apparrell, horses, rapyers, and other thinges he had. All which hath principally beene consumed by Hunt himselfe, who lyveth wholy vppon my sonnes purse, in all shewe, and course of expence lyke a noble man, himselfe neyther having any meanes, or maintenance, nor his father able to afford him any.

Besydes many other base, and vnworthy shifftes they haue made to procure money (which as yett are kept secrett from me) Hunt hath bene a principall instrument to borrowe and morgage iewells of my Lady Willoughby his aunt [=Oxford's sister Mary] worth 700li or 800li which they pawned for two hundreth poundes, or there abouts. ffor which his pencion in the Eschequer is now assigned to Sir Ewstace Hart till 300li be payd him. Hunts host, and hostes sonne in law[15] being the only witnesses to the deede of assignement.

He hath moved, and persuaded my sonne to misinforme the Kinge, that I receaue and dispose his Anuity out of the Eschequer to myne owne vse, and vppon that misinformation to procure his Maiesties Lettres for his owne receaving it. Whereas I haue yearely (for diuers yeres past) disbursed not only that and all other his owne proper maintenance, but alsoe a greate parte of my owne estate in his education. he hath alsoe of late vsed diuers meanes to procure six hundreth poundes due in Iune now last past [=June 1611] out of the low Countreyes for two yeares annuity to be paid vnto my sonne himselfe, and not to me. The end of all which Hunts endeuors is to gett the money into his owne handes that soe he may make what pray [=prey] thereof he pleaseth, and then turne my sonne home empty to me, to be maintained by me out of myne owne estate, as already in parte he hath begonne to doe.

Hunt daily draweth my sonne from my house to his the said Hunts lodging in Milford Lane at the ordinary aforesaid: where he causeth him to spende all his tyme with him in play, and other lyke exercises, soe as my sonne for 14 nightes together now last past hath not come home vntill twelue, one, two, or three of the Clock at night. At which houres I am driven (night after night) to be disquieted for the keys to lett him into my house. Soe as euerie day (by this Hunts allurement) my sonnes courses growe more, and more exorbitant.

Hunt had been with Henry on and off since the latter was sixteen, tempting him away from his studies – possibly a recapitulation of the circumstance that prompted Lawrence Nowell to declare the 17th Earl incapable of further instruction. Hunt and Henry earned the King's displeasure by neglecting Prince Henry and the King himself, and by coursing greyhounds in Waltham Forest. When the Dowager tried to restrict Henry to her house in Canon Row, London, he would run off to Essex; when she was in Essex, he would run off to London. Hunt presumed to become Henry's 'bedfellow' – an occasion for homosexual acts, though the term does not necessarily denote this. Henry might be cheated by tradesmen (in this case a shoemaker), but Hunt advised him 'that Lords might lye by authoryty' – that is, an Earl might promise to pay a tradesman but not do so.

By the age of eighteen Henry had run up debts of £700 to £800, plus £150 (pledged against his pension), plus £200 (secured with £700–800 worth of Oxford's sister's jewels), for a total of well over £1000. Henry's £200 pension was garnished for a year and a half (thus depriving him of the immediate benefit of the directive that the money should be paid to himself rather than to his mother). More recently he took a loan for another £600 from the Low Countries. The Dowager ends on a note which will strike a sympathetic chord in any parent of an unruly (or even a ruly) teenager:

> … my sonne … hath not come home vntill twelue, one, two, or three of the Clock at night. At which houres I am driven (night after night) to be disquieted for the keys to lett him into my house.

In the mother's eyes, of course, the fault lies not with the son but with his companion – so the cycle begins anew.

Indeed, Henry's younger years were to bear an uncanny resemblance to his father's. He gained a reputation in his own century as one who[16]

> was of no reputation in his youth, being very debauched and riotous, and having no means, maintained it by sordid and unworthy ways; for his Father [=Oxford] hopeless of Heirs, in discontent with his Wife [=Anne Cecil], squandred away a Princely Estate, but when she and his great Fortune were both gone, he married a young lady [=Elizabeth] of the ancient family of the Trenthams, by whom he had this young Lord, and two Daughters; she having a fortune of her own, and industry with it, after her Husband's death married her Daughters into two noble Families; the Earl of Mountgomery married the one, and the Lord Norris, after Earl of Berkshire married the other: And finding her Son hopeless, let him run his swing till he grew weary of it; and thinking he could not be worse in other Countries than he had been in his own, she sent him to travel, to try if change of Air would change his Humour. He was not abroad in France and Italy above three years, and the freedoms and extravagancies there (that are able to betray and insnare the greatest modesties) put such a bridle upon his inordinateness, that look how much before he was decried for a mean and poor spirit, so much had his noble and gallant comportment there gained, that he came over refined in every esteem; and such a Valuation was set upon his parts and merit, that he married the Lady Diana Cecil, Daughter to the Earl of Exeter, one of the most eminent Beauties and Fortunes of the time.

Although this account is not entirely accurate, especially as to Oxford's offspring by his second wife, Henry did indeed spend some years on the Continent, as we shall soon discover.

Henry so recklessly abused the King's game in 1610 and 1611 that he nearly forfeited his right to Havering Park, as revealed in a letter of 13 October 1611 from Sir Thomas Lake to Cecil:[17]

His maiesty hath commanded me to signifie to your lordship that my lord of Oxford hath been here this day a suitor for his right to Havering Parke. His maiesty is balanced in his mynde between care of his game in so fayre a ground and vnwillingnes to doe wrong. His game he doth not expect shalbe well vsed or cared for by my Lady of Oxford nor perhaps by hir sonne who both desire it but for proffitt. On the other syde his maiesty is loth to deny right to the meanest subiecte he hath much lesse to a person of his ranke. His highnes therefore desireth your lordship that for the furtherances of his own resolution my lord of Oxford may be called and his righte looked into and his maiesty advertised how it standeth whether so as that immediately the Earle may dispose of it, or whether during his minority it be not in his maiesties hande and thereby some coorse may be taken how both his maiesty may see his game provided for for the present tyme and yet doe the Earle no wrong with whom his Maiesty is purposed hereafter when his yeares make him able to contract, to agree for the whole forest to be taken into his own handes. I am willed to adde that although his maiesty knoweth your lordship to be busy enough about greater matters, yet you will not deny[?] to bestow some howres about this se[e]ing you could fynde a tyme to thinke on Arches Coate.

The matter is and is not serious. Lake, the King's distinguished servant, writes from Royston, one of James's favourite hunting estates, reporting his belief, and evidently the King's, that mother and son desire Havering merely 'for proffitt'. Hence neither can be trusted to act as a good steward. Lake compares the whole matter to the recent affair of 'Arches Coate' – a reference to James's Scottish fool, Archie Armstrong (*DNB*).

A letter from the Dowager to Sir Christopher Hatton (nephew of the Elizabethan courtier) dated 6 December 1611 reveals that she and Henry won their suit for Havering Park, but with a struggle and with conditions:[18]

Good Sir Christofer out of my assurance of your loue & well wishinge to my sonne I thincke fitt to ympart some things vnto you which much concerne him You knowe his Maiesttie hath byn pleased (though not without much difficulty) to give allowance to my sonnes hereditary interest in the Custody of Haueringe House and Parke, whereby there is made vnto him a faire entraunce for recouery of his other rightes within the Forrest if hee vse this he hath soe as may give his Maiestie Contentment. But some of his best and greatest frindes haue in private intimated to me the hazard & danger of this faire shewe of good fortune, in obteyninge the possession of that which hath byn kepte from his Auncestors soe many yeares past. They haue lett me knowe his Maiesties greate desire to compasse the disposall of the said Forrest & Parke at his owne pleasure, and haue made me vnderstand the nature & quallity of this Inheritance which standeth subiecte to forfeyture by not vsinge this office as it ought to bee. And theis Cautions I fynde are not to bee neglected. On thother parte you knowe my sonne is younge not able to advise himselfe, and I knowe he is to[o] much guided by some about him, who ayme only at their owne private endes, without respecte either of his honour or proffitt wherof some as I heare haue gotten from him grauntes or promisses of seuerall matters of benefitt within the Parke and House of Hauering without euer acquayntinge me therewith, who by the lawes of God, of nature, and of this land, haue the charge and custody of him. wherein howsoeuer my sonne forgett his duty to me, yet (hopeinge it rather proceedeth from theire ill Councell then from his owne disposi- tion) I cannott soe farre neglecte him as not to ceasse and oppose theis proceed- inges, which may soe much wronge and preiudice him with his Maiestie Good sir lett me therefore entreate you for prevention thereof to take notice from me, and as occasion shall serve, to make it knowne that my lord his father [=Oxford] for avoydinge of theis hazardes did in his life soe settle the state both of the Custody of the saide house and parke and alsoe of his rightes in the forrest as my sonne hath not to doe in either, till he come of full age. And that therefore till then noe acte or grante he shall make or doe concerninge either shall without my allowance stand good to any, hopeing that ere his full age God will giue him to vnderstand better his owne good. If you come to towne I desire to lett you knowe theis thinges more fully. In the meane tyme I shall rest vpon your loue vnto him that you will vse that interest you haue in him to perswade him to that which is truely for his owne good.

Thus the Dowager shared the general fear that Henry, left to his own devices, would misuse the House and Park at Havering, and should therefore not be given full title until his twenty-first birthday, which would occur on 24 February 1614.

On 17 June 1612 John Chamberlain wrote to Dudley Carleton, referring to the King's progress through Essex:[19]

From thence [=Wanstead] he goes to Havering, which is in the custodie of the countesse of Oxford, who intertains him likewise at hir owne charge. …

Thus the Dowager had the opportunity, for once in her life, to shine in her own right. But triumph soon turned to tragedy as Prince Henry fell ill on 10 October and died on 6 November. A letter from Chamberlain to Sir Ralph Winwood dated 6 January 1613 reports another death, doubtless also from typhoid fever:[20]

The Countess of Oxford is dead of this New Disease …

Sir Thomas Lake wrote to Dudley Carleton, on the same day:[21]

The Countesse of Oxford is lately dead and the Countesse of Bedford dangerously sicke.

The two parish registers that record Oxford's burial in 1604 record his Dowager's burial on 3 January 1613.[22] First the more succinct record:

Jan   The Lady Elizabeth: countess Dowager of Oxford: was buried the 3

Then the more expansive:

The Ladye Elizabeth Countys Dowger of Oxenforde was Buryed the Thyrde daye of Ianuarye Anno 1612 [=1613]

The Dowager's exact death-date is unknown, though it must have been on or about New Year's Day. Since typhoid fever may take a month to kill, it is likely that she was already ill on 25 November, when she signed her will.[23]

The Dowager's instructions for her burial confirm that Oxford's body had lain since 1604 without a monument:

> desiringe to be buried in the Church of Hackney within the Countie of Middlesex, as neare vnto the bodie of my said late deare and noble lorde and husband as maye bee, and that to be done as privatelie, and with as litle pompe and Ceremonie as possible [=possibly] may bee. Onelie I will that there bee in the said Church erected for vs a tombe fittinge our degree and of such chardge as shall seeme good to myne Executors hereafter named. …

The Dowager's executors were Sir Edward Moore, her brother Francis Trentham, and John Wright of Gray's Inn. Though she spares not a thought for her step-daughters Elizabeth, Bridget, and Susan Vere, she remembers many of her own friends and relatives. Her bequest of moveables to her son, couched in affectionate language, carries a sting in its tail:

> Item I give vnto my deare and lovinge sonne Henrie de Vere Earle of Oxenforde to bee kepte by him as a remembrance of my motherlie love vnto him my roape of great pearle, my newe Iewell, my thirteene diamond buttons, and all those rich garmentes, Cloakes, bedding, and houshould stuffe fyne diaper and damaske lynnen, (which are nowe in my Cosen Iohn Veres howse[)], All which Iewells and other thinges, I will shall bee delivered to my said sonne with in six monethes after the daye of his mariage or at his age of sixe and Twentie yeares which shall first happen …

Thus the Dowager has set the date for the acquisition of these treasures by her son not at the time of her death, nor on his twenty-first birthday, but on his twenty-sixth birthday, which would not arrive until 24 February 1619, more than six years following the date of the will. Her treasures are meanwhile safe in the house of her cousin (in fact, Oxford's cousin) John Vere. Henry could of course acquire the treasures earlier if he married – presumably the Dowager believed he would act more responsibly if he were to take a wife. The Dowager adds another caution:

> Alsoe I give vnto my good freind Iohn Wright of Grayes Inne within the Countie of Middlesex esquier one hundreth poundes presuminge hee will performe his best endeavor to preserve the rightes of my sonnes estate, and to assiste him with his best advise in all courses to advance his good fortunes and to increase his vertue and honor.

Rather than let Henry have free rein with his estates, as he now had with his annuity, his mother provided an overseer from the legal establishment in London.

The 17th Earl's known – or rather inferable – bequests to the poor at the time of his death amounted to 7s 6d. His Dowager was considerably more generous:

> Item I give for the releefe of the poore prisoners in the Counters in London in Newgate and Ludgate in the hospitalls of Southwarke and St Bartholomewes in the prisons of the Kinges Benche the Marshallsey and the White Lyon in Southwarke Thirtie poundes, that is to saye five markes a peece to everie of the said Counters, prisons and hospitalles. Item I will that there be distributed on the daye of my

buriall to the poore people of the parish wherein I shall happen to die Tenne poundes, and to the poore of the said parish of Hackney Twentie poundes. Alsoe I give to the poore of Castle Heningham in Essex xxli to bee distributed at the discrecion of myne Executors.

The various bequests to the poor come to a total of £80.

Now the Dowager takes up the matter of her lands, revealing that on 1 November she had 'demised leased graunted bargained and sould' her various estates at Castle Hedingham and Water Belchamp to her three executors in return for certain annual rents, for a period of twenty years, with instructions that these incomes should be used to pay her bequests and satisfy her debts. She then bequeaths the same lands to Henry, but of course these would not come to him until the bequests and debts were paid. At worst he would not have access to his estates until 1 November 1632.

Henry's prospects as reported in a letter from Chamberlain to Winwood of 6 January 1613 were bleak:[24]

> The Countess of Oxford … left her son towards £1500 in land, all her jewels and stuff, on condition he pay her legacies, which rise to £2000, and bestow £500 on a tomb for her father and her.

On 13 January Henry took letters of administration on his mother's estate 'as of St. Clement Danes' (her parish of residence); her will was probated on 15 February. On 26 June, however, administration was revoked in favour of the stipulations expressed in the will, a decision subsequently confirmed over Henry's objections.[25]

On his mother's death, therefore, Henry received little beyond the promise of her jewels in 1619 and her lands by 1632. At best his income was £200 from the exchequer and £300 from his uncle Francis Vere. Perhaps to escape his creditors, Henry spent the next six years abroad (*Peerage, DNB*). Like father, like son. On 18 March 1618, in Venice:[26]

> The Earl of Oxford, Lord Chamberlain of Great Britain, happened during the carnival to be in his gondola with a young courtesan, a thing [not] permissible at such time, and he did not know the laws. The young woman and his servants have been made prisoners. He is much distressed as he knows that they have done nothing wrong, and he begs for their release.

The arrest of the servants (though not of the courtesan) is confirmed by the English ambassador.[27]

The silence of Oxford's servant Anthony Munday in both his 1618 and his 1633 editions of Stow's *Survey of London* stands as virtual proof that on his return to England Henry did not fulfil his mother's request for a funeral monument. Though an 'ancient Table Monument' at the Hackney church has been claimed for the 17th Earl by his latter-day admirers,[28] it is seems certain that the 18th Earl by neglect consigned the mortal remains of both his parents to oblivion.

Notes

Introduction

1 Miller, ii, pp. 121–28 argues on limited evidence that the two offices were interchangeable in the popular mind.

2 Unfootnoted citations in this Introduction appear (often cited at greater length) in the main text.

3 Buc (1982), p. 170.

4 Ward, p. 214; see also p. 222: 'Whatever faults these two Earls [Leicester and Oxford] may have had they were never guilty of any unpatriotic action', while Arundel is a 'traitor' and a 'suborned informer' (pp. 222–23).

5 *CSPD*, 1581–90, pp. 38–39. Ward cites some of the libel documents (pp. 67, 99–100, 117, 128–29, 210–13), but nothing to Oxford's discredit.

6 Bossy (1959), p. 16, note 46 (citing article 41 for 42), calls the document 'Oxford's accusations'; see also Peck (1985), p. 21. Only these two have recognized that the hand is Oxford's.

7 Read (1960), p. 556, n. 21.

8 Citation from Bossy (1991), p. 100. Oxford fares little better in Hawkyard (1990), p. 260: 'Despite his great intelligence and many talents he was lazy, untruthful and self-indulgent: added to his undeniable amorality there were suspicions of homosexuality.' Oxford receives no mention whatever in Black (1959), Elton (1975), or Ridley (1987). He receives one incidental mention in MacCaffrey (1968), p. 424.

Chapter 1 Oxford's Essex

1 *CP*, xiii, 142 (334/2): '1550, 12 Aprilis Edw. Co. Oxon natus'; see also p. 431.

2 Buc (1982), p. 170.

3 Norden (1840).

4 Norden (1840), p. 20: 'Henningham, called Castle Heningham In some recordes, Hingham, or Hedingham, or Heueningham … The aunceint seat of the Earles of Oxforde.'

5 RCHM, *Essex*, i: frontispiece, pp. 51–57; church: pp. 45–51; tomb: p. 50.

6 VCH, *Essex*, ii, pp. 103–05.

7 *Peerage*, x, p. 238, note d; citing Morant, ii, p. 188, and other sources.

8 Leland (1907–10), ii, p. 25

Chapter 2 Progenitors

1 Golding (L. T.), pp. 5–16; also Morant, ii, p. 328: John Golding (d. 1527). This chapter is indebted throughout to *DNB* and *Peerage*.

2   'Memorandum that Ihon Gowldinge Esquire was buried in the temple Church in london the xxviiith of November [1547]' (p. 7).

3   See HMC *Lothian, Blickling*, p. 74, for 'An account of the manors of John de Vere, Earl of Oxford, in right of his wife Elizabeth, sister and heiress of Edward Trussel'.

4   Wilson (1936), pp. 2–4.

5   *DNB* dates the birth 'about 1512', but *Peerage*, x, pp. 247–48, note 1, cites evidence that he was '23 years old and over' on the day of his father's death on 21 March 1540.

6   *Peerage*; BL MSS Add. 6113, ff. 199v–200; 38, 133, ff. 105v–06. See also Chambers (1966), pp. 60–61: 20 June 1636: John Vere, son of Lord John de Vere and Lady Dorothy Nevell. Dispensation for marriage in any church without banns. 10s.; same day: Lord Henry Nevell and Lady Ann Maners: Dispensation for marriage without banns. 10s; preceding day: dispensation for marriage for Henry and Ann.

7   'Iohn Earle of Oxforde marryed with the ladie Dorothie Nevell sister to the Earle of Westmorland ... this examinant was at the marriage and wayted therat to which marriage Kinge Henrie the eight came in the afternoone' (Huntington Library MS EL5870 C.5 – see Chapter 3, note 2 for key).

8   Wright (1831–35), i, p. 508, dates the original castle between 1088 and 1107; the 1st Earl died in 1194.

9   Tuchman (1978), pp. 444–46.

10 Kingsford, i, p. 163; cited in Gairdner (1881), p. 163. Kingsford, ii, p. 297: the property remained in the hands of distant relations: 'John, 14th Earl, died in 1526; his second sister and co-heiress, Elizabeth, married Sir Anthony Wingfield (d. 1552), father of Sir Robert (d. 1597), who was living here in 1587' (see *CSPD*, 1581–90, p. 395: PRO SP12/199[/38], f. 71).

11 Davis (1971), p. 512.

12 Buc (1982), pp. 169–70.

13 *Peerage* cites evidence that he was 44 in 1526.

14 Ward, p. 7. Dugdale (1675–76), i, p. 189, lists as offspring of the 15th Earl: Johannes, Albericus, Galfridus, Franciscus, Horatio. In fact, Francis and Horatio were sons of Geoffrey. The date of the 15th Earl's marriage has not been established.

15 Ward, p. 7, suggests that Robert had no children, but see the 16th Earl's will of 1562, and PRO C3/251/104.

16 Markham (1888). Ursula Vere is shown as a small figure on the Castle Hedingham tomb of the 15th Earl.

17 Allen (1932), p. 16.

18 College of Arms MS L.15, p. 130.

19 Stow (1592), pp. 955 (crown), 957 (passage cited).

20 RCHM, *Essex*, i, pp. 45–51 (church), 50 (tomb).

21 *Peerage*; 16th Earl's 1552 will (see p. 16): 'Item a greate Herce Clothe of blacke velvett with Angelles Molettes & garters.'

22 Sylvester and Harding (1962), pp. 64–65.

23 *Visitations of Essex*, i, pp. 235–36. Stone, p. 602, attributes the event incorrectly to the reign of Elizabeth. Arthur Golding married Ursula Royden: Golding (L. T.), p. 59.

24 The earliest record discovered to date is 1492, during the life of the 13th Earl: Chambers (1924), ii, p. 99.

25 *CSPD*, 1547–53, No. 5.

26 *CSPD*, 1547–53, No. 7.

27 Milles (1610), sigs. F4–5v. Round (1902), p. 55: the 16th Earl 'was sharply reproved, in 1547, by an order of the Privy Council for "his pretenced claym to the said office [=of Lord Great Chamberlain], whereunto he could shewe no thing of good grounds to have the right to the same"'.

28 *CSPD*, 1547–53, No. 16; *Peerage*, citing Strype, ii, part 2, pp. 291, 123.

29 I infer Katherine's date of birth from *CPR*, Edward VI, i, pp. 376–81, which concerns her prospective marriage up to Michaelmas 1559, which I take to be the date of her majority; the same document refers to Michaelmas 1552, presumably her fourteenth birthday.

Chapter 3 Doubtful Marriage

1 ERO D/P 48/1/1, Baptisms, Burials, Marriages 1538–1701, p. 8 (on microfiche); transcript T/R 168/2 (microfilm). Belchamp St Paul's is located in NE Essex, 5 m. NW of Sudbury: RCHM, *Essex*, i, pp. 16–18.

2 Huntington Library MS EL5870. The texts of the 1585 depositions are here embedded in a document dated 39 Elizabeth (1597). Alphabetical codes refer to the successive interrogatories: A=Green; B=Anson; C=Enowes; D=Knollis; E=Walforth.

3 *APC*, x, pp. 323–24: Rook Greene of Walden – 'An Essex recusant'. Emmison (1978), p. 48: Dame Anne Wentworth of Gosfield, widow of Sir John Wentworth, knight, 20 June 1575, leaves to her 'nephew Arthur Breame of Gosfield £100 and the debt which my cousin Rooke Grene, esquire, doth owe me'; p. 49: Dame Anne leaves 'To Rooke Grene a little tablet of gold which he gave me'; p. 82: William Fitche of Little Canfield, esquire, 13 October 1577, bequeathes land 'with remainder after the expiration to the heirs of Eleanor my daughter, late the wife of Rooke Grene, esquire'.

4 A person of this name matriculated pensioner from St John's at Michaelmas 1552: Venn.

5 'Richard Enowes of Colne' is named in the 20 December 1580 will of Thomas Peaycoke of Coggeshall, clothmaker: Emmison (1978), p. 301.

6 A Thomas Knowles is named, along with his brother Samuel, in the will of Hercules Mewtas of West Ham, 9 June 1587: Emmison (1978), p. 109.

7 A William Walforde is named in the will of James Harrington of Finchingfield, 10 September 1584: Emmison (1989), No. 905. Perhaps this was the son or grandson of the elderly deponent.

8 Rooke Green suggests 1535 (A.5); Richard Enows, 1537 (C.5).

9 Not Tilbury-on-Thames, but the village of Tilbury-juxta-Clare located just south of Ridgewell, a few miles NW of Castle Hedingham: see RCHM, *Essex*, i, pp. 319–20. Tilbury Hall is now a farmhouse.

10 Various members of a Cracherode family, all Toppesfield gentry, are mentioned in wills dated 24 January 1586 and 15 February 1588: Emmison (1989), Nos. 910, 995.

11 See, for example, STC 1324 (1570?): 'A balade of a preist that loste his nose / For sayinge of masse as I suppose'; see also p. 241. For a general discussion, see Groebner (1995), pp. 1–15.

12 Thomas Darcy, only s. and h. of Roger Darcy (Esquire of the Body to Henry VII), by Elizabeth, da. of Sir Henry Wentworth, of Nettlestead, Suffolk. He succeeded his father in September 1508; was knighted at Calais, 1 November 1532; Master of the Artillery in the Tower of London, and Gentleman of the Yeomen of the Guard to Edward VI, 1550–51; and Lord Chamberlain March 1551 to 1553. He was one of the 26 Peers who signed the letters patent, 16 June 1553, settling the Crown on Lady Jane Grey (*Peerage*, iv, pp. 209–10).

13 BL MS Stowe Charter 633.

14 Noted in *CPR*, Edward VI, i, pp. 376–77. Discussed by Golding (L.T.), p. 23.

15 Chambers (1966), p. 305.

16 PRO SP10/1/45 (*CSPD* 1547–53, No. 43). Rooke Green asserts that Dorothy died 'about the second yeare of Kinge Edward the sixt', i.e. 28 January 1548 to 27 January 1549; similarly, he assigns the Earl's wedding to Margery to 3 Edward VI. Since it occurred in

fact in in 2 Edward VI, Green seems to have been one year out in his reckoning. Round (1903), p. 25, argues (incorrectly, as it turns out) that Mistress Dorothy must have been a daughter, or at least a relative, of the Mr Green of Sampford, Essex, at whose house she was residing. The Darcy letter is also printed in Townsend (1934), p. 100.

17 Golding (L. T.), p. 221.
18 Hatton (1994). For previous chaplains of the 16th Earl, see Chambers (1966), pp. 173, 228, 282.
19 *APC*, ii, pp. 221–22: 'Iohannes, Comes Oxoniensis, recognovit se debere Domino Regi, vc marcas.'
20 Golding (L. T.), p. 235, Appendix 10: 'Somerset's Hold on John de Vere' (citing Morant, p. 293). See also Golding (L. T.), pp. 40–41.
21 Golding (L. T.), p. 38, blames Katherine: 'The complete details of the vicious attack upon the validity of … Margery's marriage to John de Vere and the legitimacy of his nephew and niece … are not to be found after the lapse of nearly four hundred years, but enough has been brought to light to piece out the main facts of the story. It discloses a daughter ready to accuse her dead father of bigamy, and to stamp her half-brother and sister as bastards.'
22 Will of 1552 (settled by Parliament of 5–6 Edward VI); *CPR*, Edward VI, iv, pp. 376–77.

Chapter 4 Infancy and Childhood

1 *CSPD*, 1547–53, No. 137 (p. 55): Oxford ordered to furnish five demi-lances.
2 Cited from Golding (L. T.), p. 231, who argues (pp. 231–33) for identifying the recipient as Thomas Golding rather than the much younger Henry, as stated, for example, in *CSPD*, 1547–53, No. 371.
3 *CSPD*, 1547–53, Nos. 417.
4 BL MS Add. 5751A, f. 283 (formerly 291), addressed: 'To our loving frende Sir Anthony Aucher Knight Master of the Kinges Iuelles and plate.'
5 The family title of Lord of Badlesmere was derived from an estate in Kent.
6 BL MS Stowe Charter 633–34.
7 Jordan (1966), p. 113.
8 *CPR*, Edward VI, iv, p. 322. For more on Henry Neville, see *Peerage*, Abergavenny.
9 *CPR*, Edward VI, iv, pp. 376–77: 22 January 1553: articles of 1 February 1 Edward VI revoked.
10 BL MS Add. 5755, f. 185 (old foliation 160).
11 *CSPD*, 1547–53, No. 810.
12 Machyn, p. 329 (note for p. 32), citing College of Arms L.15, p. 130.
13 *CSPD*, 1547–80, p. 76 (PRO SP7/24); *Peerage*, x, p. 249, note a. See *DNB*, under the two conspirators.
14 Kingsford, i, p. 89.
15 Described pp. 94–97.
16 *APC*, v, pp. 104, 141, 173, 310–12; letter of commendation p. 148.
17 *APC*, v, p. 223.
18 *APC*, v, pp. 223, 232, 261, 264–65, 370.
19 BL MS Hargrave 4, f. 137v.

Chapter 5 The Education of Lord Bolbec

1 Queens' College Archives, Bk 1: f. 244 (May 1557): 'Eidem [=Master Hawsoppe] ad

domium Oxenford pro conductione equi sui et triduanis expensis vjs vjd'; f. 245
(September 1557): 'Feodario comitis Oxenfordie vt patet per acquietantiam xxxs'.

2 Queens' College Archives, Bk 1: f. 257v.

3 CUA Matriculation Book 1, p. 169.

4 Alexander Avenando, Queens' (p. 162); Roger Colte, John's (p. 163); Richard Mason,
   Christ's (p. 164); Thomas Bolton, Christ's (p. 164); Robert Wrote, Jesus (p. 165).

5 H. Crane and W. Boothe, Queens' (p. 169); Richard Wynde, Clare (p. 170).

6 Anthony Heath (9) and William Est (11) Gonville (p. 171); W. Woodroufe (12) and
   Percival Woodroufe (10) John's (p. 172); Gervis Holles (10) and W. Butler (11) Christ's (p.
   173); W. Henson (no age given) Corpus (p. 173); Wal. Harwood (11) Clare (p. 174).

7 *OED*, fellow-commoner 3, citing Grose, *Dictionary of the Vulgar Tongue* (1785).

8 St John's College Archives, Rental 1555–74, f. 123v (January–March 1559).

9 VCH, *Cambridgeshire*, iii, p. 413.

10 It has been supposed that Bartholomew Clerke served as Lord Bolbec's tutor at
   Cambridge, but Clerke was a fellow of King's College: Venn.

11 REED *Cambridge*, pp. 204–06.

12 Letters cited pp. 115, 145.

13 Cooper, ii, p. 452 (with cross-reference to p. 382).

14 PRO WARD 8/13, m. 159d: 'pro seruicio in docendo Edwardo Devere filio suo vicecomitij
   Bulbecke'.

Chapter 6 Long Live the Queen

1 *APC*, vi, p. 390.

2 Ward, p. 12, without documentation (not in *Peerage*, *DNB*, or any other obvious source).

3 *CSP Venice*, 1558–80, p. 18.

4 Round (1911), p. 122.

5 *CSP Venice*, 1558–80, p. 19.

6 Nichols, i, p. 37. Golding (L. T.), p. 32, calls her a Lady in Waiting.

7 Lysons (1792–1811), i, p. 297; Ward, p. 6.

8 Hayward (1840), p. 37.

9 *CSPD*, 1547–80, p. 140 (PRO SP12/7[/1], ff. 1–2). Heavily restored by me (original
   deteriorated).

10 *CSPD*, 1547–80, p. 140 (PRO SP12/7[/2], ff. 3–4).

11 Emmison (1970), p. 41, citing *CSPD*, 1547–80, p. 154 (PRO SP12/12[/51], ff. 107–08). For
   more such tales, see Emmison (1970), pp. 41–43; Neale (1934), p. 86; and Erickson (1983),
   p. 417, note 3 (under Chapter 22).

12 Nichols, i, pp. 92–104. Although the visit has been claimed for the Tollemache manor at
   Helmingham (Nichols, i, p. 98), see *Peerage*, x, p. 249, note d.

13 CP, i, 262 (153/88). Haynes (1992), p. 370, cites *in extenso*.

Chapter 7 The Earl is Dead

1 Nichols, i, pp. 109–10, 121–22.

2 Huntington Library HAP o/s Box 3(19); signed 'Oxynford'. This document has been
   described in *Huntingdon Papers* (1926), pt. 1, p. 127; and in HMC *Hastings*, p. 319 [1301]. It
   is entitled 'the indenture betwyxte me and my lord of Oxenford for the marryage of his
   son with a daughter of Francis Earle of Huntingdon' and endorsed 'Signatur sigillatur et
   deliberatur die et anno infrascriptis in presentia Iohannis Wentworthe et Thome Goldinge

militum Iohannis Gibon et Henrici Goldinge armigerum Iohannis Boothe Iasperi Iones et
Iohannis Lovell generosorum'. Its seal has the motto: 'EN D<IE>V EST TOVT.'

3 Stone, pp. 602–03.

4 Round (1902), p. 46: cited from the 'Devere papers', then in Round's possession.

5 Round (1902), pp. 42–58.

6 ERO D/P 48/1/1, unfoliated.

7 Machyn, pp. 290–91. I have deleted brackets from the edition recording lost text, and
   added my own brackets to clarify meaning.

8 BL MS Harley 897, f. 81. Camden, *Annals* (1625), p. 90, for 1562: 'This yeere, Iohn Vere,
   the Earle of Oxford, died, the sixteenth of that illustrious House, who, by his first Wife,
   Daughter to Ralph Neuill Earle of Westmerland, had Katherine, who was wife to Edward,
   Baron of Windsor: by his second Wife Margaret Goulding, Edw. Earle of Oxford, who
   ouer-threw and wasted his Patrimony, and Mary, who was married to Peregrine Bartie,
   Baron of Willoughbie.'

9 PRO PROB10/51 (original, dated 28 July 1562); PRO PROB11/46, ff. 174v–76 (registered
   copy); abstracted in Emmison (1980), pp. 1–4.

10 PRO C142/136/12, m. 8.

11 Loades (1989), pp. 184, 190.

Chapter 8 London Wardship

1 Machyn, p. 291.

2 CP, xiii, 107 (146/1).

3 *APC*, vii, pp. 105–30.

4 Bell (1953); Hurstfield (1958).

5 Smith (1977), p. 34: 'Edward, Lord Zouche, was a success as an administrator and
   diplomat, but never achieved significant political success.'

6 Burke (1976), p. 62.

7 Vickers (1922), pp. 384–95; *APC*, vi, p. 327. William Carr died 1 January 1589.

8 Dodds (1935), opp. p. 328. Thomas Grey died 9 April 1590.

9 Born 12 July 1549; died 14 April 1587 (he was appointed Lord Chancellor, but survived Sir
   Thomas Bromley by only two days).

10 In CP, xiii, p. 142 (334/2): '1566 December 5 inter horas 11a et 12a noctis nata est Anna
   Cecill.' This was a Saturday. In CP, v, p. 69 (140/13) Burghley gives the same date but
   identifies it incorrectly as a Sunday: 'v Decembris die Dominica Anna filia mea nata,
   postea vxor Edwardi Comitis Oxon'.

11 Robert's date of birth cannot be narrowed beyond circa 1563.

12 Kingsford, ii, p. 98. See also Wheatley (1891), i, p. 343, under 'Cecil House'.

13 Norden (1840), p. xvi.

14 *DNB*; author of STC 11748–52.

15 Way (1844), pp. 494–98 (Wheatley dates the lease, by a typographical error, 1750).

16 Hentzner (1881), p. 34. See also Colvin, iv, pp. 273–78.

17 *CSPD*, 1547–80, p. 215 (PRO SP12/26/50).

18 Golding (L. T.), p. 29: it 'would appear reasonable' that Arthur Golding was Oxford's
   tutor at Cecil House.

19 *Journals*, pp. 67, 69; pr = present; px = proxy. The first session of Elizabeth's second
   parliament sat from 11 January to 10 April 1563 (*TE*).

20 BL MS Lansdowne 6/20 (f. 69); headed 'Ihesus'.

21 BL MS Lansdowne 6/54 (f. 135): 'Verum cum neque illos adhuc tanta et tam diuturna

expectatione dignum quicque eddidisse videam: et meam operam haud fore diu Oxoniensi comiti necessariam facile intelligam ; tuae in me solitae bonitati et humanitati confisus ...' Endorsed: 'Iune 1563: Lawrence Nowell to my master Tutor to the yong Earl of Oxon, Proposing to frame an exact map of England'.

22 *CSPD*, 1547–80, p. 290 (PRO SP12/42[/38], ff. 91–92).

23 *CSPD*, 1547–80, p. 224 (PRO SP12/28/56–57, 62). The first receipt is endorsed in Cecil's hand: 'Goldyng / Er. Oxford'. Cited by Golding (L. T.), p. 234.

24 BL MS Add. 35831, ff. 204–05, 218–19, 220–21, 222–23.

25 *CSPD*, 1547–80, p. 225 (PRO SP12/29[/8], ff. 11–12), endorsed in Cecil's hand: 'Arthur Goldynges petition for my Lord of Oxford'. In Latin; translation from Golding (L. T.), pp. 38–39, omitting a superfluous 'to' before 'decree'. Golding reports his fruitless search for additional documents at Lambeth Palace and Canterbury.

26 Golding (L. T.), pp. 37–46; CP, ii, pp. 170–71 (9/91–92).

Chapter 9 Early Teens

1 *Peerage*, ix, pp. 337–38; x, pp. 249–50.

2 BL MS Add. Charter 44271 (annullment).

3 *Inquisitiones*, pp. 61–63 (esp. p. 62).

4 BL MS Lansdowne 6[/34], ff. 96–97.

5 See p. 50.

6 PRO PROB11/52, f. 105.

7 HMC *Rutland*, i, p. 89.

8 Lodged at St John's College: Nichols, i, p. 164; *The Times*, 11 March 1924.

9 Cooper, ii, p. 205.

10 REED *Cambridge*, pp. 204–06; Nelson (1994), pp. 10–14.

11 Nelson (1994), pp. 77–87; CUA U.Ac. 2(1), f. 96v; Nichols, i, pp. 180–81, 188–89.

12 See p. 236: cited at length by Ward, pp. 23–24.

13 Golding signed his dedication (to the Earl of Leicester) of his translation of Ovid's *Metamorphoses*: 'At Cecill house, the xxiij of December, Anno 1564'. See also Golding (L. T.), p. 58.

14 *CSPD*, 1547–80, p. 252 (PRO SP12/36[/47], ff. 110–11 (text f. 110)): addressed 'To the Right honorable Sir William Cicell knight master of the wardes and one of the quenys Maiesties previe counsell be these [delivered]'; signed, 'M. Oxinford'; endorsed (by Burghley): '7 Maij 1565 the Countess of Oxford. the Erl of Oxfordes monny'.

15 Leland (1774), p. 666: tournament recorded pp. 667–69, and in Holinshed (1577), p. 1835.

16 *CSPD*, Addenda 1566–79, pp. 1–2 (PRO SP15/13/5).

17 Elliott (1997), p. 71.

18 Nichols, i, pp. 215, 234; Wood, iii, p. 178. Nichols gives a more extensive list p. 229: 'Marchio Northam.; Comes Oxon.; Sussex; Lecester; Warwic; Rutland; Hunt; Ormund; Epus. Sarum; Epus. Roff; D. W. Howard; Lestrange; Graye; Patchet; Russell; Sheffield; Windsor; Stafford; Mr. Rogers; Mr. Cecill; Mr. Knolles'.

19 Venn. By the time Harvey received his MA in 1573, he had migrated to Pembroke College. He received his LL.B in 1585 from Trinity Hall.

20 Hartley (1992), p. 124.

21 Hartley (1981), i, p. 626.

22 BL MS Lansdowne 104[/76], f. 193. I overlook various corrections and false starts; I have altered the first two words in l. 12 from 'Swete nat'.

23 Oxford's admission is recorded in Foster (1889), col. 36. Prest (1972), p. 9: 'it cannot be

assumed that all entrants listed in the registers automatically came into residence immediately after joining the societies, or indeed that they ever came into residence at all. ... Most honorific admissions were made at the Lent and August readings, as a mark of respect to a man's office, rank, or person.' Compare Ward, p. 27. Other admissions about this time included Philip Sidney and John Manners.

24 Though Oxford was never listed among the governors of Gray's Inn, in 1570 the Inn purchased – and no doubt displayed – his coat of arms: Fletcher (1901), p. 484.

Chapter 10 First Blood

1 Briefly noted by Ward, pp. 28, 124. *Star*, pp. 13–16, 637, argues that Brincknell was Burghley's spy, and so (like Rosencrantz and Guildenstern) deserved to die – an argument as unfounded as it is blood-curdling.

2 A Baynam family seems to have inhabited Westminster, though they did not leave much of a mark. Burke (1914), Index, notes that a Harry Baynam married Mary Lewcacke on 14 November 1574.

3 My summary, from PRO KB9/619(part 1)/13 (Middlesex County): first reported by Feldman (1977), pp. 123–24.

4 Feldman (1977), p. 123, transcribing 'densus per oculis suis', infers that Brincknell had poor eyesight.

5 Wilson (1993), pp. 36–41.

6 Further on Waters, see p. 223. Holinshed's *Chronicles* (1577) is dedicated to Cecil, with a woodcut of his coat of arms. Further on Holinshed, see *DNB*; and Palmer (1981).

7 Document cited in full p. 152. *Se defendendo* entailed a confession of guilt usually followed by a royal pardon: see, for example, Eccles (1934), pp. 9–31; and Nicholl, pp. 178–80.

8 Burke (1914), Index. Dennys married Roger Turpin in 1573; Hugh married Margaret Holdiche in 1579; Ellen married Roman Cletan in 1580. A William who was buried in 1576 may have been either the father or yet another sibling. Hugh died of the plague in 1582; Marks, who was buried in 1583, was probably Hugh's son.

9 Burke (1914), Index. See also WCA, St Margaret's Churchwardens' Accounts, E5 (1578–80), second year, week 12: 'Item of Agnes Brincknell for her grave iijd'; 'Item of Agnes Bryncknell for the Clothe iiijd'.

10 WCA, St Margaret's Overseers Accounts, E144, 1565–66, 1568–69, Payments, 4d each year.

11 WCA, St Margaret's Churchwardens' Accounts, E4, 1566–68, second year, week 24: 'Item of Iohn Brynkenell for his graue – nil'.

12 See p. 105.

Chapter 11 Restless Youth

1 *CSP Rome*, 1558–71, pp. 265–66.

2 Ward, pp. 29–30, describes a subsequent falling-out with Oxford, citing Churchyard's *General Rehearsall of Wars* (1579); I have searched this publication in vain, however, for any reference to Oxford.

3 Morant, ii, p. 328. See *CSPD*, 1547–80, p. 364 (PRO SP12/66/47–49; February 1570): re the jointure of the late Countess of Oxford [Miller, ii, p. 359]. Article 47 is a list, in poor condition, of properties not devised; 48 is a contemporary copy of this; 49 is a list of properties devised.

4 Kingston Borough Archives, All Saints Church Parish Register, p. 129 (March 1569/70).

5 Kingston Borough Archives, KG 2/2/3. p. 17.

6 PRO PROB11/52, f. 105.

7 Ward, pp. 22, 30, asserts without evidence that Margery's remarriage offended Oxford.

8 Ward, p. 286, suggests without evidence that by 'lewd friends' Burghley meant Bohemian poets.

9 *CSPD*, Addenda 1566–79, p. 327 (PRO SP15/19/38–40); partly transcribed by Ward, pp. 32–33. PRO SP15/19[/29–36, 38–42], ff. 85v–93v; excerpts in Ward, pp. 31–34; and *Star*, pp. 16–18.

10 Some charges, for example from the second quarter, may be for non-medical items. My figure includes the following: £15–15–4; £36–5–4; £4–15–2; £10–2–0; £66–16–0.

11 *Correspondance*, i, pp. 197–98.

12 *Correspondance*, i, pp. 269–70.

13 *CSPD*, Addenda 1566–79, p. 327 (PRO SP15/19[/37], f. 88); addressed: 'To my very loving frend Sir William Damsell knight Receavour generall of the Courte of wardes & liveries'. Ogburn, p. 468, misquotes as £400.

14 Ward, p. 42, citing Sharpe, *Memorials of the Rebellion*, p. 238. Campaign is described by Ward, pp. 35–49.

15 *CSP Scotland*, 1569–71, p. 110 (cited by Ward, p. 43).

16 *CSP Scotland*, 1569–71, p. 205 (cited by Ward, pp. 46–47).

17 Discussed pp. 214–15.

18 Folger Shakespeare Library DG539.G8.H4.1565.Cage (in Oxford's characteristic binding).

19 *CPR*, 1569–72, p. 126.

20 *CSPD*, 1547–80, p. 478: PRO SP12/95/92], f. 202, apparently written about a year after the release of the Earl of Desmond in March 1574. On the Duke's removal to Charterhouse, see *Peerage*, ix, 623, note b. Edwards (1968), pp. 399–403, discusses the charges only to dismiss them.

Chapter 12 Best Friends

1 On the third sister, Margaret, see Peck (1982), p. 7; and Williams (1972), p. 264.

2 Peck (1982), p. 8. Howard's incorporation at Oxford on 19 April 1568 required no demonstration of academic accomplishment.

3 John, Baron Lumley (1534?–1609) was his only rival in this respect (*DNB*); see also Ward, p. 116.

4 Barker (1990), p. 378.

5 *DNB*, under Hicks, Michael; knighted 1604.

6 Smith (1977), p. 105 (citing BL MS Lansdowne 109, ff. 116, 114). Further on Howard's musical interests, see Bossy (1991), pp. 120–21.

7 *Peerage*. On marriages between Norfolk's sons and stepdaughters, see p. 110.

8 Ward, Table 1 (dates and pedigree not discussed in text); Peck (1985), pp. 14–15. For sustained discussions of Arundel, see Ward, pp. 215–23; and Peck (1985), pp. 13–25. Hicks (1964) traces Arundel's subsequent career.

9 Pollen and MacMahon (1919), p. 28, note; Hicks (1964), p. 38 (see also p. 128).

10 *DNB*; Vivian (1887), pp. 2–14.

11 Some authorities confuse Charles Arundel with Philip Howard, Earl of Arundel, for example CP, ii, which indexes both names under the Earl; and Lacey (1973), pp. 31–32.

12 *DNB*; also Vivian (1887), esp. pp. 4, 7, citing BL MS Harley 1079. See also BL MS Sloane 1301, f. 107; Thomas Arundel: Inq.p.m. 6 Edward VI, Pt. 2, No. 77; Charles Arundel: PRO WARDS 7/22/48 and Inq.p.m. 30 Eliz., Pt. 1, No. 89 (PRO C142/216/89: d. Paris 9

Dec 1587); will of Jane Arundel: PCC 2 Sep 1575, d. 31 Oct 1577 (PRO PROB11/59, ff. 294–94v).

13 Ward, Table 1; Peck (1985), p. 13.

14 Vivian (1887), p. 7. Philip, who was born in 1527, would have been no more than thirteen at the time of Charles Arundel's birth. The latter was certainly knighted by the then King Philip II during the summer of 1586: Peck (1985), pp. 59–60, note 94.

15 PRO SP10/18[/10], f. 19 (Jan 1552): 'but all tho she be her neyce, and gave Vc markes too her mariage'). The citation of BL MS Harley 433, art. 557, by *DNB* in the same regard is incorrect in several respects: the correct article number is 1557; but the date of that document is Richard III, not Edward VI.

16 BL MS Add. 5751, ff. 199–201 (new foliation): plate given to 'Dame Margerett Arundell' 15 Feb 1552/3.

17 *DNB*; *Peerage* (under Arundel of Wardour); *CSPD*, 1547–90 to 1595–97, indexes.

18 PRO Wards 7/22/48: 'Carolus Arundell miles nuper de Ciuitate London'. Feuillerat (1910), p. 123, note 4, seems to have been the first so to identify him. See also Chambers (1934), p. 155; and Peck (1985), Appendix F(C). Peck gives no evidence for Arundel's property in Lutton, Devonshire.

19 *DNB* (under Arundel of Cornwall, p. 613b); Morris (1872–77), i, pp. 95, 137–38; iii, esp. pp. 127–29, 365; Pollen (1921), pp. 120, 123 ('Younge Mr Arondell – At Sir Iohn Arondells at Musswell Hill').

20 BL MS Lansdowne 2[/19], ff. 50–51. Arundel is identified in an endorsement.

21 Sir William Petre served as Secretary 1544–57; Cecil 5 September 1550 until the accession of Mary July 1553 (Handbook, p. 117).

22 PRO PROB 11/64, ff. 59v–60v; evidently admitted to Gray's Inn 1559: Foster (1889), col. 29. On Francis the younger, see PRO WARDS 7/20/203; PRO C142/197/76 (f. 86: Southwark, 9 February 1582). For the Southwell pedigree, see Rye (1891), pp. 258–61; and Devlin (1956), pp. 7, 15.

23 Miles married Anne's sister Margaret, probably later than 1581: Chambers (1936), p. 151.

24 The will adds a qualifying phrase, 'then living', which may seem to imply that the nephew Francis had since died, but this is contradicted by the fact that this same Francis is named as the residual legatee.

25 *DNB*, under Sir Richard Southwell, states that Sir Robert left no children, but this is contradicted by Francis Southwell's will and by other contemporary documents: see Rye (1891), p. 261.

26 By the 1570s she had taken as her second husband William Plumbe of Northend by Fulham, Middlesex: Rye (1891), p. 261.

27 Lodge (1791), ii, p. 102 (from Talbot Papers, Vol. F, f. 79).

28 *DNB*: Wilson (1525?–81) became Secretary of State in 1577.

29 Emmison (1970), pp. 104–05: 4 April 1570; *APC*, ix, pp. 182, 187–88, 263, 373.

30 CUL MS Ii.5.31, f. 199; preceded by two notes: 'Arden in Kent [=Arden of Feversham] killed by his own wiefe'; 'one strayne(?)'.

Chapter 13 Necromancer

1 BL MS Cotton Vitellius C.vii ('A Compendious Rehearsal'), f. 4v; reported by Ward, p. 50.

2 *DNB*; *New Grove*. Parsons was born c. 1530.

3 See, for example, Morris (1872–77), pp. 129–30, concerning a deceased nobleman who appeared to Sir John Arundel, sorrowful that he had not declared the Catholic faith. See also Haynes (1992), pp. xiv, 19.

4 *Commons*; Brenan (1907), pp. 284, 341–4.

5 Brenan (1907), pp. 307, 341–44, 358. Sir George's appointment is recorded in *CPR*, 1560–63, esp. pp. 81–82. For intermediate years, see *CPR*; and *APC*, iii, p. 271; iv, pp. 193, 302, 407. For his knighthood, see Shaw (1906), i, p. 62. Two lists signed by him in 1565 are in Pepys Library MS 2878, pp. 17 (20 October) and 19–20 (2 December).

6 Young (1987), pp. 31–32.

7 Ffoulkes (1916), pp. 39, 46, 50–51, 62, 75. In 1578 the mastership was assumed by Sir Henry Lee.

8 Ffoulkes (1916), p. 50; Brenan (1907), p. 344.

9 Accession number 32.130.5 (Rogers Fund 1932), on display in Arms and Armour. See also the armour of George Clifford, 3rd Earl of Cumberland, circa 1580–85, accession number 32.130.6 (Munsey Fund 1932); and photographs in Young (1987), pp. 17, 35, 61–63, 65, 67, 142, 155, 166.

10 Brenan (1907), pp. 341–42, reports that he married Margaret, daughter of Sir John Mundy, goldsmith, Lord Mayor of London 1522–23; at the time of their marriage she was the widow of Nicholas Jennyngs (d. 1537). (The woman would have been his senior by some years, and brought money to the marriage.) But *Commons*, under Sir George Howard, declares this account inconsistent with what is otherwise known about Margaret Mundy.

11 *APC*, vii, p. 328 (13 February 1566, concerning the keeping of Lenten fasts).

12 Urry (1988), p. 85; Nicholl, p. 37. On Sayes Manor, 'originally called West Greenwich', see Dews (1884), pp. 17–40.

13 CP, ii, p. 179 (161/18). Sir George's properties may have been acquired much later by Howard, as 'Grants of the tower in Greenwich Park and of the bailiwick of the town were made in 1605' (*DNB*).

14 Ffoulkes (1916), p. 18; Young (1987): see Index, under 'armour workshops'.

15 Young (1987), pp. 108–09.

16 Folger MS L.d.256; see also L.d.294, L.d.320; Feuillerat (1914), p. 93 (full documentation pp. 87–125); *Annals*, under 1553.

17 Nichols, i, p. 115.

18 Ffoulkes (1916), who uses the illustration as a frontispiece, seems to imply, p. 75, that BL MS Harley 7457 contains the same image, but this number is currently non-existent.

19 Nichols, ii, p. 51: 'bouge of court' for bread and ale.

20 PRO SP12/99/50 (1574); SP12/106/65 (1575); CP, ii, p. 179 (161/18: 28 May 1578). The last of these items refers to his death, doubtless in anticipation. New Year's gifts: Nichols, i, p. 125 (1562); ii, pp. 89 (1578), 272 (1579).

21 *CPR*, 1578–80, No. 1332.

22 *Natural Magick in XX Bookes* (1658: Wing P2982), p. 3; cited by Traister (1984), p. 92.

23 See discussions of English Renaissance necromancy by Bradbrook (1936); West (1939); Reed (1965); Rowse (1974); Traister (1984); and Mebane (1989). On the Elizabethan underworld, see Salgado (1977). On alchemists, see Read (1947); Rowse (1971–72); Chapman (1979); and Webster (1979). Bibliographies in Traister (1984), pp. 181–92; Mebane (1989), pp. 250–96.

24 Folger MS X.d.234. I have not always been able to distinguish between formal and familiar second person singular. On necromantic copulation, see West (1939), esp. pp. 26–27.

25 Folger MS V.b.26, pp. 121–22. The ghost in the winding-sheet generated puns relative to the recently deceased Christopher Marlowe: see Nicholl, p. 70.

26 MS: *sca* or *sta*: I expand following STC 4722.

27 Traister (1984), pp. 33–56.

28 Pictures of other spirits and demons occur on pp. 85–92, 137, 141, 164–65, 168–69, 175, 178,

181, 184–85, 203–05. Translation from the Latin is mine.

29 Bossy (1991), pp. 24–25, 98–101.

30 Nicholl, p. 185; story pp. 185–88, from documents investigated by Eccles (1934), pp. 145–61.

31 Manningham (1976), p. 97.

32 Manningham (1976), p. 343.

Chapter 14 Oxford's Letters

 1 Information in this chapter is summarized from http://socrates.berkeley.edu/~ahnelson/.

 2 See *OED*, 'oft'; 'ought', v.III.5.ba.β (c. 1590). I have been unable to locate the passage cited under 'oft' from *Paradise of Dainty Devices*: 'If I may of wisedome oft define'.

 3 I disregard the distinction between 'v' and 'u'; I take as my authority *BLD*. For 'writ of elegit', see under 'elegit'. Ward, p. 304, overlooks postscript; Fowler, p. 366, mistranscribes as *eligit*.

Chapter 15 Majority and Marriage

 1 *Correspondance*, iii, p. 443.

 2 *CSP Rome*, 1558–71, pp. 400, 411–12.

 3 Hartley (1981), i, pp. 194–95; *TE*. Ward, p. 55, identifies this as Oxford's first parliament, but he sat as a minor in the parliament that opened 1 January 1563 (see p. 15).

 4 Ward, p. 51, citing D'Ewes, *Journals* (1682), p. 136.

 5 *Journals*, i, pp. 667–702; Ward, p. 351.

 6 *Journals*, i, p. 672.

 7 CP, xiii, p. 142 (334/2).

 8 Stow, *Annals* (1602) p. 669; see also Holinshed (1577), iii, p. 1225, cited in Nichols, i, p. 276.

 9 Segar (1590), p. 94; (1602), pp. 194–95; and BL MS Harley 6064, ff. 87–90. Defenders' prizes were won by Henry Grey, Henry Seymour, and Thomas Cecil.

10 A similar table occurs in BL MS Harley 6064, f. 90.

11 *Correspondance*, iv, pp. 88–89.

12 HMC *Rutland*, i, p. 92.

13 HMC *Rutland*, i, p. 94.

14 See pp. 379–80.

15 *Correspondance*, iv, pp. 155–56.

16 *Correspondance*, iv, p. 186.

17 HMC *Rutland*, i, p. 94.

18 CP, i, p. 415 (156/41–42).

19 See also Nichols, i, p. 291.

20 HMC *Rutland*, i, p. 95.

21 Stone, pp. 656–69.

22 HMC *Rutland*, i, p. 96.

23 Cooper, ii, pp. 278, 389.

24 Cooper, ii, p. 278.

25 CUA U.Ac.2(1), f. 124; and *DNB* (under Seymour). See also f. 123: 'Item in expensis quorundam nobilium ex superiori germania xij s iiij d.'

26 Digges, *Compleat Ambassador* (1655), p. 134.

27 Joseph Hunter, *Hallamshire*, p. 83, cited by Nichols, i, p. 291.

28 Nichols, i, p. 291.

29 William Parr and his third wife (*Peerage*, ix, 673).

30 Kemp (1898), p. 33.

31 CP, xiii, p. 104 (25/105).

32 CP, xiii, p. 107 (146/1): 'Payments of Sir William Damsell, Receiver General of the Court of Wards, of money for Edward, Earl of Oxford, himself, his tutors, and servants. From 4 Eliz. to 13 Eliz.'

33 CP, xiii, p. 107 (146/4).

34 For the amount of the dowry, see pp. 101, 141. Stone, p. 638.

35 Walsingham, *Diary*, p. 12.

36 See pp. 95–96.

37 *CSP Scotland (Foreign Office)*, i, p. 333 (PRO Scotland, 21/89).

38 Digges, *Compleat Ambassador* (1656), p. 164. Burghley dates to December 1571 in CP, v, p. 70 (140/13).

39 ERO (Colchester) MS D/DRg/2/24, f. 7.

40 CP, xiii, p. 109 (298/2); Ward, pp. 60–61, 64.

41 *CSP Ireland*, 1509–73, p. 464: PRO SP Ireland 35/4.

42 *CSP Spanish*, 1568–79, p. 358.

43 *Correspondance*, iv, pp. 315, 319.

44 *Correspondance*, iv, pp. 311–12. 'Instruction au Sr de Sabran'. Ralph Lane was afterwards the first Governor of Virginia (Ward, p. 66).

45 Kingsford, ii, p. 95 (full history pp. 92–95). See also Colvin, iii, pp 116–206.

46 Discussed further pp. 97–98.

47 Old Ford, Bethnal Green, Middlesex: *VCH Essex*, vi, pp. 58–59.

48 See pp. 326–27.

Chapter 16 Country Muses

1 Ward, p. 87, note 1, dates this letter in error to 1571. The Queen's New Year's gifts this year included none either to or from Oxford or Anne: Nichols, i, pp. 294–96.

Chapter 17 Country Matters

1 HMC, 14th Report, Appendix, ix (1895), p. 276.

2 *History of Queen Elizabeth* (1625), p. 297.

3 Brydges (1805), i, pp. 110–11.

4 Hazlitt (1869–70), i, p. 393; full poem pp. 384–94.

5 CRS, xxi, p. 7.

6 CSPD, Addenda 1566–79, pp. 386–87 (PRO SP15/21[/23], ff. 42–43).

7 CP, xiv, pp. 19–20 (179/134), mis-assigned to 1597.

8 *OED* defines as a tuft of feathers or spray of gems (from 'egret'), with earliest citation from 1645.

9 François Duc de Montmorency (1530–79), leader of the French Huguenots (*EB*)

10 CSPD, 1547–80, pp. 445–46.

11 *Correspondance*, iv, pp. 422–23.

12 CSPD, Addenda 1566–79, pp. 400–01.

13 APC, viii, pp. 80–143.

14 See full citation p. 3.

15 *CSP Foreign*, 1583 and Addenda, No. 451 (PRO SPF Elizabeth 146/13, p. 64).

16 CPR, 1569–72, p. 159 [3094–95].

17 BL MS Add. 5758, f. 73; cited at length in Hartley (1981), i, p. 267. See also Nichols, i, pp. 299–301 (citing BL MS Harley 853, f. 112); and *TE*.

18 *Journals*, i, pp. 703–28. Ward, p. 351, mistakenly lists Oxford as present on 30 June.

19 CP, ii, p. 18 (7/38); cited from Murdin, ii, p. 217. Gresham's letter also refers to money lent the Queen by Spinola.

20 *CPR*, 1569–72, p. 159.

21 Duncan-Jones (1991), pp. 54–56.

22 CP, i, p. 146 (152/28; misdated 1557); first(?) noted by Wallace (1915), p. 116.

23 Though 'paye de West' might suggest 'county of West[morland]', 'West Country' is more likely.

24 *DNB*; Lacey (1973), p. 16.

25 Osborn (1972), p. 27. Nichols, i, pp. 301–02, assigns the departure to 26 May

26 *Correspondance*, iv, p. 467.

27 Edwards (1968), pp. 368–69.

28 BL MS Cotton Titus E.10, cited by Nichols, i, p. 306. Participants included Mr Mack-williams.

29 Ward, pp. 193, 395–96, from a Wenceslas Hollar engraving of 1666.

30 Nichols, i, pp. 307–08. Ogburn, p. 508, citing Morant: 'When Queen Elizabeth was here in 1572 it was the property of the Lord High Chamberlain, Edward de Vere. ... The park contained 1000 acres.' See, however, pp. 203, 424.

31 CP, xiii, pp. 110–11 (140/18).

32 Kemp (1898), pp. 86, 95–96 (also in *Bibliotecha Topographica Britannica*, iv; and Nichols, i, pp. 309–20).

33 Philip Sidney's experiences in Paris are described by Duncan-Jones (1991), pp. 56–62.

34 Æneas was forced to flee Troy when it was conquered by the Greeks.

35 *OED*, under Sicilian (Vesper): 'A general massacre of all the French in Sicily, 1282'.

36 Oxford wrote *affectuesement* in his earliest letter (LL-1), in French.

37 MS note: 'This Madder, or Mather, was he, who together with Barny & Herle, as Cambden relates under this year, 1572, had conspired to take off some of the Privy Councel, wherof Burghley was one, & to deliver the Duke of Norfolke, then committed for treason about the Queen of Scots. The two former were executed.'

38 CP, xiii, pp. 112–13 (132/9).

Chapter 18 Murder

1 Nichols, i, p. 323.

2 *APC*, viii, p. 80.

3 Nichols, i, p. 325.

4 Digges (1655), p. 347: date of April 1572 is conjectural.

5 *APC*, viii, p. 91: 'Murder in London'.

6 *APC*, viii, p. 92: 'A charge of murder'.

7 *APC*, viii, p. 94: 'The rack in the Tower'.

8 *APC*, viii, p. 96 : 'The prisoners in the Tower'.

9 Golding would enter the Inner Temple on 25 January 1574, as noted by Miller, ii, p. 486. Not in Cooke ([1878]), but see Golding (L. T.), p. 266.

10 Hunter (1962), pp. 71–72, notes that John Lyly married Beatrice Browne of Mexborough, Yorkshire. Could she have been the sister of George and Anthony Brown? Could Ann Drury have been Thom Drury's sister?

11 LMA MJ/SR/179/2; identified and summarized in Jeaffreson (1886–92), i, pp. 81–82.

12 Hopkinson (1913); Wine (1973), esp. pp. xxxv–xliii.
13 Registered 17 November 1599 (Arber, iii, p. 151): see Bibliography for full title.

Chapter 19 Mayhem

1 *CSPD*, 1547–80, p. 459 (PRO SP12/91[/18], ff. 27–28); endorsed: '30 April 1573 Lord North./ Booth'; addressed: 'To the right honorable my singvlar good Lord the Lord Burleigh Lord Tresorer of England'.
2 Venn: Josias's brother Samuel, also of Corpus, did not become MA until July of this year.
3 Named in PRO STAC 5/O5/08 (17 June 1580); see also p. 100.
4 Lettehove (1882–1900), vi, p. 723.
5 Lodge (1791), ii, pp. 100–01 (from Talbot Papers, Vol. F, f. 79).
6 Elsewhere Wotton appears as one of Oxford's men: see LIB-3.1/4@65; 4.2/4.5.
7 Ward, pp. 90–92; *CSPD*, 1547–80, p. 461 (PRO SP12/91[/36], f. 64). *OED* caliver: 'it seems to have been the lightest portable fire-arm, excepting the pistol, and to have been fired without a "rest"'.
8 *CSPD*, 1547–80, p. 466 (PRO SP12/92/16).
9 *CPR*, 1572–75, No. 377.
10 Kingsford, i, p. 316, citing *Letters and Papers*, xiv, p. 1192 (8); i, p. 89.
11 Gairdner (1881), p. 137; see also Bowen (1971), pp. 9–10 (note Ogburn, p. 434).
12 Kingsford, i , p. 224. Marginal note: 'Prior of Torrington his Inne. Oxford place by London stone. Empson and Dudley.' Ward, p. 49, incorrectly identifies this as 'Lord Oxford's principal London dwelling until 1589'.
13 *CSP Foreign*, 1572–74, No. 1093.
14 BL MS Lansdowne 20, f. 75.
15 There is no evidence, as implied by Ward, p. 86, and claimed outright by Miller, ii, p. 486, that Oxford paid (or failed to pay) rent 'on behalf of writers'.
16 Loftie (1878), p. 125.

Chapter 20 Wanderlust

1 CP, ii, p. 58 (159/110–11); addressed: 'To the Right honorable my singuler good Lord and Master the Lord Threasurer of England.' Part of a 'packet' endorsed '<September 2> 1573 / Master of the Rolls / Erl of Oxfordes answer to the articles'. Dewhurst is mentioned again in 1580: see p. 469, note 24. For the Queen's progress, including Canterbury, see Nichols, i, pp. 332–54; also *APC*, viii, pp. 134–35.
2 Andrew Trollopp to Burghley, 6 October 1587: *CSP Ireland*, 1586–88, p. 424 [51]. Trollopp describes himself as Gent's deputy 'from the 10th to the 21st years of Her Majesty [=1568 to 1579]'.
3 *DNB*; Murdin, ii, p. 452, Thomas Morgan to MQS, July 1585: 'I hear that Dr. Atslowe was racked twice, almost to death, in the Tower, about the Earl of Arundell his matters, and intention to depart Englande.' Further, see Emmison (1973), p. 319: 'In 1589 Edward Arteslowe esquire (of Downham, who was the Earl of Oxford's physician) was thus charged with keeping an unnamed and unlicensed schoolmaster ...' Doubtless the 'unlicenced schoolmaster' was a Catholic or at least a Catholic sympathizer.
4 Probably not the Richard Baines involved with Marlowe, who was evidently still at Cambridge: see Nicholls, pp. 122–23.
5 Mentioned again p. 151: identified in PRO C93/4/9, No. 7.
6 CP, ii, p. 58 (159/112). Cordell's handwriting is so obscure that I cannot vouch for every word.

7 CP, ii, p. 58 (159/113–14): articles f. 113, replies ff. 113v–14. Endorsed: '2 septembre 1573. Master of the Roolls. Erl of Oxfordes answer to the articles.'

8 CP, xiii, p. 114 (146/6): Endorsed: 'Mr Lowyn Brewster and Egerts for my Lord of Oxford'.

9 See CP, xiii, p. 121 (146/7–10): Valuations of Countess Anne's properties March 16 Elizabeth; endorsed: 'The particular value of the Landes assigned for the Ioynture of the Countesse of Oxford, with all the reprises and the Clere remayne'.

10 Near Kingston-upon-Thames, valued at £800, Burghley's gift to Oxford and Anne at the time of their marriage (I am grateful to Daphne Pearson for this information).

11 CP, xiii, p. 121 (146/13).

12 Ward, p. 101, attributes this document to early 1575, transcribes 'payemaster' incorrectly as 'payend', omits the cook, and mistranscribes 'horskeper' as 'housekeeper'. Ward is followed by Star, p. 81; and by Ogburn, p. 539.

13 CP, ii, p. 58 (202/110).

14 My translation of MS insert in BL Printed Book C.24.b.6, 20th unnumbered leaf verso following p. 424 (whole narrative ff. [18v–23]); printed in Nichols, i, p. 349 (whole narrative pp. 347–52).

15 Nichols, i, pp. 355–57.

16 CSP Ireland, 1509–73, p. 527 (PRO SP63/42[/69], f. 149); complete document ff. 148–49.

17 APC, viii, p. 158 (Commissioners for Victuals).

18 Emmison (1970), p. 241.

Chapter 21 Desperadoes

1 CP, ii, p. 68 (159/80); CP summary cited by Ogburn, pp. 529–30.

2 DNB. On Rowland York, see also Ogburn, pp. 563–64.

3 See p. 48.

4 CSPD, 1547–80, p. 684 (PRO SP12/143[/42], f. 127).

5 DCAD, vi, p. 543 (C. 7935); Seal of arms. Endorsed with signatures of witnesses and note of enrolment on the Close Roll.

6 CP, xiii, p. 121 (146/7).

7 Chambers (1923), iv, p. 90.

8 Nichols, i, pp. 385–86 ('The following particulars were communicated to Archbishop Herring by Dr. Birch'); see also BL MS Lansdowne 18[/37], f. 73: 'The Names of all suche as be Lodged within the Courte: ... The Lord of Oxford ...'; f. 73v: 'Sir Georg Howard' (endorsed by Burghley, f. 74v: 'Lodgyng at Grenwych 1574').

9 Cited from (lost) Colchester MS by Ward, p. 93.

Chapter 22 Flight

1 Nichols, i, pp. 388–89, from 'Unpublished Talbot Papers'.

2 ERO (Colchester) D/DRg/2/24, cover flap; also reveals George Golding's identity as Oxford's auditor.

3 Correspondance, vi, p. 177.

4 BL MS Harley 6991[/42], ff. 84–85; excerpted passage f. 84v. Early marginal note against 'Oxfordes': 'Who went away without the knowledg of his father in law, the Lord Treasurer, or any other, & vpon some discontent. Which created some ielousies of his departure.'

5 Sharp (1840), p. 300.

6 Lambeth Palace MS 697, ff. 47–48.

7 BL MS Harley 6991[/44], ff. 88–89 (text f. 88).

8 BL MS Cotton Titus B.2, f. 295: 'Addressed: To the right honorable my very good Lord the Earle of Sussex Lord Chamberlen to hir Maiestie'.
9 Ward, p. 94, reads 'part [in]' for 'privat'.
10 *CSP Foreign*, 1572–74, No. 1496.
11 *CSPD*, Addenda 1566–79, p. 469.
12 *DNB* (under his father, also Edward Seymour). Edward wrote to his elder brother from Paris, 18 September 1574 (BL MS Add. 32091, f. 277).
13 *CSP Rome*, 1572–78, No. 336.
14 Motley (1904), ii, pp. 572–98.
15 BL MS Harley 6991[/49], ff. 98–99; citation from f. 98v.
16 *Diary*, pp. 19–20; citation from p. 19.
17 CP, xiii, p. 144 (140/15(2)).
18 BL MS Harley 6991[/50], ff. 100–01 (text ff. 100–100v).
19 Ogburn, p. 533, thinks 'your Lordships letters' were a secret file!
20 *CSPD*, 1547–80, p. 484 (PRO SP12/45, p. 59).
21 *Correspondance*, vi, p. 204.
22 *CSPD*, 1547–80, p. 485 (PRO SP12/98[/2], ff. 5–6v).
23 CP, xiii, p. 144 (140/15(2)).
24 *Correspondance*, vi, p. 209.
25 Nichols, i, pp. 391–410.
26 *CSPD*, 1547–80, p. 485 – dating 7 August, at least a week too early (PRO SP45, p. 59).
27 CP, xiii, p. 144 (140/15(2)).

Chapter 23 Preparation for Travel

1 Colchester MS (lost); cited by Ward, pp. 97–98.
2 CP, xiii, p. 144 (140/15(2)).
3 Document cited at greater length p. 145.
4 See pp. 121–23.
5 BL MS Lansdowne 19[/50], ff. 116–17; addressed: 'To the right honorable my verie good Ladie the Ladie Burghley'; endorsed: '7 Dec: [D *changed from* N] 1574: Mr Secretary Smyth to my lady with a water for the stomack'. I am grateful to Nina Green for having called this letter to my attention.
6 CP, ccxxvi, f. 66v.
7 Cornwall Record Office (Arundel Archive), AR 10/3. I am grateful to Daphne Pearson for notice of this letter, and for a transcript.
8 Nichols, i, p. 412.
9 *CSPD*, 1547–80, p. 493 (PRO SP12/103/4).
10 *CSPD*, 1547–80, p. 479 (PRO SP12/96, p. 251).
11 CP, xiii, p. 144 (140/15(2)).
12 PRO E157/1. f. 1.
13 Registered copies in CUL MS Dd.3.20, ff. 98v–99, 99–99v.
14 *Correspondance*, vi, pp. 360–61.
15 Round (1902), p. 47, citing ERO D/DRg 2/25 (transcript supplied by Daphne Pearson). Also noted in HMC, 14th Report, Appendix, ix (1895), pp. 276–77.
16 See p. 403.
17 See pp. 135, 138.
18 Ogburn, pp. 539–40, uncritically adopts Aubrey's suggestion. *DNB* suggests Hill was born about 1570.

19 See p. 153.

20 *Stiffkey*, p. 185; see also p. 304 for dating Oxford's departure 7 February 1575.

Chapter 24 To Italy

1 *CSP Foreign*, 1575–77, Nos. 35, 43.

2 CP, xiii, p. 144 (140/15(2)).

3 *CSP Venice*, 1558–80, No. 619.

4 BL MS Lansdowne 19[/83], ff. 181–82.

5 Retention (i.e., cessation) of the menses, and (the date of her) consorting with the Earl (of Oxford).

6 CP, xiii, p. 144 (140/15(2)).

7 The 'St Albans' portrait is reproduced in colour by Miller, i, frontispiece. Miller also reproduces the 'Welbeck' in colour, ii, following p. 416. An unattributed portrait which may be Oxford is currently in the possession of Katherine Chiljan: see her '"By this Hat, then ...": New Evidence about the 1580s "Portrait of a Gentleman"', *Shakespeare Oxford Newsletter*, 34 (Summer 1998), p. 2.

8 Thieme-Becker (1907–50), xiii, pp. 326–27.

9 *CSP Foreign*, 1575–77, No. 55 (PRO SP78/55).

10 *CSP Foreign*, 1575–77, No. 51 (PRO SP78/51).

11 *CSP Foreign*, 1575–77, No. 54 (PRO SP78/54); *CSP Foreign*, 1575–77, No. 61 (PRO SP78/61).

12 CP, xiii, p. 144 (140/15(2)).

13 BL MS Harley 6992, f. 4. For more on Shelley, see Ward, p. 105, note 5; and *DNB*, under Sir William Shelley (1480?–1549?).

14 *CSP Ireland*, 1574–85, p. 66 (PRO SP63/51[/32], ff. 92–93).

15 *CSP Spanish*, 1568–79, p. 494

16 CP, v, p. 70 (140/14v): 'Anna filia mea Comit' Oxon peperit Elizabetham filiam. que postea nupta est Willelmo Derby' (see Chapter 68). See also CP, xiii, p. 143 (334/2): '1575 Elizabetha Veere filia Edw. Co. Oxon. et Anne vxoris nata 20 Iulij 1575'.

17 See p. 141.

18 CP, ii, p. 101 (8/35). Mildman's sign-off: 'from London the iijd of Iuly 1575'.

19 CP, v, p. 70 (140/14v): 'eadem Elizabetha filia Anne Comitisse Oxon' baptizata apud Theobald'.

20 BL MS Add. 4827 (roll), m. 4 (in margin: 'The Erle of Oxfordes doughter'). The 'aforesaid year' is 17 Elizabeth (17 November 1574 to 16 November 1575). Noted by Rye (1885), pp. 292–96.

21 *CSP Foreign*, 1575–77, No. 209; in Latin; 3 pp., signed 'Guiliet Leuinces'.

22 *CSP Foreign*, 1575–77, No. 246.

23 CP, ii, p. 114 (160/74–5).

24 *CSP Foreign*, 1575–77, No. 368.

25 CP, xiii, p. 144 (160/115); cited by Ward, p. 117.

26 CP, xiii, p. 362 (140/124); 'Ad Illustris. fœminam D. Annam Veram Comitissam Oxonii in transmarinis partibus versaretur. Scriptu in fronte Novi Testamenti'; translation from Ward, pp. 108–09. Not a Greek Testament (*pace* Ward).

27 *CSPD*, 1547–80, p. 504 (PRO SP12/105/50).

28 *CSP Foreign*, 1575–77, No. 495.

29 CP, ii, p. 115 (160/76).

30 CP, ii, p. 118 (8/72).

Chapter 25 Journey Home

1. See headnote to deposition cited on p. 182.
2. 'to kick against the cows[?]' (the standard Italian proverb requires *stimolo* = 'thorn, prick').
3. CP, xiii, p. 144 (140/15(2)).
4. HMC *Rutland*, i, p. 107.
5. PRO E157/1, f. 1v.
6. *CSP Foreign*, 1575–77, No. 685.
7. CP, ii, p. 145 (160/91). The same amount is recorded in CP, xiii, p. 137 (146/12), endorsed March 1576.
8. *CSP Foreign*, 1575–77, No. 707.
9. *CSP Foreign*, 1575–77, No. 708.
10. *CSP Foreign*, 1575–77, No. 709.
11. *CSP Venice*, 1558–80, No. 653.
12. *CSP Foreign*, 1575–77, No. 729.
13. *APC*, ix, p. 102 ('On pirates'). On this and related cases, see Read (1960), ii, pp. 133–34, 175.
14. *CSP Foreign*, 1575–77, No. 737; full text printed in Lettenhove (1882–1900), viii, pp. 339–40.
15. *CSP Foreign*, 1575–77, No. 735; text cited from Lettenhove (1882–1900), viii, p. 340, note 1.
16. PRO 31/3/27 ('Baschet Transcripts'), No. 75; noted by Read (1925), p. 557, note 64.
17. *CSP Foreign*, 1575–77, No. 799.

Chapter 26 Inglese Italianato

1. L. P. Smith (1907), ii, p. 123, note 3.
2. Bodleian MS Tanner 309, ff. 54v–55 (full letter ff. 53v–55v); cited by Stern (1992), pp. 81–84 (excerpt p. 83).
3. Bodleian MS Tanner MS 309 (see Stern).
4. Lorenzi (1870–72), p. 24.
5. Pages 266, 268; complete description pp. 261–71; see also pp. 247–48 on playhouses and courtesans.
6. Bodleian MS Tanner 309, ff. 17–21v; excerpt ff. 19–19v.
7. Perrucci (1961), pp. 201–02; cited from Altrocchi (1959) without her embellishments.

Chapter 27 A Stranger to his Wife

1. CP, ccxxvi, f. 66v.
2. CP, xiii, p. 143 (334/2).
3. CP, ii, pp. 131–32 (160/99–100).
4. Similar expenses were incurred on behalf of Anne's second daughter, Bridget: see p. 293.
5. Named as receiver-general in Indenture of 30 January 1575 (ERO D/DRg2/25).
6. BL MS Lansdowne 102[/2], ff. 2–3; in Burghley's hand; endorsed: 'Copy. To the Queens Maiestie. Delivered by Mr Edward Cavir of the Chambre.' I cite from Ward, pp. 118–20, with corrections as marked by asterisks.
7. This clause has been rewritten from 'is to gain some part of that which she deserveth that is to have some portion of love in recompence of all that she can bestow' (spelling modernized).
8. BL MS Harley 6992[/21] (bifolium, ff. 41–42), f. 41v. Mentioned by Dewar (1964), p. 77.
9. CP, xiii, p. 144 (140/15(2)). Ward, p. 115, mistakes 3 January 1576 as the date of Burghley's writing.

10 *CPR*, 1575–78, No. 54 (PRO C66/1137, m. 28).

11 Read (1960), p. 135.

12 CP, xiii, p. 128 (146/11), dated '29 April 157<.>'.

13 Moore (1991), pp. 8–10, flatly: 'As for the five year break in Oxford's first marriage, it appears that Lord and Lady Burghley's domineering habits caused that'.

14 CP, ii, pp. 144–45 (160/115).

15 CP, xiii, p. 149 (226), 'Lord Burghley's Household Book', f. 74v.

16 CP, ii, p. 133 (9/6); addressed: 'To the honorable his verie goode Lorde the Lorde Treasurer of England'; endorsed: '27 Maij 1576 / Dr Avbry / Erl. of Oxford'.

17 See p. 123.

18 CP, ii, p. 134 (9/8): dated at top-left corner.

19 CP, ii, p. 171 (9/91).

20 Ward, pp. 126–27, thinks Burghley means Francis and Horatio; but he must also mean Robert.

21 CP, ii, p. 171 (9/92); endorsed in modern hand: 'about 1577 Memorandum of Lord Burghley respecting his good offices for the E of Oxford & his subsequent ungratefulnes ...'

22 PRO C2/Eliz/C22/42 (Cole vs. Cardynall).

23 CP, i, p. 474 (157/131–32); editors date incorrectly to 1570. Endorsed by Cecil: 'Concerning the Earl of Oxford'. First paragraph transcribed somewhat inaccurately by Ward, pp. 124–25.

24 *APC*, ix, pp. 156–70.

Chapter 28 Orazio Coquo

1 Venice, Archivio di Stato, MS Santo Ufizzio, busta 41, fasc. 'Cocco Orazio'.

Chapter 29 Oxford's Poetry (1)

1 See STC 7517 *et seq.*, and Rollins (1927), pp. xiv–xxxi. May (1975) has reconstructed the lost 1577 edition from Bodleian MS Douce.e.16.

2 I follow the numbering of Oxford's editor, May (1980).

3 If *bis* is taken to indicate a repetition, then the line becomes 'And sing wo worthe wo worthe on me forsaken man', and thus perhaps a regular hexameter. I am grateful to Professor May for this suggestion.

4 CP 170/126, 20 March 1595 (unpublished). Latin letters in Bartholomew Clerke's translation of Castiglione's *Courtier* (1571) may have been written by Clerke (translations in Ward, pp. 80–83).

5 May (1980), p. 72.

6 BL MS Harley 7392(2), f. 67. I have normalized lineation and supplied punctuation.

7 Cited from Rollins (1927), [76]; see also Ma, f. 28v: 'No joy is greater toe than this'.

8 Bodleian MS Rawlinson poet. 85, f. 14v.

Chapter 30 The Lure of Rome

1 *APC*, ix, p. 192 ('Lewd words').

2 Charles Tyrrell's will of 1570 (see p. 50): 'Item I giue vnto mistress Walgraues wife vnto mr William Walgrave of Smalle Bridge in the countie of Suff' ...'

3 *APC*, ix, p. 292.

4 *Zurich Letters*, pp. 282–83.

5 ERO, Account Books of Sir John Petre, 1576–94, D/DP A18–22; noted by Edwards (1975), p. 28: marginal note: 'Mr Lichfeld therle of Oxfords man'.

6 PRO C47/3/39.

7 BL MS Lansdowne 238, ff. 129–29v (whole collection ff. 80–161): registered transcript, year assigned by conjecture: 'A Letter to my Lord of Oxford from the Lord Burgheley Lord Treasurer of England.' Signed (in the hand of the copyist): 'Your Lordships truly affected, W. Burg[hley]'.

8 Essex's father died on 22 September 1576 (*Peerage*).

9 Nichols, ii, p. 55, reports that Elizabeth was at Theobalds on the 14th, a Tuesday, and proceeded to Gorhambury on Saturday the 18th.

10 Translation cited from Ward, pp. 207–09.

11 LIB-2.1.5/1; 3.1/5; 3.5.2; 4.1.1; see also 2.3.1/1. 2.1.5/3 refers (in error?) to *Richard* Southwell's chamber.

12 Ward, p. 20; also *DNB*, Laurence Nowell, where Oxford's first name is given incorrectly as Richard. Nowell was dean of Lichfield; *DNB* gives his death as 'in or about October 1576'.

13 Pollen and MacMahon (1919), p. 34; Bossy (1959), p. 2; Knox (1878), pp. 103, 311.

14 Knox (1878), p. 125: 'Redierunt ex Anglia Mr Stevens theolog. baccal. et Franciscus Cottonus nobilis adolescens.'

15 *CSPD*, 1547–80, p. 576 (PRO SP12/120/[/26–7], f. 44; copy f. 45).

16 Devlin (1956), p. 9; see also recusant list of 1588: 'Essex: Mrs Awdley of Colchester, widowe' (Pollen, 1919), p. 122).

17 Reaney (1935), p. 372: 'In the 16th century *Berechurch* is used as the name of a manor, a messuage, the parish, and the church.'

18 Cockburn (1978), No. 798. For the same or another John Love, mariner, see CP, iii, p. 310 (15/93–94: 19 February 1587–88); and 399 (166/8: 20 March 1589).

19 Knox (1878), p. 113; also p. 124: 15 June 1577 'de Parisiis venit Mr Tho. Smytheus theol. baccal. cum suis discipulis claris adolescentibus Sowthwelle et duobus Audleiis'.

20 CP, ii, p. 154 (160/129), first leaf verso.

21 Laboureur (1731), iii, 521, 532.

22 Paris, Bibliothèque Nationale MS Cinq Cents de Colbert, 337, f. 661v (Roncière (1908), p. 202): 'Jay esté bien ayse d'entendre de Viestre magesté son Intention pour Les cinque nauires que lon m'auoit offert & m'offre Lon encores tous les Jours de la part du Ieune seigneur qui Jai cy'deuant nommé'.

23 Laboureur (1731), iii, p. 534.

24 Bossy (1959), p. 3, citing these documents.

25 Ogle (1866), p. 55; also referenced as *CSP Foreign*, 1577–78, No. 22. For another reference, see PRO E157/1, f. 2v: 'Edward Denny for (*blank*) xxvjo Aprill 1577'.

26 Ogle (1866), pp. 117–19; also referenced as *CSP Foreign*, 1577–78, No. 256.

27 Ogle (1866), p. 199; supplemented from *CSP Foreign*, 1577–78, No. 447.

28 See p. 235.

29 Letter to Robert Cecil: CP, xvii, pp. 493–94 (113/16).

30 HMC *Rutland*, i, p. 111.

31 HMC *Rutland*, i, p. 115.

32 CP, ccxxvi, f. 190v.

33 CP, xiii, pp. 146–47 (202/136). She married first, Charles Brandon, Duke of Suffolk (d. 1545); second, Richard Bertie.

34 CP, ii, p. 156 (160/135).

35 CP, ii, p. 157 (9/70).

Chapter 31 Murder by Hire

1   LIB-3.1/4@60; references are collected at 4.2/4.4, note 46.
2   LIB-4.3/4. In 4.2/4.3–4 Arundel reports that Oxford 'caused Wekes to murther Sankie bycause he wold not kill Rowland Yorke'.
3   *APC*, x, p. 103.
4   LMA MJ/SR/210/30. The regnal date is not legible, but the document was orignally bound and has now been rebound with other documents from the appropriate term.
5   Guildhall Library MSS 6667/1 (baptisms: marked '1240'); and 6673/1 (burials: marked '5458' – Mistress Tomlynson wife of John Tomlynson; '5369').
6   WCA, parish register of St Clement Danes. My lack of full confidence in matching William Weekes with William Wylkes is based on the fact that a Robart Weekes (so spelled), in his own right or as the father of children baptized and buried 1560–80, appears in the same register: was William Wylkes therefore still a boy?
7   PRO PROB10/95; PROB11/60, f. 124; probated 24 April 1578.
8   Hertfordshire Record Office (Hertford) maintains a microfilm copy of the East Barnet parish church register along with a broken series of bishops' registers, both void for the years 1568–82; but since no Sankeys appear in any surviving register, it seems that William did not hail from East Barnet, nor did Mary or their offspring remain there.
9   *CPR*, 1558–60, p. 360.
10 Golding (L. T.), pp. 74, 77–82, citing PRO C2/Eliz/W26/37, W15/16; and STAC 5/c7/3.
11 Golding (L. T.), pp. 77–81. George Foster had been a tenant of the manor of Little Birch. Henry Golding's will confirms his wife's rights in the estate, with reversionary rights to Arthur Golding.
12 *CSP Foreign*, 1577–78, No. 202.
13 HMC *Rutland*, i, p. 115.
14 HMC *Ancaster*, p. 4. See also letter from Peregrine's mother, 14 July 1577, Ward, pp. 152–53.
15 *CSP Foreign*, 1577–78, No. 469.
16 BL MS Lansdowne 25[/27], f. 56 (entire letter ff. 56–58). The orthography of the original is so eccentric that I have followed Ward, pp. 154–56, except where noted.

Chapter 32 Put Away your Feeble Pen

1   *CPR*, 1575–78, No. 2691 (PRO C66/1165, mbs. 34–36); cited from Ward, p. 149. Ward, pp. 148–49, and Ogburn, pp. 599, 604, mention Castle Rysing without further comment.
2   CP, ii, p. 173 (160/119); *Peerage*, xii (part 2), p. 678 (and note).
3   *CSP Foreign*, 1578, No. 12.
4   CP, ii, p. 183 (10/4)
5   *CSP Foreign*, 1578, No. 86.
6   *CSP Foreign*, 1578, No. 48.
7   CP, ii, p. 220 (161/87).
8   CP, ii, p. 223 (10/70).
9   CP, ii, p. 205 (161/61).
10 Nichols, ii, p. 110, citing vol. 1, pp. 93-94, 253, 307, 387.
11 Cooper, ii, p. 365; citing Nichols, ii, p. 111.
12 Jameson (1938), translation of part IIII, p. [3].
13 On Oxford's 'Castiglione' letter, see p. 237.
14 Ward, p. 168: 'shakes a spear' (=Shakespeare); but Harvey uses the plural *tela, telum*, meaning any projectile weapon.

15 Nichols, ii, pp. 113–16.
16 *CSP Spanish*, 1568–79, p. 607.
17 Ward rejects a literal understanding of Oxford's words, noting that Queen Elizabeth called John of Austria her 'most mortal enemy' (Camden, *Queen Elizabeth*, p. 222).
18 *APC*, x, p. 323.

Chapter 33 In the Chiefest of his Royalty

1 College of Heralds MS M.4. Further on Elizabethan tournaments, see Young (1987).
2 PRO C2/Eliz/R8/29.
3 Foster, *Alumni Oxonienses*. The fact that Lyly was incorporated MA at Cambridge in 1579 tells us little more than that he visited Cambridge that year.
4 Bond (1902), i, p. 17, citing Harvey (1593).

Chapter 34 The Lure of Gold

1 Quinn (1977), p. 376 (see also pp. 484–85). Quinn (1940), p. 96: 'Dee ... was closely associated with Adrian Gilbert and John Davis in his chemical, astrological and spirit-ualistic experiments, and it is probable that he early took them into partnership for the exploration of the northerly regions. It was not until 23 January 1583, when Walsingham visited Dee's house and found Adrian Gilbert there, that "talk was begonne of Northwest straights discovery".'
2 Quinn (1974), pp. 285–86. Gilbert's map of 1580 is BL MS Cotton Augustus I.i.1.
3 *CSP Colonial*, 1513–1616, No. 106.
4 *CSP Colonial*, 1513–1616, No. 105: 'Names of Adventurers who have not paid their parts for the third voyage to the North-west. The total amount, 4,115*l.* 10s, includes 460*l.* due from Michael Lok, 450*l.* from the Earl of Oxford, Martin Frobisher 270*l.*, Sir Thos. Gresham 180*l.* ...'
5 *CSPD*, 1547–80, p. 616 (PRO SP12/129[/12], ff. 26–27): addressed: 'To the right honorable Sir ffrancis Walsingham Knight her Maiesties principall Secretarie / at the Court'; endorsed: '14 Ianuarie 1578. From Mr Michaell Locke / Towchyng the money which he was written vnto to pay to Mr Allen for his aduenture in Mr Furbishars viage.'
6 *CSP Colonial*, 1513–1616, No. 156, citing BL MS Cotton Otho E.viii, f. 87; original reads: 'but my Lord of Oxforde who beres me in hande he wolde beye the Edwarde Bone a uentar & mr Bouland & I haue offrede feyftene hondrethe poundes for here but tha houlld her at eyghtene hondrethe ...'
7 Ward, p. 241, note 2.
8 Matus (1994), pp. 158–60.

Chapter 35 Superlative in the Prince's Favour

1 See p. 195.
2 *CSPD*, 1547–80, p. 461 (PRO SP12/91/44).
3 Emmison (1970), p. 48.
4 Lodge (1791), ii, p. 209 (from Talbot Papers, F, 295). May (1991), p. 76, assigns this event to Shrovetide 1578, but 5 March 1578 fell in 1579.
5 *CSP Spanish*, 1568–79, p. 662.

Chapter 36 Alienations

1 Wilson (1936), p. 22.
2 PRO C142/136/12 (Essex): 18 January 1563; C142/286/165 (Essex) (see also WARD7/37/12): 27 September 1604.
3 PRO WARD 8/13, mbs. 506–48d.
4 Pearson, p. 40, reckons Oxford's Cornish estates at six rather than seven.
5 On Margery's inheritance, see Pearson, p. 15.
6 On the deaths of the 16th Earl's brothers (Aubrey died in 1579), see Pearson, pp. 37, 45, 50.
7 Stone, pp. 332–33. Pearson (p. 3) notes the relative success of the earls of Shrewsbury.
8 Discussed by Pearson, p. 14.
9 Castle Camps, Cambridgeshire, was acquired by Thomas Skinner through a mortgage: see Pearson, p. 30.
10 PRO C2/Eliz/C19/36/2. See Pearson, p. 49, for further discussion of long leases.
11 See Pearson, p. 57, on the pattern of Oxford's land sales.
12 *DCPR*, 1584–85 (Index covers 23–27 Elizabeth).

Chapter 37 Oxford vs. Sidney

1 Ward, pp. 165–74, cites Greville, *Life* (1652: Wing B4899), esp. pp. 38–41; and Languet (1646), excerpted and translated into English by Pears (1845), pp. 164–66, and (without independent authority) by Bradley (1912), pp. 182–83. Ward, p. 174, also cites a passage from Languet's letter of 14 November 1579 omitted by Pears, pp. 166–69; and by Bradley, pp. 183–86. Ward was unaware of the contemporary letter from Sidney to Hatton; allusions to Sidney in the Oxford–Arundel libels; and Arthur Throckmorton's Diary. Peck (1978), pp. 427–29, who examined the sheaf for Sidney references, fails to cite the Languet letter and LIB-3.1/4@68; Duncan-Jones (1991), pp. 163–67, was unaware of 3.1/4@68 and the additional Languet material cited by Ward.
2 Cited from N. C. Smith (1907), pp. 63–69, edited from a Trinity College, Cambridge, MS, and Wing B4899.
3 I am grateful to David Harris Sacks for helping me to 'decode' the exchange of insults.
4 May (1991), p. 361, states that in 1579 Ralegh was named among Oxford's retainers, though a few months later he was in the train of Leicester: Lefranc (1968), p. 29.
5 BL MS Add. 15981, f. 31v; printed by Nicolas, pp. 128–29; and by Feuillerat (1922–26), iii, p. 128 (letter No. 29); also cited in Wright (1831–35), ii, p. 101, 'from a private collection'.
6 Ward, p. 172, selectively translates *provocationem adjecisti* as 'sent him a challenge', thus blaming Sidney.
7 Ward, p. 172 note 1, identifies the *procus* as Alençon rather than Oxford. Languet uses *procus* ironically, perhaps signifying 'seducer' i.e., 'tempter'.
8 Languet (1646), pp. 399–406; translation cited from Pears (1845), pp. 167–68.
9 LIB-4.3/4@120; see also 4.2/5.5: 'His savage and inhumayne practice at Grenewidge to make awaye Phillipe Sidneye'.
10 LIB-3.1@68; see also 3.5.1/2@127: 'His practise to murder Sidney in his bedde, and to scape by barge with caliueres ready for the purpose'.

Chapter 38 Oxford vs. Leicester

1 Error for Julio, i.e., Leicester's physician Dr Guilio Borgarucci (LIB-1/1.6)?
2 Allusions to Oxford's confinement to his chamber at Greenwich: LIB-2.1.5/24; 2.3.1/3; 3.2@90; 3.6.2@146; 3.7 (by inference); 4.3/2; 4.4/1–2, 4–5.

3 *APC*, xi, pp. 346–49.
4 *CSP Foreign*, 1579–80, No. 308.
5 CP, xiii, p. 173 (146/14; see also articles 15, 16).

Chapter 39 Table, Gallery, Garden

1 *OED* sb. 2.b; see also LIB-4.3/1.3@110.
2 Either Bommel, or Bouwel, about 15 miles E.S.E. of Antwerp, and separated from it by four rivers.
3 Henry Borough was no longer alive by 1580: see LIB-4.2/4.1.
4 Don John of Austria and Giovanni Morone, 1509–80 (*EB*).
5 The three captains named are Bernardino de Mendoza (later Spanish ambassador), Colonel Cristobal de Mondragon, and Sancho d'Avila.
6 Probably 'valour' – courage; possibly a variant of 'vallum' – a defensive curtain-wall (see LIB-3.1/3@41).
7 *Peerage*: formally 'Lord Compton' only from 2 February 1589.
8 Philip Howard, ceremonially installed in January 1581 (see also LIB-4.2/8.6).
9 In August 1579 (the specified year and a half prior to this reply) Elizabeth spent thirteen days at Greenwich entertaining Anjou (Ridley, 1987, p. 207).

Chapter 40 Atheist

1 On atheism in the Renaissance, see Buckley (1932); Kocher (1946); Strathman (1951); Hunter and Wootton (1992).
2 Athanasian Creed, *Book of Common Prayer*, cited by *OED*, under 'incomprehensible': 'the father incomprehensible, the sonne incomprehensible: and the holy gost incomprehensible ...'
3 BL MS Harley 6848, ff. 187–89 (in reverse order): Wraight (1965), pp. 237–39 (with photographs).
4 I follow Stow rather than *DNB*, which puts both events on the 20th.
5 Hamont, Lewis, and Cole, see *DNB* (Hamont, Matthew). Kett: *DNB*; Wallace (1974).
6 Grosart (1881), i, pp. 259–61.
7 Wilbur (1952), esp. pp. 175–76.
8 BL MS Harley 6849, ff. 183–90; cited from Harrison (1926), pp. 255–71, but re-punctuated; discussed (among many others) by Strathman (1951); Coote (1993), pp. 185–92, 219–22, 228–29.
9 Nicholl, pp. 43–44, 266, 284–91, 314–15.
10 Davidson (1992), p. 75.
11 Coryate (1611), 'The Jews of Venice', pp. 230–37; citations from pp. 235–36.

Chapter 41 Sodomite

1 LIB-4.2/6; see also 4.3/3; 4.4/11.
2 Aretino (1969), p. 177 ('il "pascipecora"').
3 Howard: LIB-3.6.1/3; Southwell: LIB-3.6.2.
4 Folger Shakespeare Library STC 2106, issued in three parts: OT (1570); NT (1568 [=1569]); Psalms (1569). For an argument that the hand is Oxford's, see Stritmatter (1993).
5 du Maurier (1975), p. 66.
6 CUA V.C.Ct.I.3, f. 111v.

7   *APC*, x, pp. 118–74.
8   BL MS Harley 6848, ff. 185–86; fair copy BL MS Harley 6853, ff. 307–08; photo and transcript in Wraight (1965), pp. 308–09; much discussed by Nicholl, esp. pp. 307–13, 352.
9   On Mirandola, see also LIB-3.1/3@45; Valois citation from du Maurier (1975), p. 58 (see also LIB-3.1@46).

Chapter 42 Prophet

1   V.b.232; Film Fo. 64.1 (colour microfilm). The Folger holds a colour microfilm of a similar manuscript, dated 1616 (Film Acc. 413.2); both described by Nevison (1966–68).
2   V.b.26; discussed further p. 61.
3   STC 12909.7 and subsequent editions, all 1583; supplemented by John Harvey (STC 12907); satirized by Thomas Heth (STC 13255, 13255.3).
4   Ockenden (1936), including Bibliography, pp. 7–14; Haynes (1979a).
5   Peck (1982), p. 12.
6   Gabriel, John, and Richard Harvey are all implicated (*DNB*; STC). On Dee, see *DNB*; French (1972); and Sherman (1995).
7   Black (1959), pp. 184–85, 197–98; Haynes (1992), pp. 59–60. See also the notebooks of Simon Forman, described by Rowse (1974).
8   LIB-4.2/2.13 (Arundel); see also LIB-3.1/3@51 (Howard).
9   For Twyne, see STC 24413. Gabriel Harvey, another protégé, composed a more rationalistic interpretation, published in Spenser's *Three Familiar Letters* (1580).
10 Haynes (1979a), pp. 542–44.   ˋ
11 Bossy (1991), pp. 59, 77, 107; *CSPD*, 1581–90, p. 575 (SP12/222/35: Geffray le Brument to Walsingham); *CSPD*, Addenda 1580–1625, p. 78 (SP15/27A/122, ff. 196–97, letter of 31 October 1582).
12 *DNB*; and see STC (other entries under this name).
13 Eccles (1982), pp. 78–79; see also *APC*, v, p. 383 ('Laurence Kemys'; 'Kemes of Salisbury').
14 Freshfield (1887), p. xxxii.
15 Bond (1902), i, p. 29.

Chapter 43 A Passing Singular Odd Man

1   Lines 1–23 occur in BL MS Sloane 93, ff. 51v–2v. Discussed by Stern (1979), pp. 64–66.
2   For another allusion to Oxford in *Strange Newes*, see p. 45.
3   See, for example, Ward, pp. 192, 395–96.
4   Ward, pp. 193–94; *Star*, pp. 365–66; Ogburn, pp. 642–43 (with reservations). See also Miller, i, p. 509; ii, pp. 121, 518 (note).
5   I have slightly altered capitalization and punctuation.

Chapter 44 Oxford's Folly

1   Nichols, ii, p. 289.
2   HMC *Bath*, iv, p. 186.
3   Canterbury Cathedral Archives, Hales Collection, U85 box 38, volume 1; noted by Rowse (1962), p. 78.
4   *APC*, xi, pp. 356–57.
5   Duncan-Jones and van Dorsten (1973), pp. 33–57.
6   Kingsford, i, pp. 165–66; see also ii, pp. 74, 289–90. Couplet cited by Harington (1615).

Barrell (1945), p. 25b, incorrectly takes 1584 to be the year of Oxford's move to Fisher's Folly from Vere House.

7 Johnson (1607), sigs. B1–iv. Apart from his reference to William Cornwallis, Johnson follows Stow (1590).

8 PRO SPD Warrant Book, i, p. 86; cited by Chambers (1934), p. 151, note 4.

9 CP, xiii, pp. 61–62 (238/3).

10 On the court's stay at Oatlands, see p. 232.

11 *APC*, xi, p. 421; see also pp. 384, 388–89, concerning a February 1580 fray between 'Walter Rawley' and Sir Thomas Perrot. The latter, knighted by the Lord Justice of Ireland Sir William Drurye in September 1579 (Shaw, 1906), married Dorothy Devereux in 1583: *CSPD*, 1581–90, p. 114.

12 *APC*, xi, p. 429.

13 *APC*, xi, p. 422. For the life and works of Gorge, see Sandison (1953).

14 Kingsford, ii, p. 102.

15 Edward Wingfield of Kimbolton, Huntingdonshire, born circa 1562, must be distinguished from his cousin Edward Maria Wingfield of Stoneley near Fotheringay, Huntingdonshire, born circa 1550. P. W. Hasler apparently regards Edward Maria as the more likely candidate, the other being relatively young at the time; the Stoneley Wingfields having had a reputation as 'a fighting family'; about 1586 the Queen named 'one Wingfield' as a man willing to murder Mary Queen of Scots: see *Commons*, under Edward Wingfield and Edward Maria Wingfield respectively. In 1606 Edward Maria became the first governor of Virginia: see Deane (1860), from Wingfield's holograph MS in Lambeth Palace Library.

16 *CSPD*, 1547–80, pp. 663–64, 667; *CSP Ireland*, 1574–85, p. 229.

17 *CSPD*, 1547–80, p. 663 (PRO SP12/140[/1], f. 1). The letter begins by condoling Walsingham on the death of a daughter, and ends with an expression of grief over the death of his own son-in-law, who was buried at St Albans on 30 June (*Peerage*, under Kildare): 'my Lord garrets sodayne & vntymely deathe hathe disordred all my howse, whereof I have wrytten sumwhat more to mr vicechamberlayne.'

18 A kind of master of riot: *OED* revel sb. 4 (1566, 1576).

19 PRO STAC 5/O1/24 (chancery petitions), noted by Emmison (1970), p. 114.

20 Lambeth Palace (Carew) MS 597, ff. 406–07, dated 1617; headed 'A Copie of the vicounte Baltinglasses letter, to the Earl of Ormound; reseived from the said Earl the xxvij Iulie, and sent the xxx daie from my lord Iustice to the Counsell in England by Mr Markham.'; endorsed 'To the Right honourable lord the Earle of Ormound this be delivered with truste': excerpted in *CSP Carew*, 1575–80, pp. 289–90.

21 Bossy (1991), pp. 35, 108, 213, 216–18. See also *CSPD*, 1581–90, pp. 299 (PRO SP12/185/105), 343 (PRO SP12/192/11), for a Philip Curtis who was a recusant-hunter (either the same man turned, or another).

22 *CSP Foreign*, 1583 and Addenda, No. 602 (p. 569): 'Occurrences in Spain'.

23 Norden (1840), p. 30 ('Broadokes ... William Wiseman recus'); see also p. 37: 'Mayland hall. William Wiseman, E.' Emmison (1973), p. 96, note 3: 'For the full story of the capture at Widow Wiseman's house, Broadoaks, Wimbish, in 1598, see Ess. Rev., xxvii, 22–34.' See also Pollen (1921), p. 122; and Morris (1872–77) – see Indexes. Anne and Barbara Wyseman were English Bridgettine nuns in exile: Knox (1878), p. 362.

24 *CSPD*, 1547–80, p. 685 (PRO SP12/144[/6], f. 9): 'This is a trewe copy of a warraunt delyuered vnto me Edward Hubbert by Barnard Dewhurst vppon the payment of one hundreth poundes for the said Michelmas 1580' (signed 'Edward Hubbert').

25 *CSPD*, 1581–90, p. 153 (PRO SP12/167[/28], ff. 81 (cover letter), 82–83 (examination)). Mynors's name does not occur in surviving Inns of Court membership lists.

Chapter 45 Literary Patronage (1)

1 In the interest of bibliographical completeness, some redundancy has been admitted into this chapter, whose topic is continued in Chapter 75. On dedications generally, see Franklin W. Williams, Jr, *Index of Dedications and Commendatory Verses in English Books before 1641* (London: Bibliographical Society, 1962).

Chapter 46 Oxford's Players (1)

1 REED *Devon* (pp. 507–08), *Norwich* (p. 366), *Shropshire* (p. 712); and *Somerset* (pp. 1001–02).
2 Chambers (1923), iv, p. 156.
3 *MSC*, i, p. 46 (from Remembrancia, 9); cited from Chambers (1923), iv, p. 279.
4 *APC*, xi, p. 445; xii, pp. 37, 112. The case was referred on 9 June and again on 21 June.
5 Nungezer, p. 124; see also entries for Leveson and Chesson, known only from *APC*.
6 BL MS Harley 7392, f. 59 (formerly 97); cited in Chambers (1923), ii, pp. 98–99.
7 Nungezer (1929), pp. 123–24, 311.
8 The epicentre lay in the Channel off the coast of Kent. See Ockenden (1936), pp. 14–17.
9 See also S. Gardiner, *Doomes-day Booke* (1606), 'The earthquake ... shaked not only the scenicall Theatre, but the great stage and theatre of the whole land' (cited in Chambers (1923), iv, p. 208).
10 Arber, ii, p. 381. For a connection to Munday, see Chambers (1923), iv, p. 208 (item xxvi).
11 Cited from Chambers (1923), iii, p. 444.
12 CUA Lett. 9 (B.18); cited from REED *Cambridge*, p. 290.
13 PRO SP 12/139, f 76*; cited from REED *Cambridge*, pp. 290–91.
14 Provisional touring lists from REED and *MSC*, as supplemented by REED volumes in progress.
15 McMillen and MacLean (1998), p. 195.
16 BL MS Harley 286, ff. 102–03; printed in Chambers (1923), iv, pp. 303–04. Chambers supplies the date, but no author; Read (1925), ii, pp. 327–28, identifies the author, but no date.
17 PRO E.351/3218; cited from *MSC*, x, p. 11; see also Chambers (1923), ii, p. 100.
18 Hunter (1962), pp. 47–48, 67–77.
19 Wallace (1912), pp. 175–76, citing Loseley MSS, Bundle 425.
20 Chambers (1923), ii, p. 101: 'probably the same who in 1600 set up the Chapel plays'.
21 Cited by Gair (1982), p. 109, from Bodleian MS Tanner 169, f. 169v; and by Hunter (1962), p. 75.
22 Chambers (1923), ii, p. 101.
23 Chambers (1923), iv, pp. 158–63.
24 Nicolas, p. 321.
25 Chambers (1923), ii, p. 101, note 1. This excerpt has still to be verified by REED editors.
26 REED *Devon*, p. 45.

Chapter 47 Denunciations

1 Henry Howard (LIB-3.1/4), circa 30 December: 'friday night was a fortnight in the presence chamber'.
2 References to Oxford's hatred of the Howard family, including Philip, are collected at LIB-4.2/8.6, note 81.

3 Ward, pp. 207–09, translating from Pollen and MacMahon (1919), pp. 228–30.

4 Ward, p. 214. Ogburn, p. 638, suggests without evidence that Anthony Munday had supplied Oxford with intelligence regarding Spain.

5 Bossy (1959), p. 8.

6 Peck (1985), pp. 16, 19–20.

7 The letter is 6.3. Noted by Bossy (1959), p. 15, note 33; Peck (1985), p. 57, note 69.

8 *CSP Spain*, 1580–86, p. 78.

9 Colvin, ii, pt. 2, pp. 309–18.

10 On 19 April 1586 he is called 'D. Rich. Stephens, doctor theologus' (Knox, 1878, p. 210).

11 *CSP Spain*, 1580–86, p. 246, 25 December 1581, misdated by Ward, pp. 209–10, to 1580.

12 Von Klarwill (1924), p. 53. A second Fugger letter, dated 29 April and cited at greater length p. 266, similarly reports that Oxford was 'also arrested but soon set at liberty'.

13 Is Anne Vavasor implicated here? Compare LIB-2.3.1/4.

14 Simier brought jewels as gifts and bribes: Haynes (1987), p. 133.

15 If a priest would say mass only for those who were reconciled, then attendance at mass would constitute dangerous evidence of reconciliation.

16 Paget was a notorious Catholic exile and conspirator.

17 For a clarification, see LIB-2.1.5/24.

18 See answer LIB-2.1.5/25.

19 In his reply (LIB-2.1.5/25) Arundel identifies Dacre House as Howard's residence.

20 That is, home of Henry Percy. Peck (1985), p. 21, identifies this as Petworth in West Sussex, but Northumberland House in London, near St Andrew's Hill, Blackfriars, seems more likely.

21 Evidently Thomas or Hugh Swift (see LIB-2.2.3/4).

22 Louis Bussy-d'Ambois, killed in a duel 1579 (*GLE*; *OCEL*).

23 Evidently a son or kinsman of Sir Henry Jerningham, d. 1571 (*DNB*).

24 The steeple of St Paul's Cathedral in London was destroyed by lightning in 1561 (*EB*).

25 On English lotteries, see Haynes (1979b), pp. 610–13.

26 Leith and Newhaven were ports of Edinburgh (Ekwall); 'wares' might signify wares, wars, or wharves.

27 That is, short journies? petty juries (as opposed to grand juries)?

28 That is, too long to list in detail. The rebellion was presumably the rising of 1569–70.

29 La Mothe Fénélon, French ambassador to England 1568–75, active into the 1580s (*EB*).

30 Oxford seems to suggest that Pike's cover would have been maintained better if he had not quit Arundel's service so precipitously.

31 Either 'faithful households' as an extension of *OED* very A. adj. I.1.a; or an error for every household.

32 The interrogatories may be reconstructed from Arundel's depositions (LIB-2.2.3).

Chapter 48 Tables Turned

1 *CSP Spanish*, 1580–86, p. 78.

2 Cited from Ward, p. 209.

3 Name, obscure in the original, taken from Berry (1991), p. 30, ff. 9v, 10, 40.

4 Cited from Ward, p. 209.

Chapter 49 Knight of the Tree of the Sun

1 *Journals*, ii, pp. 21–54. Ward, p. 351, lists Oxford as present on 19 rather than 20 January.

2 Hartley (1981), i, p. 538.

3 PRO E351/3216, as cited in *MSC*, x, p. 10 (from annual account beginning 31 March 1581).

4 CP, xiii, p. 199 (333). The original continues: 'Sir Thomas parrott, cum vuwares [=viewers?]'. Further on tournaments, see Ward, pp. 56–61; and Young (1987), esp. p. 202. The events are described at length by Segar (1590), pp. 95–96; (1602), pp. 195–96.

5 Evidently the son of Sir William Drury, president of Munster from 1576 (d. 13 October 1579), and Margaret, daughter of Thomas Lord Wentworth (m. 10 October 1560) (*DNB*).

6 *Pforzheimer Library* (1940), iii, pp. 995–98, contains a photo facsimile of the speech, along with collateral information on the tournament.

7 *Pforzheimer Library* (1940), iii, p. 995, contains a lengthy discussion of authorship, in which Lyly finally wins out over Munday.

Chapter 50 Anne Vavasor

1 Huntington Library HA13066, transcribed in *Huntingdon Papers* (1926), pt. 2, p. 68; and in HMC *Hastings*, ii, pp. 29–30. Noted by Matus (1994), p. 240, citing HMC *Hastings*.

2 Von Klarwill (1926), p. 55.

3 Facts concerning Anne Vavasor and Edward Vere were established by Chambers (1936), pp. 151–58; and Barrell (1941–42), pp. 28–33.

4 Harington (1615), No. 300 (p. 51, sig. C4v): noted by May (1980), p. 146.

5 May (1980), p. 80.

6 *APC*, xiii, p. 74 (on Gorges, see Ward, p. 211).

7 CP, xiii, p. 200 (333).

8 See p. 279.

9 Is this the same as Edward Hamnun mentioned in 1596 (p. 359)?

10 BL MS Add. Charter 41712, bearing Oxford's signature and large wax seal.

11 See p. 216.

12 Ward, p. 216, unaccountably names Thomas Vavasour as one of Arundel's witnesses against Oxford.

13 BL MS Add. 15891, f. 77 (Nicolas, pp. 177–78).

14 PRO SP12/149[/69], ff. 160–61.

15 PRO C115/91 (formerly C115/L2/6697), f. 76, from Arnold (1980), no. 324; noted by Chiljan (1998), p. 2.

16 CP, xiii, p. 200 (333).

Chapter 51 Prisoners

1 Chambers (1936), p. 155, and Peck (1985), p. 272, argue that Arundel's 'Lady' may have been Anne Vavasor, but Arundel's letters to the lady (LIB-6.1–9) make such a hypothesis untenable.

2 *CSP Spanish*, 1580–86, p. 172.

3 See Peck (1985), p. 31, discussing the authorship of *Leicester's Commonwealth*. My own belief is that Arundel wrote only the 'Continuation' (pp. 228–48).

4 Nicolas, p. 137, misidentifies Ivy Bridge as the town of that name in Devonshire.

Chapter 52 Starting Over

1 PRO PROB11/61, ff. 96–97v, probated 27 March 1582.
2 PRO C2/Eliz/B22/18. I am grateful to Katherine Chiljan, from whom I first learned of this suit.
3 Von Bülow (1999), pp. 258–59. For an alternative translation, see von Wedel (1928).
4 BL MS Lansdowne 104[/63], ff. 164–65; in Burghley's hand; endorsed by him, 'A copy of a lettre from the Countess of Oxford to hir Husband the Erle'.
5 BL MS Lansdowne 104[/64], ff. 166–67; in Burghley's hand; endorsed by him, 'A copy of the Countess of Oxfords lettre for answer to hir husbondes lettre'.
6 CP, v, p. 70 (140/13); discussed by Read (1947), pp. 271–73.
7 CSPD, 1581–90, p. 71 (PRO SP12/155/54); see MSC, x, p. 10; and Chambers (1923), iv, pp. 98–99.
8 BL MS Cotton Appendix 47, f. 5; cited from Donno (1976), pp. 80–81. On 14 April Henry Percy wrote to Burghley from Orleans (CSPD, Addenda 1580–1625, p. 41 (PRO SP15/27/11)): 'Thanks for the benefits, and for your desire to see me prosper in piety and learning. I am most indebted to you, after the Queen and my parents. Thanks for your exquisite and rare counsel, and your directions for my travels, which I would gladly recompense. ... Commend me to Lady Burghley, and your daughter, the Countess of Oxford.'

Chapter 53 Quarrels and Killings

1 BL MS Cotton Appendix 47, f. 7v; cited from Donno (1976), pp. 90–91. Marginal note: 'Lord of Oxford hurte'.
2 Commons; DNB; Chambers (1934), p. 151. Not to be confused with Sir Thomas Knyvett of Ashwellthorpe: Commons (Thomas II), DNB; Jayne (1956), p. 151.
3 Lambeth Palace MS 647, f. 123.
4 DNB; Commons. Townshend was secretary to Philip Howard, a kinsman of Peregrine Bertie (Ogburn, p. 651).
5 Nicolas, pp. 256–57; BL MS Add. 15891, f. 69v.
6 Nicolas, pp. 258–59; DNB; Commons.
7 Guildhall Library MS 4515 (unfoliated); printed in Hallen (1889–95), i, p. 289.
8 Guildhall Library MS 4524/1 (Churchwardens Accounts, St Botolph Bishopsgate), ff. 50, 51v.
9 Nicolas, pp. 321–24; BL MS Add. 15891, ff. 53–54v.
10 BL MS Add. 15891, ff. 55–55v; printed in Nicolas, pp. 325–26: 'From my house in Westminster'.
11 Nicolas, pp. 326–27; original untraced (Nicolas incorrectly cites BL MS Add. 15891).
12 Stone, pp. 223–34; citation from p. 234.

Chapter 54 Oxford's Literary Circle

1 Noted by Woudhuysen (1996), pp. 93–94. BL MS Harley 3277, dated 1633, is a copy of uncertain provenance.
2 CSP Foreign, 1583 and Addenda, No. 249 (France, ix, p. 90), dated 26 April N.S. Further on Bonetti, see Aylward (1950); Butler (1950); and Berry (1991), pp. 12, 37. Probably not 'Rocco in Brodstrete' (LIB-4.2/6.2).
3 CSP Foreign, 1581–82, No. 700.
4 BL MS Lansdowne 36[/76], ff. 192–93; cited by Bond (1902), i, pp. 28–29. Addressed: 'To

the right honorable, the Lord Burleigh, Lord high Tresorer of England'; endorsed: 'Iulij 1582. Iohn Lilly to my Lord'.

5 *CSPD*, 1581–90, p. 71 (PRO SP12/155[/61], f. 111).

6 Emmison (1966), p. 79, citing Chelmsford Churchwardens Accounts D/P 94.

Chapter 55 To Give the Earl Warning

1 Lambeth Palace MS 647, f. 150 (from bifolium letter ff. 150–53). Compare Birch (1754), i, p. 31: 'that the earl of Oxford, who married Anne, another of his lordship's daughters, had a son borne, who died soon after his birth'.

2 Read (1960), pp. 273–74, 276.

3 ERO D/P 48/1/1.

4 Smith (1994), pp. 446–50. Miller, ii, p. 188, note, cites Barrell (1943), pp. 71–75 (Miller gives page incorrectly as 61); letter cited p. 72; information on Dennys the Frenchman pp. 72–73.

5 BL MS Lansdowne 39[/22], f. 130. Edwards (1868), ii, pp. 21–22, gives a faulty transcription. The letter concludes, 'thus beinge unfenedly [=unfeignedly] willinge to deserue your Lordships good favor I humble [=humbly] take my leue, Grenwich this present fridai / Your Lordships most willing to be cummanded. (signed) W. Rauley'.

6 Tilley (1950), No. S229.

7 HMC *Rutland*, i, p. 150.

8 Birch (1754), i, p. 37.

9 HMC *Rutland*, i, p. 150.

10 Ward gives a biographical sketch, pp. 245–46.

11 Emmison (1973), p. 52 (citing Archdeacon's Court records; see also Quarter Sessions and Assizes).

12 Emmison (1973), p. 96.

Chapter 56 I Am that I Am

1 *CSP Foreign*, 1583–84, p. 406 (Germany, States, iii, p. 6).

2 See p. 322.

3 *CSPD*, 1581–90, p. 188 (PRO SP12/172[/3], ff. 5–6), endorsed: 'Lady Oxfords Charges for one whole yere in the Court. And for wages and liveries per Annum …'

4 Labanoff (1844), vi, pp. 52–53 (full letter pp. 50–58); undated (November 1584). Citation from Nicolas, p. 15, who cites Murdin, ii, pp. 558–60 (citation p. 559).

5 PRO C2/Eliz/O2/29; Emmison (1970), p. 110 (from Tilbury-juxta-Clare); pp. 86, 176 (as J.P.); p. 289 (as J.P., from Tilbury Hall). See also p. 307.

6 Milles (1610), sig. G3v.

7 *Journals*, ii, pp. 61–110. Ward, p. 351, assigns Oxford's first attendance to the 24th in place of the 23rd.

8 *DCPR* PRO, 1584–85, No. 1267/6; ERO D/DPr/158: Licence of Alienation to Roger Harlakenden, 1 September 1584, of the manor of Earls Colne; rent in EC, White Colne, Wakes Colne, Colne Engaine, Halstead, Markshall, Great Gey, Little Tey and Feering. Noted by Emmison (1970), p. 170: Harlackenden purchased Earls Colne from 'the notorious Edward Earl of Oxford'.

9 Guildhall Library MS 4524/1 (Churchwardens Accounts, St Botolph Bishopsgate), f. 58 (1584–85).

Chapter 57 Use not thy Birth for an Excuse

1 BL MS Lansdowne 99[/93] ff. 252–53. Described by Bennett (1942), esp. p. 358.
2 *CSP Spanish*, 1580–86, p. 533.
3 HMC *Bath*, iv, p. 159.
4 Nichols, ii, p. 441 (full letter pp. 440–42).
5 Ward, pp. 250–54, describes this episode, but vastly exaggerates Oxford's role.
6 *CSP Spanish*, 1580–86, pp. 545–46. Letter dated 11 September N.S.
7 Ward, p. 252, citing from ten Raa and de Bas (1911), i, p. 189.
8 *CSP Spanish*, 1580–86, p. 547.
9 *CSP Foreign*, 1585–86, p. 104 (Holland, iv, p. 80).
10 *CSP Foreign*, 1585–86, p. 163 (Flanders, i, p. 42).
11 BL MS Cotton Galba C.viii.206–7 (ff. 184–85).(Chapter 59).

Chapter 58 Maintenance for his Nobility

1 *CSPD*, 1581–90, p. 335 (PRO SP12/190[/47], ff. 97–98).
2 Ward, p. 251, misdating to 1585, misrepresents Oxford's suit as 'a request to be given a command in the impending war'.
3 Thomas Bellott is named in Burghley's will, as cited pp. 370–73.
4 PRO E403/2597, ff. 104v–05. For 1597–98, 1598–99, see PRO E403/2655, Part 1, f. 75, Part 2, f. 100.
5 See p. 197.
6 See pp. 379–80. Stone, p. 582, estimates that Oxford spent at least £7000 per year.
7 Heton was consecrated on 3 February 1600. For all three bishops of Ely, see *HBC*, p. 245.
8 See p. 427.
9 CP, xvi, pp. 395–98 (134/56); citation from p. 397. For a more detailed analysis, see Matus (1994), p. 260.
10 *CSP Foreign*, 1586–87, p. 69 (Flanders, i, p. 92).
11 HMC, Appendix 14, part 5: Manuscripts of Lord Kenyon (1894), pp. 621–22; see also *TE*, p. 64.
12 List of participants in HMC *Bath*, v, pp. 73–74.
13 *Journals*, ii, pp. 112–43; Ward, p. 351.

Chapter 59 No Enemy can Envy this Match

1 *CSP Foreign*, 1586–87, p. 407 (Flanders, i, p. 114).
2 CP, iii, p. 250 (15/111).
3 *CSPD*, 1581–90, p. 409 (PRO SP12/201[/3, 3.1], ff. 4–4v); complete document, with attachment, ff. 4–6.
4 For the date of Susan's birth, see p. 322.
5 BL MS Lansdowne 53[/48], f. 102.
6 *CSPD*, 1581–90, p. 410 (PRO SP12/201[/16], f. 28).
7 BL MS Add. 12497, ff. 409–10v, 411–12.
8 *DCPR*, 1585–87 (2 vols); PRO C66/1291/5–8.
9 See CP, ix, p. 124 (61/73): letter from Hugh Beeston to Sir Robert Cecil, March 1599.
10 *CSPD*, 1598–1601, p. 373 (PRO SP12/273[/103], f. 185v (full document ff. 185–86)), endorsed: 'The speeches vsed by Iohn Poole in Newgate to Gunstone'; misdated in *CSPD* to 1599.

11 Parish Register of All Saints, Edmonton; LMA DRO 40/A1/1, f. 76.

12 Presumably Frances was born between January 1585 (nine months after Bridget, 6 April 1584) and September 1586 (when Susan was conceived).

13 Robinson (1819), p. 69.

14 BL MS Lansdowne 103[/38], ff. 91–92; endorsed, '15 December 1587 / Copy of my lettre to the Erle of Oxford'.

15 PRO C2/Eliz/M5/14.

Chapter 60 Another Grissel for her Patience

1 *CSP Foreign*, 1588, part 1, p. 132 (Holland, xxi, f. 242).

2 *CSP Foreign*, 1588, part 1, p. 145 (Flanders, ii, f. 156).

3 Murdin, ii, p. 746: '5 Junii Anna Com. Oxon. fil. mea ob. Grenovici'. CP, v, p. 71 (140/15): 'v Iunij Anna filia mea Co Oxon obijt Grenewick; 25 Iunij eadem sepulta in eccl. Westmon'.

4 Cited in *Bibliographica Britannica*, vi, part i, p. 4031. See also Murdin, ii, p. 788: 'Anna, Comitissa Oxoniae filia mea charissima obiit in Domino Grenwici, et 25 Sepult. Westminster'.

5 Read (1960), p. 408.

6 Photo in Miller, i, opp. p. 515. My translation from the original Latin.

7 PRO SP12/211[/56], f. 56; noted by Read (1960), p. 408.

8 Cited in Smith (1977), p. 32. Thomas, however, was not always in his father's good books.

9 *CSP Foreign*, 1588, part 4, p. 462 (London) (Holland, xxiv, f. 69); p. 499 (Flanders, iv, f. 120); p. 501 (Holland, xxiv, f. 149).

10 *CSP Foreign*, 1588, part 4, p. 496 (Flanders, iv, f. 118).

11 *CSP Foreign*, 1588, part 4, p. 533 (Holland, xxiv, f. 210).

12 BL MS Egerton 2804, f. 52, cited in Jeayes (1906), pp. 37–38.

13 *CSP Foreign*, 1588 January–June, p. 548 (Holland, xxiv, f. 45).

14 BL MSS Lansdowne 104, ff. 195–214; Cotton Julius F.10, ff. 112–15v.

15 CP, xiii, p. 362 (277/8– English; 140/124 – Latin).

Chapter 61 Rid of my Lord Oxford

1 Hart-Davis (1988), pp. 166–67.

2 Stow (1615), p. 746a: '… the Queen forthwith commands more Ships to the sea, whereupon, yet in voluntary manner, the Earles of Oxford, Northumberland, and Cumberland, sir Thomas Cecill, Sir Robert Cecill, Sir Walter Rawleigh, maister Thomas Gerard, maister Arthur Gorge, Sir Thomas Vauasor … were suddenly imbarked, committing themselues vnto the present chaunce of warre'. Camden (1625), Booke 3, p. 277: 'But so far was the title of Inuincible, or their terrible aspect vnable to affright our English shores; that the Youth of England … with Ships hyred at their owne charges, ioyned themselues in great numbers with the Fleete, with generous alacrity, and incredible courage; and amongst others, the Earles of Oxford, Northumberland …'

3 National Maritime Museum, Greenwich, PAD 0178–224 (c. 1675–1700): eight cards (none showing Oxford) are reproduced in Padfield (1988), pp. 172–75. Another set, Victoria and Albert Museum, Prints and Drawings E1184–1219–1921, preserves only 36 cards, none showing Oxford. A more reliable pictorial device is the 'Pine tapestries': see Pine (1739).

4 Laughton (1894), i, pp. lxxvi–lxxvii.

5 Edwards (1868), i, p. xxxvii.

6 McKerrow (1910), under Field, Vautrollier.

7 Read (1960), p. 432; see also Whitehead (1994), pp. 145–52.

8 BL MS Lansdowne 103, ff. 134–49 (draft in Burghley's hand); ff. 150–64 (fair copy, with corrections and additions in Burghley's hand).

9 *CSPD*, 1581–90, p. 515 (PRO SP12/213[/55], f. 92v; full letter ff. 92–94).

10 *CSPD*, 1581–90, p. 515 (PRO SP12/213[/57], f. 99).

11 Weaver (1975), pp. 24–25.

12 *CSPD*, 1581–90, p. 520 (PRO SP12/214[/1], ff. 2–3), cited by Ward, p. 292; and by Matus (1994), pp. 245–46 (my source).

13 *CSPD LPH8*, xx(1), No. 926; *APC*, iv (1552–54), pp. 93, 150, 237, 351, 353, 365, 376, 378, 390, 392–93, 398, 421; vi (1556–58), pp. 298, 300.

14 BL MS Lansdowne 104[/37], f. 89: 'Persons mete to be trusted with the view and repayr of the fortes followyng: ... Essex: for Harwych and E[a]st Mersey: Thomas Lord Darcy; Sir Thomas Lucas; Edmund Pyrton; Thomas Tay'.

15 Original not traced; cited by Ward, pp. 293–94: 'The ballad was first printed in *Life's Little Day*, pp. 277–281, by A. M. W. Stirling, and published by Messrs. Thornton Butterworth in 1924'. The procession and the service of thanksgiving at St Paul's are described more prosaically by Stow (1605), p. 1260.

16 *CSPD*, 1581–90, p. 560 (PRO SP12/218[/38], f. 60 (whole document ff. 59–60)).

Chapter 62 City House, Country House

1 CP, iii, p. 377 (166/80).

2 CP, iii, p. 378 (17/60).

3 Guildhall Library MS 4524/1 (Churchwardens Accounts, St Botolph Bishopsgate), ff. 72v, 74v.

4 PRO REQ2/388/28.

5 *Journals*, ii, pp. 145–67. Ward, p. 351, gives the somewhat misleading dates 4, 6, 10, and 22 February.

6 *CSPD*, Addenda 1580–1625, p. 275 (PRO SP15/31[/32], f. 40; whole article ff. 38–40). This and related documents are published at length by Pollen and MacMahon (1919), pp. 165–302. For Oxford's presence among the peers, see BL MSS Add. 15916, f. 5v; and Cotton Julius F.vi., f. 209.

7 Murdin, ii, p. 790. Elsewhere (Murdin, ii, p. 746) Burghley names a different day: '7 Apr. die Veneris obdormivit in Domino Mildreda Domina Burleigh uxor mea'. CP, v, p. 71 (140/15): '4 Aprilis Domina Mildr. vxor mea obdormavit in Deo Westmon'. 4 April, being a Friday, seems the more likely day.

8 CP, v, p. 71 (140/15): '21 Aprilis sepulta Westmon' iuxta comit' Oxonie filiam suam'; in Murdin, ii, p. 790.

9 My translations from the original Latin. Photo in Miller, i, opp. p. 515.

Chapter 63 I Have not Had my Health

1 CP, xiii, pp. 432–33 (41/45); I have corrected CP's 'harder' to 'better'.

2 BL MS Egerton 2618, ff. 11–12 (in the hand of an amanuensis but signed by Burghley).

3 *CSPD*, 1581–90, p. 680 (PRO SP12/233[/11], f. 24); discussed by Akrigg (1968), pp. 31–32.

4 *Stonyhurst MSS., Angl.*, i, No. 82, cited from Foley (1877–83), iv, p. 49 (endorsed 19 November [1594]).

5 On Latin formulae, see p. 66.

6 PRO SP12/234, ff. 8–9 (Henry Lok to Burghley, 6 November 1590) (partly damaged).

Addressed: 'To the Right Honorable his very good Lord, the Lord Burleigh Lord hight Thesorer of Ingland'; endorsed: '6 Nou. 159<o> / Henry Lock to my Lord'.

7   Did chains and nails, like lute-strings, serve as a cover for loans from loan sharks?

Chapter 64 Weary of an Unsettled Life

1   Eccles (1933), p. 464.
2   BL MS Lansdowne 68[/113], f. 252. Mrs Penn is described by Smith (1977), pp. 87–88. She exchanged gifts with Queen Elizabeth in 1562 (Nichols, i, pp. 116, 126): 'Mrs. Penne, a perre of silk knytt hoose'; 'To Mrs. Penne, eight guilt spones'.
3   BL MS Lansdowne 68[/113], ff. 253–54.
4   BL MS Lansdowne 68[/115], f. 257.
5   BL MS Lansdowne 68[/114], ff. 255–56.
6   PRO PROB 11/89, ff. 394–95v.
7   CSPD, Addenda 1580–1625, p. 520 (PRO SP15/39[/105], f. 141). Document dated 26 November 1609. Original badly damaged.
8   PRO C66/1387, 1392; terms recorded in PRO SP12/266, f. 137. Ward, pp. 306–07: 'The Castle had probably remained uninhabited since the day the Earl and his Countess had buried their four-day-old son in the parish churchyard in 1583'. It is unlikely that Oxford ever spent much time at Hedingham.
9   Transcript in Majendie (1796), p. 9.
10 For Wilson, see pp. 379–80. Ward, pp. 306–07, interprets Oxford's intervention as a 'perfectly natural precaution'. Though perhaps no 'savage act of vandalism', Oxford, rather than his daughters, profited from the sale of used building materials.
11 Emmison (1970), plate 21 (opp. p. 241).

Chapter 65 Mistress Elizabeth Trentham

1   HMC Rutland, i, p. 134.
2   PRO E179/266/13. Both Norfolk and Nottinghamshire had a Thurgarton.
3   From Thomas's will of 8 April 1605: PRO PROB11/105, ff. 259–60.
4   Huntington Library MS EL 3057 (also recorded in PRO C66/1383): 'We whose names are hereunder written deputies to the right honorable the Lord Burghlie high Treasurer of England and Iohn Fortescue Esq. Chauncellor of the Exchequer ... 2 March 1591 [=92] / Licence Alienated Er. Oxforde'.
5   Countess's letter of 20 November 1602, p. 408.
6   PRO E403/2559, f. 341.
7   BL MS Add. 5751A, ff. 225–25v.
8   CSP Foreign, May 1592 to June 1593, p. 2, No. 470 (editor misidentifies 'Lady Vere' as Anne Cecil). For Reziers, see Stevenson (1847), pp. 440–43.
9   HMC Rutland, i, p. 300. I have changed the penultimate word from 'like' to 'liked'.
10 CSPD, Addenda 1580–1625, p. 339 (PRO SP15/32[/51], f. 101); addressed: 'To the right honorable my singular good Lord the Lord Treasurer'; endorsed: 'primo September 1592 / Raff Bowes'.
11 CSPD, 1591–94, p. 270 (PRO SP12/243[/11], ff. 18–19; copy ff. 20–21).

Chapter 66 Oxford's Grammar School

1   Emden: 'Swalowe (Swalow), (blank). Quest., adm. 1497–8; Inc. A.; adm. HT 1502; M.A. University preacher 1506–7. Probably same as Chris. Swallowe, M.A., r. of Heydon,

Cambs., in 1513; r. of S. Rumbald's, Colchester, adm. 13 July 1513; vac. by June 1516; r. of Little Tey, Essex, vac. Mar. 1519; r. of Margaretting, Essex, adm. 17 Mar. 1519; vac. 1533'. *Pace* Emden, Swallow's Messing was in Essex (not Lincs), 1535–36: see *CSPO LPH8*, viii, p. 240; x, p. 327. On the school generally, see Merson (1975). Documents consulted include PRO C78/116, mbs 18–21 (Item 5); and C93/4/9, Nos. 7–8.

2 Original not traced; from photograph in Merson (1975). A nineteenth-century transcript is ERO D/Q 6/1/2.

3 Venn, *Register*, i, p. 174: 'Church, Bartholomew … Born in Colchester. School, Earls Colne, under Mr. Stockbridge. Age 16. … B.A. 1602–3: M.A. 1606 …'

4 Venn, *Register*, i, p. 245: Erasmus Russell, of Suffolk, son of George Russel, yeoman (schoolmaster Mr Rayne).

5 Venn, *Register*, i, p. 58.

Chapter 67 A New Lord Bolbec

1 *Journals*, ii, pp. 168–90. Ward, p. 351, overlooks Oxford's return for the closing session.

2 LMA P94/MRY/1 (mfm. X87/39), Parish Register of St Mary, Stoke Newington, f. 5.

3 CP, iv, pp. 394–95 (143/69, 71, 72v).

Chapter 68 A Husband for Lady Elizabeth

1 CP, iv, p. 527 (170/142).

2 Cited by Wilson (1994), p. 176; entire letter pp. 174–76, partly modernized. Original is Gloucestershire Record Office, MF 1161 Letter Book no. 2.

3 PRO SP12/249[/92], ff. 152–55, item 'R'; noted by Hotson (1937), p. 154; and thence by Wilson (1994), p. 176.

4 Bagley (1985), pp. 68–70.

5 *Stonyhurst MSS., Angl.*, i, No. 82, cited from Foley (1877–83), iv, p. 49.

6 Huntington Library MS 5872 (catalogued as 'Hartackerley'): 'xvto die Maij Anno Regni Elizabethe Regina xxxvjto Inter Edwardum Comitem Oxon complainantem & Rogerum Harlakenden defendantem'.

7 Huntington Library MS EL 5871 (each sheet signed by Barnabe Worthy).

8 Candidates include William and Marcus Ive of London, admitted to Inner Temple November 1583 and November 1584 respectively: Cooke ([1878]), pp. 107, 111.

9 BL MS Lansdowne 76[/76], ff. 172–73; see also Norden (1840), p. xvii: 'Darbye howse in Channon Row'.

10 BL MS King's 120, f. 14; similar letters ff. 12–13v, all registered copies. Translation cited from Ogburn, pp. 741–42, who cites Clarke (1931), pp. 131–32.

Chapter 69 Some Say my Lord of Oxford is Dead

1 BL MS Stowe 1047, f. 264v, with marginal note: 'the mariage of William erle of Darbye anno 1594'; more briefly in Stow (1600), p. 1279: 'The 26. of Ianuarie, the Earle of Darby married the Earle of Oxfords daughter at the court then at Greenwich, which marriage feast was there most royally kept'. On Derby's wealth, see Miller, i, p. 151. Further on this marriage, see Bagley (1985), pp. 69–71.

2 PRO E315/3229: see *MSC*, x, pp. 15–16, for speculation on the identity of this play.

3 *CBP*, ii, part 1, pp. 11–12 (PRO SP59/29, ff. 247–48; excerpt p. 247v).

4 *DNB* gives no date of birth; John died in 1617. Burghley granted 'The Chamberlayneshipe

of Barwick … to John Carey, Esq.' in September 1585 (Murdin, ii, p. 783); in September 1595 Burghley approved 'A Warrant to Mr. John Carey to appoint a Provost Marshall under him' (Murdin, ii, p. 802).

5 Excerpts cited p. 357.

6 Sir Thomas Heneage, d. 17 October 1595 (*DNB*).

7 WKCRO U1475/12/22; cited from HMC *De L'Isle and Dudley*, ii, p. 184; see also iii, pp. 40, 352–53.

8 CP, v, pp. 524–25 (37/16); endorsed: '1595 without date / Dr Paddy to my Master'.

Chapter 70 The Lure of Tin

1 Lewis (1924), pp. 142, 144–45. See also Haslam (n.d.). Many documents relevant to preemption are indexed in *CSPD*, 1591–94, 1595–97, and CP, xiii.

2 Edwards (1868), ii, pp. 21–22; Lewis (1924), pp. 145–46.

3 *CSPD*, 1595–97, p. 58 (PRO SP12/252[/77], ff. 140–41); endorsed: 'xvijth Iun 1595 / Copy of my lettre to the Erle of Oxford for tyn workes'.

4 Lewis (1924), pp. 145–46, concluding: 'The whole subject is extremely obscure'.

5 CP, ix, p. 382 (74/62).

Chapter 71 Oxford not to be Touched

1 Bath Record Office, Chamberlain's Account Roll No. 35 (1595–96).

2 CP, vi, p. 87 (30/109, ff. 110–10v; full document ff. 109–11).

3 CP, vi, p. 252 (42/27): 'To the lords of the Councell'; endorsed: 'The Lord Archbishop & Counsell at Yorcke to the Lords / Concerning Atkinson'.

4 *APC*, xxv, pp. 468, 485–86; xxvi, p. 20.

5 See pp. 402–03.

6 *APC*, xxv, p. 326, to xxvi, p. 198.

7 Document cited at length pp. 182–86.

Chapter 72 I Have not an Able Body

1 Oxford anticipates the change of year: letter endorsed '12 Ianuary 1596'.

2 CP, vii, p. 48 (173/27): CP editors misdate 1586–87 for 1596–97.

3 PRO REQ2/388/28 (answer).

4 WKCRO, U1475/C12/72 (HMC E, 72; Cal. II, 250–52); cited from Lillie (1848–50), ii, p. 176.

5 CP, vii, p. 327 (54/110).

6 *CSPD*, 1598–1601, p. 38 (PRO SP12/266[/99], f. 137), doubtfully assigned to March 1598.

7 CP, xiv, p. 20 (179/140).

8 Read (1960), p. 587, note 60; Hammer (1999), pp. 319–21.

9 Robinson (1842), p. 10; VCH *Middlesex*, x, pp. 78–79. Photo in Miller, ii, p. 234.

10 Colvin, iv, pp. 124–25, citing PRO E318/1685, m. 16. An inventory from Henry VIII is E 101/421/19. Details recorded in PRO SC.6/Hen. VIII/2103, mbs. 2d–3 ('Manerium Hackney').

11 BL MS Sloane Roll XXXI(8), cited by Robinson (1842), pp. 110–14 (with incorrect reference number).

12 VCH *Middlesex*, x, pp. 115–21; description pp. 119–20.

Chapter 73 The Death of Father Burghley

1 CP, xiv, p. 73 (99/40), evidently 1596–98.
2 *CSPD*, 1598–1601, p. 38 (PRO SP12/266, ff. 137 (1591–2) and 137v (3 March 1598)).
3 PRO PROB11/92, ff. 241v–45v (original will is PRO PROB1/3). Will probated 13 November 1598.
4 Chamberlain, *Letters*, i, p. 41.
5 CP, xvii, p. 646 (192/56–57), 17 June 1604; endorsed '1605: A Note of the Lady Susans Portion'. See also p. 429.
6 BL MS Lansdowne 87[/34], ff. 96–96v (whole letter ff. 96–97); endorsed: 'Mr Secretary 1598 / The Erl of Oxford requiring the Custody of his daughtters, vpon the Lord Treasurers their Grandfathers death'.
7 *CSPD*, 1598–1601, p. 104 (PRO SP12/268[/74], f. 120).

Chapter 74 A Husband for Lady Bridget

1 Folger Shakespeare Library MS Z.d.17.
2 CP, ix, p. 51 (38/13).
3 HMC *Ancaster*, p. 345.
4 *CSPD*, 1598–1601, p. 165 (PRO SP12/270[/48], f. 78v).
5 CP, ix, p. 130 (178/144); addressed (in Bridget's hand): 'To the right honourable my verie good Vnckle Mr Secretarye at the Court giue thes'; endorsed: 'Lady Bridgett Vere to my Master'.
6 *CSPD*, 1598–1601, p. 182 (PRO SP12/270[/82], f, 147). Top right corner torn away; emendations supplied by PRO staff. Addressed: 'To my very lovinge fren<d> Mr Mainard at his house in Westminster or elles where geue these'; endorsed: '16 April 1599. The Lady Bridgett Vere to Mr Maynerd. / In fauour of Mr Arnold Chapleyn to the Countesse of Bedford'.
7 *CSPD*, 1598–1601, p. 186 (PRO SP12/270[/91], f. 159). Body of letter in hand of an amanuensis.
8 *CSPD*, 1598–1601, p. 189 (PRO SP12/270[/101], f. 176). Body of letter in hand of an amanuensis.
9 *CSPD*, 1598–1601, p. 217 (PRO SP12/271[/23], f. 58).
10 *CSPD*, 1598–1601, p. 316 (PRO SP12/272[/95], f. 150).
11 CP, xxiii, p. 94 (P.229).
12 Chamberlain, *Letters*, i, p. 85.
13 CP, ix, p. 401 (74/107).
14 *CSPD*, 1601–03, p. 60 (PRO SP12/280); cited from Wilson (1936), p. 22.

Chapter 75 Literary Patronage (II)

1 CP, ii, pp. 534–35 (12/102). Translations by Nicholas include STC 16807, 26123, and (doubtfully) 5141.
2 Pollen (1908), pp. 54–55, 57–61; citation p. 61 (also noted by Nicholl, p. 175). See also Munday (1582).
3 Ward fails to document his claim (pp. 298, 336 note 1) that Lok gave Oxford an inscribed copy.
4 Translation by Dana F. Sutton, *Philological Museum* (http://e3.uci.edu/~papyri/anagrams/).

Chapter 76 Oxford's Poetry (11)

1 Breton repudiated the *Bowre* shortly after its publication: see Rollins (1933), Introduction.
2 STC 378, 379, 379.5, 380 (all 1600). For various misattributions, see May (1980), pp. 83–84.
3 May (1980), pp. 33–35, 41–42, 118, 121–22. For poems 1–9, see p. 158.
4 May (1980), p. 5.
5 See p. 181.
6 Brink (1999), pp. 19–30, following May (1981).
7 STC 17834, sig. Oo3v; compare Ward, p. 264: 'The best for Comedy among us be Edward Earl of Oxford'.
8 This obvious inference is necessarily rejected by Oxfordians, for example *Star*, pp. 1034–35.
9 New York, NY: PBS, 1985.
10 Courthope (1895–1910), ii, pp. 312–13.
11 Rowse (1983), p. 90.
12 Duncan–Jones (1999), p. 27. I have excised the phrase, 'discontented at the rising of a mean gentleman in the English Court circa 1580', independently derived from *Desiderata Curiosa* (London 1779), i, p. 270, where it is introduced as 'a pleasant conceit of Vere, Earl of Oxford'.
13 Rollins (1933), pp. 94–97.
14 Rollins (1927), p. 95.
15 Hannah (1875), pp. 147–48, citing Chetham MS Mun. A.15: 'A copy of the first two epigrams [here, the second], without distinction of authors, is printed from "an ancient MS. Miscellany" in Lord Orford's "Works", vol. i, p. 551, as Lord Oxford's, signed "Vere"'. Hannah refers to Walpole (1798–1825), i, p. 551: 'from an ancient MS. Miscellany …'
16 May (1975), p. 389.

Chapter 77 Oxford's Players (11)

1 *MSC*, vii, p. 63.
2 REED, *Coventry*, p. 348.
3 London, Guild Hall, Remembrancia, ii, p. 189, cited from *MSC*, i, p. 85; also in Chambers (1923), iv, pp. 334–35.
4 Berry (1986), p. 51.
5 Levenson (1980), esp. pp. 15–20.
6 The three entertainments are discussed on pp. 85–86, 190, 262–65.
7 *CSPD*, 1598–1601, p. 227 (PRO SP12/271[/34], f. 79): George Fenner to his partner Baltazar Gybels, Antwerp; similarly, PRO SP12/271[/35], f. 80, Fenner to Hum. Galdelli or Guiseppe Tusinga, Venice: 'Our Earle of Derby is busye in Penning Commedyes, for the commonn players.'
8 HMC *L'Isle and Dudley*, ii, p. 415.
9 CP, xiii, p. 609 (186/24); addressed: 'To the right honorable my verye good vncle Mr Secretayre'; endorsed: 'Lady Darby to my master'. Cited by Chambers (1923), ii, p. 127.
10 McMillen and MacLean (1998), p. 195.

Chapter 78 Deep Abyss and Bottom of Despair

1 Nichols, ii, p. 460.
2 CP, x, p. 251 (251/25), endorsed: 'Minute to my Lord Norreys from my Master concerning Mr Francis Norreis'; the date may be inferred from the reply (see next note). I have not noted all corrections.

3 CP, x, pp. 251–52 (251/13).

4 Jeaffreson (1886–92), i, p. 264: LMA MJ/SR/385/43 (summary translation mine).

Chapter 79 The Weakness of my Lame Hand

1 *CSPD*, 1598–1601, p. 22 (PRO SP12/266[/54], f. 75).

2 PRO E372/446 (1600–01), London, Midd., m. 2.

3 Chambers (1930), ii, pp. 87–90.

4 PRO E372/446 (1600–01), London, Midd., m. 1.

5 *Journals*, ii, p. 226; Ward, pp. 351–52.

6 *Journals* (1682), p. 535 (calling Oxford Chamberlain rather than Great Chamberlain); cited by Ward, p. 352.

7 Ward, p. 336. Lists occur in *APC*, xxxi, pp. 151, 169; HMC *Rutland*, i, p. 371 (narrative summary pp. 371–73).

8 CP 35/84. Burghley urged cooperation, but for Oxford that was 'A thinge I cannot do in honor, sythe I have alredie receyved diverse iniuries and wronges from him, which bare [=bar] me of all suche basse [=base] courses'.

9 BL MS Harley 7393, f. 13. MSS circulated so widely that the BL alone holds twelve copies (BL Index of MSS). Text printed as *Fragmenta Regalia* (1641: Wing N249–53). Ward, p. 245, cites inaccurately: 'Naunton adds that this "savours more of his Lordship's humour than of the truth"'. On Naunton, see *DNB*.

10 See *OED* emulation; *OLD*, 'æmulatio'.

11 Ward and thence Fowler date this letter March 1601: actual month is conjectural.

12 *CSPD*, 1601–03, p. 56 (PRO SP12/279/123), endorsed: 'The opinion of Serjt. Harris and Mr. Hele, Mr. Tanfield, and Mr. Diggs, what proceedings are best for Danvers' escheat for entitling the Queen's Majesty'.

13 *CSPD*, 1601–03, p. 81 (PRO SP12/281[/45], f. 90): addressed: 'To my lorde Mr attorny generall'; endorsed '1601'.

14 CP, xiii, p. 179 (206/63); see also *CSPD*, 1601–03, pp. 294–95 (PRO SP12/287[/42], ff. 63–64; also f. 65): February 1603; reference to Michael Cawley, Sir Edmund Carey, Sir Charles Danvers.

15 Language of a provisional or conditional grant.

16 to do me good in all that she cane: English translation of *de bene esse* ... see next note.

17 On correct Latin formulae, see p. 66.

18 CP, xi, p. 586 (787): endorsed '1601'.

Chapter 80 Nothing more Precious than Gold

1 CP, xii, p. 43 (85/8).

2 Manningham (1976), p. 182.

3 BL MS Stowe 557, f. 26v. Frances Cobham of Kildare received clothing and jewels for the same occasion (ff. 26, 48v).

4 *DNB*, under Charles Danvers and Henry Danvers; Burke (1883), pp. 154–55.

5 HAD MS D/F/TYS/1 (transcript of Parish Vestry Minute Book 1581–1613), pp. 45–47.

6 BL MS Add. 12506, f. 161, addressed: 'To my verie good frend Mr Doctor Caesar at St Katherines'; endorsed: 'The Countess of Oxford Against one [Thomas] Coe a tenant to her husbond that will neither pay his rent nor goo out of the house ...'

7 PRO C2/Eliz/O2/13.

Chapter 81 Missing Person

1 PRO C47/3/41.
2 Manningham (1976), p. 208, specifies 3:00 a.m.; Stowe (1605), p. 1425, about 2:00 a.m.
3 SRP, No. 1. Manningham (1976), p. 388: see STC 7759 and 8301 for lists. The (unique?) surviving copy of the first issue (2a) is Princeton University Library Ex DA391.F67q. CANT2 is provisionally reported as a ghost.
4 Stow (1605), p. 1425.
5 CP, xv, p. 1: proclamation, in Cecil's hand, is 99/43; letter to Payton is 99/43.
6 Carey had made and revised his will in 1599 and 1601, and died on 9 September 1603, about the age of fifty-six; Herbert, by contrast, was not yet twenty-three and on the verge of becoming the King's favourite (*Peerage*, *DNB*).
7 STC 8297 (note) identifies 'Norreys' as Sir Edward Norris – but the absence of a first name suggests a baron. Norreys proclaimed the King's accession at Oxford: *Peerage*.
8 O'Connor (1934).
9 *CSPD*, 1603–10, p. 40 (PRO SP14/3, f. 134 (77)). On the French ambassador, see O'Connor (1934), p. 103, citing Firth and Lomas (1906), 'List of Ambassadors'.
10 *CSPD*, 1598–1600, p. 169.
11 *DNB*, s.v. Parsons, Robert, p. 415.
12 For full identifications, see *CSPD*, 1601–03 and 1603–10 (indexes); and *Peerage*.
13 *CSPD*, 1603–10, p. 45 (PRO SP14/4/14, 14/i), ff. 27–27v (letter), 28–29 (report): letter addressed: 'To the Right honorable the lorde Cycell princypall Secretory to his maiestie and one of the lords of his hyghnes moste honorable pryuye Councell at the Cowrte'; endorsed: '10 Octob. 1603; Sir Iohn Payton to my Lord with a relation of certaine speeches passed betwixt my L. of Lyncolne and his sonne / Sir Iohn Peytons relation of such speeches as passed between him and the Erle of Lyncolne some feaw dayes before her maiesties death'.

Chapter 82 This Common Shipwrack

1 Ward, pp. 338–39, surmises without evidence that Oxford was one of these six.
2 PRO E351/3145, Funeral of Elizabeth, m. 3d.
3 PRO AO3/1186, Sir John Fortescue's accounts for funeral of Elizabeth. Similar entries in PRO LC 2/4/4.
4 BL MS Add. 20778, f. 1; Folger Shakespeare Library MS X.d.30 (42).
5 Nichols, i, pp. 107–11. See also Turner (1927), and Willson (1940).
6 See Countess Elizabeth's letter of 20 November 1602, p. 408.
7 Nichols, i, p. 107.
8 CP, xv, p. 164 (100/149); not signed; addressed: 'To the right honorable the Lord Cecill, principall Secretary: to his Maiestie'; endorsed: 'Mr Hickes to my Lord'. CP prints the endorsement incorrectly as 'Mrs. Hickes to my Lord', but she died in 1592: Smith (1977), p. 100.
9 CP, xv, p. 391 (206/6): addressed: 'To the right honorable and my very good vnckle the Lord Ciscell giue thes'; endorsed: '1603 Lady Susan to my Lord'.
10 *CSPD*, 1603–10, p. 24 (summary); PRO SP14/2[/76], ff. 189v–90v (full document is ff. 187–207); translation of original law French cited from Ward, p. 346.
11 Akrigg (1962), p. 30, assumes, without giving evidence, Oxford's presence in the coronation procession of 25 July as Lord Great Chamberlain.
12 *CSPD*, 1603–10, p. 112 (PRO SP14/8/36+ (Docquet)).

13 Huntington Library MS EL1170, f. [41].

14 Round (1911), pp. 134–35.

15 PRO C66/1612, mbs. 27–28 (starting on mb. 28). A document in English describing his rights is *CSPD*, 1603–1610, p. 22 (PRO SP14/2[/63], f. 160), endorsed: 'The state of the Erl of Oxfords place'.

16 PRO E403/2598 (Pells), part 1, f. 27v.

Chapter 83 But a Grave

1 Nichols, *James*, i, p. 327: 'From a MS. of the late John Meyrick, Esq., collated with a copy in the Cotton Library.'

2 *Journals*, ii, pp. 263–66. Ward, p. 351, does not mention this parliament.

3 Nichols, *James*, i, p. 424.

4 PRO REQ 2/388/28.

5 Jeaffreson (1886–92), ii, p. 7.

6 LMA P79/JN1/22, unfoliated.

7 LMA P79/JN1/21, f . 197v (old foliation 248v); under 'Julye 1604'. Ward's reference (p. 347), 'Newcombe MSS, Hackney Public Library', is obsolete. Ogburn, p. 762, prints a photo of the church tower; the church was demolished in 1798.

Chapter 84 A Husband for Lady Susan

1 CP, xvi, p. 392 (146/17).

2 CP, xvi, p. 258 (189/147); addressed: 'To the Right honorable my good Lord the Lord Cycell one of his Maiestes priuie Counsaile these delivered'; endorsed: 'Countesse of Oxford'. Discussed by Matus (1994), pp. 260–61.

3 Peck (1982).

4 PRO C66/1637, m. 25; subsequent 'livery' or order to pay is recorded in C66/1657, m. 11.

5 Jeayes (1906), pp. 147–48 (from BL MS Egerton 2804, f. 185): Jeayes adds, n. 2, that Philip was privately contracted to Susan on 12 October.

6 Lodge (1791), iii, pp. 100–01 (citing Talbot Papers, vol. K, f. 225).

7 Jeayes (1906), p. 150 (from BL MS Egerton 2804, f. 187).

8 CP, xvii, p. 646 (192/56–57) 17 June 1604; endorsed '1605: A Note of the Lady Susans Portion'.

9 *CSPD*, 1603–10, p. 186 (PRO SP14/12[/6], f. 8), re 'Christmas games' (p. 66). On 18 December Chamberlain wrote to Ralph Winwood 'of maskes and revells against the mariage of Sir Phillip Harbert and the Lady Susan Vere which is to be celebrated on St. Johns day': Chamberlain, *Letters*, i, p. 198.

10 *CSP Venice*, 1603–07, No. 323.

Chapter 85 The Dowager and the Heir

1 Hackney Archives Department, HAD D/F/TYS/1 (transcript of parish vestry minute book 1581–1613), p. 53.

2 PRO REQ2/388/28, Bill of Complaint of Edward Johnson. Emmison (1980), p. 1: '*Edward, 17th Earl of Oxford*. The existence of his will or administration is not mentioned in the *D. N. B.* or other biography. The editor has made a fresh attempt to trace it but it is not among any of the central or Essex probate courts; although the Earl was buried in Hackney parish church (Middlesex), he died in Stoke Newington (Middlesex) within the

probate jurisdiction of the Dean and Chapter of St Paul's Cathedral, whose records yield no reference. Burke's *Complete Peerage* (x, 253) states that he died, 24 June 1604, intestate.' Emmison's presumption that Oxford died in Stoke Newington is incorrect.

3   Essex, 2 James: PRO C142/286/165; WARD7/37/12; London, 6 James (August 1608), PRO C142/305/103; WARD7/41/35.

4   BL MS Harley 41, f. 89; copy in College of Arms, MS Vincent 445, p. 51.

5   CP, xvi, p. 310 (107/16): addressed: 'To the right honorable the Erle of Nottingam, Lord Highe Admirall of England at Haylinge giue these'; endorsed: '17 Sept. 1604 / Erl of Oxford to my Lord Admirall'.

6   Hackney Archives Department, HAD D/F/TYS/1 (transcript of parish vestry minute book 1581–1613).

7   PRO C66/1819, mbs. 29–30.

8   Hedingham: HMC, 14th Report, Appendix, ix (1895), p. 277; garden: *CSPD*, Addenda 1580–1625, p. 520.

9   HMC *Downshire*, ii, p. 241.

10 *CSPD*, 1611–18, p. 61 (PRO SP38/10, by date – Doquet).

11 Letter: PRO SP14/65[/49], ff. 76–77 (22 July 1611); addressed: 'To the right honorable my very good Lord the Earle of Salisbury lord highe Treasourer of England and the Earle of Northampton lord privie seale'; endorsed: '22° Iulij 1611 / Countesse of Oxenford to my Lord and Lord Priuy Seall / Concerning hir Sonn'; articles: ff. 78–79.

12 So identified in *Peerage*, x, p. 254, note f.

13 *OED* sb.14.b: 'An eating-house or tavern …; In the 17th cent. the more expensive ordinaries were frequented by men of fashion and the dinner was usually followed by gambling; hence the term was often used as synonymous with "gambling-house".'

14 A lane leading from the Strand to the river between Essex House and Arundel House: Kingsford, ii, p. 92.

15 Presumably the husband of the daughter of the tennis-court keeper and his wife.

16 Wilson (1653), p. 161.

17 *CSPD*, 1611–18, p. 81 (PRO SP14/66[/70], ff. 135–36).

18 BL MS Add. 29549, ff. 31–32: addressed: 'To my very loving frind Sir Christopher Hatton Knight give theis'; no endorsement.

19 *CSPD*, 1611–18, pp. 135 (PRO SP14/69[/71]; full letter ff. 114–15; citation from f. 114).

20 Nichols, *James*, ii, p. 450, note 4, citing Winwood's *Memorials*, iii, p. 422.

21 *CSPD*, 1611–18, p. 166 (PRO SP99/12, f. 18; full letter ff. 18–19).

22 LMA P79/JN1/22, unfoliated, 3 January 1612 [=1613]; P79/JN1/21, f. 208v (old foliation 260v).

23 PRO PROB11/121, ff. 74–75v.

24 Nichols, *James*, ii, p. 450, note 4, citing Winwood's *Memorials*, iii, p. 422.

25 PRO PROB11/121, ff. 74–75v; *Peerage*.

26 *CSP Venice*, xv, No. 282. The report concludes: 'I add my intercession to his. The ambassador was told that the matter would be considered, and so he took his leave.'

27 L. P. Smith (1907), ii, pp. 110–11, 113–14, 119–20.

28 Miller, ii, p. 39, citing John Strype, lecturer in the Church from 1689 to 1723, on the ancient Table Monument: 'On the north side of the chancel, first an ancient Table Monument with a fair grey marble. There were coats-of-armes on the sides, but torn off. This monument is concealed by the schoolmaster's pew.'

APPENDIX
Manuscript References for LL and LIB Documents

Full transcriptions of most documents indicated below are posted on the author's website: socrates.berkeley.edu/~ahnelson/. Computer printouts have been deposited in the Edward de Vere Collection at Concordia University, Portland, Oregon; and in the Massachusetts Center for Renaissance Studies at the University of Massachusetts, Amherst. See Abbreviations for sigla.

LL: Oxford's Letters and Memoranda
Personal Letters

LL-01: BL Lansdowne 6[/25], f. 79; 19 August 1563 (in French)
LL-02: BL Lansdowne 11[/53], ff. 121–22; 24 November 1569
LL-03: BL Harley 6991[/5], ff. 9–10; [September 1572]
LL-04: BL Lansdowne 14[/84], ff. 185–86; 22 September [1572]
LL-05: BL Lansdowne 14[/85], ff. 186–87; 31 October [1572]
LL-06: CP 8/24; 17–18 March 1575
LL-07: CP 160/74; 24 September [1575]
LL-08: CP 8/76; 27 November [1575]
LL-09: CP 8/12; [3 January 1576]
LL-10: CP 9/1; 27 April [1576]
LL-11: CP 9/15; [13 July 1576]
LL-12: PRO SP12/149[/42(15)], f. 108v; 21 May 1578
LL-13: BL Lansdowne 33[/6], ff. 12–13; [13? July 1581]
LL-14: BL Lansdowne 38[/62], ff. 158–59; [?20 June 1583]
LL-15: BL Lansdowne 42[/39], ff. 97–98; [30 October 1584])
LL-16: BL Lansdowne 50[/22], ff. 49–50; [25 June 1586]
LL-17: BL Lansdowne 63[/71], ff. 181–82; 5 August [1590]
LL-18: BL Lansdowne 63[/76], ff. 191–92; 8 September [1590]
LL-19: BL Lansdowne 68[/6], ff. 12–13; 18 May [1591]
LL-20: BL Lansdowne 68[/11]; ff. 23, 28; [30 June 1591] (see also 47)
LL-21: BL Harley 6996[/22], ff. 42–43; 25 October 1593

LL-22: BL Lansdowne 76[/74], ff. 168–69; 7 July 1594
LL-23: CP 31/106; 24 April 1595
LL-00: PRO SP12/253[/60], ff. 100–01; 7 August 1595 (see 60)
LL-24: CP 35/84; 20 October 1595
LL-25: CP 172/81; 21 October 1595
LL-26: CP 44/63; 6 September 1596
LL-27: CP 44/101; 17 September 1596
LL-28: CP 37/66(b); 11 January 1597 (see also 46)
LL-29: PRO SP12/264[/111], ff. 151–51A; 8 September 1597
LL-30: CP 251/28; [July 1600]
LL-31: CP 76/34; 2 February [1601]
LL-32: CP 181/80; [?May 1601]
LL-33: CP 182/23; 11 May 1601
LL-34: CP 88/101; 7 October 1601
LL-35: CP 89/124; 22 November 1601
LL-36: CP 89/148; 4 December 1601
LL-37: CP 181/99; [January 1602]
LL-38: CP 85/103; 22 March [1602]
LL-39: CP 99/150; 25, 27 April 1603
LL-40: CP 99/161; 7 May [1603]
LL-41: Cecil Papers 100/93; 12 June 1603
LL-42: Cecil Papers 100/99; 16 June 1603
LL-43: CP 100/108; 19 June 1603
LL-44: Essex Record Office MS D/DMh C1; 30 January 1604

Draft Interrogatories

LL-45: PRO SP12/151[/42], ff. 96–96v; [?18 January 1580]
LL-46: PRO SP15/28[/2], f. 3; [18 January 1580]

Memoranda

LL-47: BL Lansdowne 68[/11], f. 22 (see also 20)
LL-48: BL Lansdowne 108[/14], ff. 25–26; July 1592
LL-49: CP 37/66(a); 11 January 1597 (see also 28)
LL-50: CP 146/19, ff. 146/19 [1601–02]

Tin-mining Letters

LL-51: CP 170/126; 20 March 1595
LL-52: CP 25/106; 23 March 1595

LL-53: CP 31/45; 25 March 1595
LL-54: CP 31/52; 28 March 1595
LL-55: CP 31/54; 28 March 1595
LL-56: CP 31/68; 1 April 1595
LL-57: CP 31/79; 9 April 1595
LL-58: CP 31/83; 13 April 1595
LL-59: CP 31/93; 17 April 1595
LL-60: PRO SP12/252[/57], ff. 108–09; 7 June 1595
LL-61: PRO SP12/252[/69], ff. 133–34; 13 June 1595
LL-62: PRO SP12/252[/70], ff. 135–36; 14 June 1595
LL-63: PRO SP12/252[/76], ff. 144–45; 15 June 1595
LL-64: PRO SP12/253[/60], ff. 100–01; 7 August 1595 (also personal note)
LL-65: CP 31/11; 14 March 1596
LL-66: CP 71/23; June 1599 (a Saturday)
LL-67: CP 71/26; June 1599
LL-68: Huntington Library EL 2337; undated: 'this afternoon'; 2–3 years since request for farm

Tin-mining Memoranda

LL-69: BL Lansdowne 86[/66], ff. 169–70
LL-70: CP 25/76; ?9 March 1595
LL-71: PRO SP12/252[/49], ff. 96–97; 4 June 1595
LL-72: Huntington Library EL2335
LL-73: Huntington Library EL2336
LL-74: Huntington Library EL2338
LL-75: Huntington Library EL2344 'this tyme of Easter'
LL-76: Huntington Library EL2345
LL-77: Huntington Library EL2349

LIB: Libel Documents 1580–81 involving Oxford, Henry Howard, and Charles Arundel

Further extensions of LIB numbers, numerical or otherwise, refer to document subdivisions, often marked in the source manuscripts.

LIB-1: PRO SP12/151[/50], f. 110
LIB-2.1.1: BL Add. 15891, ff. 79–79v
LIB-2.1.2: PRO SP12/147[/4] f. 5
LIB-2.1.3: PRO SP12/147[/4] f. 6

LIB-2.1.4: PRO SP12/151[/47], ff. 105–06
LIB-2.1.5: PRO SP12/151[/48], ff. 107–08
LIB-2.2.1: PRO SP12/151[/42], ff. 96–96v
LIB-2.2.2: PRO SP15/28[/2], f. 3
LIB-2.2.3: PRO SP12/151[/43], ff. 95–95v, 97–97v
LIB-2.3.1: PRO SP12/151[/44], ff. 98–99
LIB-2.3.2: PRO SP12/151[/44], f. 99
LIB-2.3.3: PRO SP12/151[/44], ff. 99–99v
LIB-3.1: BL Cotton Titus C.6, ff. 7–8
LIB-3.2: BL Cotton Titus C.6, ff. 5–6
LIB-3.3: PRO SP12/147[/6], ff. 6–7
LIB-3.4: CP 98/129 [ii, 193]
LIB-3.5: BL Add. 15891, f. 119v–20
LIB-3.6.1: PRO SP12/151[/57], ff. 118–19
LIB-3.6.2: (continuation of preceding)
LIB-3.7: PRO SP12/155[/44], ff. 84–84bis
LIB-3.8: PRO SP12/150[/51], ff. 97–98
LIB-3.9: PRO SP12/150[/81], ff. 150–51
LIB-3.10: BL Add. 15891, ff. 43v–44
LIB-4.1.1: PRO SP15/27A[/46], ff. 81–82
LIB-4.1.2: (follows 4.1.1, outside back leaf)
LIB-4.2: PRO SP12/151[/46], ff. 103–04
LIB-4.3: PRO SP12/151[/45], ff. 100–02
LIB-4.4: PRO SP12/151[/49], ff. 109–09v
LIB-5.1: BL Add. 15891, f. 99
LIB-5.2: BL Add. 15891, ff. 94–94v
LIB-5.3: PRO SP12/151[/51], f. 111
LIB-5.4: BL Add. 15891, f. 73
LIB-5.5: BL Add. 15891, ff. 83v–84
LIB-5.6: BL Add. 15891, ff. 77v–78
LIB-5.7: PRO SP12/151[/53], f. 114
LIB-5.8: BL Add. 15891, f. 61
LIB-5.9: PRO SP12/151[/55], f. 116
LIB-5.10: PRO SP12/151[/56], f. 117
LIB-5.11: PRO SP12/150[/43], ff. 84–85
LIB-5.12: PRO SP12/151[/52], f. 113
LIB-6.1: PRO SP12/151[/51], f. 112
LIB-6.2: (follows preceding, f. 112)
LIB-6.3: (follows preceding, with change of ink, ff. 112–12v)
LIB-6.4: PRO SP12/149[/3], f. 3
LIB-6.5: PRO SP12/149[/3A], f. 4

LIB-6.6: PRO SP12/151[/54], f 115
LIB-6.7: (follows 6.3, f. 112v)
LIB-7.1: Huntington Library HA13066
LIB-7.2: PRO SP12/149[/67], ff. 156–57
LIB-7.3: PRO SP12/149[/68], ff. 158–59
LIB-7.4: BL Lansdowne 33[/6], ff. 12–13
LIB-7.5: BL Add. 15891, f. 77
LIB-7.6: PRO SP12/149[/69], ff. 160–61
LIB-7.7: PRO SP12/154[/11], ff. 20–21
LIB-7.8: PRO SP12/154[/12], ff. 22–22bis
LIB-7.9: PRO SP12/154[/13], ff. 23–24
LIB-7.10: BL Lansdowne 99[/93] ff. 252–53

Bibliography

Imprints to 1640 (in order of STC number)

Books printed in Great Britain – usually London – between 1475 and 1640 are listed in *A Short-Title Catalogue of Books Printed in England, Scotland, and Ireland, and of English Books Printed Abroad, 1475–1640*, comp. A. W. Pollard and G. R. Redgrave; 2nd edn, Katharine F. Pantzer, 3 vols (London, 1976–91), generally abbreviated as STC. Photographic facsimiles are available in the UMI microfilm series, available at most scholarly libraries and institutions of higher learning; or through EEBO http://wwwlib.umi.com/eebo/

In addition to titles listed below, see books noted in Chapters 45 and 75.

[Arden, Thomas] (1592), *The Lamentable and True Tragedie of M. Arden of Feversham in Kent* (STC 733 et seq.)

Ascham, Roger (1570), *The Scholemaster. Or plaine and perfite way of teaching children … the Latin tong* (STC 832 et seq.)

Axiochus, see under Plato (pseud.)

Bacon, Francis (1625), *Apophthegemes New and Old* (STC 1115 et seq.)

Baker, George (1574), *The Composition or making of the … Oil called Oleum Magistrale* (STC 1209), see also Gesner, Conrad

Baxter, Nathaniel (1606), *Sir Philip Sidneys Ouránia* (STC 1598)

Burton, William (1592), *Dauid's Euidence* (STC 4170 et seq.)

Camden, William (1615), *Annales rerum Anglicarum … regnante Elizabetha* (STC 4496)
_____ (1625), *Annales The True and Royall History of Elizabeth Queene of England* (STC 4497)

Cardano, Girolomo (1573), *Cardanus Comforte*, tr. Thomas Bedingfield (STC 4607; 2nd edn 1576: STC 4608)

Carleton, George (1624), *A Thankfull Remembrance of Gods Mercy* (STC 4640 et seq.)

Castiglioni, Badassare (1571), *Balthasaris Castilionis comitis de Curiali* [*The Courtier*], tr. Bartholomew Clerke (STC 4782 et seq.)

Chapman, George (1613), *The Revenge of Bussy d'Ambois. A Tragedie* (STC 4989)

Churchyard, Thomas ([1579]), *A Generall Rehearsall of Warres* (STC 5235 et seq.), see also Meteren, Emanuel van

Coryate, Thomas (1611), *Coryates Crudities* (STC 5808)

Edwards, Richard (1576), *The Paradyse of daynty deuises* (STC 7516 et seq.)

Fioravanti, Leonardo (1580), *A Short Discours … vppon Chirurgerie*, tr. John Hester (STC 10881 et seq.)

Fleming, Abraham (1580), *A Bright Burning Beacon ... Conteining a generall Doctrine of Sundrie Signes Specially of Earthquakes* (STC 11037).

Gesner, Conrad (1576), *The newe jewell of health*, tr. George Baker (STC 11798); also Baker's 2nd edition, *The practice of the new and old phisicke* (1599: STC 11799)

Gilbert, Humphrey (1576), *A Discourse of a Discouerie for a New Pasage to Cataia* (STC 11881)

Golding, Arthur (1573), *A Briefe Discourse of the late murther of master George Saunders* (STC 11985; 2nd ed. 1577: STC 11986)

_____ (1580), *A Discourse vpon the Earthquake that hapned the sixt of Aprill 1580* (STC 11987)

Hackluyt, Richard (1598–1600), *The Principall Navigations ... of the English Nation*, 2nd ed. (STC 12626; anr. issue 12626a)

Harington, John (1615), *Epigrams both Pleasant and Serious* (STC 12775 et seq.)

[Harvey, Gabriel] (1592), *Foure Letters* (STC 12900 et seq.), see also Spenser, Edmund, *Three Proper, and Wittie, Familiar Letters* (1580)

_____ (1593), *Pierces Supererogation* (STC 12903)

Harvey, Richard (1583), *An Astrological discourse vpon the Coniunction of Saturne & Iupiter* (STC 12909.7 et seq.)

Hill, Thomas ([1574?]), *A Contemplation of Mysteries: Contayning the rare Effectes of certayne Comets* (STC 13484)

Holinshed, Raphael ([1577]), *The Chronicles of England* (STC 13568 et seq.; 2nd edn enlarged, 1587: STC 13569 et seq.). For continuation, see Stow, *Annales* (1592)

Howard, Henry (1583), *A defensatiue against the poyson of supposed Prophesies* (STC 13858 et seq.)

[Howard, Philip] ([1581]), *Callophisus* (STC 13868.5)

Johnson, Richard (1607), *The Pleasant Walkes of Moore-fields* (STC 14690)

Leigh, Richard (1588), *The Copie of a Letter sent out of England to Don Bernardino de Mendoza. Ambassador in France for the King of Spain, declaring the State of England* (STC 15412 et seq.)

Lichfild, Henry (1613), *The First Set of Madrigals of 5. Parts, Apt both for Viols and Voyces* (STC 15588)

M., D. F. R. de (1589), *Respuesta y Desengano contra las falsedades pvblicadas e impresas en Espana enbituperio de la Armada Inglesa ...* (STC 17131)

_____ (1589), *An Answer to the vntruthes, pvblished and printed in Spaine*, tr. John Lea (STC 17132)

Markham, Gervase (1624), *Honour in his Perfection: or, A Treatise in Commendation of the Vertues of Henry Earle of Oxendord, Henry Earle of Southampton [etc.]* (STC 17361)

Marprelate, Martin (pseud.) (1589), *Pap with a Hatchet*, attributed to John Lyly (STC 17463 et seq.)

Marston, John (1598), *The Metamorphosis of Pigmalions Image. And Certaine Satyres* (STC 17482)

_____ (1598), *Scourge of Villanie. Three Bookes of Satyres* (STC 17485 et seq.)

Meteren, Emanuel van (1602), *A True Discourse Historicall , of the Succeeding Governours in the Netherlands*, tr. Thomas Churchyard and R. Robinson (STC 17846)

Milles, Thomas (1610), *The Catalogue of Honor or Tresury of True Nobility Peculiar to Great Britaine* (STC 17926)

Munday, Anthony (1582), *A breefe and true reporte, of the execution of certaine traytours at Tiborne, the xxviii. and xxx. dayes of Maye. 1582. Gathered by A.M. who was there present. The names of them executed on Monday, the xxviii. of Maye. Thomas Foord. Iohn Shert. Robert Iohnson. The names of them executed on Wednesday, the xxx. of Maye. VVilliam Filbie. Luke Kirbie. Lawrance Richardson. Thomas Cottom* (STC 18261)

_____ (1582), *A discouerie of Edmund Campion, and his confederates, their most horrible and traiterous practises, against her Maiesties most royall person and the realme* (STC 18270)

_____ ([1580]), *A View of sundry Examples. Reporting many Straunge murthers … Also a short discourse of the late Earthquake the sixt of Aprill* (STC 18281)

Nash, Thomas (1596), *Have With You to Saffron-Walden* (STC 18369)

_____ (1592), *Strange Newes, of the Intercepting of Certaine Letters* (STC 18377 et seq.)

_____ (1594), *The Unfortunate Traveller; or, The Life of Jacke Wilton* (STC 18380 et seq.)

Norden, John (1593), *Speculi Britanniae. The first parte an historicall discription of Middlesex* (STC 18635)

Ovid (1565), *The fyrst fower bookes of P. Ouidius Nasos worke, intitled Metamorphosis,* tr. Arthur Golding (STC 18955); followed by 2nd ed. with 15 books (1567: STC 18956 et seq.)

Painter, William (1566), *The Palace of Pleasure* (STC 19121 et seq.)

Plato (pseud.) (1592), *Axiochus. A most excellent dialogue, written in Greeke by Plato. Tr. by Edw.* [sic] *Spenser. Heereto is annexed a speech spoken at the tryumphe at White-hall by the page to the earle of Oxenforde.* (STC 19974.6)

Proctor, John (1549), *The Fal of the Late Arrian* (STC 20406)

Rich, Barnaby (1581), *Riche his Farewell to Militarie Profession* (STC 20996 et seq.)

Segar, William (1590), *The Booke of Honor and Armes* (STC 22163)

_____ (1602), *Honor Military, and Civil* (STC 22164)

Soowthern, John (1584), *Pandora, the Musyque of the Beautie, of his Mistresse Diana* (STC 22928)

Spenser, Edmund (1590), *The Faerie Queene* (STC 23080 et seq.), see also Harvey, Gabriel, *Foure Letters* (STC 12900)

_____ (1580), *Three Proper, and Wittie, Familiar Letters* (STC 23095)

Stow, John ([1580]), *The Chronicles of England, from Brute vnto this present yeare 1580* (STC 23333)

_____ ([1592]), *The Annales of England* (STC 23334)

_____ ([1600]), *The Annals of England* (STC 23335)

_____ ([1605]), *The Annals of England* (STC 23337)

_____ (1615), *The Annals of England* (STC 23338)

_____ (1598), *A Suruay of London,* 1st edn (STC 23341 et seq.)

_____ (1618), *A Survay of London,* 3rd edn Anthony Munday (STC 23344)

_____ (1633), *A Survay of London,* 4th edn Anthony Munday (STC 23345 et seq.)

Stubbes, Philip (1583), *The Anatomie of Abuses* (STC 23376 et seq.)

Twyne, Thomas (1580), *A shorte and pithie discourse, concerning earthquakes* (STC 24413)

A Warning for Faire Women. Containing, The most tragicall and lamentable murther of Master George Sanders of London Marchant, nigh Shooters hill. Consented vnto by his owne wife, acted by M. Browne, Mistris Drewry and Trusty Roger agents therin: with their seuerall ends. As it hath beene lately diuerse times acted by the right Honorable, the Lord Chamberlaine his Seruantes (1599: STC 25089)

Watson, Thomas ([1582]), *The Hekatompathia [in Greek] or Passionate Centurie of Loue* (STC 25118a)

The Weakest goeth to the Wall. As it hath bene sundry times plaide by the right honourable Earle of Oxenford, Lord great Chamberlaine of England his seruants (1600: STC 25144 et seq.)

Imprints 1641–1700 (in order of Wing number)

Books printed in Great Britain – usually London – between 1641 and 1700 are listed in *Short-title Catalogue of Books Printed in England, Scotland, Ireland, Wales, … 1641–1700,* comp. Donald Wing, 2nd edn, 3 vols (New York: Index Society, 1972–88), generally referred to as 'Wing'. Photographic facsimiles are available in the UMI microfilm series, available at most scholarly libraries and institutions of higher learning; or through EEBO http://wwwlib.umi.com/eebo/

D'Ewes, Simonds (1682), *The Journals of all the Parliaments during the Reign of Queen Elizabeth* (Wing D1250)

Digges, Leonard (1655), *The Compleat Ambassador* (Wing D1453)

Dugdale, William (1675–76), *Baronage of England* (Wing D2480)

Languet, Hugo (1646), *Huberti Langueti Epistolae Politicae et Historicae ad Philippum Sydnaeum* (non-Wing), excerpted and translated into English by Pears (1845), pp. 164–66, and (without independent authority) by Bradley (1912)

Porta, Giambattista della (1658), *Natural Magick in XX Bookes* (Wing P2982)

Wilson, Arthur (1653), *The History of Great Britain, being the Life and Reign of King James the First* (Wing W2888)

Post-1700 Imprints (see also Abbreviations)

Place of publication is London unless otherwise noted.

Akrigg, G. P. V. (1962), *Jacobean Pageant; or, The Court of King James I* (Cambridge, MA)

_____ (1968), *Shakespeare and the Earl of Southampton* (Cambridge, MA)

Allen, Percy (1932), *The Life Story of Edward de Vere as 'William Shakespeare'*

Altrocchi, Julia Cooley (1959), 'Edward de Vere and the Commedia dell'Arte', *Shakespeare Authorship Review,* 2 (Autumn)

Aretino, Pietro (1969), *Sei Giornate,* ed. Giovanni Aquilecchia (Bari)

Arnold, Janet (1980), 'Lost from Her Majesties Back', *Costume Society Extra Series,* 7

Aubrey, John (1949), *Brief Lives,* ed. Oliver Lawson Dick

Aylward, J. D. (1950), 'The Inimitable Bobadill [=Rocco Bonetti]', *N&Q,* 195, pp. 2–4, 28–31

Bagley, J. J. (1985), *The Earls of Derby 1485–1985*

Barker, Felix, and Peter Jackson (1990), *The History of London in Maps*

Barker, Nicholas (1990), 'The Books of Henry Howard, Earl of Northampton', *Bodleian Library Record,* 13, pp. 375–81

_____ (1990), 'A "Lost" Sidney Document', *Bodleian Library Record,* 13, pp. 353–59

Barrell, Charles Wisner (1941–42), '"Shake-speare's" Own Secret Drama: Discovery of Hidden Facts in the Private Life of Edward de Vere, Proves Him Author of the

Bard's *Sonnets*', *Shakespeare Fellowship Newsletter*, 3, pp. 1–5, 13–17, 23–33, 45–52, 57–65, 69–77

———— (1943), 'Who was John Soothern? New Facts Relating to the Identification of the Mysterious Author of *Pandora*, 1584', *Shakespeare Fellowship Newsletter*, 5, pp. 71–75

———— (1945), 'Earliest Authenticated "Shakespeare" Transcript …', *Shakespeare Fellowship Quarterly*, 6, pp. 22–26

Bell, H. E. (1953), *An Introduction to the History and Records of the Court of Wards and Liveries*, Cambridge Studies in English Legal History (Cambridge)

Bennett, Josephine Waters (1942), 'Oxford and *Endimion*', *PMLA*, 57, pp. 354–69

Berry, Herbert (1986), *The Boar's Head Playhouse*, illustrated by C. Walter Hodges (Washington DC: Folger Shakespeare Library)

———— (1991), *The Noble Science: A Study and Transcription of Sloane Ms. 2530, Papers of the Masters of Defence of London, Temp. Henry VIII to 1590* (Newark: University of Delaware Press)

Birch, Thomas (1754), *Memoirs of the Reign of Queen Elizabeth*, 2 vols

Black, J. B. (1959), *The Reign of Elizabeth, 1558–1603*, Oxford History of England, 8, 2nd edn (Oxford)

Bond, R. Warwick (1902), *Life, Essays, Notes in the Complete Works of John Lyly*, 3 vols (Oxford: Clarendon Press)

Bossy, J. A. (1959), 'English Catholics and the French Marriage 1577–1581', *Recusant History*, 5, pp. 2–16

Bossy, John (1991), *Giordano Bruno and the Embassy Affair* (New Haven, CT)

Bowen, Gwynneth (1971), 'What Happened at Hedingham and Earls Colne', *Shakespeare Authorship Review*, 24 (Spring), pp. 9–10.

Bradbrook, Muriel (1936), *The School of Night: A Study in the Literary Relationships of Sir Walter Ralegh* (Cambridge)

Bradley (1912), see Languet, Hugo

Bray, Alan (1988), *Homosexuality in Renaissance England* (Boston, MA, Gay Men's Press)

Brenan, Gerald, and Edward Phillips Statham (1907), *The House of Howard*, 2 vols

Brink, Jean R. (1999), 'Manuscript Culture Revisited', *Sidney Journal*, 17, pp. 19–30

Brockhaus Enzyklopädie, 25 vols (Wiesbaden, 1966–81)

Brydges, Samuel Egerton (1805), *Censura Literaria*

Buc, George (1982), *History of Richard the Third*, ed. Arthur Kincaid

Buckley, George Truett ([1932]), *Atheism in the English Renaissance* (Chicago, University of Chicago Press)

Burke, Arthur Meredyth (1914), *Memorials of St. Margaret's Church Westminster: The Parish Registers 1539–1660*

Burke, Bernard (1883), *A Genealogical History of the Dormant, Abeyant, Forfeited, and Extinct Peerages of the British Empire* [*Burke's Dormant and Extinct Peerages*]

———— (1976), *Burke's Irish Family Records*, ed. Hugh Montgomery-Massingberd and Charles Kidd (New York)

Butler, K. T. (1950), 'Some Further Information about Rocco Bonetti', *N&Q*, 195, pp. 95–97

Chambers, D. S. (ed.) (1966), *Faculty Office Registers 1534–1549* (Oxford)

Chambers, Edmund K. (1923), *The Elizabethan Stage*, 4 vols (Oxford)

———— (1930), *William Shakespeare: A Study of Facts and Problems*, 2 vols (Oxford)

[_____] (1934), *An Index, Compiled by Beatrice White, to 'The Elizabethan Stage' and 'William Shakespeare: a study of facts and problems', by Sir Edmund Chambers* (Oxford)

_____ (1936), *Sir Henry Lee: An Elizabethan Portrait* (Oxford)

Chapman, Allan (1979), 'Astrological Medicine', in Charles Webster (ed.). *Health, Medicine and Mortality* (Cambridge), pp. 275–300

Chiljan, Katherine (1998), '"By this Hat, then ...": New Evidence about the 1580s "Portrait of a Gentleman"', *Shakespeare Oxford Newsletter*, 34 (Summer), p. 2

Clarke, Eva Turner (1931), *Hidden Allusions in Shakespeare's Plays* (New York)

Cockburn, J. S. (ed.) (1978), *Calendar of Assize Records; Essex Indictments Elizabeth I* (London: HSMO)

Cooke, W. H. (ed.) ([1878]), *Students Admitted to the Inner Temple 1547–1660*

Coote, Stephen (1993), *A Play of Passion: The Life of Sir Walter Ralegh*

Courthope, William John (1895–1910), *A History of English Poetry*, 2 vols (Oxford)

Davidson (1992), see Hunter and Wooton

Davis, Norman (ed.) (1971), *Paston Letters and Papers of the Fifteenth Century*, Part I (Oxford)

Dawson, Giles E. (1965), *Records of Plays and Players in Kent 1450–1642*, Malone Society Collections, 7

Deane, Charles (ed.) (1860), *A Discourse of Virginia* (Boston, MA)

Devlin, Christopher (1956), *The Life of Robert Southwell, Poet and Martyr* (New York)

Dewar, Mary (1964), *Sir Thomas Smith: A Tudor Intellectual in Office* (London: Athlone)

Dews, Nathan (1884), *The History of Deptford in the Counties of Kent and Surrey*

Dodds, Madeline Hope (ed.) (1935), *A History of Northumberland*, vol. 14 (Newcastle-upon-Tyne)

Donno, Elizabeth Story (ed.) (1976), *An Elizabethan in 1582: The Diary of Richard Madox, Fellow of All Souls*, Hakluyt Society, 2nd series, vol. 147

du Maurier, Daphne (1975), *Golden Lads: A Study of Anthony Bacon, Francis, and their Friends*

Duncan-Jones, Katherine (ed.) (1991), *Sir Philip Sidney* (New Haven, CT)

_____ (1999), 'The Sound of Broken Glass', *TLS* (25 June), pp. 26–27

_____ (1973), and Jan van Dorsten (eds.), *Miscellaneous Prose of Sir Philip Sidney* (Oxford)

Eccles, Mark (1933), 'Sir George Buc, Master of the Revels', in *Thomas Lodge and Other Elizabethans*, ed. Charles J. Sisson (Cambridge, MA.: Harvard UP), pp. 409–506

_____ (1934), *Christopher Marlowe in London* (Cambridge, MA)

_____ (1982), *Brief Lives: Tudor and Stuart Authors*, in *Studies in Philology*, Texts and Studies (Fall)

Edwards, A. C. (1975), *John Petre: Essays on the Life and Background of John, 1st Lord Petre, 1549–1613* (London: Regency)

Edwards, Edward (1868), *The Life of Sir Walter Ralegh*, 2 vols

Edwards, Francis, SJ (1968), *The Marvellous Chance: Thomas Howard, Fourth Duke of Norfolk, and the Ridolphi Plot, 1570–1572*

_____ (1994), 'William Shakespeare: Why Was His True Identity Concealed?', *The Elizabethan Review*, 2, pp. 23–48

Edwards, Richard (2001), *The Works of Richard Edwards: Politics, Poetry and Performance in Sixteenth-Century England*, ed. Ros King (Manchester UP)

Elliott, Jr, John R. (1997), 'Early Staging in Oxford', in *A New History of Early English Drama*, ed. John D. Cox and David Scott Kastan (New York: Columbia UP), pp. 68–78

Elton, Geoffrey R. (1975), *England Under the Tudors*, A History of England, 4, 2nd edn

Emmison, F. G. (1966), *Catalogue of Essex Parish Records, 1240–1894* (Chelmsford)

_____ (1970), *Elizabethan Life: Disorder* (Chelmsford)

_____ (1973), *Elizabethan Life: Morals and the Church Courts, Mainly from Essex Archidiaconal Records* (Chelmsford)

_____ (1978), *Elizabethan Life: Wills of Essex Gentry and Merchants*, Essex County Council Publication 71 (Chelmsford)

_____ (1980), *Elizabethan Life: Wills of Essex Gentry and Yeomen* (Chelmsford)

_____ (ed.) (1989), *Essex Wills: The Archdeaconry Courts 1583–1592* (Chelmsford)

Erickson, Carolly (1983), *The First Elizabeth* (New York)

Feldman, Bronson (1977), *Hamlet Himself* (Philadelphia: Lovelore Press)

Feuillerat, Albert (1910), *John Lyly: Contribution à l'Histoire de la Renaissance en Angleterre* (Cambridge)

_____ (ed.) (1914), *Documents relating to the Revels at Court in the time of King Edward VI and Queen Mary (The Loseley Manuscripts)*, vol. 2, Materialien zur Kunde des älteren Englischen Dramas, 21 (Louvain)

_____ (1922–26), *The Complete Works of Sir Philip Sidney*

_____ (1962), *The Prose Works of Sir Philip Sidney*, 4 vols (Cambridge: Cambridge UP)

Ffoulkes, Charles J. (1916), *Inventory and Survey of the Armouries of the Tower of London*, vol. 1 (London: HMSO)

Firth, C. H., and H. C. Lomas (1906), *Diplomatic Relations of England and France, 1603–88* (Oxford)

Fletcher, Reginald J. (1901), *The Pension Book of Gray's Inn, 1569–1669*

Foley, Henry (ed.) (1877–83), *Records of the English Province of the Society of Jesus*, 7 vols in 8 pts

Foster, Joseph (1889), *Register of Gray's Inn: Admissions 1521–1889*

French, Peter J. (1972), *John Dee: The World of an Elizabethan Magus*

Freshfield, Edwin (1887), *The Vestry Minute Book of the Parish of St Margaret Lothbury in the City of London 1571–1677*

Greville, Fulke (1986), *Fulke Greville's Life of the Renowned Sir Philip Sidney* [1652: Wing B4899], ed. John Gouws (Oxford UP)

Gair, W. Reavley (1982), *The Children of Paul's: The Story of a Theatre Company, 1553–1608* (Cambridge and New York: Cambridge UP)

Gairdner, James (ed.) (1881), *Three Fifteenth-Century Chronicles, with Historical Memoranda by John Stowe*, Camden Society, n.s., 28

Groebner, Valentin (1995), 'Losing Face, Saving Face: Noses and Honour in the Late Medieval Town', *History Workshop Journal*, 40, pp. 1–15

Grosart, Alexander B. (ed.) (1881), *The Life and Complete Works in Prose and Verse of Robert Greene, M.A.*, 15 vols; vol. 1: *Storojenko's Life of Robert Greene* ([London])

Hallen, A. W. C. (ed.) (1889–95), *The Registers of St. Botolph, Bishopsgate*, 3 vols (Alloa)

Hammer, Paul E. J. (1999), *The Polarisation of Elizabethan Politics: The Political Career of Robert Devereux, 2nd Earl of Essex, 1585–1597* (Cambridge: Cambridge UP)

Hannah, John (ed.) (1875), *The Poems of Sir Walter Raleigh; Collected and Authenticated with those of Sir Henry Wotton and other Courtly Poets from 1540 to 1650*

Harrison, George B. (ed.) (1926), *Willobie his Avisa, 1594, with an Essay …*

Hart-Davis, Duff (1988), *Armada*

Hartley, T. E. (ed.) (1981), *Proceedings in the Parliaments of Elizabeth I*, vol 1: *1558–1581* (Leicester)

_____ (1992), *Elizabeth's Parliaments: Queen, Lords, and Commons, 1559–1601* (Manchester)

Haslam, Graham (no date), 'An Administrative Study of the Duchy of Cornwall, 1500–1650', PhD dissertation, Louisiana State University. Copy at the Huntington Library

Hatton, David (1994), *Clare, Suffolk: An Account of Historical Features of the Town, its Priory and its Parish Church* (Clare: Clare Parish Council, Suffolk)

Hawkyard, Alasdair (1990), 'Councillors to Queen Elizabeth: the Cecils', in David Starkey (ed.), *Rivals in Power: Lives and Letters of the Great Tudor Dynasties*, pp. 250–69

Haynes, Alan (1979a), 'The Elizabethan Earthquake, 1580', *History Today*, 29, pp. 542–44

_____ (1979b), 'The First English National Lottery [1567]', *History Today*, 29, pp. 610–13

_____ (1987), *The White Bear: Robert Dudley, the Elizabethan Earl of Leicester*

_____ (1992), *Invisible Power: The Elizabethan Secret Services 1570–1603* (Stroud, Gloucestershire)

Hayward, Sir John (1840), *Annals of Queen Elizabeth* (Camden Society)

Hazlitt, William C. (ed.) (1869–70), *Gascoigne's Works*, 2 vols

Hentzner, Paul (1881), *A Journey into England in the Year MDXCVIII*, ed. Horace Walpole, Aungervyle Society, first series, 1 (Edinburgh)

Hicks, Leo (1964), *An Elizabethan Problem: Some Aspects of the Careers of Two Exile Adventurers*

Hope, Warren (1992), *The Shakespeare Controversy: An Analysis of the Claimants to Authorship, and their Champions and Detractors* (Jefferson, NC: McFarland)

Hopkinson, A. F. (1913), *Play Sources: The Original Stories on Which are Founded the Tragedies of* Arden of Feversham *and* A Warning for Fair Women ...

Hotson, Leslie (1937), *I, William Shakespeare* (London: Cape)

Hunter, George K. (1962), *John Lyly: The Humanist as Courtier*

Hunter, Michael, and David Wootton (eds.) (1992), *Atheism from the Reformation to the Enlightenment* (Oxford); includes Nicholas Davidson, 'Unbelief and Atheism in Italy, 1500–1700', pp. 55–85

The Huntingdon Papers (The Archives of the Noble Family of Hastings), 6 pts (London: Maggs Bros., 1926)

Hurstfield, Joel (1958), *The Queen's Wards; Wardship and Marriage under Elizabeth I* (Cambridge, MA: Harvard UP)

Jameson, Thomas Hugh (ed.) (1938), 'The "Gratulationes Valdinenses" of Gabriel Harvey', PhD dissertation, Yale

Jayne, Sears Reynolds (1956), *Library Catalogues of the English Renaissance* (Berkeley and Los Angeles)

Jeaffreson, John Cordy (ed.) (1886–92), *Middlesex County Records*, 4 vols

Jeayes, Isaac Herbert (ed.) (1906), *Letters of Philip Gawdy ... 1579–1616*

Jordan, W. K. (ed.) (1966), *The Chronicle and Political Papers of King Edward VI*

Kemp, Thomas (ed.) (1898), *The Black Book of Warwick* (Warwick)

Knox, Thomas F. (ed.) (1878), *The First and Second Diaries of the English College, Douay*, Records of the English Catholics under the Penal Laws, 1

Kocher, Paul H. (1946), *Christopher Marlowe: A Study of his Thought, Learning, and Character* (Chapel Hill, NC)

Labanoff, Alexandre (ed.) (1844), *Lettres, instructions et mémoires de Marie Stuart, reine d'Écosse*, 7 vols

Laboureur, Jean Le (1731), *Les Memoires de Messire Michel de Castelnau Seigneur de Mauvissiere*, 3 vols (Brussels)

Lacey, Robert (1973), *Sir Walter Ralegh*

Laughton, John Knox (ed.) (1894), *State Papers Relating to the Defeat of the Spanish Armada*, 2 vols (London: HMSO)

Lefranc, Pierre (1968), *Sir Walter Ralegh Écrivain*

Leland, John (1774), *De Rebus Britannicis Collectanea*, ed. Thomas Hearne

_____ (1907–10), *The Itinerary of John Leland in or about the Years 1535–1543*, ed. Lucy Toulmin Smith, 5 vols

Lettehove, M. C. Baron Kervyn de (ed.) (1882–1900), *Relations politiques des Pays-Bas et de l'Angleterre sous le règne de Philippe II*, 11 vols

Levenson, Jill L. (1980), *A Critical Edition of the Anonymous Elizabethan Play The Weakest Goeth to the Wall* (New York: Garland)

Lewis, George (1924), *The Stannaries: A Study of the English Tin Miner* (Cambridge, MA)

Lillie, George (1848–50), *The Romance of the Peerage*, 2 vols

Loades, David (1989), *Mary Tudor: A Life* (Oxford)

Lodge, Edmund (1791), *Illustrations of British History*, 3 vols

Loftie, W. J. (1878), *Memorials of the Savoy* (Edinburgh)

Lorenzi, G. B. (ed.) (1870–72), *Leggi e memorie venete sulla prostituzione fino alla caduta della republica*, 2 vols (Venice)

Lysons, Daniel (1792–1811), *Environs of London*, 4 vols

MacCaffrey, Wallace T. (1968), *The Shaping of the Elizabethan Regime* (Princeton, NJ)

Majendie, Lewis (1796), *An Account of Castle Hedingham*

Manningham, John (1976), *The Diary of John Manningham of the Middle Temple 1602–1603*, ed. Robert Parker Sorlien (Hanover, NH: University Press of New England)

Markham, Clements R. (1888), *The Fighting Veres*

Matus, Irvin (1994), *Shakespeare, in Fact* (New York)

May, Steven W. (1975a), 'The Authorship of 'My Mind to me a Kingdom is'', *RES*, n.s., 26, pp. 385–94

_____ (1975b), 'William Hunnis and the 1577 *Paradise of Dainty Devices*', *Studies in Bibliography*, 28, pp. 63–80

_____ (ed.) (1980), *The Poems of Edward DeVere, Seventeenth Earl of Oxford, and of Robert Devereux, Second Earl of Essex, Studies in Philology*, 77, part 5

_____ (1981), 'Tudor Aristocrats and the Mythical "Stigma of Print"', *Renaissance Papers* (Durham, NC: Southeastern Renaissance Conference, 1981 for 1980), pp. 11–18

_____ (1991), *The Elizabethan Courtier Poets: The Poems and their Contexts* (Columbia, MO: University of Missouri Press)

McKerrow, R. B. (1910), *A Dictonary of Printers and Booksellers ... 1557–1640*

McMillen, Scott, and Sally-Beth MacLean (1998), *The Queen's Men and their Plays* (Cambridge)

Mebane, John S. (1989), *Renaissance Magic and the Return of the Golden Age: The Occult Tradition and Marlowe, Jonson, and Shakespeare* (Lincoln, NE)

Merson, A. D. (1975), *Earls Colne Grammar School, A History* (privately published by the School Governors)

Moore, Peter (1991), 'The Fable of the World, Twice Told', *SOS Newsletter*, 27, No. 3 (Summer), pp. 8–10

Morris, John (ed.) (1872–77), *The Troubles of our Catholic Forefathers Related by Themselves*. First [–third] series

Motley, John Lothrop (1904), *The Rise of the Dutch Republic: A History*, 3 vols

Neale, J. E. (1934), *Queen Elizabeth*

Nelson, Alan H. (1994), *Early Cambridge Theatres* (Cambridge)

Nevison, J. L. (1966–68), 'Embroidery Patterns of Thomas Trevelyon', *The Walpole Society*, 41, pp. 1–38

Norden, John (1840), *Speculi Britanniae Pars: An Historical and Chorographical Description of the County of Essex, 1594; Edited from the Original Manuscript in the Marquess of Salisbury's Library at Hatfield*, Camden Society, 9

Ockenden, R. E. (1936), *Thomas Twyne's Discourse on the Earthquake of 1580* (Oxford: Pen-in-Hand Publishing Co.)

O'Connor, Norreys Jephson (1934), *Godes Peace and the Queenes* (London: Oxford UP)

Ogle, O. (ed.) (1866), *Copy-book of Sir Amias Poulet's Letters, Written during his Embassy to France (A.D. 1577)* (London: Roxburghe Club)

Osborn, James M. (1972), *Young Philip Sidney, 1572–1577*, Elizabethan Club, 5 (New Haven)

Padfield, Peter (1988), *Armada: A Celebration of the Four Hundredth Anniversary of the Defeat of the Spanish Armada, 1588–1988*

Palmer, Alan (1981), *Who's Who in Shakespeare's England* (Brighton)

Pears (1845), see Languet, Hugo.

Peck, D. C. (1978), 'Raleigh, Sidney, Oxford, and the Catholics, 1579', *Notes and Queries*, n.s. 25, no. 5 (vol. 223), pp. 427–31

‾‾‾‾‾ (ed.) (1985), *Leicester's Commonwealth: The Copy of a Letter Written by a Master of Art of Cambridge (1584) and Related Documents* (Athens, OH)

Peck, Linda Levy (1982), *Northampton, Patronage and Policy at the Court of James I* (London and Boston)

Perrucci, Andrea (1961), *Dell' Arte Rappresentative Premeditata ed all'Improviso* (Naples, 1699; ed. Anton Giulio Bragaglia, Florence)

The Carl H. Pforzheimer Library: English Literature, 1475–1700, 3 vols (New York, 1940)

Pine, John (1739), *The Tapestry Hangings of the House of Lords: Representing the Several Engagements between the English and Spanish Fleets [1588]*

Pollen, John Hungerford (1908), *Unpublished Documents Relating to the English Martyrs, Vol. 1, 1584–1603*, Catholic Record Society, 5

‾‾‾‾‾ (1919), 'Recusants and Priests, March 1588', *Miscellanea, XII*, Catholic Record Society, 22, pp. 120–29

‾‾‾‾‾ (1921), *Sources for the History of Roman Catholics in England, Ireland and Scotland, from the Reformation Period to that of Emancipation, 1533 to 1795*

Pollen, John Hungerford, and William MacMahon (eds) (1919), *The Venerable Philip Howard Earl of Arundel, 1557–1595*, Catholic Record Society, 21

Prest, Wilfred (1972), *Inns of Court under Elizabeth I and the Early Stuarts. 1590–1640*

Quinn, David B. (1940), *The Voyages and Colonising Enterprises of Sir Humphrey Gilbert*, 2 vols, Hakluyt Society, 2nd series, nos. 83–84

‾‾‾‾‾ (1974), *England and the Discovery of America*

‾‾‾‾‾ (1977), *North America from Earliest Discovery to First Settlements* (New York)

Read, Conyers (1925), *Mr. Secretary Walsingham and the Policy of Queen Elizabeth*, 3 vols
_____ (1955), *Mr. Secretary Cecil and Queen Elizabeth*
_____ (1960), *Lord Burghley and Queen Elizabeth*
Read, John (1947), *The Alchemist in Life, Literature and Art*
Reaney, P. H. (ed.) (1935), *The Place-Names of Essex*, English Place-Name Society, 12 (Cambridge)
Reed, Robert R., Jr (1965), *The Occult on the Tudor and Stuart Stage* (Boston, MA)
Ridley, Jasper (1987), *Elizabeth I*
Robinson, William (1819), *History and Antiquities of the Parish of Edmonton, in the County of Middlesex*
_____ (1842), *History and Antiquities of Hackney*
Rollins, Hyder E. (ed.) (1927), *The Paradise of Dainty Devices (1576–1606), by Richard Edwards* (Cambridge, MA)
_____ (ed.) (1933), *Brittons Bowre of Delights, 1591*, by Nicholas Breton (Cambridge, MA)
Ronciere, Charles Germain Bourel de la (1908), *Catalogue des manuscrits de la Collection des Cinq Cents de Colbert* (Paris)
Round, J. Horace (1902), 'The Lord Great Chancellor', *The Monthly Review* (June)
_____ (1903), 'Notes on the Great Lord Chamberlain Case', *The Ancestor*, 4 (January)
_____ (1911), *The King's Sergeants and Officers of State* (London: James Nisbet)
Rowse, A. L. (1962), *Ralegh and the Throckmortons*
_____ (1971–72), 'Mentality and Belief: Witchcraft and Astrology', in *The Elizabethan Renaissance*, 2 vols, pp. 227–72
_____ (1974), *Simon Forman: Sex and Society in Shakespeare's Age*
_____ (1983), *Eminent Elizabethans* (Athens, GA)
Rye, Constance E. B. (1885), 'Queen Elizabeth's Godchildren', *The Geneaologist*, n.s. 2, pp. 292–96
Rye, Walter (ed.) (1891), *The Visitacion of Norffolk*, Harleian Society Publications, vol. 32
Salgado, Gamini (1977), *Elizabethan Underworld*
Sandison, Helen Estabrook (ed.) (1953), *The Poems of Sir Arthur Gorges* (Oxford)
Sharp, Cuthbert (ed.) (1840), *Memorials of the Rebellion of 1569*
Shaw, William A. (1906), *The Knights of England*, 2 vols
Sherman, William H. ((1906)), *John Dee: The Politics of Reading and Writing in the English Renaissance* (Amherst, MA)
Smith, Alan G. R. (1977), *Servant of the Cecils: The Life of Sir Michael Hickes, 1543–1612* (London: Jonathan Cape)
Smith, Logan Pearsall (ed.) (1907), *Life and Letters of Sir Henry Wotton*, 2 vols (Oxford)
Smith, Nowell C. (ed.) (1907), *Sir Fulke Greville's Life of Sir Philip Sidney* (Oxford: Clarendon Press)
Smith, Rosalind (1994), 'The Sonnets of the Countess of Oxford and Elizabeth I: Translations from Desportes', *Notes and Queries*, 239, pp. 446–50
Stern, Virginia F. (1979), *Gabriel Harvey: His Life, Marginalia and Library* (Oxford)
_____ (1992), *Sir Stephen Powle of Court and Country: Memorabilia of a Government Agent for Queen Elizabeth I, Chancery Official, and English Country Gentleman* (Selinsgrove, PA, London, Toronto: Susquehana UP)
Stevenson, J. (ed.) (1847), *The Correspondence of Sir Henry Unton … 1591 and 1592*
Strathman, Ernest A. (1951), *Sir Walter Ralegh: A Study in Elizabethan Skepticism* (New York)

Stritmatter, Roger (1993), 'A Quintessence of Dust: An Interim Report on the Marginalia of the Geneva Bible of Edward de Vere, the Seventeenth Earl of Oxford, Owned by the Folger Shakespeare Library,' *The Shakespeare Oxford Society, Newsletter*, vol. 29, no. 2A (Spring), pp. 1–2

Sylvester, Richard S., and Davis P. Harding (eds) (1962), *Two Early Tudor Lives* (New Haven, CT: Yale UP)

ten Raa, F. J. G., and F. de Bas (1911), *Het Staatsche Leger*, part 1

Thieme-Becker (1907–50), *Allgemeines Lexikon der bildenden Künstler*, 37 vols

Tilley, Morris Palmer (1950), *Dictionary of the Proverbs in England in the Sixteenth and Seventeenth Centuries* (Ann Arbor, MI)

Townsend, G. J. W. (1934), *History of the Great Chamberlainship of England*

Traister, Barbara Howard (1984), *Heavenly Necromancers: The Magician in English Renaissance Drama* (Columbus, MO)

Tuchman, Barbara (1978), *A Distant Mirror: The Calamitous Fourteenth Century* (New York)

Turner, Edward Raymond (1927), *The Privy Council of England in the Seventeenth and Eighteenth Centuries 1603–1784* (Baltimore: Johns Hopkins UP)

Urry, William (1988), *Christopher Marlowe and Canterbury*

Vickers, Kenneth H. (ed.) (1922), *A History of Northumberland*, vol. 11 (Newcastle-upon-Tyne)

Vivian, J. L. (ed.) (1887), *The Visitations of Cornwall, Comprising the Heralds' Visitations of 1530, 1573, and 1620* (Exeter)

von Bülow, Gottfried (1999), 'Journey through England amd Scotland made by Lupold von Wedel in the years 1584 and 1585, *Transactions of the Royal Historical Society*, n.s., 9, pp. 223–70

von Klarwill, Victor (ed.) (1924), *The Fugger News-Letters; Being a Selection of Unpublished Letters from the Correspondents of the House of Fugger during the Years 1568–1605*, tr. Pauline de Chary (New York)

––––––– (ed.) (1926), *The Fugger News-Letters, Second Series; Being a Further Selection from the Fugger Papers Specially Referring to Queen Elizabeth … 1568–1605*, tr. L.S.R. Byrne (New York)

von Wedel, Lupold (1928), 'A Knight Errant', in *Queen Elizabeth and Some Foreigners*, ed. Victor von Klarwill, tr. T. H. Nash (London: Bodley Head)

Wallace, Charles William (1912), *The Evolution of the English Drama up to Shakespeare* (Berlin)

Wallace, Dewey D. (1974), 'From Eschatology to Arian Heresy: The Case of Francis Kett (d. 1589)', *Harvard Theological Review*, 67, pp. 459–73

Wallace, Malcolm William (1915), *The Life of Sir Philip Sidney* (Cambridge)

Walpole, Horace (Earl of Orford) (1798–1825), *The Works of Horatio Walpole*, 9 vols

Way, Albert (1844), 'Lease of the Earl of Bedford to Sir William Cecil', *Archaeologia*, xxx, pp. 494–98

Weaver, Leonard T. (1975), *The Harwich Story* (Harwich)

Webster, Charles (ed.) (1979), *Health, Medicine and Mortality in the Sixteenth Century, Cambridge Monographs on the History of Medicine* (Cambridge)

West, Robert H. (1939), *The Invisible World* (Athens, GA)

Wheatley, Henry B. (1891), *London Past and Present*, 3 vols

Whitehead, Bertrand T. (1994), *Brags and Boasts: Propaganda in the Year of the Armada* (Stroud, Gloucestershire, and Dover, NH)

Wilbur, Earl Morse (1952), *A History of Unitarianism, in Transylvania, England, and America* (Cambridge, MA)

Williams, Neville ([1972]), *All the Queen's Men: Elizabeth I and her Courtiers*

Willson, David Harris (1940), *The Privy Councillors in the House of Commons, 1604–1629* (Minneapolis)

Wilson, Ian (1994), *Shakespeare, The Evidence: Unlocking the Mysteries of the Man and his Work* (New York)

Wilson, Luke (1993), '*Hamlet*, Hales v. Petit, and the Hysteresis of Action', *ELH*, 60, pp. 36–41

Wilson, Thomas (1936), 'The State of England Anno Dom. 1600', in *Camden Society Miscellany*, XVI, Camden Society, 52

Wine, M. L. (ed.) (1973), *The Tragedy of Master Arden of Faversham*, Revels Plays

Woudhuysen, H. R. (1996), *Sir Philip Sidney and the Circulation of Manuscripts, 1558–1640* (Oxford)

Wraight, D. A. (1965), *In Search of Christopher Marlowe, A Pictorial Biography* (rpt. 1993)

Wright, Thomas (1831–35), *The History and Topography of the County of Essex*, 2 vols

Young, Alan (1987), *Tudor and Jacobean Tournaments*

Zurich Letters, tr. Hastings Robinson, Parker Society, 2nd ser., 51 (1845)

Index

Individuals whose connection to the narrative is remote are generally indexed, if at all, under last name only, for example, Brincknell family, following Brincknell, Thomas. Notes are generally indexed only for those proper names which do not appear on the footnoted page in the main text. The chronology of and topics important to Oxford's life are indexed under Vere, Edward de.

Bourg (Burge), ___, Captain du 202–03
Bowen, Gwynneth 5
Bowes, Jerome 84
Bowes, Ralph 84, 338–39
Bowland, Mr ___ 188–89
Bowyer, S. 107
Brackenbury, Captain ___ 303
Brakinbury, R. 171–72
Bray, Alan 217
Brekeley, Mistress ___ 281
Brenings, Robert 283, 286
Breton, Nicholas: *Brittons Bowre of Delights*
    384–86, 482
Bridges, Eleanor 134
Bridgewater 246
Brigham, ___ 358
Brincknell, Thomas 47–49, 51, 57, 72, 105,
    152, 223
    Brincknell family 48, 450
Bristol 113, 115, 245, 247
Brittons Bowre of Delights, see Breton
Broad Street 182, 215
Bromley, Henry 412
Bromley, (Sir) Thomas 120, 239, 259, 268,
    282–83, 412
Brooke *alias* Cobham, Henry 288
Brooke, Henry, Lord Cobham 112, 179–80,
    308, 312–13, 367, 370
Brooke, John 130
Brooke, William, Lord Cobham 67, 367
Brooke, Lord, *see* Greville, Fulke
Brooke House, *see* Hackney (House)
Brooke, ___ (servant in Anne's household)
    293
Brooke of Ashe, John 237
Brown, Anthony 184
Brown, George 89–92, 105, 167
    Brown family 92, 456
Browne, Anthony, 1st Viscount Montague
    26, 68, 302
Browne, Edward 393
Browne, Margaret 293
Browne, Thomas 40
Browne, ___ (sergeant) 23
Browning, James? (physician) 292
Bruce, Edward, Lord Kinloss 416–17
Bruno, Giordano 61
Brydges, Edmund, 2nd Baron Chandos 74, 83
Brydges, Giles, 3rd Baron Chandos 83, 370

Buc, (Sir) George 2, 11, 287
Buckhurst, Lord, *see* Sackville, Thomas
Buckley, William 387
Buckway, Maynard (and Mary) 183, 185–86
Bull, Richard 33
Bullocke family 276–77
Bulmer, (Sir) Bevis 358
Burge, *see* Bourg
Burghley, Lady, *see* Cooke, Mildred
Burghley (Cecil) House 34, 36, 39, 43, 47,
    49, 51, 76, 99, 166, 177, 184, 201, 285–
    86, 296, 327, 350, 370, 371, 378, 448
Burrough, *see* Borough
Bussy d'Ambois, Louis 126, 256
Burton, William 210
Butler, Thomas, Earl of Ormond 45, 180,
    126–27, 233–34, 281–82, 407
Byfleet 353, 357

Cadman, Thomas 313
Caesar, Dr Julius 408
Cage, Anthony 191
Cage, Daniel 423
Caishio 406
Caius College, Cambridge 341–42
Calais 11, 26, 84, 108–10, 135–36, 298, 311,
    321
Calfhill, James: *Progne* 44–45
Callophisus 262
Calvin, John 236, 380
Camarden, ___ 331
Cambridge (town and university) 23–25, 42,
    44–45, 54–56, 72–73, 92–93, 104, 180,
    215–16, 224–25, 335, 339–42, 386, 449
Camden, William 48, 79, 105, 312, 314
Campion, Edmund 244, 250, 381
Canon Row 349, 353, 359, 432, 436
Canterbury 99, 104
Cantillon, ___ 176
Capuano, Alvise 212
Cardano, Girolomo: *Cardanus Comforte*
    77–79, 237
Cardinall, William 152
Carey, (Sir) Edmund 399
Carey, (Sir) George 73
Carey, George, 2nd Lord Hunsdon 345,
    350–51, 370, 392, 410
Carey, Henry, 1st Lord Hunsdon 42, 74,
    180, 312, 350